PATENT REMEDIES AND COMPLEX PRODUCTS

Through a collaboration among twenty legal scholars from eleven countries in North America, Europe, and Asia, *Patent Remedies and Complex Products* presents an international consensus on the use of patent remedies for complex products such as smartphones, computer networks, and the Internet of Things. It covers the application of both monetary remedies like reasonable royalties, lost profits, and enhanced damages, as well as injunctive relief. Readers will also learn about the effect of competition laws and agreements to license standards-essential patents on terms that are "fair, reasonable, and nondiscriminatory" (FRAND) on patent remedies. Where national values and policy make consensus difficult, contributors discuss the nature and direction of further research required to resolve disagreements. This title is also available as Open Access on Cambridge Core at doi.org/10.1017/9781108594981.

C. Bradford Biddle is Principal at Biddle Law PC and Faculty Fellow at the Center for Law, Science and Innovation, Sandra Day O'Connor College of Law, Arizona State University (ASU). He has taught courses on technology standard setting and internet law as an Adjunct Professor at ASU and elsewhere, and was a Fellow with Stanford Law School's Center for Internet and Society.

Jorge L. Contreras is a Professor of Law at the S. J. Quinney College of Law, University of Utah. He is the editor of five books, has published more than 100 articles and book chapters, and has served on high-level advisory boards at the US National Institutes of Health, National Academies of Science and American National Standards Institute, among others.

Brian J. Love is an Associate Professor of Law at School of Law, Santa Clara University, California, where he serves as Co-Director of the School's High Tech Law Institute and teaches courses in intellectual property law and remedies. Prior to joining Santa Clara, Brian was a Teaching Fellow at Stanford Law School a patent litigator, and a law clerk at several courts.

Norman V. Siebrasse is a Professor of Law at the University of New Brunswick, Canada. His research focuses on pharmaceutical patent law, patent remedies and the intersection of intellectual property law and commercial law. His writing is regularly cited by the Canadian courts, including the Supreme Court of Canada. He served as a law clerk at the Supreme Court of Canada.

Patent Remedies and Complex Products

TOWARD A GLOBAL CONSENSUS

Edited by

C. BRADFORD BIDDLE

Arizona State University, Sandra Day O'Connor College of Law

JORGE L. CONTRERAS

University of Utah, S. J. Quinney College of Law

BRIAN J. LOVE

Santa Clara University, School of Law

NORMAN V. SIEBRASSE

University of New Brunswick (Canada), Faculty of Law

CAMBRIDGE
UNIVERSITY PRESS

CAMBRIDGE
UNIVERSITY PRESS

University Printing House, Cambridge CB2 8BS, United Kingdom

One Liberty Plaza, 20th Floor, New York, NY 10006, USA

477 Williamstown Road, Port Melbourne, VIC 3207, Australia

314-321, 3rd Floor, Plot 3, Splendor Forum, Jasola District Centre, New Delhi - 110025, India

103 Penang Road, #05-06/07, Visioncrest Commercial, Singapore 238467

Cambridge University Press is part of the University of Cambridge.

It furthers the University's mission by disseminating knowledge in the pursuit of
education, learning and research at the highest international levels of excellence.

www.cambridge.org
Information on this title: www.cambridge.org/9781108445498
DOI: 10.1017/9781108594981

First published 2019
First paperback edition 2022

A catalogue record for this publication is available from the British Library

Library of Congress Cataloging in Publication data
NAMES: Biddle, Brad, 1968– editor. | Contreras, Jorge L., editor. | Sibrasse, Norman, 1961– editor. | Love,
Brian J. (Law teacher), editor.
TITLE: Patent remedies and complex products : toward a global consensus / edited by Brad Biddle,
Arizona State University College of Law ; Jorge Contreras, University of Utah College of Law; Norman
Sibrasse, University of New Brunswick (Canada) Faculty of Law; Brian J. Love, University of Santa
Clara School of Law
DESCRIPTION: Cambridge, United Kingdom ; New York, NY, USA : Cambridge University Press, 2019. |
Includes bibliographical references and index.
IDENTIFIERS: LCCN 2019012481 | ISBN 9781108426756 (hardback)
SUBJECTS: LCSH: Patent laws and legislation. | Remedies (Law) | BISAC: LAW / Intellectual Property /
General.
CLASSIFICATION: LCC K1505 .P379 2019 | DDC 346.04/86–dc23
LC record available at https://lccn.loc.gov/2019012481

ISBN 978-1-108-42675-6 Hardback
ISBN 978-1-108-44549-8 Paperback

Contents

Contributors

Colleen V. Chien
Professor of Law, *Santa Clara University School of Law*

Chien is an associate professor at Santa Clara University School of Law where she teaches, writes, and mentors students. From 2013 to 2015, she served in the Obama White House as a senior advisor, Intellectual Property and Innovation, working on a broad range of patent, copyright, technology transfer, open innovation, educational innovation, and other issues. Professor Chien is nationally known for her research and publications on domestic and international patent law and policy issues. She has testified on multiple occasions before Congress, the DOJ, the FTC, and the U.S. Patent and Trademark Office on patent issues, frequently lectures at national law conferences, and has published several in-depth empirical studies, including of patent litigation, patent-assertion entities (PAEs) (a term that she coined), and the secondary market for patents. Prior to joining the Santa Clara University School of Law faculty in 2007, Professor Chien prosecuted patents at Fenwick & West LLP in San Francisco, as an associate and then Special Counsel, and was a fellow at the Stanford Center for Law and the Biosciences. In 2017, Professor Chien was awarded the American Law Institute's Early Career Medal; she also has received the Vanguard Award for Public Service, and has been named Eric Yamamoto Emerging Scholar, a Tech Law Leader, one of Silicon Valley's "Women of Influence," and one of the 50 Most Influential People in Intellectual Property in the world. Chien is a graduate of Stanford (engineering) and Berkeley Law School and lives in Oakland with her husband and their two sons, Max and Benjie.

Jorge L. Contreras
Professor of Law, *University of Utah S.J. Quinney College of Law*

Contreras is a professor of law at the University of Utah S.J. Quinney College of Law and a senior fellow of the Centre for International Governance Innovation (CIGI). He has written and spoken extensively on institutional structures and policy implications of intellectual property, technical standardization, and scientific research. Professor Contreras serves as Co-Chair of the ABA Section of Science & Technology Law's Interdisciplinary Division and is a member of the American National Standards Institute (ANSI) IPR Policy Committee and of NIH's Council of Councils. He previously served as a member of the U.S. National Academy of Science's (NAS) Committee on IP Management in Standard-Setting Processes, which produced the 2013 report *Intellectual Property Challenges for Standard-Setting in the Global Economy.* Professor Contreras edited the ABA's *Technical Standards Patent Policy Manual* (2007) and the *Cambridge Handbook of Technical Standardization Law* (vol. 1, 2017; vol. 2, 2019 forthcoming) and has published more than one hundred scholarly articles, reports, white papers, and book chapters in publications including *Science, Nature, Georgetown Law Journal, University of Illinois Law Review, North Carolina Law Review, Antitrust Law Journal, Harvard Journal of Law and Technology,* and *Berkeley Technology Law Journal.* He is the founding editor of SSRN's *Law, Policy and Economics of Technical Standards* e-journal, and was the winner of the Standards Engineering Society's (SES) 2011 and 2015 scholarly paper competitions. Before entering academia, Professor Contreras was a partner at the international law firm Wilmer Cutler Pickering Hale and Dorr LLP, where he practiced international corporate and intellectual property transactional law.

Thomas F. Cotter
Briggs and Morgan Professor of Law, *University of Minnesota Law School*

Cotter is the Briggs and Morgan Professor of Law at the University of Minnesota Law School. He received his bachelor's and master's degrees in economics from the University of Wisconsin, and in 1987 graduated *magna cum laude* from the University of Wisconsin Law School, where he served as Senior Articles Editor of the Wisconsin Law Review. From 1987 to 1989, Cotter clerked for the Honorable Lawrence W. Pierce, United States Court of Appeals for the Second Circuit. He practiced law at Cravath, Swaine & Moore from 1988 to 1990, and at Jenner & Block from 1990 to 1994. From 1994 to 2005, he taught at the University of Florida College of Law and from 2005 to 2006 at Washington and Lee University School of Law. He joined the Minnesota faculty in 2006. Professor Cotter's research and teaching focuses on intellectual property law, antitrust, and law and economics. He is the author of four books – *Law and Economics: Positive, Normative, and Behavioral Perspectives* (co-authored with Jeffrey L. Harrison) (3d ed., 2013); *Comparative Patent Remedies: A Legal and Economic Analysis* (2013); *Trademarks, Unfair Competition, and Business Torts* (co-authored with Barton Beebe, Mark A. Lemley, Peter S. Menell, and Robert P. Merges) (2011); and *Intellectual Property: Economic and Legal Dimensions of Rights and Remedies* (co-authored with Roger D. Blair) (Cambridge University Press 2005). He has authored or co-authored over fifty other scholarly works, including articles in the *California Law Review,* the *Georgetown Law Journal*, the *Iowa Law Review*, and the *Minnesota Law Review*.

Damien Geradin
Professor of Competition Law & Economics, *Tilburg Law School, Tilburg University*
   Geradin is a professor of competition law and economics at Tilburg University (the Netherlands) and at George Mason University School of Law (Washington, D. C). He is also a visiting professor at University College London. Professor Geradin has also held visiting professorships at Columbia Law School, Harvard Law School, the University of Michigan Law School, UCLA School of Law, and the College of Europe, Bruges. He was a visiting lecturer at the University of Paris II (Assas) and at King's College London, and also a Fulbright scholar and visiting lecturer at Yale Law School. He is also the founding partner of EDGE | Legal Thinking, a Brussels-based boutique law firm specialized in EU competition law and intellectual property law. Over the past twenty years, he has authored, co-authored, or edited over twenty books and one hundred scientific papers in the field of competition law, IP law, and the regulation of network industries – including *EU Competition Law & Economics* (with Nicolas Petit and Anne Layne-Farrar) (2012) and *Global Antitrust Law & Economics* (with Einer Elhauge) (2nd ed., 2012). Professor Geradin is a co-editor-in-chief of the *Journal of Competition Law & Economics*, a nongovernmental advisor to the International Competition Network (ICN), and a member of the International Task Force of the ABA's Section of Antitrust. His work has been cited by the Court of Justice of the EU, the Supreme Court of the United States, and various U.S. Courts of Appeals, and in regulatory proceedings.

John M. Golden
Loomer Family Professor in Law, *University of Texas at Austin School of Law*
   Golden is the Loomer Family Professor in Law at the University of Texas at Austin, where he has taught administrative law, contracts, patent law, and seminars relating to innovation and intellectual property. Since 2011, he has served as faculty director of the Andrew Ben White Center in Law, Science and Social Policy. Professor Golden has a JD from Harvard Law School, a PhD in physics from Harvard University, and an AB in physics and history from Harvard College. After law school, he clerked for the Honorable Michael Boudin of the United States Court of Appeals for the First Circuit and for Associate Justice Stephen Breyer of the Supreme Court of the United States. Professor Golden also worked as an associate in the intellectual property department of Wilmer Cutler Pickering Hale and Dorr LLP.

Haijun Jin
Professor of Law, *Renmin University of China School of Law*
   Jin is a professor of law at Renmin University of China School of Law. He also studied and worked in foreign institutions for the last decade as, among others, a visiting professor at the University of Frankfurt am Main and the University of

Washington, and a visiting scholar at Harvard Law School and the Max-Planck Institute for Intellectual Property and Competition Law in Munich. His research covers various aspects in the field of intellectual property and private law, including specific issues on patent and trade secrets, IP licensing, and technology transfer. He has published articles, monographs, and book chapters, including several articles in English: "Reality and Potentiality: Compulsory Patent Licensing in China from a Comparative Perspective," *European Intellectual Property Review* (2009); "Government-Backed Patent Funds in China: Their Roles as Policy Tools to Promote Innovation by SMEs," *Asia-Pacific Tech Monitor* (2013); and "From Status to Contract: Employee Invention System in China," *Science, Technology and Law* of Korean Chungbuk National University (2016). Professor Jin serves as executive council member of the China Intellectual Property Law Society (CIPL), and a member of the China Intellectual Property Society (CIPS).

Alison Jones
Professor of Law, *Dickson Poon School of Law, King's College London*
    Jones is Professor of Law at King's College London and a solicitor at Freshfields Bruckhaus Deringer LLP. Prior to joining King's in 1992, Professor Jones read law at Girton College, Cambridge, worked at Slaughter & May, and completed a BCL at Christ Church, Oxford. Since joining King's, she has taught competition law (EU, UK, and U.S.), trusts, property, and EU law. Her main research interests are currently in the area of EU competition and U.S. antitrust law. Professor Jones is co-author of Jones and Sufrin on *EU Competition Law* and a regional editor for *the Restitution Law Review*; and writes two of the Centre of European Law's modules for the Diploma in EU competition law. She is also Director of the LLB Law with European Legal Studies programme.

Sang Jo Jong
Professor of Law, *Seoul National University School of Law*
    Jong is a professor of law at Seoul National University and has served as Dean of the School of Law, SNU. Professor Jong is a graduate of Seoul National University and received his PhD from the London School of Economics, with a doctoral thesis titled "The Legal Protection of Computer Programs." His research and teaching mostly center on copyright, trademark, patent, unfair competition, antitrust, and Internet laws. He has published more than one hundred scholarly articles in law journals (mostly in Korean) and has submitted several policy papers to government agencies. Professor Jong taught Korean Law at Harvard Law School in 2015 and at the University of Washington School of Law in 2014 and also taught comparative intellectual property laws at Georgetown University Law Center in 2007 and at Duke Law School in 2003. He has served as a civilian member of the Presidential Council of Intellectual Property, the President of the Korea Game Law & Policy Society, the Director of the SNU Center for Law & Technology, and a panel member of the WIPO Arbitration and Mediation Center.

Oskar Liivak
Professor of Law, *Cornell Law School, Cornell University*

Liivak, Professor of Law at Cornell Law School, graduated from Rutgers College with highest honors in 1994, received a PhD in 2000 in physics from Cornell University focusing on techniques for determining protein structure, and received a JD from the Yale Law School in 2005. From 2000 to 2001, he was a post-doctoral scientist working on physical realization of quantum computing in the Quantum Information Group at IBM's Almaden Research Center in San Jose, California. Prior to law school, he served as a patent agent in the Boston office of Fish and Richardson P.C. Most recently, Professor Liivak served as a law clerk to Judge Sharon Prost on the United States Court of Appeals for the Federal Circuit. Professor Liivak has published articles on patents and intellectual property law in the *Cornell Law Review*, the *Harvard Journal of Law & Technology*, the *UC Davis Law Review*, and many other publications.

Brian J. Love
Associate Professor of Law, *Santa Clara University School of Law*

Love is an associate professor at the Santa Clara University School of Law, where he serves as Co-Director of the High Tech Law Institute and teaches courses in patent law, intellectual property law, and remedies. His research focuses on patent law and policy, with an emphasis on the empirical study of patent litigation. His academic writing has been published by the law reviews of Stanford University, the University of Chicago, the University of Pennsylvania, the University of California Berkeley, the University of Virginia, and Washington University in St. Louis, among others. His articles have been cited by the U.S. Court of Appeals for the Federal Circuit, the U.S. Federal Trade Commission, the U.S. Department of Justice, the U.S. Council of Economic Advisers, and the U.S. Congressional Research Service. Love is also a frequent media commentator, with op-eds appearing in *The Wall Street Journal, USA Today, Los Angeles Times, The Hill, Wired,* and *TechCrunch.* Prior to joining Santa Clara, Professor Love was a lecturer and teaching fellow at Stanford Law School, where he oversaw the LLM Program in Law, Science & Technology. He also practiced law in Fish & Richardson's litigation department and served as a law clerk to the Hon. Dorothy W. Nelson of the U.S. Court of Appeals for the Ninth Circuit and to the Hon. David C. Godbey of the U.S. District Court for the Northern District of Texas.

Renato Nazzini
Professor of Law, *Dickson Poon School of Law, King's College London*

Nazzini joined King's College London as Professor of Law in 2012. Previously, he was Professor of Competition Law and Arbitration at the University of Southampton, which he joined from the Office of Fair Trading, then the UK competition authority (now the Competition and Markets Authority), where he was Deputy Director of the Legal and Policy Department and led or advised on major areas of enforcement and policy. His work included the review of the policy on abuse of dominance under Article 102 TFEU, which led to the adoption of the Commission Guidance Paper on Article 102 TFEU, and the formulation of the policy on actions for damages for competition infringements, which led to major reforms in the UK and in the EU. Professor Nazzini is currently a nongovernmental adviser to the International Competition Network (ICN), where he has been particularly active on the Unilateral Conduct Working Group and on the Merger Working Group. Professor Nazzini's research interests are in the areas of competition law, commercial arbitration, and ADR. His work on competition law has focused extensively on enforcement, remedies, and procedure. He is the author of *Competition Enforcement and Procedure* (2016), *The Foundations of European Union Competition Law: The Objective and Principles of Article 102* (2011), and *Concurrent Proceedings in Competition Law: Procedure, Evidence and Remedies* (2004). He is a general co-editor of Global Competition Litigation Review and a member of the editorial board of the European Business Law Review.

Yogesh Pai
Assistant Professor of Law, *National Law University, Delhi*

Pai specializes in intellectual property law and has research interests at the interface of intellectual property with competition, trade, and economic policy. He is the Co-Director of the Centre for Innovation, Intellectual Property and Competition (CIIPC) at National Law University, Delhi (NLU, Delhi). He is also the Thomas Edison Fellow (2017–18) at George Mason University, Washington D.C. Before joining NLU, Delhi, Professor Pai was coordinator of the Ministry of Human Resource Development Chair on IPR at NLU, Jodhpur. He was also the Faculty-in-Charge of *Trade, Law and Development*, rated among the top journals in international trade worldwide. His international work experience involved working with the South Centre, Geneva. He previously has worked with Centad, New Delhi, and has taught as a guest on the faculty at Indian Law Institute, New Delhi. Professor Pai consults with the World Trade Organization for Regional Trade Policy Courses and is a tutor with the WIPO Academy Distance Learning Programme. He has been a speaker on intellectual property issues in India and abroad. His distinguished academic paper presentations include those at the Intellectual Property Scholars Conference (New York 2017); ACRIALA – IPSA, Singapore Management University (2016, 2017); and the Centre for Asian Legal Studies, NUS, Singapore (2015). He has published in national and international journals, including *Oxford Journal of Antitrust Enforcement, Journal of World Intellectual Property, Journal of Indian Law Institute, Journal of Intellectual Property Rights, Journal of Indian Society of International Law, NUJS Law Review*, and *Jindal Global Law Review*.

Nicholas Petit
Professor of Law, *University of Liège School of Law*

Petit is Professor of Law at Liege University, Belgium and a research professor at the School of Law of the University of South Australia in Adelaide (UniSA). Professor Petit's research focuses on antitrust law, intellectual property, and law in a context of technological change. His recent written works deal with the legal challenges created by the introduction of artificial intelligence and robotics in society. He is also working on a book on technology platforms' competition. Professor Petit holds a PhD from the University of Liege (Belgium), an LLM from the College of Europe (Bruges), a master's degree from the University of Paris II, and an LLB from the University of Paris V. He practiced law with a leading U.S. law firm in Brussels and served as a clerk at the Commercial Chamber of the French Supreme Court. In 2005 he attended Harvard Law School's Visiting Researchers Programme. Professor Petit is a co-author of *EU Competition Law and Economics* (2012) and the author of *Droit européen de la concurrence* (2013), a monograph that was awarded the prize for the best law book of the year at the Constitutional Court in France. In 2017, he received the Global Competition Review award for academic excellence.

Peter George Picht
Professor, *University of Zurich*

Picht studied law at Munich University and Yale Law School, did his PhD (*summa cum laude*) at Munich University/the Max Planck Institute for Innovation and Competition, and holds a master's degree from Yale Law School. He has worked with the EU Commission's DG for Competition, with the Max Planck Institute for Innovation and Competition as a senior research fellow, and with other institutions, as well as with the law firms Allen & Overy LLP and Linklaters LLP. Professor Picht now holds a chair for commercial law at the University of Zurich and is head of the University's Centre for Intellectual Property and Competition Law (CIPCO). He remains affiliated with the Max Planck Institute as a research fellow. Professor Picht's academic teaching and writing, as well as his counseling activity, focus on intellectual property law, competition law, and international private and procedural law, in particular commercial arbitration (mainly IP and competition), trusts, and estates. In these fields, he has advised governments, companies, foundations, trusts, and other legal entities, as well as private persons and families. Professor Picht is admitted to the bar in Germany and Switzerland.

Christopher B. Seaman
Associate Professor of Law, *Washington and Lee University School of Law*

Seaman joined the Washington and Lee law faculty in 2012. His research and teaching interests include intellectual property, property, and civil procedure, with a particular focus on intellectual property litigation and remedies for the violation of intellectual property rights. Seaman's intellectual property-related scholarship has appeared or is forthcoming in a variety of law reviews and journals, including the *Virginia Law Review*, the *Iowa Law Review*, the *Washington Law Review*, the *BYU Law Review*, the *Harvard Journal of Law and Technology*, the *Yale Journal of Law and Technology*, and the *Berkeley Technology Law Review*. His empirical study of willful patent infringement and enhanced damages was selected as a winner of the Samsung-Stanford Patent Prize competition for outstanding new scholarship related to patent remedies, and his co-authored article on patent injunctions at the Federal Circuit was chosen as a winner of the Federalist Society's Young Legal Scholars Paper Competition. Seaman received his BA in 2000 from Swarthmore College and his JD in 2004 from the University of Pennsylvania Law School, where he was an executive editor of the *University of Pennsylvania Law Review* and a recipient of the Edwin R. Keedy Award. After a judicial clerkship with the Honorable R. Barclay Surrick of the U.S. District Court for the Eastern District of Pennsylvania, he practiced intellectual property law at Sidley Austin LLP in Chicago from 2005 to 2009. Prior to joining Washington and Lee's faculty, Professor Seaman was a visiting assistant professor at IIT Chicago-Kent College of Law and an adjunct professor at Loyola University Chicago School of Law.

Norman V. Siebrasse
Professor, *University of New Brunswick Faculty of Law*

Siebrasse joined UNB Law in 1993, after receiving an LLM from the University of Chicago and clerking at the Supreme Court of Canada for the Honorable Madam Justice McLachlin during the 1991 to 1992 term. His research and writing focuses on patent law, particularly pharmaceutical patent law, patent remedies, and the intersection of intellectual property law and commercial law. His blog, Sufficient Description, comments on recent Canadian patent law cases, and is widely read by the Canadian patent bar. His writing, including his blog, is regularly cited by the Canadian courts. He is an active member of the Intellectual Property Institute of Canada (the national association of intellectual property lawyers) and is a member of Life Sciences and Patent Legislation Committees.

Rafal Sikorski
Assistant Professor, *Adam Mickiewicz University in Poznań*

Sikorski is an assistant professor at the Adam Mickiewicz University in Poznań. He is also Senior Partner at SMM Legal in Poland, where he manages the Intellectual Property Department, advising clients on IP disputes and transactions, industrial property law, combating unfair competition, and the intricacies of competition law. Sikorski graduated from the Faculty of Law and Administration of Adam Mickiewicz University in Poznań in 1999. In 2000, he received the title of LLM in International Business Transactions from the Central European University in Budapest. Since 2005 he has held a PhD in legal science awarded by the Faculty of Law and Administration of Adam Mickiewicz University in Poznań. His scientific accomplishments include a number of publications on copyright law, industrial property law, unfair competition law, competition law, and private international law. He is currently co-editing a series entitled *An Outline of Intellectual Property Law* (*Zarys Prawa Własności Intelektualnej*). Within his scientific work, he mainly focuses on relations between competition law and intellectual property law, with a particular emphasis on standardization and patent pools. Additionally, Professor Sikorski deals with issues in determining the governing law for intellectual property contracts and infringements of such.

Masabumi Suzuki

Dean and Professor of Intellectual Property Law, *Nagoya University Graduate School of Law*

Suzuki is Dean and a professor of intellectual property Law at Nagoya University Graduate School of Law in Japan. Professor Suzuki is a member of the Intellectual Property Committee of the Industrial Structure Council at the Ministry of Economy, Trade and Industry (METI), and Deputy-Chair of the Subdivision on Copyright of the Council for Cultural Affairs at the Agency for Cultural Affairs in the Japanese Government. He also serves as a director of the Japan Association of Industrial Property Law, the Copyright Law Association of Japan, and the Japan Association of International Economic Law. Professor Suzuki has written and lectured widely on intellectual property law in Japanese and English. His publications in English include "Injunctive Relief for Patent Infringement: A New Trend in Japan?," "Enforcement of FRAND-encumbered SEPs," "International Investment Agreements, Intellectual Property Rights and Public Health," "Domestic Measures for Public Health Policy and International IP/Trade Law: The Case of the Australian Plain Packaging Act," and "Patent Enforcement in Japan" (co-written with Yoshiyuki Tamura). He also has edited several books including *Preventive Instruments of Social Governance* (2017), *Realization of Substantive Law through Legal Proceedings* (2017), and *Commentary on Trademark Act* (2015). Prior to entering academia, Professor Suzuki was an official at METI, where he served as Director of the Office of Intellectual Property Policy and in other positions.

David O. Taylor

Associate Professor of Law and Co-Director of the Tsai Center for Law, Science and Innovation, *Dedman School of Law, Southern Methodist University*

Taylor is an associate professor and founding Co-Director of the Tsai Center for Law, Science and Innovation at SMU Dedman School of Law. He serves on the Advisory Council of the U.S. Court of Appeals for the Federal Circuit, the Executive Board of the Institute for Law and Technology at the Center for American and International Law, the Amicus Committee and Patentable Subject Matter Task Force of the American Intellectual Property Law Association, and the Advisory Board of *The International Lawyer*. He has written and spoken extensively on patent law and policy, patent litigation, and civil procedure. He has published numerous articles in journals including the *Berkeley Technology Law Journal*, the *New York*

University Law Review, the *Connecticut Law Review*, the *Georgia Law Review*, and the *University of California Davis Law Review*, and has given presentations at law schools across the United States, including Boston College, Berkeley, Cardozo, Stanford, and Texas, and internationally in China, Taiwan, and Vietnam. He also serves as an expert and consultant in intellectual property disputes. Taylor is the recipient of a Thomas Edison Innovation Fellowship from George Mason University Antonin Scalia Law School's Center for the Protection of Intellectual Property. Before entering academia, Taylor clerked for the Honorable Sharon Prost of the U.S. Court of Appeals for the Federal Circuit, and engaged in patent litigation, licensing, and prosecution at the international law firm Baker Botts LLP. He earned his bachelor of science, *magna cum laude*, in mechanical engineering from Texas A&M University and his juris doctor, *cum laude*, from Harvard Law School.

Jacques de Werra

Professor of Contract and Intellectual Property Law, *University of Geneva*

de Werra has been Professor of Contract Law and Intellectual Property Law at the Law School of the University of Geneva since 2006 and Vice-Rector of the University since 2015. He completed his PhD thesis in copyright law while a visiting scholar at the Max-Planck Institute for IP, Competition and Tax Law in Munich in 1996. He was admitted to the Swiss bar (1999) and the New York bar (2002), and holds an LLM degree from Columbia Law School (2001). He was a faculty associate at Harvard's Berkman Center for Internet and Society and has held visiting professor positions at Stanford Law School, Nagoya University, and City University of Hong Kong. Professor de Werra's scholarly interests cover IP law, contract law, and Internet/IT and technology law. He has developed a particular expertise in IP commercial law and in ADR mechanisms for IP and technology disputes (specifically arbitration). He has published widely in leading law reviews (including the *Harvard Journal of Law and Technology* and the *Columbia VLA Journal of Law and the Arts*) and has authored or edited various books of reference, including the *Research Handbook on Intellectual Property Licensing* (2013) and (co-edited with Prof. Irene Calboli) *The Law and Practice of Trademark Transactions* (2016). He organizes the joint WIPO – University of Geneva Summer School on IP and the Geneva Internet law summer school. He is the scientific editor of an IP books series containing the proceedings of the annual IP conferences that he organizes at the University of Geneva.

Foreword

Patent systems are designed to provide incentives to innovate by temporarily protecting the intellectual property to which those innovations give rise. While not always perfectly calibrated, most patent systems historically have accomplished that goal. But as the nature of innovation has changed over the years, patent systems have struggled to adapt to those changes. Legal principles that were once quite good at striking a balance between too much patent protection and too little when applied to simple patented technology are less pertinent in our modern world of increasingly complex technology. We no longer live in a world of simple inventions where the patented technology provides most, if not all, of the value of an end product. We no longer live in a world where reasonable royalties for past infringement are readily calculable or where an injunction against ongoing infringement almost always makes sense.

We now live in a world of complex technology – computers operating with sophisticated software, smartphones and similar multifunction devices, interactive televisions, autonomous vehicles, virtual reality, and the "Internet of Things." Such complex technology creates complexities of a different sort for patent systems. A single end product (or even a single component of an end product) may contain multiple patented technologies, sometimes exponentially more than traditional machines or products. The law of patent remedies was crafted for simpler inventions; it does not neatly address the realities of current innovation.

Determining how our concepts of injunctions, reasonable royalties, lost profits, and enhanced damages should be applied in this new era is challenging. This is particularly true when it comes to properly valuing individual contributing pieces of patented technology. Assessing the value added by a patented invention to complex technology is necessary, but far from easy. And these challenges are magnified by the interaction of those remedies derived from patent law with those stemming from competition and contract law, particularly those contracts that patent holders enter into in return for designation of their patent as a standard-essential patent.

Compounding these challenges is the fact that, while patent laws and their attendant remedial principles are national, technology sales and, thus, a desire to encourage innovation, are global. Individual systems for patent remedies tailored to complex technologies on a national basis thus seem inadequate and short-sighted. Imposing one country's attempted solution on jurisdictions with different legal and economic traditions cannot be done, however. That is not the solution. Cross-fertilization of ideas presents an opportunity to search out best practices, which can then both be adopted and adapted as appropriate. Finding consensus on what those best practices are is no small task. Such an undertaking would require an international coalition of patent law and economic experts focused on harmonizing disparate patent systems while maintaining respect for each nation's values and policy goals.

The International Patent Remedies for Complex Products (INPRECOMP) project – involving an impressive group of twenty scholars from distinguished academic institutions in eleven countries – is taking aim at rethinking patent enforcement systems on a global scale. This book is an ambitious attempt to wrestle with the intricacies of intellectual property protection around the world and to seek international consensus on issues affecting patent remedies in the context of complex products.

The INPRECOMP participants have approached their challenging task in a thoughtful manner that is both academically rigorous and practical. I have had the pleasure of watching the INPRECOMP project in action. In March 2017, the INPRECOMP group presented its ideas and proposals for possible international harmonization to a panel of judges and patent law practitioners. I had the privilege to be among those before whom the group tested its concepts and from whom the group sought feedback. The work of the INPRECOMP participants, now reflecting that very feedback, is set forth in this work. This book represents substantial thought and effort directed to an important but very challenging goal. Careful consideration of the group's ideas will be edifying for judges, legislators, and practitioners alike, as patent disputes relating to complex technology become increasingly more international in scope.

Hon. Kathleen M. O'Malley
U.S. Court of Appeals for the Federal Circuit

Preface and Acknowledgments

This project on International Patent Remedies for Complex Products (INPRECOMP) has an ambitious objective – to engage intellectual property scholars worldwide on the topic of patent remedies for complex products, in order to identify areas of consensus along with topics needing further research and discussion. This project was made possible by a gift from Intel Corporation to the Center for Law, Science & Innovation (CLSI) at the Sandra Day O'Connor College of Law at Arizona State University. Intel provided the funding for a project (with the details to be determined by the CLSI) to advance and broaden scholarly research and dialogue on patent remedies for complex products. Intel encouraged us to involve scholars from as many different perspectives and countries as feasible. Other than that general direction, Intel played no role in the design, participant selection, topic choice, or work product of this project. We appreciate Intel's support of independent research, and we thank it for making this project possible.

A number of individuals played a central and indispensable role in this project, and each deserves accolades for the commitment, patience, and expertise he or she brought to the project. First and foremost, Brad Biddle, a Faculty Fellow of the ASU Center for Law, Science & Innovation, was key to both launching and administering the project. Brad first broached the subject of this project and made the initial contact with Intel. He operated as our de facto project coordinator, convening meetings and conference calls of our steering committee, which he chaired, pushing gently but firmly to ensure we stayed on schedule, and stepping in to help resolve any disagreements or problems along the way. Brad's enthusiasm and leadership for this project were, respectively, infectious and effective.

One of the most important things that Brad did at the outset was to recruit two subject matter experts to be the thought leaders of this project. These are law professors Jorge Contreras of the S.J. Quinney College of Law at the University of Utah and Norman Siebrasse of the University of New Brunswick, Faculty of Law. Jorge and Norman are not only tremendously knowledgeable experts on patents and patent remedies, but they are also committed to balance, objectivity, and scholarly excellence. Jorge's and Norman's impressive expertise, extensive contacts in the field, enthusiasm for the subject matter, and good-natured commitment to the project were critical for the project's success.

In addition to serving on the INPRECOMP steering committee over the two-plus years of the project's duration, Jorge and Norman were central in selecting the other faculty members of this project, whose biographies can be found above. They assembled an outstanding team of twenty leading intellectual property scholars from eleven countries in North America, Europe, and Asia. These scholars attended two 2-day meetings, one in London and one in Phoenix. After the London meeting, the group split into six working groups with overlapping membership, each dedicated to an individual chapter. The teams participated in numerous conference calls and email exchanges to develop and reach consensus on the material in this book, which was then circulated for comment to the entire group. Their time, expertise, and perspective gave this project its intellectual richness, breadth, and depth, for which we are enormously grateful.

Some of these academic participants did even more. We particularly appreciate the additional work of the following working group chairs: Tom Cotter (Chapter 1), Chris Seaman (Chapter 2), Colleen Chien (Chapter 3), Norman Siebrasse (Chapter 4), Jorge Contreras (Chapter 5), and Alison Jones and Renato Nazzini (Chapter 6). We also thank Alison Jones and Renato Nazzini for hosting and helping to organize the London meeting.

As the working groups began drafting the chapters that ended up being this book, we quickly realized that we needed a lead editor, someone who was knowledgeable about the subject matter and able to work with the author teams to coordinate consensus where it was possible and to identify and manage differences. We found the perfect person for this important role in Brian Love, Associate Professor of Law and Co-director of the High Tech Law Institute at the Santa Clara University School of Law, who was already a member of the INPRECOMP team. Brian did yeoman's work in collaborating with the teams of authors for each chapter, bringing the discussions to completion, and putting into writing for each chapter the text and recommendations upon which each chapter's authors could agree. This process involved a tremendous commitment of time and skill, which Brian provided with enthusiasm and excellence.

The other key player in bringing this book to fruition was Jay Jenkins, the Intellectual Property Director of the CLSI at ASU. Jay served as line editor, working closely with Brian to go through each chapter line-by-line to edit the text for clarity, consistency, and impact. Jay also worked in completing all the references, a daunting task given the different nations and languages of the primary materials used in the production of this work. Without Jay's tireless efforts, this book never would have seen the light of day, and we are very grateful for his dedication and effort.

Another important component of this project was the opportunity to "stress test" our initial ideas with a panel of eminent judges and a panel of leading practitioners. We provided the initial drafts of our chapters and then invited these legal experts to critique, question, and challenge our initial work at the Phoenix meeting. Our judicial panel consisted of the Hon. Marsha Berzon of the U.S. Court of Appeals for the Ninth Circuit, the Hon. Klaus Grabinski of the German Federal Court of Justice (Bundesgerichtshof), the Hon. Kathleen O'Malley of the U.S. Court of Appeals for the Federal Circuit, and the Hon. James Robart of the U.S. District Court for the Western District of Washington. The practitioner panel consisted of Tina Chappell from Intel, Luke McLeroy from Avanci, Mark Selwyn from WilmerHale, and Richard Stark from Cravath, Swaine & Moore. The feedback received from these experts in private practice and the judiciary were extremely insightful and helpful, and greatly assisted the project team in understanding the practical and legal issues presented by patent damages for complex products. We additionally thank Judge O'Malley for writing the preface to this book.

Finally, I would like to thank the staff of the Center for Law, Science & Innovation for their administrative support of this project. Center Director Lauren Burkhart negotiated the agreement with Intel, was in charge of the budgeting for the project, participated on the project steering committee, and organized the meetings, conference calls, and other activities involved with the project. She was ably assisted by Center Coordinator Debb Relph, who among other things coordinated travel arrangements, reimbursement, and logistics. Their excellent assistance was essential for the smooth and successful implementation of this project.

Typically, at the end of a long list of acknowledgments like this, there would be a statement that all errors and misunderstandings are the sole responsibility of the author. That is not possible here because there is no single "author" of this book. Rather, it represents a group process involving a disparate set of knowledgeable experts that produced its chapters as consensus documents, not an easy or simple achievement. In fact, it is probably safe to say that no single member of the team is perfectly satisfied, or even fully agrees with, everything said and how it is said in this book. Rather, this book is part of what we hope will be an ongoing and worldwide consensus-building process. This work does not aspire to represent the final word on these important issues. Rather, by advancing areas of consensus and identifying areas needing further research, we hope we have produced something that can be studied, referenced, quoted, critiqued, agreed or disagreed with, and ultimately further advanced, all with the goal of improving patent remedies for complex products around the world.

Gary Marchant
Regent's Professor of Law and Faculty Director of the
Center for Law, Science and Innovation
Arizona State University
Sandra Day O'Connor College of Law

Executive Summary

In each of the first five chapters of this volume, we summarize the current state of the law of patent remedies among leading jurisdictions, articulate the principal arguments for and against different remedies-related practices adopted in various countries, and provide consensus-based recommendations for improving (and generally harmonizing) the award of remedies for patent infringement. In addition, we identify areas where further research is needed. Below, we briefly summarize the principal recommendations made in each chapter.

CHAPTER 1: REASONABLE ROYALTIES

Chapter 1 addresses "reasonable royalty" damages.

BASIC PRINCIPLES FOR CALCULATING A REASONABLE ROYALTY:

Chapter 1 principally recommends that courts replace the so-called *Georgia-Pacific* factors used in the United States (and analogous factors used outside the United States) with the following three steps for calculating reasonable royalty damages:

(1) ***Calculate the incremental value of the invention and divide it appropriately between the parties.*** A license for the use of a patented technology typically requires the licensee to share with the licensor some portion of the incremental value the licensee derives or expects to derive from the use of that technology. To ensure that a reasonable royalty for the unauthorized use of a patented technology accurately reflects this incremental value, ideally a court would (1) estimate the difference between the value the infringer derived from the use of the patented invention (as distinct from the value contributed by other features of the infringing end product), and the value the infringer would have derived by using the next-best available noninfringing alternative instead; (2) divide that differential value between the patent owner and the infringer; and (3) as an aid in carrying out this division, consider any relevant evidence, including possibly

the use of a rebuttable presumption that the parties would have agreed, *ex ante*, to an even (50/50) split.

(2) **Assess market evidence.** In negotiating licenses for the use of patented technologies, parties often consider the rates and other terms disclosed in relevant comparable licenses (or, where applicable, the rates charged by relevant patent pools or disclosed in publications of industry standard rates). Courts also should consider such evidence for purposes of calculating reasonable royalties for the unauthorized use of patented technologies, albeit subject to appropriate adjustments and with due appreciation for the potential limitations of such evidence.

(3) **Comparison.** When it is feasible and cost justified, courts should carry out both steps described above – each one acting as a "check" on the accuracy of the other – and then attempt to reconcile or adjust the results, as the evidence warrants. That said, one can expect only that courts do the best they can with the evidence available to them. Thus, when the evidence necessary to carry out step 2 is available but the evidence necessary to carry out step 1 is not – as will likely often be the case in litigation involving complex products – courts may need to rely exclusively on market evidence. (The converse will be true when the available evidence relates only to step 1, not 2.)

PATENTED ALTERNATIVES:

A conceptual difficulty with step 1 of the above framework arises if the next-best noninfringing alternative is, itself, also patented. It is not at all uncommon that the best substitutes for a patented technology are also patented, as several inventors devise different solutions to the same problem. One possibility is that in such a case the value of the patented invention is zero, on the view that the infringing user in the hypothetical negotiation should be imagined to play one patentee off against another until the patentee is haggled down to its minimum willingness to accept. By the same token, if the infringed technology was not quite as good as the patented alternative, the value of the infringed technology would be zero. Chapter 1 recommends that courts reject this approach, on the ground that although it makes sense from a static welfare perspective, it provides a facially inadequate incentive to invent (zero compensation) and therefore appears inconsistent with the conventionally understood purpose of the patent system.

DIVIDING INCREMENTAL VALUE:

Chapter 1 additionally recommends that, to the extent possible, a split of the incremental profit should reflect the value of any ancillary services (such as marketing) or risks that either the patent owner or the infringer, in fact, undertook. While courts should permit the parties to introduce any competent evidence on this issue, a fact finder may also wish to consider empirical findings that people in Western societies generally view a 50/50 split of benefits as fair, and that economists often use the Nash Bargaining Solution in modeling bargaining behavior.

Moreover, when courts use a hypothetical bargaining construct to split incremental value, Chapter 1 recommends that courts adopt a "contingent *ex ante* approach" under which the hypothetical negotiation is generally assumed to take place before any sunk costs are incurred, but with the benefit of *ex post* information. The rationale for this approach is that the bargain must be assumed to take place *ex ante*, so that the patentee is not entitled to extract any holdup value; but at the same time, using *ex post* information more accurately reflects the true incremental value of the invention, and so provides a more accurate reward to the patentee.

In addition, courts should consider comparables and other market evidence with caution. Such evidence often may be the best that is available, and even when there is other evidence of the value of the technology over alternatives, it may still be useful to consider market evidence by way of comparison. But courts should be cognizant that there are significant practical and conceptual problems involved with using comparable licenses – even "established" ones – as evidence of a reasonable royalty.

EVIDENTIARY GATEKEEPING AND THE ENTIRE MARKET VALUE RULE:

Chapter 1 also recommends that in jurisdictions employing juries to decide patent cases, courts should require patentees to present royalty evidence using the smallest saleable patent-practicing unit, rather than the entire market value of a larger complex end product, as the royalty base. Framing damages by reference to the value of the entire accused product may have an undue influence on jurors (sometimes known as "anchoring") in cases where the asserted patent covers just one of many components or features that comprise the entire product, and in such cases may lead to damages awards that are overcompensatory.

Finally, Chapter 1 recommends that courts consider whether individual pieces of expert evidence satisfy a basic threshold of quality in addition to separately examining the overall sufficiency of all relevant evidence. In the absence of a jury or other fact finder distinct from the trial-level adjudicator of questions of law, there is probably less significance to the distinction between (1) the ultimate assessment of the overall sufficiency of evidence to support a damages award and (2) gatekeeping for the relevance and reliability of expert testimony. But although the particular standard for expert testimony gatekeeping has been controversial within the United States, something like *Daubert*-style review might generally be useful even in jurisdictions that do not try patent cases to juries.

CHAPTER 2: LOST PROFITS AND DISGORGEMENT

Chapter 2 addresses remedies that either (1) award as damages the profits that the patent owner would have earned absent infringement (lost profits), or (2) award to the patent owner the profits earned by the infringing party (disgorgement).

AVAILABILITY OF LOST PROFITS:

Chapter 2 recommends that a patentee's lost profits (including from lost sales and price erosion) should be the preferred measure of damages when a patentee can establish harm in a product market due to the infringement.

CAUSATION AND NONINFRINGING ALTERNATIVES:

Chapter 2 additionally recommends that lost profits should generally be available whenever a practicing patentee can demonstrate "but for" causation by a preponderance of the evidence, rather than only when the patentee can satisfy more detailed standards or requirements, such as the *Panduit* factors presently used in the United States. This chapter further recommends that courts should consider the availability and substitutability of noninfringing alternatives when analyzing "but for" causation, and overrule decisions (such as *United Horse-Shoe* in the UK) that hold to the contrary. If the infringer could have competed with the patentee by offering a noninfringing alternative to the patented invention, the patentee would have lost fewer sales (and thus profits) absent the infringement. Even an imperfect substitute that provides some, but not all, of the functionality of the patented invention can affect both the price of the patented product and consumer choice.

LOST PROFITS FOR UNPATENTED PRODUCTS:

In addition to profits on lost sales of patented products, Chapter 2 recommends that patentees should be permitted to recover losses associated with (1) sales of products that incorporate both infringing and noninfringing components, (2) additional contemporaneous sales of distinct but related items, and (3) anticipated future sales of replacement or repair parts, provided that the patentee can demonstrate that such sales were reasonably foreseeable by an infringing competitor in the relevant market.

AVAILABILITY OF DISGORGEMENT:

In jurisdictions where disgorgement is an available remedy, Chapter 2 recommends that the grant of accounting be within the discretion of the court, rather than automatic, given the potential burden on the infringer in taking an accounting.

Courts also should require patentees to elect between an accounting and damages; they should not be permitted to pursue both simultaneously.

DIFFERENTIAL PROFIT METHOD:

Chapter 2 additionally recommends that jurisdictions permitting disgorgement adopt a differential profit approach to calculating the infringer's profits. Rather than requiring the infringer to disgorge the entire profit made on an infringing product, courts should limit disgorgement recoveries to the difference between the infringer's actual profits and the profits it would have made had it used the best noninfringing alternative. A contrary rule – such as the accounting profit approach or the U.S. approach in design patent cases – can result in disgorgement of profits that are not causally attributable to the infringement, and thus will put the patentee in a better position than it would have been but for the infringement.

CHAPTER 3: ENHANCED DAMAGES, LITIGATION COST RECOVERY, AND INTEREST

Chapter 3 addresses remedies beyond reasonable royalties and profits.

ENHANCED DAMAGES:

Chapter 3 recommends that when enhanced (or "punitive") damages are awarded, they should be calculated consistent with the objectives of the patent system – for example, by weighing the ability of such awards to deter opportunistic infringement against their countervailing tendency to discourage the dissemination of technological information via patent disclosures – rather than on the basis of subjective notions of retributive punishment.

LITIGATION COST RECOVERY:

Chapter 3 additionally recommends that when litigation costs are awarded to prevailing parties, such awards should aim to compensate for the reasonable and proportionate costs actually incurred by the prevailing party in a meaningful manner unless equity prescribes otherwise, rather than only partially (as is often the case in practice). Moreover, in countries in which fee shifting is not presently the norm, legislatures and courts should consider experimenting with more generous fee shifting rules, as well as discovery reforms designed to reduce the risk that the stronger party will make unnecessary and excessive expenditures with the expectation of reimbursement.

INTEREST:

Chapter 3 recommends that courts be required to award pre- and post-judgment compound interest, nominally at rates that reflect the infringer's cost of borrowing. To the extent such reforms would be difficult to implement in the short run, legislatures should (as a second-best solution) periodically reconsider statutory interest rates to ensure that they do not differ substantially from market rates.

CHAPTER 4: INJUNCTIVE RELIEF

Chapter 4 addresses the law and policy of injunctive relief, focusing primarily on permanent injunctions.

BASIC PRINCIPLES FOR INJUNCTIVE RELIEF:

Chapter 4 principally recommends that courts should not automatically issue injunctive relief in all cases in which a patentee prevails in a suit for infringement. Instead, courts should have and, in appropriate circumstances, exercise discretion to deny injunctive relief when issuance of an injunction would otherwise generate costs or burdens for others that are disproportionate to the nature of the adjudged infringement and to the noncompensable harms the patentee would suffer in the absence of an injunction. Further, courts should be afforded the flexibility and discretion to tailor injunctive relief in appropriate circumstances to avoid imposing unnecessary hardship on infringers or the general public.

PROPORTIONALITY:

In assessing whether the negative effects of the injunction on enjoined parties would be disproportionate to the nature of the infringement and any noncompensable harm that the patentee will experience without injunctive relief, Chapter 4 additionally recommends that: (1) courts consider only those relevant negative effects on enjoined parties or the general public that have some reasonable likelihood of actually occurring if adjudged infringers and third parties take reasonable mitigating measures in relation to an injunction; and (2) courts consider only the relative, as opposed to absolute, sizes of the patentee's harm and an injunction's negative effects.

TAILORING INJUNCTIVE RELIEF:

Chapter 4 additionally recommends that courts consider whether tailoring injunctive relief – for example, by staying an injunction for a period of time to allow redesign of an infringing component of a complex product – may avoid or mitigate the negative effects an injunction otherwise might impose. Moreover, courts should consider tailoring injunctions in the normal course, even when a proportionality-based test is otherwise satisfied.

ONGOING ROYALTY IN LIEU OF INJUNCTIVE RELIEF:

Chapter 4 recommends that when injunctive relief is not granted (and damages have not separately compensated for future infringement) courts should award as a substitute additional monetary damages in the form of an "ongoing reasonable royalty." This ongoing royalty should be calculated in accordance with the principle for determining a "reasonable royalty" for past infringement, without any special enhancement due to the ongoing reasonable royalty's association with activity that occurs after the judgment of infringement.

CHAPTER 5: THE EFFECT OF FRAND COMMITMENTS ON PATENT REMEDIES

Chapter 5 addresses a special category of cases in which an asserted patent is, or has been declared to be, essential to the implementation of a collaboratively developed voluntary consensus standard, and the holder of that patent has agreed to license it to implementers of the standard on terms that are fair, reasonable, and nondiscriminatory (FRAND). Both as a matter of patent law, contract law, and competition law, the existence of such a FRAND commitment may affect a patent holder's entitlement to monetary damages and injunctive relief.

MONETARY DAMAGES:

Chapter 5 recommends that courts assessing FRAND royalty rates should reject strict application of the *Georgia-Pacific* framework, and instead select whatever methodology for calculating FRAND rates is best supported by the available evidence. Depending on the evidence available, courts may choose to rely on sufficiently comparable license agreements covering the same patents, general consensus on aggregate royalty rates for an overall standard or technology, and one or both of the "bottom-up" and "top-down" royalty calculation methodologies.

INJUNCTIONS:

Chapter 5 additionally recommends that courts place reasonable conditions on the issuance of injunctions against the infringement of standards-essential patents – such as those discussed in Chapter 4 – even absent a violation of competition law. When balancing equities between the parties, this chapter additionally recommends that courts incorporate the procedures laid out in *Huawei* v. *ZTE* or under the law of Japan or Korea. While these procedural analyses were developed with potential violations of competition law or contract law in mind, they nonetheless model a well-functioning bilateral relationship within the standard-setting context and, thus, are relevant to a full and fair assessment of the appropriateness of equitable relief.

Introduction

Information and communications technology products are indispensable tools of modern life across the globe. Smartphones and laptops connect to a vast global computing infrastructure. Sophisticated medical equipment is ubiquitous in hospitals. Robotics increasingly enable manufacturing of every kind of product. Sensor networks facilitate the flow of urban traffic. The emergence of autonomous vehicles, products enabling augmented and virtual reality, the broad array of "Internet of Things" devices, and countless other innovations suggest that these kinds of products will continue to play an ever-growing role in the modern global economy.

These products are technological marvels, comprising thousands of different technologies, developed over decades by hundreds of different companies, all working together seamlessly. In a sense, they are legal marvels as well. Their design, manufacture, and utilization take place in a legal and economic environment that is itself complex and full of hazards.

One crucial part of this environment is the global patent system. Just as smartphones include thousands of technologies, they incorporate inventions claimed in not just thousands, but tens or even hundreds of thousands of individual patents issued by patent offices across the globe. For that reason, smartphones and most other information and communications technology products can be viewed as "complex products" from a legal perspective as well – particularly when considered relative to pharmaceuticals and mechanical devices that, while equally advanced technologically, are often covered by just a handful of patents.

The reality that innovative companies now routinely bring these kinds of complex products to market in the midst of this daunting patent landscape raises a number of challenging questions with respect to how the law should value patents and provide remedies for their infringement.

For example, how should courts and, where applicable, juries calculate damages for infringement of one patent out of the thousands of (often complementary) inventions incorporated in a device? How can courts and juries tell if one feature among hundreds drove the sale of the entire product? Should patent law take into consideration that it might not be possible, let alone cost effective, for a product manufacturer in a fast-moving field to license all of the thousands of patents embodied in its product, even prior to beginning development? Should an injunction be granted to prevent the use of a patented technology that covers a minor feature of a complex product, when the effect of the injunction would be to keep the entire product itself off the market? How (if at all) can the risks of patent holdup be reduced without generating substantial error costs or other unintended negative consequences?

Our aim in this book is to begin to address these questions systematically by setting forth both the current state of the law and an agenda for future research. We identify areas of existing consensus; build new consensus where possible; identify areas of disagreement; and specify the nature and direction of research that would be required to help resolve those disagreements. We hope that this book will assist policymakers, judges, lawyers, and others throughout the world to address these and other issues in a rational, predictable, and cost-effective manner, and that it will stimulate fruitful discussion of our recommendations and research proposals.

Before we begin that process, however, we flag for readers some important premises that underlie the analysis in this volume.

First, we take an instrumental view of the patent system. The most commonly articulated policy justifications for having a patent system are that patents provide an incentive to invest in the creation of novel, useful, and nonobvious inventions, as well as an incentive to disclose those inventions to the public so that others may learn from them, improve upon them, design around them, license them, and, once they expire, freely practice them. At the same time, patents give rise to a variety of social costs, sometimes including monopoly and other access costs, transaction costs, and administrative costs. The ideal patent system therefore would maximize the surplus of social benefits over social costs, in comparison with alternatives such as public or private funding, grants, prizes, tax credits, first-mover advantages, trade secrecy, and contract. All of these sometimes conflicting objectives are based on an instrumental view of the patent system, in which patents are justified as private rights granted in order to advance the public good. While this view is not universally accepted, it is the mainstream position, and we adopt it accordingly.

That said, we harbor no illusions that the current patent system is ideal, according to that definition, or even that the ideal system is practically attainable. Although the state of both theoretical and empirical economics continues to advance, the accurate quantification of benefits and costs with regard to any social policy often remains elusive. Given these limitations, as well as individuals' often differing value systems and the difficulty of reducing these values to any common metric, reasonable minds frequently will disagree over whether the likely effect of a proposed modification to existing patent law on balance would be beneficial or detrimental. Nevertheless, some general idea that patent rights are intended to serve the public good that comes from invention is helpful. We thus believe that, its limitations notwithstanding, the legal policy analysis that we offer here can assist policymakers in predicting whether various applications or modifications of patent law, particularly the law of patent remedies, are likely to move toward or away from the hypothetical ideal.

Second, we take substantive (i.e., non-remedial) patent law as given. Though we acknowledge that the existing patent system is imperfect, for the purposes of this project we take substantive patent law as given, and seek to identify remedies that operate in tandem with the substantive law. For example, it is not clear whether the existing patent system provides the optimal incentive to invent. Perhaps the patent term should be shorter, or longer, or the scope of patents narrower, or broader. We do not delve into these contentious issues. Rather our approach is to consider how the law of remedies, when applied to patent law, may improve the overall patent system.

We take the view that legislatures and courts should address perceived flaws in substantive patent law by modifying it directly, not by modifying the law of remedies to mitigate substantive flaws indirectly. For example, it is not our view that courts should seek to correct for flaws in the law of patent scope by awarding minimal or nominal damages for the infringement of a patent that is valid only because the law of nonobviousness is too weak to prevent the grant of a weak patent. Granted, legislative change can be difficult to achieve in practice; and there may be cases in which correcting a problem through modulation of remedies would be the best practical solution. But there is at this point nothing approaching a consensus as to which aspects of substantive patent law are flawed, much less which of those flaws are best corrected by modifying the law of remedies.

We thus address patent remedies as a field unto itself. There are many difficult remedial issues to be addressed even taking substantive patent law as given. Our aim in this book is to make the current remedial system the best it can be. Consequently, while we do not reject this alternative approach in principle, we do not pursue it in this book.

Third, we try to balance the theoretical with the practical. In making the recommendations found in the chapters that follow, we strive to embrace the tension between optimal and realistic reforms in at least two important ways. First, we recognize that there is generally a trade-off between accuracy and administrability. For example, as more effort is devoted to improving the accuracy of damages calculations, administrative costs are likely to rise, and at some point the cost may outweigh the benefit. The law of patent remedies must negotiate various trade-offs among several important considerations, among them accuracy, predictability, administrability, and the risk of error and other unintended consequences. Second, we acknowledge that complete harmonization across the globe is unlikely. The patent laws of many nations are infused with long-standing, generally applicable legal traditions and rules that, in practice, are unlikely to change in the foreseeable future. For example, as discussed in Chapter 3, while enhanced damages are regularly awarded in the United States for willful or bad-faith infringement, most other countries have not traditionally awarded enhanced damages to any great extent; conversely fee shifting is the default in many jurisdictions, but it is exceptional in in the United States. In addition, the United States routinely uses juries to assess damages, while most other countries never do. Legal systems also differ significantly with regard to the use of expert witnesses and the extent of pretrial discovery, both of which affect the information available to fact finders assessing monetary remedies. Given these differences, what may appear to be the best practice for one legal system may not be optimal for another. Accordingly, the best practical approach to various issues may differ among jurisdictions.

Further, we recognize that complete harmonization may not be desirable even if it were possible. We cannot always confidently predict the consequences of our own recommendations, and some degree of experimentation among jurisdictions may be useful in testing what works and what does not. In our experience, courts adjudicating patent matters concerning complex products in different jurisdictions are generally aware of what their counterparts in other parts of the world are doing and at least occasionally consider alternative approaches when novel issues arise. Thus, an experimentalist approach that invites a diversity of solutions to common problems may eventually result in the adoption of optimal solutions around the world.

Our proposals therefore attempt a balance. While we will generally suggest what we believe to be the best reform, we also will provide alternatives where that first-best solution is likely not attainable.

Fourth, we do not consider extraterritorial application of national law. Though our project is international in scope, we take no position on how nations should handle infringing conduct that crosses territorial borders. A common scenario raising these concerns is when product supply chains involve more than one nation, and thus plausibly give rise to causes of action for infringement in multiple jurisdictions, as well as to the prospect that a patentee may try to enforce in one jurisdiction a remedy obtained in another jurisdiction. Yet another scenario arises when harm occurring outside a nation's territory is plausibly caused by infringing conduct that itself took place within the nation. We consider the legal issues raised in such circumstances (among them, international exhaustion, proximate causation, conflicts of law, comity principles, and international trade agreements) to be beyond the scope of this project.

Fifth, the focus of this book is on remedies for the infringement of what are generally known as "utility" patents, which cover inventions. We do not address so-called design patents, which are also known as industrial designs and design rights, and which are themselves subject to a rich body of law and ongoing debate and discussion. Nor do we cover utility models (sometimes referred to as petit patents), which are generally understood to convey protection without active examination or review by a national patent office. While we acknowledge that all of these additional patent-like rights may be implicated in complex products, along with copyrights, trade secrets, trade dress, trademarks, and the like, and it may be fruitful to pursue a cross-border analysis of other intellectual property rights in the future, such an analysis is beyond the scope of our current project.

Finally, we note that the chapters that follow assume a degree of familiarity with theoretical concepts such as patent "holdup" and "holdout," as well as a basic understanding of competition law. Readers who are not familiar with these concepts may wish first to skip ahead to Chapters 6 and 7 before returning to Chapter 1. Chapter 6 provides a general overview of the intersection of patent law and competition law, and Chapter 7 summarizes the academic literature on holdup and holdout. Both chapters are different from the initial five, in that they are primarily descriptive in nature and do not make normative recommendations. That said, both chapters do recommend avenues for future research.

1

Reasonable Royalties

Thomas F. Cotter, John M. Golden, Oskar Liivak, Brian J. Love,
Norman V. Siebrasse, Masabumi Suzuki, and David O. Taylor

1.1 PRELIMINARY MATTERS

This section will briefly describe (a) the extent to which reasonable royalties are awarded in the major jurisdictions for which descriptive statistics are available; (b) the principal theoretical justifications for awarding them; and (c) at a very general level, the principal methods for calculating them.

1.1.1 *Empirical Literature*

The empirical literature on reasonable royalties consists largely of descriptive statistics reporting median, average, or largest-ever patent damages awards for selected countries. These statistics provide insight into different jurisdictions' approaches and priorities related to awarding damages.

The most extensive literature on this subject pertains to the United States. According to a 2014 Lex Machina Patent Litigation Damages Report, for example, in 708 U.S. patent cases filed and terminated from 2000 to 2013, district courts awarded over $8 billion in reasonable royalties, slightly less than $3 billion in lost profits, and slightly more than $2 billion in compensatory lump sum damages for which "the specific sub-type (reasonable royalties or lost profits) is not specified or the apportionment of the award between sub-types is not specified."[1] Lex Machina's list of median reasonable royalty, lost profit, and compensatory lump sum awards from 2000 to 2013 indicates that reasonable royalty awards are more common than lost profits awards, but that in some years the median lost profit award exceeded the median reasonable royalty award.[2] Lex Machina's Patent Litigation Year in Review 2016 reports median reasonable royalty damages in 2016 of $3,552,600, based on

---

[1] Byrd et al. 2014, 1–4.
[2] *See id.* at 6.

thirty-six cases; median lost profits damages of $1,631,231, based on eight cases; and median "Other/Mixed Damages" of $67,785, based on eighteen cases.[3]

PricewaterhouseCoopers (PwC) also publishes annual patent litigation reports. However, PwC reports median patent damages awards in the United States (excluding summary and default judgments) without separately accounting for lost profits and reasonable royalties. Interestingly, PwC's reported median award for 1997–2016 ($5.8 million in 2016 dollars) is considerably higher than the medians reported by Lex Machina for 2000–2015, most likely due to methodological differences between the two studies.[4] PwC also reports that in 80 percent of the cases in which courts awarded damages to practicing entities from 2007 to 2016 they awarded reasonable royalties.[5] (Courts awarded lost profits in 40 percent of these cases; the percentages exceed 100 percent because courts sometimes award lost profits on a portion of infringing sales and reasonable royalties on the remainder.) Further, although nonpracticing entities (NPEs) had a lower win rate than practicing entities during the time period studied, the median award to NPEs that prevailed at trial from 2012 to 2016 was almost four times the median award to practicing entities ($15.7 million versus $4.1 million).[6] Awards to NPEs almost always consist of reasonable royalties, rather than lost profits.

For other countries, less data is available, and the data that is available is generally less precise. Studies of Japanese damages awards indicate that reasonable royalty awards make up a plurality of all such awards[7] but that the amounts awarded tend to be low by U.S. standards. For example, according to a 2014 study of all sixty-eight cases from January 1, 1999, to March 5, 2013, in which Japanese courts awarded reasonable royalties, in only five cases did the award exceed ¥200,000,000 (equal to about U.S. $1.7 million).[8] The royalty rate was 5 percent in 28 percent of cases, 3 percent in 22 percent, and 10 percent in 16 percent (based on the value of the infringer's sales revenue from the infringing product). Like the PwC studies of U.S. damages, the reports of which we are aware on average or median damages awards in France do not distinguish between royalty and lost

[3]   *See* Howard & Maples 2016, 32.

[4]   For discussion of some differences in methodology, *see* Cotter & Golden 2018, 15 n.65.

[5]   We use the phrase "courts award" above even though in the majority of U.S. cases a jury awards damages. A judge ultimately must decide whether or not to enter final judgment in accordance with the verdict and the applicable rules of civil procedure.

[6]   *See* Barry et al. 2017, 9–11, 16.

[7]   *See* Matsunaka 2004, based on a review of all cases "published in the list of IPR related judgments on the Supreme Court website, in which the right holder claimed damages relating to IP ... and for which judgment affirming all or part of the claim was rendered during the period from January 1, 1998, to December 31, 2003," reporting that reasonable royalty awards made up the plurality in both patent (forty out of seventy-nine) and utility model (twenty-two out of forty-two) cases from 1999 to 2003.

[8]   Second Subcommittee of the Second Patent Committee 2014 (in Japanese); Cotter 2015 (discussing this article). *See also* Nakamura 2014, 407–10 (listing all Japanese patent damages judgments from January 1, 2003 to January 30, 2014); Yamaguchi 2016, 136 (reporting that there were thirteen first instance patent damages judgments in 2014, the top one being in the amount of ¥1,568,040,000, equal to about $13.3 million as of December 21, 2016).

profits awards.[9] In China, statutory damages predominate and awards of reasonable royalties are comparatively rare.[10]

1.1.2 *Theoretical Justifications*

As noted in the Introduction, for purposes of this project we take the substantive law of patents as a given, and do not advise courts to use the law of remedies to correct for perceived flaws in the substantive law. It follows from this premise that, in general, the law of patent damages should work to preserve the patent incentive, such as it is, by restoring the patent owner to the position it would have occupied, but for the infringement. Consistent with this rationale, courts and other observers often view reasonable royalty awards as a substitute for the royalty the patent owner would have earned, and that the infringer would have paid, absent the infringement. Commentators nevertheless sometimes express concern that such a standard threatens to encourage infringement (and to discourage *ex ante* negotiation), since it leaves the infringer no worse off for having infringed. This concern is particularly applicable if the royalty award is exactly the same as the royalty the patent owner would have negotiated, if the infringement was intentional, and if the infringer rationally could expect to avoid detection some nonzero percent of the time.[11] In addition, the infringer may avoid some of the risks that a real-world licensee would incur[12] – though of course, if the infringer is sued, it may wind up incurring substantial attorney fees, which it otherwise could have avoided, to

[9] *See, e.g.,* Dumont 2015 (reporting mean and median damages of €323,270 and €60,000, respectively, based on analysis of "483 patent infringement suits encompassing 673 patents" filed in the Tribunal de la grande instance de Paris from 2008 to 2013). *But see* République Française, Ministère du Redressement Productifs 2014, 58, 154–56 (in a study comparing awards in France, Germany, and the United Kingdom from January 1, 2010 to August 1, 2013, and believed to cover approximately 25 percent of all decisions rendered during the applicable time periods, reporting inter alia that 36 percent of reasonable royalty awards in France and 50 percent of such awards in Germany were for more than €100,000). For discussion of other French studies, *see* Cotter & Golden 2018, 17.

[10] *See* Cotter & Golden 2018, 18 (citing literature).

[11] This underdeterrence concern is likely to be less pronounced in cases in which the patent owner seeks an award of lost profits rather than reasonable royalties, because a patent owner presumably would seek lost profits only when it would have refused to license the infringer at all, due to the patent owner's or its exclusive licensee's superior efficiency in producing the patented product. *See* Blair & Cotter 2005, 58. In addition, concerns that a reasonable royalty might discourage patent owners from commercializing their technology, by not taking the value of commercialization efforts into account, should be alleviated if the fact finder considers the impact such investments would have had on the bargain the patentee would have struck *ex ante*, including its timing and the relevant information set; the appropriate division of the value of the invention between the parties; and the selection of appropriate comparator licenses. *See infra* Sections 1.3.1 through 1.3.6.

[12] For example, in many countries a licensee may be able to avoid paying royalties once the patent is invalidated, but it would be unable to recover back the royalties it paid prior to invalidation. By contrast, an infringer who challenges validity can avoid paying royalties altogether if the patent is invalidated (and in some countries with bifurcated infringement and validity proceedings, the "infringer" may even be entitled to recover back any damages it paid prior to invalidation). In addition,

defend itself.[13] To the extent that restorative damages risk underdeterring infringement, the law in the United States already ensures that royalty awards will not be exactly the same as what would have been negotiated, because the royalty awards must be calculated based on an assumption that the patent in question is valid and infringed, whereas in actual negotiations the parties commonly reduce the royalty based on the possibility of invalidity and noninfringement.[14] In addition, to address the risk of underdeterrence due to nondetection, policymakers could authorize courts to (1) grant injunctions, (2) award the disgorgement of the infringer's profits, (3) shift fees to the prevailing party, (4) impose criminal sanctions, or (5) award enhanced damages. Other chapters of this book discuss these alternatives in depth. However, as specifically discussed in Chapter 3, many countries decline to award enhanced or punitive damages on public policy grounds – though in some of these countries, courts occasionally award reasonable royalties above the "normal" rate to reflect the infringer's avoidance of risks that a good-faith licensee would have incurred.[15]

Alternatively, one could view reasonable royalties as a form of restitution, in the sense that the award forces the infringer to pay back the royalty it wrongfully withheld from the patentee.[16] Whether the characterization of royalties as restorative or restitutionary makes any practical difference may depend on whether the focus is on awarding the royalty the parties *would have* negotiated absent the infringement, or the royalty the infringer *should be required to pay* in light of some normative criterion. The "hypothetical bargain" or "willing licensor-willing licensee" approach, as it is often applied in the United States, might seem to be an example of the former approach, insofar as it attempts to construct the terms of the bargain the parties themselves would have negotiated prior to the date of infringement. But even that approach does not construct the exact bargain the parties would have made, because the hypothetical negotiation assumes the patent in question was valid and infringed, as discussed above. Without these assumptions, there would appear to be little difference between

---

an intentional infringer may be aware from the time it begins infringing that there is a market for the patented product – unlike a licensee, who at the time the license is concluded may face an uncertain demand for the product – and may avoid other disadvantages, such as upfront royalty payments or submitting to periodic inspections by the patentee.

[13] See AIPLA 2015, I-105–8 (reporting that the median cost of litigating a patent infringement suit with less than $1 million at risk through to judgment is $600,000; for a suit with between $1 million and $10 million at risk, $2 million; for a suit with between $10 million and $25 million at risk, $3.1 million; and for a suit with over $25 million at risk, $5 million). For estimates of the cost of litigating a patent infringement action in other countries, see generally Elmer & Gramenopoulos 2016; Heath 2015.

[14] See generally Taylor 2014.

[15] For discussion, see, e.g., Cotter 2013a, 269–70 (discussing this possibility under French and German law). Although the theory is economically sound, courts and commentators in France and Germany have not universally embraced such awards due to their resemblance to disfavored enhanced or punitive damages.

[16] See RESTATEMENT (THIRD) OF RESTITUTION AND UNJUST ENRICHMENT § 42 cmt. a.

characterizing reasonable royalties as restorative or restitutionary. The royalty the court believes the patent owner would have earned absent the infringement is identical to the infringer's gain (i.e., the royalty it withheld, if not adjusted upward to reflect certainty as to validity and infringement).[17] On the other hand, an approach that attempts to determine the royalty the infringer *should* be required to pay does not necessarily entail restoring the parties to the positions they actually would have occupied but for the infringement – though any such approach needs to specify just what the appropriate normative criterion *is*. Some recent scholarship recommends focusing more on the benefit the infringer *actually* derived from the use of the invention (as opposed to its *expected* benefits *ex ante*), so that the resulting award will more closely correlate with the invention's contribution to the art. As discussed in Sections 1.2 and 1.3, one would then have to determine how to divide that benefit between the parties. In theory, the division could be based on what the parties likely would have negotiated *ex ante*, or on industry custom or other criteria.[18] Other recent scholarship also suggests that a restitutionary approach to patent damages would provide courts with more flexibility to adjust the requisite level of proof based on factors such as the stakes involved and the extent to which the infringer was at fault.[19]

---

[17] *See* Cotter 2013b. One drawback of an approach that attempts to construct the bargain the parties would have struck is that it does not provide much guidance in cases in which (1) *no* bargain would have been struck, because the patentee preferred exclusivity and would not have licensed the infringer at any rate the infringer would have accepted, but (2) the plaintiff cannot, or chooses not to, prove its own lost profits. It also does not provide much guidance on what to do when the parties' evidence is defective but the court is statutorily obligated to award *some* royalty anyway, as is arguably the case for example under 35 U.S.C. § 284. In such instances, reliance on industry standard rates or other nonspecific evidence may be the only available fallback.

   Note also that when the infringer is required to give up the *entire* profit or cost saving it derived from the use of the patented invention, the remedy is more appropriately characterized as "disgorgement" or an "accounting of profits," as opposed to a reasonable royalty. For further discussion, *see* Chapter 2.

[18] *See, e.g.*, Risch 2018 (arguing that reasonable royalties should reflect the value of the use of the patented invention to the infringer); Siebrasse & Cotter 2016 (proposing that, consistent with the standard sometimes articulated by German courts, U.S. courts aspire to construct the bargain the parties would have negotiated *ex ante* with full knowledge of all relevant information that is made known *ex post*); Taylor 2014 (arguing that reasonable royalties should reflect the value of the use of the patented technology). *Compare* BGH v. 14.3.2000 – X ZR 115/98 (Ger.) (stating that "what is owed is what reasonable contracting parties would have agreed to, at the conclusion of a licensing agreement, if they had foreseen the future development and specifically the duration and amount of the use of the patent"), with *General Tire & Rubber Co. Ltd.* v. *Firestone Tyre & Rubber Co. Ltd.* (HL 1975, p.186–87) (UK) (in a case in which the trial court had awarded a royalty of one U.S. cent per pound of tire tread stock (T.T.S.), based on evidence that the infringer's use of the patented method reduced its costs by 1.8 old pence per pound of T.T.S., holding on appeal that a proper royalty would have been only 3/8 of a U.S. cent per pound of oil extended rubber (O.E.R.), based on the "going rate" the patentee had charged others for the use of the invention).

[19] *See* Golden & Sandrik 2017. It is also conceivable that, if restitutionary awards are characterized as equitable in nature, there might not be a constitutional right to trial by jury on the amount of the award under U.S. law, though the point is highly debatable. *See* Cotter 2013b, 25–29.

1.1.3 *Principal Approaches*

Courts throughout the world often consider a range of factors in calculating reasonable royalties. One approach often used in the United States, the United Kingdom, and some other countries is to construct the hypothetical bargain to which the court believes the parties would have agreed to avoid infringement.[20] As discussed above, the hypothetical bargain approach may be viewed as either restorative or restitutionary. If the resulting royalty reflects what the parties actually would have negotiated, the patentee is rendered no worse off, and the infringer no better off, compared to the positions they would have occupied had they actually negotiated a license. As discussed in the following Sections, however, among the issues courts may need to address in constructing such a hypothetical bargain are (1) the timing of the bargain, (2) the knowledge the court should impute to the parties (including knowledge of validity and infringement of the relevant patent, as discussed above), and (3) the relevant factors that are probative of the terms of the bargain. Alternatively, as suggested above, an approach that focuses on dividing the actual gain to the infringer could still be cast as a hypothetical bargain, albeit one in which the parties agree *ex ante* on how to divide the benefit the infringer actually derives *ex post*.[21] This approach would be less concerned than the more common *Georgia-Pacific* approach with trying to accurately construct the terms the parties themselves actually would have negotiated *ex ante*.

Another option under U.S. law is the so-called analytical approach, which "focuses on the infringer's projections of profit for the infringing product."[22] The leading case is *TWM Mfg. Co. v. Dura Corp.*,[23] in which the Federal Circuit approved a damages award that involved subtracting "the infringer's usual or acceptable net profit from its anticipated net profit realized from sales of infringing devices." Although courts sometimes permit the patentee who employs the analytical approach to use the infringer's actual profits as a proxy for expected profits,[24] the approach does not appear to be used very frequently. Critiques of the analytical approach argue, among other things, that the method is indistinguishable from disgorgement; that the concept of a "usual or acceptable net profit" is not very precise; that the approach does not account for various other factors that can explain a divergence from the normal rate of return, including the presence of other product features, or for the fact that different

---

[20] *See, e.g., Georgia-Pacific Corp.* v. *U.S. Plywood Corp.* (S.D.N.Y. 1970, p.1120) (U.S.); *General Tire & Rubber Co. Ltd.* v. *Firestone Tyre & Rubber Co. Ltd.* (HL 1975, p.178–79 (opinion of Lord Wilberforce), 188–89 (opinion of Lord Salmon)) (UK).

[21] *See* Siebrasse & Cotter 2016.

[22] *Lucent Techs., Inc.* v. *Gateway, Inc.* (Fed. Cir. 2009, p.1324) (U.S.).

[23] *TWM Mfg. Co., Inc.* v. *Dura Corp.* (Fed. Cir. 1986, p.899) (U.S.). The infringer's expected profit from the sales of products incorporating the patented technology also was an important factor in the Second Circuit's modification of the royalty awarded in *Georgia Pacific*. *See Georgia-Pacific Corp.* v. *U.S. Plywood Corp.* (2d Cir. 1971, p.289–99) (U.S.). For further discussion of the analytical approach, *see* Skenyon et al. 2016, § 3.8; Cox 2017; Gooding 2012; Pedigo 2017; Rooklidge 2014.

[24] *See* Pedigo 2017.

products can have different profit margins; and that the approach can unfairly penalize an infringer who has a higher profit rate due to efficiencies in production.[25]

Where an established royalty rate exists, courts sometimes have used that rate rather than endeavoring to construct a hypothetical bargain or an appropriate division of the profits projected or earned from the use of the invention.[26] Where no such established rate exists, courts nevertheless frequently turn to comparable license rates as an aid in constructing the hypothetical bargain. In some countries, courts also make extensive use of what are believed to be industry standard rates for various technologies. For example, in Japan courts often start with the standard royalty rate for a given technological field, as reported in publications of the Japanese Institute of Inventors and Innovation (*Hatsumei Kyokai*), and then adjust the rate up or down based on factors such as "the technical or economical value and importance of the invention," the plaintiff's own high profit margin, the contribution of the invention to the infringer's profitability or to the value of the end product, the existence of alternatives, and the infringer's sales volume.[27]

A fourth possibility would be to employ some sort of "top-down" approach as in *In re Innovatio IP Ventures, LLC Patent Litigation*,[28] whereby the court identifies an appropriate royalty base, decides how much of the revenue attributable to the base should be payable as aggregate royalties, and then determines what portion of those aggregate royalties should accrue to the patents in suit, based on their relative importance. Some form of "top-down" approach may be used in cases involving complex products, but the accuracy of the approach in estimating the value of the patents in suit depends upon obtaining a considerable amount of arguably difficult-to-obtain information.[29]

---

[25] *See* Cox 2017 (arguing that the analytical approach is economically deficient, for reasons stated in the text above); Gooding 2012, 7 (critiquing the analytical approach on the ground, inter alia, that it "assumes that every penny of additional profit (above the infringer's 'usual' or 'acceptable' profit) is attributable solely to the patented invention. It therefore makes no attempt to account for the importance of the infringed technology in generating those incremental profits and does not reflect 'the invention's contribution to the infringing product or service'") (quoting *Uniloc USA, Inc.* v. *Microsoft Corp.* Fed. Cir. 2011, p.1313) (U.S.); Rooklidge 2014.

[26] *See, e.g., Rude* v. *Westcott* (U.S. 1889, p.164–65) (U.S.) (stating that, to qualify as an established royalty, the rate "must be paid or secured before the infringement complained of," "must be paid by such a number of persons as to indicate a general acquiescence in its reasonableness by those who have occasion to use the invention," "must be uniform at the places where the licenses are issued," and should not be paid in settlement of another infringement claim). For discussion, *see* Cotter 2013a, 108.

[27] *See* Second Subcommittee of the Second Patent Committee 2014 (in Japanese); Cotter 2015. *See, e.g., Fulta Elec. Machinery Co.* v. *Watanabe Kikai Kogyo K. K.* (IP High Ct. 2015) (Japan).

[28] *In re Innovatio IP Ventures, LLC Patent Litigation* (N.D. Ill. 2013) (U.S.). *See also Samsung Elecs. Co.* v. *Apple Japan LLC* (IP High Ct. 2014, p.132–38) (Japan) (applying a form of top-down analysis); *Unwired Planet Int'l Ltd.* v. *Huawei Techs. Co.* (Pat 2017, ¶¶ 475–80) (UK) (applying a top-down approach as a cross-check on the FRAND royalty derived from analysis of comparables).

[29] *See* Cotter 2018, 206–11.

This approach is discussed further in Chapter 5 on the effect of FRAND commitments on patent remedies.

1.2 REFORMULATING *GEORGIA-PACIFIC*

Judicial systems throughout the world often permit the finder of fact to consider a range of factors of arguable relevance to the calculation of reasonable royalties. In the United States, for example, damages expert witnesses frequently base their opinions on the fifteen factors first compiled in *Georgia-Pacific Co. v. U.S. Plywood Co.* (set forth below).[30] Courts in other countries,

[30]
1. The royalties received by the patentee for the licensing of the patent in suit, proving or tending to prove an established royalty.
2. The rates paid by the licensee for the use of other patents comparable to the patent in suit.
3. The nature and scope of the license, as exclusive or nonexclusive; or as restricted or nonrestricted in terms of territory or with respect to whom the manufactured product may be sold.
4. The licensor's established policy and marketing program to maintain his patent monopoly by not licensing others to use the invention or by granting licenses under special conditions designed to preserve that monopoly.
5. The commercial relationship between the licensor and licensee, such as, whether they are competitors in the same territory in the same line of business; or whether they are inventor and promoter.
6. The effect of selling the patented specialty in promoting sales of other products of the licensee; the existing value of the invention to the licensor as a generator or sales of his non-patented items; and the extent of such derivative or convoyed sales.
7. The duration of the patent and the term of the license.
8. The established profitability of the product made under the patent; its commercial success; and its current popularity.
9. The utility and advantages of the patent property over the old modes or devices, if any, that had been used for working out similar results.
10. The nature of the patented invention; the character of the commercial embodiment of it as owned and produced by the licensor; and the benefits to those who have used the invention.
11. The extent to which the infringer has made use of the invention; and any evidence probative of the value of that use.
12. The portion of the profit or of the selling price that may be customary in the particular business or in comparable businesses to allow for the use of the invention or analogous inventions.
13. The portion of the realizable profit that should be credited to the invention as distinguished from non-patented elements, the manufacturing process, business risks, or significant features or improvements added by the infringer.
14. The opinion testimony of qualified experts.
15. The amount that a licensor (such as the patentee) and a licensee (such as the infringer) would have agreed upon (at the time the infringement began) if both had been reasonably and voluntarily trying to reach an agreement; that is, the amount that a prudent licensee – who desired, as a business proposition, to obtain a license to manufacture and sell a particular article embodying the patented invention – would have been willing to pay as a royalty and yet be able to make a reasonable profit and which amount would have been acceptable by a prudent patentee who was willing to grant a license.

Georgia-Pacific Corp. v. *U.S. Plywood Corp.* (S.D.N.Y. 1970, p.1120) (U.S.). Notice that the fifteenth *Georgia-Pacific* factor is the hypothetical bargain discussed above in Section 1.2. In one view, the fourteen preceding factors are best viewed as aids in determining the fifteenth. *See* Durie & Lemley 2010, 643.

including Canada,[31] Germany,[32] and Japan,[33] sometimes look to a similar range
of factors.

Critics nevertheless have noted several potential problems with the *Georgia-
Pacific* framework. First, depending on the facts of the case, some of the *Georgia-
Pacific* factors may simply be irrelevant,[34] thus potentially distracting the trier of fact
from focusing on the economically relevant considerations.[35] Second, the framework offers little or no guidance to either the trier of fact or the judge on how to
weigh or prioritize the factors.[36] Third, and following from the first two points, it is
sometimes said that a clever expert can manipulate the factors in support of virtually

---

[31] See *AlliedSignal Inc.* v. *DuPont Canada Inc.* (Fed. Ct. 1998, ¶ 209) (Can.) (listing as potentially
relevant factors in constructing a hypothetical license: (1) whether the patentee would have need to
transfer technology to the implementer; (2) differences in the parties' practice of the invention; (3)
whether the patentee would have agreed to an exclusive or nonexclusive license; (4) the territory
covered by the license; (5) the term of the license; (6) whether there were available competing
technologies; (7) whether the patentee and the implementer are competitors; (8) the demand for
the infringing product; (9) the risk that the product would not sell; (10) the novelty of the invention;
(11) the compensation needed for research and development costs; (12) whether the invention would
result in increased revenues accruing to the licensee; and (13) whether the patentee has the capacity to
meet market demand itself). See also *Jay-Lor Int'l Inc.* v. *Penta Farm Sys. Ltd.* (Fed. Ct. 2007, ¶¶ 147,
160–73) (Can.) (approving the use of these factors).

[32] See Cotter 2013a, 268 (stating that German courts may take into account a range of factors, including
the existence of noninfringing alternatives; "the terms of comparable licenses; the significance of
the invention as suggested by the defendant's profit expectations; whether the use interferes with the
patentee's monopoly position (*Monopolstellung*); the increase in value brought about by the use of the
patented invention, including revenue from other goods that are sold and used together with it; and
whether the revenue derived from the infringement is attributable in part to the infringer's (or third
parties') technology").

[33] See *id.* at 321–22 (stating that Japanese courts often use as a starting point the standard rate for a given
technological field as reported by the Japanese Institute of Inventors and Innovation (*Hatsumei
Kyokai*), as well as "a variety of additional factors similar to those used in the United States and
Canada, including the scope and significance of the patent and the benefits the defendant derives
from its use"); Second Subcommittee of the Second Patent Committee 2014 (article, in Japanese,
discussing the factors that explain the royalty rates awarded by Japanese courts); Cotter 2015 (discussing the preceding article).

[34] See *Ericsson, Inc.* v. *D-Link Sys.* (Fed. Cir. 2014, p.1231, 1235) (U.S.) (vacating a damages judgment
where the jury were instructed, among other things, on factors that were irrelevant to the facts of the
case); Durie & Lemley 2010, 628 (stating that *Georgia-Pacific* "overloads the jury with factors to
consider that may be irrelevant, overlapping, or even contradictory").

[35] See Contreras & Gilbert 2015, 1499 (stating that "the *Georgia-Pacific* fifteen-factor analysis muddied
the water substantially in 1970, allowing litigants and courts to focus on any number of confounding
factors that distracted from the core inquiry regarding the value of the patented technology"); Durie &
Lemley 2010, 628.

[36] See Durie & Lemley 2010, 631 (stating that "a non-exclusive fifteen-factor test that requires balancing
and consideration of the interactions between the factors is likely to give little or no practical guidance
to a jury"); *Patent Reform Act of 2009: Hearing on H.R. 1260* (H. Comm. on the Judiciary 2009, p.75)
(prepared statement of Professor John R. Thomas, Georgetown University Law Center) (stating that
"the *Georgia-Pacific* factors are difficult to apply consistently" because the case "offers no recipe – that
is to say, no principles for deciding whether one of the seemingly randomly ordered elements should
be weighed more heavily than another in a given determination") (quoted in Seaman 2010, 1703–04);
Schlicher 2009, 22 (stating that "juries are not given useful guidance on how to apply the so-called
Georgia-Pacific factors").

any award.[37] As a consequence, it can be very difficult for the parties to predict how the trier of fact will apply the factors, and for a reviewing court to detect errors in their application.[38] In combination, these problems threaten not only to reduce accuracy and increase costs, but also to make settlement more difficult and to place the more risk-averse party at a disadvantage.[39]

In response to these problems, some recent scholarship and other initiatives advocate restructuring the analysis to focus on a smaller number of economically relevant factors. Most prominent, perhaps, are the Federal Circuit Bar Association's Model Patent Jury Instructions, which propose that U.S. courts instruct juries to "consider all the facts known and available to the parties at the time the infringement began," but that "[s]ome of the kinds of factors that you may consider in making your determination are: (1) The value that the claimed invention contributes to the accused product. (2) The value that factors other than the claimed invention contribute to [the accused product]. (3) Comparable license agreements, such as those covering the use of the claimed invention or similar technology."[40] In a similar vein, Durie and Lemley argue that the *Georgia-Pacific* factors largely "boil down to three fundamental questions: (1) what is the marginal contribution of the patented invention over the prior art?; (2) how many other inputs were necessary to achieve that contribution, and what is their relative value?; and (3) is there some concrete

---

[37] *See* Cotter 2018, 193 (stating that "unless the judge exerts very tight control over the presentation of evidence, a clever expert could manipulate the factors to find support for virtually any damages amount"); Durie & Lemley 2010, 632 (stating that "[t]he breadth of the available factors also means that it is difficult to exclude evidence or expert testimony espousing virtually any theory of reasonable royalty damages, no matter how outlandish," and that because *Georgia-Pacific* provides little guidance as to which factors must be accorded the most weight in any given case, the expert's ultimate conclusion, no matter how extreme, can usually be justified by at least some combination of them").

[38] *See* Durie & Lemley 2010, 628, 632 (stating that "because the jury's finding is the result of such a complex, multi-factor test, it is as a practical matter almost entirely immune from scrutiny by either district or appellate judges facing a deferential standard of review," and that "the fifteen-factor test makes it extremely difficult for judges to review a jury damage award for substantial evidence, either on judgment as a matter of law (JMOL) or on appeal"); *The Evolving IP Marketplace* (Fed. Trade Comm'n 2009, p.15) (testimony of Professor Paul M. Janicke, University of Houston Law Center) (stating that *Georgia-Pacific* leads to "erratic results" because the test is like a "grab bag" where "the judge throws the grab bag with all the factors to the jury and says, 'Do what you think is right'") (quoted in Seaman 2010, 1704); Seaman 2010, 1665, 1703 (stating that "the so-called *Georgia-Pacific* test … has become increasingly difficult for juries to apply in lengthy and complex patent trials, resulting in unpredictable damage awards," and that "*Georgia-Pacific*'s absence of guidance for balancing the various factors contributes to a lack of certainty and predictability in reasonable royalty awards"); Taylor 2014, 151–52. ("No doubt one contributing factor to inaccuracy, uncertainty, and unpredictability regarding reasonable royalties is the relatively unbounded expert testimony and evidence allowed by the *Georgia-Pacific* factors and the hypothetical negotiation construct.")

[39] *See* Cotter 2018, 168 (stating that "the greater the range of possible outcomes (that is, the greater the variance around the expected mean), the smaller the probability that the parties will settle their dispute (thus raising administrative costs), and the greater the likelihood that the more risk-averse party will be willing to settle on unfavorable terms").

[40] FCBA 2016. In a recent article, Contreras and Eixenberger advocate the uniform adoption of the Federal Circuit Bar Association's proposed jury instructions. *See* Contreras & Eixenberger 2016.

evidence suggesting that the market has chosen a number different than the calculus that results from (1) and (2)?"[41] Jarosz and Chapman also have advocated a three-step framework, focusing on the incremental value of the invention over alternatives, comparable licenses, and design-around costs.[42]

Following from the above, our principal recommendation is that, when applying a "bottom-up"[43] approach to estimating reasonable royalties, courts should replace the *Georgia-Pacific* factors (and analogous factors used outside the United States for calculating reasonable royalties) with a smaller list of considerations. More specifically, courts should collapse the *Georgia-Pacific* factors into the following three steps. (We defend each of the individual parts of this recommendation in detail in Section 3.1 below.)

1. *Calculate the incremental value of the invention and divide it appropriately between the parties.* A license for the use[44] of a patented technology typically requires the licensee to share with the licensor some portion of the incremental value the licensee derives or expects to derive from the use of that technology. To ensure that a reasonable royalty for the unauthorized use of a patented technology accurately reflects this incremental value, ideally a court would (1) estimate the difference between the value the infringer derived from the use of the patented invention (as distinct from the value contributed by other features of the infringing end product), and the value the infringer would have derived by using the next best available noninfringing alternative instead; (2) divide that differential value between the patent owner and the infringer; and (3) as an aid in carrying out this division, consider any relevant evidence, including possibly the use of a rebuttable

---

[41] Durie & Lemley 2010, 629.
[42] *See* Jarosz & Chapman 2013.
[43] This chapter uses the term "bottom-up" to refer to approaches in which the royalties due to patent holders in separate cases are for the most part determined independently of one another. As discussed *supra* note 28 and accompanying text, as an alternative to such an approach courts sometimes may employ a "top-down" approach, in which they first determine the aggregate royalty burden for a specific product or standard and then apportion that burden among the patents reading on that product or standard (*see TCL Commc'ns Tech. Holdings, Ltd.* v. *Telefonaktiebolaget LM Ericsson* (C. D. Cal. 2017) (U.S.); *Unwired Planet Int'l Ltd.* v. *Huawei Techs. Co.* (Pat 2017) (UK); *Samsung Elecs. Co.* v. *Apple Japan LLC* (IP High Ct. 2014) (Japan)). Although top-down approaches may help to reduce risks of holdup and royalty stacking, they may lend themselves more to cases involving patents declared essential to the practice of standards embodying a discrete set of technologies. Outside that context, the evidence needed to employ a top-down approach may be more difficult to obtain, given the lack of both a finite set of declared patents and a defined set of technological features for which royalties are due. Given this chapter's emphasis on complex products generally, therefore, its focus will be on improvements to the bottom-up approach, though in the end the decision whether to apply a bottom-up or top-down approach in FRAND or other complex product cases ultimately may depend on the availability and quality of the evidence before the court.
[44] As a shorthand, we employ the word "use," as in "use of the invention over alternatives," though strictly speaking the infringer's conduct at issue could consist of any selection or combination of the specific activities, such as manufacturing, use, or importation, that can constitute infringement.

presumption that the parties would have agreed, *ex ante*, to an even (50/50) split.

2. *Assess market evidence.* In negotiating licenses for the use of patented technologies, parties often consider the rates and other terms disclosed in relevant comparable licenses (or, where applicable, the rates charged by relevant patent pools or disclosed in publications of industry standard rates). Courts also should consider such evidence for purposes of calculating reasonable royalties for the unauthorized use of patented technologies, albeit subject to appropriate adjustments and with due appreciation for the potential limitations of such evidence as discussed in Section 1.3.6.

3. *Comparison.* When it is feasible and cost justified, courts should carry out both steps described above – each one acting as a "check" on the accuracy of the other – and then attempt to reconcile or adjust the results, as the evidence warrants. That said, one can expect only that courts do the best they can with the evidence available to them. Thus, when the evidence necessary to carry out Step 2 is available but the evidence necessary to carry out Step 1 is not[45] – as will likely often be the case in litigation involving complex products – courts may need to rely exclusively on market evidence. (The converse will be true when the available evidence relates only to Step 1, not 2.) Furthermore, as discussed in greater detail in Chapter 5 on the effect of FRAND commitments on patent royalties, in appropriate cases courts also may consider applying a "top-down" approach either as direct evidence or as a check on the value derived from the use of comparables and other market evidence.

Explanation. As discussed in Section 1.3.1 below, economists generally accept "incremental value" – that is, the difference between the value derived from the patented invention over the next best available noninfringing alternative – as an accurate measure of the value of patented technology.[46] By necessity, such an inquiry also requires the trier of fact to apportion the value attributable to the patented invention as opposed to other features of the infringer's product, assuming that the noninfringing alternative end product sold by the infringer would have retained those other features.[47] The first part of Step 1 above therefore combines

---

[45] See *Unwired Planet Int'l Ltd.* v. *Huawei Techs. Co.* (Pat 2017, ¶ 182) (UK). (stating that "There was ample evidence before me that … parties negotiating SEP licences in fact use methods which are based on patent counting. That is evidence which supports a finding that a FRAND approach to assessing a royalty rate is to engage in some kind of patent counting. Indeed when one thinks about it some sort of patent counting is the only practical approach at least for a portfolio of any size. Trying to evaluate the importance of individual inventions becomes disproportionate very quickly.")

[46] As is also discussed above, however, there are legitimate debates over whether the focus should be on actual or only expected advantages, and on how to proceed when the next best alternative is itself patented.

[47] The simplest example would be one in which the infringer has sold both comparable products, one containing the patented feature and one without that feature, under similar market conditions, such that it is possible to infer the incremental benefit conferred by the patent. See, e.g., *Grain Processing Corp.* v. *Am. Maize-Prods. Co.* (Fed. Cir. 1999) (U.S.); *Carson et al.* v. *American Smelting & Refining*

Georgia-Pacific factors 8, 9, 10, and 13 into one overarching concept.[48] Step 1 presumably will be easier to accomplish, however, when the infringing product embodies relatively few patented features. We defend our recommendation regarding the division of incremental value in Section 1.3.3 below.

Step 2 recommends that courts also make appropriate use of comparables and other market evidence of how actors in the real world value the technology in suit. To be sure, courts and commentators have identified numerous potential pitfalls in the use of comparables, which we discuss in greater detail in Section 1.3.6 below. These theoretical problems notwithstanding, however, we do not advocate forgoing the use of comparables (nor do we see that as a likely development, in any event), but rather emphasize the need for careful judgment in applying them. Moreover, at least in some cases a patent pool rate or other comparable may have a very high probative value, though that rate may need to be adjusted (for example, to account for the reasons why the patentee did not join the pool).[49]

Step 3 recommends that, where feasible, courts apply both Step 1 and Step 2, and then compare the results. To the extent the numbers generated by each step diverge, the court will then have to decide how best to reconcile them based on all of the relevant facts and circumstances. For example, a court may be more confident in the result generated by Step 1 when the end product embodies only a small number of patents or when there are few if any licenses that are closely comparable. By contrast, Step 2 may seem more probative when the product's complexity makes it difficult to distinguish the value contributed by a single patent over the next best alternative. (On the other hand, even in complex products cases it sometimes may be possible to estimate the value of a specific patented feature relative to other features, through the use of conjoint or discrete choice analysis, testimony from technical experts, or application of some form of "top-down" approach as discussed in the FRAND chapter.)[50] Further, in cases (1) involving relatively small stakes, or (2) arising in countries that impose substantial limits on pretrial discovery or the use of expert witnesses, or (3) in which the parties' evidence on damages is inadmissible or incompetent, the best practice may be to consider comparables, industry standard

---

Co. (W.D. Wash. 1928) (U.S.). To the extent the patented invention is complementary to other features of the infringer's product, however, as it often will be in complex products cases, apportionment becomes more complicated. *See infra* Section 1.3.1 (discussing a hypothetical in which the patented invention provides 20 percent longer battery life to a smartphone).

[48] See Cotter 2018, 192 n.133 (stating that among the most important *Georgia-Pacific* factors are "factors 8 through 10, all of which relate to the value of the patented technology, in terms of its effect on the implementer's profit or cost, in comparison with alternatives," and "factor 13, 'the portion of the realizable profit that should be credited to the invention as distinguished from non-patented elements, the manufacturing process, business risks, or significant features or improvements added by the infringer'").

[49] *See, e.g., Microsoft Corp. v. Motorola, Inc.* (W.D. Wash. 2013) (U.S.).

[50] For discussion of the use of conjoint and discrete choice analysis in litigation, *see, e.g.,* Platt & Chen 2013; Sidak & Skog 2016; Verma et al. 2002 (providing an accessible discussion of discrete-choice analysis).

rates, or other such market evidence, despite its potential drawbacks, rather than to award zero damages or rely on other, even more speculative, evidence of the value of the technology over alternatives.

1.3 INCREMENTAL VALUE AND OTHER ISSUES

In this Section, we present the analysis underlying our principal recommendation as described in Section 1.2. We also present our recommendations relating to various issues that may arise either in the application of our principal recommendation or in the event courts continue to employ a multifactor, *Georgia-Pacific*-like approach to reasonable royalties.

1.3.1 *Incremental Value*

1 Overview

We perceive a widespread consensus among innovation economists and lawyers that the social value of a technology is its incremental value over the next best alternative, and that the economic value of a patented technology to an implementer is the (actual or expected) profit or cost saving the implementer derives from the use of the patented technology over the next best available noninfringing alternative.[51] We therefore recommend that policymakers adopt, subject to the systemic considerations noted in the Introduction, the guiding principle that the royalties awarded in litigation should be commensurate with the value of the patented technology as so defined.[52] We also recognize, however, that there are substantial difficulties, both practical and conceptual, in assessing that value – particularly in the case of complex products, where the patented technology contributes only a small part to the overall value of the product. In those contexts, a patented feature might be the deciding factor for a few purchasers, and it might increase the value to others, but for most purchasers it is likely to be one of a host of factors that shift buying preferences as a whole. We discuss the conceptual difficulties below.

---

[51] *See, e.g.*, Swanson & Baumol 2005, 10–11; Farrell et al. 2007, 610–11; Elhauge 2008, 541; Denicolò et al. 2008, 577–78; Layne-Farrar et al. 2009, 448; Shapiro 2010, 286; Gilbert 2011, 864; Camesasca et al. 2013, 304; Cotter 2013a, 128; Carlton & Shampine 2013, 536, 545; Jarosz & Chapman 2013, 812; Taylor 2014, 95–97; Cotter 2014a, 357; Sedona Conference 2014, 23–24; Contreras & Gilbert 2015, 1467–69, 1499–1500; Siebrasse & Cotter 2017a; Lee & Melamed 2016, 411–12; Epstein & Marcus 2003, 557–58. *See also* Taylor 2014, 91–97 (contrasting the value of the technology with the value of patent rights, where the latter might include for example the ability to use an injunction to extract holdup value.)

[52] Our recommendation that royalties should be "commensurate with" the value of the technology, however, does not amount to a recommendation that courts should aspire to award patentees the entire social value of their inventions. For discussion, *see, e.g.*, Frischmann & Lemley 2007; Golden 2010, 529–39; Lemley 2005, 1036–37; Taylor 2014, 138–41.

2 Complements

The first conceptual difficulty involves complementarity between the infringing technology and other patented technologies that are also implemented in the same product. The problem is illustrated most clearly in a case in which two versions of a complex product are sold, with no difference between the two except that one version embodies the patented technology while the other does not.[53] It may seem that this is a case in which it is easy to determine the incremental value of the patented technology; it would seem to be simply the difference between the two prices. However, this is not correct if, as is commonly the case, the patented technology depends on other patented technology. For example, suppose the patented invention provides for 20 percent longer battery life in a smartphone, and a smartphone with the longer battery life sells for $50 more than the phone would with the shorter battery life it would otherwise have. The incremental value of the patented invention would appear to be $50. But the price consumers are willing to pay for the phone depends on its patented wireless technology, and without that wireless technology the phone would be worthless, no matter how long the battery life. In that case, the $50 price difference is only partially attributable to battery technology, because it is also partially attributable to the wireless technology.[54] Put another way, the patentee holding the wireless technology might reasonably demand a higher royalty for the phone with the battery-extending technology than for the base phone, leaving only some part of the $50 to be split between the battery patentee and the phone vendor. Whether the wireless patentee actually demands a higher royalty in such a case is a different question – though it is not unlikely that it would do so. It is common for patentees, particularly those with basic technology patents, to charge an *ad valorem* royalty on the product price, with the result that the wireless royalty would be higher for the more expensive phone.

3 Patented Alternatives

A second conceptual difficulty arises from the proposition that the value of the invention is its value over the best noninfringing alternative. This proposition is uncontroversial so long as the alternative is unpatented, but its application is not so clear if the alternative is patented. It is not at all uncommon that the best substitutes for a patented technology are also patented, as several inventors devise different solutions to the same problem.[55] The problem is illustrated most clearly when the

---

[53] *See Samsung Elecs. Co. v. Apple Japan LLC* (IP High Ct. 2014, p.134) (Japan).

[54] In economic theory the independent value of the complementary technology is given by the Shapley value. *See* Siebrasse & Cotter 2017a. However, it will rarely be possible to compute Shapley pricing directly.

[55] In the standards context it also quite likely that in practice all the relevant technologies will be patented, precisely because of the incentive provided by the prospect of being included in the

inventions are near perfect substitutes,[56] and it is particularly salient in the context of standard-essential patents (SEPs), where it is often the case that multiple alternative patented technologies competed for inclusion in the standard.

One possibility is that in such a case the value of the patented invention is zero, on the view that the infringing user in the hypothetical negotiation should be imagined to play one patentee off against another until the patentee is haggled down to its minimum willingness to accept.[57] More generally, on this view the value of the invention is its incremental value over the patented alternative, ignoring the royalties that would have to be paid to use that alternative, on the rationale that those royalties do not reflect the value of the alternative technology but merely the value of the patent right.[58] By the same token, if the infringed technology were not quite as good as the patented alternative, the value of the infringed technology would be zero. We recommend rejecting this approach, on the ground that although it makes sense from a static welfare perspective, it provides a facially inadequate incentive to invent (zero compensation) and therefore appears inconsistent with the conventionally understood purpose of the patent system.

Another possibility would be to assume that a patented alternative that is on the market is available for its established market price, which is normally above marginal cost. Put another way, "[t]he proper comparison is between the cost and value of the patentee's component and the cost and value of the alternative, including patent royalties that would have to be paid on the alternative where appropriate."[59] This approach has some support in the case law, though it cannot be considered established law.[60] Nevertheless, although this approach might seem appealing when both technologies are mature and both have an established price, it might be difficult to apply if both technologies are new to the market and neither has an established price. This suggestion is therefore likely to be unhelpful in the SEP context, where alternative technologies competed for inclusion in the standard *ex ante*, and the alternative that was not selected may not have a market presence at all *ex post*, or will have a value that is much lower than if it had been selected for inclusion in the standard. Another problem arises when the alternative technology is mature and has an established price, and the infringed technology is new. If the technologies are close substitutes, we would expect the new technology to drive down the price of the established technology, even in the absence of infringement. Thus, if the established price of the alternative is used for comparison purposes, the

---

standard; *see, e.g.,* Layne-Farrar 2014 (discussing the competition among patentees to have their technology included in the standard).

[56] Consider, for example, the near-simultaneous invention of Viagra (sildenafil) and Cialis (tadalafil).

[57] Swanson & Baumol 2005, 10–21 (auction model).

[58] Taylor 2014, 161.

[59] Lemley & Shapiro 2007a, 2039 n.153.

[60] *See In re Innovatio IP Ventures, LLC Patent Litigation* (N.D. Ill. 2013, p.20) (U.S.) (stating that the court would consider patented alternatives, but "that they will not drive down the royalty in the hypothetical negotiation by as much as technology in the public domain").

patentee will be overcompensated in comparison with the royalties it would have received but for the infringement. Perhaps, then, the proper approach in principle would be to assess how the price of the patented alternative would have evolved in response to the introduction of the infringed technology, in the absence of infringement. On the other hand, simply using the established price has clear advantages in terms of ease of proof.

We are not aware of any literature providing a thorough theoretical analysis of this problem.[61] We therefore propose further research on this issue.

1.3.2 *Hypothetical Bargain*

In the United States, the most common approach to assessing a reasonable royalty is usually referred to as the "hypothetical negotiation" approach:[62]

> The hypothetical negotiation tries, as best as possible, to recreate the *ex ante* licensing negotiation scenario and to describe the resulting agreement. In other words, if infringement had not occurred, willing parties would have executed a license agreement specifying a certain royalty payment scheme.[63]

While this approach is now deeply entrenched, the leading cases emphasize that the goal of the hypothetical negotiation framework is not to replicate the bargain that actual willing parties would have arrived at; that would be "inaccurate, and even absurd,"[64] given that "[t]here is, of course, no actual willingness on either side, and no license to do anything, the infringer being normally enjoined ... from further manufacture, use, or sale of the patented product."[65] The hypothetical negotiation is a "legal fiction,"[66] "employed by the court as a means of arriving at reasonable compensation,"[67] and it is to be "flexibly applied as a 'device in the aid of justice.'"[68]

We recommend that courts embrace this view of the hypothetical bargain framework as a tool – a proxy for the issues of how to split the surplus from the invention – rather than as a goal in and of itself.[69] For example, it is well established in U.S. law that the parties to the hypothetical negotiation are assumed to have known that the

---

[61] For a brief discussion, *see* Siebrasse & Cotter 2017a.

[62] *Lucent Techs., Inc. v. Gateway, Inc.* (Fed. Cir. 2009, p.1324) (U.S.). It is also sometimes referred to as a "hypothetical bargain" or "willing licensor/willing licensee" approach.

[63] *Id.* at 1325.

[64] *Rite-Hite Corp. v. Kelley Co.* (Fed. Cir. 1995, p.1554 n.13) (U.S.) (en banc).

[65] *Panduit Corp. v. Stahlin Bros. Fibre Works Inc.* (6th Cir. 1978, p.1159) (U.S.).

[66] *Id.*

[67] *Hanson v. Alpine Valley Ski Area, Inc.* (Fed. Cir. 1983, p.1081) (U.S.) (quoted with approval in *Rite-Hite Corp. v. Kelley Co.* (Fed. Cir. 1995, p.1554 n.13) (U.S.)).

[68] *TWM Mfg. Co., Inc. v. Dura Corp.* (Fed. Cir. 1986, p.900) (U.S.) (quoted with approval in *Rite-Hite Corp. v. Kelley Co.* (Fed. Cir. 1995, p.1554 n.13) (U.S.)).

[69] *See similarly* Janicke 1993, 726–27 ("The engrafted 'assumptions' of validity, infringement, and business information would be better viewed as reminders to the decisionmaker on reasonable royalty to help him or her reach a just result, rather than as facts artificially deemed 'known' at an artificial negotiation.").

patent was valid and infringed, even though actual parties would not. This rule is required to achieve just compensation, because the opposite view – that the parties should be assumed to discount the royalty to allow for the probabilistic nature of the patent (as would presumably be done by parties to an actual negotiation) – would result in so-called double discounting;[70] not only would the court-approved royalty derived from the hypothetical negotiation include a discount for the risk of non-liability, but then pre-litigation negotiations in which royalties were based on the expectation of such a court award occurring with a less than 100 percent probability would include a further discount for risk of non-liability. For that reason, we agree that this well-established principle of U.S. law is sound. Moreover, based on similar reasoning, the hypothetical negotiation should include an assumption of liability, not just validity and infringement, as well as entitlement to relief and enforceability.[71] And more generally, departures from a strict attempt to reconstruct what real parties would have done had they actually bargained are justified whenever such a departure would be a better means of arriving at reasonable compensation – in particular, compensation that reflects the value of the patented technology over its best noninfringing alternative. Indeed, if sound principles of reasonable compensation require an unwieldy number of departures from a hypothetical negotiation framework, the proper course would be to abandon the framework rather than the sound principles.[72]

1.3.3 *Dividing Incremental Value*

The second and third parts of Step 1 involve identifying the appropriate division of the incremental value. Both sides often can make a substantial claim to at least a portion of the incremental value – the patentee because this value results from use of the claimed invention, and the adjudged infringer because it made complementary or supplementary investments that resulted in a commercial embodiment of that invention. How then should the value be divided?

In theory, an invention can give rise to pure economic rents, reflecting the value of the invention over the best noninfringing alternative. If two parties, such as

---

[70] Cotter 2013a, 135–36; *see also* Choi 2009, 154–55 (arguing that the use of *ex post* information is necessary to cure this problem); Taylor 2014, 115–16 (reviewing the development of the law on this point, and arguing that the problem is not only one of double discounting, but circularity, because the discounted value that the parties would negotiate would itself then be reflected in the damages award, and the parties, anticipating this, would further discount the negotiated price, and so on).

[71] Taylor 2014, 127–29.

[72] *See* Janicke 1993, 726 (suggesting that "[i]n view of the increasing number of assumptions engrafted onto the underlying fiction of hypothetical negotiation, the Federal Circuit should consider whether the time has come to abolish the fiction altogether . . . "); Taylor 2014, 125–26. Similarly, although real-world negotiations sometimes might result in a degree of royalty stacking in cases involving complex products, for purposes of awarding reasonable royalties courts could make the assumption that the parties would have bargained to avoid this outcome, in order better to align royalties with the value of the technology.

a patent owner and a licensee, must cooperate to realize those rents, there is no simple theoretical answer as to how the parties will split the rents between them, since even a very lopsided split, in either direction, would leave both parties better off as compared with using the noninfringing alternative. The most prominent solution to the problem is the Nash Bargaining Solution (NBS), which implies a 50/50 split. However, the NBS requires unrealistically restrictive assumptions about the parties, such as that they are identical in every way. Economic theory is relatively underdeveloped in terms of fleshing out how pure rents would be split when the parties are modeled more realistically.[73] The Nash Bargaining Solution is sometimes used, not because it is a particularly accurate model, but for lack of anything better.

Moreover, the division of the incremental profit due to the invention is unlikely to be a split of pure rents. Turning a patented invention into a commercialized innovation that actually commands a premium in the market-place requires some or all of manufacturing, distribution, marketing, process refinement, technical support to the licensee by the patentee, end-user support, and so on, all of which involve risk and investment by one party or the other. The royalty paid by the licensee to the patentee does not reflect a split of pure rents, but also, or even instead, compensation to the party who made the investments and shouldered the risks relating to these ancillary services.[74] *Georgia-Pacific* factor 13 recognizes this possibility,[75] as have cases such as *Tights, Inc.* v. *Kayser-Roth Corp.*:

> The Court finds, in the context of this case, that the patentee would have been reasonably entitled to receive from 25% to 50% of the cost saving as reasonable royalties. This Court finds that 25% of the cost saving is a reasonable entitlement where the parties anticipate that the licensee will have to make substantial con-tributions to practical commercialization. This Court finds that 50% of the cost

---

[73] The main theoretical refinement is by Ariel Rubinstein, who shows that under certain conditions, a party with a higher discount rate (higher time value of money) will have less bargaining power. Rubinstein 1982.

[74] *See* Siebrasse & Cotter 2016, 954–55:

> In an actual license agreement, both parties bring something to the table in the process of turning an invention into a commercially valuable revenue-generating product. The patentee's most obvious contribution is the invention, but bringing the final product to market generally requires further development and technical implementation, such as clinical trials, as well as marketing, manufacturing, and distribution, all of which require further investment at risk beyond the investment made by the patentee in the invention itself. Either of the parties may provide these further services, and the way the parties split the incremental profit in an actual negotiation depends on who provides what services and the relative importance and cost of those services.

[75] *Georgia-Pacific Corp.* v. *U.S. Plywood Corp.* (S.D.N.Y. 1970, p.1120) (U.S.) ("13. The portion of the realizable profit that should be credited to the invention as distinguished from non-patented ele-ments, the manufacturing process, business risks, or significant features or improvements added by the infringer.").

saving is a reasonable entitlement where the parties anticipate that the licensee will have to make only routine creative contributions toward commercialization.[76]

We therefore recommend that, to the extent possible, the split of the incremental profit should reflect the value of any such ancillary services or risks that either the patent owner or the infringer, in fact, undertook. In our view this is consistent with the hypothetical bargaining construct because it reflects the agreement the parties themselves would have arrived at in similar circumstances. Recall that the principal justification for the hypothetical bargain is that it preserves the patent incentive by restoring the patent owner to the position it would have occupied absent the infringement. That position would depend in part on how the parties would have agreed, *ex ante*, to divide the value to be derived from the use of the patented invention, in comparison with alternatives. However, we emphasize that we recommend taking such services into account to the extent they are actually incurred. Even if an actual licensee would have provided marketing for the invention, and an actual royalty would have reflected that value, the reasonable royalty award should only reflect that if in fact the infringer undertook the marketing.[77]

More broadly, we propose further research to unpack and refine the nature of "bargaining power" as it relates to the division of the incremental value of the invention.[78] We suspect that the division in any given case is determined in part by compensation for ancillary services and in part by industry norms (which may themselves reflect reflect standard practices about provision of ancillary services). To some extent this unpacking is a matter of obtaining better evidence as to what factors actually drive the division of the incremental profit in practice. In addition, there are some conceptual or normative issues to be resolved. In particular, one intuitive understanding of "bargaining power" is that a party with deeper pockets has greater bargaining power, and so would be able to extract a greater share of the incremental value in an actual licensing negotiation. For example, if the patent owner was a small cash-strapped start-up, and the potential licensee was a large company, the licensee might in practice be able to extract very favorable terms. It can be argued that it would be appropriate to replicate that unequal division in a reasonable royalty assessment, on the view that the patentee should not be made better off than it would have been had the parties actually licensed. On the other hand, the favorable terms might be considered to be an illegitimate holdout by the licensee, which should not be replicated in a reasonable royalty, on the view that it does not reflect the incremental value of the invention, just as the courts should not give the patentee a higher royalty if it would have been able to engage in holdup in an actual negotiation. These questions deserve further exploration.

---

[76] *Tights, Inc.* v. *Kayser-Roth Corp.* (M.D.N.C. 1977, p.164) (U.S.).

[77] *See* Siebrasse & Cotter 2016, 989–90.

[78] In economic theory, "bargaining power" is used largely as a label rather than an explanatory variable. If the observed split is 80/20, and there is no evident reason for an uneven division, then we say that one of the parties has greater bargaining power than the other.

Having decided which factors should be relevant to the division of the incremental profit, the second question is what evidence should be used to establish that
division. A few possibilities come to mind. First, comparables may shed light, either
explicitly or implicitly, on how the parties would have agreed to divide the surplus.
As discussed above, evidence also could reflect any ancillary services or risks that
either the patent owner or the infringer, in fact, incurred, so as to adjust the royalty
derived from the comparable license. Second, there may be evidence of what the
parties would have agreed to based on their own prior negotiations, the patentee's
course of dealing with other parties, or the custom of the industry. To illustrate, in
United States Frumentum Co. v. Lauhoff, the U.S. Court of Appeals for the Sixth
Circuit held that evidence was admissible as to what share of the profits or of the
selling price "it may be customary in that or similar business to allow for the use of
such an invention."[79] (Of course, questions may arise as to just how similar a "similar
business" must be.) When there is no such evidence of how the parties would have
agreed to split the incremental value, however, what then? On the one hand, it
would seem wrong to award the patent owner nothing – and in any event U.S. law
normally would preclude such a result because section 284 of the U.S. Patent Act
requires courts to award "damages adequate to compensate for the infringement, *but
in no event less than a reasonable royalty* for the use made of the invention by the
infringer."[80] Indeed, one of the reasons for the gradual adoption of the reasonable
royalty remedy in the United States in the early to mid-twentieth century was
precisely to avoid situations in which courts could award only nominal damages,
due to difficulties in quantifying the owner's loss or the infringer's gain with
sufficient certainty.[81] Rather, as Judge Learned Hand expressed it back in 1933, "[t]
he whole notion of a reasonable royalty is a device in aid of justice, by which that
which is really incalculable shall be approximated, rather than that the patentee,
who has suffered an indubitable wrong, shall be dismissed with empty hands."[82] By
the same token, it would seem equally wrong to award the patentee 100 percent of
the profit the infringer earned from the use of the claimed invention simply because

---

79   *U.S. Frumentum Co. v. Lauhoff* (6th Cir. 1914, p.617) (U.S.); *see also Georgia-Pacific Corp. v. U.S.
     Plywood Corp.* (S.D.N.Y. 1970, p.1120) (U.S.) (listing factor 12, which refers to "[t]he portion of the
     profit or of the selling price that may be customary in the particular business or in comparable
     businesses to allow for the use of the invention or analogous inventions," and is likely based on
     Frumentum).
80   U.S. Patent Act, 35 U.S.C. § 284 (emphasis added); *see also Apple, Inc. v. Motorola, Inc.* (Fed. Cir.
     2014, p.1328) (U.S.) (stating that, even when a patent owner fails to introduce admissible evidence
     quantifying its loss, the court is obligated to "determine what constitutes a reasonable royalty from the
     record evidence"); Schönknecht 2012, 311–13 (discussing the German courts' "free discretion" to
     estimate damages under § 287 of the Code of Civil Procedure, and stating that "[t]he injured party
     is not required to prove the exact amount of its damage; rather, it is sufficient if it presents a factual
     basis on which the court can establish 'at least a rough estimate' of the damage.") (citing BGH
     v. 6.3.1980 – X ZR 49/78 – *Tolbutamid* (Ger.)).
81   Taylor 2014, 97–101, 112–13 (describing this history of the development of reasonable royalties).
82   *See, e.g., Cincinnati Car Co. v. New York Rapid Transit Corp.* (2d Cir. 1933, p.594–95) (U.S.).

the infringer couldn't prove the appropriate division (unless the patentee was seeking, and was entitled to under the relevant substantive law, an award of the infringer's profits).[83]

Arguably then, the best practice would be to permit the parties to introduce whatever competent evidence they have on the division of profits, including comparables, while also permitting the fact finder to take note of, for example, findings from behavioral psychology and economics (e.g., the ultimatum game) suggesting that people in Western societies generally view a 50/50 split of benefits as fair. (Similarly, the Nash Bargaining Solution, application of which often may result in a 50/50 split, is a widely used construct in game theory – albeit with economists often employing the 50/50 split as a plausible assumption, rather than substantiating it as an empirical fact of how two actual parties would have bargained.)[84] For example, in *Summit 6, LLC v. Samsung Electronics Co.*, the Federal Circuit recently affirmed a damages judgment based on an expert witness's purported isolation of the incremental profit Samsung had derived from the use of the patented invention, and his subsequent division of that profit between the parties based on analysis of Samsung's bargaining power and application of the Nash Bargaining Solution.[85]

We therefore recommend that, when faced with the question of how to divide the incremental value derived from the use of the invention over the next best alternative, courts permit the parties to introduce any competent evidence on this issue – including, where necessary to estimate a royalty "in aid of justice," empirical findings that people in Western societies generally view a 50/50 split of benefits as fair, and that economists often use the Nash Bargaining Solution in modeling bargaining behavior. Further to this point, policymakers may wish to consider adopting a rebuttable presumption that the parties would have agreed to a 50/50 split – which presumption, however, should come into play only after there has been an initial determination of the incremental profit derived from the use of the invention, and should not be difficult for the parties to rebut by means of more specific evidence (comparables, industry practice, risk allocation, etc.).[86]

---

[83] Such awards are no longer available in the United States other than in design patent cases, as discussed in Chapter 2.

[84] *See, e.g.*, Henrich 2015, 191–92, 358–59; Stout 2011, 52–54.

[85] *Summit 6, LLC v. Samsung Electronics Co.* (Fed. Cir. 2015, p.1297) (U.S.). *Compare VirnetX, Inc. v. Apple Inc.* (Fed. Cir. 2014, p.1333–34) (U.S.) (disapproving of the use of the Nash Bargaining Solution on the ground that use of a 50–50 split as the proposed starting point for a damages calculation was "insufficiently tied to the facts of the case").

[86] Various bodies of law, including patent law, make use of presumptions in a variety of contexts in which a fact of interest (call it X) is difficult to prove but likely correlated with the presence of some other, more easily provable, fact (call it Y). In such cases, presuming the existence of fact X upon proof of fact Y may reduce adjudication costs and better promote the goal of accurate fact finding than would a rule requiring that, absent competent proof of fact X, the trier of fact must find *not-X*. Relatedly, a rebuttable presumption encourages the party against whom the presumption operates to come forward with evidence justifying a departure from the presumption, which makes sense if that party is likely to be better positioned than its counterpart to have access to such information. For

By contrast, we would not recommend use of a stronger presumption (e.g., one that can be rebutted only by clear and convincing evidence) out of concern that, inter alia, the trier of fact (particularly a lay jury) might accord such a presumption too much weight. Further, a weak presumption of this sort should be sharply distinguished from the 25 percent rule of thumb previously used by U.S. courts and rejected by the Federal Circuit in *Uniloc USA, Inc.* v. *Microsoft Corp.*[87] Unlike that rule of thumb, under which a damages expert was permitted to presume that "the licensee pay a royalty rate equivalent to 25 per cent of its expected profits for the product that incorporates the IP at issue,"[88] the presumptive value split suggested here would apply only after the incremental profit properly attributable to use of the claimed invention has been isolated from all other portions of overall revenue and profit. In complex product cases, there are likely to be multiple innovations besides the claimed invention that have contributed to overall revenue and profit. Consequently, in such cases, 50 percent of the incremental profit attributable to the claimed invention can be expected to often be only a small percentage or even only a small fraction of a percent of the overall profit from the complex product.

1.3.4 *Timing of Hypothetical Negotiation*

The standard view in U.S. case law is that the hypothetical bargain occurs just prior to the date on which the infringement began.[89] This timing has been controversial in two main respects. First, it is the basis for the mainstream view in U.S. law that the hypothetical bargain should be based only on information that is available to the parties *ex ante*, and that *ex post* information is relevant only as indirect evidence of what the parties would have expected *ex ante* (the "book of wisdom" approach).[90] The standard in Germany, by contrast, states that the court should consider the bargain the parties would have reached *ex ante* had they foreseen all relevant *ex post* information;[91] and a few commentators argue for the expanded use of *ex post* information in U.S. law as well, on the view that this allows for a more accurate

---

discussion of the function and working of presumptions generally, *see, e.g.*, Mueller & Kirkpatrick 1999, 126–31; McGowan 2010, 582; Posner 1999, 1503–04.

[87] *Uniloc USA, Inc.* v. *Microsoft Corp.* (Fed. Cir. 2011) (U.S.).

[88] Goldscheider et al. 2002, 123.

[89] *See Lucent Techs., Inc.* v. *Gateway, Inc.* (Fed. Cir. 2009, p.1324–25) (U.S.) (stating that "the hypothetical negotiation or the 'willing licensor-willing licensee' approach . . . attempts to ascertain the royalty upon which the parties would have agreed had they successfully negotiated an agreement just before infringement began," recreating "as best as possible . . .the ex ante licensing negotiation scenario and . . . resulting agreement"); *Georgia-Pacific Corp.* v. *U.S. Plywood Corp.* (S.D.N.Y. 1970, p.1120) (U.S.). In the SEP context, courts have begun to shift the time frame for the hypothetical negotiations, from just before the patent was infringed to just before the standard was adopted. *See In re Innovatio IP Ventures, LLC Patent Litigation* (N.D. Ill. 2013, p.19) (U.S.); *Microsoft Corp.* v. *Motorola, Inc.* (W.D. Wash. 2013, p.19) (U.S.); *Apple, Inc.* v. *Motorola, Inc.* (N.D. Ill. 2012, p.913) (U.S.).

[90] *See infra* Section 1.3.5.

[91] *See* Schönknecht 2012.

valuation of the patented technology.[92] Second, there is substantial scholarly commentary, particularly in the SEP context, suggesting that the timing of the hypothetical negotiation should be earlier, just prior to the time when sunk costs[93] were incurred; this commentary reflects the view that the user would inevitably have incurred sunk costs by the time of the first infringement, so that a license negotiated at that time would allow the patentee to hold up the user for part of those sunk costs, leading to a royalty in excess of the value of the invention.[94]

With these critiques in mind, we recommend that, to the extent courts continue to employ a hypothetical bargaining construct at all, they should apply a flexible approach that takes into account the hypothetical bargain's status as a legal fiction employed as an aid to arriving at reasonable compensation, rather than as a foundational principle in its own right to be applied strictly and literally. With regard to timing in particular, in many cases the *precise* date of the hypothetical negotiation does not have any impact on the reasonable royalty, and the early U.S. decisions invoking the hypothetical negotiation approach did not usually specify the time when the negotiation took place. On the other hand, in the cases establishing the time of the first infringement as the appropriate date, courts have chosen the infringement date not because it reflects the time of a negotiation between truly willing parties, but because that timing does justice on the facts of the particular case. As discussed in Sections 1.2 and 1.3.5, our preferred approach is not to employ a hypothetical negotiation as such, but rather to identify the surplus that the parties are negotiating over, and to divide that surplus in an appropriate manner. But whichever construct is used, the ultimate goal is to ensure that the division does not reflect lock-in but that it does reflect any ancillary services or risks that either party has shouldered.

To illustrate our recommendation, consider a case in which the court deems the hypothetical negotiation to have taken place at the time of first infringement, but after the infringer has incurred sunk costs. In such a case, the patentee might be able to extract some of the value associated with those sunk costs even if it has no substantial relation to the value of the patented technology, contrary to the consensus view that the patentee normally should not be able to extract such unrelated value.[95] Fortunately, we are not aware of any cases in which the courts have approved of allowing the patentee to extract value associated with such sunk costs specifically on the basis that this would have happened had the parties bargained on the infringement date. In our view, the key point is to ensure that the evidence used

---

[92] *See* Siebrasse & Cotter 2016.

[93] We use the term "sunk costs" throughout in the *economic* sense of costs that have been incurred and cannot be recovered, rather than in the accounting sense of fixed costs.

[94] *See, e.g.,* Taylor 2014, 129 (noting that "[t]o avoid extraction of value from patent holdup, the time period for the hypothetical negotiation should be assumed to be just prior to any investment by the infringer in developing or using the patented technology").

[95] Unless there is some specific reason for allowing a supracompensatory remedy, such as the need to deal with the problem of opportunistic infringement, as discussed in Chapter 3.

to establish the reasonable royalty avoids problems associated with sunk costs. If, for example, the bargain is constructed using comparable licenses, a strict adherence to the principle that the bargain takes place prior to infringement would bar the use of any comparable licenses entered into after that date. But if the party to the relevant comparable had negotiated its license prior to incurring any sunk costs, then neither that license nor a royalty based on it would reflect sunk-costs holdup, and there would be no reason to reject the use of that comparable based on its date of execution.

Further, while the view that a reasonable royalty should not reflect the infringer's sunk costs is generally sound, it doesn't necessarily require that the royalty be based on evidence that predates those sunk costs. The previous example highlights one such scenario. As another example, often it may be easier to determine the date on which infringement began than the date on which the infringer began incurring sunk costs, in which case – as long as the sunk costs are not *too* large – the marginal increase in accuracy resulting from moving up the date of the hypothetical negotiation may not be justifiable in view of the additional administrative expense. Alternatively, consider the facts of *Tights, Inc.* v. *Kayser-Roth Corp.*,[96] in which the court noted that a licensee would pay a lower royalty if it would be required to make substantial contributions to practical commercialization, and a higher royalty if it made less contributions toward commercialization. The timing of the hypothetical negotiation was important because the product market was relatively mature by the time of the first infringement, and so the reasonable royalty was higher than it would have been had the infringer entered a nascent market.[97] If the bargain date were moved back to avoid sunk-costs holdup, this would imply that the reasonable royalty in *Tights* would have to be reduced correspondingly. In our view, *Tights* was correctly decided on its facts, and a lower royalty to notionally avoid sunk-costs holdup – which was not in issue – would be inappropriate.

This illustrates the importance of addressing the underlying issue rather than focusing solely on the date of the hypothetical negotiation. A negotiation date that is appropriate for some purposes (avoiding sunk-costs holdup) may be inappropriate for others (ensuring that the royalty reflects the infringer's contribution to commercialization). Moving the negotiation date back to solve one problem might simply create other problems, when all that is really necessary is to ensure that the specific evidence on which the royalty is based does not inappropriately incorporate sunk-costs holdup.

1.3.5 *Information Set*

We now turn our attention to the issue of changed information. Suppose that at the time of the first infringement, the parties anticipated that the invention would be

---

[96] *Tights, Inc.* v. *Kayser-Roth Corp.* (M.D.N.C. 1977) (U.S.).
[97] *See id.* at 164.

a great success, and so they would have contracted for a very high royalty, but in fact the invention was a failure. If the royalty is to be based only on the information that was available to the parties at the time of the first infringement, the damages award would be very high; but if it is based on the knowledge that the invention is in fact worthless, then the royalty would be very low. For example, following a jury trial in 2012, a federal district court entered judgment in the amount of $1 billion in favor of Monsanto in a patent infringement dispute against DuPont. This amount reflected the jury's best estimate of the lump-sum amount that DuPont would have agreed to pay and that Monsanto would have accepted, just before the infringement began, even though DuPont never sold any of the infringing seed at all.[98] Notably, the opposite story may also be told. A technology expected to be worthless may prove to be valuable. The mainstream view in U.S. law nevertheless is that *ex post* information can be used only to establish what the parties believed at the time of first infringement, and if it can be established that their views turned out to be wrong, then the reasonable royalty will be calculated on the basis of those wrong views, and not on the basis of what actually transpired.

We recommend, however, that contrary to the mainstream U.S. approach, courts should adopt what Siebrasse and Cotter refer to as the "contingent ex ante approach" under which the hypothetical negotiation is generally assumed (subject to the caveats noted in the preceding section) to take place before any sunk costs are incurred, but with the benefit of *ex post* information.[99] The rationale for this approach is that the bargain must be assumed to take place *ex ante*, so that the patentee is not entitled to extract any holdup value; but at the same time, using *ex post* information more accurately reflects the true incremental value of the invention, and so provides a more accurate reward to the patentee. This is not really inconsistent with a hypothetical negotiation framework, because parties often negotiate on a contingent basis. For example, it is routine to negotiate a running royalty, the effect of which is to make the return to the patentee contingent on *ex post* information. Using *ex post* information in the hypothetical negotiation posits that the parties would contract on a broadly contingent basis, taking into account all relevant factors, not just the volume sold. This approach would not exclude evidence that the parties actually would have agreed upon a lump sum royalty, but merely presumes that the parties would have preferred a royalty that took into account the risk of lack of success of the patented technology. This approach is also consistent with the established rule that the parties to the hypothetical negotiation are assumed

---

[98] *Monsanto Co. v. E.I. DuPont De Nemours & Co.* (E.D. Mo. 2013) (U.S.). No reported opinion followed the entry of judgment, and the case settled shortly thereafter. For discussion, *see* Chao & Gray 2013.

[99] *See* Siebrasse & Cotter 2016; Sidak 2016a. The Sedona Conference also discusses expanded use of *ex post* information: *see* Sedona Conference 2016, 22–28. Note, however, that as discussed in the preceding subsection, there may be cases in which the timing of the hypothetical negotiation to avoid sunk costs may not be particularly relevant.

to know that the patent is valid and infringed even though during actual negotiations they would have discounted the royalty for risk of non-liability.

This view also has some support in U.S. case law, most prominently in the statement by Justice Cardozo in *Sinclair Refining* that:

> An imaginary bid by an imaginary buyer, acting upon the information available at the moment of the breach, is not the limit of recovery where the subject of the bargain is an undeveloped patent. Information at such a time might be so scanty and imperfect that the offer would be nominal. The promisee of the patent has less than fair compensation if the criterion of value is the price that he would have received if he had disposed of it at once, irrespective of the value that would have been uncovered if he had kept it as his own.[100]

This is often said to reflect only the principle that *ex post* information may be used as evidence of what the parties would have believed at the time of the first infringement, but on its face it supports the use of *ex post* information more generally. Similarly, in *Georgia-Pacific*, the district court actually did consider post-infringement evidence, and on appeal the Second Circuit held that the district court had not erred in so doing.[101] More recently, it appears that the courts have begun to be more liberal in the use of *ex post* evidence.[102]

On the other hand, one objection to the use of *ex post* information is that courts have tended to invoke the "book of wisdom" asymmetrically to benefit patentees but not infringers.[103] One obvious response to this objection is that it is wrong to do so. Presumably clarifying that the use of *ex post* evidence is generally permissible would help avoid an unprincipled asymmetric approach.[104] Lee and Melamed further argue that using *ex post* information substantively, rather than merely as evidence of what the parties would have known or believed at the time of the first infringement, leads to two mistakes:

> First, the rationale assumes that the actual profits would have been unforeseen entirely at the time of the hypothetical negotiation, when the parties negotiating ex ante would likely have understood that there would be a range of possible outcomes (some leading to higher profit and some leading to little or no profit for the infringer) and would have taken all of them into account in selecting

---

[100]   *Sinclair Ref. Co. v. Jenkins Petroleum Process Co.* (U.S. 1933, p.699) (U.S.).
[101]   *Georgia-Pacific Corp. v. U.S. Plywood Corp.* (2d Cir. 1971, p.297) (U.S.).
[102]   *See* Lee & Melamed 2016, 414 (reviewing the cases and suggesting that "following [*Fromson v. W. Litho Plate & Supply Co.* (Fed. Cir. 1988, p.1575) (U.S.)], courts have regularly relied on the book of wisdom doctrine to permit the consideration of ex post developments, regardless whether those ex post developments provided any insight into the parties' ex ante bargaining positions or whether the case involved willful infringement").
[103]   *See* Janicke 1993, 725–27.
[104]   *See id.* (criticizing the court for using *ex post* information asymmetrically, and arguing that the appropriate response is to formally recognize that "the court should examine the business realities at the time infringement began and subsequently, independent of any theory that a hypothetical negotiation has occurred").

a reasonable royalty ex ante. Second, . . . a royalty determined on the basis of ex post evidence will generally include a premium based on ex post economic developments that increase the infringer's reliance on the patent – in particular, lock-in costs – and that are unrelated to the incremental benefit the patent confers.

The first objection, however, misses the point. When the parties' expectations are accurate *ex ante*, there is no difference between an approach that uses *ex post* information and one that does not.[105] The rationale for the use of *ex post* information is that it allows more accurate determination of the royalty when the parties are mistaken. The second objection is sound so far as it goes, though it actually applies equally to the standard position that the negotiations are assumed to take place at the time of first infringement, by which time the infringer will normally have already incurred lock-in costs. The response is the same whether or not *ex post* information is to be taken into account; it is to refuse to award royalties that reflect lock-in costs. Put another way, Lee and Melamed implicitly assume that in order to take into account *ex post* information, it is necessary to assume that the hypothetical negotiation takes place *ex post*; but under the Siebrasse and Cotter proposal, the hypothetical negotiation is assumed to take place before sunk costs have been incurred, but in light of all *ex post* information, not just information regarding validity and infringement.

In short, rather than excluding *ex post* information entirely, the better response is to clearly articulate the rationale, which is not simply to increase the patentee's reward, and thereby make it clear that *ex post* information is admissible no matter what effect it has on the reasonable royalty damages. Consequently, we are of the view that the contingent *ex ante* approach is sound.

1.3.6 *Comparable Licenses*

If we imagine a reasonable royalty as the product of a hypothetical negotiation between the parties using certain assumptions, the use of comparable licenses – what similarly situated parties "did in fact agree to"[106] – as an aid in making this determination seems quite sensible.[107] Indeed, when a license meets the stringent

---

[105] Unless there is a bias in which cases get litigated: *see* Siebrasse & Cotter 2016.

[106] Durie & Lemley 2010, 641; *see also* Masur 2015, 120 ("At first blush this approach makes sense; if the courts must reconstruct a hypothetical royalty negotiation, actual preexisting royalty agreements might well constitute the best available evidence of the contours of such a negotiation. Not surprisingly, scholars, commentators, and courts nearly unanimously bless the use of existing licenses to calculate patent damages.").

[107] The first two *Georgia-Pacific* factors, for example, focus specifically on prior licensing agreements. *See Georgia-Pacific Corp.* v. *U.S. Plywood Corp.* (S.D.N.Y. 1970, p.1120) (U.S.) (listing "1. The royalties received by the patentee for the licensing of the patent in suit, proving or tending to prove an established royalty" and "2. The rates paid by the licensee for the use of other patents comparable to the patent in suit"). Other factors refine the relevance of prior licenses by adding context. For example, the third and fourth factors consider the nature of the patentee's licensing program by weighing the exclusivity of the prior licenses and any geographic restrictions or other special conditions found in them. *See id.* Courts outside the United States also frequently look to comparable licenses, or sometimes industry standard

requirements to qualify as an "established" one, its probative value might seem clear.[108] There are nonetheless significant practical and conceptual problems involved with using comparable licenses – even "established" ones[109] – as evidence of a reasonable royalty. Although we do not suggest that courts should forgo the use of comparable licenses, we recommend that courts should be aware of the problems discussed below, and to the best of their ability take these considerations into account when using comparables.

1 Comparability

The most obvious hurdle in using comparable licenses is to ensure comparability. It is rare to find actual licenses entered into in exactly the circumstances of the hypothetical negotiation. In theory, a license may be sufficiently comparable to be considered as evidence of a reasonable royalty even though it was not negotiated in circumstances exactly corresponding to the hypothetical negotiation, though adjustments then may have to be made to allow for the differences. And if the license is too dissimilar, it may be properly excluded – particularly in U.S. practice, in which judges play an important gatekeeper role by excluding evidence from consideration by juries.

While licenses involving different patents for related technologies may in principle be useful comparators, there are evident problems in determining whether a different technology is sufficiently comparable. Consequently, courts prefer to rely on licenses granted by the patent owner for the same patent,[110] but even then

---

rates, as an aid in calculating reasonable royalties. For discussion of practice in Germany and Japan, *see* Cotter 2013a, 268, 321–22; Second Subcommittee of the Second Patent Committee 2014. Our discussion in the text above to "comparables" therefore should be understood to apply to other analogous forms of evidence, such as industry standard rates.

[108] *Dowagiac Mfg. Co. v. Minn. Moline Plow Co.* (U.S. 1915, p.648) (U.S.) (stating that where the patentee undertakes "a course of granting licenses" then those "established royalties … [afford] a basis for measuring damages"); *Rude* v. *Westcott* (U.S. 1889, p.164–65) (U.S.) (stating that, to qualify as an established royalty, the rate "must be paid or secured before the infringement complained of," "must be paid by such a number of persons as to indicate a general acquiescence in its reasonableness by those who have occasion to use the invention," "must be uniform at the places where the licenses are issued," and should not be paid in settlement of another infringement claim); *Nickson Indus., Inc. v. Rol Mfg. Co.* (Fed. Cir. 1988, p.798) (U.S.) ("Where an established royalty exists, it will usually be the best measure of what is a 'reasonable' royalty.").

[109] *See, e.g., Consol. Rubber Tire Co.* v. *Diamond Rubber Co. of NY* (S.D.N.Y. 1915, p.459) (U.S.) (describing the inappropriateness of awarding established royalties in circumstances where the licensed patent was widely believed to be invalid); Taylor 2014, 101–04 (explaining that, "[i]n an unbroken line of succession, later courts have followed Judge Hand's reasoning [in *Consol. Rubber Tire Co.*] by awarding reasonable royalties rather than diminished royalties established during periods of 'disrepute' and 'open defiance' of patents").

[110] *See* Masur 2015, 123–24 (noting the difficulties with using different technologies); *see also* Cotter 2011, 748 ("Strictly speaking, then, for a license to be economically comparable it should relate to the same patent or patents at issue … "); Weinstein et al. 2013, 553 ("In view of *ResQNet* and *Lucent*, comparable licenses can only include licenses to the patent-in-suit itself, essentially removing from consideration licenses contemplated under *Georgia-Pacific* Factors 2 and 12.").

problems arise. Licenses often bundle many patents together, including the patent of interest, which makes it difficult to separate out the value of the technology protected by the patent in suit. Licenses involving technology transfer, as opposed to a mere promise not to sue, routinely include other forms of supporting IP such as trademarks or trade secrets relevant to the patented technology, as well as other obligations on both sides such as grantback clauses or obligations to provide ongoing technical support. In litigation, the hypothetical negotiation concerns a very different transaction, often one involving a bare license to the patent itself. Nevertheless, it may be possible to make adjustments to compensate for the value attributable to other factors.[111] At least U.S. courts appear generally well attuned to this problem, and commonly exclude licenses including substantial non-patent benefits.[112]

Moreover, even licenses to the same patent with similar ancillary clauses are not necessarily comparable in terms of the royalty, because patentees are likely to price discriminate – that is, to charge different users prices that reflect the variation in value among those users.[113] A few square centimeters of Gore-Tex may save a life when used in a vascular graft, while a square meter of it may be needed for added comfort in a rain jacket. If the patent owner charged the same amount per unit area to the raincoat manufacturer as to the stent manufacturer, it would either forego substantial profits on the license for the stent, or forgo the raincoat license entirely. Price discrimination is consistent with the principle, enunciated at the outset of this chapter, that the patentee should be entitled to a reward commensurate with the value of its technology over the next best alternative. If that value varies between applications, the patentee is likely to charge a different price for those applications. This means that the royalty in a license for the use of the patented technology in a raincoat is probably not a valid comparable in litigation of the use of the technology in a stent, even if the ancillary clauses (and even the licensee) are exactly the same. (Indeed, even licensees that manufacture both stents and raincoats may well pay a different royalty to the patentee for the different uses.)[114] Similarly, a patentee may also price discriminate between different users, even for the same application, if for example one of the users has access to complementary technology while the other does not.[115]

---

[111] *See, e.g., Microsoft Corp.* v. *Motorola, Inc.* (W.D. Wash. 2013, p.79–92) (U.S.) (quantifying the value to Microsoft of access to the technology in the pool); *Unwired Planet Int'l Ltd.* v. *Huawei Techs. Co.* (Pat 2017) (UK) (awarding FRAND royalties based on adjustments to the royalties earned by the assignor of the relevant patent families).

[112] *See* Hovenkamp & Masur 2017, 407 n.48.

[113] *See, e.g., id.* at 12.

[114] *See Samsung Elecs. Co.* v. *Apple Japan LLC* (IP High Ct. 2014, p.134) (Japan) (awarding different royalties for the same technology to the same manufacturer of phones and tablets).

[115] *See* Hovenkamp & Masur 2017, 395–96.

2 Circularity

Another possible problem with using comparable licenses is circularity. Because the use of comparables to determine a reasonable royalty is one of the most predictable aspects of a reasonable royalty assessment, one would expect the parties to anticipate the use of comparables if the matter were to proceed to litigation, and to factor this into their bargaining. Thus, if there is any systematic and predictable error in the courts' assessment of the royalty, this error will then be amplified through the use of comparables. Moreover, circularity can arise even if the parties never litigate, as it depends only on the parties' expectation of the litigation outcome.[116]

Circularity can come in two distinct forms, which we will refer to as "holdup/ holdout circularity" and "probabilistic circularity." First, if the prior licenses being used as comparables were negotiated in circumstances where the licensee was subject to holdup or the patentee subject to holdout, the comparable will reflect holdup or holdout value, not just the value of the patented technology over the noninfringing alternative.[117] One cure for holdup circularity would be to eliminate the risk of holdup itself by denying injunctive relief, though the question of whether denying injunctions in a broader class of cases is desirable, is a significant issue in and of itself (and one that probably should not be driven by the problem of holdup circularity). Alternatively, courts can avoid holdup circularity even if they grant injunctions by excluding evidence of licenses that were negotiated in circumstances giving rise to holdup. This implies excluding evidence of licenses that were negotiated after the licensee had incurred sunk costs. But this may not be easy, as it requires knowledge not just of the prior license itself, but the circumstances under which it was negotiated. In addition, Lemley and Shapiro argue that a form of holdup arises when the user would have had to keep its product off the market after litigation to allow for redesign, and this form of holdup also can be magnified by circularity. This "redesign holdup circularity" can be avoided by excluding licenses negotiated in those circumstances, but this rule too would seem difficult to implement, since it would require knowledge of what the licensee would have thought its best option was in the counterfactual world in which its licensing negotiations failed. The problem of redesign holdup circularity nevertheless can be mitigated if stays are normally granted to allow redesign, as discussed in Chapter 4 on injunctions.[118]

---

[116] *See* Masur 2015, 133; Taylor 2014, 112–15.

[117] *See* Shapiro 2010, 314–15; Lemley & Shapiro 2007a, 2021–22. As discussed in Chapter 4, the Lemley & Shapiro model assumes that a court will always grant a permanent injunction to the successful patentee, and reasonable royalties for the prejudgment infringement. The longer the trial takes as a proportion of the term of the patent, the greater the effect of the reasonable royalty on the litigation outcome, and so the larger the multiplier. In Shapiro's formal model, if litigation always takes the same amount of time, the circularity effect will result in a multiplier that is inversely proportional to the post-trial patent term. *See* Shapiro 2010, 314.

[118] Lemley and Shapiro also argue that the probabilistic nature of patents can give rise to holdup, even when a license is negotiated *ex ante*: *see* the discussion of "probabilistic holdup" in Chapter 7.3.1.

A different kind of circularity can arise due to the probabilistic nature of patents. As discussed in Section 7.3.1, parties to an actual negotiation would discount the value of the patented technology by the probability of liability, thus potentially giving rise to the double discounting problem if courts use a negotiated royalty as the basis for a reasonable royalty. (The doubly discounted reasonable royalty awarded by the court then would serve as background to the negotiation of the next license, which would then be trebly discounted and so on.)[119] In contrast with the problem of holdup circularity, which potentially *inflates* negotiated royalties as compared with the benchmark value of the patented technology, this problem of "probabilistic circularity" *deflates* negotiated royalties as compared with the benchmark. (Note too that it is likely to infect even established royalties, notwithstanding their more elevated status in the hierarchy of comparables as noted above.) Furthermore, unlike holdup circularity, which does not arise if the parties do not anticipate that a permanent injunction will be granted, probabilistic circularity arises whether or not the parties expect a permanent injunction to be granted.

Conceivably, holdup circularity and probabilistic circularity may offset one another in some cases, but given the difficulty in assessing the magnitude of both types of circularity, it will be impossible to determine the degree to which this is so. The most that might be said is that when the prior license involved a license to a patent that was not already known to be valid and infringed, and it was negotiated after the licensee had incurred sunk costs, the negotiated royalty might be too high or too low, depending on which effect dominates.

In principle, the problem of probabilistic circularity can be avoided by suitably enhancing the actual royalties to compensate for discounting.[120] There are two problems with this response, however. The first is that, in practice, it seems that such an enhancement is rarely made.[121] The second, and more fundamental, problem is the difficulty of making an appropriate adjustment. The ideal multiplier would turn on the belief of the parties to the comparable license as to the probability of liability at the time they negotiated the license. But this will be very hard to prove, as it turns "upon private information, available only to the parties to the first licensing agreement, about the plaintiff's probability of success in litigation."[122] The information may not exist at all outside the minds of the negotiators, and

---

Probabilistic holdup, however, does not result in circularity, because the overcharge arises because the potential licensee's threat point is not to use the patented technology entirely; that is to say, the licensee acts as if the patent was valid and infringed. But that is the appropriate assumption once validity and infringement have been established at trial.

[119] *See* Taylor 2014, 115–16.

[120] *See id.* at 130–31.

[121] *See* Masur 2015, 132 n.76; Taylor 2014, 144–48 (explaining why this is so). For a rare exception, *see* St. Lawrence (E.D. Tex. Feb. 21, 2017) (permitting St. Lawrence's expert to offer an opinion that the royalty rate that St. Lawrence had previously negotiated with Samsung for the use of the patents in suit in the pending case against ZTE and Motorola should be increased by 50 percent to reflect a "settlement discount" and 18 percent to account for an "invalidity discount").

[122] Masur 2015, 120; *see also* Taylor 2014, 147.

because the prior licensee is not a party to the current litigation, any internal memoranda shedding light on the licensee's view of the probability of liability probably would not be discoverable. (In some cases, the patentee's internal memoranda might shed light on the issue, but even using this information would be problematic, as it would normally represent only the patentee's view.)[123] And in any event, this inquiry would require time-consuming and expensive satellite litigation. An alternative would be for the court to try to estimate the discount based on objective factors relative to the particular prior license, such as the testimony of experts as to the probability of liability. But this would be a difficult inquiry on a new issue that would not otherwise have to be litigated, and that does not seem especially susceptible to the production of reliable results.[124] Thus, in many situations, courts might be better off without adjusting for the implicit discount, and instead simply being mindful that the comparable license provides "a floor for valuing the patent, not [necessarily] a reasonable estimate."[125]

Finally, one could imagine using a standard multiplier. For example, if "any given patent owner has a 25% chance ex ante of prevailing against any given alleged infringer, then the appropriate multiplier is four."[126] But a standard multiplier not calibrated to evidence of discounting in a particular case merely recasts the circularity problem.[127] This is because a standard multiplier will overcompensate patentees with strong patents. Anticipating this, parties bargaining in the shadow of the expected trial outcome will negotiate a royalty based on the inflated damages value, and that inflated royalty will feed back into future awards, and so on.[128] This would result, in effect, in a new source of holdup that would allow a patentee with a strong patent to extract more than the value of its invention. The same spiral would happen in the other direction with patents that are weaker than average.[129]

---

[123] Though it is not unreasonable to assume the patentee's estimated probability of liability would be in the same ballpark as the licensee's, or they would not have been able to come to an agreement.

[124] *See* Masur 2015, 149–52 (arguing persuasively that an inquiry of this type would be unsatisfactory); Taylor 2014, 147–48 (same).

[125] Masur 2015, 131.

[126] *Id.* at 149–52; *see also* Taylor 2014, 146 ("If infringement and validity are independent variables, then the multiplier resulting from the assumption of liability should be four; that is, the jury should multiply the negotiated royalty reflecting 50% probability of validity and 50% probability of infringement by four to obtain a reasonable royalty reflecting certainty as to liability.").

[127] A separate problem with the standard multiplier is that it would probably not be admissible in U.S. law as not being tied to the facts of the case. *See* Masur 2015, 146. Regardless, even in instances of reliable evidence tied to the facts of the case, there is reason to think a jury in particular would not use an appropriate multiplier. Taylor 2014, 146 ("[D]oes anyone really think that in a *close* case a jury will multiply pre-litigation royalties by *four*, while in a case of *blatant liability* a jury will *not increase pre-litigation royalties at all*?").

[128] For example, if the parties to the actual negotiation thought there was a 90 percent chance of liability, the royalty in the prior comparable license will hardly be discounted at all, and a reasonable royalty based on that prior license, augmented by a standard multiplier of four, will therefore be almost four times too large. *See* Masur 2015, 154.

[129] *See id.* at 155.

It therefore would appear very difficult in most cases to reliably enhance the actual royalty arrived at in prior comparable licenses, even though the licenses are themselves otherwise very similar to that at issue in litigation. An alternative approach would be to try to select licenses in which the royalty was not discounted, because they were negotiated in circumstances in which the probability of liability is high. One example would be licenses negotiated after a patent had been held to be valid in other litigation. But even then, the previous judgment of validity would not be binding in litigation involving a different infringer, so it is likely there would still be some discount for the probability of invalidity. And unless the implementation was exactly the same (as might be the case in the SEP context), there might be substantial discounting as to infringement as well, let alone discounting due to risks of invalidity or unenforceability. Further, this approach would severely restrict the cases in which comparables could be used.

In the same vein, some authors have suggested that prior settlements, which courts in the United States normally (though not always) exclude from evidence,[130] actually should be preferred, particularly if the settlement was entered into when the patent owner appeared to be winning the underlying litigation.[131] This proposal is again only helpful in a relatively narrow range of cases, as prior settlements are not always available. Moreover, it must be clear that the patentee was winning on the basis of objective factors, such as preliminary motions favoring the patentee, or the discounting problem will not be addressed.[132] Further, if the patentee in the prior litigation would have expected to obtain an injunction if successful, the settlement may reflect holdup value – thus solving the problem of probabilistic circularity at the expense of inviting the problem of holdup circularity. Another concern with settlements is that they may reflect the value of avoiding litigation costs rather than the value of the patented technology, though this would be a significant problem only when litigation costs are at least comparable to the value of the patented technology.[133]

3 Dynamic Considerations

Some of these problems are likely to get worse in contexts where patentees can predict that a reasonable royalty will be the primary remedy, because we would

[130]   *See, e.g., Rude* v. *Westcott* (U.S. 1889, p.164) (U.S.); *but see ResQNet* (Fed. Cir. 2010, p.868) (approving use of settlement as a comparable, on the facts of the case); Narechania & Kirklin 2012.

[131]   *See* Taylor 2014, 131 (suggesting that "to the extent settlement agreements reflect more certainty regarding liability, economists may be able to use them, rather than other agreements, to identify more easily the true value of patented technology"). This suggestion is more fully developed by Masur 2015, 145–46. *See also Prism Techs.* (Fed. Cir. 2017) (approving the use of a settlement license on the facts of the case, and discussing the circumstances under which settlements are more or less likely to be probative).

[132]   *See* Masur 2015, 145–46, 148.

[133]   In such a case, it may even be that the royalty will be too low, not too high. If the patent is weak, litigation value settlement may make sense, but once it is adjudged to be valid and infringed, those low-value settlements no longer reflect the true value of the patented technology.

expect them to adjust their licensing practices to reflect this expectation.[134] These adjustments might have two kinds of unwanted effects. First, they may make determining accurate damages in the particular case even more difficult. A patentee worried about probabilistic discounting depressing its recovery in future litigation may insist on artificially bundling unnecessary trade secrets or other sham terms into a license solely to ensure that it cannot subsequently be used as a comparable. This is wasteful in itself, though if the parties are careful to include terms that they know are in fact of no value, it will not otherwise distort the transaction.[135] Another possibility is that a patentee would include self-indulging statements in license agreements about large discounts in light of significant risks of non-recovery.[136] Conversely, the patentee may try to game the system by negotiating licenses with artificially high rates, in hopes that these will be used as comparables.[137] This tactic is also wasteful in terms of increased transaction costs, but again it will not affect the licensing terms more generally if courts can detect and exclude such licenses from being used as comparables (which, however, is debatable).

Second, such adjustments may distort the general licensing behavior of the patentee in ways that will have more general effects. As discussed above, price discrimination means that a patentee will rationally charge a high royalty to a high-value user and a low royalty to a low-value user. But if the patentee anticipates that its license to a low-value user will be used as a comparable in subsequent litigation against a high-value user, it may prefer not to license the low-value user at all. This hurts both parties, and society as a whole.[138] The cure for this, in principle, would be for courts to exclude licenses negotiated with a low-value user as comparables in subsequent litigation with the high-value user, but it is far from clear that courts could reliably and predictably differentiate the two cases.[139] And of course, the first step would be for courts to acknowledge the need to do so. Otherwise, the use of comparable licenses to assess reasonable royalties may actually result in restricted licensing of the technology. This would be highly undesirable if it is now, or is likely to become, a problem in practice.

All of this is not to say that comparables are not probative at all, or that the above problems can never be mitigated or avoided. For example, Judge Robart's use of the

---

[134] As discussed in Chapter 4, awarding ongoing royalties in lieu of injunctions generates a risk of error in the calculation of such royalties – though whether such errors systematically favor one party or the other, and whether they are justified in view of the holdup risk resulting from injunctions, are debatable questions.

[135] *See* Hovenkamp & Masur 2017, 406.

[136] Taylor 2014, 149.

[137] *See* Hovenkamp & Masur 2017, 406–09; Cotter 2018, 195 (noting that this seems to have been the case in *Microsoft Corp. v. Motorola, Inc.* (W.D. Wash. 2013) (U.S.)).

[138] *See* Hovenkamp & Masur 2017, 403–04.

[139] *See id.* Note that it is not enough that the courts *could* make the distinction; they would have to do so in practice with sufficient predictability that the patentee would not need to worry about the low-value license affecting its recovery in a high-value lawsuit.

MPEG LA H.264 patent pool rate in *Microsoft* v. *Motorola* probably did not trigger a serious probabilistic discounting problem, because even if *some* individual patents in the pool might have been invalid or not infringed, parties to the pool could be highly confident that it was necessary to take a pool license to practice the technology in question. The price discrimination problem also did not appear to arise in that case, because the pool did not price discriminate other than on the basis of volume,[140] and a pool license would have been available to the infringer. Sunk-costs circularity also probably did not arise because, at least as it appears, the pool rates were set to attract licensees who had not yet incurred sunk costs. Moreover, it may be the case that the circularity problems noted above are more theoretical than practical. Although the annual patent litigation studies produced by PwC and Lex Machina, discussed above in Section 1.1.1, reveal some variations from year to year, there does not appear to be any trend toward consistently higher (or lower) median damages awards in the United States over the past decade. Theoretical difficulties aside, therefore, it may be that courts already are adequately counteracting the potential spiraling effects of circularity.

Overall, then, we recommend that courts should apply comparables and other market evidence with caution. Such evidence often may be the best that is available, and even when there is other evidence of the value of the technology over alternatives, it may still be useful to consider market evidence by way of comparison. Nonetheless, courts probably could make more accurate determinations if more license terms were publicly accessible. We therefore recommend (and propose further research devoted to) ongoing efforts to encourage such disclosure.[141]

1.3.7 *Entire Market Value Rule and Smallest Saleable Unit*

Another practical concern that often arises when applying a multifactor approach to reasonable royalties is that the parties may make strategic choices with respect to the royalty base and royalty rate that they present to fact finders. To reach a specific reasonable royalty award, a patentee could argue (or a fact finder could determine) that a relatively small rate should be applied to a relatively large base, or conversely that a relatively large rate should apply to a relatively small base. For example,

---

[140] *See Microsoft Corp.* v. *Motorola, Inc.* (W.D. Wash. 2013, p.78) (U.S.) (stating that "[t]he MPEG LA H.264 patent pool charges royalties to licensees for products that incorporate an H.264 codec according to the following schedule: • the first 100,000 units are royalty-free; • for unit volumes between 100,000 and 5 million, the royalty is $0.20 per unit; and • for unit volumes above 5 million, the royalty rate is $0.10 per unit").

[141] *See, e.g.,* Contreras et al. 2016 (proposing a study aimed at providing "researchers, litigants, judges, policy makers, regulators and the public with previously unavailable information regarding commercial patent licensing practices, including royalty rates, in a manner that does not compromise firm-level confidential information"); *see also* Ward 2017 (discussing recent German case law intended to increase the disclosure, subject to confidentiality order, of comparables for use in FRAND licensing disputes).

a 1 percent royalty rate applied to a \$10,000 base and a 25 percent rate applied to a \$400 base both lead to a \$100 reasonable royalty award.

In theory, it should be irrelevant which method a litigant elects when presenting a damages case in court, and a fact finder should be able to determine an appropriate royalty employing either method. In line with this observation, in many jurisdictions courts routinely use the value of the end product as the royalty base.[142]

In recent years, however, U.S. law has placed limits on patentees' ability to introduce evidence of the profit or revenue derived from sales of the entire accused product. These restrictions have been motivated at least in part by the long-recognized need to ensure that damages are properly apportioned to the patented features of the accused device, and not to other elements.[143] Concerns over large bases resulting in overcompensation thus have led the Federal Circuit to articulate a general rule that the royalty base should be the "smallest saleable patent-practicing unit" (SSPPU) in the accused product, and that use of the "entire market value" of the end product as the base is permissible only when the patent drives the demand for the end product.[144] In yet more recent cases, however, the Federal Circuit has permitted use of the entire market value when the parties themselves negotiated *ex ante* on the basis of the entire accused product,[145] or comparable licenses were negotiated on the basis of entire products.[146]

---

[142] In Germany, for example, even when the patent covers only a portion of an end product, courts consider what reasonable parties would have selected as the royalty base, and often though not invariably use the value of the end product, taking into account such factors as industry custom; the convenience of the parties; whether the invention accounts for all or most of the value of the end product; whether the component is often sold separately; and whether it invests the product with its own distinctive stamp (*kennzeichnendes Gepräge*). See Cotter 2013a, 268; Kühnen 2015, 700–02; Schönknecht 2012, 322–24. Similarly, in Japan courts typically use the value of the end product as the base. *See* Second Subcommittee of the Second Patent Committee 2014; Cotter 2015; *Samsung Elecs. Co. v. Apple Japan LLC* (IP High Ct. 2014) (Japan).

[143] *Garretson v. Clark* (U.S. 1884, p.121) (U.S.) ("The patentee ... must in every case give evidence tending to separate or apportion the defendant's profits and the patentee's damages between the patented feature and the unpatented features.").

[144] *See, e.g., VirnetX, Inc. v. Apple Inc.* (Fed. Cir. 2014) (U.S.) (reversing a damages award based on the entire value of accused smartphone, rather than the smallest saleable infringing component); *LaserDynamics, Inc. v. Quanta Comp., Inc.* (Fed. Cir. 2012, p.67) (U.S.) ("[I]t is generally required that royalties be based not on the entire product, but instead on the 'smallest salable patent-practicing unit.'"). Though the term "entire market value rule" is generally now understood to have this meaning, earlier case law gave the doctrine much broader application. *See* Love 2007, 272 (discussing older case law under which the entire market value rule acted as "a broad exception to the general rule of apportionment").

[145] *See CSIRO v. Cisco Sys., Inc.* (Fed. Cir. 2015, p.1301–04) (U.S.) (holding that it was permissible for a court to consider evidence of the parties' previous negotiations, which were based on the entire value of the accused product).

[146] *See Ericsson, Inc. v. D-Link Sys.* (Fed. Cir. 2014, p.1225–29) (U.S.) (holding that it was permissible for a court to admit evidence of comparable licenses that were based on the entire value of allegedly infringing products). *See also* Teece & Sherry 2016 (criticizing case law requiring litigants to use a smallest saleable unit royalty base on the grounds that "very few real-world licenses comport with the SSPPU doctrine, making it difficult to appeal to the terms of real-world licenses in assessing reasonable royalties").

In addition to concerns over apportionment, the Federal Circuit justifies its preference that the royalty base be the smallest saleable unit on the grounds that the value of the entire accused product will tend to have an undue influence on jurors in cases where the asserted patent covers just one of many components or features that comprise the entire product, and in such cases may lead to damages awards that are overcompensatory.[147] The concern may stem from a cognitive bias known as "anchoring," i.e., the human tendency to give undue weight to the first data point one encounters, even if that data point is arbitrary or irrelevant.[148] In the context of U.S. litigation, anchoring tends to reinforce the importance of the plaintiff's damages case,[149] which is virtually always presented first and in some cases is not countered at all by the infringer.[150] Experimental studies using fact patterns involving personal injury cases and punitive damages awards have found evidence of an anchoring effect and suggest that, all else equal, a plaintiff that requests more damages will tend to receive a larger award.[151] Thus, there is a risk that reasonable royalty awards based on the entire value of the accused multicomponent products will systematically overvalue patent rights that cover just a fraction of the products' components or features.

A related problem is that, according to one study based on royalties awarded from 1982 to 2005, U.S. juries tend to award royalty rates that are within the general vicinity of 10 percent, regardless of the size of the base that the rate is applied to.[152]

---

[147] *See VirnetX, Inc. v. Apple Inc.* (Fed. Cir. 2014, p.1327) (U.S.) (noting that the "smallest saleable unit" requirement is based on a "fundamental concern about skewing the damages horizon" by "misleadingly suggest[ing] an inappropriate range" of damages); *LaserDynamics, Inc. v. Quanta Comp., Inc.* (Fed. Cir. 2012, p.68) (U.S.) ("Admission of ... overall revenues, which have no demonstrated correlation to the value of the patented feature alone, only serve to make a patentee's proffered damages amount appear modest by comparison, and to artificially inflate the jury's damages calculation beyond that which is 'adequate to compensate for the infringement.'").

[148] *See, e.g.*, Furnham & Boo 2011, 35 (defining the "anchoring effect" as "the disproportionate influence on decision makers to make judgments that are biased toward an initially presented value").

[149] *See* Greene & Bornstein 2003, 149–73 (reviewing the literature on anchoring's effect on juries). *See also* Posner & Sunstein 2005, 593 ("Juries lack reference points, so their judgments will depend heavily on the presentation of evidence by lawyers, and on whatever anchors, prejudices, and expectations citizens bring to the jury box.").

[150] *See* Chao 2012, 136–37 (noting that the anchoring effect of the plaintiff's royalty base "is often exacerbated by the tactics defendants use at trial," including failure to offer a counter-anchor due to "fear that presenting a damages case will be interpreted as an admission of liability").

[151] *See* Campbell et al. 2016, 546 (finding in an experimental study of mock jurors deciding a medical malpractice case that "powerful anchoring effects dominate much smaller but still statistically significant credibility effects" that result from presenting "outrageous[ly]" large anchors); Chapman & Bornstein 1996, 519 (finding in an experimental study of mock jurors deciding a personal injury case that "anchoring occurs in legal applications, and that plaintiffs would do well to request large compensation awards"); Hastie et al. 1999, 445 (finding in an experimental study in which mock jurors were asked to award punitive damages that "plaintiff's requested award values had a dramatic effect on awards: the higher the request, the higher the awards").

[152] *See* Lemley & Shapiro 2007a, 2034 (finding in a study of fifty-eight patent verdicts awarded between 1982 and 2005 that "[t]he royalty rate for components is approximately 10.0%, compared with 13.1% for all inventions and 14.7% for integrated product claims").

Combined with anchoring, this finding (if it is still valid) suggests that a patentee who is permitted to present large revenue figures to a jury or judge[153] might receive a larger damages award as a result, even if the revenue figures themselves bear little relation to the value of the patented technology. On the other hand, we are not aware of any more recent studies on the issue, and it is possible that the effect has diminished over time (due, perhaps, to the abolition of the 25 percent rule of thumb). There is also concern that juries prefer whole-number rates even when the evidence suggests that the appropriate rate is less than 1 percent. We therefore propose further research on the question of whether juries are susceptible to awarding inappropriately high damages given concerns with apportionment, anchoring, and preferences for particular royalty rates.

In addition, there may be a risk that use of the entire market value as the royalty base will skew litigation outcomes by encouraging patentees to sue downstream parties that are ill suited to defend patent cases. Imagine for example, an allegedly infringing component that is produced by manufacturer M, incorporated into a consumer electronics product produced by company C, shipped to retailer R, and sold to user U. Because infringement can occur by making, selling, or using patented technology, M, C, R, and U are all potential targets for suit. However, in all likelihood it is M that is best positioned to defend a patent suit.[154] R and U, in particular, may well know nothing about how the component operates, not to mention the intricacies of patent law. Nonetheless, the effect of anchoring will tend to inflate the amount of damages a patentee can expect to recover from C, R, or U. While M may sell the chip to C for pennies or a few dollars, C may earn dozens or hundreds of dollars per unit in sales to R, and R may sell the final product to users for several hundred dollars more per unit.[155] In addition, U may use the product as part of a business that generates many thousands of dollars a year. Given the option to choose, a patentee will find it advantageous (for reasons that have little to do with the value of the patented technology) to seek damages from component purchasers, retailers, or even users, all of whom have suboptimal incentives to test the patent's

---

[153] Generally speaking, we think it is likely that judges, by virtue of their legal training and experience, will be less susceptible to this effect than lay jurors. As a result, this concern may be particularly acute in countries in which juries award damages, and less of a concern in countries where damages are calculated by judges. However, we do not believe that judges are completely immune. Indeed, experimental studies have shown that judges are susceptible to anchoring effects when awarding damages and determining criminal sentences. *See* Rachlinski et al. 2015, 695 (finding "that the presence of misleading numeric reference points (or 'anchors') affected judges' decisions in a series of hypothetical cases").

[154] *See* Love & Yoon 2013, 1620–35 (explaining that, compared to their downstream customers, manufacturers are less susceptible to litigation cost holdup and are better positioned to both test the merits of infringement allegations and appropriately value infringed patent rights). *See also* Europe Economics 2016, 5, 28, 48 (noting that European PAEs tend to target telecom companies, "the most vulnerable segment of the supply chain").

[155] Consider, for example, an allegedly infringing $6.50 3G wireless chipset installed in a smartphone that retails for $500. *See* Love & Yoon 2013, 1634 n.104 (using the example of a new iPhone 4S in 2013).

validity and the patentee's infringement contentions.[156] On the other hand, if patentees are suing retailers and users who are ill-positioned to defend themselves in an effort to obtain inappropriately high royalties, the first best solution may be to rein in the ability to maintain patent infringement lawsuits down the chain of distribution, rather than to alter damages law.

Finally, limiting damages to the smallest saleable unit may have certain practical benefits. For example, defaulting to a smaller royalty base will tend to reduce the effect of error in royalty rate selection.[157] It will also tend to narrow the range of possible trial outcomes, which benefits risk-averse parties and increases the likelihood of pretrial settlement.

At the same time, there are several economic arguments in favor of using the entire market value as the royalty base. First, limiting damages calculations to the component level may undervalue patented technology by failing to share with the patentee a portion of the spillover value created by its invention.[158] A new high-resolution computer screen, for example, may be undervalued by U.S. patent law because, though demand for computers is not primarily driven by their screens, better screens enable or improve other computer functionality, such as video gaming and movie watching.[159] While in many circumstances we would expect spillover value to be reflected in the sales price of the patented component, it may not be in

---

[156] Love & Yoon 2013, 1628 (arguing that "[a]s between a similarly situated customer and manufacturer, it is virtually always the manufacturer that is best suited to vigorously litigate the case in a manner that challenges the patent's validity and delineates its claim scope" because customers are often "compan-[ies] outside the technology industry that . . . have no expertise in the accused technology[,] . . . were not involved in the design, development, or manufacture of the accused technology[, and] . . . have no understanding of the field of the patent and no knowledge of the prior art to the patent"). Though it is true that a patentee will generally find it more costly to sue multiple downstream parties rather than a single manufacturer, experience suggests that many patentees will nonetheless make this choice. In the United States, retailers are commonly sued for selling allegedly infringing products. For example, according to Lex Machina, Wal-Mart, Target, and Best Buy were each sued for patent infringement more than eighty times between 2012 and 2016. Moreover, some patentees have even pursued large numbers of end users of allegedly infringing products. *Id.* at 1610–11 (describing patent monetization campaigns undertaken by patentees like Innovatio IP Venutres, LLC, MPHJ Technology Investments, LLC, and ArrivalStar S.A., which collectively sued hundreds of end users and threatened to sue thousands more).

[157] *See* Stern 2015, 554 n.26 ("[C]onsider a $1 chip in a $500 smartphone. Suppose the invention contributes 10% of the value of the chip and that the reasonable royalty is half of that or 5 cents, i.e., 5% of the $1 chip price. In principle, the reasonable royalty based on the smartphone price would be the same 5 cents or 0.02% of $500. But how is a jury or judge to determine the difference between a royalty of 0.02% and 0.01% or even 0.1%? Yet the cash value of the error is multiplied greatly by starting out with an inflated royalty base. Choosing between infinitesimals is an inherently error-prone exercise.").

[158] *See* Petit 2016 (arguing that use of a "smallest saleable unit" benchmark for patent damages may undervalue "general purpose technologies" that "yield countless positive production externalities"); Geradin & Layne-Farrar 2010, 774–76 (arguing that a strict application of the U.S. entire market value rule may undervalue patent rights to a component of a complex product "if the component in question 'enables' other components but does not rise to the level of driving demand").

[159] *See* Geradin & Layne-Farrar 2010, 775 (using this same example).

some instances. Thus, as Petit has argued, "general purpose" technologies with many relatively low-value uses may be undervalued in patent suits against parties that use the technology for less common applications that produce especially large cost savings or profits.[160]

Relatedly, to the extent price discrimination is economically efficient, it makes sense to allow patent owners to extract a higher royalty from implementers who market comparatively expensive end products for which the patent confers substantial value. In addition, as noted above, in real-world licensing transactions parties often, though not invariably, use the entire market value as the base. To the extent reasonable royalty awards should mimic real-world licenses, use of the entire market value often would seem unexceptional.[161]

Given the wide variety of arguments for and against the entire market value/ SSPPU rules as employed in the United States, we first propose further research, both with regard to the economic issues highlighted above and into the psychology of judges and juries (e.g., can anchoring and other biases be overcome in other ways?). Given the likelihood that anchoring does play a role in jury deliberations, however, we further recommend that, for now at least, the Federal Circuit retain rules substantially restricting the use of the entire market value. By the same token, given the likelihood that professional judges are less affected (though perhaps not unaffected) by anchoring, for now we do not recommend that other countries (which do not employ juries to decide patent cases) alter their more liberal approach to the use of the entire market value.

1.4 PRACTICAL CONSIDERATIONS

In this final Section, we briefly address three remaining practical issues that courts in some countries either have considered or may devote further attention to in the future, namely (1) the evaluation of individual pieces of expert evidence to satisfy a basic threshold of quality; (2) the enhancement of reasonable royalty awards to achieve additional deterrence; and (3) the calibration of damages awards based on context-specific factors.

---

[160] *See* Petit 2016 (using the example of wireless technology that, when adopted for use in airplanes, led to substantial cost savings by reducing aircraft weight and, consequently, fuel costs). *See also* Régibeau et al. 2016, 77 (comparing wireless technology in a smartphone, which "do[es] appear to influence a number of important functionalities," to wireless technology in a car, which "it would be rash to argue ... contribute to a very substantial share of the value that consumers place on specific cars"); Layne-Farrar 2017 (recommending that courts focus on valuing the use of a technology to the implementer, not on trying to pinpoint its location in a particular component; and that they should permit experts to use as the royalty base the implementer's properly apportioned revenue, without disclosing to the jury the infringer's overall revenues or profits).

[161] *See also* Baron & Pentheroudakis 2017, 93–94 (noting that "[t]he practicability (and traceability) of the SSPPU is questionable in the context of portfolio licensing: it is often not possible to map a portfolio of hundreds or even thousands of diverse patents to a single SSPPU").

1.4.1 *Expert Evidence and* Daubert *Gatekeeping in the United States*

In the United States, there are two main ways by which judges can police proof of reasonable royalty damages. First, they can enforce and, as appropriate and necessary, develop legal doctrine directly regulating what constitutes adequate evidence for reasonable royalty damages. Second, they can enforce and, as appropriate and necessary, develop legal doctrine regulating the admissibility of evidence for purposes of such proof.

The second, admissibility oriented mechanism looms large in the United States, where the primary fact finder is commonly a jury, rather than the trial judge. Under the United States' Federal Rule of Evidence 702, which essentially embodies a requirement previously articulated by the Supreme Court of the United States in *Daubert* v. *Merrell Dow Pharmaceuticals, Inc.*,[162] trial judges police the admissibility of expert testimony to ensure that this evidence "will help the trier of fact to understand the evidence or to determine a fact in issue," "is based on sufficient facts or data," and results from the application of "reliable principles and methods."[163] Because expert testimony is often a vital component of the proof of reasonable royalty damages, judicial gatekeeping under *Daubert* has become a powerful tool for limiting the permissible evidentiary bases for such damages. The U.S. Court of Appeals for the Federal Circuit has reversed or vacated a number of damages verdicts in patent cases on *Daubert* grounds.[164]

In the absence of a jury or other fact finder distinct from the trial-level adjudicator of questions of law, there is probably less significance to the distinction between (1) the ultimate assessment of the overall sufficiency of evidence to support a damages award and (2) gatekeeping for the relevance and reliability of expert testimony. But although the particular standard for expert testimony gatekeeping has been controversial within the United States,[165] something like *Daubert*-style review might generally be useful even in the absence of juries. We recommend that courts consider whether individual pieces of expert evidence

---

[162] *Daubert* v. *Merrell Dow Pharm. Inc.* (U.S. 1993) (U.S.); *see also* Bernstein & Lasker 2015, 6 ("In 2000, the Judicial Conference of the United States ... amended Federal Rule of Evidence 702 for the express purpose of resolving conflicts in the courts about the meaning of *Daubert*.").

[163] FED. R. EVID. 702.

[164] *See, e.g.*, *VirnetX, Inc.* v. *Apple Inc.* (Fed. Cir. 2014, p.1329, 1333–34) (U.S.) (holding that damages expert's testimony on the royalty base and in support of a fifty-fifty split of profits was inadmissible); *LaserDynamics, Inc.* v. *Quanta Comp., Inc.* (Fed. Cir. 2012, p.79) (U.S.) (holding that a damages expert's testimony on the value of a reasonable royalty rate "was unreliable under Federal Rule of Evidence 702 and should have been excluded"); *Uniloc USA, Inc.* v. *Microsoft Corp.* (Fed. Cir. 2011, p.1318) (U.S.) (affirming grant of a new trial on damages where expert testimony based on a "25% rule of thumb" for the proportion of product value constituting a reasonable royalty "fail[ed] to pass muster under *Daubert*").

[165] *See, e.g.*, Bernstein & Lasker 2015, 9 (reporting "continued divisions among federal courts over the proper standards for admission of expert testimony ..."); Faigman & Imwinkelreid 2013, 1695 ("Even if *Daubert* is the right choice for the federal judiciary, a state could reasonably conclude that it is not the right path for it to take.").

satisfy a basic threshold of quality in addition to separately examining the overall sufficiency of all relevant evidence.

1.4.2 *"Kickers" for Reasonable Royalties*

There has been discussion in the United States about whether there should be the possibility of a "kicker" that increases damages beyond a straight reasonable royalty for any of multiple reasons: for example, compensation for litigation costs,[166] deterrence,[167] compensation for lost profits that a royalty rate might not ordinarily reflect,[168] and correction for pre-existing royalty rates' incorporation of a discount because of uncertainty about patent claim validity or scope.[169] The U.S. Court of Appeals for the Federal Circuit has indicated that courts may combine a reasonable royalty award with compensation for other damages that the royalty does not cover – for example, lost profits from depression of royalties obtained from others because infringement has bred "widespread and open disregard of [relevant] patent rights."[170] But the Federal Circuit has also held that monetary awards to compensate for litigation expenses or to punish an infringer may only be awarded in accordance with statutory provisions and precedent specific to awards of attorney fees or enhanced damages.[171] Thus, under current law in the United States, courts may not include a kicker for such purposes when assessing standard compensatory damages.

Consideration of awarding a kicker beyond reasonable royalties generally seems best addressed under other rubrics, which we explore in other parts of this book. In this chapter, we have already addressed questions about the need to correct for pre-litigation uncertainty in the context of the hypothetical negotiation framework. Likewise, questions about when and how to award lost profits are addressed in Chapter 2, and questions about when and how to punish infringement or compensate for litigation costs are discussed in Chapter 3. Rather than handle such concerns obliquely through the use of kickers added to reasonable royalties, we

---

[166] Cotter 2004, 316 (noting a "Federal Circuit decision stating that courts may not incorporate into the reasonable royalty award a damages 'kicker' so as to compensate the patentee for litigation and other expenses").

[167] *Id.* (indicating that a damages "kicker" might advance goals of deterrence).

[168] Lee & Melamed 2016, 459 ("[S]ince the royalty may include a 'kicker' based on *Georgia-Pacific* Factor 4 (the patent holder's policy of licensing or not licensing the patent), patent holders are generally compensated at least to some extent for their loss of market exclusivity."); Yang 2014, 655 (noting scholarly speculation that "[c]ourts, worried about undercompensating patentees who could not prove lost profits, added 'kickers' to reasonable royalty awards . . . ").

[169] Lemley & Shapiro 2007a, 2019–20 (contending that "[c]ourts have recognized [the discount] problem and periodically seek to modify the market-based royalty data by adding 'kickers,' either expressly or sub rosa."); *see also supra* note 15 (noting the occasional practice in France and Germany of increasing royalties to account for risks the infringer has avoided).

[170] *Maxwell* v. *J. Baker, Inc.* (Fed. Cir. 1996, p.1109) (U.S.) (quoting jury instruction).

[171] *Whitserve, LLC* v. *Computer Packages, Inc.* (Fed. Cir. 2012, p.34 n.18) (U.S.).

recommend that they be addressed directly through remedial doctrines created for those particular purposes.

1.4.3 *Calibrated Evidentiary Burdens or Royalty Measures*

As an alternative to applying the same standards for measuring or proving reasonable royalty damages in every case, courts could apply standards for measuring or proving reasonable royalty damages that are responsive to context-specific factors. These factors could include (1) the relative blameworthiness of the parties; "(2) the state of the art or the availability of evidence for proving damages," including one or another party's status as a cheaper information provider; and "(3) the amount of damages alleged."[172] Calibration of damages measures or evidentiary burdens based on context-specific factors has occurred in other legal areas, such as contract law[173] and the law of restitution.[174] In these areas of law, doubts are often resolved against parties viewed as blameworthy,[175] and courts have relaxed "demands of reasonable certainty when ... the state of the art or other circumstances do not permit more precise or robust proof of damages."[176] Extension of such calibration to encompass sensitivity to "the amount of damages alleged" seems plausible and perhaps even natural for a form of monetary relief that uses the word "reasonable" in its very name. At least if the law wishes to ensure that smaller claims for damages are practically enforceable, the law should not generally demand that a claimant for such limited damages expend more on proving these damages than the claimant alleges the damages to be worth. Nonetheless, because there is enough immediate challenge in articulating basic principles for computing reasonable royalties, we propose further research on more context-specific calibration.

---

[172] Golden 2017, 274; *see also* Chiang 2017 (advocating two principles for the assignment of evidentiary burdens in damages law: (1) "courts should only require a party to produce information when the social benefit of the information ... exceeds the costs of producing the information" and (2) "courts should impose the burden of proof on the party that can produce the required evidence at lower cost").

[173] Golden 2017, 272 (observing that, in contract law, "courts have allowed for pragmatic or fairness-oriented tuning of certainty standards on a retail as well as a wholesale basis").

[174] Golden & Sandrik 2017 ("The law of restitution illustrates how, in addressing difficult-to-quantify monetary relief, courts can develop a context-sensitive yet coherent approach that ... deploys both [monetary-relief] measures and burdens of proof or production in ways that distinguish between levels of relative responsibility or fault.").

[175] *See* Golden 2017, 271 (discussing treatments of doubts and blameworthiness in the First and Second Restatements of Contracts); Golden & Sandrik 2017 (discussing how the Restatement (Third) of Restitution and Unjust Enrichment assigns evidentiary burdens in accordance with "'the equitable disposition that resolves uncertainty in favor of the claimant against the conscious wrongdoer'" (quoting RESTATEMENT (THIRD) OF RESTITUTION AND UNJUST ENRICHMENT § 51 cmt. i)).

[176] Golden 2017, 272.

2

Lost Profits and Disgorgement

Christopher B. Seaman, Thomas F. Cotter, Brian J. Love,
Norman V. Siebrasse, and Masabumi Suzuki

2.1 INTRODUCTION

This chapter addresses two particular types of monetary remedies for patent infringement: (1) recovery of the patentee's lost profits and (2) disgorgement of the infringer's profits. In one respect, these remedies are mirror images of each other.[1] Both analyses make a comparison between the actual world in which the patent was infringed and a hypothetical "but for" world in which no infringement occurred. The patentee's lost profits represent the difference between the amount the patentee would have made without any infringement, and the amount the patentee actually made. For disgorgement, it is the opposite – an accounting of the infringer's profits is based on the difference between the amount the infringer actually made, and its (necessarily lower) profit in a "but for" world where it did not infringe.[2]

Despite this parallel, there are important differences in both the theoretical justifications for lost profits and disgorgement and their acceptance in patent systems around the world. As discussed in more detail below, the two remedies have different objectives: Lost profits are intended to restore the patentee to the position it would have occupied absent infringement (i.e., to make the patentee whole), while disgorgement may serve other purposes, including deterring infringement, recapturing wrongful gains made by the infringer, and encouraging prospective users of patented technology to bargain for a license.[3] In addition, while all major jurisdictions permit

---

[1] *Cf.* Eisenberg 2006, 561 (noting that the disgorgement remedy in contract law "is the mirror image of the expectation interest" – that is, to put the nonbreaching party in the position it would have occupied absent breach); *see also infra* note 210 and accompanying text (explaining in greater detail why recovery of the patentee's lost profits and disgorgement of infringer's profits represent mirror images in terms of methodology).

[2] Although disgorgement typically refers to the infringer's profits, strictly speaking it is not necessarily limited to cases in which the infringer actually made a profit. The disgorgement remedy also could be applicable to cases where the infringer actually lost money from sales of infringing products or services, but the infringer's losses "would have been even greater but for the infringement." Cotter 2013a, 68. This might occur, for example, if use of the patented technology resulted in cost savings, without which the infringer's losses would have increased.

[3] *See* Roberts 2010, 655–56, 671–72, 684–85; Cotter 2013a, 68–69 (further explaining why disgorgement would create an incentive to negotiate because it can make infringers "at least incrementally worse off

a practicing patentee to recover lost profits (at least in theory, although in practice it is more common in some countries than others), there is more divergence between major patent systems regarding whether and when the infringer can be required to disgorge its profits.

2.2 LOST PROFITS

2.2.1 *Introduction*

Patent systems around the world principally rely on monetary damages awards to compensate patentees for past acts of infringement.[4] For patentees that sell goods or services that practice the patented technology,[5] damages awards typically may include profits from sales lost due to the infringer's sales of its own competing products or services.[6] They may also include "price erosion," which are profits lost by the patentee on sales that it actually made, but at a lower price point than would have occurred absent competition from the infringer.[7] In both situations, the patentee must demonstrate causation – namely, that it would have made the sales that the infringer actually made,[8] or (for price erosion claims) that the patentee's actual sales would have been at a higher price absent infringement and thus would have resulted in a higher profit margin.[9] As a result, the lost profits inquiry requires a hypothetical reconstruction of the market as it would have existed "but for" the infringement.[10]

---

than they would have been if they had entered voluntary negotiations … "). In addition, in some jurisdictions like Japan, the infringer's profits are presumed to be equal to the amount of the patentee's actual damages. *Id.* at 323. In such situations, the infringer's profits serve as a proxy (albeit an imperfect one) for the restorative purpose of the lost profits remedy.

[4] Cotter 2013a, 63; *see also* Lemley 2009, 669 (explaining "[t]he purpose of … patent damages rules is ultimately … to compensate the inventor for losses attributable for the infringement … .").

[5] Lost profits generally are not available to nonpracticing entities (NPEs) and other patentees that primarily or exclusively monetize their patents through licensing and/or litigation. *See* Lee & Melamed 2016, 398 ("An increasing number of suits are brought by nonpracticing entities that cannot claim lost profits because they do not make or sell any products or services.").

[6] *See* Cotter 2013a, 63 ("[T]he patent owner should be entitled to recover at least her own lost profit resulting from the infringement.").

[7] *See, e.g.,* Thiele et al. 2010, 207 ("Price erosion occurs when a defendant's infringing activities force a patent owner to sell the patented product at a lower price than it would have set in the absence of the infringing product.").

[8] *See, e.g., BIC Leisure Prod, Inc. v. Windsurfing Int'l, Inc.* (Fed. Cir. 1993, p.1218) (U.S.) ("To recover lost profits … a patent owner must prove a causal relation between the infringement and its loss of profits.").

[9] *See* Parr & Smith 2005, 621 (noting that the patentee must demonstrate "a causal link between the actions of the infringer and the price erosion of the patent holder's patented product"); *see also* Marchese 1994, 749 ("No matter the form of lost profits sought, the patentee must establish causation – i.e., a nexus between the infringing activity and the patentee's lost profits.").

[10] *See, e.g., Grain Processing Corp. v. Am. Maize-Prods. Co.* (Fed. Cir. 1999, p.1350) (U.S.).

In this Section, we first discuss the availability and standard for awarding lost profits in major patent systems. This includes, for instance, the standard for determining entitlement to lost profits and whether the patentee must establish some degree of fault by the infringer as a prerequisite to recovery. Second, we address the role of noninfringing alternatives in this analysis, including whether the availability of a noninfringing alternative should limit or preclude an award of lost profits. As discussed below, major patent systems have taken divergent approaches to this issue. Third, we discuss whether and under what circumstances the patentee can recover lost profits for unpatented goods or services that are related in some way to the patented product. Fourth, we consider the issue of apportionment, most notably the question of whether lost profits awards for complex products should be apportioned to distinguish between the value of the patented feature(s) and other, unpatented aspects of the product. And fifth, we evaluate whether patentees should be entitled to recover for other sorts of harms related to market competition by an infringer, such as moral prejudice, loss of goodwill, and loss of chance.

2.2.2 *Specific Issues Regarding Lost Profits*

1 Availability and Standard

Most major patent systems recognize that a patentee's lost profits are an appropriate measure of damages, although there are differences regarding both the standard for awarding lost profits as well as the implementation of this methodology. Here, we first summarize the availability and (where ascertainable) the standard for proving entitlement to lost profits in key jurisdictions and then offer several recommendations.

In the United States, Section 284 of the Patent Act provides that a "court shall award the [prevailing patentee] damages adequate to compensate for the infringement, but in no event less than a reasonable royalty for the use made of the invention by the infringer."[11] Courts recognize two types of compensatory damages under Section 284: (1) "the patentee's lost profits" and (2) "the reasonable royalty [the patentee] would have received through arms-length bargaining."[12]

---

[11] 35 U.S.C. § 284.

[12] *Lucent Techs., Inc. v. Gateway Inc.* (Fed. Cir. 2009, p.1324) (U.S.); *see also* Lemley 2009, 655 ("Courts interpreting this provision have divided patent damages into two groups": (1) lost profits, which are available to patent owners who can prove they "would have made sales in the absence of infringement," and (2) "reasonable royalties, a fallback for everyone else.") We note that lost profits and reasonable royalties are not necessarily exclusive methodologies; for instance, in the United States, hybrid awards where a patentee recovers lost profits on some lost sales and reasonable royalties on the remaining sales are also possible. *See* Lemley 2009, 673 ("[T]here are also cases in which a patentee can prove that it would have made some but not all of the defendant's sales. In that case a hybrid award makes sense, with the patentee receiving lost profits on provable losses and a reasonable royalty on other sales."). This is not the case in all jurisdictions, however.

The classic type of lost profits damages are from lost sales of a product or service that practices the patent.[13] "Lost sales constitute sales that the patent owner failed to make due to the infringement, as well as sales the infringer made that the patent owner would have made but for the infringement."[14] For instance, in *Seymour v. McCormick* (1853), the Supreme Court of the United States held that a prevailing patentee "is entitled to the actual damages he has sustained by reason of the infringement, and those damages may be determined by ascertaining the profits which ... he would have made, provided the defendants had not interfered with his rights."[15] However, the Court rejected the trial court's presumption "that if the [infringer] had not made and sold machines, all persons who bought the [infringer]'s machines would necessarily have been compelled to go to the patentee and purchase his machines."[16] Instead, the Court required proof the patentee would have actually made these sales absent infringement – a burden that it was unable to carry.[17]

Modern U.S. case law follows a broadly similar approach, holding that lost profits are not presumed,[18] and instead requiring the patentee to "show a reasonable probability that, 'but for' the infringement, it would have made the sales that were made by the infringer."[19] This is most commonly achieved using the four-factor *Panduit* test,[20] which requires "the patent owner to prove: '(1) demand for the patented product, (2) absence of acceptable non-infringing substitutes, (3) his manufacturing and marketing capability to exploit the demand, and (4) the amount of the profit he would have made.'"[21] The first three of these requirements are best viewed as proxies to establish causation in fact. The first,

[13] See *Rite Hite Corp. v. Kelley Co.* (Fed. Cir. 1995, p.1545) (U.S.) (explaining the "general rule for determining actual damages to a patentee that is itself producing the patented item is to determine the sales and profits lost to the patentee because of the infringement"). Lost profits due to lost sales are sometimes called "diverted sales." See Chisum 2017, § 20.05[2][a].

[14] Skenyon et al. 2016, § 2:3.

[15] *Seymour v. McCormick* (U.S. 1853, p.486) (U.S.).

[16] *Id.* at 487–88.

[17] *Id.* at 490 (holding that the court "can find only such damages as have actually been proved to have been sustained" and that "[a]ctual damages must be actually proven, and cannot be assumed as a legal inference from any facts which amount not to actual proof of the fact").

[18] See, e.g., *Kaufman Co. v. Lantech, Inc.* (Fed. Cir. 1991, p.1141) (U.S.) ("The loss of profits is not presumed to result automatically from infringing sales.").

[19] *Rite-Hite Corp. v. Kelley Co.* (Fed. Cir. 1995, p.1545) (U.S.); *see also Aro Mfg. Co. v. Convertible Top Replacement Co.* (U.S. 1964, p.507) (U.S.) ("The question to be asked in determining damages is how much had the Patent Holder ... suffered by the infringement. And that question [is] primarily: had the Infringer not infringed, what would the Patentee Holder–Licensee have made?" (internal quotations omitted)).

[20] See *State Indus., Inc. v. Mor-Flo Indus., Inc.* (Fed. Cir. 1989, p.1577) (U.S.) (referring to *Panduit* as the "standard way of proving lost profits," but also mentioning that it is "nonexclusive").

[21] *Id.* (quoting *Panduit Corp. v. Stahlin Bros. Fibre Works Inc.* (6th Cir. 1978) (U.S.)); *see also Mentor Graphics Corp. v. EVE-USA, Inc.* (Fed. Cir. 2017, p.1284) (U.S.) (explaining that *Panduit* is a "useful, but non-exclusive method to establish the patentee's entitlement to lost profits" (internal quotations and citation omitted)).

demand for the patented product, demonstrates that at least some consumers would have preferred the patentee's product because of the patented technology. The second, which will be discussed in more detail below, asks whether consumers would have been willing to substitute a noninfringing alternative for the patentee's product.[22] If so, the substitution effect will make it more difficult for the patentee to obtain supra-competitive profits.[23] The third asks whether the patentee would have been able to increase production in order to make (at least some of) the sales that the infringer actually made.[24] The fourth and final element encompasses the "but for" market reconstruction – i.e., what would have been the patentee's profits absent infringement? Courts in the United States have viewed this as a relatively demanding element, requiring "reliable economic proof of the market" that would have developed "'but for' the infringement" to establish the amount of lost profits with sufficient accuracy.[25]

U.S. courts also allow recovery for other foreseeable profits lost by the patentee due to the infringement.[26] These may include, for instances, losses due to price erosion,[27] lost sales of unpatented products sold by the patentee that directly compete with the infringing product,[28] and (explained in more detail below) lost sales of unpatented components and products that are "functionally associated" with

---

[22] This requirement was subsequently modified by the so-called market share rule announced in *State Industries, Inc.* v. *Mor-Flo Industries, Inc.*, which allows the patentee to recover lost profits on a portion of the infringer's sales even if there is a noninfringing alternative by dividing the infringer's sales among the patentee and the noninfringing firm(s) in proportion to their respective market shares, and to recover a reasonable royalty on the remainder. *State Indus., Inc.* v. *Mor-Flo Indus., Inc.* (Fed. Cir. 1989, p.1578) (U.S.); *see also* Blair & Cotter 2001, 25 ("Subsequent case law has recognized that [*Mor-Flo's*] market-share principle in effect creates an exception to *Panduit* factor two.").

[23] *See* Blair & Cotter 1998, 1634 ("When there are substitutes for the patented invention, the elasticity of demand is altered and the patentee's monopoly power diminishes."); *cf.* DOJ & FTC 2017, 4 (noting that "there will often be sufficient actual or potential close substitutes" for a patented "product [or] process" that will "prevent the exercise of market power").

[24] Note that this does not necessarily require that the patentee have been able to make *all* of the infringer's sales – if the patentee would have market power in the absence of the infringer, there would be some loss in total sales due to higher per-unit cost charged by the patentee, and thus fewer overall sales (i.e., deadweight loss). In addition, it does not require that the patentee itself necessarily have to be able to increase production – for instance, it would be sufficient if the patentee could contract with a third-party to make the additional patented products. *See, e.g., Ristvedt-Johnson, Inc.* v. *Brandt, Inc.* (N.D. Ill. 1992, p.562) (U.S.).

[25] *Grain Processing Corp.* v. *Am. Maize-Prods. Co.* (Fed. Cir. 1999) (U.S.); *see also* Lemley 2009, 658 (noting that "courts take [the *Panduit*] requirements seriously and quite often reject claims for lost profits").

[26] *See Rite-Hite Corp.* v. *Kelley Co.* (Fed. Cir. 1995, p.1546) (U.S.) ("If a particular injury was or should have been reasonably foreseeable by an infringing competitor in the relevant market, broadly defined, that injury is generally compensable absent a persuasive reason to the contrary.").

[27] *See, e.g., Yale Lock Mfg. Co.* v. *Sargent* (U.S. 1886, p.551) (U.S.) ("Reduction of prices, and consequent loss of profits, enforced by infringing competition, is a proper ground for awarding of damages."); *Minn. Min. & Mfg. Co.* v. *Johnson & Johnson Orthopaedics, Inc.* (Fed. Cir. 1999) (U.S.) (affirming the trial court's award of nearly $29 million in lost profits due to price erosion).

[28] *See, e.g., King Instruments Corp.* v. *Perego* (Fed. Cir. 1995) (U.S.) (affirming award of lost profits for the patentee's sales of an unpatented tape loader).

the patented item.[29] In addition, if a patentee can prove entitlement to lost profits for only some of its lost sales, it can "recover a mixed award of lost profits on some sales and an established or reasonable royalty on other sales."[30]

Despite this, awards of lost profits are increasingly uncommon in the United States. A recent study by consulting firm PricewaterhouseCoopers found that lost profits alone represented 26 percent of patent damages awards from 1997 to 2006, compared to nearly 60 percent that awarded damages based exclusively on a reasonable royalty.[31] This trend continued from 2006 to 2015, where only 21 percent of patent damages awards were based solely on lost profits.[32] In addition, the study's authors note that "price erosion claims have become almost nonexistent in recent years."[33] Several explanations have been offered for this development. First, lost profits are available only in a subset of patent disputes – namely, cases where both "the patent owner and infringer actively compete in the same market."[34] Thus, cases brought by nonpracticing patentees – which represent a considerable share of patent infringement lawsuits filed in the United States[35] – are ineligible for a lost-profits recovery. Second, in the context of complex, multifunction products, it may be difficult for a patentee to demonstrate that the infringer's inclusion of a patented feature caused it to lose sales.[36] Third, some patentees who might be eligible to recover lost profits appear to be eschewing them in favor of reasonable royalty damages.[37] This may be the case for several reasons: because the patentee is skeptical that it can satisfy *Panduit*'s rigorous requirements; because the patentee wishes to avoid disclosing detailed financial information regarding its business to a competitor; or because the patentee believes that it can obtain at least as large of an award using the more flexible reasonable royalty approach.

The UK and Commonwealth countries, like Canada and Australia, similarly permit awards of lost profits damages. Section 61 of the UK Patent Act authorizes

---

[29] See *Am. Seating Co.* v. *USSC Group, Inc.* (Fed. Cir. 2008, p.1268–69) (U.S.) (describing "convoyed sales").

[30] Chisum 2017, § 20:05.

[31] Berry et al. 2017, 11. Another 14 percent of awards involved a mix of both lost profits and reasonable royalties.

[32] *Id.* (reporting that 61 percent of patent damages awards were based on a reasonable royalty alone, while the remaining 19 percent of awards represented a mix of lost profits and reasonable royalties).

[33] Berry et al. 2015, 8.

[34] Lee & Melamed 2016, 394; *see also* Lemley 2009, 658 ("[P]atentees cannot possibly meet [the *Panduit*] requirements unless they participate in the market in direct competition with the infringer.").

[35] See Cotropia et al. 2014, 674 figure 1 (finding that less than half of patent cases filed in the United States in 2012 were brought by operating companies).

[36] See *Mentor Graphics Corp.* v. *EVE-USA, Inc.* (Fed. Cir. 2017, p.1289) (U.S.) ("With [complex], multi-component products, it may often be the case that no one patentee can obtain lost profits on the overall product – the *Panduit* test is a demanding one."). For example, buyers may have preferred the infringer's product for reasons entirely unrelated to the patented feature, such as a lower price or other, unrelated aspects of the infringer's product.

[37] See Lemley 2009, 657–61 (detailing various reasons that a patentee may not be able to establish lost profits, even if it directly competes in a product market with the infringer).

the patent owner to claim "damages in respect of the infringement," and like in the United States, case law in the United Kingdom has explained that the objective of patent damages is to restore the patentee to the position it would have occupied but for the infringement.[38] In general, this extends to all losses by the patentee (including lost profits and price erosion) that are: (1) foreseeable, (2) caused by the infringement, and (3) not excluded from recovery by public or social policy.[39] In practice, this standard appears to be more flexible and less demanding than *Panduit*; the High Court of Justice has specifically noted that although the burden of proof is on the patentee, "[d]amages are to be assessed liberally."[40] Both Canada and Australia permit the recovery of actual damages suffered by the patentee due to infringement as well,[41] including lost profits and price erosion subject to the foreseeability principle.[42] In Canada, for example, to recover lost profits, the patentee "must show on a balance of probabilities that 'but for' the defendant's wrongful conduct, [it] would not have suffered loss."[43]

One significant area of divergence between the United States on one hand, and the United Kingdom and Australia on the other, is that the latter may decline to award damages (including lost profits) against an infringer who was not aware, and had no reason to believe, that the patent existed.[44] In other words, in these jurisdictions, an unwitting infringer may only be subject to injunctive relief. In contrast, direct patent infringement in the United States is a strict liability offense, and damages can be awarded against even an innocent infringer.[45] This distinction may not be as sharp in practice, however, because "in the typical lost profits case, the defendant is a competitor of the plaintiff and thus unlikely to qualify as an innocent infringer."[46] In addition, in these countries the fact that a patentee marked

---

[38] *Gerber Garment Tech. v. Lectra Systems Ltd.* (Civ 1997, p.445) (UK).

[39] *Id.* at 444; *see also Ultraframe Ltd. v. Eurocell Building Plastics Ltd.* (Pat 2006, ¶ 47) (UK) ("Where a claimant has exploited his patent by manufacture and sale he can claim (a) lost profit on sales by the defendant that he would have made otherwise [and] (b) lost profit on his own sales to the extent that he was forced by the infringement to reduce his own price … ").

[40] *Ultraframe Ltd. v. Eurocell Building Plastics Ltd.* (Pat 2006, ¶ 47) (UK).

[41] *See Patents Act 1990*, § 122(1) (Austl.); Patent Act, R.S.C. 1985, c. P-4 (Can.), § 55.

[42] *See Cotter 2013a*, 187 n.87 and cases cited therein.

[43] *Apotex Inc. v. Merck & Co.* (Fed. Ct. 2015, ¶ 45) (Can.).

[44] The UK statute prohibits any monetary award in those circumstances, while the Australian statute states that the trial court has discretion whether to award damages or not in such cases. *Compare* Patents Act, 1977, c. 37, § 62(1) (UK) ("In proceedings for infringement of a patent damages shall not be awarded … against a defendant or defender who proves that at the date of the infringement he was not aware, and had no reasonable grounds for supposing, that the patent existed … "), *with* Patents Act 1990, § 123(1) (Austl.) ("A court may refuse to award damages … in respect of an infringement of a patent if the defendant satisfies the court that, at the date of the infringement, the defendant was not aware, and had no reason to believe, that a patent for the invention existed.").

[45] *See Commil USA, LLC v. Cisco Sys., Inc.* (U.S. 2015, p.1926) (U.S.) ("Direct infringement is a strict-liability offense."); *Global-Tech Appliances, Inc. v. SEB S.A.* (U.S. 2011, p.761 n.2) (U.S.) ("Direct infringement has long been understood to require no more than the unauthorized use of a patented invention. Thus, a direct infringer's knowledge or intent is irrelevant." (internal citations omitted)).

[46] Cotter 2013a, 190.

its products[47] with the patent number(s) or an Internet link containing patent information can undermine a claim of innocent infringement.[48]

Lost profits are similarly available as a matter of principle in every EU country,[49] although in practice they appear to be considerably less common than in the United States and the United Kingdom.[50] For example, in Germany, patent owners may recover the difference between the profit they would have earned absent infringement and their actual profits.[51] This may include "both profits lost on sales lost to the infringer and damages for price erosion," as well as "more remote harms" like market confusion provided that such harms were likely caused by the infringement.[52] Similarly, in France, the patentee can recover lost profits on lost sales of patented goods as well as price erosion.[53] However, the amount of lost profits awarded in France appears to be considerably lower than in the United States, even after accounting for the larger size of the U.S. economy.[54]

In Asia as well, lost profits are available in most major jurisdictions, although many also require some degree of culpability by the infringer. For example, in its 1998 amendments to Japan's patent law, the Diet "intended for awards of lost profits . . . to be the general or default remedy in patent infringement matters."[55] As a result of these changes, the owner or exclusive licensee of a Japanese patent can claim damages "against an infringer . . . sustained as a result of the intentional or negligent infringement of the patent right."[56] Japan's Patent Act also presumes that the amount of the patentee's lost profits is the same as the infringer's profits.[57]

---

[47] Some working group members question the desirability of patent marking requirements and their relationship to an infringer's mental state.

[48] For instance, in Australia, if the patented product is marked with the patent information and widely sold prior to infringement, the infringer is presumed "to have been aware of the existence of the patent . . . " *Patents Act 1990*, § 123(2) (Austl.); *cf.* Patents Act, 1977, c. 37, § 62(1) (UK) (providing that "a person shall not be taken to have been . . . aware [of the patent] or to have had reasonable grounds for so supposing by reason only of the application to a product of the word 'patent' or 'patented,' . . . unless the number of the patent or a relevant internet link accompanied the word or words in question").

[49] For example, the EU IP Rights Directive provides that judicial authorities in member states pay the IP rightsholder (here, the patentee) "damages appropriate to the actual prejudice suffered . . . as a result of the infringement . . . including lost profits . . . which the injured party has suffered." Directive 2004/48/EC, art. 13(1).

[50] *See, e.g.,* Pitz & Hermann 2007, 190 (explaining that "[t]he calculation of damages based on lost profits plays little part in German court practice" because "the most commonly used method to determine damages in Germany [is] a reasonable royalty on the infringer's sales").

[51] Cotter 2013a, 262.

[52] *Id.*

[53] *Id.* at 264.

[54] *See id.* at 259 & n.150 (describing Pierre Véron's empirical studies of French patent litigation, which found a median damage award of €40,000 from 2000 to 2009, compared to the median award in the United States of over $5 million during a similar time frame).

[55] *Id.* at 313 (citing Takenaka 2009, 478).

[56] Tokkyo-hō [Patent Act], No. 121 of 1959, art. 102(1) (Japan).

[57] Cotter 2013a, 308.

Despite these changes, one study found that lost profits represented the minority approach to compensating the patentee: about 20 percent of all patent damages claims in Japan were based on lost profits, and a mere 17 percent of successful claims.[58] Korea's patent law is highly similar to Japan's, providing that lost profits shall be awarded only for intentional or negligent infringement.[59]

In China, Article 65 of the Patent Law establishes a statutory preference for awarding "the patentee's actual losses caused by the infringement," although it also permits use of the infringer's profits as a proxy for the amount of the patentee's loss if it is difficult to determine.[60] In addition, while "article 65 does not expressly condition damages liability on the defendant's intent or negligence ..., as a general matter, Chinese law accepts the principle that damages liability is conditional upon the defendant's fault."[61] Despite this preference, lost profits are rarely awarded in China; in over 90 percent of cases, statutory damages are awarded instead.[62] Several empirical studies also have found that the amount of Chinese patent damages awards tend to be low, particularly by U.S. standards.[63]

India's law regarding patent damages has been influenced by that of the United Kingdom.[64] The Indian Patent Act authorizes the patentee to elect to recover either actual damages or an accounting of the infringer's profits.[65] Similarly, India precludes any damages, including lost profits, in cases where the infringer "was not aware and had no reasonable grounds for believing that the patent existed."[66] However, there appears to be little precedent from Indian courts that provides specific guidance regarding damages.[67]

In light of the foregoing discussion, we make several recommendations regarding the availability and standard for awarding lost profits damages. First, we recommend that lost profits (including from lost sales and price erosion) should be the preferred measure of damages when a patentee can establish harm in a product market due to the infringement. As the Supreme Court of the United States explained in *Aro Manufacturing* v. *Convertible Top Replacement Co.*, the patentee's loss from patent infringement is "'the difference between [the patentee's] pecuniary condition after the infringement ... and what his condition would have been if the infringement had not

---

58 Matsunaka 2004, 170.
59 Patent Act, Act No. 14691, March 31, 2017, art. 128(1) (Kor.).
60 Cotter 2013a, 353.
61 *Id.* at 354 (citing Jingjing Cao).
62 Cotter & Golden 2018, 17 n.77.
63 Cotter 2013a, 354–55; Love et al. 2016, 733–34; *but cf. WatchData Co.* v. *Hengbao Co.* (Beijing IP Ct. 2016) (China), *discussed in* Ge 2017 (awarding lost profits damages of RMB 49 million – approximately U.S. $7 million – for infringement of USB security token technology).
64 Cotter 2013a, 375.
65 The Patents Act, No. 39 of 1970, § 108(1) (India).
66 *Id.* § 111(1). *Compare to* Patents Act, 1977, c. 37, § 62(1) (UK).
67 Cotter 2013a, 375.

incurred.'"[68] Lost profits best serve this make-whole objective by compensating the patentee's actual losses caused by the infringer's market entry. Although available in all major jurisdictions, in practice lost profits are less commonly awarded than other methodologies for determining damages, such as a reasonable or established royalty or an award of the infringer's profits. In particular, we are concerned about authority suggesting that a patentee could potentially obtain *greater than* its lost profits under an alternative measure of damages (such as a reasonable royalty), as this would tend to overcompensate the patentee.[69]

Second, we recommend that lost profits should be awarded whenever a practicing patentee can demonstrate "but for" causation by a preponderance of the evidence.[70] The focus on causation is central to the lost-profits analysis, but some jurisdictions such as the United States have articulated more detailed standards or requirements as part of this inquiry (i.e., the *Panduit* factors). Rigorous adherence to such standards might make it more difficult in practice for a patentee to establish entitlement to lost profits.[71] We recommend that jurisdictions instead focus on "but for" causation as the central inquiry for lost profits claims.

Third, as previously noted, jurisdictions differ on whether some degree of fault or culpability is required to support an award of lost profits. We were unable to reach a consensus about whether lost profits should be available regardless of the infringer's degree of fault. However, this may be a worthwhile topic for further research.[72]

Fourth, we were unable to reach a consensus regarding some jurisdictions' (rebuttable) presumption that the amount of the patentee's loss is equal to the amount of the infringer's profits. Arguments in favor of this approach include that it may simplify the damages calculation and thus reduce adjudication costs,[73] and

---

[68] *Aro Mfg. Co. v. Convertible Top Replacement Co.* (U.S. 1964, p.507) (U.S.) (quoting *Yale Lock Mfg. Co. v. Sargent* (U.S. 1886, p.582) (U.S.)).

[69] *See* Love 2009, 915–23 (criticizing decisions by the U.S. Court of Appeals for the Federal Circuit suggesting that overcompensation through reasonable royalty awards may be appropriate in some circumstances); *see also Rite-Hite Corp. v. Kelley Co.* (Fed. Cir. 1995, p.1576–78) (U.S.) (Nies, J., dissenting) (arguing that a "reasonable royalty" in excess of a patented product's sales price is inappropriate). We discuss the appropriateness of non-compensatory damages that may exceed the patentee's actual loss in Chapter 3.

[70] Our recommendation is limited to remedies for infringing conduct taking place within a particular jurisdiction. We take no collective position on the issue of whether a patentee should be entitled to recover lost profits that it would have earned outside of a particular jurisdiction but for infringing conduct within that jurisdiction (i.e., extraterritorial lost profits), which is an issue currently (as of early May 2018) before the Supreme Court of the United States. *See WesternGeco LLC v. Ion Geophyiscal Corp.*, No. 16–1011 (U.S.).

[71] *See generally* Lemley 2009.

[72] *See* FTC 2011, 131–34 (discussing potential modifications to liability for inadvertent infringement). For example, some scholars have suggested that independent invention should be a defense to patent infringement. *See, e.g.*, Shapiro 2006; Vermont 2006.

[73] *See* Cotter 2016b (describing the potential benefits and drawbacks of Japan's presumption that the patentee's profits presumptively are the same as the infringer's profits).

that the patentee may prefer to rely on the infringer's profits because it would not require disclosure of the patentee's sensitive financial information (such as net revenue, fixed costs, variable costs, and research and design costs) to a competitor. Arguments against this approach include that the infringer's profits may represent a poor proxy for the amount of the patentee's lost profits, potentially resulting in over- or under-compensation. For example, if the infringer is more efficient than the patentee (and thus has a higher per-unit profit on its sales), then using the infringer's profits as a basis for determining the patentee's loss will result in overcompensation.[74] In contrast, if the infringer is less efficient than the patentee (and thus has a lower per-unit profit on its sales), then using the infringer's profits will result in under-compensation unless the patentee can overcome this presumption. It is unclear, however, to what extent this presumption actually results in over- or under-compensation. We propose further research on this issue from both theoretical and empirical perspectives.

2 Noninfringing Alternatives

A specific issue worth further discussion is the role that noninfringing alternatives play in the lost-profits analysis. If the infringer could have competed against the patentee just as effectively by offering a noninfringing alternative to the patented invention, the patentee would have lost just as many sales (and thus profits) absent the infringement. In such a case, the patentee has not lost any profits *caused* by the infringement, since it would have lost those profits anyway, and it should recover at most a reasonable royalty reflecting some portion of the value of the patented technology to the infringer (e.g., its profit-enhancing or cost-reducing advantages over the next best alternative). Put another way, an award of lost profits if a noninfringing alternative exists would render the patentee better off than it would have been "but for" the infringement, and thus would enable the patent owner to reap a reward in excess of the economic value of its invention.[75] Courts in the United States[76]

---

[74] In such cases, from an efficiency perspective, we would prefer the infringer be the producer than the patentee. This might occur, for instance, though a license.

[75] Alternatively, if the patentee is entitled under domestic law to recover the infringer's profits attributable to the infringement – a topic discussed in depth in Section 2.3 below – those profits should reflect the value of the patented technology over the next best alternative, rather than the entire profit derived from sales of the infringing product. To award the entire profit would render the infringer worse off as a result of the infringement, and thus would be difficult to justify in terms of patent policy absent a compelling reason for additional deterrence, such as those discussed in Chapter 3.

[76] *See, e.g., Grain Processing Corp.* v. *Am. Maize-Prods. Co.* (Fed. Cir. 1999, p.1350–51) (U.S.) ("A fair and accurate reconstruction of the 'but for' market … must take into account, where relevant, alternative actions the infringer foreseeably would have undertaken had he not infringed. Without the infringing product, a rational would-be infringer is likely to offer an acceptable non-infringing alternative, if available, to compete with the patent owner rather than leave the market altogether."); *SmithKline Diagnostics, Inc.* v. *Helena Labs. Corp.* (Fed. Cir. 1991, p.1166) (U.S.) (analyzing the

and France[77] have long recognized the relevance of noninfringing alternatives in these contexts, as more recently has Canada,[78] while courts in the United Kingdom and Germany have not.

The United Kingdom in particular continues to abide by an 1888 decision of the House of Lords, *United Horse-Shoe & Nail Co. v. John Stewart & Co.*,[79] which rejected the relevance of noninfringing alternatives to damages calculations.[80] With all due respect to the House of Lords, we think that *United Horse-Shoe* fails to grasp the economic logic embodied in the noninfringing alternative concept, and that there is little reason for contemporary patent systems to continue adhering to the decision. We therefore recommend that *United Horse-Shoe* and other similar decisions elsewhere be overruled, and that courts explicitly recognize the importance of considering noninfringing alternatives to the accurate calculation of patent damages.[81]

Relatedly, to the extent that domestic law permits the recovery of the infringer's profits attributable to the infringement,[82] we also recommend that courts or legislatures explicitly define the term "profit" to mean the benefit derived from the infringement over the next best alternative. Although that benefit most commonly takes the form of an increase in the infringer's profits compared to what it would have earned using a noninfringing alternative, in a case in which the infringer winds up losing money (for example, because it did not sell enough infringing products to cover costs) the infringer nonetheless benefits if its losses would have been even greater absent the infringement. Thus, to the extent disgorgement is permitted, the infringer also should be required to disgorge the cost saving it enjoyed as a result of the infringement, even if it earned no "profit" in an accounting sense.

---

availability of noninfringing alternatives to the patented technology and reasoning that "if the realities of the market are that [non-infringing third parties] would likely have captured sales made by the infringer, despite a difference in the products, it follows that the 'but for' test" for lost profits "is not met").

[77] Cotter 2013a, 265 n.171 (citing French cases regarding noninfringing alternatives in the lost profits analysis).

[78] *See Apotex Inc. v. Merck & Co.* (Fed. Ct. 2015, ¶ 1) (Can.) (concluding that "as a matter of law, the availability of a non-infringing alternative is a relevant consideration" in calculating damages for patent infringement); *see also* Crowne 2015.

[79] *United Horse-Shoe and Nail Co. Ltd. v. John Stewart & Co.* (HL 1888) (UK).

[80] Notably, Lord Watson's opinion in *United Horse-Shoe* does appear (in contrast to the other Lords) to recognize that noninfringing alternatives are relevant in the lost profits analysis, although he ultimately ruled against the infringer on the basis that the alternative was not proven. *See id.* at 267 ("[I]n estimating [the patentee's] damage, there must be taken into account all legitimate competition to which they would have been exposed if [the infringing] nails had not been on the market ... [T]o ignore it would be tantamount to giving [patentee] not compensation merely, but profits which they would never have earned ...").

[81] *See, e.g., Grain Processing Corp. v. Am. Maize-Prods. Co.* (Fed. Cir. 1999, p.1356) (U.S.) ("The availability of substitutes will influence the market forces defining th[e] 'but for' marketplace ..."). We agree that *Grain Processing* was correctly decided and recommend that it be generally followed.

[82] *See infra* Section 2.2.2 (explaining jurisdictions' recognition of the disgorgement remedy).

Another matter is what qualifies as a noninfringing alternative to the patented technology. For example, U.S. case law establishes that an alleged alternative must have similar functionality and a comparable price to the patented technology.[83] This definition, however, fails to recognize that substitution is a matter of degree in product markets,[84] particularly for multifunctional products where consumers may value certain features more than others. Even an imperfect substitute that provides some, but not all, of the functionality of the patented invention can none-theless affect both the price of the patented product as well as consumer choice.[85] As a result, we recommend that courts focus on the substitutability of noninfringing alternatives in evaluating how many of the infringer's sales the patentee would have made in the "but for" analysis.

In addition to these recommendations, there remain several issues regarding non-infringing alternatives that deserve further research. First, as discussed in Chapter 1, to date there has been little discussion in the legal and economic literature of how courts should proceed when the next best alternative itself is patented.[86] In the reasonable royalties context, the principal question raised by the presence of patented alternatives is whether one should assume that the owners of the two patents engage in Bertrand competition – which ultimately could drive the price of both patents down to zero, if neither is better than the other – or whether such an assumption threatens to undermine the patent incentive. In the present context, the question that arises from the presence of patented alternatives is whether courts should presume that the patented alternative was not available to the infringer, or instead should require proof that the patent covering the alternative was either invalid or would have been licensed (and if so, at what price). The problem with the latter option is that it risks greatly increasing the cost of adjudication for comparatively little benefit.[87] Further research to address the issue would be welcome.

Second, further research on which party should be required to prove the absence of noninfringing alternatives would be helpful, as there is an apparent conflict among jurisdictions on this issue. In the United States, the case law is a bit muddled, but the patentee generally must make this showing as part of the *Panduit* test for lost

---

[83] See *BIC Leisure Prod, Inc. v. Windsurfing Int'l, Inc.* (Fed. Cir. 1993, p.1219) (U.S.) (holding that to be acceptable, "the alleged alternative 'must not have a disparately higher price than or possess char-acteristics significantly different from the patented'" technology); *TWM Mfg. Co., Inc. v. Dura Corp.* (Fed. Cir. 1986, p.901–02) (U.S.) ("A product lacking the advantages of that patented can hardly be termed a substitute for the consumer who wants those advantages." (internal quotations omitted)).

[84] See *In the Matter of Mahurkar Double Lumen Hemodialysis Catheter Patent Litig.* (N.D. Ill. 1993, p.1389–90) (U.S.) ("Competition is not an all-or-none process. There are degrees of substitutability.").

[85] See Blair & Cotter 2005, 214 ("Whether one product substitutes for another depends not only upon the function of the two products, but also upon the prices at which they are offered to the public."); *see also* Seaman 2010, 1715–18 (advancing a similar argument).

[86] See also Sichelman 2018, 319–20 (mentioning this issue).

[87] For a brief discussion of the issue, *see* Cotter 2018, 191–92.

profits.[88] This effectively requires the patentee to prove a negative – namely, that there was no feasible noninfringing alternative during the period of infringement. In contrast, in Canada, the infringer bears the burden of demonstrating the existence of a noninfringing alternative.[89] To our knowledge, there is little discussion in the legal or economic literature addressing which of these approaches is optimal. One might speculate that the infringer often would be better placed than the patentee to propose and substantiate the existence of noninfringing alternatives, particularly if, as in *Grain Processing*, the infringer had the capacity to create and implement a noninfringing design around without much difficulty. But perhaps patent owners have unique insights into the matter that are not apparent at first blush, or maybe the allocation of the burden of proof on this issue does not matter much in practice because both parties have sufficient motivation to present the evidence that best favors their position.

Third, the degree of certainty needed to establish that a noninfringing alternative was in fact available to the infringer is not always clear. The U.S. decision in *Grain Processing*, for example, held that a noninfringing alternative was available during the period of infringement – even though it was not actually on the market – because it would have been simple for the infringer to develop a noninfringing (but slightly costlier) process to produce the (unpatented) end product. Other cases addressing this issue turn on their unique facts,[90] and of course having to establish the availability of an alternative that was not actually on the market at the time of

---

[88] *See, e.g., Presidio Components, Inc. v. Am. Tech. Ceramics Corp.* (Fed. Cir. 2017, p.1381) (U.S.) (reversing the jury's award of lost profits because the patentee "failed to provide evidence that [a non-infringing product] was either not an acceptable or available substitute" to the patentee's product); *Datascope Corp. v. SMEC, Inc.* (Fed. Cir. 1989, p.822–23) (U.S.) (affirming district court's denial of lost profits because the patentee "failed to prove element . . . two . . . of the *Panduit* test – absence of acceptable noninfringing substitutes"); *see also Panduit Corp. v. Stahlin Bros. Fibre Works Inc.* (6th Cir. 1978, p.1156) (U.S.) ("[A] patent owner must prove . . . absence of acceptable noninfringing substitutes . . . "). But in *Grain Processing Corp. v. Am. Maize-Prods. Co.* (Fed. Cir. 1999) (U.S.), the Federal Circuit shifted the burden to the infringer, explaining that "[w]hen an alleged [non-infringing] alternative is not on the market during the [period of infringement], a trial court may reasonably infer that it was not available as a non-infringing substitute at that time. The accused infringer then has the burden to overcome this inference by showing that the substitute was available during the [period of infringement]." *Id.* at 1353. Moreover, when there are only "two suppliers in the relevant market" (i.e., the patentee and the infringer were the only sellers), there is "a presumption of 'but for' causation" for lost profits, and "the burden . . . then shifts to the infringer" to demonstrate that the patentee would not have made some or all of the diverted sales. *Micro Chem., Inc. v. Lextron, Inc.* (Fed. Cir. 2003, p.1125) (U.S.). The infringer can rebut this presumption, for example, "by showing that it sold another available, noninfringing substitute in the relevant market." *Id.; see also Integrated Tech. Corp. v. Rudolph Tech., Inc.* (Fed. Cir. 2013) (U.S.) (holding that in a market with only two suppliers, the fact finder may infer that any sales made by the infringer would have been made by the plaintiff, notwithstanding evidence that the infringer could have competed by means of a noninfringing alternative).

[89] *See, e.g., Apotex Inc. v. Merck & Co.* (Fed. Ct. 2015, ¶ 74) (Can.) ("As a matter of principle, the burden lies on the defendant to establish the factual relevance of a non-infringing alternative on a balance of probabilities.").

[90] *See, e.g., Kidd 2014. For discussion of the relevant Canadian law on this issue, *see Siebrasse 2017.

infringement poses some risk of increasing adjudication and error costs.[91] Nonetheless, we are inclined to agree with the *Grain Processing* framework on the basis that the increase in accuracy justifies the cost, though further research might help to structure this analysis so that courts can apply it in a consistent, predictable, and cost-efficient fashion.

3 Lost Profits on Sales of Related but Unpatented Products

Another important issue is whether a prevailing patentee can recover lost profits damages for unpatented products that are related to sales of the patented product.

In the United States, courts have applied three (at least partially overlapping) doctrines to determine which kinds of potential lost sales can be compensated for in a lost profits award. Generally, these doctrines apply respectively to (1) sales of products that incorporate both infringing and noninfringing components, (2) additional contemporaneous sales of distinct but related items, and (3) anticipated future sales of replacement or repair parts.

First, in the context of complex products, courts have applied the so-called entire market value rule to define the scope of the primary lost "sale" for which profits may be owed. Though the majority of modern case law on the entire market value rule has come in the context of reasonable royalty awards,[92] courts have also discussed the doctrine in relation to lost sales of infringing products or assemblies that have both patented and unpatented components. In such cases, the entire market value rule dictates that lost profits damages may be recovered for lost sales of all components that operate as part of the same "functional unit" as the infringing component or part, such that they are "analogous to components of a single assembly or parts of a complete machine."[93] Thus, for example, a patentee that sells paper winding equipment can recover lost profits for lost sales of the entire line of equipment – including the unpatented stand, loader, embosser, and sealer – because all three work together with the infringing rewinder as part of a single assembly that the patentee virtually always bundled into a single sale.[94]

Second, courts have also developed the related concept of "convoyed" or "collateral" sales. Convoyed sales are sales of items that, though physically separate from the infringing product, are nonetheless typically sold along with the infringing product. Though case law in this area is muddled, courts have sometimes suggested that patentees may recover damages for lost sales of items simply because they were traditionally purchased at the same time as the infringing device.[95] For example, in

---

[91] *See* Kidd 2014.
[92] *See* Chapter 1.
[93] *Rite-Hite Corp.* v. *Kelley Co.* (Fed. Cir. 1995, p.1550) (U.S.).
[94] *Paper Converting Mach. Co.* v. *Magna-Graphics Corp.* (Fed. Cir. 1984, p.22–23) (U.S.).
[95] *See Kaufman Co.* v. *Lantech, Inc.* (Fed. Cir. 1991, p.1144) (U.S.) ("In determining whether a patentee should be awarded lost profits on unpatented accessory sales, the deciding factor is whether the patentee could normally anticipate the sale of unpatented items as well as the patented ones."); *Paper*

Golden Blount, Inc. v. *Robert H. Peterson Co.*, the Federal Circuit affirmed an award of lost profits damages that included profits lost on aesthetic artificial logs and grates in addition to profits lost on infringing gas fireplace burners because it was "standard practice in the industry" to sell all three items together.[96] However, in most cases involving convoyed sales, the Federal Circuit has required that the patentee demonstrate that the unpatented component must be "functionally associated" with or related to the patented product in some way.[97]

Third, at least some case law differentiates between convoyed sales and sales of repair or replacement parts, sometimes called "derivative sales," which are often made in the future after the original infringing sale.[98] However, in principle, the same rules applicable to convoyed sales appear to apply in this context as well. As the Federal Circuit stated in *King Instrument Corp.* v. *Otari Corp.*, lost profits damages are recoverable for spare parts when the patentee "normally would have anticipated the sale of the spare parts" but for infringement.[99] Thus, for example, in *Leesona Corp.* v. *United States*, the patentee was allowed to recover damages reflecting lost sales of replacement anodes for a patented battery where in "a normal 'life cycle,' it was anticipated that the 22 anodes for each battery would each be replaced 50 times."[100]

At their core, all three doctrines focus on drawing a line between what sales were, and were not, foreseeably lost due to infringement. We recommend that losses associated with all three categories of sales should generally be recoverable provided that the patentee can demonstrate both (1) "but for" causation and (2) proximate causation, which is established by demonstrating that sales of the unpatented component, part, or good was "reasonably foreseeable by an infringing competitor

---

Converting Mach. Co. v. *Magna-Graphics Corp.* (Fed. Cir. 1984, p.23) (U.S.) (affirming district court award of damages relating to lost sales of unpatented "auxiliary equipment" that are not "integral parts" of the patented invention and holding that such losses are normally recoverable when "normally the patentee ... can anticipate [the] sale of such unpatented components as well as of the patented ones" (internal quotations and citation omitted)); *see also Rite-Hite Corp.* v. *Kelley Co.* (Fed. Cir. 1995, p.1578–81) (U.S.) (Newman, J., dissenting) (rejecting the majority's conclusion that a convoyed item must be "functionally inseparable from the patented item." (internal quotations omitted)).

96 *Golden Blount, Inc.* v. *Robert H. Peterson Co.* (Fed. Cir. 2006, p.1370–72) (U.S.).

97 *See, e.g., Am. Seating Co.* v. *USSC Group, Inc.*(Fed. Cir. 2008, p.1268) (U.S.) ("A 'convoyed sale' refers to the relationship between the sale of a patented product and a functionally associated non-patented product ... A functional relationship does not exist when independently operating patented and unpatented products are purchased as a package solely because of customer demand."); *Rite-Hite Corp.* v. *Kelley Co.* (Fed. Cir. 1995, p.1550) (U.S.) ("Our precedent has not extended liability to include items that have essentially no functional relationship to the patented invention and that may have been sold with an infringing device only as a matter of convenience or business advantage.").

98 *See Carborundum Co.* v. *Molten Metal Equip. Innovations, Inc.* (Fed. Cir. 1995, p.881 n.8) (U.S.) ("The expression 'convoyed sales' should preferably be limited to sales made simultaneously with a basic item; the spare parts here [which are sold, if ever, after the original infringing sale] should best be called 'derivative sales.'").

99 *King Instrument Corp.* v. *Otari Corp.* (Fed. Cir. 1985, p.865–66) (U.S.).

100 *Leesona Corp.* v. *United States* (Ct. Cl. 1979, p.975) (U.S.).

in the relevant market."[101] Such a change would appear to be consistent with the law in several other countries, which permit the recovery of lost profits on lost sales of collateral goods subject to normal principles of proximate causation.[102]

There is one possible qualification to the argument that patentees generally should be able to recover lost profits for lost sales of unpatented products that they would have earned, but for the infringement, as long as those losses are proximately caused by the infringement. Suppose that the patentee is not making, using, or selling *any* products covered by the patent in suit, but rather is enforcing the patent to maintain its position in the market for the unpatented product. By their nature, patents tend to suppress competition with respect to use of technology. But it is debatable whether the enforcement of a patent merely to eliminate the use of a newer and possibly superior technology is consistent with the underlying purposes of the patent system. It is at least plausible that awards of lost profits (and injunctions) in such cases disserve the public interest. On the other hand, requiring patent owners to "work" their patents in order to recover lost profits would be at odds with the traditions of countries such as the United States, which generally has eschewed such requirements. In addition, it might be easy for patent owners to circumvent such a requirement by engaging in some token use of the technology covered by their patents. We therefore recommend further research on the frequency with which patent owners seek to enforce "idle" patents, and of the appropriate legal rules for addressing such conduct.[103]

4 Apportionment

One topic that is particularly significant for complex, multifunctional products is whether the patentee is required to quantify the portion of its lost profits that are attributable to the patented feature(s), as opposed to unpatented aspects and other components of the larger product. This is known as apportionment.

Historically, apportionment was an important issue in early U.S. patent cases.[104] For example, in *Seymour v. McCormick*,[105] the Court distinguished between a patent directed to an entirely new machine and a patent that merely claimed an improvement on an existing machine. In the former situation, a patentee "would be entitled to the entire lost profit on any sales to an infringer because those sales would

---

[101] *Rite-Hite Corp. v. Kelley Co.* (Fed. Cir. 1995, p.1546) (U.S.).

[102] Cotter, 2013a, 187 (discussing applicable rules in the United Kingdom, Canada, and Australia); *see also id.* at 262 n.160, 264, 320–21 (discussing applicable rules in Germany, France, and Japan).

[103] For discussion and citation to other sources discussing both the legal issues and the broader economic topic of technology suppression, *see* Blair & Cotter 2005, 246–54; Hovenkamp & Cotter 2016.

[104] *See* Bensen 2005, 3 (noting that "between 1853 and 1915, the Supreme Court addressed apportionment more than thirty-five times in patent damages decisions, sometimes in two or three decisions in the same year").

[105] *Seymour v. McCormick* (U.S. 1853) (U.S.).

have necessarily gone to the patentee."[106] In contrast, the Court held that it would be a "grave error" to award similar damages for "an improvement of small importance when compared with the whole machine."[107] Thus, *Seymour* "recognized that if patent damages were not calculated after apportioning value between the patented invention and the prior art," it would overcompensate the patentee.[108]

Other courts and scholars have concluded that "apportionment is not required ... because patentees need only show 'but for' causation to recover lost profits."[109] For instance, in *W. L. Gore & Associates* v. *Carlisle Corp.*, the court held that "once the fact that sales have been lost has been proven, there is no occasion for the application of apportionment."[110] In other words, the "but for" standard for lost profits largely obviates the need for further apportionment.[111]

The U.S. Court of Appeals for the Federal Circuit recently addressed the issue of apportionment for lost profits awards in *Mentor Graphics Corp.* v. *EVE-USA, Inc.*[112] Both parties in *Mentor Graphics* made and sold emulation and verification systems, which are software programs that allow one computer system to act like another, ordinarily noncompatible, system.[113] These emulation systems, which are used by chipmakers like Intel to test semiconductor designs, are highly complex and expensive. The patented technology at issue covered a method and apparatus for debugging chip designs by inserting "test probes" with the ability to measure "intermediate values" in a series of logic gates.[114] This feature was later incorporated into the infringing emulators.[115]

At trial, the jury awarded the patentee over \$36 million in lost profits.[116] On appeal, the infringer asserted that the verdict should be overturned because the district court had failed to apportion the amount of lost profits "to cover only the

---

[106]   Bensen 2005, 6 (citing *Seymour* v. *McCormick* (U.S. 1853, p.489) (U.S.)).
[107]   *Seymour* v. *McCormick* (U.S. 1853, p.490–91) (U.S.).
[108]   Love 2007, 268.
[109]   Bensen 2005, 4; *see also* Rabowsky 1996, 285, 295 ("[U]nder current law, there is never a need to apportion lost profits between patented and unpatented items ... [A]pplication of the entire market value rule and the generic 'but for' causation test eliminates the need for apportionment."); Conley 1987, 371, 373 ("[T]he concept of recovery of lost profits, as uniformly applied by the courts, does not admit to dividing the patent owner's lost profits according to any perceived value contributed by the invention ... It is submitted that the district court in *W. L. Gore* set forth the proper approach for determining the scope of damages due to lost sales.").
[110]   *W. L. Gore and Assoc., Inc.* v. *Carlisle Corp.* (D. Del. 1978, p.364) (U.S.).
[111]   *See* Cotter 2013a, 116 ("[A]pportionment makes little sense if the goal is to estimate the plaintiff's lost profits based on the plaintiff's own sales.").
[112]   *Mentor Graphics Corp.* v. *EVE-USA, Inc.* (Fed. Cir. 2017) (U.S.).
[113]   *Id.* at 1280, 1286.
[114]   U.S. Patent No. 6,240,376 (filed July 31, 1998); *see also Mentor Graphics Corp.* v. *EVE-USA, Inc.* (Fed. Cir. 2017, p.1281) (U.S.) (describing the patented technology).
[115]   The two inventors were originally Mentor employees and assigned the patent-in-suit to Mentor; they subsequently left Mentor and founded EVE-USA, Inc., the principal defendant. *Mentor Graphics Corp.* v. *EVE-USA, Inc.* (Fed. Cir. 2017, p.1280) (U.S.).
[116]   *Id.* at 1283. The jury also awarded the patentee a much smaller amount (\$242,110) as a reasonable royalty. *Id.*

patentee's inventive contribution."[117] While agreeing that "apportionment is an important component of damages law generally" and that it is "necessary in both reasonable royalty and lost profits analysis," the Federal Circuit rejected the infringer's argument, holding that "apportionment was properly incorporated into the lost profits analysis ... through the *Panduit* factors."[118] Specifically, it explained that *Panduit's* first two requirements – "that patentees prove demand for the product as a whole and the absence of non-infringing alternatives" – appropriately "ties lost profit damages to specific claim limitations and ensures that damages are commensurate with the value of the patented features."[119] Under the facts in *Mentor Graphics*, the lost profits analysis under *Panduit* was straightforward; the relevant market contained two suppliers (the patentee and the infringer), there was one purchaser (Intel), and there were no acceptable noninfringing alternatives, so each sale made by the infringer necessarily resulted in a lost sale to the patentee.[120] In addition, the infringer did not dispute any of this evidence on appeal.[121] As a result, the Federal Circuit held that "satisfaction of the *Panduit* factors satisfies the principles of apportionment."[122]

We believe that the Federal Circuit's approach in *Mentor Graphics* is correct. If the infringement caused the patentee to lose sales, the principle that patentees should be made whole requires that the patentee recover the profits it would have earned on these lost sales, even if the patented feature is only one aspect of a more complex product.[123] By contrast, an infringing sale that does not displace a patentee's

---

[117] *Id.* at 1287.

[118] *Id.* at 1288.

[119] *Id.* However, the Federal Circuit expressly declined to consider whether alternative (non-*Panduit*) methods of determining lost profits would be subject to apportionment. *See id.* ("We leave for another day whether a different theory of 'but for' damages adequately incorporates apportionment principles.")

[120] *Id.; see also id.* at 1289 ("Mentor would have made every single sale to Intel that Synopsis otherwise would have made.").

[121] *Id.* at 1286–88.

[122] *Id.* at 1288; *see also id.* at 1290 ("We hold that the district court did not err in refusing to further apportion lost profits after the jury returned its verdict applying the *Panduit* factors. We conclude that, when the *Panduit* factors are met, they incorporate into their very analysis the value properly attributed to the patented feature.").

    The Federal Circuit recently denied a petition to rehear the *Mentor Graphics* case en banc, with five judges joining an opinion by Judge Stoll declaring that the panel's decision "is consistent with longstanding patent law damages principles" and that "based on the jury's undisputed fact findings on the *Panduit* factors in this case, ... the panel [decision] properly accounted for apportionment." *Mentor Graphics Corp. v. EVE-USA, Inc.* (Fed. Cir. Sep. 1, 2017, p.1299–1300) (U.S.) (Stoll, J., concurring in the denial of rehearing en banc). Dissenting from the denial of rehearing, Judges Dyk and Hughes contended that "the panel decision ... improperly holds that when lost profits are awarded for patent infringement" under the *Panduit* test, "there is no requirement for apportionment between patented and unpatented features." *Id.* at 1300 (Dyk, J., dissenting from denial of rehearing en banc). *See also* Chao 2018, 1345 (asserting that the panel decision in *Mentor Graphics* erred by "relying exclusively on [a] 'but for' analysis" that "fails to distinguish between lost profits attributable to a feature, and lost products attributable to an entire product").

[123] *See* Cotter 2009, 1178 n.137 (noting that "any other rule renders the patentee worse off as a result of the infringement").

sale should result in a reasonable royalty, where the value of other, non-patented features is considered in determining the royalty.[124] As the Federal Circuit noted in *Mentor Graphics*, courts may grant mixed awards of lost profits and reasonable royalties in cases where some but not all lost sales are due to the infringement;[125] this is particularly likely in cases involving complex, multicomponent products, where different customers value different features in their purchasing decisions. These mixed awards obviate the need for courts to engage in further apportionment of lost profits to cover only the value of the patented feature.

5 Potential Recovery for Other Harms

A final consideration is the availability of damages to compensate for other types of harms suffered by the patentee as a result of infringer's unlawful competition that fall outside the categories previously discussed.

Although as a general matter tort law aims to restore the victim to the position it would have occupied had the tort never occurred, legal systems throughout the world often impose substantial limits on this restorative principle, both to reduce the costs of adjudication and to vindicate other social policies. Similarly, if the goal of the patent system were to fully restore the patent owner to the position it would have occupied but for the infringement, courts would permit the patentee to recover not only its lost profits on lost sales due to the infringement, but also compensation for any other proven and quantifiable harms so caused, such as: (1) future losses that the patentee may suffer due to the infringer's accelerated entry into the market; (2) losses to the patent owner's goodwill or reputation, or to the prestige of the goods embodying the patented invention, due for example to consumers confusing the infringer's product with the patentee's; (3) lost profits at subsidiaries of the patentee;[126] (4) lost profits due to cost increases from lost economies of scale; (5) the opportunity cost of having to devote time to litigation, advertising or marketing expenses incurred in response to the infringement; and (6) emotional harms resulting from the infringement.

For a variety of reasons, however, it is unlikely that any legal system would award damages for *all* of these losses, even if the patent owner were able to prove them. For example, no legal system of which we are aware allows patent owners (or other tort

---

[124] See *Georgia-Pacific Corp.* v. *U.S. Plywood Corp.* (S.D.N.Y. 1970, p.1120) (U.S.) ("The portion of the realizable profit that should be credited to the invention as distinguished from non-patented elements, the manufacturing process, business risks, or significant features or improvements added by the infringer."); see also *Lucent Technologies, Inc.* v. *Gateway, Inc.* (Fed. Cir. 2009, p.1332–33) (U.S.) (overturning a jury's $357 million damages award in part because the accused product was "an enormously complex software program comprising hundreds, if not thousands or even more, features," and the patent-in-suit covered only "one small feature" of that product).

[125] *Mentor Graphics Corp.* v. *EVE-USA, Inc.* (Fed. Cir. 2017, p.1286) (U.S.).

[126] For instance, this might occur if the patentee's subsidiary supplies an unpatented active pharmaceutical ingredient to the patentee for manufacture in the patented formulation.

victims, for that matter) to recover damages for their opportunity costs of having to devote time to litigation – a result that probably is sound, given the substantial difficulties that would surround the accurate quantification of such losses.

On the other hand, ordinary principles of proximate causation in Anglo-American jurisprudence and counterpart doctrines elsewhere do not necessarily preclude patent owners from recovering for some of these other losses where provable. For example, courts in the United States and elsewhere have approved awards of lost profits resulting from the infringer having gained an accelerated foothold in the marketplace as a result of its infringement, though such losses can be difficult to prove and awards do not appear to be common.[127]

As for injury to goodwill, reputation, or prestige, as well as emotional harms, Article 13(1) of the EU Enforcement Directive states that in setting damages for the infringement of IP rights, the judicial authorities of member states "shall take into account all appropriate aspects, such as the negative economic consequences, including lost profits, which the injured party has suffered, any unfair profits made by the infringer *and, in appropriate cases, elements other than economic factors, such as the moral prejudice caused to the rightholder* ..."[128] In its 2016 *Liffers* decision, the Court of Justice of the European Union held that under Article 13(1), an IP owner can recover damages for moral prejudice in addition to a reasonable royalty[129] – though what "moral prejudice" means in the context of patent infringement cases remains somewhat unclear. (*Liffers* itself was a copyright case, and it refers to the possibility that moral prejudice may include injury to the author's reputation.) According to Fox et al. (2015), in the patent context, the concept has met with varying interpretations throughout the EU:

> Moral prejudice has barely any constancy between European jurisdictions even under the Enforcement Directive, and so there is no clear line to follow. All of the above-mentioned jurisdictions, with the exception of Germany, have it as an available claim, though it is rare (to an extreme) in the Netherlands, and England and Wales. In France, while theoretically tied to reputation, it appears to be used as a mechanism to adjust the quantum equitably. In Italy, moral prejudice must be demonstrated (essentially, damage to reputation), and then quantified as up to as much of 50 percent of the loss of profits.[130]

---

[127]   *See* Blair & Cotter 2001, 10–11 (stating that U.S. courts have awarded or considered awarding damages for additional costs, such as advertising and marketing expenditures, incurred in response to the infringement, as well as for "lost future profits, injury to the patent owner's reputation resulting from the sale of poor-quality infringing goods, and the infringer's accelerated entry into the marketplace once the patent expires," although "[t]hese latter injuries ... are more commonly perceived either as being subsumed in one or more of the other categories, or as being too remote or speculative.") (citations omitted); *see also* Cotter 2013a, 187, 262 n.160, 314 n.110, 320–21 (discussing the possibility of recovery for more remote harms in the United Kingdom, Germany, and Japan).

[128]   Directive 2004/48/EC, art. 13(1) (emphasis added).

[129]   *See Liffers* v. *Producciones Mandarina SL* (E.C.J. 2016) (EU).

[130]   Fox et al. 2015, 572–73.

Similarly, a recent patent infringement decision of the Court of Appeal of Madrid held that "moral damages" – including "psychological suffering or distress, which is considered to exist in a variety of situations such as psychological or spiritual shock or suffering, helplessness, worry (as a mental sensation of disquiet, sorrow, fear or foreboding uncertainty), anxiety, anguish, uncertainty, shock, affliction and other similar situations" – are in theory compensable (although the patent owner had not proven the facts alleged in support of them), as well as damages for "loss of prestige," which were awarded based on evidence that the infringing products were of lower quality than the plaintiff's, having been presented "in simple cardboard boxes as opposed to the luxury image attributed to the products of the complainant."[131] In the United States, by contrast, while damages for harm to goodwill or reputation resulting from patent infringement are in theory compensable[132] (though again, apparently rare), emotional harms probably are not.[133]

A standard law-and-economics account of proximate causation suggests that infringers who have breached a duty of care should not be responsible for losses having a low *ex ante* probability of occurring because the imposition of liability in such cases would increase adjudication costs without materially decreasing the (already low) risk of harm.[134] Whether this account (or other accounts of) proximate cause counsel in favor of more generous awards of damages for "moral prejudice" in patent cases has not been much addressed (to our knowledge) in the scholarly literature; neither has the related topic of the extent of proof that should be necessary to recover for and quantify such losses, assuming they are compensable at all. Further research on these issues may be warranted.

A final question related to this body of issues is whether courts should award damages, in patent or other cases, for "loss of chance" – i.e., for the profits that would have been earned on lost sales, discounted by the probability that those sales would have been made but for the infringement. For example, if the plaintiff can prove that there was a 30 percent chance it would have made ten more sales, under the loss of chance doctrine it would be entitled to recover 30 percent of the profit it would have earned on those sales. Courts in some countries award patent owners lost profits on this basis, but the United States does not. Rather, in the United States, the patent owner would recover no damages unless it could prove that it more likely than not suffered the loss (i.e., that the probability was greater than 50 percent).[135]

The principal argument in favor of awarding damages for loss of chance is that such a rule results in more accurate compensation to patentees in the aggregate. For example, if a patent owner could show that it had a 40 percent chance of making

---

[131] *See* Cotter 2016c (quoting a translation by Miquel Montañá).
[132] *See Lam, Inc.* v. *Johns-Manville Corp.* (Fed. Cir. 1983, p.1068) (U.S.).
[133] *See Rite-Hite Corp.* v. *Kelley Co.* (Fed. Cir. 1995, p.1546) (U.S.) (stating that "remote consequences, such as a heart attack of the inventor or loss in value of shares of common stock of a patentee corporation caused indirectly by infringement are not compensable").
[134] *See, e.g.,* Landes & Posner 1983, 119–20, 125–33; Shavell 1980, 490–93.
[135] For further discussion, *see* Cotter 2014b.

each of one hundred individual sales, under the U.S. rule it would recover no lost profits, even though it is likely that it would have made at least *some* of the one hundred sales. Conversely, if the owner can show that it had a 60 percent chance of making each of the hundred sales, it would recover lost profits for all one hundred, even though it is likely it would not have made all of them. On the other hand, one might question whether courts (or juries) are well positioned to make such finely grained probability determinations, and even if they are, whether the additional cost of adjudication would be justified by the marginal accuracy gains. Further research in this area might be of more than merely theoretical interest.

2.3 DISGORGEMENT OF INFRINGER'S PROFIT

In this Section, we first discuss several theoretical justifications for disgorgement of the infringer's profits. We then describe the availability of, and requirements for, the disgorgement remedy in major patent systems around the world. Finally, we conclude with an analysis of specific issues regarding disgorgement as a remedy, including the authors' recommendations regarding its availability, methods of calculation, and burden of proof.

2.3.1 *Theoretical Justifications*

As discussed in Section 2.2.2, disgorgement of the infringer's profits serves a different objective than the make-whole rationale of awarding the patentee its actual losses due to the infringement. In particular, "awards of defendant's profits threaten to undermine the principle that courts should not overcompensate patent owners."[136] For instance, where the infringer is more efficient than the patentee (i.e., it has a higher per-unit profit), the patent owner may be better off under a disgorgement remedy than if the infringement had never occurred.[137]

Several justifications have been offered for disgorgement of an infringer's profits. First, the disgorgement remedy prevents unjust enrichment by ensuring the infringer is no better off as a result of the infringement. In other words, it "correct[s] the imbalance created by the infringer retaining a benefit for which it would be unjust ... to retain without paying the patent owner."[138] For example, in 1888, the Supreme Court of the United States awarded the patentee recovery of the infringer's profit, reasoning that equity would not permit "the wrongdoer to profit by his own wrong."[139]

---

[136] Cotter 2013a, 68.
[137] For example, if the patentee makes $3 profit per unit sold, the infringer makes $5 profit per unit sold, and the patentee lost one hundred units of sales to the infringer (assuming no other changes), then disgorgement of the infringer's profits results in a $200 surplus to the patentee above its lost profits compared to the hypothetical "but for" world where infringement never occurred.
[138] Roberts 2010, 670.
[139] *Tilghman v. Proctor* (U.S. 1888, p.145) (U.S.).

The *Restatement (Third) of Restitution and Unjust Enrichment* articulates a similar rationale for the disgorgement remedy more generally. It explains that "[t]he object of restitution . . . is to eliminate profits from wrongdoing while avoiding, so far as possible, the imposition of a penalty. Restitution remedies that pursue this object are often called 'disgorgement' or 'accounting.'"[140] Under the *Restatement* approach, "the unjust enrichment of a conscious wrongdoer . . . is the net profit attributable to the underlying wrong."[141] "Conscious wrongdoer," in turn, is defined as one who acts either "with knowledge of the underlying wrong" or "despite a known risk that the conduct in question violates the rights of the claimant."[142]

Second, disgorgement may deter patent infringement by ensuring that the infringer is not better off as a result of infringing. Absent disgorgement, a prospective user of patented technology may opt to infringe rather than take a license,[143] particularly if the make-whole remedy for the patentee (lost profits and/or a reasonable royalty) will leave the infringer with some profit.[144] Disgorgement also may be combined with make-whole damages to the patentee, ensuring that the wrongdoer will be worse off than if it had not infringed, although this also runs the risk of over-rewarding the patentee and over-deterring potential infringers.[145]

Third, disgorgement may encourage patent licensing. Without the disgorgement remedy, potential users of patented technology may "lack an incentive to negotiate" *ex ante* because, as explained above, they may be no worse off if they infringe, get caught, and pay the patentee's losses, and they will be better off if they can infringe and avoid detection.[146] As a result, disgorgement "ensure[s] that defendants are at least incrementally worse off than they would have been if they had entered into voluntary negotiations."[147]

---

[140] RESTATEMENT (THIRD) OF RESTITUTION AND UNJUST ENRICHMENT § 51(4); *see also id.* at cmt. a ("The principal focus of § 51 is on cases in which unjust enrichment is measured by the defendant's profits, where the object of restitution is to strip the defendant of a wrongful gain . . . Restitution measured by the defendant's wrongful gain is frequently called 'disgorgement.'").

[141] *Id.* at § 51(4).

[142] *Id.* at § 51(3).

[143] *See* Lemley 2005, 1045 (arguing that, in the United States, "[p]atent law emphasizes deterrence least among the intellectual property regimes" because "it does not require disgorgement of profits").

[144] This may occur, for instance, when the infringer is more efficient than the patentee (i.e., because the infringer does not incur the patentee's R&D costs), and thus the infringer's profit from infringement exceeds the patentee's losses.

[145] *See* Cotter 2013a, 69 ("A rule permitting awards of defendants' profits nevertheless does pose some risk of overdeterrence; moreover, to the extent patent holdup is a concern, overcompensatory damages awards threaten to exacerbate the problem.").

[146] *Id.* Of course, this simplifies the analysis because the infringer may want to avoid litigation for other reasons, such as litigation costs, the possibility of paying the patentee's attorney's fees and costs, and the possibility of enhanced damages for conscious infringement where available (as in the United States).

[147] *Id.; see also* Lemley 2005, 1046 (explaining that disgorgement "helps intellectual property owners internalize the positive externalities of their invention by preventing unauthorized uses and therefore encouraging licensing").

2.3.2 Comparative Approaches to Disgorgement

1 North America

In the United States, historically, recovery of the infringer's profits was possible as an equitable remedy for patent infringement.[148] The Patent Act of 1819 created federal jurisdiction for actions in equity under the patent laws, thus authorizing federal courts to issue injunctions and other equitable relief, including "an equitable account of the infringer's illicit profits."[149] The Patent Act of 1870 explicitly extended disgorgement to actions at law as well, providing that "the claimant shall be entitled to recover . . . the profits to be accounted for by the defendant."[150]

However, in the Patent Act of 1946, Congress dropped all references to the infringer's profits.[151] The legislative history suggests that Congress was concerned by the time and expense needed to calculate the infringer's profits, which in some cases took many years of litigation.[152] In *Aro Manufacturing Co. v. Convertible Top Replacement Co.*, Justice Brennan of the Supreme Court concluded that the purpose of the 1946 amendment was "precisely to eliminate the recovery of profits as such and recovery of damages only,"[153] in an opinion concurred in by a total of four of the nine Justices.[154] Although it was "only a plurality opinion and arguably constituted dictum,"[155] later court decisions have interpreted the amendment in the same manner.[156] Therefore, most

---

[148] *See* Chisum 2017, § 20:02[3] ("Neither the earliest [U.S.] patent acts (1790 and 1793) nor the 1819 Act conferring equitable jurisdiction in patent infringement actions on the federal courts mentioned recovery of profits or any other monetary recovery in equity. Nevertheless, the courts recognized the power of a court of equity, which had acquired jurisdiction over a case by virtue of the complainant's request for injunctive relief, to grant full and complete relief by ordering an accounting of the infringer's illicit profits. Although an infringer was not a true trustee for the patent owner, the remedy of an accounting for profits, a familiar device in the equitable law of trusts, was readily adopted and applied to patent cases. Finally, the 1870 Act expressly referred to a complainant's entitlement to recover 'the profits to be accounted for by the defendant.'"(citation omitted)).

[149] *Id.; see also Stevens* v. *Gladding* (U.S. 1854, p.455) (U.S.) ("The right to an account of profits is incident to the right to an injunction in copy and patent-right cases."); Roberts 2010, 657–58.

[150] Act of July 8, 1870, § 55, 206.

[151] Congress's intent in the 1946 amendments is said to be "unclear." *See* Chisum 2017, § 20.02[4][a] ("[The Report of the House and Senate Patent Committees] stresses the intricate and insolvable problem of apportionment and the expense and delay of complex and technical accounting procedures before masters. However, the last paragraph of the Report states that the bill 'would not preclude the recovery of profits as an element of general damages.' This suggests an alternative and narrower intent, to wit, to eliminate a mandatory accounting of profits where the patent owner is willing to have recovery based on a reasonable royalty." (citation omitted)).

[152] *See* Roberts 2010, 662–63 (explaining that "[t]he majority of the legislative history [of the 1946 Patent Act] provides support for the general proposition that Congress eliminated the recovery of the infringer's profits" because of the "wasted time and expense generated by the profit apportionment problem").

[153] Chisum 2017, § 20.02[4][b].

[154] *Aro Mfg. Co.* v. *Convertible Top Replacement Co.* (U.S. 1964, p.505) (U.S.).

[155] Chisum 2017, § 20.02[4][c].

[156] *See, e.g., Zegers* v. *Zegers, Inc.* (7th Cir. 1972) (U.S.). For other examples, *see* Chisum 2017, § 20.02[4][c].

commentators believe that an award of the infringer's profits is not possible for utility patents in the United States.[157]

For design patents, however, Section 289 of the Patent Act provides that the infringer shall "be liable to the owner to the extent of his total profit, but not less than $250."[158] The Patent Act of 1887 introduced a provision to the same effect,[159] and when Congress abolished the recovery of the infringer's profits in 1946, they retained the special "total profit" provision for design patents.[160]

While Section 289 makes it unlawful to manufacture or sell an "article of manufacture" to which a patented design or a colorable imitation thereof has been applied and makes an infringer liable to the patent holder "to the extent of his total profit,"[161] in the case of a design for a multicomponent product, a question arises how to identify an "article of manufacture": whether it must always be the end product or it can also be a component of the product. In a case involving the infringement of designs for smartphones, the U.S. Court of Appeals for the Federal Circuit took the former interpretation and identified the entire smartphone as the only permissible "article of manufacture" for the purpose of calculating the infringer's "total profit" because "[t]he innards of Samsung's smartphones were not sold separately from their shells as distinct articles of manufacture to ordinary purchasers."[162] However, in *Samsung* v. *Apple*, the Supreme Court recently reversed the Federal Circuit's judgment and remanded the case.[163] In a unanimous opinion written by Justice Sotomayor, the Court stated that "the term 'article of manufacture' is broad enough to encompass both a product sold to a consumer as well as a component of that product."[164] Thus, the Supreme Court adopted the interpretation under which a patent holder would "sometimes be entitled to the infringer's total profit from a component of the end product."[165] The Court left it up to the lower courts to determine how to define the relevant "article of manufacture" and how to calculate the profit attributable to that article.[166]

In Canada, a successful patentee is entitled to damages, but may request an accounting of the infringer's profits.[167] The grant of an accounting is within the

---

[157] See Roberts 2010, 665 (contending that the relevant part in *Aro Mfg.* was arguably *obiter dictum*, but acknowledging that "subsequent courts, including the Supreme Court" have treated it as authoritative regarding the elimination of disgorgement as a remedy).

[158] 35 U.S.C. § 289.

[159] Act of Feb. 4, 1887, § 1, 387–88.

[160] See Chisum 2017, § 23.05[1][a] (explaining that the reason for the distinction between utility and design patents is "less than clear").

[161] 35 U.S.C. § 289.

[162] *Apple, Inc.* v. *Samsung Elecs. Co., Ltd.* (Fed. Cir. 2015, p.1002) (U.S.).

[163] *Samsung Elecs. Co., Ltd.* v. *Apple, Inc.* (U.S. 2016) (U.S.).

[164] *Id.* at 435.

[165] *Id.* at 434.

[166] See *id.* at 436 (declining to "set out a test for identifying the relevant article of manufacturing at the first step of the § 289 damages inquiry ...").

[167] Patent Act, R.S.C. 1985, c. P-4 (Can.), § 55 (damages), § 57 (accounting).

discretion of the court, though it is normally granted when sought, in the absence of some reason why it should not be permitted.[168] There are no fixed criteria for denying an accounting, though traditional equitable criteria will be considered.[169] In practice, "an accounting of profits has been the dominant monetary remedy for patent infringement in Canada," with at least twelve reported decisions since 1990.[170]

2 Europe

In the EU, Article 13 of the IP Enforcement Directive (2004/48/EC) stipulates:

1. Member States shall ensure that the competent judicial authorities, on application of the injured party, order the infringer who knowingly, or with reasonable grounds to know, engaged in an infringing activity, to pay the rightholder damages appropriate to the actual prejudice suffered by him/her as a result of the infringement. When the judicial authorities set the damages:

    (a) they shall take into account all appropriate aspects, such as the negative economic consequences, including lost profits, which the injured party has suffered, any unfair profits made by the infringer . . .[171]

As the provision requires the judicial authorities of Member States to "take into account . . . any unfair profits made by the infringer," a state "arguably would be in compliance with the Directive if it merely permitted courts to consider the defendant's profit in estimating the plaintiff's own 'actual prejudice.'"[172] The Commission Staff Working Document "Analysis of Enforcement Directive" published in December 2010[173] states:

> The profits unlawfully made by the infringer ("unjustified enrichment") constituted a new aspect for assessing damages in some Member States and it has been implemented into the national legislation in very different ways.
>   Many Member States require a rightholder to prove that profits were made with or as a result of the infringing products (causal link). Infringers may sometimes make higher profits with the infringing products than the rightholders with their

---

[168] *See* Siebrasse 2016 (reviewing the cases).
[169] *See, e.g., J.M. Voith GmbH* v. *Beloit Corp.* (Fed. Ct. 1997, ¶¶ 110, 113, 119) (Can.); *Philip Morris Prod. S.A.* v. *Marlboro Canada Ltd.* (Fed. Ct. 2015) (Can.).
[170] Siebrasse et al. 2008, 85; *see also* Cotter 2013a, 198 n.129 (listing cases).
[171] Directive 2004/48/EC, art. 13(1).
[172] Cotter 2013a, 257. For a similar analysis of apportionment of a breaching party's profits in contract disputes to reflect the nonbreaching party's expectancy interest, *see generally* Anderson 2015 (arguing in favor of a compensatory remedy for nonpecuniary loss in breach of contract cases, where the remedy is apportionment of the breaching party's profits based on evidence indicating nonpecuniary loss). Notably, this approach does not depend on the state of mind of the breaching party, and thus represents a compensatory rather than punitive approach.
[173] European Commission, at 22–23, COM (2010) 779 final (Dec. 22, 2010).

branded goods. Rightholders appear to find it very difficult to prove that they would have earned the same profits as the infringers, particularly where the infringers offer their products under conditions that significantly differ from those of the legal channels (e.g., lower prices, lower manufacturing costs, and absence of related services). Furthermore, in some Member States[174] it appears that infringers' profits can only be taken into consideration once, either as a recovery of unfair profits or as damages (or part of damages), but not in a cumulative way. In other Member States[175] the transfer of infringers' profits are awarded as an alternative, when the profits are higher than the rightholder's calculated damages (e.g., the rightholders' lost profits). Finally, in some Member States,[176] in addition to damages, also the transfer of the infringer's profits may be ordered.

In Germany, damages awarded for patent infringement are intended to be compensatory in nature and may be recovered for negligent or intentional infringement.[177] Surrender of the infringer's profits has been generally accepted as a method for calculating patent infringement damages for decades and, in 2008, its availability was codified in Section 139, para. 2 of the German Patent Act.[178] Under this provision, a patentee may choose among three methods for calculating damages (i.e., lost profits (actual damages suffered), license analogy (royalty), and the infringer's profits), but may not combine or cumulate them with respect to any single act of infringement.[179]

Traditionally, patentees rarely elected to calculate damages by reference to infringers' profits, primarily because courts liberally allowed infringers to deduct production costs from the revenue they earned on sales of infringing products. However, the decision by Federal Court (BGH) in the *Gemeinkostenanteil* case in 2000[180] brought about a fundamental change. In that decision, the Court held that, while the variable costs of manufacturing and marketing the infringing products may be deducted, an infringer's fixed costs may no longer offset its revenue. Though

---

[174] *Id.* at 22 n.52 ("E.g., Slovak Republic.").

[175] *Id.* at 23 n.53 ("E.g., Germany and Italy.").

[176] *Id.* at 23 n.54 ("E.g., Benelux countries in cases of bad faith.").

[177] Kamlah 2014, 904.

[178] *Id.* at 915. Article 139 of the Patent Act was amended in response to Article 13 of the EU Enforcement Directive. The theoretical ground for surrender of the infringer's profits was unclear and controversial. The pervasive view seems to have been to understand the remedy as a result of an analogous application of the rules on false agency (angemaßte Eigengeschäftsführung; Section 687, para. 2 of BGB (the Civil Code)). Some scholars have criticized this view, pointing out that false agency requires an intentional act while patent infringement can be committed negligently. *Id.* After the codification of para. 2 of Article 139, a view to take the surrender of the infringer's profits as just one of different methods for calculation of damages for the compensatory purpose seems to be getting more support from scholars and practitioners. *See* Melullis 2008, 679; Grabinski 2009, 260–61 (stating that a recourse to the law of false agency is not necessary any more, at least for the new Article 139, para. 2). *See also* Schönknecht 2012, 311 (stating that the methods based on the infringer's profits and license analogy are merely different forms of liquidation of a unitary damages claim). For an argument about the characterization of the three methods in Germany, *see* Cotter 2013g.

[179] Kamlah 2014, 907; Schönknecht 2012, 311.

[180] BGH v. 2.11.2000 – I ZR 246/98 – *Gemeinkostenanteil* (Ger.).

this case dealt with infringement of design rights, courts have applied the same rule to damages awarded for patent infringement. Post-*Gemeinkostenanteil*, Germany has seen a marked increase in requests for damages based on alleged infringers' profits.[181]

In France, Code de la propriété intellectuelle Article, L. 615–7, provides for two different methods of calculation: actual damages and an analogy to licenses. It stipulates that "[t]o set the amount of damages, the court distinctly takes into account: the negative economic consequences of the infringement, including the loss of earnings and any loss suffered by the injured party, the moral prejudice caused to the latter and the profits made by the infringer, including the savings in intellectual, material and promotional investments that it achieved from the infringement."[182] It is said that "[t]he place of the infringer's profits in the calculation of damages is not yet clear in case law," and "[s]ome decisions have considered that the claimant can be granted the infringer's profits, while others take a different position."[183]

In the United Kingdom, "it is standard to allow the successful patentee to elect for either an inquiry as to damages or an account of profits for past infringements."[184] The patentee is entitled to limited disclosure of the infringer's financial information in order to choose between damages or profits.[185] An account of profits is an equitable and restitutionary remedy whose purpose is to deprive the infringer of the profits that it has improperly made by wrongful acts committed in breach of the claimant's rights and transfer those profits to the claimant.[186] Requesting of profits is said to be a "much rarer choice than requesting damages because the outcome is much more uncertain."[187]

---

[181] Kamlah 2014, 907. Grabinski 2009, 262, reports that in recent years the method based on the infringer's profits has been used in at least three-fourths of the cases for damages for the infringement of patents or utility models before LG Düsseldorf (the regional court in Düsseldorf). For the details of the calculation method of the infringer's profits, *see, e.g.,* Kühnen 2017, 863–78; Kamlah 2014, 916–20. *See also* Cotter 2013d (discussing BGH v. 24.7.2012 – X ZR 51/11 – *Flaschenträger*).

[182] Romet et al. 2015, 170; Fox et al. 2015, 569.

[183] Romet et al. 2015, 170. In the accompanying footnotes, the authors cite *TYC Europe v. Valeo* (CA Paris 2013) (Fr.); *Hydr Am v. Gimaex and Weber Hydraulik* (TGI Paris 2013) (Fr.) and *Time Sport International v. JCR* (TGI Paris 2013) (Fr.) as decisions taking the former position, while citing *Saint Dizier Environment v. Materiel Santé Environment and CME* (TGI Paris 2013) (Fr.) as a decision taking the latter.

[184] *Glaxosmithkline UK Ltd. v. Wyeth Holdings LLC* (Pat 2017, ¶ 31) (UK); *see also,* Birss et al. 2016, ¶ 21–52.

[185] Birss et al. 2016, ¶ 21–53 (citing *Island Records Ltd. v. Tring Int. Plc.* (Ch 1995) (UK)).

[186] Birss et al. 2016, ¶ 21–136; Rennie-Smith 2015, 81, 104. As to the calculation of profits, *see* Birss et al. 2016, ¶¶ 21–137 to –140 ("Where only part of a product or process infringes, profits are to be apportioned between those which were caused by or attributable to the use of the invention (and which the patentee may thus recover) and those which were not. However, where the invention is the essential ingredient of the defendant's whole product or process it may be appropriate not to apportion." (citing *Celanese Int'l Corp. v. BP Chemicals Ltd.* (Pat 1999, ¶ 46) (UK)). For a discussion on the recent decision *Design & Display Ltd. v. OOO Abbott & Anor* (Civ 2016) (UK), *see* Cotter 2016a.

[187] Fox et al. 2015, 568.

3 Asia

Article 102 of the Japanese Patent Act provides for three special methods for calculating damages: methods using the patentee's profit margin, the infringer's profits, or hypothetical royalty. Paragraph 2 of that Article provides: "Where a patentee or an exclusive licensee claims against an infringer compensation for damage sustained as a result of the intentional or negligent infringement of the patent right or exclusive license, and the infringer earned profits from the act of infringement, the amount of profits earned by the infringer shall be presumed to be the amount of damage sustained by the patentee or exclusive licensee." Though courts initially limited this form of damages to patentees that were practicing the patented invention, the Grand Panel of the Intellectual Property High Court softened this requirement in 2013, holding that disgorgement is available anytime the patentee lost profits as a result of infringement, even if those profits did not result from lost sales of goods or services covered by the patent-in-suit.[188] For example, it is now generally accepted that disgorgement is an available remedy for patentees that sell unpatented products that compete with the infringing products supplied by the infringer. It is still unclear and disputed, however, whether patentees that only license the patent-in-suit to third parties may request disgorgement as a remedy. Moreover, when disgorgement is awarded, at least some courts have apportioned the infringer's profits to reflect the percentage of infringing sales attributable to the infringing feature.[189]

Section 65 of the Patent Act of China provides for several methods for determination of the amount of damages: the actual loss incurred by the patentee, the infringer's profits, and reasonable royalties – though, in practice, the vast majority of patentees in Chinese patent suits pursue statutory damages.[190] Though disgorgement is rarely awarded, the Chinese Supreme People's Court (SPC) has held that an infringer's profits may be calculated by multiplying the profits per unit of infringing product and the quantity of the infringing products that have sold in the market.[191] The SPC also held in 2009 that disgorgement awards may be apportioned "to deduct profits led by factors other than the infringed patent from the whole amount of the infringing profits."[192]

Australia follows a similar approach to the United Kingdom and Canada and permits disgorgement of an infringer's profits.[193] The leading authority makes clear

---

[188] *Sangenic Int'l Ltd. v. Aprica Children's Prod. Inc.* (IP High Ct. 2013) (Japan) (Waste Storage Device).
[189] For example, the court in Case No. 2014 (Ne) 10022 (IP High Ct. 2014) (Japan) (Telephone Number Automatic Creation Device) admitted 65 percent "partial reversal of the presumption" based on the infringer's profits, taking into account the contribution of the patented invention to the profits.
[190] Pattloch 2015, 315, 343. *See also* Hu 2016, 5, 8 (showing that out of the patent (invention patent) infringement cases that awarded damages between June 1, 2008 and Dec. 31, 2011, 5.26 percent, 2.26 percent, 0 percent, and 92.48 percent were based on losses of patentees, infringers' profits, analogies of royalties, or statutory damages, respectively).
[191] Hu 2016, 16 (citing Wu 2014).
[192] *Id.* (citing Supreme People's Court of the People's Republic of China 2009, art. 16).
[193] Cotter 2013a, 198.

that, like in the United Kingdom, a patentee may elect an accounting in lieu of seeking monetary damages.[194]

2.3.3 *Specific Issues Regarding Disgorgement*

1 Availability

We were unable to reach consensus regarding the question of whether disgorgement should be available in all major patent systems. We acknowledge the divergence in approaches between jurisdictions on this issue,[195] as well as the competing policy arguments for and against disgorgement. Group members who favor disgorgement point to several potential benefits. First, it creates an incentive for potential infringers to engage in *ex ante* licensing of patent rights, while not being as serious of a sanction as punitive damages. While an accounting will not incentivize a truly innocent infringer (i.e., an infringer that was unaware of the patent-in-suit and could not have reasonably identified all patents covering a product prior to market entry)[196] into negotiating *ex ante*, it can incentivize a negligent or deliberate infringer to do so. Second, disgorgement may be advantageous for a patentee who wishes to avoid divulging financial information to a competitor in a damages assessment. This appears to be a motivation for pharmaceutical companies routinely electing an account in countries such as Canada, even when damages based on the patentee's loss would be greater.[197]

In contrast, group members who are less enthusiastic about disgorgement as a remedy point to several potential drawbacks of the remedy. First, disgorgement may create a significant risk of over-deterrence, causing firms to be less willing to introduce new and innovative products, particularly complex products that incorporate numerous different technologies.[198] In addition, non-compensatory damages awards like disgorgement threaten to exacerbate the holdup problem.[199] Furthermore, there may be substantial litigation costs associated with calculating the amount of profit due to infringement that is to be disgorged.[200] Finally,

---

[194] *Dart Indus. Inc. v. Decor Corp. Pty Ltd.* (HCA 1993) (Austl.)).

[195] *See supra* notes 148–194 and accompanying text.

[196] *See* FTC 2011, 55–56 (explaining the contention that for IT products, "the enormous number of potentially relevant, overlapping patents make identifying the applicable rights prior to product launch prohibitively costly").

[197] Siebrasse et al. 2008; *cf.* Michel 2010, 11 (noting that the need for protective orders is "particularly acute in the context of damages discovery, which often includes extremely sensitive financial information concerning a party's costs, revenues, profits, and the like. Disclosure of such information publicly could severely harm a party's business or competitive position.").

[198] Cotter 2013a, 69; *see also* Cotter 2011, 740 n.69 (expressing similar concerns about the risk of over-deterrence posed by restitutionary awards in patent cases).

[199] Cotter 2013a, 69.

[200] *See supra* note 153 and accompanying text (describing litigation costs and delays in the United States for disgorgement of profits from utility patents prior to 1946).

disgorgement in the context of complex, multifunction products may amplify the risk of error in calculating a remedy, as courts will be required to determine the share of infringer's profit due to infringement of patented feature(s), as opposed to unpatented or licensed components, as well as the infringer's own contributions to the infringing product.

In light of this lack of consensus, the recommendations in the rest of this Section are oriented at jurisdictions where disgorgement is an accepted remedy. In countries like the United States that do not currently award disgorgement as a remedy, we propose further research on whether an accounting may be desirable as an alternative to enhanced damages to deter willful infringement.

2 Discretionary or As of Right

In jurisdictions where disgorgement of the infringer's profits is available as a remedy, one question is whether it should be awarded automatically or at the trial court's discretion. Though an accounting is an equitable remedy, in UK law, a successful patentee is entitled to an accounting if it so elects.[201] Similarly, when the remedy was available in U.S. law, it appears to have been routinely granted, perhaps as of right. In Canadian law, in contrast, the remedy is clearly discretionary, though it is normally granted.[202]

In view of the potential burden on the infringer in taking an accounting, particularly in complex product cases, we recommend that in jurisdictions that choose to allow an accounting, the grant of accounting be within the discretion of the court. One factor that should be considered is whether an accounting will place an undue burden on the infringer, recognizing that the costs of discovery in an accounting are likely to fall disproportionately on the infringer.[203] That is, an accounting should not be granted when it is used primarily as a tool to harass the infringer.

---

[201] *See, e.g., Siddell v. Vickers* (Civ 1892, p.162) (UK) (reviewing the cases and stating that "the Plaintiff in an action for infringement of a patent, having succeeded, is entitled at his election either to damages or an account of profits, and that is the state of the law"); *Celanese Int'l Corp. v. BP Chemicals Ltd.* (Pat 1999, ¶ 35) (UK) ("A plaintiff who is successful in patent litigation has an entitlement to elect between damages and an account."); *Hollister Inc. & Dansac AS v. Medik Ostomy Supplies Ltd.* (PCC 2011, ¶ 7 (UK) (quoting *Celanese*). However, neither damages nor an accounting is available against an innocent infringer. Patents Act, 1977, c. 37, § 62(1) (UK). In Australian law, it appears that an accounting is routinely granted if requested, but the court "may" refuse to order either damages or an accounting against an innocent infringer. *Patents Act 1990*, § 123(1) (Austl.).

[202] A successful patentee is presumptively entitled to an accounting in the sense that an accounting, if sought, is normally granted in the absence of some reason why it should not be permitted. *See* Siebrasse 2016 (reviewing the cases). Traditional equitable factors will be considered in making the decision to deny an accounting. *See, e.g., J.M. Voith GmbH v. Beloit Corp.* (Fed. Ct. 1997, ¶¶ 110, 113, 119) (Can.); *Philip Morris Prod. S.A. v. Marlboro Canada Ltd.* (Fed. Ct. 2015) (Can.).

[203] *See, e.g., Eurocopter v. Bell Helicopter Textron Canada Ltée* (Fed. Ct. 2012, ¶ 412) (Can.) (refusing to grant an accounting in part because of the difficulty of calculating the accounting in a case in which the patented invention, helicopter landing gear, "although essential for the proper functioning and security of a helicopter, represents just a small part of the total cost of a helicopter").

This is not to say that we are recommending that an accounting be granted sparingly. It should also be recognized that when damages are sought, particularly in the form of lost profits, the discovery burden will fall disproportionately on the patentee, and the desire to avoid that burden is an entirely legitimate reason for the patentee to elect an accounting in lieu of lost profits. As explained in more detail below, the patentee will often pay an implicit price in the form of foregone damages when electing an accounting,[204] and this is an inherent disincentive to abuse of the accounting remedy. The concern that an accounting will unduly burden the infringer will be further mitigated in jurisdictions with limited discovery. Therefore, an accounting should not be denied solely because of the burden it places on the infringer, but only when that burden is disproportionate to the amount at issue, as compared with the alternative of assessing damages.

We would also emphasize that the concern for the burden on the infringer is not necessarily the only consideration that should be taken into account in determining whether an accounting should be granted. We focus on this point because it is one lesson to be taken from the history of the accounting remedy in U.S. law. Because an accounting of profits is not available in the United States and it is not the primary remedy in most jurisdictions in which it is available, the broader question of when an accounting should be granted has not received sustained attention, either in the cases or in the literature. We propose further research on this issue.

3 Calculating the Infringer's Profits

A) DIFFERENTIAL PROFIT METHOD. In our view, the fundamental principle in calculating an accounting of the infringer's profits is that the "the inventor is only entitled to that portion of the infringer's profit which is causally attributable to the invention."[205] In order to implement this causation requirement, the correct approach to calculating the profits to be disgorged is the "differential profit" approach, in which "[a] comparison is to be made between the defendant's profit attributable to the invention and his profit had he used the best non-infringing option."[206] The profit causally attributable to the infringement is the difference between the infringer's actual profits and the infringer's profits in the "but for" world in which it did not infringe. The differential profit approach was established as the correct approach to an accounting of profits by the Supreme Court of Canada in

---

[204] *See infra* note 238 and accompanying paragraph of text.
[205] *Monsanto Canada Inc. v. Schmeiser* (Sup. Ct. 2004, ¶ 101) (Can.).
[206] *Id.* at ¶ 102; *see* Cotter 2013a, 197 (noting that "the profit attributable to the infringement is, strictly speaking, only the profit the defendant earned over and above what he would have earned from using the next-best available alternative"). *See also Monsanto Canada Inc. v. Schmeiser* (Sup. Ct. 2004, ¶ 101) (Can.) (noting that "the inventor is only entitled to that portion of the infringer's profit which is causally attributable to the invention").

Monsanto Canada Inc. v. *Schmeiser* (2004) and is now well established in Canadian patent law.[207]

The increased profit due to the invention may take the form of increased sales, increased profits, or reduced costs:

> If the presence of the infringing feature caused the infringer to earn ten sales that it otherwise would not have earned, the proper measure of the benefit derived from the use of the patent is the profit earned on the ten additional sales. Similarly, if the infringer would have made the same number of sales at the same prices, but at higher production costs, the benefit derived from the use of the patent is the cost saving.[208]

The infringer's differential profit is very closely related to the value of the invention over the best noninfringing alternative, which is widely acknowledged to be the social value of the invention.[209] The difference between the two is only that the differential profit represents the profit attributable to the patented technology in the hands of the infringer, which may be less than its true social value (if, for example, the infringer is particularly inefficient at implementing the invention). In many cases, however, the two concepts will coincide.

The differential profit approach to an accounting of profits is the mirror image of the approach we recommend to damages. In *Aro Manufacturing Co.* v. *Convertible Top Replacement Co.*, the Supreme Court of the United States stated that the statutory measure of "damages" is "the difference between [the patentee's] pecuniary condition after the infringement, and what his condition would have been if the infringement had not occurred."[210] Substituting the words "the infringer's" for the bracketed phrase gives the differential profits approach to an accounting. This symmetry arises because the causation inquiry is fundamentally the same in either context. If the patentee is entitled to damages in the form of lost profits, the inquiry is the same, with the only difference being whether the focus is on the patentee's profits or the infringer's profits.

The differential profit approach to an accounting of profits is also closely related to the incremental profit approach we recommend as the appropriate approach to reasonable royalty damages.[211] The hypothetical negotiation approach to a reasonable royalty considers a negotiation between the patentee and the infringer in which the infringer's maximum willingness to pay is determined by its profits if it

---

[207] *See, e.g., Apotex Inc.* v. *ADIR* (Fed. Ct. 2017) (Can.); *Monsanto Canada Inc.* v. *Rivett* (Fed. Ct. 2010) (Can.); *Frac Shack Inc.* v. *AFD Petroleum Ltd.* (Fed. Ct. 2017) (Can.).

[208] Cotter 2013a, 205.

[209] *See* Chapter 1.

[210] *Aro Mfg. Co.* v. *Convertible Top Replacement Co.* (U.S. 1964, p.507) (U.S.) (plurality opinion) (quoting *Yale Lock Mfg. Co.* v. *Sargent* (U.S. 1886, p.552) (U.S.)); *see also id.* (stating that the primary question is "had the Infringer not infringed, what would Patent Holder-Licensee have made?" (quoting *Livesay Window Co., Inc.* v. *Livesay Indus., Inc.* (5th Cir. 1985, p.471) (U.S.))).

[211] *See* Chapter 1.

had used the best noninfringing alternative. The only difference between this and the differential profits approach to an accounting of profits is that an accounting awards all of the value of the invention to the patentee, while reasonable royalty damages splits that value between the parties.[212]

The differential profit approach contrasts with the approach to disgorgement of profits under U.S. law of design patents, in which the infringer is required to disgorge the entire profit made on an infringing "article of manufacture,"[213] even though that profit may be only partially attributable to the invention. This approach, as set out by the Supreme Court in *Samsung v. Apple*,[214] turns on the specific wording of the relevant U.S. statutory provision rather than any general principle regarding disgorgement, and consequently we will not explore the reasoning in detail. Suffice it to say that this approach is contrary to the sound economic principle that the plaintiff should recover damages reflecting only the value of the patented feature. The U.S. approach in design patent cases can result in disgorgement of profits that are not causally attributable to the infringement, and thus will put the patentee in a better position than it would have been but for the infringement.[215] Indeed, if, as is common, there is more than one patented design in a product, an infringer might be liable for its entire profits to multiple parties.[216] Consequently we recommend that the U.S. design patents approach to disgorgement of the infringer's profits should not be adopted in patent law.

The differential profit approach also contrasts the accounting profit approach, in which the infringer's profit is calculated as the difference between its revenues and costs attributable to the infringing product, without any consideration of whether some or all of that profit might have been made using a noninfringing alternative. Like the U.S. approach to disgorgement in design patents, the accounting profits approach is contrary to the sound economic principle that the plaintiff should recover damages reflecting only the value of the patented feature, and it will often result in disgorgement of profits that are not causally attributable to the infringement. The U.S. design patents approach ignores value contributed by other aspects of the infringing product, while the accounting profit approach ignores the value that the infringer might have derived from a noninfringing alternative. Consequently, we recommend that the accounting profits approach should not be adopted in patent law.

---

[212] *See* Taylor 2014, 140 ("[A]warding all of the infringer's profit as a categorical rule governing all awards of reasonable royalties would effectively reinstitute disgorgement of profits as a remedy for patent infringement.").

[213] U.S. Patent Act § 289.

[214] *Samsung Elecs. Co., Ltd. v. Apple, Inc.* (U.S. 2016) (U.S.); *see also supra* notes 161–166 and accompanying text (discussing the *Samsung* decision on design patent remedies in more detail).

[215] *See, e.g.,* Lemley 2013, 221 (arguing that disgorgement under § 289 "drastically overcompensates the owners of design patent," in cases involving "a modern, multicomponent product").

[216] *See id.* at 231–32 (explaining that under the U.S. system of design patent remedies, "we may have multiple parties lining up, each entitled to collect the defendant's entire profit … ").

In sum, we recommend that the correct approach to calculating an accounting of profits is the differential profit approach, in which the profits to be disgorged by the infringer are equal to the difference between its actual profits, and the profits it would have made had it used the best noninfringing alternative.

B) DIFFICULTY OF ASSESSMENT. As previously explained, disgorgement of the infringer's profits was eliminated from U.S. law as a remedy for infringement of utility patents by the 1946 Patent Act,[217] largely because of the difficulty of apportioning profits in the case of complex products.[218] Two general difficulties arise. One is how to allocate overhead expenses that support both infringing and noninfringing products. The second is the problem of apportionment "where the [infringer's] profits were not attributable solely to the patented invention."[219]

The first problem arises regardless of whether the product is simple or complex. It is also more tractable, both conceptually and practically. The infringer's profits are its revenues less its costs. The direct costs of producing the infringing goods are clearly deductible, but what about general overhead, such as rent, and other fixed costs that would be spent whether or not the infringing product was made? The argument against deducting fixed costs is that they would have been incurred in any event and thus are not costs caused by the infringement. This is reflected in the so-called incremental profits approach,[220] in which the profits are the difference between those actually earned and those that would have been earned but for the infringement in the short run. On the other hand, the functions paid for by overhead are necessary to operation of the business in the longer run, and so those costs, while indirect, must have contributed something to the production of the infringing product.[221] In the long run, a business cannot run profitably without covering its fixed costs; for instance, if the infringer produced five different products, all of which infringed patents held by different patentees, and deduction of fixed costs was not permitted, the infringer would be required to account for far more profit than it actually made.

The same issue of deducting fixed costs arises in the context of damages in the form of lost profits. In both contexts, deducting fixed costs would benefit the infringer by reducing the profits that the infringer must disgorge, or which the

---

[217] Act of Aug. 1, 1946, § 70, 778; *see also supra* notes 151–57 and accompanying text.
[218] *See supra* note 152 and accompanying text; *see also* H.R. REP. No. 79–1587, at 2 (1946) ("Frequently a suit for patent infringement involves the infringement of only an improvement in a complex machine, and it is impossible to apportion profits due to the improvement. In such circumstances the proceedings before masters, which are conducted in accordance with highly technical rules and are always expensive, are often protracted for decades and in many cases result in complete failure of justice.").
[219] Chisum 2017, § 20.02[3].
[220] The "incremental profits" approach must be distinguished from the "differential profits" approach that looks to the value of the invention over the best noninfringing alternative; the incremental profit approach looks to the incremental profit of production.
[221] Cotter 2013a, 206–07.

patentee claims as damages. In the United States, "[t]he incremental income approach to the computation of lost profits is well established in the law relating to patent damages," and therefore "fixed costs – those costs which do not vary with increases in production, such as management salaries, property taxes, and insurance – are excluded when determining profits."[222] UK and Australian courts, on the other hand, are willing to allow deduction of some part of the overhead if it can be shown on the facts that, but for the infringement, "the infringer would have devoted his capacity to the manufacture and/or marketing of non-infringing products."[223] This essentially amounts to considering fixed costs as opportunity costs, except rather than allowing a deduction for opportunity costs as such, a proportion of the general overhead is allocated to the infringing activity if and only if there was a foregone opportunity.[224] The infringer is not, however, entitled to simply allocate a proportion of general overheads to an infringing activity.[225]

The economic analyses of the question of whether the overhead should be deducted is divided. The argument against deduction is that fixed costs would have been incurred in any event, and so cannot be attributed to the infringement. The argument in favor of deduction is that it is fair to assume that the infringer would have earned something from the use of equipment and other assets that in fact were deployed for infringing purposes.[226] We do not take a position on this debate, as it does not raise issues peculiar to complex products (or even to patent law, as the same question exists in debates over remedies for breach of contract), which is the focus of this project. However, we see no reason in principle why the issue should be treated differently in the two contexts. Consequently, we recommend that the same approach to fixed costs be taken in the context of both lost profits damages and an account of the infringer's profits.

The second major area of difficulty is peculiar to complex products, where the infringing technology contributes only a relatively small part of the overall value of the infringing product. The challenge is to apportion the infringer's profits between the patented invention and the noninfringing aspects of the product.[227] Exactly the same problem arises in the context of damages. In our view, the solution in principle is the same in both contexts, namely the differential profits approach; the profit attributable to the infringing technology is the difference between the profit the infringer actually made and the profit it would have made but for the infringement.

---

[222]   *Paper Converting Mach. Co. v. Magna-Graphics Corp.* (Fed. Cir. 1984, p.22) (U.S.); *see also State Indus., Inc. v. Mor-Flo Indus., Inc.* (Fed. Cir. 1989, p.1579–80) (U.S.) (approving the award of incremental profits); Chisum 2017, § 20.05[4][b].

[223]   *Design & Display Ltd. v. OOO Abbott & Anor,* (Civ 2016, ¶ 40) (UK) (citing *Dart Indus. Inc. v. Decor Corp. Pty Ltd.* (HCA 1993) (Austl.)).

[224]   *Dart Indus. Inc. v. Decor Corp. Pty Ltd.* (HCA 1993, p.114–15) (Austl.); *Hollister Inc. & Dansac A/S v. Medik Ostomy Supplies Ltd.* (Civ 2012, ¶¶ 82–86) (UK).

[225]   *Hollister Inc. & Dansac A/S v. Medik Ostomy Supplies Ltd.* (Civ 2012, ¶ 85) (UK).

[226]   Cotter 2013a, 206–09.

[227]   Chisum 2017, § 20.02[3].

And, as in the context of damages, actually applying this approach is often extremely difficult,[228] for exactly the same reasons discussed in the damages context.[229]

Given that at least some of the problems that led the United States to eliminate the remedy of an accounting of profits also arise in the context of damages, the question arises as to why the accounting remedy was singled out for abolition. The answer (at least in part) is that damages were also often denied, but on a case-by-case basis, rather than via legislative mandate. Damages had to be proved, not presumed,[230] and in a complex products case, the patentee often cannot establish lost profit damages, as it has difficulty proving causation – i.e., that it lost sales due to the patented technology.[231] In early U.S. law, damages for lost royalties were generally not available in the absence of an established royalty, and consequently a prevailing patentee would commonly receive only nominal damages despite substantial infringement.[232] The harshness of this result was mitigated by the recognition of reasonable royalty damages,[233] which relaxed the standard of proof required to establish entitlement to a royalty.[234] However, in the current understanding of reasonable royalty damages, where the value of the invention over the best non-infringing alternative is split between the patentee and the infringer, even reasonable royalty damages require apportionment of the value between the patented invention and other aspects of a complex product, which has proven very difficult in that context as well.[235] Thus an accounting of the infringer's profits is not in general more (or less) difficult than assessing damages in either the form of lost profits or a reasonable royalty, but any of these may be less difficult than the others on the facts of a particular case. With that said, all will typically be fairly difficult in the context of a complex product.

---

[228] See *Westinghouse Electric & Mfg. Co.* v. *Wagner Electric & Mfg. Co.* (U.S. 1912, p.615–20) (U.S.) (discussing the difficulty of apportioning profits); *Siddell* v. *Vickers* (Civ 1892, p.162–63) (UK) (same); *see also generally* Chisum 2017, § 20.02[3], and cases cited therein.

[229] See *infra* Section 2.2.2; Chapter 1.

[230] Chisum 2017, § 20.02[2].

[231] Except in relatively rare cases where the patented technology drives market demand for the product. Under U.S. law, the so-called entire market value rule will allow the patentee to recover lost profits on the sale of the entire product in such cases. See *generally* Love 2007; *see also supra* notes 92–94 and accompanying text (further explaining the entire market value rule). A similar rule was applied in early U.S. accounting of profits cases. Chisum 2017, § 20.02[2][c].

[232] Chisum 2017, § 20.02[2].

[233] *Id.* § 20.02[3][c] ("To this general rule, the cases recognized an exception where the sold article derived its entire marketable value from the patented improvement." (citing Robinson 1890, 505–07)).

[234] See *generally* Taylor 2014, 97–99 (describing the development of the law governing reasonable royalties in response to undercompensation associated with nominal damages).

[235] *Glaxosmithkline UK Ltd.* v. *Wyeth Holdings LLC* (Pat 2017, ¶ 34) (UK) (noting "In many cases, when assessing a reasonable royalty for damages, the court considers what profits have been made by the defendant and apportions what it regards as a fair share by way of royalty. Therefore, damages inquiries already involve, to some extent, the complexity that also occurs in the case of accounts of profits."); *see also* Chapter 1.

Other considerations also may have motivated the U.S. decision to abolish the accounting remedy. An accounting, though a monetary remedy, was available to the successful patentee as of right if it brought suit in equity.[236] A successful patentee could use the cost and time of an accounting as a weapon to harass the infringer.[237] There is no symmetry in this respect with damages, where the practical burden of proving its lost profits would fall on the patentee.

This problem was exacerbated because in old U.S. law, the patentee could seek both damages and an accounting at the same time.[238] In other systems derived from English law, including the United Kingdom, Canada, and Australia, the patentee must elect either damages or an accounting. The quantum of lost profit damages will commonly be greater than the infringer's profits that would be disgorged in an accounting because the infringer often prices below the patentee. When a patentee is required to make such an election, the opportunity cost of foregoing damages makes it unpalatable to elect an accounting solely to harass the infringer. We recommend that if an accounting is permitted, the patentee should be required to elect between an accounting and damages, and should not be permitted to pursue both simultaneously.

In summary, the concerns that led the United States to entirely eliminate the accounting remedy are shared by the damages remedy, and these concerns were exacerbated by the unique ability of patentees to harass infringers by requesting both damages and an accounting of profits under the U.S. regime that existed prior to 1946. U.S. history does not support the view that an accounting of profits, by itself, is a uniquely problematic remedy.

c) BURDEN OF PROOF. The final issue to consider is the burden of proof regarding the proper amount of disgorgement. The difficulty of apportioning the infringer's profits to the patented technology in complex product cases means that the burden of proof is of the utmost importance. As with apportionment, there is no easy solution to this problem.

---

[236] *See, e.g., Tilghman* v. *Proctor* (U.S. 1888, p.144) (U.S.) ("But upon a bill in equity by the owner against infringers of a patent, the plaintiff is entitled to recover the amount of gains and profits that the defendants have made by the use of his invention."); *Stevens* v. *Gladding* (U.S. 1854, p.455) (U.S.) ("The right to an account for profits is incident to the right to an injunction, in copy and patent-right cases."). This right was confirmed by the Patent Act of 1870. *See* Act of July 8, 1870, § 55, 206 (providing that a successful patentee "shall be entitled to recover, in addition to the profits to be accounted for by the defendant, the damages the complainant has sustained thereby ...").

[237] *See Kori Corp.* v. *Wilco Marsh Buggies & Draglines, Inc.* (Fed. Cir. 1985, p.654) (U.S.) ("The legislative history of the 1946 amendments clearly indicates that one of its purposes was to eliminate the necessity of the traditional accounting to determine the infringer's profits in all damages determinations, and to deter the use of such proceedings by successful patentees to harass the infringer.").

[238] Act of July 8, 1870. Double recovery, however, was not permitted, as the patentee's actual damages were recoverable only to the extent that they exceeded the infringer's profits. *See Rite-Hite Corp.* v. *Kelley Co.* (Fed. Cir. 1995, p.1561) (U.S.) (Nies, J., dissenting-in-part).

One possible approach is to put the burden of apportionment on the infringer, on the view that the patentee should not be restricted to a nominal award because of the difficulty of apportionment.[239] On the other hand, in cases where it is clear that the patented technology contributes only a small part of the value of the product, awarding the entire profit to the patentee because of the difficulty of apportionment will unjustly overcompensate the patentee.[240] It is possible to further parse the burden according to particular considerations, such as whether the difficulty of apportionment was the fault of the infringer (e.g., by not keeping adequate books), or whether the patent is for the whole product, or only for an improvement, and so on. The question of the burden of proof was extensively debated in U.S. law when the disgorgement remedy was available, but no fully satisfactory solution was ever developed.[241] Nor has the question been resolved in other jurisdictions in which disgorgement is still permitted, in part because the issue is pressing in only complex product cases, and relatively few of these have been decided so far.[242] Consequently, if an accounting of profits is to be permitted as a remedy in the context of complex products, further research is required on the issue of the burden of proof of apportionment.

We note that the issue of the burden of proving apportionment is distinct from the burden of proving the availability of a noninfringing alternative.[243] As previously discussed in the lost profits section, further research would be helpful on this issue.

---

[239] *See Westinghouse Electric & Mfg. Co. v. Wagner Electric & Mfg. Co.* (U.S. 1912, p.615, 618–19) (U.S.) (noting that if the difficulty of an apportionment "could only be converted into an impossibility, the defendant retained all of the gains, because the injured patentee could not separate what the guilty infringer had made impossible of separation," and that "[t]he inseparable profit must be given to the patentee or infringer. The loss had to fall on the innocent or the guilty. In such an alternative the law places the loss on the wrongdoer.").

[240] *Dowagiac Mfg. Co. v. Minn. Moline Plow Co.* (U.S. 1915, p.647) (U.S.).

[241] Chisum 2017, § 20.02[3][d][iii] (discussing lower court cases interpreting the Supreme Court of the United States cases in *Westinghouse* and *Dowagiac*).

[242] An accounting is regularly granted in Canada, but usually in the context of pharmaceuticals, where the entire value of the product is normally attributable to the patented invention. *Celanese Int'l Corp. v. BP Chemicals Ltd.* (Pat 1999) (UK) is a UK case in which apportionment was addressed in some detail, but not in a very satisfactory manner, and without discussing the burden of proof issue. *See* Cotter 2013a, 201–02.

[243] *See supra* notes 88–89 and accompanying text.

3

Enhanced Damages, Litigation Cost Recovery, and Interest

Colleen V. Chien, Jorge L. Contreras, Thomas F. Cotter, Brian J. Love,
Christopher B. Seaman, and Norman V. Siebrasse

3.1 INTRODUCTION

In an ideal world, parties to patent suits behave efficiently and always act in good faith, knowledge is symmetric and perfect, and litigation is cost-free and accurate. In the real world, of course, none of these assumptions hold. Sometimes patentees bring weak cases that stretch claim language beyond the pale or assert claims that are almost certainly invalid. Conversely, sometimes accused infringers are found to have intentionally copied the patented technology or otherwise willfully refused to license patent rights they very likely infringe. How courts deal with opportunistic behaviors like these varies considerably from country to country, and to an even greater degree than in other areas of patent law, each country's approach reflects broader cultural and legal norms. In the United States, for example, enhanced damages – also referred to as "punitive" or "exemplary" damages – are an accepted way of sanctioning and deterring socially undesirable behavior, while in continental Europe punitive damages are often considered contrary to sound public policy. Likewise, while the "American rule" is that each party to a suit pays its own attorney, most other countries follow in some form or fashion the "English rule" of "loser pays," a practice with roots in the judicial system of the Byzantine Empire.[1] In addition, much like fee awards and punitive damages, the availability of pre- and post-judgment interest can have a significant impact on parties' incentives to license, litigate, and settle.

In this chapter we describe the approaches countries have devised to supplement compensatory patent damages in order to deter willful copying, weak claims and defenses, and opportunistic holdout behavior. We consider the impact that these policy choices have on innovators, including their willingness to pursue or defend against allegations of infringement and their incentives to read and clear prior patents during the R&D process.

---

[1] Pfennigstorf 1984, 41.

3.2 ENHANCED DAMAGES

We begin with a discussion of enhanced damages in the United States, where punitive awards for patent infringement are most common.[2] We then take a comparative look at how other nations approach enhanced damages. Next, we consider normative arguments regarding enhanced damages, and conclude with recommendations and topics for further research.

3.2.1 *Approaches to Enhanced Damages*

1 The United States

In the United States, enhanced damages for patent infringement have been available as a matter of judicial discretion since 1836.[3] The current statutory language regarding enhanced damages is found in § 284 of the Patent Act, which provides in relevant part that courts "may increase the damages up to three times the amount found or assessed."[4] The Supreme Court of the United States described this provision (albeit in dicta) as providing that "punitive or 'increased' damages" could be recovered "in a case of willful or bad-faith infringement."[5] Prior to the creation of the Federal Circuit, the regional U.S. Courts of Appeals similarly required willful infringement for imposing enhanced damages under § 284.[6]

For the first twenty-four years of the Federal Circuit's existence, the court defined willfulness as a form of negligent infringement, holding that when "a potential infringer has actual notice of another's patent rights, he has an affirmative duty to exercise due care to determine whether or not he is infringing."[7] However, in 2007

---

[2] We are not aware of any existing data comparing the prevalence of enhanced damages awards across the globe. In our experience, such awards are more common in the United States than anywhere else in the world. This is almost certainly true in terms of the absolute number of exemplary awards, and it may well also be true relative to the number of patent infringement suits filed in each nation.

[3] *See* Act of July 4, 1836, ch. 357, § 14, 5 Stat. 117, 123 (U.S.) ("[I]t shall be in the power of the court to render judgment for any sum above the amount found by such verdict as the actual damages sustained by the plaintiff, not exceeding three times the amount thereof, according to the circumstances of the case, with costs ... "). Prior to 1836, treble damages were automatically awarded to a prevailing patentee. Act of Feb. 1, 1793, ch. 11, § 5, 1 Stat. 318, 322 (U.S.); *see also Birdsall v. Coolidge* (U.S. 1876, p.68–69) (U.S.) (discussing the history of the patent statutes in the 1800s).

[4] U.S. Patent Act, 35 U.S.C. § 284.

[5] *Aro Mfg. Co. v. Convertible Top Replacement Co.* (U.S. 1964, p.508) (U.S.); *see also Dowling v. United States* (U.S. 1985, p.227 n.19) (U.S.) ("willful infringement").

[6] *See, e.g., Lam, Inc. v. Johns-Manville Corp.* (10th Cir. 1982, p.474) (U.S.) ("Courts have limited the increase to instances in which the infringement was willful, and even then it is committed to the trial court's discretion."); *Am. Safety Table Co. v. Schreiber* (2d Cir. 1969, p.378) (U.S.) ("Awards of increased damages are made sparingly and only when a clear showing of deliberate infringement justifies the exercise of the Court's discretion. Where, however, a patent infringement is willful, intentional, and deliberate an award is proper." (internal quotations omitted)).

[7] *Underwater Devices Inc. v. Morrison-Knudsen Co.* (Fed. Cir. 1983, p.1389–90) (U.S.), overruled by *In re Seagate Tech., LLC* (Fed. Cir. 2007) (U.S.) (en banc).

the court changed course, holding in *In re Seagate* that to prove willful infringe-ment, a patentee must make "at least a showing of objective recklessness" by the accused infringer.[8] This "objective recklessness" standard involved a two-part test:

> [T]o establish willful infringement, a patentee must show by clear and convincing evidence that the infringer acted despite an objectively high likelihood that its actions constituted infringement of a valid patent. The state of mind of the accused infringer is not relevant to this objective inquiry. If this threshold objective standard is satisfied, the patentee must also demonstrate that this objectively-defined risk ... was either known or so obvious that it should have been known to the accused infringer.[9]

Subsequently, the Federal Circuit clarified that the first part of the *Seagate* test – the so-called objective prong – was "best decided by the judge as a question of law subject to *de novo* review."[10] Under *Seagate* and subsequent Federal Circuit deci-sions, an infringer was not objectively reckless if it "raised a 'substantial question' as to the validity or noninfringement of the patent."[11] This was true even if the infringer "was unaware of the arguable defense when he acted."[12]

Despite this apparently substantial change in the relevant legal standard, will-fulness findings remained relatively common even after *Seagate*. According to one empirical study, findings of willful infringement in patent cases that reached final judgment went from 48 percent in the three-year period prior to *Seagate* to 37 per-cent for a similar period after the decision.[13] However, when willfulness was found, the district court awarded enhanced damages only 55 percent of the time after *Seagate*, compared to over 80 percent of the time before it.[14] In addition, over 70 percent of enhanced-damages awards were for double damages or less, consider-ably below the statutory maximum of treble damages.[15]

The Supreme Court again weighed in on the appropriate standard for enhanced damages in *Halo Electronics, Inc. v. Pulse Electronics*.[16] While recognizing that the statutory text granted discretion to the trial courts in determining enhanced damages, it also explained that such discretion "'should be exercised in light of the considerations' underlying the grant of that discretion."[17] Specifically, it explained that enhanced damages under § 284 were "designed as a 'punitive' ... sanction for

---

8   *In re Seagate Tech., LLC* (Fed. Cir. 2007, p.1371) (U.S.) (en banc).
9   *Id.*
10 *Bard Peripheral Vascular, Inc. v. W. L. Gore & Assocs., Inc.* (Fed. Cir. 2012, p.1007) (U.S.).
11 *Bard Peripheral Vascular, Inc. v. W. L. Gore & Assocs., Inc.* (Fed. Cir. 2015, p.844) (U.S.).
12 *Halo Elec., Inc. v. Pulse Elec., Inc.* (U.S. 2016, p.1930) (U.S.) (citing *In re Seagate Tech., LLC* (Fed. Cir. 2007, p.1371) (U.S.)); *Spine Sol., Inc. v. Medtronic Sofamor Danek USA, Inc.* (Fed. Cir. 2010, p.1319) (U.S.).
13 Seaman 2012, 441 tbl.1.
14 *Id.* at 466 tbl.6.
15 *Id.* at 469 fig.3.
16 *Halo Elec., Inc. v. Pulse Elec., Inc.* (U.S. 2016) (U.S.).
17 *Id.* at 1932 (quoting *Octane Fitness, LLC v. ICON Health & Fitness, Inc.* (U.S. 2014, p.1756) (U.S.)).

egregious infringement behavior," including "willful, wanton, malicious, bad-faith, deliberate, consciously wrongful [or] flagrant" infringement.[18]

Turning to the standard in *Seagate*, the Court held that while it "reflects, in many respects, a sound recognition that enhanced damages are generally appropriate under § 284 only in egregious cases," the Federal Circuit's two-part test was "unduly rigid, and it impermissibly encumbers the statutory grant of discretion to district courts."[19] In particular, the Court explained, the *Seagate* test "insulates the infringer from enhanced damages, even if he did not act on the basis of the defense or was even unaware of it."[20] As a result, under *Seagate*, "someone who plunders a patent . . . can nevertheless escape any liability under § 284."[21] *Halo* changed the standard to correct for this, making it possible for the "subjective willfulness" of an alleged patent infringer to lead to enhanced damages, "without regard to whether his infringement was objectively reckless."[22] Furthermore, a patentee need only prove willfulness by a preponderance of the evidence (unlike *Seagate*, which required clear-and-convincing evidence).[23]

Evidence that the infringer has copied the patented technology, when coupled with knowledge of the patent (in contrast to mere knowledge, discussed below), can be sufficient for a court to impose enhanced damages.[24] For instance, in *Apple Inc. v. Samsung Electronics Co., Ltd.*,[25] the district court held that the infringer's continued sale of a product containing a copied feature (Apple's swipe-to-unlock functionality) was substantial evidence to support the jury's finding of willfulness, at least once the infringer had knowledge of the patent through the filing of plaintiff's complaint.[26] Considering the *Read* factors,[27] the district court then imposed a 30 percent enhancement of the jury's compensatory damages award, again basing its decision in part on undisputed evidence that the infringer had copied the

---

[18] *Id.*

[19] *Id.* (quoting *Octane Fitness, LLC v. ICON Health & Fitness, Inc.* (U.S. 2014, p.1755) (U.S.))

[20] *Id.* at 1932–33.

[21] *Id.* at 1933.

[22] *Id.*

[23] *Id.*

[24] *See, e.g., Imperium IP Holdings (Cayman), Ltd. v. Samsung Elecs. Co.* (E.D. Tex. 2016, p.763–64) (U.S.) (finding infringer engaged in egregious infringement and awarding the maximum enhancement of triple damages in part because of evidence of infringers' copying); *PPC Broadband v. Corning Optical Commc'ns RF, LLC* (N.D.N.Y. 2016, p.6) (U.S.) (Memorandum Decision and Order) (finding that "the evidence supports the conclusion that Corning deliberately copied PPC's patents" and awarding double damages as an enhancement).

[25] *Apple, Inc. v. Samsung Elecs. Co., Ltd.* (N.D. Cal. 2017) (U.S.); *See also Dominion Res. Inc. v. Alstom Grid, Inc.* (E.D. Pa. 2016, p.21) (U.S.) (finding that the infringer "had the means and opportunity to copy [the] patent" and awarding double enhanced damages); *R-BOC Reps., Inc. v. Minemyer* (N.D. Ill. 2017) (U.S.) (awarding maximum enhanced damages in light of the infringers' "deliberate copying").

[26] *Apple, Inc. v. Samsung Elecs. Co., Ltd.* (N.D. Cal. 2017, p.1027–29) (U.S.); *see also id.* at 1028 ("The fact that Samsung copied is evidence of willfulness.").

[27] *See supra* note 66.

patented feature.[28] Similarly, efforts by the infringer to conceal its conduct may warrant enhanced damages.[29]

2 Europe

While awarding enhanced damages in patent disputes is largely an American phenomenon, punitive damages for patent infringement are theoretically available in Europe. For example, in the United Kingdom, in *Rookes* v. *Barnard*, the House of Lords held that exemplary damages are generally available where, inter alia, "the Defendant's conduct has been calculated by him to make a profit for himself which may well exceed the compensation payable to the Plaintiff,"[30] but the same court subsequently explained that the award of punitive damages in civil cases is an "undesirable anomaly," that ought to be limited as much as possible.[31] In *Catnic Components Ltd.* v. *Hill & Smith*,[32] the Patents Court went so far as to hold that exemplary damages could not be awarded for patent infringement.[33] But while exemplary damages are now apparently available in patent cases,[34] we are not aware of any UK patent decisions actually awarding exemplary damages.[35]

The EU Enforcement Directive, adopted in 2004, outlines three measures of compensatory damages for knowing infringement: hypothetical license, lost profits, and disgorgement.[36] All methods aim, in principle, only to compensate the patentee; indeed, although the Directive specifically directs Member States to encode provisions to prevent further infringement of property rights, it also states that the scope of this obligation does not extend to punitive damages but instead aims to

---

[28]   *Apple, Inc.* v. *Samsung Elecs. Co., Ltd.* (N.D. Cal. 2017, p.1030) (U.S.) ("Evidence of copying weighs in favor of enhanced damages ... On appeal, Samsung did not even dispute that it copied Apple's slide-to-unlock feature ... [T]his factor weighs in favor of enhanced damages.").

[29]   *See PPC Broadband* v. *Corning Optical Commc'ns RF, LLC* (N.D.N.Y. 2016, p.8) (U.S.) (finding that "Corning concealed its infringement" and concluding that "this factor strongly supports enhancement"); *see also Dominion Res. Inc.* v. *Alstom Grid, Inc.* (E.D. Pa. 2016, p.24) (U.S.) (holding that the infringer "decided internally not to share information," "did not admit its ongoing actions," and was "less than fully candid" to the patentee, and finding that this misconduct favored enhancing damages).

[30]   *Rookes* v. *Barnard* (HL 1964, p.37) (UK). The *Rookes* case did not involve intellectual property rights.

[31]   *Cassell & Co. Ltd.* v. *Broome* (HL 1972, p.837) (UK).

[32]   *Catnic Components Ltd.* v. *Hill & Smith Ltd.* (Pat 1983) (UK).

[33]   *See id.* at 541 ("In my judgment, the claim to exemplary damages is not open to the plaintiffs in the absence of any authority that exemplary damages had been awarded for infringement of patent prior to the decision of the House of Lords in *Rookes* v. *Barnard*.").

[34]   *See Kuddus* v. *Chief Constable of Leicestershire Constabulary* (HL 2001, ¶ 119) (UK) (holding that the categories of cases in which exemplary damages are available are not closed, while emphasizing again that the "exemplary damages principle is itself an anomaly in the civil law.").

[35]   *See* Cotter 2013f; *see also* Bayliss et al. 2005, 2 ("We are not aware of any exemplary damages having been sought in any patent case since the decision in *Kuddus*."). In *Catnic Components Ltd.* v. *Hill & Smith Ltd.* (Pat 1983, p.540–41) (UK), Falconer J noted no prior case awarding exemplary damages in a patent case had been cited to him, and between *Catnic* and *Kuddus*, such awards were not available as a matter of law.

[36]   Directive 2004/48/EC, rec. 26.

"allow for compensation based on objective criteria."[37] In practice, however, disgorgement can go beyond mere compensation as the patentee may receive more than she would have received under an *ex ante* license. This tension is generally accepted because of the difficulty of otherwise determining an amount adequate to provide sufficient compensation.

Punitive damages are rare in continental Europe, as most EU nations "consider punitive damages to be against public policy, and for the most part this view applies to IP infringement just as it does to other torts."[38] However, courts in Germany and France have occasionally awarded royalty amounts 25 percent to 100 percent higher than those compared to what the parties would have actually negotiated,[39] which may serve as a form of deterrence.[40]

3 Australia, Canada, and Asia

In Australia, since 2006, courts have been able to increase damages upon consideration of the following: (1) "the flagrancy of the infringement"; (2) the need for deterrence; (3) the infringer's conduct after infringement; (4) any benefit accrued to the infringer due to infringement; and (5) "all other relevant matters."[41] Despite this, few reported decisions in Australia have granted enhanced damages under this provision.[42] Similarly, in Canada, punitive damages may be awarded "in exceptional cases of high-handed, malicious, arbitrary or highly reprehensible misconduct that represents a marked departure from the ordinary standards of decent behavior."[43] But they have rarely been awarded in Canadian patent cases.[44]

In China, courts may award compensatory damages that are "one to three times the patent licensing fee"[45] even though, strictly speaking, punitive damages as such

---

[37] *Id.*

[38] Cotter 2013a, 275.

[39] *Id.* at 269–70 & n.187. Based on, for example, considering factors that increase the award beyond the amount a hypothetical licensee would have paid (e.g., the fact that an infringer did not have to "open its books" to the patentee).

[40] *Id.*

[41] Patents Act 1990 § 122(1A) (Austl.).

[42] Cotter 2013a, 210. The only decision the authors are aware of is *Pacific Enter. (Aust) Pty Ltd.* v. *Bernen Pty Ltd.* (Fed. Ct. 2014) (Austl.), where the Federal Court awarded $40,000 in additional damages (on top of $355,487.16 in compensatory damages) in a patent infringement proceeding.

[43] *Eurocopter* v. *Bell Helicopter Textron Canada Ltée* (Fed. Ct. App. 2013, ¶ 163) (Can.).

[44] *See* Siebrasse 2013 ("Punitive damages are very rarely awarded in Canadian patent cases ... "). For a recent, notable exception, *see Eurocopter* v. *Bell Helicopter Textron Canada Ltée* (Fed. Ct. App. 2013) (Can.) (affirming the patentee's entitlement to punitive damages) and *Airbus Helicopters, S.A. S.* v. *Bell Helicopter Textron Canada Ltée* (Fed. Ct. 2017) (Can.) (assessing punitive damages).

[45] *Id.* at 358 (quoting Article 21 of China's Patent Trial Guidelines). In 2015, the Chinese Supreme People's Court provided the second amendment to this Guidelines of 2001, which deleted the specific words "one to three times" the patent licensing fee and replaced them with "times" the fee, affording Chinese judges broad discretion. However, it is unclear whether this provision is compensatory or punitive in nature. There is some suggestion that this provision was first introduced for compensatory purposes. However, "the nature and the circumstances of the infringement" factor implies that this

are not currently permitted.[46] In Japan, damages awarded for patent infringement are governed by general rules applicable in all tort actions, according to which, damages are to be compensatory in nature, and not for sanction or general deterrence. Therefore, punitive damages are not available.[47] That said, the Japanese Patent Act contains special provisions that partly shift the burden of proof for the calculation of damages to infringers, which allows courts to award damages that likely exceed the actual loss to patentees. Still, courts seldom take into account the subjective mental state of infringers (e.g., gross negligence, willfulness, or bad faith) in the calculation of damages.[48] Taiwan is one of the few jurisdictions that, like the United States, currently awards up to treble damages for intentional infringement.[49]

3.2.2 *Criminal Sanctions*

Criminal sanctions are another potential deterrent to deliberate infringement; however, they are imposed even less frequently than punitive civil damages. While the TRIPS Agreement requires member countries to provide criminal penalties for certain forms of copyright and trademark infringement, it is silent on the criminalization of patent infringement.[50] As a result, jurisdictions have taken differing approaches. For example, while the United States has no "criminal penalties for the distribution of goods infringing valid patents,"[51] the EU Enforcement Directive authorizes (though does not require) criminal penalties for IP infringement generally,[52] and a number of jurisdictions in Europe, South America, and Asia have criminal patent infringement laws on the books.[53] However, actual criminal prosecutions for patent infringement appear to be extremely rare across the globe.

---

provision also encompasses punitive considerations. The same ambiguity characterizes the statutory damages provisions in the same Guidelines. *See* Li & Wang 2017, 215.

[46] The draft fourth Patent Law amendment, which is still under consideration, proposes authorizing treble damages for willful infringement. Cotter 2013c; *see also* Covington & Burling LLP 2015.

[47] The Japanese Supreme Court refused to recognize and enforce a decision by a court in California that awarded punitive damages to the plaintiff based on the Civil Code of the State of California, saying that the decision was against public policy and had no effect in Japan. *Northcon I v. Mansei Kogyo* (Sup. Ct. 1997) (Japan).

[48] While damages are granted only against intentional or negligent infringers, negligence is presumed by the Patent Act and infringers are rarely successful in rebutting the presumption. *See* Suzuki & Tamura 2011, 438–39.

[49] Cotter 2013a, 372; *see also* Cotter 2013c.

[50] TRIPS Agreement, art. 61.

[51] *Dowling v. United States* (U.S. 1985, p.227) (U.S.).

[52] Directive 2004/48/EC, rec. 28. After vigorous opposition, a proposal to require criminal sanctions for all intentional IPR infringements on a commercial scale as part of a Second Intellectual Property Rights Enforcement Directive ("IPRED2") was rejected. *See, e.g.,* Manta 2011, 471, 491.

[53] *See, e.g.,* Patentgesetz [PatG] [Patent Act], 1980 § 142 (Ger.); Manta 2011, 471–72 n.8.

3.2.3 *Policy Considerations Relating to Enhanced Damages*

1 Enhanced Damages and Opportunism

There are two principal rationales for enhanced damages: to punish bad behavior and to discourage willful infringement by making the infringer pay more if caught. However, these rationales must be understood in context. In the pharmaceutical industry, the copying of discrete drugs by generic firms is a routine way of doing business that is regulated outside of enhanced damages as discussed below. In contrast, in component industries, non-willful or inadvertent infringement is common due to the difficulty of identifying with certainty all relevant prior art, the cumulative nature of innovation, and the weakness of certain issued patents. In addition, as discussed further below, enhanced damages have the potential to interfere with one of the primary rationales behind the patent system: the disclosure and dissemination of technical information.

The award of enhanced damages in often justified in moralistic terms. As noted above, in *Halo Electronics, Inc.* v. *Pulse Electronics*,[54] the Supreme Court of the United States explained that enhanced damages were "designed as a 'punitive' ... sanction for egregious infringement behavior" that is "willful, wanton, malicious, bad-faith, deliberate, consciously wrongful, flagrant, or – indeed – characteristic of a pirate."[55] The Court emphasized the role of "subjective bad faith," saying that the "subjective willfulness of a patent infringer" may in itself warrant enhanced damages, and rejected the objective prong of the Federal Circuit's prior test.[56] UK and Canadian courts have justified enhanced damages in similar language, as addressing conduct that is "oppressive, high-handed, malicious, wanton or [the] like."[57] However, while there is considerable agreement as to the role of enhanced damages, it appears that there is a significant divergence among jurisdictions with respect to whether this goal is properly the domain of civil law, rather than criminal law. The House of Lords has remarked that "the objections to allowing juries to go beyond compensatory damages are overwhelming. To allow pure punishment in this way contravenes almost every principle which has been evolved for the protection of offenders," and consequently the use of enhanced damages in civil cases ought to be strictly limited.[58]

We prefer to frame the question in terms of the patent system's primary purpose of promoting innovation efficiently. Moral considerations aside, enhanced

---

[54] *Halo Elec., Inc.* v. *Pulse Elec., Inc.* (U.S. 2016) (U.S.).
[55] *Id.* at 1932.
[56] *Id.* at 1933.
[57] *Cassell & Co. Ltd.* v. *Broome* (HL 1972, p.837) (UK); *see also Whiten* v. *Pilot Ins. Co.* (Sup. Ct. 2002, p.617) (Can.), in which the Supreme Court of Canada stated that "[p]unitive damages are awarded against a defendant in exceptional cases for 'malicious, oppressive and high-handed' misconduct that 'offends the court's sense of decency.'"
[58] *Cassell & Co. Ltd.* v. *Broome* (HL 1972, p.837) (UK).

damages can be justified in an economic sense as a mechanism to redress and deter opportunistic infringement. Without the possibility of increased damages (or some other enhanced monetary remedy), prospective infringers may be insufficiently deterred from appropriating a patented technology.[59] At worst, if the copier is caught and adjudged to infringe, it will have to pay the patentee's actual damages for past infringement (plus face a possible injunction against future use),[60] an amount that may in some cases be less than the infringer's own profit.[61] At best, the infringer avoids detection and pays nothing. This is sometimes described as a "catch-me-if-you-can" problem[62] or "heads-I-win-tails-you-lose" scenario.[63]

One particularly salient variation of the catch-me-if-you-can scenario arises in connection with standards-essential patents (SEPs), which are discussed in greater detail in Chapter 5.[64] An opportunistic manufacturer of standardized products may determine that the most efficient course of action is not to seek a FRAND license, but instead to delay in taking a license until sued for infringement, at which point its maximum liability will be the FRAND royalty it otherwise would have paid. This scenario has been referred to in the literature as "reverse holdup" or "holdout."[65] This kind of opportunistic behavior can impair the incentive to innovate by undermining the compensatory role of damages and unduly limiting the return to the patentee. Punitive damages serve as a counterweight and move

---

[59] *See* Cotter 2013a, 145 ("[F]rom an economic perspective, an award of enhanced damages might be socially optimal in a case in which awarding lost profits or foregone royalties alone would underdeter infringement of the type in suit.").

[60] As discussed below, until recently, attorney fees were rarely awarded in U.S. patent cases.

[61] For instance, if the infringer is more efficient than the patentee.

[62] *See Monsanto Canada Inc. v. Rivett* (Fed. Ct. 2009, ¶ 23) (Can.). For further discussion, *see also* Chapter 7.

[63] *See Panduit Corp. v. Stahlin Bros. Fibre Works Inc.* (6th Cir. 1978, p.1158) (U.S.). One commonly alleged variation of the catch-me-if-you-can scenario arises in connection with standards-essential patents (SEPs), which are discussed in greater detail in Chapter 5. An opportunistic manufacturer of standardized products may determine that the most efficient course of action is not to seek a FRAND license, but instead to delay in taking a license until sued for infringement, at which point its maximum liability will be the FRAND royalty it otherwise would have paid. This scenario has been referred to in the literature as "reverse holdup" or "holdout." The availability of enhanced damages, however, can change the opportunistic manufacturer's calculus, as it would have a significant risk of exposure to enhanced damages owing to its awareness (through the standards-development and SEP disclosure process) that it is infringing.

[64] Over the past several years, significant litigation has arisen in the United States, Europe, and Asia regarding the appropriate level of such FRAND royalty rates. As discussed in Chapter 6, courts in several U.S. cases have determined that such FRAND royalty rates should be calculated in more or less the same manner as "reasonable royalty" damages for patent infringement (i.e., using a modified form of the Georgia-Pacific fifteen-factor analytical framework). Moreover, in the context of SEPs subject to FRAND commitments, it is often the case that SEP holders are quite limited in their ability to seek injunctive relief against infringers (both as a matter of contract law and under applicable competition and antitrust principles – see Chapters 5 and 6). *See* Chapters 1 and 6; *see also* Contreras & Gilbert 2015 (analyzing convergence of FRAND royalty determination and reasonable royalty damages calculations).

[65] *See, e.g.,* Chien 2014.

the infringer's calculus back in the direction of infringement avoidance.[66] Indeed, U.S. courts consider whether an infringer has attempted to conceal its infringement – and thus reduce its risk of detection – in determining whether and how much to enhance damages under the so-called *Read* factors.[67]

2 Calibrating Responses to Opportunism

Though the possible application of multipliers to damages can help deter opportunistic infringement, there are a variety of other penalties that also may serve to make the infringer worse off if it is caught than if it had licensed *ex ante*. These include litigation costs, injunctive relief, and disgorgement of the infringer's profits. Since the availability of fee shifting, injunctive relief, disgorgement, and enhanced damages all vary across jurisdictions, the general policy question is which of these provides the optimal response.

One difficulty is that while all of these alternatives to enhanced damages potentially make the infringer worse off than if it had licensed *ex ante*, none is well calibrated to the problem of opportunistic infringement. For example, the prospect of being sued, even in the United States where the risk of paying the other party's fees is relatively low, may be costly enough to deter the "catch-me-if-you-can" strategy. However, it is not clear whether litigation cost exposure is sufficiently related to the frequency and magnitude of opportunistic infringement.[68] Similarly, the prospect of injunctive relief may also deter infringement, if an injunction allows the patentee to extract holdup value from the infringer. In effect, injunctive relief operates as a form of enhanced damages – an "injunction penalty" – in which the holdup value that is extracted with the aid of injunction constitutes the enhancement. However, as with the litigation cost "penalty," the injunction "penalty" is unrelated to the magnitude of the "catch-me-if-you-can" problem, which is determined by the probability of detection. The remedy of disgorgement of the infringer's profits will also often make

---

[66] *See generally* Polinsky & Shavell 1998; *see also BMW of N. Am., Inc. v. Gore* (U.S. 1996, p.582) (U.S.) (explaining that higher punitive damages "may . . . be justified in cases in which the injury is hard to detect").

[67] These factors, first enunciated in *Read Corp. v. Portec, Inc.* (Fed. Cir. 1992, p.827) (U.S.) are (1) "whether the infringer deliberately copied the ideas of another"; (2) "whether the infringer, when he knew of the other's patent protection, investigated the scope of the patent and formed a good-faith belief that it was invalid or that it was not infringed"; (3) "the infringer's behavior as a party to the litigation"; (4) the "[d]efendant's size and financial condition"; (5) the "[c]loseness of the case"; (6) the "[d]uration of the defendant's misconduct"; (7) "[r]emedial action by the defendant"; (8) the "[d]efendant's motivation for harm"; and (9) "[w]hether the defendant attempted to conceal its misconduct."

[68] For example, if there is a 30 percent probability of detection for royalties that would have been $10m, then litigation costs would have to be $7m to make the "catch-me-if-you-can" strategy unprofitable. The incentive to bargain *ex ante* is increased with fee shifting, but the problem remains that it is not clear whether even this heightened incentive is generally sufficient to encourage *ex ante* bargaining. Of course, at a higher probability of detection, the incentive provided by avoiding litigation costs may be adequate.

the infringer worse off than if it had licensed *ex ante*, particularly if the patentee did not compete with the infringer and so would be entitled only to a reasonable royalty. A negotiated royalty will normally split the licensee's profit from the use of the invention between the licensee and the patentee, while a disgorgement of the infringer's profits will give the entire profit due to the infringement to the patentee.[69] While an accounting makes the infringer worse off than if it had licensed *ex ante*, again the difficulty is that the magnitude of the extra penalty is unrelated to the frequency of opportunistic behavior by infringers.[70]

In contrast with the three foregoing remedies, enhanced damages can in principle be calibrated to efficiently deter intentional infringement. However, this does not appear to be attempted in practice in U.S. law, and it is not clear that it would be practical to do so with sufficient accuracy to make enhanced damages superior to the alternatives. For example, a 50 percent probability that infringement will be detected and proven would imply that damages should be doubled to provide the right incentive, but it is not clear how to assess the probability of detection. As noted above, U.S. courts do consider the likelihood of underdetection as a factor in assessing the magnitude of enhanced damages, but it is normally used as but one factor among many, and there is no attempt to determine its likelihood even approximately, so as to allow the penalty to be appropriately calibrated.

3 Incentives to Challenge and Learn from Patents

Another problem is that enhanced damages may deter otherwise-beneficial challenges to the validity of issued patents. For example, in the pharmaceutical context, there is a very large social benefit to invalidating a blockbuster pharmaceutical patent, even when the patent is likely valid. If detection is almost certain (as in the pharmaceutical context), the infringement will not impair the incentive to invent in those cases in which the patent is ultimately held to be valid, because the patentee

---

[69] An accounting of profits is regularly awarded in Canada, and Canadian courts have expressly recognized its role in deterring the "catch-me-if-you-can" strategy. *See Monsanto Canada Inc. v. Rivett* (Fed. Ct. 2009) (Can.); *Eli Lilly and Co.* v. *Apotex Inc.* (Fed. Ct. 2009) (Can.); *Varco Canada Ltd. v. Pason Systems Corp.* (Fed. Ct. 2013, ¶ 399) (Can.).

[70] Enhanced damages are not normally available if an accounting of profits has been granted, reflecting the view that these are different mechanisms for addressing the same problem: *see Eli Lilly and Co. v. Apotex Inc.* (Fed. Ct. 2009, ¶ 663) (Can.) (noting that the "egregious" nature of the infringer's conduct had already been weighted in affording the patentee with the right to elect for an accounting of the infringer's profits). Similarly, in *Kuddus v. Chief Constable of Leicestershire Constabulary* (HL 2001, ¶ 109) (UK), Lord Scott suggested that the need for exemplary damages "has been largely overtaken by developments in the common law. Restitutionary damages are available now in many tort actions as well as those for breach of contract. The profit made by a wrongdoer can be extracted from him without the need to rely on the anomaly of exemplary damages," citing the discussion by Lord Nicholls of Birkenhead in *Attorney General v. Blake* (HL 2000, p.394–98) (UK). In the one patent-law context in which U.S. courts do award disgorgement of profits (for design patent infringement), the statute is understood to forbid the court from awarding both disgorgement and enhanced damages. *See Braun Inc. v. Dynamics Corp. of Am.* (Fed. Cir. 1992, p.824) (U.S.).

will be fully compensated in damages. The profit to be made from the infringement in cases in which the patent turns out to be invalid therefore provides an incentive to undertake potentially socially beneficial patent challenges. Awarding enhanced damages in such cases risks unduly chilling desirable patent challenges. Consistent with this, deemed infringement under the U.S. pharmaceutical patent linkage system cannot give rise to enhanced damages in U.S. law.[71] However, the same basic problem may arise outside the pharmaceutical industry.

Relatedly, and more relevant with respect to complex products, the availability of enhanced damages may induce innovators to engage in socially wasteful efforts to locate and license existing patent rights. For products covered by many patents, each covering an incremental innovation, preclearance of patent rights will often not be cost effective and, in fact, may be practically impossible.[72]

Yet another significant problem with enhanced damages is that knowledge of asserted patents has historically made it more likely that infringers will owe them. As a result, seeking out and reading patent disclosures – acts that the patent system is supposed to facilitate – are instead discouraged by the possibility that they will give rise to a significant liability enhancement. In the U.S. reading patents can increase both one's risk of treble damages *and* one's risk of an attorney fees award.[73] As a number of commentators have noted, in the tech sector, it has been the practice of in-house attorneys to discourage the reading of patents, at least historically.[74] Perhaps as a result, one study found that knowledge of the asserted patent was only alleged in 30 percent of U.S. patent infringement complaints.[75]

---

[71] See *Glaxo Group Ltd.* v. *Apotex, Inc.* (Fed. Cir. 2004, p.1350–51) (U.S.) (holding that a technical act of infringement under section 271(e) of the Hatch-Waxman Act cannot form the basis of a willfulness finding).

[72] See Mulligan & Lee 2012, 289, 304 (estimating that "[i]n software, for example, patent clearance by all firms would require many times more hours of legal research than all patent lawyers in the United States can bill in a year" because "there are around twenty-four billion new [software] patent-firm pairs each year that could produce accidental infringement").

[73] U.S. Patent Act, 35 U.S.C. § 285 (specifying that "[t]he court in exceptional cases may award reasonable attorney fees to the prevailing party"). One way to show that a case is "exceptional" is by showing that the infringer engaged in "willful infringement." *See, e.g., Minks* v. *Polaris Indus.* (Fed. Cir. 2008, 1375) (U.S.) (upholding exceptional case determination and award of attorney fees based on jury finding of willful infringement); *Tate Access Floors, Inc.* v. *Maxcess Techs., Inc.* (Fed. Cir. 2000, p.972) (U.S.) (noting an express finding of willful infringement is a sufficient basis for classifying a case as "exceptional," and that when a trial court denies attorney fees in spite of a finding of willful infringement, the court must explain why the case is not "exceptional" within the meaning of the statute).

[74] For a review of this literature, *see* Means 2013, 2012–14 (describing reports by the National Research Council (2004), Federal Trade Commission (2003) and to WIPO from the Computer & Communications Industry Association documenting the *in terrorem* impact of willfulness on reading patents).

[75] See Cotropia & Lemley 2009, 1442 (reporting that, "[o]f … 193 cases, only 60 (or 31.1%) involved allegations that the defendant was even aware of the patent before the lawsuit").

Not all innovators are deterred from reading patents. A recent study of 832 corresponding authors of scientific articles found that the majority of respondents reported that they sometimes read patents,[76] both for technical (~80 percent) and legal reasons (~64 percent–76 percent),[77] and that only 9 percent of patent-reading respondents and only 4 percent of nonreaders said that they had been instructed to not read patents. However, the survey was limited to researchers who publish scientific articles, which excludes industrial researchers in many sectors, particularly those where publishing is not the norm, and the results varied by technology.[78] And while post-*Halo* case law has clarified that mere knowledge of a patent is insufficient to award enhanced damages, it is not clear that this will provide adequate comfort against the prospect of treble damages.[79] Thus, the risk remains that enhanced damages may discourage innovators from using patent disclosures as a source of technical information to a socially undesirable degree.

---

[76] Ouellette 2017. The literature on the gains to innovation from reading patents is summarized in Chien 2016, 1859–65. According to Hall & Harhoff 2012, 550, patent reading varies greatly by industry. When inventors from the United States, Europe, and Asia were asked to quantify the time saved in their respective invention processes due to the availability of patent information, the answer depended on the industry. However, the median time savings was 5.9 hours and the mean was 12.2 hours. *Id.* In the field of organic chemistry, the average time savings from reading a patent was thirty-six hours. *Id.* In contrast, survey takers reported an average saving in digital communication technology of only one hour. *Id.* The use of chemistry patents as technical sources of information is also reflected in studies of citation patterns by scientific researchers. In their study of the thirty thousand PTO patents cited by research articles, Glänzel & Meyer 2003, 415–19, found that chemical patents captured a majority of the citations. Drug and medical patents were also highly cited. *Id.* Among individual patents, content mattered. When surveyed, researchers found the inclusion of details from practice – for example, the choice of equipment, implementation protocols, and recipes – to be most useful. *Id.*

[77] For example, to determine if the researcher's invention was patentable or infringing. Ouellette 2017, 421–22.

[78] *Id.* at 423 (reporting about concerns that 37 percent of industry researchers in electronics and software had been instructed not to read patents, the highest among all sectors). By contrast, in other fields like chemistry, patents are seen as an important part of the literature. *Id.*

[79] *See, e.g., Cont'l Circuits LLC v. Intel Corp.* (D. Ariz. 2017, p.11) (U.S.) (stating that "under *Halo*, knowledge is a necessary condition of willfulness, but not a sufficient one," and granting the alleged infringer's motion to dismiss the claim for enhanced damages because "[p]laintiff has alleged sufficient facts to show knowledge, but not to show the additional element of egregiousness"); *CG Tech. Dev., LLC v. Big Fish Games, Inc.* (D. Nev. 2016, p.14) (U.S.) (holding that allegations that defendant was "made aware of" the patents-in-suit and "continued use of its infringing products constitutes willful and blatant infringement" was inadequate for enhanced damages because "they fail to allege any facts suggesting that Defendant's conduct is egregious ... beyond typical infringement" (internal quotations omitted)); *Finjan, Inc. v. Cisco Sys. Inc.* (N.D. Cal. 2017) (U.S.), at 1–2, 5 (finding that the accused infringer's awareness of the plaintiff's patent portfolio, including through unsuccessful pre-suit licensing negotiations, did not state a plausible claim for willful infringement after *Halo*); *see also Varian Med. Sys., Inc. v. Elekta AB* (D. Del. 2016, p.4–8) (U.S.) (holding that knowledge of a patent by a foreign subsidiary, and "formulaic recitation of the pre-*Halo* elements of a willful infringement claim," are insufficient to plead egregious infringement). *But see Blitzsafe Texas, LLC v. Volkswagen Grp. of Am., Inc.* (E.D. Tex. 2016) (U.S.) (holding that alleged infringer's pre-suit knowledge of the patent, through a citation to the patent application that later issued as the patent during an inter partes reexamination, alleged a plausible case of pre-suit willful infringement).

4 Conclusion

In principle, then, whether enhanced damages should be available is not a question that can be addressed in isolation. It turns on numerous other features of the patent system, including the availability of fee shifting, permanent injunctions, preliminary injunctions, and administrative review of granted patents. While all of these features of the patent system interact with enhanced damages, they also have independent justifications and there is considerable jurisdictional variation on all these issues. This makes it difficult to provide any firm recommendations related to enhanced damages in isolation.

It may be that the variation between jurisdictions that we observe with respect to awarding enhanced damages is justified by the variations in other relevant aspects of the patent system. For instance, in the United States, disgorgement of the infringer's profits is not an available remedy for utility patent infringement,[80] fee shifting is neither mandatory nor common,[81] permanent injunctive relief is not automatic,[82] preliminary injunctions against patent infringement are rarely granted,[83] and inter partes review (among other procedures) is available to challenge granted patents. All of these features point in the direction of relatively greater use of enhanced damages.[84] This may explain why enhanced damages are used so much more in the United States than in other jurisdictions. On the other hand, the contrast between U.S. practice and that of other jurisdictions is sufficiently strong that it may be driven by a basic philosophical difference over the appropriateness of inserting moralistic considerations into civil law remedies, rather than by an accumulation of technical differences.

3.2.4 *Recommendations and Further Research*

We recommend that the availability of enhanced damages be assessed with reference to the objectives of the patent system, rather than by moral criteria. In particular, we recommend that in jurisdictions in which enhanced damages are regularly awarded, namely the United States, the award of enhanced damages be assessed in light of its efficacy in addressing the problem of opportunistic infringement and, accordingly, that courts should consider as a factor in awarding enhanced damages the intentional "holdout" conduct of a potential licensee.

We further recommend the evaluation of how enhanced damages, in combination with other mechanisms, such as cost shifting, discussed above, can deter

---

[80]   *See* Chapter 2.
[81]   *See infra* Section 3.3.2.
[82]   *See* Chapter 4; *see also* Seaman 2016 (reporting empirical data on injunction grant rates post-*eBay*).
[83]   Gupta & Kesan 2016, 15 fig.3 (finding that preliminary injunctions are granted less than 20 percent of the time they are requested following *eBay*).
[84]   As a result, as Mark Lemley has argued, U.S. "patent law emphasizes deterrence least among [all] the intellectual property regimes." Lemley 2005, 1045.

copying and other types of deliberate infringement, and encourage *ex ante* bargaining (to the extent that is a desirable goal). This evaluation should also take into account the risk of deterring socially beneficial patent challenges, inducing excessive patent searching and licensing, and patent learning. In addition, further empirical research into the question of how often researchers read patents, and whether they are deterred from doing so by the availability of enhanced damages and other sanctions, would be useful, particularly for technological fields and jurisdictions outside the United States that have not been addressed by prior studies.[85]

Beyond that, it is difficult to make firm recommendations in light of the complex interplay of relevant mechanisms. We have not reached a consensus as to the desirability of enhanced damages generally. It is probable that if we take all the other features of the patent system in different jurisdictions as given, significant jurisdictional variation in the use of enhanced damages would be justified. It is even possible that the current divergence between the United States and most other jurisdictions can be justified in light of differences in other aspects of the patent system. Conversely, if we assume that all the relevant factors discussed above are available policy levers, designing a patent system that optimizes each of these mechanisms both in its own terms and in combination, is a major research project. We propose that further research be conducted on both fronts. That is, it would be useful to investigate the extent to which the variation in existing practice related to enhanced damages can be justified in light of the existing variations among patent systems; and it would also be useful to investigate what a holistically optimized system might look like.

3.3 LITIGATION COST RECOVERY

In many countries, awards of attorney fees and disbursements are governed by general fee-shifting statutes that generally allow the prevailing party to recover some or all of its attorney fees and additional costs. In this section, we provide a brief summary of cost recovery regimes in place around the world and review the existing scholarly research related to the award of litigation expenses (principally attorney fees).

3.3.1 *Approaches to Litigation Cost Recovery*

1 Europe

Article 14 of the EU Enforcement Directive states that "Member States shall ensure that reasonable and proportionate legal costs and other expenses incurred by the successful party shall, as a general rule, be borne by the unsuccessful party, unless

---

[85] *See supra* notes 77–82 and accompanying text.

equity does not allow this."[86] Individual practice nevertheless differs among EU members. In some states, for example, fees are awarded according to statutory rates that in practice are not fully compensatory, while in others fees more closely approximate the amount the prevailing party actually and reasonably incurred.[87] Overall, however, some practitioners believe that the amounts awarded generally have increased since the implementation of the Directive.[88] In addition, a 2016 judgment of the Court of Justice for the European Union (CJEU) arising from a copyright action holds that, under the Directive, member state rules requiring that the prevailing party be reimbursed at a flat rate are permissible only if those rules result in the compensation of "a significant and appropriate part of the reasonable costs" actually incurred, and also that fees for technical advisers also must be compensated if they are "directly and closely linked to" the judicial proceeding at issue.[89]

2 Asia

In the major Asian jurisdictions the situation is somewhat different. In Japan, for example, although the prevailing patentee is in principle entitled to recover any attorney fees it incurred as a result of the infringement, it appears that parties often do not claim such fees. Moreover, even when fees are awarded, they usually are based on a percentage (often 10 percent) of the compensatory damages awarded, rather than on an hours-worked basis. Commentators generally agree that these awards do not fully compensate the prevailing party . . . .[90]

In China, Article 65 of the Patent Law states, inter alia, that the compensation due for infringement "shall include the reasonable expenses paid by the patentee for putting an end to the infringement."[91] In practice, however, attorney fees arc not awarded as a matter of right, and when they are awarded they tend to be low.[92] Nonetheless, in one recent case the Beijing IP Court awarded the prevailing plaintiff 1 million RMB in costs (equal to about $144,000 as of January 2, 2017); according to

---

[86] Directive 2004/48/EC, art. 14.

[87] *See* Cotter 2013a, 276 n.210. For other discussions, see generally Elmer & Gramenopoulos 2016; Osterrieth 2015, 142–43; Rennie-Smith 2015, 109; Romet 2015, 174. In yet other circumstances, parties can recover costs as part of a damages claim despite statutory limits on fee shifting.

[88] *See* Cotter 2013a, 276 n.210 (citations omitted).

[89] *United Video Properties, Inc.* v. *Telenet* NV (CJEU 2016) (EU). For brief discussion, *see* Cotter 2016d.

[90] Cotter 2013a, 328 (citations omitted); see also Suzuki & Tamura 2011, 450 (stating that "[t]he amount of attorney fees compensated is usually approximately 10% of the amount of damages granted to the winning party (as held in many court decisions). However, if the amount of damages is relatively high, the percentage amount of attorney fees compensated will be lower. Conversely, if the amount of damages awarded is low, the respective amount of attorney's fees that the winning party may claim may be higher depending on the special circumstances of each case" (citations omitted)).

[91] Patent Law of the People's Republic of China, art. 65.

[92] *See* Cotter 2013a, 360 (noting, in addition, that courts sometimes award the costs of investigation) (citations omitted); Cui & Shen 2016, 16–34 to –35; Pattloch 2015, 347 (stating that, "in practice, only about one-third of the real costs will be awarded by the court").

commentators, this may have been China's first patent case in which a court based a fee award on the time billed by the prevailing party's attorneys.[93] Fee awards also tend to be nominal in Korea.[94]

3 The United States

The United States provides a further point of contrast with other jurisdictions. While the United States does provide for the routine recovery by the prevailing party of at least some litigation expenses,[95] the general rule in the United States (hence known as the "American Rule") is that each party bears its own attorney fees. There are some exceptions to this rule, for example by statute in the antitrust and civil rights contexts.[96] Moreover, courts have the inherent authority to award attorney fees for "willful disobedience of a court order" or "when the losing party has 'acted in bad faith, vexatiously, wantonly, or for oppressive reasons.'"[97] Aside from this inherent authority, awards of fees in patent cases are governed by 35 U.S.C. § 285, which states that "[t]he court in exceptional cases may award reasonable attorney fees to the prevailing party."[98]

---

[93] For an English language discussion of the case, *WatchData Co. Ltd.* v. *Hengbao Co. Ltd.* (Beijing IP Ct. 2016) (China), *see* SIPO 2016 ("The court also supported the demand of the litigation cost, commonly known as attorney fees, considering the necessity of hiring agents, the difficulty of the case and the actual contribution of the lawyers. For the first time, the Beijing Intellectual Property Court recognized the above three factors as the principles to judge attorney fees."). *See also* Cotter 2016f (citing two other sources discussing *Watchdata*).

[94] *See* Cotter 2013a, 370 (citations omitted); Kim et al. 2016, 30–19; Kim 2015, 436.

[95] 28 U.S.C. § 1920 ("A judge or clerk of any court of the United States may tax as costs the following: (1) Fees of the clerk and marshal; (2) Fees for printed or electronically recorded transcripts necessarily obtained for use in the case; (3) Fees and disbursements for printing and witnesses; (4) Fees for exemplification and the costs of making copies of any materials where the copies are necessarily obtained for use in the case; (5) Docket fees under section 1923 of this title; (6) Compensation of court appointed experts, compensation of interpreters, and salaries, fees, expenses, and costs of special interpretation services under section 1828 of this title."). While conventional wisdom suggests that cost recoveries in U.S. civil litigation are relatively small, *see* Cotter 2013a, 146–47 n.283, that is not always the case, particularly in patent suits involving court-appointed expert witnesses. *See VirnetX, Inc.* v. *Apple, Inc.* (E.D. Tex. 2017, p.2) (U.S.) (Plaintiff's uncontested notice of costs, attorneys' fees, and prejudgment interest – later granted by stipulated order – requesting more than $300,000 in costs and approximately $1.8 million in attorneys' fees).

[96] *See, e.g.,* 15 U.S.C. § 15(a) ("[A]ny person who shall be injured in his business or property by reason of anything forbidden in the antitrust laws may sue therefor . . . and shall recover threefold the damages by him sustained, and the cost of suit, including a reasonable attorney's fee."); 42 U.S.C. § 1988 ("In any action or proceeding to enforce a provision of sections 1981, 1981a, 1982, 1983, 1985, and 1986 of this title, title IX of Public Law 92–318 [20 U.S.C. 1681 et seq.], the Religious Freedom Restoration Act of 1993 [42 U.S.C. 2000bb et seq.], the Religious Land Use and Institutionalized Persons Act of 2000 [42 U.S.C. 2000cc et seq.], title VI of the Civil Rights Act of 1964 [42 U.S.C. 2000d et seq.], or section 12361 of title 34, the court, in its discretion, may allow the prevailing party, other than the United States, a reasonable attorney's fee as part of the costs.").

[97] *Octane Fitness, LLC* v. *ICON Health & Fitness, Inc.* (U.S. 2014, p.1758) (U.S.) (quoting *Alyeska Pipeline Serv. Co.* v. *Wilderness Soc'y* (U.S. 1975, p.258–59) (U.S.)). *See also* FED. R. CIV. P. 11.

[98] Until fairly recently, the governing Federal Circuit precedent construing § 285 has been summarized as follows: The burden is on the moving party to establish the exceptional nature of the case by clear and convincing evidence, and "[o]nly a limited universe of circumstances warrants a finding of

Until recently, Federal Circuit precedent interpreting § 285 recognized "[o]nly a limited universe of circumstances warrant[ing] a finding of exceptionality in a patent case: 'inequitable conduct before the PTO; litigation misconduct; vexatious, unjustified, and otherwise bad faith litigation; a frivolous suit or willful infringement.'"[99] Furthermore, a court would award fees to the prevailing alleged infringer based on the weakness of the patentee's case only if the claims asserted were "objectively baseless" and brought "in subjective bad faith"[100] – a standard that mirrored the stringent requirements for stripping litigants of *Noerr-Pennington* immunity for claims of attempted monopolization premised on sham litigation.

In 2014, however, the Supreme Court of the United States in *Octane Fitness, LLC v. Icon Health & Fitness, Inc.* overruled this body of precedent, holding that courts should consider whether a case is "exceptional" for purposes of § 285 based on the "totality of the circumstances."[101] In a companion case, the Court also held that, contrary to Federal Circuit precedent, "an appellate court should review all aspects of a district court's § 285 determination for abuse of discretion."[102]

Since the Supreme Court's decision in *Octane Fitness*, the number of patent cases in which U.S. courts have awarded attorney fees has increased, though given the exceptionality requirement even under the more lenient standard that number remains small; and in most cases, courts have awarded only a fraction of the entire fees incurred in prosecution or defense of the action. Jiam (2015), for example, reports that from the date of the *Octane Fitness* decision through March 31, 2015, courts granted fee petitions in twenty-seven out of sixty-three cases – more than double the proportion reported in a 2011 study by Chien – but the awards themselves mostly ranged from just $200,000 to $300,000.[103] Similarly, Flanz (2016) reports a statistically significant higher percentage of successful fee petitions post-*Octane Fitness*,[104] while Barry et al. (2016) report

---

exceptionality in a patent case: 'inequitable conduct before the PTO; litigation misconduct; vexatious, unjustified, and otherwise bad faith litigation; a frivolous suit or willful infringement.'" Once the movant establishes exceptionality, the court then determines whether a fee award is appropriate, taking into account such factors as "the closeness of the case, the tactics of counsel, the conduct of the parties, and any other factors that may contribute to a fair allocation of the burdens of litigation as between winner and loser." The court alone determines whether a case is exceptional, subject to review for clear error; the amount of fees awarded, if any, is reviewed under the abuse of discretion standard. Cotter 2013a, 147–48 (citations omitted).

[99] *Wedgetail, Ltd. v. Huddleston Deluxe, Inc.* (Fed. Cir. 2009, p.1304) (U.S.).

[100] *Brooks Furniture Mfg., Inc. v. Dutailier Int'l, Inc.* (Fed. Cir. 2005, p.1381) (U.S.), abrogated in part by *Octane Fitness, LLC v. ICON Health & Fitness, Inc.* (U.S. 2014) (U.S.).

[101] *Octane Fitness, LLC v. ICON Health & Fitness, Inc.* (U.S. 2014, p.1756) (U.S.).

[102] *Highmark Inc. v. Allcare Health Mgmt. Sys., Inc.* (U.S. 2014, p.1747) (U.S.). In a footnote, however, the Court added that "[t]he abuse-of-discretion standard does not preclude an appellate court's correction of a district court's legal or factual error … " *Id.* at 1748 n.2.

[103] *See* Jiam 2015, 624, 627.

[104] *See* Flanz 2016.

that the average number of fee award decisions "increased from about 4 per month to 7 per month."[105] The latter source also reports, however, that the median fee award post-*Octane Fitness* has been approximately $0.3 million, with the maximum award amounting to $12.5 million.

3.3.2 *Economic Theory and Empirical Research on the Effects of Cost Recovery*

There is general agreement in the theoretical literature that awarding expenses to prevailing parties in civil litigation will, all else equal, have two primary effects: first, that it will enhance the overall quality of the pool of lawsuits that are filed, and second that it will increase the intensity of litigation in suits that are filed.[106] The first effect is based on the theory that the availability of cost recovery will discourage the filing of weak (i.e., low-probability-of-winning) cases by reducing the plaintiff's total expected recovery and, conversely, encourage the filing of strong (i.e., high-probability-of-winning) cases by increasing the plaintiff's expected total award.[107] In effect, the risk of paying the infringer's costs acts as a potential penalty for bringing weak claims, while the prospect of having one's own costs covered by the infringer serves as a potential reward for bringing strong claims.

At the same time, however, theory suggests that cost recovery can increase the duration and complexity of legal disputes. Given that litigants typically disagree at least marginally about the likely outcome of a case, the availability of awards of attorney fees and litigation expenses will tend to exaggerate the gap between the parties' estimates of the expected value of their respective recovery or payout if the case is litigated to a decision on the merits. The wider this gap, the less likely parties are to reach a mutually agreeable settlement. In addition to extending litigation, cost recovery can encourage well-resourced parties to devote more resources to litigation. By raising the stakes of litigation, cost awards increase the marginal benefit of additional spending on litigation. Additionally, by raising the prospect that one's opponent will wind up paying additional amounts spent on litigation, cost awards also decrease the marginal cost of doing so. Finally, because cost shifting increases the stakes of the dispute, a party that is risk-averse may be more willing than it otherwise would be to forgo a valid claim or agree to less favorable terms of

---

[105] Barry et al. 2016, 7. Barry et al., additionally report that this median award "represented 82% of the median amount requested." *Id.* For further discussion of the empirical studies on post-*Octane Fitness* fee awards to date, *see* Cotter & Golden 2018, 15–16 n.71.

[106] For an overview of the theoretical literature related to the effect that attorney fee awards (the primary driver of litigation expenses) have on litigation, *see* Spier 2007, 300–03.

[107] This effect assumes that the parties have relatively symmetric information about the lawsuit. Fee shifting can also have the opposite effect when the parties have asymmetric information. Polinsky & Rubinfeld 1998.

settlement.[108] In practice, however, the limits on the fees and disbursements recovered and the uncertainty associated with litigation outcomes dampen some of these theoretical effects.

Existing empirical studies, though limited in number, tend to support these conclusions, but not uniformly.[109] Studies by Edward Snyder and James Hughes of medical malpractice litigation in Florida found that, after the state's introduction of fee shifting in this area of law, plaintiffs won more often and received higher damages on average.[110] A recent study by Helmers et al. (2018) of intellectual property cases litigated in the United Kingdom also supports the prediction that fee shifting tends to weed out weaker suits, as well as cases involving smaller entities, and thus decreases the number of suits that are filed.[111] In addition, descriptive statistics collected by Love et al. (2017) suggest a link between the prevalence of fee shifting in Europe and the continent's relative lack of suits by patent "trolls" that file large numbers of low-value suits.[112] When cases are actually filed, a study of U.S. litigation by Fournier and Zuehlke suggests that fee shifting tends to reduce the likelihood of settlement, all else being equal.[113] On the other hand, two studies of litigation in Alaska (the only U.S. state that routinely awards attorney fees to prevailing parties),[114] and one experimental study,[115] have failed to find that fee shifting has significant effects on litigation incentives and behavior. Again, in practice, the decisions of individual litigants depend heavily on other factors external to the availability of attorney fees, such as the availability of insurance, third-party litigation financing, and the relationship between the cost of litigation and the value of the technology at stake.

---

[108]   A risk-averse person "when faced with a choice between two gambles with the same expected value, will usually choose the one with a smaller variability of return." Nicholson & Snyder 2008, 207; *see also* Pindyck & Rubinfeld 2013, 166–67.

[109]   For an overview of the empirical literature related to attorney fee awards, *see* Kritzer 2002.

[110]   Snyder & Hughes 1990; Hughes & Snyder 1995. *But see* Williams 2001 (finding that U.S. states with one of several forms of fee shifting rules had a higher ratio of bodily injury claims to property damage claims in suits following car accidents, and concluding that this finding contradicts the hypothesis that fee awards discourage frivolous claims).

[111]   Helmers et al. 2018 (studying IP cases filed before and after the introduction of a cap on the level of costs recoverable in suits litigated in the United Kingdom's Intellectual Property Enterprise Court).

[112]   Love et al. 2017 (finding in a study of patent suits brought in Germany and the United Kingdom a high rate of accused infringer-filed actions and a low rate of settlement relative to the United States, and concluding from these findings that fee shifting may deter patent monetization); Helmers et al. 2014 (studying patent suits filed in the United Kingdom and making similar findings).

[113]   Fournier & Zuehlke 1989, 193 (studying cases litigated in U.S. federal courts between 1979 and 1981).

[114]   Di Pietro et al. 1995, ES-11 ("The major conclusion of this report is that attorney fee shifting in Alaska seldom plays a significant role in civil litigation."); Rennie 2012 (comparing cases filed in the District of Alaska with cases filed in other districts, and finding no significant differences).

[115]   Inglis et al. 2005 (finding no significant difference in settlement outcomes in an experiment comparing settlements negotiated in legal environments that do and do not award attorney fees to prevailing parties).

3.3.3 *Recommendations for Best Practices and Future Research*

On one hand, mandatory cost shifting ensures that the prevailing patent owner is compensated to some degree for what can be a huge expense,[116] and helps to deter weak assertions of patent rights. On another, cost shifting may also encourage litigating parties to increase the duration and complexity of their disputes. In addition, there is some risk that mandatory fee shifting may lead risk-averse parties with strong claims or defenses to abandon them, which might seem both socially inefficient and substantively unfair. Finally, shifting can require additional, costly adjudication to determine which fees and expenses are reasonable and thus compensable. While some jurisdictions like Germany set statutory rates that minimize such adjudication costs, other systems condition fee or cost awards on other factors (e.g., whether the infringement was willful), which adds to the expense of this "satellite litigation." Consequently, it is hard to draw strong conclusions about whether fee shifting in the abstract is desirable or not, and resolution of the issue may depend as much on cultural expectations as on theoretical or empirical economics. As a practical matter, it is highly unlikely that the United States will adopt mandatory fee shifting in the foreseeable future, or that other countries in which fee shifting is commonplace will abandon it.

That said, we recommend the following: First, in countries in which fee shifting is an established part of the legal landscape, fee shifting rules should aim to compensate for the reasonable and proportionate costs actually incurred by the prevailing party in a meaningful manner unless equity prescribes otherwise (as, for example, the EU Enforcement Directive mandates), rather than only partially (as is often the case in practice). As a general rule, fee awards should not be calculated based upon a specified portion of the amount awarded, as is sometimes the case in Japan. Second, in countries in which fee shifting is not the norm, legislatures and courts arguably should consider experimenting with somewhat more generous fee shifting rules – for example, as proposed in the Innovation Act (which would have required courts to award fees to the prevailing party, "unless the court finds that the position and conduct of the nonprevailing party or parties were reasonably justified in law and fact or that special circumstances (such as severe economic hardship to a named inventor) make an award unjust")[117] – perhaps coupled with discovery reforms to reduce the risk that the stronger party will make unnecessary and excessive expenditures with the expectation of reimbursement.

Further research might center on, among other things, proposals for constraining the cost of satellite litigation over fees and other litigation expenses; and on an

---

[116]   *See* AIPLA 2017, I-118 to –122 (reporting mean costs through appeal of $627,000 for cases with less than $1 million at stake, $1.456 million with $1–$10 million at stake, $2.374 million with $10–$25 million at stake, and $3.831 million with more than $25 million at stake).

[117]   In 2013, the Innovation Act, H.R. 3309, 113th Cong. (2013), passed the U.S. House of Representatives, but ultimately stalled in the Senate. It was introduced again in the next session, Innovation Act, H.R. 9, 114th Cong. (2015), but again failed to pass.

empirical determination of (1) how often courts in the United States award fees under the Equal Access to Justice Act, after which the Innovation Act proposal was to some degree modeled, and (2) whether settlements are more or less common in countries with mandatory fee shifting. We also would welcome further empirical studies of the availability of fee shifting that take into account the practical aspects of fee shifting both with respect to market options such as insurance or third-party litigation financing and the design of fee-shifting regimes, vis-à-vis methods and procedures for determining awards, the percentage of fees that are actually awarded in practice, and the relationship between the value of the suit and the fees, though it is unclear whether or not the data are just too noisy for such analysis.

3.4 PRE- AND POST-JUDGMENT INTEREST

If damages are to fully compensate the patent owner for the losses attributable to the infringement, damages awards should take into account the time value of money. To this end, it would seem straightforward to require courts to award adequate pre- and post-judgment interest to ensure that the patent owner is no worse off than it would have been, absent the infringement.[118] Nonetheless, awards of prejudgment interest are not standard in every country; and even in countries in which they are awarded, if the rates are not carefully chosen or interest is not compounded, they may wind up either over- or undercompensating the prevailing patentee. The problem is particularly acute when the litigation is protracted, and undercompensatory prejudgment interest can encourage a defendant to delay and prolong litigation.[119] Consequently, undercompensatory prejudgment interest can exacerbate the problem of "holdout," in which a user of patented technology unduly delays licensing, by effectively giving the infringer the benefit of a low-interest loan.

3.4.1 *Approaches in Selected Countries*

In the United States, the Supreme Court's decision in *General Motors Corp. v. Devex Corp.*[120] interprets § 284 of the Patent Act as creating, in effect, a presumption that the prevailing patentee is entitled to prejudgment interest on the compensatory portion of a damages award. More specifically, *Devex* holds that, in enacting § 284 of the Patent Act, "Congress sought to ensure that the patent owner would in fact receive full compensation for 'any damages' he suffered as a result of

---

[118] An interesting question, albeit one beyond the scope of the present project, is whether defendants who ultimately prevail in infringement litigation but who are temporarily excluded from the market or required to incur other costs (e.g., due to a preliminary or permanent injunction that is subsequently vacated) should be entitled to some form of compensation, and if so whether they should be entitled to pre- and post-judgment interest on any such award. For brief discussion of the compensation issue, *see, e.g.,* Cotter 2014c; Cotter 2016e.

[119] *See Eli Lilly and Co. v. Apotex Inc.* (Fed. Ct. 2014, ¶ 113) (Can.).

[120] *General Motors Corp. v. Devex Corp.* (U.S. 1983) (U.S.).

the infringement," and that courts therefore should award prejudgment interest on the compensatory portion of an award "absent some justification for withholding" it (such as when the patent owner has delayed prosecution of the suit).[121] Note, however, that "[b]ecause prejudgment interest has no punitive purpose, it must be applied only to the compensatory damages, not enhanced or other punitive damages."[122] In addition, U.S. courts are obligated to award post-judgment interest running from the date on which the judgment is entered until the date on which the award is paid.[123]

Courts nevertheless have wide discretion to determine the appropriate interest rate and whether to award simple or compound interest, and these choices can have a substantial impact on the amount actually paid.[124] Awarding compound interest is necessary to ensure that the patentee is not rendered worse off than she would have been absent the infringement. For example, suppose that the patent owner suffers a $1 million loss on March 1, 2008, and is awarded $1 million plus simple interest at an annual rate of 5 percent on March 1, 2018 (the date of judgment). The total award will be $1.5 million. If the interest had been compounded annually instead at the 5 percent rate, the total award would come to $1,628,890, which "reflects more accurately the wealth the patentee would have had as of 201[8], had the infringement never occurred and had she invested the $1 million profit in a relatively safe venture."[125]

---

[121] Blair & Cotter 2001, 24, 51. Earlier in time, interest ran only from the time that damages were actually determined or, when courts submitted the damages calculation to a special master, "from the day when the master's report was submitted to the court." *Crosby Steam Gage & Valve Co. v. Consol. Safety Valve Co.* (U.S. 1891, p.458) (U.S.). Under this rule, "interest from the date on which damages were liquidated" effectively meant little or no prejudgment interest.

[122] *Humanscale Corp. v. CompX Int'l Inc.* (E.D. Va. 2010, p.1) (U.S.) (citing *General Motors Corp. v. Devex Corp.* (U.S. 1983, p.355) (U.S.)).

[123] *See* 28 U.S.C. § 1961(a) ("Interest shall be allowed on any money judgment in a civil case recovered in a district court ... Such interest shall be calculated from the date of the entry of the judgment, at a rate equal to the weekly average 1-year constant maturity Treasury yield, as published by the Board of Governors of the Federal Reserve System, for the calendar week preceding the date of the judgment."); *id.* at § 1961(b) (stating that post-judgment "[i]nterest shall be computed daily to the date of payment except as provided in section 2516(b) of this title and section 1304(b) of title 31, and shall be compounded annually"); FED. R. APP. P. 37(a) ("Unless the law provides otherwise, if a money judgment in a civil case is affirmed, whatever interest is allowed by law is payable from the date when the district court's judgment was entered."). *See also* Michel 2010, 3 ("[T]he court may award pre-judgment interest under 35 U.S.C. § 284 on the compensatory portion of the damages award, pre-judgment interest on any award of attorney fees, and post-judgment interest under Fed. R. [App.] P. 37 on the entire award.").

[124] *See, e.g., ActiveVideo Networks, Inc. v. Verizon Comm'ns, Inc.* (E.D. Va. 2011, p.3) (U.S.) (stating that courts have "wide latitude" in selecting a prejudgment interest rate, with most opting for "either prime rate or the U.S. Treasury rate," while post-judgment interest is calculated under 28 U.S.C. § 1961 "at a rate equal to the weekly average 1-year constant maturity Treasury yield ... for the calendar week preceding the date of the judgment"); Epstein 2006; Fish & Richardson, P.C. 2018.

[125] Cotter 2013a, 277; *see also* Epstein 2006, 10 ("From the point of view of economics, interest should always be compounded because a plaintiff would earn interest on interest when lending money. The only substantial justification for simple interest is greater ease of computation. But

As for the rate chosen, however, Epstein argues that courts generally should select a rate that reflects the infringer's cost of short-term borrowing (i.e., a restitutionary award) rather than the plaintiff's opportunity cost of capital (i.e., a compensatory award), because among other problems the latter conclusively presumes that the money the plaintiff would have had available to invest absent the infringement would have earned a positive return. Epstein further argues that courts should avoiding using both the prime rate, which is often higher than the rate the infringer would have to pay to borrow an amount in excess of $1 million, and the risk-free rate available on Treasury bills, which is unavailable to most private entities. Instead, he urges courts in the United States to use Federal Reserve survey rates to estimate the infringer's cost of borrowing in an objective (and comparatively nonintrusive) manner.[126] We are inclined to agree with Epstein's proposal.[127]

The rules in other countries vary considerably. First, some countries don't award prejudgment interest at all,[128] or only sparingly.[129] Second, some countries (including Germany and the United Kingdom) routinely award prejudgment interest but do not compound it.[130] A third model is presented by Japan, where courts generally award prejudgment interest at a statutory rate of 5 percent, and post-judgment

---

this rationale is archaic in an age of spreadsheets. Moreover, nearly all market interest rates involve compounding.").

[126] *See* Epstein 2006, 9–11. On the question of whether to use the plaintiff's expected rate of return, Epstein further argues that doing so could induce plaintiffs to protract litigation, and that such a rate would be premised on the assumption that the plaintiff could not have borrowed the money to invest from another source.

[127] Ideally, it might be best for a legislative body to mandate a uniform policy so as to decrease the risk of forum shopping, though whether litigants would actually choose an otherwise inconvenient forum for such a benefit alone is debatable. *See Arctic Cat Inc.* v. *Bombardier Recreational Prod., Inc.* (S.D. Fla. 2017, p.8) (U.S.) (expressing concern that applying the Florida interest rate "would encourage forum-shopping by patent litigants hoping to take advantage of states with high interest rates on judgments").

[128] *See* Cotter 2013a, 276; *see also* Elmer & Gramenopoulos 2016, 9–12 to –13 (noting the unavailability of prejudgment interest in Russia and Mexico); *id.* at C-48 tbl. A (table listing information on pre- and post-judgment interest in selected countries).

[129] *See* Cotter 2013a, 276 n.211 (stating "while post-judgment interest is awarded in France, prejudgment interest generally is not," and quoting a translation of Code Civil [C. civ.] art. 1153–1 (Fr.): "In all matters, the award of a compensation involves interest at the statutory rate even failing a claim or a specific provision in the judgment. Save as otherwise provided by legislation, that interest runs from the handing down of the judgment unless the judge otherwise rules."); *see also, Knight* v. *AXA Assurance* (QB 2009) (UK) (reporting experts' agreement that prejudgment interest generally is not available in France). However, there are exceptions to this rule. *See, e.g., S.A. Technogenia* v. *S.A.R. L. Martec* (TGI Paris 2010) (Fr.) (awarding prejudgment interest calculated yearly at the legal interest rate, from 1990). In addition, "French judges also are authorized to increase the amount of a damages award to reflect the increase in the inflation rate from the date of infringement." Cotter 2013a, 276 n.211 (citations omitted).

[130] *See* Cotter 2013a, 277 n.212–13 (citations omitted). Relatedly, when German courts award lost profits, they compute them from the date on which the plaintiff demands payment, not from the date on which the injury is suffered, thus risking substantial undercompensation. *See id.* at 277 (citations omitted).

interest following a one-year grace period.[131] This flat rate can, depending on the time value of money, lead to over- or undercompensation.[132] Of course, any such risk of overcompensation should be taken with a grain of salt, given the typically low damages awards rendered by Japanese courts as discussed in the Reasonable Royalties Paper.

3.4.2 *Recommendations for Best Practices and Future Research*

Consistent with the above discussion, we recommend that courts be required to award pre- and post-judgment compound interest, nominally at rates that reflect the infringer's cost of borrowing. Such a requirement would prevent the rules with respect to interest from either over- or undercompensating patent owners (and from either over- or underdeterring implementers) and would require courts to award pre- and post-judgment compound interest, arguably at rates that reflect the infringer's cost of borrowing. To the extent such reforms would be difficult to implement in the short run (e.g., due to cultural resistance to awards based on compound interest, as may be the case in Germany) we recommend as a second-best solution the periodic reconsideration of statutory interest rates in countries such as Japan in which those rates may differ substantially from market rates.

As for future research, to our knowledge there has been no systematic empirical study of the interest rates U.S. courts select in patent infringement cases, or the frequency with which they award simple versus compound interest. Such research would be helpful in evaluating whether or to what extent the choices courts make with regard to interest likely result in systematic over- or undercompensation, or enable infringers to benefit from delay. Resolution of these matters in turn would help to illuminate, among other things, the debate over "patent holdout" discussed in Chapter 7.[133]

---

[131] *Id.* at 328 (describing the availability of compound interest under Civil Code Article 405 if payment is delayed by one year or more after the creditor demands payment). Somewhat analogous to German practice, *see also supra* note 27, "although interest 'theoretically' accrues from the date of the commission of a tortious act, in practice the plaintiff demands interest only from the date following service of the complaint." *Id.* (citing Hoshi 1998, 12). The 5 percent rate comes from Minpō [Civ. C.] art. 404 (Japan), which states that "[u]nless the parties otherwise manifest their intention with respect to a claim which bears interest, the rate of such interest shall be 5% per annum."

[132] Cotter 2013a, 328.

[133] *See General Motors Corp.* v. *Devex Corp.* (U.S. 1983, p.655 n.10) (U.S.) ("A rule denying prejudgment interest not only undercompensates the patent owner but may also grant a windfall to the infringer and create an incentive to prolong litigation. There is no reason why an infringer should stand in a better position than a party who agrees to pay a royalty and then fails to pay because of financial difficulties."). The same could be said for a rule that awards inadequate pre- or post-judgment interest.

4

Injunctive Relief

*Norman V. Siebrasse, Rafal Sikorski, Jorge L. Contreras, Thomas F. Cotter,
John Golden, Sang Jo Jong, Brian J. Love, and David O. Taylor*

4.1 INTRODUCTION

Patent systems commonly empower courts to order accused or adjudged infringers
to refrain from continuing infringing conduct in the future. Some patentees file suit
for the primary purpose of obtaining and enforcing an injunction against infringement by a competitor, and even in cases in which the patentee is willing to license an
invention to an accused infringer for an agreed price, the indirect monetary value of
an injunction against future infringement can dwarf the amount a finder of fact is
likely to award as compensation for past infringement. In some of these cases, an
injunction, if granted, would impose costs on accused infringers or third parties that
go well beyond the more intrinsic value of the patented technology. In this chapter,
we explore the theory behind injunctive relief in patent cases, survey the availability
of this remedy in major patent systems, and suggest a general framework for courts to
use when deciding whether injunctive relief is appropriate in individual cases.

4.2 THEORY

As a matter of general theory, there are two frequently invoked rationales for issuing
injunctions against patent infringement: first, formal or moral arguments that such
relief follows from – or is necessary to vindicate – the property-like nature of patent
rights, and second, economic arguments that, relative to purely monetary relief,
injunctions better advance social welfare in circumstances commonly characteristic
of patent cases. Neither theory is absolute, however, and it is generally accepted that
both suggest that injunctive relief should be limited or denied in a number of
circumstances.

4.2.1 *Nature of Patent Rights and Injunctions*

To many, the nature of patent rights as "rights to exclude" is determinative of
a strong, if not overwhelming, presumption in favor of injunctive relief, particularly

when a final determination of infringement has been made.[1] The language and structure of international agreements, for example, is sometimes invoked in support of arguments that the nature of patent rights justifies a robust presumption in favor of injunctive relief.[2] The TRIPS agreement, to which the over 150 members of the WTO are subject, provides that members must give a patent owner rights "to prevent third parties not having the owner's consent from" acts such as using the invention, subject only to "limited exceptions" or the satisfaction of specific requirements for situations "[w]here the law of a Member allows for other use of the subject matter of a patent without the authorization of the right holder."[3]

Some also justify a strong presumption in favor of injunctive relief by analogy to remedies for violation of rights in tangible property, whether real or personal.[4] One factor contributing to liberal use of injunctive relief to remedy real property harms is a general assumption that each parcel of real property is unique – not just in an objective sense, but also often for subjective personal reasons unique to its owner – and thus not readily replaceable via the market for real estate.[5] A similar argument can be made with respect to patent rights. Because each patent claim is uniquely associated with a novel invention, as well as one or more inventors who may feel strongly invested in the novel idea they introduced to the world, monetary remedies can be difficult to calibrate properly[6] and cannot return a patent holder to its rightful position by enabling the patent holder to purchase an essentially perfect substitute for what the infringer has taken.[7]

Still others justify such a presumption through a mixture of formal and pragmatic concerns that points to practical difficulties in "protecting a right to exclude through monetary remedies that allow an infringer to use an invention against the patentee's wishes."[8] According to this view, the availability of injunctions to protect property-like "rights to exclude" might, as a practical

---

[1] Balganesh 2008, 638 ("[I]t remains common in modern times to equate the right to exclude with an entitlement to exclusionary or injunctive relief."). In contrast, in rejecting any simple "general rule that courts will issue permanent injunctions against patent infringement absent exceptional circumstances," *eBay Inc.* v. *MercExchange, L.L.C.* (U.S. 2006, p.391) (U.S.), the Supreme Court of the United States made clear its view that "the creation of a right is distinct from the provision of remedies for violations of that right," *id.* at 392.

[2] Keyhani 2008, 11–12; cf. Mace 2009, 264 (discussing different potential interpretations of TRIPS).

[3] TRIPS Agreement, arts. 28(1), 30, 31.

[4] Epstein 2010, 456.

[5] *See, e.g.*, RESTATEMENT (SECOND) OF TORTS § 946(b) cmt. b ("The relative adequacy of injunction ... must be considered with reference to the question whether the plaintiff's need for the particular chattel in question would be satisfied by the substitute which could be purchased in the market ... This test is not limited to ascertaining that the chattel is unique. The term 'unique chattel' connotes an absolute irreplaceability, such as would be true of a painting by Rembrandt, or a family heirloom valued for its associations. Obviously, the damage remedy is futile in such cases.").

[6] Merges 1994, 2664 ("Because each asset covered by an [intellectual property right] is in some sense unique ... it is difficult for a court in an infringement case to properly value the right-holder's loss.").

[7] *See* Oppenheimer 2015, 262 n.33.

[8] *Cf. eBay Inc.* v. *MercExchange, L.L.C.* (U.S. 2006, p.395) (U.S.) (Roberts, C.J., concurring) (emphasis omitted).

matter, be critical to secure the benefit of such rights following a trespass or infringement. An injunction backed by potentially punitive sanctions for contempt might be presumed to have a greater deterrent effect on future infringement than would result from a mere repeat of compensatory monetary sanctions for past infringement.[9] At least in jurisdictions that do not permit an award of ongoing royalties, this added deterrence can help spare a rightsholder from the need to sue the same infringer again to obtain compensation for substantially the same form of infringement, and thus reduces the risk that uncompensated costs associated with repeat litigation will lead the rightsholder to eventually cease defending its rights altogether. It similarly prevents repeat damages awards or ongoing royalties, even fully compensatory ones, from serving as informal compulsory licenses, which are (formally) constrained by international accords, such as TRIPS.[10] Indeed, these arguments may be even stronger in the context of patent rights than property rights because patents protect publicly disclosed information (i.e., the enabling information disclosed in a patent), which the rightsholder has little ability to defend by means of self-help.[11] That is, having disclosed the patented invention to the public in exchange for state-backed rights to exclude, a patentee has substantially surrendered a capacity to "fence in" that information in the manner of a real property owner building a fence to help prevent future trespass.

That said, even those advocating for strong property-like protection of patent rights commonly concede that the property-like nature of patent rights does not mandate injunctive relief in all situations.[12] Indeed, TRIPS itself makes clear that "Members may limit the remedies available against [infringing] use to payment of remuneration,"[13] a provision that some commentators argue gives member nations broad discretion to limit injunctions.[14] In addition, even in the context of trespass to real property rights, common law countries have historically subjected injunctive relief to exceptions that consider whether awarding such relief inflict a burden on the trespasser or public that is disproportionate to the harm that the trespass has inflicted upon the property owner.[15] A quintessential example is found in the legal treatment of encroaching structures. Despite the nature of the underlying property right at stake, courts will generally refuse to order the demolition of buildings that were inadvertently built so that they extend slightly over the boundary with

---

[9]   See, e.g., Golden 2012, 1414–15.

[10] See, e.g., Keyhani 2008, 11–12.

[11] See, e.g., Gergen et al. 2012, 236.

[12] See, e.g., Epstein 2010, 489–90.

[13] Id. at art. 44(2).

[14] See, e.g., Cotropia 2008, 580; see also Kapczynski 2009, 1608 n.223 (summarizing the debate).

[15] See, e.g., Balganesh 2008, 646 (contending that "[c]ourts never abdicated their discretion [to deny injunctions against trespass], but merely came to limit it to exceptional circumstances"); Epstein 2010, 494 ("[T]he boundary conditions on land have themselves never been treated as absolute and inviolate either.").

a neighboring property.[16] As courts have recognized, awarding such an injunction would allow the neighboring property owner to leverage the building's entire value to extract a settlement from the building's owner that is disproportionately large relative to the neighbor's actual harm from losing a sliver of land.[17]

Similar concerns arise as well in the context of patent infringement when an injunction might allow a patent holder to prevent, or at least to substantially tax, the use of much more than the patented technology itself. This can happen if, for example, an infringer must undergo high "switching costs" (e.g., from retooling or closing a factory) in order to terminate an ongoing course of infringement.[18] Awarding an injunction in such a circumstance can allow the patent holder to negotiate a settlement derived in part on the value of technology located outside the scope of his claims, extending the effective reach of patent rights potentially far beyond the scope of the inventor's contribution to society. Even for those who believe that injunctions should generally issue against patent infringement, such extension of patents' effective reach can outrun rights-based rationales for injunctive relief and lead to concessions that court practices in issuing injunctions should be qualified or tailored accordingly.[19]

4.2.2 *Economic Analysis and Complex Products*

Economic arguments for or against injunctions often draw on more general debates about the relative economic efficiency of protecting legal entitlements through "property rules" associated with grants of injunctive relief or "liability rules" associated with awards of compensatory damages.[20] As suggested by the discussion above of how rationales for injunctions can mix formal and pragmatic perspectives, these economic arguments can overlap with arguments that might at least initially be viewed as more fundamentally tied to the nature of patent rights. Sometimes the difference between more purely economic and more fundamentally rights-based arguments can appear to revolve principally around the extent to which an argument looks to vindication of underlying purposes of patent law, as opposed to vindication of patent rights that are assumed generally to serve those underlying purposes. Sometimes the difference can seem to reflect to a large degree the level of generality

---

[16]   *See, e.g.*, Fennell 2006, 1042 n.21 ("Although the specifics vary from jurisdiction to jurisdiction, and exceptions can be found, most modern American courts will deny injunctive relief in good faith encroachment situations where the injunction would impose a disproportionately heavy burden on the encroacher."); *see also* the discussion in Section 4.3.3 below noting that in the United Kingdom the most common type of property case in which an injunction is refused are those where the plaintiff has sought a mandatory injunction to pull down a building that infringes his right to light or that has been built in breach of a restrictive covenant.

[17]   *See Isenberg v. East India House Estate Co. Ltd.* (Ct Ch 1863) (UK) (before Lord Westbury LC); *see also Jaggard v. Sawyer* (Civ 1995) (UK), both discussed in Section 4.3.3 below.

[18]   *See, e.g.*, Cotter et al. 2019; Heald 2008, 1183–87.

[19]   *See, e.g.*, Epstein 2010, 493–94.

[20]   Calabresi & Melamed 1972, 1092; Cotter 2013a, 53; Cotter & Golden 2018.

at which argument is conducted – for example, whether one primarily looks to achieve "right" outcomes in individual cases or on-average "right" outcomes in great masses of cases.

For purposes here, a more fundamentally economic approach is taken to be one that is concerned less with protecting rights to exclude as such and more with ensuring that rights are valued as accurately as possible. Proper judicial remedies for patent infringement can help secure this end by helping set properly calibrated expected values for rights that can then stimulate innovative activity in line with social goals. To this end, the primary benefit of "property rules" associated with a strong presumption of injunctive relief arises not from bare enforcement of the "right to exclude," but rather from the fact that such a rule effectively demands that "someone who wishes to remove the entitlement from its holder . . . buy it from [the holder] in a voluntary transaction" at a price to which the holder agrees.[21] In contrast, a "liability rule," generally associated with no more than compensatory damages, can effectively enable (litigation costs aside) a party to "destroy the initial entitlement" in exchange for payment of "an objectively determined value" to which the entitlement holder need not agree.[22]

Typical economic analysis suggests that property rules – and, hence, the presumptive issuance of injunctive relief – is socially desirable when the obstacles to voluntary transactions "are relatively low compared to the information and error costs associated with government determinations of proper amounts" of damages under a liability rule.[23] As indicated above, it is generally accepted that the relative uniqueness of individual patent rights, combined with the lack of a thick public market for patent rights to which potential damages awards could be compared,[24] makes it difficult for courts and jurors to assign a value to patent infringement. In addition, the public nature of the patent document and patents' restriction to new technologies provide (at least in theory) some reason to hope that a private party looking to use a patented technology will be able to identify the relevant patent holder and to contract to use the technology in advance of any infringement. With these considerations in mind, some scholars have concluded that conventional economic analysis suggests that patent rights are good candidates for property-rule enforcement.[25] Proponents of such treatment often also argue that injunction-enforced exclusivity will spur patent holders to improve and exploit the patented technology, as well as allow them to

---

[21] Calabresi & Melamed 1972, 1092.

[22] *Id.*

[23] Cotter & Golden 2018.

[24] *See, e.g.*, Lemley & Myhrvold 2007, 257–59 (describing problems created by the "blind market" for patents and proposing mandatory publication of patent license and sale terms as a solution); Kelley 2011, 116–17 ("[B]oth scholars and practitioners are seeking ways to improve how patents are valued, with scholars often calling for greater disclosure of sale terms to aid in setting market prices and practitioners focusing on refining methods for predicting a patent's value to their own clients.").

[25] *See, e.g.*, Merges 1994; Schoenhard 2008.

coordinate follow-on development in a way that limits wastefully duplicative downstream activities.[26]

Other scholars have called these contentions into question, however, particularly in light of the complexity of modern technology and the realities of the current patent landscape.[27] Today, new products often incorporate a multitude of technologies, and when a relevant individual patent is likely to cover just one of these myriad technologies, achieving clearance of patent rights through voluntary transactions becomes problematic. For one, identifying all the patents that a new complex product might infringe can become a particularly difficult and expensive task – one that in many circumstances may not be possible at a cost that makes sense from a social welfare standpoint.[28] In addition, the difficulty of determining the portion of the value of a complex product that should be attributed to a single patented technology can make it hard for private parties to agree on an appropriate license value, even if they are bargaining in good faith to agree on such a value (though by the same token, it makes it difficult for a court to accurately assess a reasonable royalty).

The concepts of "holdup" and "holdout" offer another, related lens through which to view economic debates about the propriety of injunctions. Parties on both sides of a patent transaction face strong temptations for strategic reasons to insist on payment of an amount that is higher or lower than a good-faith estimate of patented technology's true value.[29] One such temptation is for a patent owner to leverage the availability of injunctive relief to extract "holdup" value from potential licensees that have already incorporated the patented technology in a larger, complex product. By threatening to seek an injunction to shut down production and sale of the licensee's entire product, a patent holder can effectively place at risk not just the value that the licensee derives from the patented technology, but also the value of all the other technologies bundled into the product. In other circumstances, a potential licensee might be tempted to adopt a "holdout" strategy by refusing to strike a deal either at all or at anything but an unreasonably low licensing rate, not just to delay eventual payment but perhaps in hopes of establishing a reputation as a tough negotiator or of leveraging the costs and risks of litigation against a smaller, less sophisticated patent holder.

---

[26] See Kitch 1977, 266.

[27] See Lemley & Weiser 2007, 797–98.

[28] See Mulligan & Lee 2012, 289, 304 (estimating that "[i]n software, for example, patent clearance by all firms would require many times more hours of legal research than all patent lawyers in the United States can bill in a year" because "there are around twenty-four billion new [software] patent-firm pairs each year that could produce accidental infringement"). See generally Sterk 2008, 1304 (concluding that, "compared with a liability-rule regime, a property-rule regime creates excessive incentives to search even when search costs are high, the probability of encroachment is relatively low, and the likely harm to the property owner is low").

[29] See Chapter 7.

Consequently, determining when injunctions should be available can at least in part be viewed as an exercise of efficiently weighing the risk that they will enable "holdup" against the prospect that they will deter "holdout." Substantially because an injunction could deprive a potential infringer of more than the portion of the value of a patented technology that corresponds to a "reasonable royalty" or a patentee's lost profits, the threat of injunctive relief can act as a strong deterrent to holdout. If an injunction is unavailable and patent damages simply require an infringer to pay an amount essentially equivalent to what an advance license would cost, a potential user of a patented technology might well be tempted to hold out and refuse to pay for such a license in advance.[30] The possibility that the patent holder will not detect infringement or will ultimately decline to undergo the costs of enforcement might make holding out an economically sound strategy. Injunctions can check the temptation to engage in such a strategy. But as is commonly a risk with deterrence, there is danger that the deterrence from threatened injunctive relief will overreach, particularly where the complexity of a product or process has the dual effects of (1) making advance patent clearance difficult to achieve and (2) making a patent's potential holdup value much greater than the properly apportioned value of the patented technology. Hence, especially with respect to complex products, there can be a significant danger that the holdup potential of injunctive relief will chill investment in innovation to a socially undesirable degree.

As a result, from an economic perspective, there is good reason to believe that neither a pure property rule nor a pure liability rule is an ideal fit for patent infringement. As discussed in greater detail below in Section 4.4, one way to help thread the needle – that is, to substantially retain the relative advantages of injunctive relief while limiting the likelihood of injunctive "over-reach" that places a greater burden on innovative activities than is socially desirable – is to make decisions on the issuance and tailoring of injunctions with particular attention to concerns about proportionality. Among those who favor greater emphasis on liability rules for patent infringement, the potentially disproportionate nature of injunctive relief, particularly when complex products are involved, is one of the main concerns with a property-rule approach.[31] Even scholars who are among the strongest proponents of property rules tend to acknowledge that it can make little economic sense to issue an injunction that provides a basis for "economic extortion" by placing at the patentee's mercy the continued viability of a "complex product [that] has thousands of different components of which only one is covered by the plaintiff's patent."[32] Likewise, there is common concern about the risk of socially excessive holdout by potential infringers, with a threat of injunctive relief being one of the means by which such parties can be encouraged to clear others' rights *ex ante*, rather than *ex*

[30] We discuss this topic further in Chapter 3.
[31] *See, e.g.,* Lemley & Weiser 2007, 793–96.
[32] *See, e.g.,* Epstein 2010, 490.

post.[33] Hence, for a broad range both of theorists and of theories, there seems at least a baseline common ground: Courts or other enforcers of patent rights should have some power to issue injunctions or other, potentially supra-compensatory remedies, but economic analysis argues against injunctive relief in at least some situations where that relief will have effects disproportionate to the underlying rights at issue.

As Sections 4.2 and 4.3 will make clear, there are a variety of ways by which courts might try to alleviate such disproportionality, including not only denying injunctive relief altogether but also by delaying or otherwise tailoring injunctive relief to make it less burdensome. For purposes here, however, the key point is that, from a variety of theoretical viewpoints, engaging in such alleviation is something that can make good sense, whether the concern is respecting property rights, achieving fairness, or advancing overall social welfare.

4.2.3 Preliminary *v.* Permanent Injunctions

The above analysis focuses on the question of whether and to what extent injunctive relief is appropriate as a general matter, albeit at least sometimes with a background presumption that a patent has been adjudged to have been infringed. Further theoretical wrinkles come from considering the question of *when* in the context of patent infringement litigation such relief should go into effect. While "permanent" injunctions are almost universally available as a remedy for patent infringement, many patent systems also permit courts to award "preliminary" injunctive relief while a patent suit is pending.[34]

A preliminary injunction can play an important role in preventing irreparable harm to a patent holder's market position during the months or years that elapse before a case is litigated to a final judgment. But preliminary injunctions are generally harder to justify on practical and theoretical grounds than their permanent counterparts. For one, at the time of a preliminary injunction an accused infringer is still only accused: there has not yet been a final judgment of actual infringement on the merits.[35] Because it has not yet been determined that the activity to be enjoined falls within the scope of a valid patent right, the case for a preliminary injunction based on nature-of-the-right analysis is generally diluted. Moreover, under an economic analysis, the risks of inflicting a disproportionate burden on an accused infringer and of providing a disproportionate reward to a patent holder are also inflated by the possibility that the patent holder will not necessarily win on the merits. As Hoffmann J has said:

---

[33] *See, e.g.,* Heald 2008, 1175 ("An efficient system of remedies would provide all parties with incentives to negotiate when that is the optimal strategy from the standpoint of social welfare.").

[34] It is also common in some jurisdictions, most notably Germany and China, for injunctions to issue after a finding of infringement, but before the asserted patent's validity has been adjudicated in a separate administrative action. *See* Cremers et al. 2016; Love et al. 2016.

[35] Laycock 2002, 445.

The principal dilemma about the grant of interlocutory injunctions, whether prohibitory or mandatory, is that there is by definition a risk that the court may make the "wrong" decision, in the sense of granting an injunction to a party who fails to establish his right at the trial (or would fail if there was a trial) or alternatively, in failing to grant an injunction to a party who succeeds (or would succeed) at trial. A fundamental principle is therefore that the court should take whichever course appears to carry the lower risk of injustice if it should turn out to have been "wrong" in the sense I have described.[36]

More formally, we can say that the court should focus on comparing the expected harm to each of the parties. The expected harm to the patentee can be expressed as $P \times H_P$ where P is the probability that the plaintiff will prevail on the merits and H_P is the harm that the patent holder is expected to suffer if the injunction is denied. Similarly, the expected harm to the defendant is $(1-P) \times H_D$, where H_D is the harm the defendant is expected to suffer if the injunction is granted. If the expected harm to the patentee is greater than the expected harm to the infringer, the injunction should be granted; otherwise it should be refused.

One way to ensure that a preliminary injunction is not granted unless the risk of injustice is low, is to make the patent holder's likelihood of success on the merits a significant factor in the decision whether to issue a preliminary injunction.[37] If a patent holder is very likely to prevail in a patent infringement suit, the patent holder will have a greater likelihood of being able to obtain a preliminary injunction against allegedly infringing activity. In terms of the above formula, this approach focuses on ensuring the "P" is as high as possible. The difficulty with this approach is that if courts are required to make a preliminary conclusion on the merits, it may require parties to conduct, and courts to preside over, what amounts to a "mini-trial" that may well involve extensive discovery and a multiday evidentiary hearing covering topics that will be rehashed again in more detail if the case proceeds to trial. For that reason, this approach was abandoned in England forty years ago in favor of holding that the only question regarding the merits is whether the plaintiff has raised "a serious question to be tried," so that the grant of a preliminary injunction will turn largely on the balance of hardships.[38] Notably, the U.S. Court of Appeals for the

---

[36] *Films Rover Int'l Ltd.* v. *Cannon Film Sales Ltd.* (Ch 1986, p.780–81) (UK). This is similar to the principle of minimization of irreparable harm advocated in Leubsdorf 1978 and restated by Judge Posner in *Am. Hosp. Supply Corp.* v. *Hosp. Prods. Ltd.* (7th Cir. 1986, p.598) (U.S.). The difference is that the Leubsdorf-Posner approach draws a difficult distinction between irreparable and reparable harms that Hoffmann J's formulation avoids: *see generally* Laycock 1991, 118–23. Laycock ultimately endorses a rule that is essentially the same as Hoffmann J's lower risk principle: *see* Laycock's "restatement," *id.* at 273. *See also* Lichtman 2003 (arguing that the optimal decision rule may be more complex than the Posner formula, once one takes into account the variance of courts' predictions concerning the magnitude of the harms each party faces).

[37] *See* Dobbs 1993, 253 § 2.11(2); this was also true in UK law prior to the American Cyanamid decision in 1975, *Am. Cyanamid Co.* v. *Ethicon Ltd.* (HL 1975) (UK).

[38] *See Am. Cyanamid Co.* v. *Ethicon Ltd.* (HL 1975) (UK); *All. for the Wild Rockies* v. *Cottrell* (9th Cir. 2011, p.1134–35) (U.S.) ("A preliminary injunction is appropriate when a plaintiff demonstrates . . . that

Federal Circuit has taken effectively the opposite approach in patent cases; pre-liminary injunctions may be denied solely based on the *defendant* raising a *substantial* question regarding validity or infringement, a standard some judges have criticized as requiring denial if the defendant raises any defense "worthy of consideration."[39]

An alternative approach to addressing disproportionality is to require the plaintiff to agree *ex ante* to compensate the defendant, either partially or fully, should the plaintiff fail to win the case on the merits. In the United States, plaintiffs are generally required as a condition for obtaining a preliminary injunction to post a bond that may be used to compensate the defendant if it is later found to have been wrongfully enjoined.[40] However, the defendant may recover no more than the bond amount, which may result in undercompensation.[41] In many other countries, including at least the United Kingdom, Canada, France, Germany, and Spain, courts normally require a plaintiff to agree *ex ante* to fully compensate the defendant *ex post* should the plaintiff fail to win the case on the merits.[42] Whether full or partial compensation is required, this approach focuses on reducing H_D, because the harm to the defendant if the injunction is "wrongly" granted is only the difference between its true loss and the amount of the compensation. The patentee's expected loss, H_P, is similarly minimized by the prospect of an award of damages if the injunction is refused and the patentee prevails. A court in a jurisdiction that requires full com-pensation to the defendant if the injunction is wrongly granted should be more willing to grant a preliminary injunction than a court in a jurisdiction that requires only partial indemnification.

A combination of these approaches – requiring compensation to the defendant as a condition of granting the preliminary injunction, while at the same time under-taking a modest examination of the merits – is also possible and arguably desirable. Appropriate case management may allow the merits to play a more substantive role in some cases while still avoiding the problem of mini-trials.

An additional concern with preliminary injunctions is that their issuance early in infringement proceedings can, absent appropriate safeguards, sometimes impose an especially high burden on accused infringers. Once accused of patent infringement, a technology user will often explore ways of "designing around" the patent or otherwise avoiding use of potentially infringing technology in future products or

serious questions going to the merits were raised and the balance of hardships tips sharply in the plaintiff's favor." (quoting *Lands Council* v. *McNair* (9th Cir. 2008, p.987) (U.S.) (en banc))).

[39] *Kimberly-Clark Worldwide, Inc.* v. *First Quality Baby Prod., LLC* (Fed. Cir. 2011, p.1298) (U.S.) (Newman, J., dissenting from denial of en banc rehearing) ("No other circuit denies a preliminary injunction merely because the nonmovant has raised an argument worthy of consideration.").

[40] *See* FED. R. CIV. P. 65(c) ("The court may issue a preliminary injunction or a temporary restraining order only if the movant gives security in an amount that the court considers proper to pay the costs and damages sustained by any party found to have been wrongfully enjoined or restrained.").

[41] *See* Grosskopf & Medina 2009, 907–09.

[42] *See* Heath 2008; Montañá 2013; Véron 2012; Dobbs 1993, 263 § 2.11(3).

processes. The grant of a preliminary injunction early in the litigation process may make it expensive and disruptive for the accused infringer to shift to a less legally vulnerable position. If the accused infringer has to entirely suspend production and sale of a complex product during a period of redesign in order to comply with a preliminary injunction, this may allow the patentee to hold up the accused infringer, in the same manner as the grant of a permanent injunction. Refusing a preliminary injunction entirely mitigates the potential for this type of holdup, but may not adequately protect the interests of the patentee. An intermediate approach is to grant the preliminary injunction, subject to a stay. As with permanent injunctions, staying a preliminary injunction to allow more time for such switching can mitigate the possibility of disproportionate hardship to an accused infringer. But of course, a court needs to weigh this potential benefit of delay against the harm that a patent holder is expected to suffer in the meantime.

4.3 COMPARATIVE OVERVIEW OF INJUNCTION PRACTICES

4.3.1 *Overview*

A permanent injunction is an available form of relief in all patent law systems.[43] In all major legal systems injunctions have traditionally been available almost automatically in case of patent infringement, so long as there is some real threat of future infringement. This tradition has come under pressure recently, with the confluence of several factors, including the rise of patent assertion entities (PAEs), litigation over standard-essential patents subject to FRAND commitments, and the general rise in litigation involving complex products, where an injunction to prevent infringement by a minor feature may keep the entire product off the market.

For comparative purposes, the various legal systems can be divided into three broad categories: the United States, other common law countries, and civil law countries. In most civil law countries, such as Germany, a successful patentee is considered to be entitled to an injunction as a matter of right.[44] The ability to obtain injunctive relief may be restrained, however, through various types of generally applied defenses, such as abuse of rights or lack of good faith, as well as by competition law. In countries with a common law tradition, such as England and the United States, injunctive relief has long been recognized as being discretionary in principle, notwithstanding the traditional practice of granting injunctions almost automatically in patent cases. However, since the Supreme Court of the United States decision in *eBay*, practice in the common law countries has diverged. In most countries, including England, there remains a strong presumption in favor of

---

[43] Indeed, the TRIPS Agreement provides that a permanent injunction must be an available remedy: *see* TRIPS Agreement, art. 44(1).

[44] *See* Cotter 2013a, 245–46.

granting injunctive relief. In contrast, in the United States since *eBay*, there is no longer a presumption in favor of injunctive relief.

One noteworthy aspect of the divergence between England and Germany, for example, is that (for the time being) both nations are subject to the EU Enforcement Directive,[45] which deals with civil remedies for violation of IP rights. It is directed to member states, which are left free to decide how they ensure that IP remedies are applied in a manner that complies with the rules prescribed by the directive. The general principles governing application of injunctions may be perfectly respected within a patent system that requires balancing patentees' and implementers' interests in each case, as is the case with systems where injunctive relief is rooted in equity. Equally, these principles may be respected in a patent system where injunctive relief may be denied by resorting to defenses placed "outside" of patent law, such as abuse of rights, breach of rules of good faith, or antitrust/competition law.

Substantively, Article 3 provides that remedies "shall ... be effective, proportionate and dissuasive," Article 11 requires that injunctive relief is an available remedy, and Article 12 provides that injunctive relief may be refused, and pecuniary compensation awarded instead, if the infringer "acted unintentionally and without negligence, if execution of the measures in question would cause him/her disproportionate harm and if pecuniary compensation to the injured party appears reasonably satisfactory." While Article 11 provides that member states must ensure that an injunction aimed at prohibiting the continuation of the infringement "may issue," Article 12 provides that courts "may" order pecuniary compensation in speci-fied circumstances. This appears to contemplate that an injunction will normally issue except in those circumstances. To date, the EU Enforcement Directive does not appear to have had a significant impact on the jurisprudence of the member states with regard to injunctions, perhaps because each state considers that the principles are already embodied in national law (as is the view in England, discussed in more detail below), or because cases that require a deviation from traditional principles to conform with the Directive have not yet arisen. However, it is possible that this will change in the years to come, particularly in light of recent, additional Communications from the European Commission that emphasize the Enforcement Directive's principle of proportionality.[46]

---

[45] Directive 2004/48/EC.

[46] European Commission, at 18, COM (2017) 708 final (stating, inter alia, that courts should ensure, on a case-by-case basis, that injunctions be consistent with the principle of proportionality; that injunc-tions "should have the minimal scope necessary to accomplish this objective"; and that it "is not necessary that the measures required by the injunction lead to a complete cessation of the IPR infringements"); European Commission, at 10, COM (2017) 712 final (similar).

4.3.2 *United States*

1 *eBay* Principles

The U.S. Patent Act provides that an injunction may be granted as a remedy for patent infringement, "in accordance with the principles of equity."[47] Prior to the decision of the Supreme Court of the United States in *eBay* v. *MercExchange*,[48] nearly all patentees who sought injunctive relief received a permanent injunction after prevailing on liability,[49] and the Federal Circuit in the decision on appeal had stated that "the general rule is that a permanent injunction will issue once infringement and validity have been adjudged."[50] In *eBay*, the Supreme Court held that "a plaintiff seeking a permanent injunction must satisfy a four-factor test before a court may grant such relief."[51] The Court described this test as being in accordance with "well-established principles of equity," but some scholars have disputed whether the test set out in *eBay* is consistent with traditional equitable principles previously applied by U.S. courts.[52] Whether it was a return to, or departure from, traditional principles, the *eBay* decision has had a major impact on the practice of injunctive relief, particularly in patent cases. Prior to *eBay* injunctions were granted to prevailing patentees in almost all cases, but since *eBay* motions for permanent injunctions have been granted approximately three quarters of the time.[53] This overview describes U.S. law post-*eBay*.

In *eBay* the Supreme Court rejected both a categorical rule in favor of permanent injunctions and a categorical denial of injunctions based on certain "expansive principles."[54] The Court identified a four-factor test to guide courts' exercise of their discretion to grant injunctions. Writing for the Court, Justice Thomas explained that the patent owner "must demonstrate" four factors:

> (1) that it has suffered an irreparable injury; (2) that remedies available at law, such as monetary damages, are inadequate to compensate for that injury; (3) that, considering the balance of hardships between the plaintiff and defendant,

---

[47] U.S. Patent Act, 35 U.S.C. § 283. There are some statutory exceptions, unrelated to complex products: *see, e.g., id.* at § 287(c). Patent owners may also obtain exclusion orders from the International Trade Commission. The relevant inquiry differs (*see Spansion, Inc.* v. *Int'l Trade Comm'n* (Fed. Cir. 2010, p.1359) (U.S.)), and is not considered in this overview.

[48] *eBay Inc.* v. *MercExchange, L.L.C.* (U.S. 2006) (U.S.).

[49] *See id.* at 395 (Roberts, C.J., concurring) ("From at least the early 19th century, courts have granted injunctive relief upon a finding of infringement in the vast majority of patent cases.").

[50] *MercExchange, LLC* v. *eBay, Inc.* (Fed. Cir. 2005, p.1338) (U.S.).

[51] *eBay Inc.* v. *MercExchange, L.L.C.* (U.S. 2006, p.391) (U.S.).

[52] *See* Gergen et al. 2012.

[53] Seaman 2016, 1983 (reporting on the basis of an empirical study that since *eBay* "permanent injunctions were granted slightly less than three-quarters of the time (72.5%)," and noting this is consistent with previous empirical scholarship finding grant rates ranging between 72 percent and 75 percent).

[54] *eBay Inc.* v. *MercExchange, L.L.C.* (U.S. 2006, p.393) (U.S.).

a remedy in equity is warranted; and (4) that the public interest would not be disserved by a permanent injunction.[55]

As interpreted by the Federal Circuit, all four parts of the test must be individually satisfied (i.e., proven like elements, rather than weighed as factors) for a permanent injunction to be granted,[56] and it is in any event clear that an injunction will not be granted unless the patentee can establish that it has suffered irreparable injury, regardless of the balance of hardships.[57]

Justice Kennedy, joined by three other Justices, wrote a concurring opinion that has proven influential.[58] He highlighted three concerns he viewed as new: (1) firms using patents "not as a basis for producing and selling goods but, instead, primarily for obtaining licensing fees"; (2) situations where "the patented invention is but a small component of the product the companies seek to produce and the threat of an injunction is employed simply for undue leverage in negotiations"; and (3) the "burgeoning number of patents over business methods."[59]

Indeed, as discussed in the sections below, lower courts applying the *eBay* test often appear to be influenced more by concerns similar to those expressed by Justice Kennedy than by the formal test enunciated by the Court. Accordingly, rather than orient the discussion that follows around the factors set out in *eBay* itself, we frame the discussion in terms of the factors empirically identified by Seaman (2016) as being the most important determinants of whether an injunction will be granted. Consequently, we pay little attention to factors such as the balance of hardships and the public interest, which, while prominent in the formal *eBay* test, play a relatively small role in practice in the context of complex products. The factors identified by Seaman do not correspond directly to the *eBay* factors, though they are all encompassed in the *eBay* test. For example, the status of the patentee, as a competitor or a nonpracticing entity, is not expressly a factor under *eBay*, but is raised as part of the irreparable harm analysis.

---

[55] *Id.* at 391.

[56] As interpreted by the Federal Circuit, *eBay* requires patentees to satisfy all four parts of the test in order to obtain an injunction. *Nichia Corp.* v. *Everlight Ams., Inc.* (Fed. Cir. 2017) (U.S.) (holding that an injunction should be denied unless all four factors are satisfied). Such a rule is inconsistent with traditional equitable practice, *see* Gergen et al. 2012, 207–08, and arguably also at odds with contemporaneous case law developed by at least some other U.S. Courts of Appeals, *see, e.g., Citigroup Glob. Mkts., Inc.* v. *VCG Special Opportunities Master Fund Ltd.* (2nd Cir. 2010, p.35) (U.S.) (holding that a party seeking a preliminary injunction must "show (a) irreparable harm and (b) either (1) likelihood of success on the merits or (2) sufficiently serious questions going to the merits to make them a fair ground for litigation and a balance of hardships tipping decidedly toward the party requesting the preliminary relief" (internal quotation marks omitted)).

[57] *See Winter* v. *Natural Resources Defense Council, Inc.* (U.S. 2008) (U.S.).

[58] *See* Seaman 2016, 1989.

[59] *eBay Inc.* v. *MercExchange, L.L.C.* (U.S. 2006, p.396–97) (U.S.) (Kennedy, J., concurring).

2 Irreparable Injury

A) GENERAL. Prior to *eBay*, courts applied a rarely rebutted presumption that prevailing patentees would suffer irreparable harm in the absence of an injunction, but the Supreme Court overruled that presumption in *eBay*.[60] Under what we take to be the best view of the first *eBay* factor, a patent owner must demonstrate that it would suffer irreparable injury if an injunction were not granted.[61] Confusingly, however, the Supreme Court stated that a patent owner must demonstrate "that it *has* suffered an irreparable injury."[62] The Federal Circuit has acknowledged that "by its terms the first *eBay* factor looks, in part, at what has already occurred" and accordingly held that a district court did not err in "consider[ing] evidence of past harm" in deciding whether to issue an injunction.[63]

A recent study, Seaman (2016), has shown that loss of market share is by far the most common reason for a district court finding irreparable harm.[64] Other important reasons include price erosion, loss of goodwill or damage to a brand or reputation, and loss of future business opportunities.[65] A patentee that competes in the same market as the infringer more easily establishes these reasons for irreparable harm as compared to a patentee that does not compete with the infringer. The infringer's potential inability to pay money damages is the only one of the six most important reasons for finding irreparable harm that is not related to the competitive status of the parties, and it is the least common of the six.[66] Consequently, as discussed in more detail below, a patentee that competes with the infringer is much more likely to be granted an injunction than one that does not.

The second factor asks whether legal remedies are adequate compensation. Despite the Supreme Court identifying two separate factors, the first and second factors ask essentially the same question.[67]

B) CAUSAL NEXUS. An aspect of the irreparable harm requirement as interpreted by the Federal Circuit is that there must be a causal nexus between the infringement and the irreparable harm. It is not enough that the patentee would suffer irreparable harm if the sale and distribution of the infringing product were not enjoined; the

---

[60] *Apple, Inc.* v. *Samsung Elecs. Co., Ltd.* (Fed. Cir. 2015, p.649) (U.S.) (*Apple IV*).
[61] Literally, the Court stated that the patent owner must show that it "has" suffered an irreparable injury, but despite the use of the past tense, it was initially understood conditionally by a number of courts. See Gergen et al. 2012, 209–10.
[62] *eBay Inc.* v. *MercExchange, L.L.C.* (U.S. 2006, p.391) (U.S.) (emphasis added).
[63] *i4i Ltd. Partnership* v. *Microsoft Corp.* (Fed. Cir. 2010, p.861–62) (U.S.).
[64] Seaman 2016, 1993 ("[T]he most common reason by far for finding irreparable harm was loss of market share (80%).").
[65] *Id.* at 1992–93.
[66] *Id.* (finding that inability to pay is the basis for a finding of irreparable harm in only 5 percent of cases in which irreparable harm is established).
[67] Gergen et al. 2012, 207–08 ("[T]he test redundantly states requirements of irreparable injury and inadequacy of legal remedies."); see also Seaman 2016, 1994 (revealing a very strong positive relationship between these first two factors).

patentee must suffer that harm because of the infringement. As the Federal Circuit explained in *Apple II*:

> where the accused product includes many features of which only one (or a small minority) infringe – a finding that the patentee will be at risk of irreparable harm does not alone justify injunctive relief. Rather, the patentee must also establish that the harm is sufficiently related to the infringement.[68]

As illustrated by this example, the causal nexus requirement is particularly relevant to patents covering complex products.[69]

Some Federal Circuit decisions have used language suggesting that the patented technology must "drive demand" for the product,[70] which might largely preclude injunctive relief in complex product cases. However, in *Genband US LLC v. Metaswitch Networks Corp.* the Federal Circuit explained that at least in the context of a complex product, "in which only a component of a larger product or system is covered by the patent in suit,"[71] it is not necessary for the infringing feature to be the sole driver of demand. When the patentee relies on lost sales to show irreparable harm, the causal nexus can be established by showing that the infringing features significantly increased the product's desirability,[72] or that they impact customers' purchasing decisions.[73] On the other hand, "[i]f all but an insignificant number of purchases from the infringer would have been made even without the infringing feature, the causal connection to the asserted lost-sale-based injury is missing."[74]

3 Balance of Hardships and Public Interest

The third part of the *eBay* test assesses the relative effect on the parties of granting or denying an injunction, while the fourth looks to the public interest.[75] In contrast with the requirement that the patentee establish irreparable harm, which is often the sole reason for denying injunctive relief, these factors rarely constitute the sole basis for denying injunctive relief, except in the case of medical devices.[76]

---

[68] *Apple, Inc. v. Samsung Elecs. Co., Ltd.* (Fed. Cir. 2012, p.1374) (U.S.) (*Apple II*); *see also id.* at 1373, 1374 (explaining that the causal nexus requirement is part of the irreparable harm factor).

[69] In principle, "the causal nexus requirement applies regardless of the complexity of the products," but "[i]t just may be more easily satisfied (indeed, perhaps even conceded) for relatively 'simple' products." *Apple, Inc. v. Samsung Elecs. Co., Ltd.* (Fed. Cir. 2013, p.1362) (U.S.) (*Apple III*).

[70] *See, e.g., Apple, Inc. v. Samsung Elecs. Co., Ltd.* (Fed. Cir. 2012, p.1324) (U.S.) (*Apple I*); *Apple, Inc. v. Samsung Elecs. Co., Ltd.* (Fed. Cir. 2012, p.1375) (U.S.) (*Apple II*).

[71] *Genband US LLC v. Metaswitch Networks Corp.* (Fed. Cir. 2017, p.1384) (U.S.).

[72] *Id.*

[73] *Id.* at 1383, quoting *Apple, Inc. v. Samsung Elecs. Co., Ltd.* (Fed. Cir. 2015, p.642) (U.S.) (*Apple IV*).

[74] *Genband US LLC v. Metaswitch Networks Corp.* (Fed. Cir. 2017, p.1384) (U.S.).

[75] *eBay Inc. v. MercExchange, L.L.C.* (U.S. 2006, p.392) (U.S.).

[76] Seaman 2016, 1991–92, 1995.

4 Status of the Patentee

Some commentators have suggested that injunctions should be more readily granted to patentees who would have been unwilling to license to the infringer, because the patentee is seeking to enforce market exclusivity, either for itself as a competitor in the market with the infringer, or for a handful of exclusive licensees,[77] and some district courts have relied upon the willing/unwilling licensor distinction to deny injunctive relief to patent owners deemed to be willing licensors.[78] In *eBay*, the Supreme Court rejected the proposition that a plaintiff's willingness to license its patents and its lack of commercial activity in practicing the patents would be sufficient to establish that the patent holder would not suffer irreparable harm if an injunction did not issue, but the Court gave as counterexamples patent holders such as university researchers or self-made inventors who might prefer to license rather than bring their works to market themselves.[79] As noted above, in his concurrence, Justice Kennedy suggested that injunctions should be more readily refused to firms using patents "not as a basis for producing and selling goods but, instead, primarily for obtaining licensing fees," which is to say, patent assertion entities, as distinct from other types of nonpracticing entities mentioned in the Court's opinion. Moreover, while the Federal Circuit has held that it is not error for a district court to consider evidence of past licensing behavior, the evidence must be considered in the context of all of the evidence.[80] In particular, a district court errs, according to the Federal Circuit, when it finds that monetary damages will be adequate to compensate the patent owner based on the mere fact that the patent owner "is willing to license the asserted ... patents in some circumstances," and even if there also is evidence that the patent owner "is willing to license some patents to [the infringer]."[81]

In terms of the district court practice since *eBay*, Seaman (2016) has shown that a patent owner's willingness to license the asserted patent has not, as such, proven to be a statistically significant circumstance pointing toward the denial of injunctive relief.[82] However, Seaman (2016) defines willingness to license very broadly, to

---

[77] Lee & Melamed 2016, 445; Lemley & Shapiro 2007a, 2036.

[78] *See, e.g., Telcordia Tech., Inc. v. Cisco Sys., Inc.* (D. Del. 2009, p.748 n.10) (U.S.) (noting the patent owner's "willingness to license its patents also suggests that its injury is compensable in monetary damages, which is inconsistent with the right to exclude"); *Sundance, Inc. v. DeMonte Fabricating Ltd.* (E.D. Mich. 2007, p.2) (U.S.) (stating that "licens[ing] the [infringed patent] to others, and offer[ing] to license it to [the infringer] prior to filing suit ... demonstrat[e] that money damages are adequate").

[79] *eBay Inc. v. MercExchange, L.L.C.* (U.S. 2006, p.393) (U.S.).

[80] *Apple, Inc. v. Samsung Elecs. Co., Ltd.* (Fed. Cir. 2013, p.1370) (U.S.) (*Apple III*).

[81] *Id.*

[82] Seaman 2016, 198–99 ("[S]everal other factors identified in the existing literature as relevant to the injunction calculus appear not to be statistically significant and/or do not have the anticipated impact. For instance, a patentee's willingness to license the patent(s)-in-suit is actually positively correlated with injunctive relief after controlling for all other factors, although this finding is not statistically significant.") (footnotes omitted).

include any case in which there was evidence that the patentee was willing to license to any other party in at least one instance, even if the patentee did not have a general practice of licensing. Seaman (2016) also found that the presence of competition between the patent owner and the infringer has proven to be the single most significant circumstance corresponding to the provision of injunctive relief: "Patent holders who competed with an infringer were granted a permanent injunction in the overwhelming majority of cases (84%; 150 of 179 cases), while patentees who were not market competitors rarely succeeded in obtaining injunctive relief (21%; 8 of 39 cases)."[83] PAEs in particular rarely obtain injunctive relief.[84] In fact, some commentators have gone so far as to suggest that "district courts appear to have adopted a de facto rule against injunctive relief for [patent assertion entities] and other patent owners who do not directly compete in a product market against an infringer."[85] The doctrinal mechanism turns primarily on the irreparable harm requirement; as noted above, the factors that most commonly establish irreparable harm are associated with the patentee (or its exclusive licensee) being an active competitor in the relevant market.

Broadly, all of this suggests that patentees who seek market exclusivity, either for themselves or for a small number of licensees, are able to obtain injunctive relief more easily than those who do not seek market exclusivity but instead only licensing fees, especially PAEs.

5 Behavior of the Plaintiff

The Federal Circuit recently held that laches, or undue delay, is a defense that bars injunctive relief even when courts find infringement of valid and otherwise enforceable patents.[86] Under the *eBay* approach this traditional equitable factor may be relevant to the balance of hardships or irreparable harm.[87] Presumably courts would consider other traditional equitable factors relating to the behavior of the plaintiff, such as the requirement that the plaintiff have "clean hands," in appropriate circumstances. However, these equitable factors have to date not played a major role in denial of injunctive relief in respect of an otherwise enforceable patent.[88]

---

[83] *Id.* at 1990–91 ("Patent holders who competed with an infringer were granted a permanent injunction in the overwhelming majority of cases (84%; 150 of 179 cases), while patentees who were not market competitors rarely succeeded in obtaining injunctive relief (21%; 8 of 39 cases).").

[84] Seaman 2016, 1988 (noting that PAEs received injunctions in the district court only 16 percent of the time); *id.* at 1952–53 (noting that "while the vast majority of patentees still obtain injunctive relief following eBay, [patent assertion entities] rarely do"). PAEs are somewhat more successful on appeal to the Federal Circuit, though the sample is small: *see* Holte & Seaman 2017, 200.

[85] Seaman 2016, 1953.

[86] *SCA Hygiene Prod. Aktiebolag v. First Quality Baby Prod., LLC* (Fed. Cir. 2015, p.1317) (U.S.).

[87] *Id.* at 1331.

[88] The most prominent invocation of unclean hands is in respect of the defense of "inequitable conduct," which while frequently pled is very rarely proven. *See Therasense, Inc. v. Becton, Dickinson, & Co.* (Fed. Cir. 2011, p. 1285) (en banc) ("Inequitable conduct is an equitable defense

6 Tailoring

U.S. courts have tailored injunctive relief to fit the particular circumstances of patent cases and to avoid inequitable results.[89] In particular, "[c]ourts sometimes will delay the full effectiveness of injunctions to avoid some of the special disruption or other hardship that an immediately effective order might cause."[90] Such tailoring has included a stay of the effect to allow redesign,[91] or a "sunset" provision, allowing the infringer to continue to sell into an existing market,[92] or both.[93] One court has suggested that the Federal Circuit "has expressed a preference for injunctive relief that is tailored to minimize disruptions to businesses and consumers."[94] In some of these cases a significant concern is the hardship to the infringer's customers, rather than that to the infringer itself.[95]

A stay may also be granted pending appeal, but the purpose of such a stay is to mitigate the risk of injustice if the trial decision is reversed, and the considerations are generally different – in particular, courts consider the likelihood of success on the merits when analyzing a motion for a stay pending appeal.[96] The effect of a stay pending appeal may be to allow the infringer time to design around the patent, but its purpose is different.

7 Complex Products

As already indicated in the discussion of the causal nexus requirement, U.S. courts have developed particular aspects of the law governing the provision of injunctive relief in patent cases involving complex products. In his concurrence in *eBay*, Justice Kennedy suggested that an injunction might not serve the public interest

to patent infringement that . . . evolved from a trio of Supreme Court cases that applied the doctrine of unclean hands to dismiss patent cases involving egregious misconduct.").

[89] *See generally* Golden 2012. In *Apple, Inc.* v. *Samsung Elecs. Co., Ltd.* (Fed. Cir. 2013, p.1370) (U.S.) (*Apple III*) the Federal Circuit noted that "a delay in enforcement may make an injunction more equitable and, thus, more justifiable in any given case."

[90] Golden 2012, 1461.

[91] *See, e.g.*, *B. Braun Melsungen AG* v. *Terumo Med. Corp.* (D. Del. 2011, p.524) (U.S.); *Metso Minerals, Inc.* v. *Powerscreen Int'l Distribution Ltd.* (E.D.N.Y. 2011, p.77) (U.S.).

[92] *Broadcom Corp.* v. *Qualcomm Inc.* (C.D. Cal. 2007) (U.S.) *aff'd on this point Broadcom Corp.* v. *Qualcomm Inc.* (Fed. Cir. 2008, p.704) (U.S.).

[93] *Broadcom Corp.* v. *Emulex Corp.* (C.D. Cal. 2012) (U.S.) *aff'd Broadcom Corp.* v. *Emulex Corp.* (Fed. Cir. 2013) (U.S.).

[94] *Metso Minerals, Inc.* v. *Powerscreen Int'l Distribution Ltd.* (E.D.N.Y. 2011, p.77) (U.S.), citing *Broadcom Corp.* v. *Qualcomm Inc.* (Fed. Cir. 2008, p.704) (U.S.) and *Verizon Servs. Corp.* v. *Vonage Holdings Corp.* (Fed. Cir. 2007, p.1311 n.12) (U.S.).

[95] *See, e.g.*, *Broadcom Corp.* v. *Emulex Corp.* (Fed. Cir. 2013) (U.S.); *Broadcom Corp.* v. *Qualcomm Inc.* (Fed. Cir. 2008) (U.S.).

[96] *See E.I. DuPont De Nemours & Co.* v. *Phillips Petroleum Co.* (Fed. Cir. 1987, p.278) (U.S.) ("In considering whether to grant a stay pending appeal, this court assesses movant's chances for success on appeal and weighs the equities as they affect the parties and the public."); *see also Hilton* v. *Braunskill* (U.S. 1987, p.776) (U.S.) (discussing factors relevant to granting a stay pending appeal).

"[w]hen the patented invention is but a small component of the product the [infringer] seek[s] to produce."[97] This advice appears to have taken root at the district court level: "[w]hen a patent is found to cover a small component, district courts rarely grant an injunction."[98] In such cases the district courts are reluctant to grant an injunction even when the patentee and infringer are competitors.[99]

In *Apple IV*, the Federal Circuit emphasized that the requirement that there be a causal nexus between the infringement and the irreparable harm suffered by the patentee applies even when the injunction is narrowed to apply only to an infringing feature rather than to the infringing product.[100] This implies that an injunction should not be granted if the patented technology does not significantly increase the product's desirability.

8 Standard-Essential Patents

Another relevant circumstance is whether the asserted patent is a standard-essential patent. While the Federal Circuit has rejected any per se rule that injunctions are unavailable with respect to standard-essential patents, it confirmed that commitments to license on fair, reasonable, and nondiscriminatory (FRAND) terms are relevant when analyzing the entitlement to injunctive relief.[101] The court has explained that, on the one hand, "[a] patentee subject to FRAND commitments may have difficulty establishing irreparable harm."[102] But, "[o]n the other hand, an injunction may be justified where an infringer unilaterally refuses a FRAND royalty or unreasonably delays negotiations to the same effect."[103] These issues are discussed in greater detail in Chapter 5.

4.3.3 *England*

In England, the principles on which an injunction is granted or denied in the context of patent law are the same as for property rights generally, including rights in land.[104] It is well established in English law that the grant of a permanent injunction is discretionary in principle, but a plaintiff whose legal

---

[97]   *eBay Inc. v. MercExchange, L.L.C.* (U.S. 2006, p.396) (U.S.).
[98]   Seaman 2016, 1998 (noting also that the effect is statistically significant); *see also id.* at 1998 n.304 (noting that "[d]istrict courts only granted injunctions 14% of the time (2 of 14 cases) where the district court found that the patent covered a 'small component.'").
[99]   *Id.* at 1991–92.
[100] *Apple, Inc. v. Samsung Elecs. Co., Ltd.* (Fed. Cir. 2015, p.640) (U.S.) (*Apple IV*).
[101] *Apple, Inc. v. Motorola, Inc.* (Fed. Cir. 2014, p.1331) (U.S.).
[102] *Id.* at 1332.
[103] *Id.*
[104] The power to grant injunctive relief stems from the inherent jurisdiction of the courts of equity, which was conferred on the Supreme Court of Judicature by the fusion of the courts of common law and equity in the late nineteenth century.

right has been violated is presumptively, or "prima facie," entitled to the grant of an injunction, and it is said that "the court will only rarely and reluctantly permit such violation to occur or continue."[105] The primary test is whether the effect of the grant of the injunction would be grossly disproportionate to the right protected.[106] The discretionary nature of injunctive relief is not considered inconsistent with proprietary rights, because the relief itself, as an equitable remedy, is inherently discretionary.[107]

If injunctive relief is refused, damages are normally awarded in lieu thereof.[108] If actual loss cannot be proven as a consequence of the violation of the right, damages will normally be awarded on the basis of the amount of money that could reasonably have been demanded by the plaintiff for her consent to the breach.[109] This is essentially the same "hypothetical negotiation" measure that is used when assessing damages for past infringement when the patentee does not, or cannot, claim lost profits.[110]

1 Traditional Principles

In *Shelfer* v. *City of London Elec. Lighting Co,*[111] AL Smith LJ said that as "a good working rule" an injunction might properly be refused, and damages awarded in lieu of an injunction, if the following conditions were all satisfied:

(i)   the injury to the plaintiff's legal right is small;
(ii) is one that is capable of being estimated in money;

---

[105]   *Jaggard* v. *Sawyer* (Civ 1995, p.202) (UK); *see also HTC Corp.* v. *Nokia Corp.* (Pat 2013, ¶ 8) (UK) (summarizing the law as being that a claimant is "prima facie" entitled to an injunction to restrain a person from committing an act that invades the claimant's legal right, and stating that "it is only in special circumstances that the court will exercise its discretion to award damages in lieu of an injunction"); and *Banks* v. *EMI Songs Ltd.* (No 2) (Ch 1996, p.457) (UK) ("The normal rule is that an injunction will be granted when there has been an infringement of a proprietary right, such as a copyright.").

[106]   *Navitaire Inc.* v. *easyJet Airline Co. Ltd.* (No.2) (Ch 2005, p.250) (UK), quoted with approval in *Virgin Atlantic* v. *Premium Aircraft* (Civ 2009, ¶ 24) (UK); *see also id.* at ¶ 25 (stating that for refusal of a permanent injunction "[t]he test is whether enforcement would be 'grossly disproportionate'"); *see similarly Jaggard* v. *Sawyer* (Civ 1995, p.208) (UK), per Millett LJ (referring to "a loss out of all proportion to that which would be suffered by the plaintiff if it were refused").

[107]   *See Jaggard* v. *Sawyer* (Civ 1995, p.207) (UK), per Millett LJ (stating that "references to the 'expropriation' of the plaintiff's property are somewhat overdone, not because that is not the practical effect of withholding an injunction, but because the grant of an injunction, like all equitable remedies, is discretionary").

[108]   The power to grant damages in lieu of an injunction as compensation for the future continued violation of the right stems from the Chancery Amendment Act 1858, 21 & 22 Vict. c. 27, s. 2 (Lord Cairns' Act); *see Jaggard* v. *Sawyer* (Civ 1995, p.204) (UK).

[109]   *Jaggard* v. *Sawyer* (Co Ct 1993, p.202–03, 213) (UK), relying on *Wrotham Park Estate Co.* v. *Parkside Homes Ltd.* (Ch 1974) (UK). This approach is often referred to as the "*Wrotham Park* basis" for assessing damages.

[110]   *HTC Corp.* v. *Nokia Corp.* (Pat 2013, ¶ 13) (UK).

[111]   *Shelfer* v. *City of London Elec. Lighting Co.* (Civ 1895) (UK).

(iii) is one that can be adequately compensated by a small money payment;

(iv) and the case is one in which it would be oppressive to the defendant to grant an injunction.

These are only guidelines, not a test,[112] but have been influential and are widely considered when the refusal of an injunction is in issue.

2 Proportionality

In practice, it appears that the most important consideration is the fourth.[113] The word "oppressive" is understood to mean that "the effect of the grant of the injunction would be grossly disproportionate to the right protected."[114] The harm to the defendant from the grant of an injunction must be substantial for it to be oppressive, and given that the injury to the plaintiff's legal right is small, it follows that the grant would be disproportionate. Moreover, "[t]he word 'grossly' avoids any suggestion that all that has to be done is to strike a balance of convenience."[115]

The most common type of property case in which an injunction is refused is "where the plaintiff has sought a mandatory injunction to pull down a building which infringes his right to light or which has been built in breach of a restrictive covenant,"[116] in circumstances in which the loss to the plaintiff resulting from the breach is small. Though the cases do not use the term, this is a classic case in which the defendant has incurred substantial sunk costs, and substantial value expected from that investment would be lost if the injunction were enforced.

The UK courts have recognized that the harm may be disproportionate even if the injunction is not enforced but is instead used for bargaining leverage. As was famously said, in such a case an injunction would "deliver over the Defendants to the Plaintiff bound hand and foot, in order to be made subject to any extortionate demand that he may by possibility make."[117] Thus the concern is not solely the waste that would be incurred if the building were actually torn down, but the injustice entailed by giving such bargaining leverage to the plaintiff.

---

[112] *HTC Corp.* v. *Nokia Corp.* (Pat 2013, ¶ 8) (UK) ("Subsequent cases have emphasised that AL Smith LJ's good working rule is only that: it is not a statute or straightjacket.").

[113] *Jaggard* v. *Sawyer* (Civ 1995, p.208) (UK) per Millett LJ ("The outcome of any particular case usually turns on the question: would it in all the circumstances be oppressive to the defendant to grant the injunction to which the plaintiff is prima facie entitled?").

[114] *Navitaire Inc.* v. *easyJet Airline Co. Ltd.* (No.2) (Ch 2005, p.250) (UK), quoted with approval in *Virgin Atlantic* v. *Premium Aircraft* (Civ 2009, ¶ 24) (UK); *see also id.* at ¶ 25 ("[A]lthough the case for withholding the injunction has to be strong, it is clear that a permanent injunction can be withheld, indeed even on a permanent basis. The test is whether enforcement would be 'grossly disproportionate.'"); and *see similarly Jaggard* v. *Sawyer* (Civ 1995, p.208) (UK), per Millett LJ (referring to "a loss out of all proportion to that which would be suffered by the plaintiff if it were refused").

[115] *Navitaire Inc.* v. *easyJet Airline Co. Ltd.* (No.2) (Ch 2005, p.250) (UK).

[116] *Jaggard* v. *Sawyer* (Civ 1995, p.208) (UK).

[117] *Isenberg* v. *East India House Estate Co. Ltd.* (Ct Ch 1863, p.641) (UK) per Lord Westbury LC, quoted in *Jaggard* v. *Sawyer* (Civ 1995, p.207) (UK), and referred to *id.* at 208.

3 Adequacy of Damages

The second *Shelfer* factor asks whether the value of the injury to the plaintiff's right is capable of being estimated in money. This is essentially the same question as whether damages would be an adequate remedy under the *eBay* test.[118] The second *Shelfer* factor nonetheless plays a very different role from irreparable harm under *eBay*, because it is a condition for refusing, not granting, an injunction. Under *eBay* the patentee's failure to establish irreparable harm often justifies refusal of injunctive relief. In contrast, under *Shelfer*, if the right is capable of being estimated in money, an injunction will nonetheless be granted unless doing so would be oppressive. Adequacy of damages is important only where the effect of the injunction would be grossly disproportionate, in which case an injunction might nonetheless be granted if damages would not be adequate. This scenario appears to be rare, however.

Similarly, under the first and third *Shelfer* factors, the loss to the plaintiff must be small, even if the loss to the defendant is disproportionately larger. In cases in which injunctive relief is found to be disproportionate, it is typically also the case that the objective injury to the plaintiff appears to be small, and there are few cases in which an injunction is granted even though its effect would be disproportionate, on the basis that the harm to the plaintiff is large.[119]

4 Status of the Plaintiff

The UK courts generally do not consider whether the plaintiff really wanted to enforce exclusivity, or was willing to license.[120] An exception is the Court of Appeal decision in *Gafford v. Graham*, in which the Court of Appeal refused to grant an injunction ordering the demolition of a building built in breach of a restrictive covenant, in part because the plaintiff was willing to accept money.[121] However, this was also a case in which granting the injunction was expected to have a disproportionate effect. Arnold J in *HTC Corp. v. Nokia Corp.*, a patent case, recognized the authority of *Gafford* on this point,[122] but he went on to hold that whether the patentee sought market exclusivity or leverage in licensing negotiations is irrelevant to whether an injunction should be granted.

---

[118] See *Shelfer v. City of London Elec. Lighting Co.* (Civ 1895, p.845) (UK) per Lindley LJ (remarking that an injunction might properly be refused in cases "where an action for damages is really an adequate remedy").

[119] Though *Shelfer* itself might be an example, as the injunction was granted on the basis that the injury to the plaintiff was not small, nor capable of being estimated in money, without consideration of proportionality: *see id.* at 848, per Smith LJ.

[120] Generally, as in e.g., *Jaggard v. Sawyer* (Civ 1995) (UK), there is no discussion of this issue at all.

[121] *Gafford v. Graham* (Civ 1998, p.84–86) (UK).

[122] *HTC Corp. v. Nokia Corp.* (Pat 2013, ¶ 11) (UK).

5 Behavior of the Plaintiff

As an injunction is an equitable remedy, traditional equitable bars to relief apply, including laches (unreasonable delay) and acquiescence.[123] The requirement that the party seeking relief must come to equity with clean hands applies in principle. However, there appear to be few if any cases in which this played a significant role in denying injunctive relief on the facts.

Beyond this, in one case an injunction was refused in part because the plaintiff had not sought an interlocutory injunction, though there was no question of laches or acquiescence;[124] and it has been suggested that an injunction will not be granted if the plaintiff, knowing of the defendant's actions, stands by without acting on his rights.[125] However, these have been cases in which the effect of the injunction would have been disproportionate to the harm suffered by the plaintiff. The principle here appears to be that a rights owner cannot obtain an injunction with disproportionate effect if the plaintiff, by acting more promptly, might have enforced its rights with less burden on the defendant.

6 Behavior of the Defendant

If the defendant acted "in good faith and in ignorance of the plaintiff's rights" this will weigh against an injunction.[126] That is true even if the defendant might in principle have ascertained her true rights in advance.[127] Conversely, the usual view is that a defendant who has behaved badly, in particular by proceeding with knowledge that it would be acting in violation of the plaintiff's rights, would not be entitled to relief from an injunction even if the effect would be disproportionate.[128] However, the English courts appear very reluctant to grant an injunction that would be oppressive, particularly one that would involve pulling down a building, and such injunctions have sometimes been refused even in the face of bad-faith conduct by the defendant.[129]

---

[123] *See, e.g., Gafford v. Graham* (Civ 1998) (UK) (refusing an injunction due to acquiescence).

[124] *Jaggard v. Sawyer* (Civ 1995, p.209) (UK).

[125] *Gafford v. Graham* (Civ 1998, p.73–74) (UK).

[126] *Jaggard v. Sawyer* (Civ 1995, p.209) (UK); and similarly, *Jaggard v. Sawyer* (Co Ct 1993, p.209) (UK) (refusing an injunction, in part because the defendants acted "in good faith and in the not unreasonable belief" that they were entitled to make use of road).

[127] *Jaggard v. Sawyer* (Co Ct 1993, p.199) (UK) (noting that the defendant "might have shown more care in the investigation of his position. I put that down to his inexperience in a complicated situation.").

[128] *Jaggard v. Sawyer* (Civ 1995, p.209) (UK); *Shelfer v. City of London Elec. Lighting Co.* (Civ 1895, p.848) (UK).

[129] *See Gafford v. Graham* (Civ 1998, p.79) (UK) (noting that the defendant had built "in blatant and calculated disregard of the plaintiff's rights."); *Wrotham Park Estate Co. v. Parkside Homes Ltd.* (Ch 1974) (UK) (noting that the defendant built houses after having been served with the writ claiming breach of the restrictive covenant).

7 Effect of the EU Enforcement Directive

As noted above, the EU Enforcement Directive provides that courts may issue an injunction for the infringement of IP rights and that damages in lieu may be granted under certain conditions.[130] It has not been specifically implemented in the United Kingdom, on the view that the court's existing general powers under UK law are sufficient to ensure compliance with the relevant provisions of the Directive.[131]

Even so, the EU Enforcement Directive has been referred to in several cases, and in a 2013 decision in *HTC Corp.* v. *Nokia Corp.*, Arnold J stated that in light of the EU Enforcement Directive,

> the time has come to recognise that, in cases concerning infringements of intellectual property rights, the criteria to be applied when deciding whether or not to grant an injunction are those laid down by art.3(2): efficacy, proportionality, dissuasiveness, the avoidance of creating barriers to legitimate trade and the provision of safeguards against abuse.[132]

It is doubtful whether this is significantly different from the traditional UK position, at least so far as the requirement of proportionality is concerned.[133] The factors set out in Article 13 for refusing injunctive relief have not been specifically discussed.

8 Tailoring

The leading case on staying a permanent injunction is *Virgin Atlantic* v. *Premium Aircraft*. The Court of Appeal held that the test for staying a permanent injunction is the same "grossly disproportionate" test that applies to denying the injunction.[134] On the facts, the Court of Appeal granted a two-month period of "runoff" allowing the

---

[130] Directive 2004/48/EC, arts. 11, 12.

[131] *HTC Corp.* v. *Nokia Corp.* (Pat 2013, ¶ 21) (UK).

[132] *Id.* at ¶ 26. *See also* Ohly 2009, 274 ("Although the Enforcement Directive aims at a high standard of protection, it does not unilaterally benefit right holders. While the need for effective protection of intellectual property is evident, the principle of proportionality must also be taken into account.").

[133] In *Vestergaard Frandsen A/S* v. *Bestnet Europe Ltd.* (Civ 2011, ¶ 56) (UK) Jacob LJ raised the issue of whether traditional English law principles of injunctive relief embody the concept of proportionality, and remarked "I rather think they do." In *Virgin Atlantic* v. *Premium Aircraft* (Civ 2009, ¶¶ 23–25) (UK), Jacob LJ expressly approved Pumfrey J's test in *Navitaire Inc.* v. *easyJet Airline Co. Ltd.* (No.2) (Ch 2005, p.250) (UK), which was based on traditional *Shelfer* factors, as being consistent with Article 3 of the Enforcement Directive. In *HTC Corp.* v. *Nokia Corp.* (Pat 2013, ¶ 32) (UK), Arnold J remarked that the practical effect of the approach he adopted, based on the Enforcement Directive, is likely "little different to Pumfrey J's test of 'grossly disproportionate,'" and in summarizing his conclusion at ¶ 74, Arnold J referred to the *Shelfer* factors. In *Unwired Planet Int'l Ltd.* v. *Huawei Techs. Co.* (Pat 2017, ¶ 25) (UK) Birss J stated that "when the holder of an intellectual property right has established infringement and a threat and intention to infringe in future, an injunction will normally be granted," saying this would be consistent with Art 3 of the Directive.

[134] *Virgin Atlantic* v. *Premium Aircraft* (Civ 2009, ¶ 25) (UK). The effective period of the carve-out was approximately two months; the decision was December, but until April 20 it was considered on the basis of a balance of convenience, as being a stay pending appeal. From April 20 to end of June, it was considered on the basis of proportionality: *id.* at ¶ 29.

infringer to use the patented technology to fulfill an existing order, on the condition that the infringer would pay a substantial royalty.[135] The court emphasized as an important factor in granting the stay that the infringer would not be directly competing with the patentee with infringing products during this period.[136]

In *Illinois Tool Works Inc. v. Autobars Co. (Servs.) Ltd.*[137] the court granted a three-month stay of a permanent injunction, to allow the infringer to launch a noninfringing product. This was justified primarily on general public interest grounds, namely the potential loss of employment in times of high general unemployment.[138]

9 Complex Products

Arnold J's decision in *HTC Corp. v. Nokia Corp.* is important as being the only UK case dealing with injunctive relief for infringement of a patent related to a complex product. As noted above, Arnold J considered that the key issue was whether the grant of an injunction would be "grossly disproportionate" to the right protected. He stated that "perhaps the single most important consideration," in assessing proportionality, "is the availability and cost of non-infringing alternatives,"[139] and "[i]f non-infringing alternatives are available at non-prohibitive cost . . . then there is unlikely to be a problem of patent hold up."[140]

On the facts, the patented technology was a modulator circuit, there were non-infringing chips currently available, and HTC would be able to source other noninfringing alternatives given sufficient time.[141] The cost of switching was not prohibitive.[142] HTC's main argument that an injunction would be disproportionate was that it would take a significant amount of time – though probably something less than eighteen months – to redesign its phones, and during that period an injunction would keep its phones off the market.[143] Thus it was design-around time, not design-around cost, that was at issue. On the other side of the equation, Arnold J also held that "[t]his is not a case in which the injury to the patent is small, capable of being estimated in money and adequately compensated by a relatively small money payment."[144] Consequently, he granted the injunction.

In *Unwired Planet Int'l Ltd. v. Huawei Techs. Co.* Birss J granted an injunction in the context of a SEP. At first glance this appears striking, particularly in view of the

---

[135]   *Id.* at ¶¶ 31, 33.
[136]   *Id.* at ¶ 38.
[137]   *Illinois Tool Works Inc. v. Autobars Co. (Servs.) Ltd.* (Ch 1974) (UK).
[138]   *Id.* at 375.
[139]   *HTC Corp. v. Nokia Corp.* (Pat 2013, ¶ 65) (UK).
[140]   *Id.* at ¶ 67.
[141]   *Id.* at ¶ 70.
[142]   *Id.* at ¶ 70.
[143]   *Id.* at ¶ 72.
[144]   *Id.* at ¶ 74.

great reluctance of U.S. courts to grant an injunction for a SEP. The difference is more apparent than real. Despite the injunction, there was no potential for holdup, as Birss J held the patentee, Unwired Planet, was only entitled to a license on FRAND terms, and in particular at the FRAND rate determined by Birss J in the same decision in which he granted the injunction. This means that Unwired Planet would not be able to use its injunction for bargaining leverage.

4.3.4 *Civil Law Systems*

1 Traditional Principles

As a broad generalization, countries with civil law systems tend to award injunctive relief to a prevailing patentee routinely, and in some countries, effectively as a matter of right, so long as there is a real threat of future infringement.[145] In most cases this appears to be primarily as a matter of legal tradition and an absolutist approach to property rights generally, rather than as a matter of the provisions of the civil code itself.[146] Consequently, it has been suggested that these systems do have some flexibility in principle, and that the tendency to grant injunctive relief as an entitlement might stem from an absence of perceived need to refuse injunctive relief.[147]

In addition, competition law may provide a basis for refusing injunctive relief, a fact we discuss in more detail in Chapter 6. In several countries it has been judicially recognized that injunctive relief may be denied for this reason in the context of SEPs, and injunctions have been denied to SEP holders in some countries. Competition law is limited, however, because some form of market power is normally required. While this may be established for SEPs, patents reading on complex products, like other patents, do not generally entail market power.

2 Abuse of Rights

A more general potential restraint on the grant of injunctive relief is the doctrine of abuse of rights, which may apply when IP rights are exercised in lawful, yet

---

[145] *See* Cotter 2013a, 245–46 (noting that "European courts appear to grant successful patentees permanent injunctions in the vast majority of cases," and German courts "appear to read domestic law as entitling the prevailing patent owner to a permanent injunction as a matter of right," and "the same is reputed to be true of the Netherlands and Switzerland"); *id.* at 305 (noting that Japanese courts "routinely" grant permanent injunctions); *id.* at 365 (noting that commentators indicate that courts in Taiwan and South Korea "generally award permanent injunctions to prevailing patent owners").

[146] For example, *see id.* at 245 n.109 (noting that the relevant language of the German Patent Act is permissive rather than mandatory).

[147] *See id.* at 246–47 (noting that the European attitude to injunctive relief might change if "trolling" becomes more common, and noting various commentators suggesting "that European courts may show more flexibility than is commonly believed, if and when perceived abuses arise"). In one instance China's Supreme People's Court (SPC) refused an injunction to a successful patentee on public interest grounds, in particular environmental protection. *Id.* at 349.

nonetheless abusive, ways. The doctrine serves as a corrective mechanism that resorts to such standards of behavior by the rightsholders as morality, good faith, fairness, and proportionality as well as reasonableness and social functions of rights. Its application generally leads to limiting the exercise of rights. The abuse of rights doctrine is recognized by European Union law, as well as the civil laws of many European states, including EU Members such as France,[148] Germany,[149] Italy,[150] and the Netherlands,[151] and nonmembers, like Switzerland.[152] The doctrine of abuse of rights is also recognized by many Asian nations, including Japan and Korea.[153]

In these countries, injunctive relief may be refused if sought in circumstances deemed abusive. Though various legal systems differ in the way they define abusive behavior of rightsholders, there is a significant degree of convergence. Generally speaking, the assertion of an IP right may be deemed abusive if that enforcement: (i) is undertaken for the sole purpose of harming the infringer, (ii) results in harm to the infringer that is disproportionate to the benefit that accrues to the rightsholder, (iii) upsets reasonable expectations that the rightsholder has induced in the infringer, or (iv) is contrary to the social or economics aims of IP law.[154]

Circumstances that have been found sufficiently abusive to be grounds for refusing a permanent injunction against patent infringement have so far been narrow. Courts in both Korea and Japan, for example, have held that it can constitute an abuse of right to seek injunctive relief against infringement of a patent that will clearly be invalidated in a separate invalidation proceeding.[155] Both countries have also applied the doctrine to refuse injunctive relief in cases enforcing standard-essential patents.[156]

---

[148]   The abuse of rights doctrine in France has its roots in the French Civil Code, *see* Code Civil [C. civ.] [Civil Code] art. 1382 (Fr.).

[149]   Bürgerliches Gesetzbuch [BGB] [Civil Code] § 226 (Ger.) (the exercise of a right is not permitted if its only purpose is to cause damage to another); *id.* at § 242 (requiring good faith in the execution of obligations); *id.* at § 826 (providing for restitution where damage is inflicted on another in a manner contrary to public policy).

[150]   Art. 833 Codice civile [C.c.] (It.) (prohibiting acts with no other purpose than harming or harassing others).

[151]   Artikel 3:13 BW (Neth.) (a right may be abused when: (1) it is exercised with no other purpose than to damage a third party; (2) it is exercised for a purpose other than the one for which it was granted; and (3) the exercise of the right results in disparity between the interests that are served by its effectuation and the interests that are damaged as a result thereof).

[152]   Schweizerisches Zivilgesetzbuch [ZBG] [Civil Code], SR 210, art. 2 (Switz.) (every person must act in good faith in the exercise of their rights and obligations, and the manifest abuse of a right is not protected by law).

[153]   For recent commentary on the abuse of rights doctrine, *see, e.g.*, Sganga & Scalzini 2017; Léonard 2017, 10; Léonard 2016; Steppe & Léonard 2017; Nagakoshi & Tamai 2016. *See also* Cotter 2013a, 305, 365 (noting the availability of general abuse of rights doctrine in patent cases in Japan and Korea.).

[154]   *See generally* sources cited *supra* note 147.

[155]   *See* Saikō Saibansho (S. Ct. 2000) (Japan) (Kilby patent case); *LG Electronics, Inc. v. Daewoo Electronics, Inc.* (S. Ct. 2012) (Kor.).

[156]   In the SEP context, the Japanese IP High Court, in *Samsung Elecs. Co. v. Apple Japan LLC* (IP High Ct. 2014) (Japan) (FRAND II) and *Samsung Elecs. Co. v. Apple Japan LLC* (IP High Ct. 2014) (Japan) (FRAND III), refused to grant preliminary injunctions for the infringement by Apple of Samsung's

In summary, while the abuse of rights doctrine originated as a general corrective mechanism that might therefore in principle provide flexibility to refuse injunctive relief when the burden on the infringer is disproportionate to the right protected, it has developed into a narrower remedy which, to date, is not normally invoked in such circumstances.[157]

4.3.5 *International Context and TRIPS*

Finally, we note that a network of international agreements also influences the national rules discussed above. For example, the TRIPS Agreement, to which the United States, the United Kingdom, and all other EU Members are signatories, explicitly recognizes patentees' right to demand an injunction from judicial authorities against an infringer.[158] At the same time however, TRIPS also provides that remedies "shall be applied in such a manner as to avoid the creation of barriers to legitimate trade and to provide for safeguards against their abuse,"[159] and requires that remedies be "fair and equitable,"[160] a phrase that in the context of international trade agreements is usually equated with the principle of proportionality, good faith, due process and nondiscrimination.[161]

In addition, TRIPS explicitly recognizes that signatories may deny injunctive relief in a number of circumstances, including when doing so would adversely impact competition (i.e., violate competition law),[162] when the accused infringer unwittingly acquired the infringing subject matter (e.g., the manufacturer of a complex product that is later revealed to incorporate an infringing component),[163] and when doing so would otherwise "not unreasonably conflict with a normal exploitation of the patent [or] unreasonably prejudice the legitimate interests of the patent owner"[164] (an exception in which the *eBay* standard arguably falls).[165]

FRAND-committed standard-essential patent on the basis of an abuse of right; similarly in Korea it is an abuse of patent rights for a FRAND-committed patent holder to seek an injunction when the patent holder violates its duty to negotiate in good faith and merely tries to maintain its market dominance. *Samsung Electronics Co. Ltd. v. Apple Korea Ltd.* (Dist. Ct. 2012) (Kor.).

[157] One possible exception is that the Tokyo District Court, Tōkyō Chihō Saibansho (Tokyo Dist. Ct. 2015) (Japan) (Cu-Ni-Si Alloy), stated that it would be inequitable to grant an injunction on the basis of disproportionality between the infringement and the burden on the infringer. However, this decision has little precedential value as it was a lower court decision and the legal basis for the denial of injunction was not clear.

[158] TRIPS Agreement, art. 44(1).

[159] *Id.*

[160] *Id.* at art. 44(2).

[161] Malbon et al. 2014, 628.

[162] TRIPS Agreement, arts. 40, 44(2).

[163] TRIPS Agreement, art. 44(1).

[164] TRIPS Agreement, art. 30.

[165] *See* Cotropia 2008, 580.

4.4 RECOMMENDATIONS

In light of arguments for and against injunctive relief summarized in Section 4.2, and after surveying in Section 4.3 approaches adopted around the world, we outline recommendations for how courts should approach the questions of whether to award injunctions against patent infringement and how such injunctions should be crafted. These recommendations are far from comprehensive: They do not provide precise guidance on how courts should weigh a variety of additional factors that might properly influence a decision on injunctive relief. This lack of comprehensiveness reflects partly the multiplicity of such potential factors and partly this project's focus on concerns particular to complex products. The lack of comprehensiveness also reflects the fact that, although we have found common ground with respect to certain basic principles for injunctive relief, we have a plurality of views with respect to even such fundamental questions as whether there should be a presumption in favor of granting injunctive relief after infringement has been shown and a continuing threat of infringement established.[166] Although such background disagreements limit the scope of what we affirmatively recommend, we believe they also highlight the robustness of the principles that the group as a whole embraces. These principles appear sound even to people with widely varying views about the general advisability of injunctive relief.

4.4.1 Basic Principles for Injunctive Relief

First, and perhaps foremost, we recommend against the adoption of rules resulting in the automatic issuance of injunctive relief in all cases in which a patentee prevails in a suit for patent infringement. As discussed in greater detail below, we recommend instead that courts retain, and in appropriate circumstances exercise, discretion to deny injunctive relief when issuance of an injunction would otherwise generate costs or burdens for others that are disproportionate to the nature of the adjudged infringement and to the noncompensable harms the patentee would suffer in the absence of an injunction.

Consistent with the above recommendations, we recommend that courts be afforded the flexibility and discretion to tailor injunctive relief in appropriate circumstances to avoid imposing unnecessary hardship on infringers or the general public. Examples of potential forms of tailoring include granting a stay of the injunction's enforcement to allow the infringer time to design

---

[166] We recommend the standard requirement that, for an injunction against infringement to be granted, there be some prospect of future infringement. But we will not focus on this point because it appears to be commonly satisfied in patent infringement cases, including complex product cases, in which a continuing course of conduct has been held to be infringing.

around the patent, and limiting the scope of an injunction in a case involving a complex product so that the injunction precisely targets continued use of the infringing feature(s), rather than forbidding continued use or sale of an entire product.

Finally, in cases where injunctive relief is not granted, and damages have not separately compensated for future infringement,[167] we recommend that additional monetary damages in the form of an "ongoing reasonable royalty" be normally awarded as a substitute. We recommend that this ongoing royalty be calculated in accordance with the principle for determining a "reasonable royalty" for past infringement, without any special enhancement due to the ongoing reasonable royalty's association with activity that occurs after the judgment of infringement.[168]

4.4.2 *Proportionality*

We recommend that courts use the concept of "proportionality" as a limiting principle for injunctive relief. Attention to this principle can help balance concerns about patentee holdup and implementer holdout discussed in Section 2 of this chapter, and can likewise help balance interests in vindicating a patent owner's rights and in protecting legitimate interests of the public as well as adjudged or accused infringers. We believe that this broad principle is consistent with the law of a number of jurisdictions, including the EU Enforcement Directive (especially as interpreted in *HTC Corp.* v. *Nokia Corp.*);[169] more recent Communications from the European Commission;[170] traditional equitable principles applied in common law jurisdictions, including the United Kingdom and Canada;[171] and the four-factor test for awarding

---

[167] A damages award in the form of a lump sum that compensates for both past and future use of the patented technology would involve such compensation for future infringement. Some U.S. cases have upheld awards of damages in the nature of a lump-sum royalty payment based on an infringer's expected sales. *See, e.g., Interactive Pictures Corp.* v. *Infinite Pictures, Inc.* (Fed. Cir. 2001, p.1384–85) (U.S.).

[168] While we use the term "royalty" in this sentence, we acknowledge that cases may arise in which patentees that were awarded lost-profits damages are denied injunctions due to proportionality concerns. We propose further research on the question of how ongoing damages should be calculated in such a case.

[169] *See HTC Corp.* v. *Nokia Corp.* (Pat 2013) (UK). *See also* Ohly, 2009, 274 ("Although the Enforcement Directive aims at a high standard of protection, it does not unilaterally benefit right holders. While the need for effective protection of intellectual property is evident, the principle of proportionality must also be taken into account.").

[170] European Commission, at 18, COM (2017) 708 final (stating, inter alia, that courts should ensure, on a case-by-case basis, that injunctions be consistent with the principle of proportionality; that injunctions "should have the minimal scope necessary to accomplish this objective"; and that it "is not necessary that the measures required by the injunction lead to a complete cessation of the IPR infringements"); European Commission, at 10, COM (2017) 712 final (similar).

[171] *See* Gergen et al. 2012, 246 ("Under the traditional approach, if the patentee wins on validity and infringement, the patentee will be presumptively entitled to an injunction against

permanent injunctions articulated by the Supreme Court of the United States in *eBay* v. *MercExchange*.[172] Further, some version of a proportionality principle appears consistent with the TRIPS Agreement, as noted above.[173] Accordingly, we believe that proportionality-based tests can be applied in a broad variety of jurisdictions without need for legislative action.

That said, we also acknowledge that this recommendation leaves open various substantive, evidentiary, and procedural questions that impact the extent to which injunctive relief should be granted. Though we flesh out one framework for incorporating concerns of proportionality below, a degree of vagueness in our proposal is intentional. How individual jurisdictions answer these questions will depend on a multiplicity of factors, including general legal norms and commitments relating to the enforcement of private rights, the extent to which patent enforcement is treated as involving moral stakes, and perceptions about the relative dangers of abusive behavior by patentees and potential infringers, respectively.

1 General Recommendation

We generally recommend that an injunction against infringement not issue if the negative effects of the injunction on enjoined parties would be disproportionate to the nature of the infringement and any noncompensable harm that the patentee will experience as a result of the absence of an injunction.

This recommendation applies to both preliminary and permanent injunctions. At the preliminary-injunction stage, however, "the nature of the infringement" factor might be better characterized as a factor concerned with what, at that preliminary stage, a court considers to be the likely nature of the alleged infringement.

Beyond this, there remains some work to be done in clarifying various details. Application of this recommendation requires an explication of the terms "nature of the infringement," "negative effects," "noncompensable harm" (including the public interest), and "disproportionate." This is where we turn our attention next.

---

continuing infringement. This presumption can be overcome by a showing of undue hardship – i.e., some form of disproportionate hardship – not by a mere showing that equipoise-style balancing of the equities at least ostensibly favors the infringer. The reliance from sunk investments and the hardship of potentially shutting down factories qualify as long as actual noncompensable harm to the plaintiff is relatively small. Importantly, however, the undue-hardship safety valve will only apply if the infringer has acted in good faith. Knowing violation by one who has notice or should have had notice of infringement at the time infringing conduct began will generally support a presumption that an injunction should issue.").

[172] *See* discussion *supra* Section 4.3.2.

[173] *See supra* note 152 and accompanying text.

2 The Nature of the Infringement

The "nature of the infringement" in our general recommendation is meant to encompass at least two sets of concerns: (i) the scale of the infringement in relation to the overall scope of an infringing product or process, and (ii) various circumstances relating to the relative blameworthiness of the infringing conduct or of the patent holder itself.

In the context of complex products, the scale of the infringement can be understood as relating to the extent to which the infringement involves a relatively minor or, at least, isolated component of a multicomponent product that has numerous other valuable features. Infringement in such a circumstance might be viewed as comparable to constructing a large building overwhelmingly on one's own land but, as it turns out, with a small sliver of the building's footprint encroaching on another's property.

Even a "small sliver" case of infringement might be viewed as substantially problematic if the infringement in question is willful and malicious. To deter such bad-faith conduct, courts and policymakers might want to deploy injunctions even when those injunctions inflict economic burdens much larger than the economic value of the "small sliver" of infringement itself. Accordingly, courts may wish to incorporate into their analysis of the nature of the infringement the relative blameworthiness of the enjoined party's infringing conduct. On the side of an adjudged or accused infringer, relevant factors may include the extent to which (i) the adjudged or accused infringer knew or should have known that the conduct in question would be infringing; (ii) the adjudged or accused infringer had such actual or constructive knowledge before becoming substantially invested in a course of conduct later judged or alleged to infringe; and (iii) the adjudged or accused infringer engaged in reasonable and good-faith efforts to license or otherwise preclear pertinent patent rights (assuming such action was possible and non-futile) as opposed to engaging in holdout behavior or exhibiting recklessness with respect to such rights. Taking such factors into account can help prevent our recommended proportionality limitation on injunctive relief from protecting strategic holdout behavior by patent infringers who might otherwise anticipate that they can escape injunctive relief as long as they can successfully characterize their infringement as involving only a "small sliver" of a multifeatured product or process.

But we should emphasize that, in considering *relative* blameworthiness, courts may also weigh the extent to which a patentee may have behaved badly or otherwise contributed to the course of infringement about which the patentee now complains. On the side of the patentee, relevant factors with respect to relative blameworthiness may include the extent to which (i) the patentee contributed to delay in the adjudged or accused infringer's appreciating the risk of potential infringement, whether this contribution came by the patentee's failing to assert patent rights promptly or otherwise; (ii) the patentee engaged in reasonable and good-faith efforts to license the claimed invention to the adjudged or accused infringer; and (iii) the patentee engaged in other behavior that either helps to render the infringement less blameworthy or otherwise helps to balance equities more favorably to the adjudged or accused infringer.

A traditional equitable principle related to such considerations of blameworthiness is the principle that, by acting badly, an infringer can forfeit any opportunity for relief from the effects of an injunction. Deliberate infringement of another's rights, with full knowledge that those rights were being infringed, is often cited as one traditional ground for denying relief from an injunction even when its negative effects on the infringer would otherwise be disproportionate. Given that the scope of rights under an individual patent and the validity of a patent's claims are often open to question, however, many situations involving infringement of patent rights are likely to involve a lesser degree of culpability. Further, the patent thickets that can envelop complex product markets could make patent clearance in such markets especially hard. Difficulties in evaluating the incremental worth of a claimed invention in relation to an overall complex product can likewise complicate assessment of the extent to which failures in negotiation reflect holdup, holdout, or simple good-faith disagreement. In short, the relative blameworthiness of patentee and infringer in a situation involving failed negotiations might be difficult to assess. Moreover, even when one party has clearly behaved both badly and worse than the opposing party, the level of culpability will often fall short of that of the knowingly and deliberately infringing trespasser.

Because of such murkiness, we decline to recommend any particular disqualifying rules, either strictly forbidding injunctions or strictly forbidding relief from an injunction, based on party misbehavior or lack of ideal behavior. Instead, we focus below on how such conduct can inform the disproportionality analysis for injunctive relief. Like questions about the extent to which and manner in which a patentee needs to make a threshold showing of irreparable injury, we propose further research on the advisability and contents of such disqualifying rules.

3 Negative Effects

This subsection explains what we mean by "negative effects of the injunction on enjoined parties" and how a target's ability to mitigate such negative effects should factor into the disproportionality calculus. Here, we also explain why we confine our general recommendation to negative effects on enjoined parties, rather than including negative effects on third parties or the general public.

A) NEGATIVE EFFECTS ON ENJOINED PARTIES. Negative effects on enjoined parties can include out-of-pocket expenses, opportunity costs, or other welfare losses experienced as a consequence of the injunction, whether resulting from cessation of relevant activities, payments for a patent license, product redesign, or otherwise.

Such costs can be especially large relative to the nature of any patent infringement in the context of complex products. This follows from the fact that an injunction might forbid production or distribution of an entire complex product or service even though only one of many value-adding components or aspects of the product or service is infringing. Because of the multicomponent, multiply innovative nature of the infringing product, the claimed invention is most likely only one of a large number of aspects of the product that contribute to its overall value. Hence, an injunction that stops manufacture or use of the overall product might inflict economic hardship on the infringer that is far out of proportion to the value of the product's infringing aspect. Further, the claimed invention's operation within the product might be interrelated with that of other aspects of the product in complementary, synergistic, or otherwise complicated ways that make redesign of the product to exclude the claimed invention significantly more difficult than the simple removal and replacement of a largely isolated infringing module. Thus, even aside from the out-of-pocket expense needed to develop a noninfringing redesign, the time required for a noninfringing redesign might be substantial. During that time, the entire product will be kept off the market, even when the patented technology only contributes a small part of the overall value. As a result, a generic injunction that forbids the continuation of infringing activity and goes into immediate effect can be especially likely to require an extended shutdown of infringer activity, with the extensive economic effects described above. Although the adjudged infringer may attempt to obtain a license from the patentee for its continued activity, a profit-maximizing patentee would predictably use the leverage afforded by an injunction to extract much of the benefit to the adjudged infringer of avoiding its force. Consequently, a license in the wake of such an injunction might largely maintain the size of the negative effects of an injunction while shifting their form to that of a cash payout to the patentee. Hence, the amount of such a payout might mostly reflect the "holdup" value of the injunction, rather than the more fundamental economic value of the claimed invention.[174]

B) NEGATIVE EFFECTS ON RELATED THIRD PARTIES AND THE PUBLIC. In addition to the costs imposed on enjoined parties, many jurisdictions consider the negative effects an injunction might have on third parties or the public at large. Third parties that might suffer from an injunction are suppliers to an adjudged or accused infringer, downstream consumers, and intermediaries.[175] In addition, completely unrelated third parties can suffer as well. For example, an injunction that effectively takes a widely used communications technology off the market or that

---

[174] The leading article on this issue is Lemley & Shapiro 2007a. For a discussion of the relevant literature, *see* Chapter 7.

[175] *See i4i Ltd. Partnership* v. *Microsoft Corp.* (Fed. Cir. 2010, p.861–62) (U.S.) ("Here, the relevant 'public' includes not only individual consumers, but also companies that license infringing Word products and manufacturers that are part of Microsoft's distribution channels.").

generates a substantial decrease in that technology's availability, affordability, or usability could disrupt the work and home lives not only of direct users of the technology, but also the work and home lives of virtually anyone, including government officials, who seeks to communicate with the direct users.[176] Similarly, an extended shutdown of a manufacturing plant or communications center can negatively affect not only direct employees but also a much larger community or economic ecosystem in which they exist.

That said, some negative effects to the public from the enforcement of patents are to be expected as a normal incident of patent rights, and the existence of patent laws presumably reflects a judgment that such negative effects are counterbalanced by positive effects that render the issuance and enforcement of patent rights generally in the public interest. As a result, advocacy of courts' general consideration of the public interest in issuing an injunction against patent infringement can seem to some to amount to an invitation to the courts to question or ignore general policy judgments embodied within the patent system. In light of such concerns, we have failed to reach consensus on the extent to which courts should consider the negative effects of injunctions on third parties or the general public as a basis for denying injunctive relief. Thus, we have not included such negative effects to third parties or the public in our general recommendation on proportionality.

On the other hand, we agree that, in deciding whether to issue injunctions, courts should consider, as a potential basis for denying injunctive relief, harms to the public that substantially outweigh the costs inherent in a functioning patent system – i.e., negative consequences to the public that are substantially beyond what a patentee could reasonably and legitimately have expected in vindication of its patent rights – to the extent such harms are likely to be realized. Such a requirement aligns with existing *de jure* compulsory licensing regimes, which generally take effect only in exceptional circumstances.[177] Examples of injunctions that could cause significant public harm might include those that would potentially reduce the availability of devices or products important to public health and safety, the preservation of national security, the uninterrupted operation of capital markets, and the functioning of a reliable and secure transportation, power, telecommunications, and computing infrastructure.

---

[176] For example, the permanent injunction issued in *NTP v. RIM* raised serious concern among the roughly three million individuals using BlackBerry devices in the United States at the time. Indeed, the U.S. Department of Justice filed a brief in the case warning that "a substantial public interest ... may be impaired" if the injunction were to impair BlackBerry usage by the three hundred thousand government employees using such devices at the time. *See* Noguchi 2005.

[177] *See HTC Corp. v. Nokia Corp.* (Pat 2013, ¶ 32) (UK) ("[T]he court must be very cautious before making an order which is tantamount to a compulsory licence in circumstances where no compulsory licence would be available. It follows that, where no other countervailing right is in play, the burden on the party seeking to show that the injunction would be disproportionate is a heavy one."). For further discussion of compulsory licensing regimes, *see* McManis & Contreras 2014.

c) NEGATIVE EFFECTS AND MITIGATION. Finally, we note that both adjudged infringers and third parties can often take action that mitigates the possible negative effects from an injunction, for example by switching to a close substitute product or substituting supply or customer relationships with entities who do not rely on the infringing product for relationships with entities who do. Moreover, as we discuss further below, a court itself might be able to mitigate the negative effects of an injunction by tailoring injunctive relief appropriately. Given the possibility that adjudged infringers and third parties could react in any of a number of ways to injunctive relief, a decision-maker might wonder which potential future scenarios "count" for assessing the expected negative effects of an injunction. Because the purpose of proportionality as a limit on injunctive relief is to avoid disproportionate awards to patentees and hardships to others, we recommend that relevant negative effects to adjudged infringers and, to the extent considered relevant, third parties, be limited to those that have some reasonable likelihood of actually occurring if adjudged infringers and third parties take reasonable mitigating measures in relation to an injunction. We discuss how we believe courts should proceed with respect to potential tailoring later in this chapter.

4 Noncompensable Harm to the Patentee

The noncompensable harm to the patentee encompasses the ways in which the patentee cannot be made whole through a purely monetary award, including an ongoing royalty, if appropriate. Noncompensable harms could include competitive or other business harms that are difficult to quantify, loss of an ability to choose licensing partners or to structure licensing terms, and a potential need to file suit again if an ongoing royalty is not provided and the course of infringement continues or resumes.

Even patentees who might be characterized as "willing licensors" can suffer noncompensable harm. For one, even if a patentee is an indiscriminate licensor whose typical or desired licensing arrangement is in the nature of a bare lump-sum payment or running royalty, equity has commonly recognized that uncertainty about the proper value of damages (such as a reasonable royalty) and courts' common lack of aptitude in price setting mean that monetary awards are an inadequate replacement for the capacity to license on privately agreed terms or not to license at all.[178] In addition, patent licenses are often structured in ways that channel licensee behavior, whether by explicitly limiting what a licensee may do or by providing incentives for licensees to meet certain goals. Monetary awards for past infringement necessarily fail to replicate such structure, and ongoing royalties generally lack them as well. Further, an attempt to replicate such more complicated arrangements between unwilling partners and through a court order might be problematic for all sides and could upset a more targeted licensing program.

---

[178]   Golden 2007, 2152; Calabresi & Melamed 1972.

Finally, at least where the relevant patentees are business entities, patents are fundamentally held only to make money and, consequently, a so-called willing licensor is not so distinct from a supposedly "unwilling licensor" or competitor in terms of its ability to be satisfied with a large enough money payment.[179]

Nonetheless, in the wake of the Supreme Court of the United States's decision in *eBay*, U.S. district courts appear to have often treated patentees who are not competitors of adjudged or accused infringers, especially patentees who qualify as patent assertion entities (PAEs), as not suffering substantial noncompensable harm from the absence of an injunction and thus as subject to "a de facto rule against injunctive relief."[180] The legal status of this de facto rule is murky,[181] but it does raise the question of whether there should be a rule at least presumptively disqualifying PAEs or other forms of presumptively willing licensors from obtaining injunctive relief for patent infringement. This is another iteration of the question of whether there should be threshold tests or disqualifying rules for injunctive relief that adopt a more categorical approach than our recommended proportionality principle. As above, we propose further research on these questions.

5 Disproportionality

The final key term to define is "disproportionate," the fulcrum term that determines when the negative effects to the enjoined party are such, relative to the nature of the infringement and threatened noncompensable harm to the patentee, that an injunction should be denied. Here we define this term for purposes of our general recommendation and discuss why our recommendation is not limited only to situations in which harm to the patentee is not great.

A) DISPROPORTIONALITY DEFINED. For purposes of our general recommendation, disproportionality should be understood to require that the expected negative effects of an injunction substantially outweigh, rather than merely incrementally outweigh, the expected noncompensable harm to the patentee if an injunction is denied. This substantial outweighing should be such that a court believes that the resulting negative consequences threatened to the infringer are beyond what a patentee could reasonably and legitimately have expected in vindication of its patent rights.

However, we make no recommendation with respect to the precise formulation of such a rule. At least one jurisdiction has adopted a rule that injunctions be denied

---

[179]   *HTC Corp. v. Nokia Corp.* (Pat 2013, ¶¶ 54–56) (UK).

[180]   Seaman 2016, 1953; *see also* Section 4.3.1.

[181]   Holte & Seaman 2017 (concluding that, on appeal, the Federal Circuit is more favorable toward injunctive relief for PAEs than district courts are at the trial level); *cf. eBay Inc. v. MercExchange, L.L.C.* (U.S. 2006) (U.S.) (language generally rejecting categorical treatment and suggesting that, under certain circumstances, a nonpracticing entity may have a legitimate claim to injunctive relief).

only when their negative effects are "grossly disproportionate,"[182] and signaled that "the burden on the party seeking to show that the injunction would be disproportionate is a heavy one."[183] It is not clear whether such differences in language or stated burden are associated with substantial practical differences in how a proportionality principle is applied and whether any such practical differences point in favor or against these variations on a proportionality principle. We propose further research on these issues.

Though we take no position on the exact degree of disproportionality required, we do intend for the disproportionality highlighted by our general recommendation to contrast with a more "equipoise-style balancing of the equities" to determine whether to grant injunctive relief.[184] Though a case could be made for something more in the nature of a "preponderance of the hardships" standard for issuing injunctions, various objections to equipoise-style balancing can be made in the context of permanent injunctions. For example, equipoise-style balancing may (i) insufficiently respect the legislative judgment that a patentee should have a "right to exclude"; (ii) provide insufficient assurance to patentees or would-be patentees that patent rights will be respected; and (iii) insufficiently deter holdout behavior and other forms of inadequate attentiveness to patent clearance. Equipoise-style balancing might be more justified in relation to preliminary injunctions and is the general approach followed by the United Kingdom, for example, with respect to such preliminary relief. But because justified denial of an injunction based on disproportionality will a fortiori mean that an injunction would have been denied under equipoise-style balancing, we choose to focus on a point of common ground with respect to both preliminary and permanent injunctions – namely, our view that injunctions should be denied when disproportionality, as we define it above, has been found.

B) DISPROPORTIONALITY REGARDLESS OF WHETHER PATENTEE'S HARM IS SMALL OR GREAT. Another potentially relevant consideration in the disproportionality analysis is the absolute, as opposed to relative, size of the patentee's harm. Some Anglo-American cases have suggested that if the harm, or at least the noncompensable harm, to the plaintiff is substantial, an injunction should be granted even if its effect would be disproportionate.[185] That is, disproportionality is a ground for

---

[182] *Virgin Atlantic v. Premium Aircraft* (Civ 2009, ¶ 25) (UK); this derives from Pumfrey J's statement in *Navitaire Inc. v. easyJet Airline Co. Ltd.* (No.2) (Ch 2005, p.250) (UK), quoted with approval in *Virgin Atlantic v. Premium Aircraft* (Civ 2009, ¶ 24) (UK).

[183] *HTC Corp. v. Nokia Corp.* (Pat 2013, ¶ 32) (UK) ("[W]here no other countervailing right is in play, the burden on the party seeking to show that the injunction would be disproportionate is a heavy one. I suspect that the practical effect of this approach is little different to Pumfrey J's test of 'grossly disproportionate.'").

[184] Gergen et al. 2012, 246 (contrasting "equipoise-style balancing" to the traditional question of whether a permanent injunction would inflict "undue hardship").

[185] *See, e.g., Shelfer v. City of London Elec. Lighting Co.* (Civ 1895) (UK).

refusing an injunction only if the damages or noncompensable harm to the plaintiff is small. We recommend against any such limitation on the proportionality principle. Harm to a plaintiff from the lack of an injunction can be substantial yet nonetheless dwarfed by much greater negative effects to an adjudged infringer from issuance of the injunction, with the result that issuance of the injunction is contrary to both the specific purposes of patent law and the purposes of law more generally. We likewise recommend against an opposite approach that would deny an injunction unless harm to the patentee is substantial, regardless of disproportionality. Failure to vindicate patentees' interests even in small-value cases can have a negative impact on operation of the patent system as a whole when such failure is aggregated across the full spectrum of small-value disputes.

6 Burdens of Proof or Production

A further consideration worth addressing is who, between the patent holder and the accused or adjudged infringer, should bear the burden of proof on disproportionality and whether any facts, if proven, should give rise to a presumption of proportionality or disproportionality.

In all jurisdictions the patentee bears the burden of proving liability in order to obtain an injunction. In some jurisdictions this gives rise to a presumption that injunctive relief be granted. In other jurisdictions, the patentee bears a further burden to establish entitlement to injunctive relief. We take no position on this issue. Nonetheless, we acknowledge that an adjudged or accused infringer is likely to be in a better position than the patentee to produce evidence of the negative effects that it (and, depending upon the implementation, related third parties, and, through ripple effects, the general public) is likely to suffer from an injunction against infringement. Thus, we believe that it is reasonable for courts to place some burden of production with respect to such effects on the infringer. Otherwise, the patentee could be left to speculate about potential negative effects and then seek to prove their limited size or absence even when an adjudged or accused infringer would perceive little basis for alleging them.

As suggested above, we have, in general, not reached consensus on the extent to which there should be presumptions for or against injunctive relief after various showings have been made. On the other hand, while disproportionality may generally be more likely when patents are enforced against complex products, we do recommend against a general presumption of disproportionality in complex product cases. First, practically speaking, such a presumption might place undue pressure on the precise definition of what constitutes a "complex product." Second, even in cases in which the claimed invention indisputably constitutes a minor component of a complex product, disproportionality is by no means inevitable. For example, a minor feature of an end product might be very cheap and easy to design around, so that the end product itself does not need to be kept off the market and redesign costs are small even if a court were to grant an injunction.[186] Further, as discussed below, injunctions in complex product cases may be specifically tailored to avoid disproportionality even when an immediately effective injunction of generic scope, such as one forbidding any further manufacture, use, sale, or importation of an infringing product by an adjudged infringer, would have disproportionate effect.

4.4.3 *Tailoring Injunctive Relief*

As a corollary to our general recommendation on proportionality, we recommend that a proportionality-based test like the one described above be deployed in a system that gives courts latitude to construct injunctions that are tailored to avoid or mitigate disproportionate effects. In short, we do not envision a proportionality test that generally consists of a simple up-or-down vote on the appropriateness of a one-size-fits-all formulation of enjoined activities. Rather, we envision a process in which a court may consider the potential negative effects of an injunction *together with* ways in which those effects can be mitigated by tailoring injunctive relief. Put another way, tailoring should not necessarily be seen as a restriction on an injunction that would have been granted in any event; by mitigating the effects of an injunction, tailoring may enable an injunction to be granted when it would otherwise have been refused for disproportionality.

The two primary ways in which an injunction can be tailored to help ensure a proportionate effect are modifications to its scope or timing. For example, a court might stay an injunction or delay its effective date to allow time for an adjudged infringer to design around the patent.[187] Alternatively, a court might exclude already existing products from the scope of the injunction. This proposal has been made by some commentators,[188] and occasionally applied or at least considered by courts in the United States, the United Kingdom, and Canada.[189] In at least some

---

[186]   *See HTC Corp.* v. *Nokia Corp.* (Pat 2013, ¶ 67) (UK) ("If non-infringing alternatives are available at non-prohibitive cost, however, then there is unlikely to be a problem of patent hold up. Accordingly, other things being equal, an injunction is unlikely to be disproportionate.").

[187]   One possible objection to staying injunctive relief is concern that the possibility of such delay can discourage an accused or even adjudged infringer from acting reasonably to avoid future infringement or to prepare for such infringement avoidance until the date that an injunction issues. In *HTC Corp.* v. *Nokia Corp.* (Pat 2013) (UK), Arnold J refused to grant a stay on the basis that the infringer was aware of the likelihood of proceedings for over eighteen months, and this was ample time for it to have made contingency plans. An argument against such an approach is that many asserted patents are invalid or not infringed, and requiring the alleged infringer to start redesign when it is first put on notice may allow the owner of a weak patent to extract an excessive royalty. We express no view on this issue, and recommend further research.

[188]   *See* Lemley & Shapiro 2007a, 2037–38; Chien & Lemley 2012 (making a similar proposal in respect of the USITC); Golden 2012.

[189]   *See, e.g., i4i Ltd. Partnership* v. *Microsoft Corp.* (Fed. Cir. 2010, p.861–62) (U.S.) ("In light of the record evidence, we conclude that the district court erred by ordering Microsoft to comply with the injunction within sixty days. The only evidence about how long it would take . . . gave an estimate of 'at least' five months."); *Cincinnati Car Co.* v. *New York Rapid Transit Corp.* (2d Cir. 1933) (U.S.)

jurisdictions, however, tailoring along the lines we propose might require a substantial shift in judicial philosophy – though within the European Union some such movement may be possible in the years to come.[190]

Tailoring generally, and a stay in particular, can be especially impactful in the context of complex products, where infringement of a patent covering a minor component of the end product might result in the entire product being held off the market during the period of redesign. Such a consequence might allow the patentee to force a license that extracts not just the value of the patented technology, but also the value of the entire product line over the period during which it would otherwise be held off the market.[191] Consequently, we recommend that courts generally be willing to consider such tailoring whenever injunctive relief is sought in relation to a complex product.

In fact, we recommend that courts should consider tailoring injunctions in the normal course, even when a proportionality-based test like that in our general recommendation is otherwise satisfied. While the argument for tailoring an injunction may be particularly strong when the injunction would otherwise be refused as having a disproportionate effect, we recommend against any requirement that tailoring be permitted only after disproportionate harm is shown.

(recounting that earlier in the case "we suspended the injunction to allow the defendant to substitute another device[,] ... [i]t did so, and when the new structure came before us, we held that it escaped the claims of the patent"); *Illinois Tool Works Inc.* v. *Autobars Co. (Servs.) Ltd.* (Ch 1974) (UK) (granting a three-month stay to allow the infringer to launch a noninfringing product); *Virgin Atlantic* v. *Premium Aircraft* (Civ 2009) (UK) in which the Court of Appeal tailored the injunction by allowing the infringer to use the patented technology to fulfill an existing order, on the condition that the infringer would pay a substantial specified sum, that the infringer's parent company would provide a guarantee, and that the infringer would give an undertaking that the infringing product would not be used in competition with the patentee: *id.* at ¶¶ 31, 33. The effective period of the carve-out was approximately two months. *See also AbbVie Corp.* v. *Janssen Inc.* (Fed. Ct. 2014) (Can.) *set aside on other grounds AbbVie Corp.* v. *Janssen Inc.* (Fed. Ct. App. 2014) (Can.) (granting an injunction in relation to a pharmaceutical biologic, while allowing the infringer's product to be sold to treat a subset of disorders for which the patentee's product was ineffective).

[190] *See, e.g.,* sources cited *supra* note 46. *See also* BGH v. 10.5.2016 – X ZR 114/13 (Ger.) (stating that a court may grant an *Aufbrauchfrist,* or transition period, when "in consideration of the interests of the patent owner and the infringer, the immediate enforcement of the injunction would result in a disproportionate and undue hardship and thus would be in bad faith," and citing academic literature recommending that courts should consider granting such a transition period on a case-by-case basis, taking into account all of the participants' interests; the infringer's good or bad faith; whether the patented invention formed just a small but functionally necessary component of a complex product; and whether an unpatented or licensed product could be substituted within a reasonable time). The German court describes these conditions as applying only under narrow conditions (*engen Voraussetzungen*), however, and denied such a transition period on the facts presented; and legislation might be necessary clearly to authorize courts to award interim royalties pending such a transition period.

[191] *See* Lemley & Shapiro 2007a, 2000–02.

4.4.4 *Ongoing Royalty in Lieu of Injunctive Relief*

When a permanent injunction is refused, U.S. courts routinely grant monetary compensation that is to be paid to the patentee by the infringer for post-judgment infringing uses of the patented invention.[192] This compensation is known as an ongoing royalty. An ongoing royalty is awarded at the request of the patentee, who, in the absence of an injunction against further infringement, might otherwise be expected to bring a second lawsuit for infringement occurring after entry of final judgment in the initial lawsuit. The ongoing royalty may in principle be awarded as a lump sum, or on a per unit basis, calculated either as a fixed dollar amount or as a percentage of, for example, the sale price. Typically, the ongoing royalty is initially assessed on the basis of the same principles as reasonable royalty damages for past infringement (discussed in Chapter 1), but U.S. courts will often enhance that royalty on the view that any continuing infringement is automatically willful.[193]

We recommend that, at least when an injunction is refused on grounds of the disproportionality of negative effects on enjoined parties, the governing principles for ongoing royalties should generally be the same as those governing awards of past damages, without further enhancement.[194] When an injunction is denied on grounds of disproportionality to enjoined parties, the general implication is that the infringer has become effectively "locked into" a course of infringement from which it is difficult to extricate itself at a reasonable cost. Such "lock-in" might be properly considered to constitute extenuating circumstances for continued use of the patented invention. Further, such circumstances suggest that further-enhanced damages for continued infringement might themselves impose a disproportionate burden that the infringer will be unable to contract around.[195] It has been suggested that a modest increase in the ongoing (forward-looking) royalty rate may be needed if the royalty rate for past infringement would be inadequate to fully compensate the patentee.[196] This may be appropriate in cases where future uses of the patented technology are more economically valuable than past uses.[197] But the royalty rate should not be increased simply to compensate for the patentee's loss of bargaining power that occurs when an

[192] Because injunctions are almost always granted to a successful patentee in other jurisdictions, the question has so far arisen primarily in U.S. law. We are not aware of case law from other jurisdictions directly addressing this issue.

[193] *See generally* Seaman 2015.

[194] We take no position on whether an ongoing royalty should be enhanced, or even awarded, when injunctive relief is denied for other reasons, such as litigation misconduct, or undue delay (laches), as our focus is on problems of disproportionality that may arise in the context of a complex product. Nor do we take any specific position on enhancement of ongoing royalties in unusual cases, such as where lost profit damages were awarded, but an injunction was denied nonetheless, except that in such cases the general governing principles we have articulated should remain applicable.

[195] *See* Seaman 2015, 244.

[196] *Id.* at 245–46.

[197] This is consistent with our recommendation in Chapter 1 that the assessment of a reasonable royalty should use all information available at the time of trial, including *ex post* information: *see* Chapter 1.

injunction is denied. If it is indeed desirable on the facts of the case to force the infringer to negotiate a license as opposed to paying an ongoing royalty, we anticipate that it will commonly be preferable to do so by granting an injunction, stayed or otherwise, that is appropriately tailored to minimize any disproportionality to those burdened by it.

We further recommend that when a permanent injunction is not granted on grounds of disproportionality, an ongoing royalty should normally be granted in lieu thereof.[198] Denying a sought-after ongoing royalty and forcing a patentee to relitigate a continuing course of infringement from scratch would threaten to unduly dilute the incentives that the patent system means to provide.[199] Failure to award an ongoing royalty might also leave an adjudged infringer in a situation of uncertainty about its potential future liability.

We do not rule out the possibility that an ongoing royalty might be denied in some circumstances in which an injunction has been refused on grounds of disproportionality. However, we note that, even the fact that a patented technology is important to the public interest, as for example in the case of life-saving drugs or devices, does not provide generally sufficient grounds for refusing an ongoing royalty, just as it does not provide generally sufficient grounds for refusing past damages for infringement. General refusal to award ongoing royalties for important inventions would arguably undermine the patent incentive where it is needed most.

While we recommend against routine enhancement of ongoing royalties solely on the basis of the willfulness of the ongoing infringement, as just discussed, we do not rule out the possibility that ongoing royalties might be enhanced in exceptional circumstances, based on relevant equitable considerations, such as those discussed in Chapter 3 on enhanced damages.

Finally, we recommend that the assessment of an ongoing royalty take into account all information available at the time of trial, as well as any reasonably foreseeable changes to market demand or structure that might affect the royalty. This is consistent with our recommendation in Chapter 1 that the hypothetical negotiation used to assess a reasonable royalty for past infringement should take place with the benefit of *ex post* information. If that recommendation regarding reasonable royalties is followed, there will be no difference between the award for reasonable royalties and an ongoing royalty. If courts ignore *ex post* information in assessing reasonable royalty damages, we are nonetheless of the view that they

---

[198] One exception to this general recommendation arises in cases in which damages awarded already represent a lump-sum, fully paid license for both past and future use of the patented technology. However, we take no position on whether the courts should award a lump sum for both past and future use of the patented technology in circumstances in which the parties would have done so: *see* Siebrasse & Cotter 2016, 978–88 (arguing that a court should not attempt to replicate a lump sum that similarly situated parties would have agreed to in a hypothetical negotiation because an award of damages ex post cannot functionally replicate an actual lump sum received ex ante.)

[199] Seaman 2015, 219.

should take such information into account in assessing an ongoing royalty, in which a divergence between the two rates would occur. Further, to the extent an ongoing royalty is paid out on a continuing basis, rather than in a lump sum, there might be grounds, under some circumstances, for a court to revisit the ongoing-royalty order on grounds that later developments have made it manifestly inappropriate.

5

The Effect of FRAND Commitments on Patent Remedies

Jorge L. Contreras, Thomas F. Cotter, Sang Jo Jong, Brian J. Love, Nicolas Petit, Peter Picht, Norman V. Siebrasse, Rafal Sikorski, Masabumi Suzuki, and Jacques de Werra

5.1 INTRODUCTION

The rules and policies of many standards-development organizations (SDOs) require SDO participants to offer to license patents that are essential to the SDO's standards (standards-essential patents or SEPs) on terms that are "fair, reasonable, and non-discriminatory" (FRAND). This requirement is generally viewed as creating a binding obligation on the patent holder to offer or grant such licenses, though the precise content of that obligation may not be consistent across jurisdictions or SDOs. It is sometimes the case, however, that despite the existence of a FRAND obligation, the holder of a SEP and the manufacturer, seller, or user of a standardized product (an "implementer") do not enter into a license agreement, thereby causing the product to infringe the SEP. In such cases, if the parties cannot resolve their dispute privately, questions of legal liability and remedies arise.

The complex set of questions concerning the imposition of duties and liability for alleged breaches of FRAND commitments is beyond the scope of this chapter. We cover certain aspects, such as potential antitrust or competition law liability relating to such breaches, in Chapter 6. Here, we focus instead on the remedies that may be awarded once such liability is established. Such liability may be found either (or both) with respect to the SEP holder's failure to offer or grant a license on FRAND terms to the implementer, and/or the implementer's infringement of the SEPs prior to the SEP holder's granting of a license.

Assuming that liability is established, potential remedies for FRAND violations or patent infringement include monetary damages, specific performance, and injunctive relief. Monetary damages typically take the form of compensatory damages[1] paid by the implementer to the SEP holder for past infringement (i.e., the implementer's use of the patented technology prior to the issuance of a license), as well as enhanced damages under certain circumstances.[2] In return, implementers may seek specific

---

[1] *See* Chapters 1 and 2.
[2] *See* Chapter 3.

performance requiring the SEP holder to grant a license complying with the relevant FRAND conditions, as well as monetary damages to compensate for the SEP holder's breach of its FRAND commitment.[3] In addition, a SEP holder may pursue injunctive relief of its own to prevent an implementer from continuing to infringe until a license is granted.

Because specific performance is contractual or pseudo-contractual in nature and thus focuses primarily on *the terms* of the SEP holder's FRAND commitment, we consider it beyond the scope of this project. We ask instead what effect, if any, *the existence* of a prior FRAND commitment should have on the patent law remedies that a SEP holder might otherwise be able to obtain from an infringer.

5.2 FRAND COMMITMENTS AND MONETARY PATENT DAMAGES

In general, a patent holder is entitled to monetary compensation when its patent is infringed. As described in the preceding chapters, the measure of damages varies from country to country. In this section we first consider whether a FRAND commitment affects the level of monetary damages to which a SEP holder is entitled when an unlicensed implementer infringes the SEP, as compared with an award of damages assessed on general patent law principles. For example, is the "reasonable" in FRAND the same as the "reasonable" in reasonable royalty damages awarded by U.S. courts? A related question is whether the existence of a FRAND commitment precludes a monetary award based on lost profits, or a disgorgement of infringer profits, which might be available in the absence of a FRAND commitment, particularly in jurisdictions that do not base patent damages on the award of a reasonable royalty. We begin by surveying the applicable law in the United States and the European Union, and then make recommendations.

We do not address the question whether an award of "reasonable" royalties to the holder of an infringed SEP who has not made a FRAND commitment should equate to "reasonable" royalties awarded to a SEP holder that has made a FRAND commitment. The question of how to treat such SDO "outsiders" is beyond the scope of this chapter.[4]

---

[3] For example, in *Microsoft Corp.* v. *Motorola, Inc.* (9th Cir. 2015) (U.S.), Microsoft was able to collect approximately $15 million in damages for Motorola's breach of its FRAND commitment, which were primarily attributable to the costs Microsoft incurred in moving a facility out of Germany.

[4] For a discussion of the extent to which outsiders enforce SEPs, *see* Contreras 2016; *Rembrandt Wireless Tech., LP* v. *Samsung Elects. Co., Ltd.* (E.D. Tex. 2016) (U.S.) (awarding reasonable royalty damages to a holder of SEPs covering the Bluetooth standard, even though SDO participants who developed the standard committed to grant licenses on a royalty-free basis); *CSIRO* v. *Cisco Sys., Inc.* (Fed. Cir. 2015) (U.S.) (awarding "reasonable royalty" damages to SEP holder that did not make a FRAND commitment).

5.2.1 *United States*

1 Reasonable Royalty

As discussed in Chapter 1, in the United States the primary statutory measure of damages for patent infringement is a "reasonable royalty."[5] As a result, several U.S. courts that have calculated FRAND royalty rates for SEPs have looked to traditional methodologies for determining reasonable royalty damages.

For the past several decades, the calculation of reasonable royalty damages in the United States has generally followed the fifteen-factor "bottom-up" methodology[6] introduced in *Georgia-Pacific Corp. v. U.S. Plywood Corp.*[7] However, because this framework assumes that the patent holder and the infringer have no pre-existing relationship or duty toward one another, many of the assumptions underlying this analysis do not hold in cases involving FRAND-committed SEPs. This disconnect has been pointed out in several cases including *Microsoft Corp. v. Motorola, Inc.* and *Ericsson, Inc. v. D-Link Sys.* In *Microsoft*, the court expressly modified twelve of the fifteen factors as follows:

  (i)   The lack of comparability of negotiated royalty terms that fail to account for RAND obligations. (Factors 1 and 12);

 (ii)   The importance of the value of the patented technology apart from the value associated with incorporation of the patented technology into the standard. (Factors 6, 8, 10, 11, and 13);

(iii)   The importance of alternatives that could have been written into the standard instead of the patented technology, with the focus on the period before the standard was adopted and implemented. (Factor 9);

 (iv)   The purpose of the RAND commitment to encourage widespread adoption of the standard through avoidance of holdup and stacking. (Factor 15);

  (v)   The irrelevance of some of the factors because they do not relate to the RAND context (e.g., whether patentee has a policy to license others, relationship of the licensor and licensee, and the patent term). (Factors 4, 5, and 7).[8]

In *Ericsson*, the Federal Circuit noted several respects in which the *Georgia-Pacific* factors were both irrelevant and contrary to the RAND commitment under consideration.[9] Thus, as the lower court did in *Microsoft*, the Federal Circuit criticized the use of *Georgia-Pacific* Factors 4, 5, 8, 9, and 10 when considering royalties subject to a RAND commitment.[10] Though the court did not hold that

---

[5] U.S. Patent Act, 35 U.S.C. § 284.

[6] For a discussion of bottom-up versus top-down royalty calculation methodologies, *see* Section 5.2.4 below.

[7] *Georgia-Pacific Corp. v. U.S. Plywood Corp.* (S.D.N.Y. 1970, p.1120) (U.S.). *See* Chapter 1.

[8] *Microsoft Corp. v. Motorola, Inc.* (W. D. Wash. 2013, ¶¶ 99–110) (U.S.).

[9] *Ericsson, Inc. v. D-Link Sys.* (Fed. Cir. 2014, p.1230–32) (U.S.).

[10] *Id.*

a modified version of the *Georgia-Pacific* factors must always be used in cases involving SEPs, it found that the combination of errors in the lower court's instructions to the jury was significant enough to warrant remand.[11]

These changes suggest that the *Georgia-Pacific* framework, as originally conceived, is not well suited to the determination of FRAND royalty levels.[12] Moreover, there appears to be nothing in U.S. law that compels courts to utilize either the *Georgia-Pacific* framework, or patent damages law in general, to determine royalties complying with a SEP holder's FRAND commitment. What's more, the inconsistent and ad hoc application of the *Georgia-Pacific* factors to different FRAND royalty calculations has led to significantly different outcomes in different courts in the United States, even in cases concerning the same technical feature of a single standard.[13]

2 Enhanced Damages

As discussed in Chapter 3, another important element of U.S. patent damages law is the availability of "enhanced" (i.e., up to treble) damages when infringement is found to have been willful. The standard for willfulness supporting an award of enhanced damages has recently been clarified, and somewhat liberalized, by the Supreme Court of the United States in *Halo Elecs. v. Pulse Elecs.*[14] It is currently debated whether a manufacturer's implementation of a technical standard in a product without a license from the holder of a FRAND-committed SEP should be considered willful if the SEP is, indeed, infringed. On one hand, the manufacturer is clearly aware of the standard and, in many cases, the patents declared to be essential to the standard are listed in a public database. What's more, the manufacturer may even have received a notification of the patent from the patent holder. These factors might weigh in favor of a finding that the manufacturer's infringement was willful.[15] But on the other hand, independent analysts have determined that a large number of patents declared to be essential to various standards are not, in their view, actually essential,[16] and obtaining a reliable legal opinion (see Chapter 3) regarding which among hundreds or thousands of patents listed in a public database are essential to a standard is likely prohibitive in terms of cost and time. Moreover, even patents that are essential to a standard are sometimes found to be invalid or not infringed by a particular product

---

[11]   *Id.* at 1235.

[12]   Nor, as argued in Chapter 1, in the general damages context either.

[13]   *See* Bartlett & Contreras 2017 (discussing five different U.S. decisions arriving at divergent FRAND royalty rates for aspects of the IEEE Wi-Fi standard).

[14]   *Halo Elec., Inc. v. Pulse Elec., Inc.* (U.S. 2016) (U.S.).

[15]   *See* Sidak 2016b, 1109–12 (discussing criteria for enhanced damages in the context of SEPs).

[16]   For example, Goodman & Myers 2005, Fairfield 2007, and Fairfield 2010 found that only 27, 28, and 50 percent of patent families declared as "essential" to ETSI's GSM, WCDMA, and LTE standards, respectively, were actually essential to implementation of those standards.

implementing the standard.[17] These factors tend to weigh against a finding of willfulness with respect to the infringement of SEPs by standard implementers. However, even if weighing strongly against a finding of willfulness, it is not clear that such factors should amount to a categorical exclusion of enhanced damages in the case of SEP infringement.[18]

To date, we are aware of only one U.S. district court decision enhancing damages for the infringement of SEPs.[19] However, at least one member of the Court of Appeals for the Federal Circuit has acknowledged their potential availability, at least when a potential licensee has negotiated in bad faith.[20]

Beyond the threshold question whether enhanced damages may be available for the infringement of SEPs is a further question regarding the ways that the availability of enhanced damages may affect the conduct of parties in the standardization environment. As noted above, the standard measure of damages for patent infringement in the United States is a "reasonable royalty." A "reasonable" royalty is also what is required to be paid under a FRAND commitment. Thus, an opportunistic manufacturer of standardized products could decide that the most efficient course of action is not to seek a FRAND license from a SEP holder at all, but instead to delay until it is sued for infringement, at which point its maximum liability (assuming that both patent validity and infringement are established) would only be the FRAND royalty it otherwise would have paid *ex ante*. As discussed elsewhere, this form of conduct by standards implementers has been termed "holdout."[21]

The availability of enhanced damages (in addition to awards of attorney's fees and pre- and post-judgment interest) could change a standard implementer's calculus somewhat. That is, if the implementer willfully infringes SEPs under the relevant legal standards and refuses to pay royalties under a FRAND license offered by the SEP holder, then enhanced damages may be awarded in an eventual infringement

[17] *See, e.g.*, Netgear, Inc., Annual Report (Form 10-K) (Feb. 16, 2018), p.86 (reporting that the three patent claims covering 3G wireless telecom standards that were found to be infringed by a jury in *Ericsson, Inc. v. D-Link Sys.* (E.D. Tex 2013) (U.S.), *aff'd* (Fed. Cir. 2014) (U.S.) were subsequently found by the PTAB to be invalid in a series of 2015 inter partes review proceedings that were subsequently affirmed by the Federal Circuit in 2017).

[18] *See* Sidak 2016b, 1105–07 (arguing that a FRAND commitment should not per se foreclose the possibility of enhanced damages in SEP infringement cases).

[19] *See Core Wireless Licensing S.A.R.L. v. LG Electronics, Inc.* (E.D. Tex. 2016, p.2) (U.S.) (court enhanced damages by 20 percent following jury finding of willful infringement). *See also* Sidak 2016b, 1101–02 (discussing case).

[20] The prospect of enhanced damages for the intentional violation of a FRAND commitment has been noted by Chief Judge Prost of the U.S. Court of Appeals for the Federal Circuit, who wrote in the context of a dispute over the issuance of an injunction for SEPs, that "if a trial court believes that an infringer previously engaged in bad faith negotiations, it is entitled to increase the damages to account for any harm to the patentee as a result of that behavior." *Apple, Inc. v. Motorola, Inc.* (Fed. Cir. 2014, p.1342) (U.S.) (Prost, J., concurring). For additional discussion of relevant literature, *see* Chapter 7 n.177.

[21] This is sometimes also referred to as the "catch-me-if-you-can" problem: for more discussion, *see* Chapters 3 and 7.

suit by the SEP holder. If so, the cost of holding out could far exceed the FRAND royalty that would originally have been payable. Accordingly, the availability of enhanced damages, at least in the United States, could reduce the risk that opportunistic standards implementers will hold out and refuse to pay FRAND royalties that are legitimately due.

5.2.2 *European Union – Applicability of* Huawei v. ZTE *to Monetary Remedies*

As discussed in Chapter 6 and in Section 5.3 below, the Court of Justice of the European Union (CJEU) in *Huawei Techs. Co. Ltd.* v. *ZTE Corp.* lays out a procedure that a SEP holder must follow in order to avoid committing an abuse of its dominant position under Article 102 of the Treaty on the Functioning of the European Union (TFEU) when it seeks an injunction to prevent infringement of a SEP. The CJEU's decision in *Huawei*, however, does not explicitly address the issue of monetary damages. In fact, the CJEU states in *Huawei* that Article 102 of the TFEU does not prohibit a SEP holder "from bringing an action for infringement against the alleged infringer of its SEP and seeking the rendering of accounts in relation to past acts of use of that SEP or an award of damages in respect of those acts of use."[22] This suggestion has been followed in subsequent decisions rendered by German courts. In *NTT DoCoMo* v. *HTC*, for instance, the Mannheim District Court noted that a SEP holder that has made a FRAND commitment must follow the *Huawei* rules of conduct only with regard to an action for injunction or the recall of products. It is, however, free to bring an action seeking monetary remedies in relation to past acts of infringement.[23] Comparable statements regarding the rules of conduct derived from *Huawei* v. *ZTE* were made by the Mannheim District Court in *Pioneer* v. *Acer*[24] and *Philips* v. *Archos*[25] and by the Düsseldorf District Court in *Unwired Planet* v. *Samsung.*[26] Accordingly, a SEP holder does not commit an abuse under Article 102 of the TFEU even if it brings an action for damages without having notified the implementer of an infringement and without having offered it a FRAND license.

This said, the obligations developed by the CJEU in *Huawei* v. *ZTE* do have an *indirect* impact on the extent to which damages and the rendering of accounts are due. Where the SEP holder fails to grant a FRAND license although it has made a FRAND commitment and the implementer has expressed its readiness to take a license, damages are limited to the FRAND royalty level (presumably excluding other forms of damages such as lost profits and disgorgement of infringer's profits)

---

[22]   *Huawei Techs. Co. Ltd.* v. *ZTE Corp.* (CJEU 2015, ¶ 76) (EU).
[23]   LG Mannheim v. 29.1.2016 – 7 O 66/15 – *NTT DoCoMo* v. *HTC,* ¶ II, 1 (Ger.).
[24]   LG Mannheim v. 8.1.2016 – 7 O 96/14 – *Pioneer* v. *Acer,* ¶ 79 (Ger.).
[25]   LG Mannheim v. 1.7.2016 – 7 O 209/15 – *Philips* v. *Archos,* ¶ III, IV, 1 (Ger.).
[26]   LG Düsseldorf v. 19.1.2016 – 4b O 120/14 – *Unwired Planet* v. *Samsung,* ¶ VII, 6, b, aa, bb (Ger.).

but *only* for the period after the SEP holder's abusive refusal to license.[27] Claims for information and the rendering of accounts must, in this event, be limited to what is necessary for determining these FRAND-based damages.[28]

What's more, implementers of standards who have been refused a license in violation of a SEP holder's FRAND commitment may themselves be entitled to monetary damages under some interpretations of these cases.[29] Though this theory has not yet been tested in court, such claims could be similar to U.S. breach of contract claims that have been brought successfully against SEP holders in cases such as *Microsoft Corp.* v. *Motorola, Inc.* Moreover, it is possible that if a standards implementer fails to comply with the procedures outlined in *Huawei* v. *ZTE*, a SEP holder, without violating Article 102 of the TFEU, may be permitted to seek damages in excess of reasonable royalties, including lost profits or disgorgement of the infringer's profits.[30]

5.2.3 *National Damages Laws*

The courts of every country will, in general, evaluate claims for FRAND damages in view of its national rules and precedents regarding contractual interpretation and remedies. A full discussion of the rules of every country is beyond the scope of this chapter. However, in the Appendix we provide a discussion of several exemplary countries (Germany, Switzerland, Korea, Japan, and China) for illustrative purposes. It is important to note, however, that while we discuss the potential impact of FRAND commitments on monetary patent damages under a variety of national laws, we do not necessarily believe that FRAND royalties negotiated under global license agreements, which are increasingly viewed as the norm,[31] should specify royalties on a country-by-country basis, or that the interpretation of FRAND under the policy of a particular SDO should vary based on the patent damages laws of the country in which parties to a dispute may adjudicate the level of FRAND royalties.[32]

---

[27]   *Id.* at ¶ VII, 6, b, dd.

[28]   *Id.* at ¶ VII, 6, b, ee.

[29]   LG Düsseldorf v. 19.1.2016 – 4b O 120/14 – *Unwired Planet* v. *Samsung*, ¶ 353 (Ger.); LG Düsseldorf v. 19.1.2016 – 4b O 122/14 – *Unwired Planet* v. *Samsung*, ¶ 370 (Ger.); Picht 2018, 42.

[30]   *See id.* at ¶ VII, 6, b, cc, dd.

[31]   *See, e.g., Unwired Planet Int'l Ltd.* v. *Huawei Techs. Co.* (Pat 2017) (UK); *TCL Commc'ns Tech. Holdings, Ltd.* v. *Telefonaktiebolaget LM Ericsson* (C.D. Cal. 2017) (U.S.). For a discussion of issues surrounding national versus global FRAND licensing, *see* Contreras 2017b.

[32]   *See* Teece et al. 2012, 34 ("[T]o suggest that RAND-reasonable is to be interpreted in accordance with the vagaries of different countries' patent infringement damages law could make what is and what is not RAND-reasonable different from country to country."). This being said, recent cases have appropriately (if imperfectly) attempted to adjust determined FRAND royalty rates based on varying market factors, patent coverage, and patent strength in different regions of the world (e.g., United States/Europe v. China and so-called minor markets). *See, e.g., Unwired Planet Int'l Ltd.* v. *Huawei Techs. Co.* (Pat 2017) (UK); *TCL Commc'ns Tech. Holdings, Ltd.* v. *Telefonaktiebolaget LM Ericsson* (C.D. Cal. 2017) (U.S.).

5.2.4 Discussion and Analysis: Monetary Damages and FRAND

The fact that courts in the United States have chosen to determine FRAND royalty rates using the methodology of patent damages calculations (including the *Georgia-Pacific* framework) is, most likely, the result of the fact that the term "reasonable royalty" is used in both the U.S. Patent Act and the SDO policies establishing FRAND commitments. Yet these two concepts (patent damages and FRAND royalty rates) arose via different historical pathways[33] and are intended to achieve different goals. FRAND royalty rates are created through private agreements among SEP holders and SDOs, or public promises made by SEP holders in the market-place. As pointed out in Chapter 1, in the vast number of license agreements made outside the shadow of litigation, royalty rates are not determined using the analytical framework that courts employ to calculate damages in litigation. No SDOs of which we are aware have pointed to the *Georgia-Pacific* framework, or patent damages analysis in general, as guideposts for determining FRAND rates.[34] To the extent that SDO participants have suggested FRAND rates for different standards, these rates have been developed based on industry norms and market factors,[35] rather than the hypothetical negotiation framework mandated under *Georgia-Pacific*.[36]

But because the term "reasonable" is used in these two different contexts – patent damages and FRAND licenses – the temptation to recruit one (the extensive body of case precedent relating to patent damages) for use when addressing the other (the proper level of FRAND royalties) has proven too tempting to resist for U.S. courts. As a result, U.S. courts determining FRAND royalty rates regularly invoke the case law and methodologies of reasonable royalty damages, including the imperfect *Georgia-Pacific* framework and all of its baggage, when calculating a FRAND royalty or instructing the jury in doing so, leading to an apparent convergence of contractual FRAND damages and "reasonable royalty" patent infringement damages.[37]

Outside of the United States, where patent damages are not so closely tied to a "reasonable royalty," there is less temptation for courts to tie FRAND royalties to patent damages calculations, though this has on occasion occurred, for example, in *Samsung v. Apple Japan*.[38] In other jurisdictions such as Korea, however, patent

---

[33] The historical origins of modern FRAND commitments in the United States can be traced to a series of antitrust remedial orders entered from the 1940s to the 1970s that required that patent holders found to have engaged in anticompetitive conduct make licenses to those patents available on terms that were "reasonable." This language was later adopted by ANSI and other SDOs around the world. *See* Contreras 2015b.

[34] *See also* Teece et al. 2012, 33–34 ("[W]e are not aware of any SSO that has explicitly announced that [RAND royalties and 'reasonable' royalty patent damages] are intended to be synonymous.").

[35] *See* Contreras 2015a.

[36] Chapter 1 critiques the *Georgia-Pacific* factors for much the same reason in respect of reasonable royalty determinations more generally.

[37] *See* Contreras & Gilbert 2015 (observing this convergence but arguing that both FRAND royalty calculations and the U.S. reasonable royalty damage framework should be revamped to focus on the "incremental value" of the patented technology to the infringing product).

[38] *See Samsung Elecs. Co. v. Apple Japan LLC* (IP High Ct. 2014) (Japan).

damages are based on the disgorgement of profits of the infringer, which bear little relation to reasonable royalties.[39] To be sure, in the non-U.S. cases that have resulted in written decisions concerning FRAND royalty determinations to date, none have made reference to *Georgia-Pacific* or its fifteen-factor analytical framework.

The *Georgia-Pacific* framework supports what has been termed a "bottom-up" approach to calculating patent royalties. Under a bottom-up approach, royalties are determined case by case depending on the determined value of the patents in suit, without significant regard for the value of other patents that may cover the same technology or standard. Such approaches are discussed in Chapter 1, both with and without application of the *Georgia-Pacific* framework.

One promising alternative to a bottom-up approach in the area of standards-essential patents is what has been termed a "top-down" approach to determining FRAND royalties. Such top-down mechanisms begin by determining the aggregate royalty burden associated with a standard when considering the royalties owed to any particular patent holder.[40] As the U.S. District Court for the Northern District of Illinois noted in *In re Innovatio IP Ventures, LLC Patent Litigation*, "the determination of a [F]RAND royalty must address the risk of royalty stacking by considering the aggregate royalties that would apply if other [SEP] holders made royalty demands of the implementer."[41] Top-down approaches recognize that when multiple patents cover a single standard, the rate charged by one SEP holder will necessarily affect the rates that the other SEP holders are able to obtain from a single manufacturer.[42] Once an aggregate royalty is determined, various methodologies can then be used to allocate that total among individual SEP holders.[43] As explained by the European Commission in a recent communication, "an individual SEP cannot be considered in isolation. Parties need to take into account a reasonable aggregate rate for the standard, assessing the overall added value of the technology."[44]

---

[39] *See Samsung Elecs. Co. v. Apple Korea Ltd.* (Dist. Ct. 2012) (Kor.).

[40] *See* Cotter 2018, 206–07 (discussing the *Innovatio* top-down analysis); Pentheroudakis & Baron 2017, 95–96 (analyzing top-down approaches in *Innovatio* and other cases); Bartlett & Contreras 2017 (discussing the benefits of top-down approaches).

[41] *In re Innovatio IP Ventures, LLC Patent Litigation* (N.D. Ill. 2013, p.9) (U.S.) (internal quotes omitted). It is worth noting that the specific top-down royalty approach used by the court in *Innovatio*, which was based on the deemed profit of a hypothetical component supplier, was somewhat unusual and has not been followed by other courts, nor do we endorse it.

[42] *See* Lemley & Shapiro 2007a, 2011 ("[T]he royalty rate negotiated by one patent holder is affected by the rates the downstream firm pays to other patent holders, so a proper analysis must account for the joint determination of all the royalty rates.").

[43] Allocation methodologies, while critical to the determination of FRAND royalties, are subject to an extensive literature, a discussion of which is beyond the scope of this chapter. *See generally* Bartlett & Contreras 2017, 208–09 (cataloging a range of patent valuation and allocation methodologies, including numerical proportionality/headcount, citation count, cost recovery, real option value, substitute cost, footprint, discounted cash flow, and comparable license analysis).

[44] European Commission, COM (2017) 712 final.

Such a top-down approach was used by the Japanese IP High Court in *Samsung v. Apple Japan*, which held that the aggregate royalty burden for the 3G UMTS standard should not exceed 5 percent, based on four public statements and informal agreements among industry participants relating to the standard.[45] The court then allocated a portion of this total royalty to Samsung's asserted UMTS-essential patent based on the total number of SEPs likely to be essential to the standard.[46]

The English Patents Court used two methods to calculate a FRAND royalty in *Unwired Planet v. Huawei*:[47] one based on comparable licenses and one (used to check the former result) based on a top-down methodology similar to that of the Japanese IP High Court in *Samsung v. Apple Japan*. In *Unwired Planet*, the court determined the aggregate royalty attributable to a standard under all applicable SEPs and then allocated an appropriate amount to the SEP holder asserting the patents-in-suit. Under the court's top-down methodology, the FRAND royalty was calculated as the aggregate SEP royalty burden of a particular standard on a product (e.g., the portion of a smartphone's price that is attributable to the 4G standard) multiplied by the percentage of 4G SEPs held by the plaintiff.[48] To calculate the aggregate royalty burden attributable to the various standards in suit, the court considered public statements made by other holders of SEPs with respect to royalties on those standards.[49] It then calculated the plaintiff's share of the total SEP pool, using a variety of counting and filtering methodologies, including a filter for the likely essentiality of the patents in the asserted portfolio.[50] The result calculated by the court was consistent with the result that it obtained using a methodology based on comparable licenses.

Top-down approaches can avoid both the potential inconsistencies associated with ad hoc adaptations of damages frameworks such as *Georgia-Pacific* and contrast with other "bottom-up" royalty approaches, in which royalties due to individual patent holders are determined independently of one another, whereby the total royalty burden emerges only as the sum of its individual components.[51] Courts applying bottom-up approaches have used different royalty calculation criteria and

---

[45] *Samsung Elecs. Co. v. Apple Japan LLC* (IP High Ct. 2014, p.131) (Japan) (FRAND I).

[46] *Id.* at 132, 137–38 (noting that out of 1,889 patent families declared as essential to UMTS, an independent research report issued by Fairfield Resources International, Inc. found that only 529 of these patent families "are or are likely to be essential" to the standard. Accordingly, the court based the royalty due to Samsung on a total pool of 529, rather than 1,889, SEP families). For a more detailed discussion of the methodology, *see* Siebrasse & Cotter 2017b, 384–85.

[47] *Unwired Planet Int'l Ltd. v. Huawei Techs. Co.* (Pat 2017) (UK).

[48] *Id.* at ¶ 178.

[49] *Id.* at ¶¶ 264–72. While such statements are not ideal data points on which to base aggregate royalty determinations and can be, as the court acknowledged, both unreliable and self-serving, they are, to date, the most useful data available. *But see* Contreras 2017a (suggesting that joint negotiation of such rates within SDOs would yield better data on which to base such determinations).

[50] *Unwired Planet Int'l Ltd. v. Huawei Techs. Co.* (Pat 2017, ¶¶ 325–29) (UK). For a more detailed discussion of the methodology, *see* Siebrasse & Cotter 2017b, 384–86.

[51] *See* Bartlett & Contreras 2017, 293–95 (discussing and providing examples of bottom-up calculations).

factors on a case-by-case basis, even when patents covering the same features of the same standard have been involved, thus yielding inconsistent and potentially excessive results.[52] For example, in 2013 and 2014, five different U.S. district courts, either in bench trials or through a jury, calculated royalties for a total of thirty-five SEPs covering Wi-Fi standards. The aggregate royalty for these thirty-five patents amounted to approximately 4.5 percent of the total sale price of a typical $50 Wi-Fi router.[53] Yet it has been estimated that there are approximately 3,000 patents covering the Wi-Fi standard,[54] nearly one hundred times the number subject to adjudication thus far. Were the royalty for each of these patents to be calculated in a similarly uncoordinated, bottom-up manner, the aggregate patent royalty on a Wi-Fi router could easily surpass the product's total selling price by an order of magnitude or more.

This being said, implementing top-down approaches is not without its challenges and practical difficulties. Most notably, there is not yet a uniformly accepted methodology for determining the aggregate royalty level for all patents covering a particular standard. In the *Apple Japan* and *Unwired Planet* cases discussed above, the courts relied on public statements made by SEP holders, statements that at least one court acknowledged to be of limited reliability and manifestly "self-serving."[55] What's more, even once an aggregate royalty for all patents covering a standard is determined, a methodology must be developed to allocate that aggregate royalty among the many different holders of SEPs covering that standard. In most cases to date, courts using top-down methodologies have simply allocated the aggregate royalty among SEP holders on a simple "numerical proportionality" or one-patent-one-share basis.[56] While this methodology is easily applied, it overlooks inherent value differences among patents such as those identified in *Microsoft Corp. v. Motorola, Inc.*

More broadly, while in principle a top-down methodology has several attractive features as compared with a bottom-up approach, its application to a given case is only as good as the available evidence. Because the top-down and bottom-up approaches rely on different types of evidence, one or the other might be preferable in a particular case, given the evidence at hand.

---

[52] *See id.* at 295–96 and table 2.

[53] *Id.*

[54] *In re Innovatio IP Ventures, LLC Patent Litigation* (N.D. Ill. 2013, p.41) (U.S.).

[55] *Unwired Planet Int'l Ltd.* v. *Huawei Techs. Co.* (Pat 2017) (UK). *See also TCL Commc'ns Tech. Holdings, Ltd.* v. *Telefonaktiebolaget LM Ericsson* (C.D. Cal. 2017) (U.S.) (court similarly relying on public statements); Contreras 2017a (discussing methodologies for aggregate royalty determination). This being said, unlike patents other than SEPs, such public statements do exist in the context of SEPs, at least giving some indication what relevant parties have concluded about aggregate value. In *In re Innovatio* the court relied on the profit margin on the smallest salable patent practicing unit: for a discussion and critique, see Siebrasse and Cotter 2017b, 381–82 who suggest that the methodology used in *Innovatio* was flawed in various respects.

[56] As Birss. J, noted in *Unwired Planet Int'l Ltd.* v. *Huawei Techs. Co.* (Pat 2017) (UK), "patent counting" may be unavoidable when large numbers of patents are involved.

For the foregoing reasons, we recommend that (1) consistent with the recommendations in Chapter 1, courts assessing FRAND royalty rates, particularly outside the United States, reject strict application of the *Georgia-Pacific* fifteen-factor hypothetical negotiation framework when making that assessment, and (2) courts assessing FRAND royalty rates select a methodology for calculating these rates that is best supported by the available evidence, whether such evidence be sufficiently comparable license agreements covering the same patents, or general consensus on aggregate royalty rates for an overall standard or technology, and, if the evidence would support using multiple approaches, consider utilizing both bottom-up and top-down royalty calculation methodologies and comparing the results. We also propose that further research be conducted regarding suitable methodologies for determining the aggregate top-down royalty burden for particular standards and for allocating aggregate royalties among individual holders of SEPs, with the understanding that if a reliable method for determining such an aggregate royalty burden can be developed, it would result in a desirable methodology for calculating FRAND royalty rates.

Finally, we recognize that there may be a potential role for enhanced damages in deterring intentional "holdout" conduct of a potential licensee, and thus propose that further research be conducted regarding the potential deterrent effect of such damages on holdout behavior in the SEP context. We take no position regarding the potential availability of patent damages in excess of FRAND levels under German or EU case law.

5.3 FRAND COMMITMENTS AND INJUNCTIVE RELIEF

5.3.1 *United States*

The judicial framework for injunctive relief in patent cases in the United States is set forth in the Supreme Court of the United States's 2006 decision in *eBay v. MercExchange*, which is discussed at length in Chapter 4. Under *eBay*, a court considering whether to grant an injunction to a SEP holder must balance four equitable factors: whether the SEP holder would suffer irreparable harm absent issuance of the injunction, whether the SEP holder would adequately be compensated by monetary damages, whether a balancing of interests of the parties favors granting the injunction, and the effect of the injunction on the public interest.

In *Microsoft Corp. v. Motorola, Inc.*, Motorola sought an injunction to prevent Microsoft's continued infringement of Motorola's patents covering two standards (IEEE's 802.11 and ITU's H.264). The court found that Motorola made FRAND commitments with respect to these patents, and that Microsoft agreed to accept a license on reasonable terms. The court evaluated these facts in view of the four *eBay* factors and determined that Motorola did not suffer an irreparable injury or show that monetary damages would be inadequate to compensate it for the infringement. Accordingly, the court denied Motorola's request for an injunction. In *Realtek Semiconductor Corp. v. LSI Corp.*,[57] the U.S. District Court for the Northern District of California held that a SEP holder breached its FRAND commitment by seeking injunctive relief against an implementer of a standard *before* the patent holder offered a license to the implementer. Again, the injunction was denied.

These district court decisions laid the groundwork for the Federal Circuit to consider the issue of permanent injunctive relief in FRAND-related cases. In *Apple, Inc. v. Motorola, Inc.*, the Federal Circuit analyzed Motorola's request for an injunction against the sale of Apple products allegedly infringing Motorola's FRAND-committed SEPs.[58] The trial judge denied Motorola's request, reasoning that a patent holder making a FRAND commitment, by definition, has acknowledged that a monetary royalty would be adequate compensation for a license under the patent, thereby eliminating any argument that the infringement would cause the patent holder irreparable harm under *eBay*.[59]

Though the Federal Circuit panel was divided on some issues, all three members of the panel concurred that "[t]o the extent that the district court applied a *per se* rule that injunctions are unavailable for SEPs, it erred."[60] The court reasoned that the *eBay* framework "provides ample strength and flexibility for analyzing FRAND-committed patents and industry standards in general," and found no reason to create "a separate rule or analytical framework for addressing injunctions for FRAND-committed patents."[61] The court acknowledged that under the *eBay* framework, "a patentee subject to FRAND commitments may have difficulty establishing irreparable harm."[62] Nevertheless, "an injunction may be justified where an infringer unilaterally refuses a FRAND royalty or unreasonably delays negotiations to the same effect."[63] With this in mind, the Federal Circuit affirmed the district court's rejection of Motorola's request for an injunction.[64]

Chief Judge Rader, dissenting-in-part, argued that a genuine issue of material fact existed regarding Apple's conduct with respect to the acceptance of a FRAND

---

[57] *Realtek Semiconductor Corp. v. LSI Corp.* (N.D. Cal. 2014) (U.S.).

[58] *Apple, Inc. v. Motorola, Inc.* (Fed. Cir. 2014) (U.S.).

[59] *Apple, Inc. v. Motorola, Inc.* (N.D. Ill. 2012) (U.S.).

[60] *Apple, Inc. v. Motorola, Inc.* (Fed. Cir. 2014, p.1331) (U.S.).

[61] *Id.* at 1331–32.

[62] *Id.* at 1332.

[63] *Id.* (citing DOJ & USPTO 2013). As discussed above in Section 5.2.1.2, this phenomenon is known as "holdout" or "reverse holdup" and is said to occur when an infringer refuses in bad faith to accept the FRAND license terms offered by a SEP holder.

[64] *Apple, Inc. v. Motorola, Inc.* (Fed. Cir. 2014, p.1332) (U.S.). Interestingly, even though *Apple v. Motorola* did not involve antitrust issues (and despite the fact that the Department of Justice (DOJ) is required to uphold the law as it is fashioned by the courts of the United States), in 2017 the head of the DOJ's Antitrust Division sharply critiqued the Federal Circuit's reasoning in *Apple v. Motorola*, implying that it transformed FRAND commitments into a "compulsory licensing scheme." Delrahim 2017.

license from Motorola (i.e., potential holdout) and that the case should have been remanded for further fact finding on this issue.[65] In sharp contrast, Judge Prost, concurring-in-part and dissenting-in-part, disagreed with the majority's suggestion that an alleged infringer's refusal to negotiate a license could ever serve as a basis for issuing an injunction on a FRAND-committed patent.[66] She reasoned that while a potential licensee's bad faith negotiation might justify an award of enhanced damages (see discussion above), the *eBay* "irreparable harm" test would nevertheless militate against granting an injunction on a FRAND-committed patent.[67] However, Judge Prost conceded that an injunction might be appropriate if the patentee were unable to collect the damages to which it was entitled, for example, if the infringer refused to pay an adjudicated damage award or was beyond the jurisdiction of the court.[68]

The U.S. Department of Justice (DOJ) and Federal Trade Commission (FTC) have also taken an interest in the propriety of parties bound by FRAND commitments seeking injunctive relief. In 2011, the FTC issued guidelines specifying that under *eBay*, injunctive relief might not always be justified in the FRAND context, writing that "[a] prior [F]RAND commitment can provide strong evidence that denial of the injunction and ongoing royalties will not irreparably harm the patentee."[69] And in 2012, the DOJ approved three large patent acquisition transactions only after the involved parties (Apple, Google, and Microsoft) committed not to seek injunctions preventing the use of FRAND-committed SEPs.[70]

In late 2012 and 2013, the FTC brought two actions under Section 5 of the FTC Act to address suspected violations of FRAND commitments.[71] In the first such action, the FTC investigated Robert Bosch GmbH in connection with its proposed acquisition of a firm called SPX.[72] According to the complaint, SPX participated in an SDO developing standards for automotive cooling systems.[73] Despite having made a FRAND commitment to the SDO, SPX asserted two patents covering the SDO's standards against suspected infringers and then sought injunctive relief to prevent future sales of infringing products.[74] The FTC argued that SPX's attempt to obtain injunctive relief in the face of its FRAND commitment was inherently coercive and oppressive, and thereby constituted an unfair method of competition in violation of Section 5. Bosch settled the action by committing that SPX would no longer seek injunctive relief in this context.

---

[65]   *Apple, Inc. v. Motorola, Inc.* at 1333–34.
[66]   *Id.* at 1342.
[67]   *Id.*
[68]   *Id.* at 1343.
[69]   FTC 2011, 235.
[70]   *See* Contreras 2012.
[71]   Under Section 5 of the FTC Act, 15 U.S.C. § 45(a)(1), the FTC may prosecute "unfair methods of competition" and "unfair or deceptive acts or practices."
[72]   *In the Matter of Robert Bosch GmbH* (FTC Apr. 23, 2013) (U.S.).
[73]   *Id.* at 715–19.
[74]   *Id.* at 718–19.

The FTC again took action to address a patent holder's attempt to obtain injunctive relief in the face of a prior FRAND commitment in *Motorola Mobility LLC and Google, Inc.*[75] In that case, Motorola (later acquired by Google) held patents essential to practice standards promulgated by IEEE, ITU, and ETSI. Motorola participated in, and made FRAND commitments to, each of these SDOs. Nevertheless, in separate suits asserting these patents against Apple and Microsoft, Motorola sought exclusion orders at the ITC and injunctions in federal court to prevent future sales of standards-compliant products, even though both defendant implementers were allegedly willing to acquire licenses to Motorola's patents. The FTC asserted that Motorola's attempt to enjoin sales of Apple and Microsoft products using its standards-essential patents constituted an unfair method of competition in violation of Section 5.[76] The dispute was settled after Google agreed not to seek injunctive relief against an infringer of certain FRAND-committed patents unless the infringer was beyond the jurisdiction of the U.S. courts, stated in writing that it would not accept a license of the patent, refused to enter into a license agreement determined to meet the FRAND requirement by a court or arbitrator, or failed to provide written confirmation of an offer of a FRAND license.[77]

As discussed in Chapter 4, U.S. courts considering the issuance of an injunction must also consider the potential effect of the injunction on the public interest. While public interest considerations have not yet played a major role in the injunction analysis undertaken by courts adjudicating FRAND disputes, the public interest has played a large role in certain SEP-related proceedings before the U.S. International Trade Commission (ITC), an independent federal agency. Similar to a court's power to issue an injunction to prevent future infringement of a patent within the United States, the ITC has the authority to issue exclusion orders to prevent the importation of infringing products into the United States.[78] In considering whether to grant such an exclusion order, the ITC is required, among other things, to consider "the effect of such exclusion upon the public health and welfare, competitive conditions in the United States economy, the production of like or directly competitive articles in the United States, and United States consumers."[79] This requirement has generally been referred to as the ITC's "public interest" requirement.

In several recent cases, the ITC has considered requests for exclusion orders against products infringing one or more FRAND-committed SEPs. In 2013, the ITC issued an exclusion order prohibiting Apple from importing devices allegedly infringing certain Samsung FRAND-committed SEPs into the United States.[80] But

---

[75] *In the Matter of Motorola Mobility LLC and Google Inc.* (FTC July 23, 2013) (Decision and Order).
[76] *Id.* at 2–3.
[77] *Id.* at 8.
[78] Tariff Act of 1930, 19 U.S.C. § 1337(a)(1)(A).
[79] *Id.* at § 1337(d)(1).
[80] *In the Matter of Certain Electronic Devices, Including Wireless Communication Devices, Portable Music and Data Processing Devices, and Tablet Computers* (ITC June 4, 2013) (U.S.). Samsung could invoke an ITC proceeding because it has substantial operations in the United States. Apple was

in a surprising reversal, the U.S. Trade Representative (USTR) disapproved (vetoed) the ITC's exclusion order citing, among other things, the importance of standardized products to the U.S. economy.[81]

In 2013, the DOJ and the U.S. Patent and Trademark Office (PTO) issued a joint Policy Statement relating to the consideration of the public interest with respect to ITC exclusion orders. They state that "the remedy of an injunction or exclusion order may be inconsistent with the public interest ... where an exclusion order based on a F/RAND-encumbered patent appears to be incompatible with the terms of a patent holder's existing F/RAND licensing commitment."[82] In this Policy Statement, the DOJ and PTO consider circumstances in which an injunction or exclusion order *may* be an appropriate remedy, including cases in which an implementer refuses to accept the FRAND license being offered, refuses to pay a reasonable royalty, refuses to engage in negotiation, or is not subject to the jurisdiction of a court that could award damages.

The FTC has reached similar conclusions regarding circumstances under which the public interest would, and would not, be served by the issuance of an ITC exclusion order against a product infringing a FRAND-committed SEP. In a written Statement to the ITC, the FTC reasoned that the ITC's public interest considerations "support denial of an exclusion order unless the holder of the RAND-encumbered SEP has made a reasonable royalty offer" that has not been accepted by the implementer.[83] The FTC has also suggested that the ITC consider ways to lessen the harmful impact of exclusion orders, for example, by delaying their effectiveness to give the infringer time to design around the asserted patent, and circumscribing the scope of exclusion orders to cover only infringing articles.

5.3.2 *European Union*

Much of the European Union's law regarding injunctions and SEPs stems from the CJEU's 2015 decision in *Huawei* v. *ZTE*.[84] *Huawei* establishes that in order to comply with EU competition law, a SEP holder that wishes to seek an injunction against an unlicensed implementer without committing an abuse of dominance under Article 102 of the TFEU must engage in a series of procedural steps including (i) alerting the unlicensed implementer of the infringement; and (ii) issuing an initial FRAND offer if the implementer manifests interest in the conclusion of a licensing agreement (these steps are described in greater detail below).

subject to an exclusion order against its products because they were manufactured in China and other countries.

[81] Froman 2013.

[82] DOJ & USPTO 2013, 6.

[83] FTC 2012.

[84] *Huawei Techs. Co. Ltd.* v. *ZTE Corp.* (CJEU 2015) (EU). In addition to member states of the European Union, it is likely that the *Huawei* ruling would be followed in non-EU member states, such as Switzerland.

There is some disagreement among commentators regarding the circumstances under which *Huawei* applies. *Huawei* involved alleged conduct that is termed an "exclusionary" abuse under Article 102 of the TFEU. That is, the holder of a FRAND-pledged SEP seeks to "prevent products manufactured by competitors from appearing or remaining on the market and thereby reserve to itself the manufacture of the product in question."[85] In the view of some commentators who rely on the literal wording of the opinion, *Huawei* can only be read to encompass such exclusionary conduct,[86] and does not contemplate antitrust liability for so-called exploitative abuses (i.e., against firms that use injunctions on FRAND-pledged SEPs to extract unfair licensing terms, a problem often described as "patent holdup," as described in Chapter 7). Others, however, take the position that, because Article 102 of the TFEU deals with both exclusionary and exploitative abuses, there is no reason to assume that the CJEU in *Huawei* intended to limit its ruling to exclusionary abuses, a point that is important in the ongoing discussion of conduct by patent assertion entities (PAEs) that largely seek monetary remedies.[87]

There is also disagreement over the effect that *Huawei* seeks to achieve. Some argue that under *Huawei* the nature of a pledge to grant a license on FRAND terms is purely procedural. Under this interpretation, FRAND may be understood as a "comity device" that generates bilateral fair play obligations on patent holders and prospective licensees.[88] This understanding differs from the alternative interpretation of FRAND as imposing substantive limits on the royalty that may be charged.

1 *Huawei* v. ZTE – Procedure

The question whether and to what extent a FRAND undertaking given by a dominant SEP holder to an SDO limits its right to bring an action for prohibitory injunction (or for the recall of products) is clarified in *Huawei v. ZTE*. According to the CJEU the SEP holder is still able to seek an injunction, but "in order to prevent an action for a prohibitory injunction . . . from being regarded as abusive [under EU competition law], the [SEP holder] must comply with conditions which seek to ensure a fair balance between the interests concerned."[89] These conditions include the following:

i. The SEP holder is not allowed to bring such action against the implementer without prior notice to or prior consultation with the implementer, even if the SEP has already been used by the implementer.[90] The SEP holder's notification

---

[85] *Id.* at ¶ 52.
[86] Petit 2017, 301.
[87] *See* Contreras & Picht 2017 and Chapter 6.
[88] *See* CEN-CENELEC 2015.
[89] *Huawei Techs. Co. Ltd. v. ZTE Corp.* (CJEU 2015, ¶ 55) (EU).
[90] *Id.* at ¶ 60.

should alert the implementer of the infringement by designating the SEP and specifying the way in which it has been infringed. This is because, owing to the large number of SEPs incorporated in some standards, it is not certain that an implementer will necessarily be aware that it is using a patent that is both valid and essential to the standard.[91]

ii. After the implementer has expressed its willingness to conclude a licensing agreement, it is for the SEP holder to present a specific, written offer for a license on FRAND terms, in accordance with the undertaking given to the SDO, specifying, in particular, the amount of the royalty and the way in which that royalty is to be calculated.[92]

iii. The implementer, in turn, must diligently respond to that offer, in accordance with recognized commercial practices in the field and in good faith. The required conduct must be established on the basis of objective factors and implies, in particular, that there are no delaying tactics. Should the implementer not accept the offer, it may rely on the abusive nature of an action for prohibitory injunction or for the recall of products only if it has submitted to the proprietor of the SEP in question, promptly and in writing, a specific counteroffer that corresponds to FRAND terms.[93] Furthermore, where the implementer is using the teachings of the SEP before a licensing agreement has been concluded, it must, from the point at which its counteroffer is rejected, provide appropriate security, for instance by providing a bank guarantee or by placing the amount necessary on deposit. The calculation of the security must include, inter alia, the number of the past acts of use of the SEP, and the alleged infringer must be able to render an account in respect of those acts of use.[94]

iv. Where no agreement is reached on the details of the FRAND terms following the counteroffer of the implementer, the parties may, by common agreement, request that the amount of the royalty be determined by an independent third party, by decision without delay.[95]

2 Cases Interpreting *Huawei* v. ZTE

The rules of conduct developed by the CJEU in *Huawei* v. ZTE were a response to the restrictive framework developed under the German *Orange-Book-Standard*[96] and *Standard-Spundfass*[97] cases. The *Huawei* framework, which offers an approach that better balances the interests of SEP holders and standards implementers, serves

---

[91] *Id.* at ¶ 61–62.
[92] *Id.* at ¶ 63.
[93] *Id.* at ¶ 65–66.
[94] *Id.* at ¶ 67.
[95] *Id.* at ¶ 68.
[96] BGH v. 6.5.2009 – KZR 39/06 – *Orange-Book-Standard* (Ger.).
[97] BGH v. 13.7.2004 – KZR 40/02 – *Standard-Spundfass* (Ger.).

as general guidance for FRAND licensing negotiations. While the framework under *Huawei* appears procedural in nature, it also embodies important substantive concerns of EU competition law. The steps required by the parties under *Huawei*, as well as certain issues that require further clarification and that national courts (principally, but not exclusively, in Germany) are in the process of working out, are discussed below.

A) RESPONSE BY IMPLEMENTER. As regards the SEP holder's infringement notification, there are two issues of particular interest. First, German courts have considered the time limits within which the alleged infringer has to express its willingness to conclude a licensing agreement on FRAND terms.[98] The Düsseldorf District Court found in *Saint Lawrence v. Vodafone*[99] that the more details the infringement notification contains, the less time remains for the implementer to examine the patent(s) at issue and to express its willingness to conclude such an agreement. The findings of the lower court were confirmed by the Düsseldorf Higher Regional Court because the implementer, by waiting more than five months after the infringement notification was given, reacted belatedly and in an evasive manner.[100] In the case of *Saint Lawrence v. Deutsche Telekom* the Mannheim District Court held that there was no sufficient expression of willingness to conclude a licensing agreement on FRAND terms because the supplier of an implementer, acting as intervenor in the proceedings, needed more than three months to submit a license request after it became aware of the action for prohibitory injunction.[101] As the Düsseldorf District Court found in *Saint Lawrence v. Vodafone*, an infringement notification can be omitted if the implementer already disposes of all necessary information and lacks willingness to license.[102]

B) CONTENT OF INFRINGEMENT NOTIFICATION. As to the minimum content of the infringement notification, the Düsseldorf District Court found in the case of *Saint Lawrence v. Vodafone*[103] that the notification has to indicate at least the number of the patent, the contested embodiments, and the alleged acts of use performed by the implementer.[104] There is, however, no obligation to provide

---

[98]   *Cf.* LG Mannheim v. 27.11.2015 –12 O 106/14 – *Saint Lawrence v. Deutsche Telekom*, ¶ 214 (Ger.) (short time limit as a general rule because implementer must only have the opportunity to make first sight assessment, in particular since it remains possible to challenge the patents during the negotiations or even to reserve the right to do so after the conclusion of a license contract); LG Düsseldorf v. 31.3.2016 – 4a O 73/14 – *Saint Lawrence v. Vodafone*, ¶ 218 (Ger.) (network operator needs to be given time for consulting with its suppliers); *Id.* at ¶ 216, 218 (information received from patentee, market position, experience of implementer ought to play a role).

[99]   LG Düsseldorf v. 31.3.2016 – 4a O 73/14 – *Saint Lawrence v. Vodafone* (Ger.).

[100]   OLG Düsseldorf v. 9.5.2016 – I-15 U 36/16 – *Saint Lawrence v. Vodafone* (Ger.).

[101]   LG Mannheim v. 27.11.2015 – 2 O 106/14 – *Saint Lawrence v. Deutsche Telekom*, ¶¶ 146–49 (Ger.).

[102]   LG Düsseldorf v. 31.3.2016 – 4a O 73/14 – *Saint Lawrence v. Vodafone*, ¶¶ 208–10 (Ger.).

[103]   *Id.*

[104]   *Id.* at ¶ 193.

additional information, in particular regarding the interpretation of the patent claims or on which part of the standard the patent reads.[105] Whether the infringement notification must indicate only the patent for which an injunction is sought or whether it must include reference to other IP rights with respect to which a license is offered was left undecided by the Düsseldorf District Court in *Sisvel v. Haier*.[106] The Mannheim District Court determined in *NTT DoCoMo v. HTC*,[107] as well as in *Philips v. Archos*,[108] that the SEP holder has to identify the (allegedly) infringed patent by reference to its patent number and by indicating that the patent-in-suit has been declared standard essential. Furthermore, the SEP holder is not only obliged to clarify the relevant standard but also to specify the pertinent part of the standard and the infringing element of the implementer's products in a way that enables the implementer to assess whether its use of the standard infringes on the patent-in-suit.[109] In this respect, the Mannheim District Court found in both *NTT DoCoMo v. HTC* and *Philips v. Archos* that presenting claim charts corresponding to recognized commercial practice for licensing negotiations is, in principle, an acceptable way to give notice of the alleged infringement.[110] On the other hand, a mere statement that the implementer infringed the patent-in-suit by producing or marketing products implementing the standard is not adequate.[111]

c) LICENSING OFFER. The third step under *Huawei v. ZTE* involves the SEP holder's making an offer that is FRAND.[112] In order to understand the relationship between the steps described by *Huawei*, reference can be made to the findings of the Düsseldorf Higher Regional Court in *Saint Lawrence v. Vodafone*.[113] According to this decision, the conduct of the parties required by the CJEU constitutes a mechanism of alternating, consecutive steps in which no subsequent conduct requirement is triggered unless the other party performed the previous "step." As

---

[105]   *Id.*
[106]   LG Düsseldorf v. 3.11.2015 – 4a O 93/14 – *Sisvel v. Haier* (Ger.).
[107]   LG Mannheim v. 29.1.2016 – 7 O 66/15 – *NTT DoCoMo v. HTC* (Ger.).
[108]   LG Mannheim v. 1.7.2016 – 7 O 209/15 – *Philips v. Archos* (Ger.).
[109]   LG Mannheim v. 29.1.2016 – 7 O 66/15 – *NTT DoCoMo v. HTC* (Ger.); *cf. also* LG Mannheim v. 1.7.2016 – 7 O 209/15 – *Philips v. Archos* (Ger.). It is worth noting that this obligation to specify is required by some SDO disclosure policies (e.g., IETF) and under consideration by additional SDOs.
[110]   LG Mannheim v. 29.1.2016 – 7 O 66/15 – *NTT DoCoMo v. HTC* (Ger.); LG Mannheim v. 1.7.2016 – 7 O 209/15 – *Philips v. Archos*, ¶ IV.1. (Ger.).
[111]   LG Mannheim v. 1.7.2016 – 7 O 209/15 – *Philips v. Archos*, ¶ IV.1. (Ger.).
[112]   Some indication as to what comprises a FRAND offer is found in the EU Commission guidelines on horizontal cooperation agreements. European Commission, 2011 O.J. (C11/01) 1. The Commission specifies that fair and reasonable royalties should bear some relationship to the value of licensed IPRs. It suggests for example that the *ex ante* value of licensed IPRs, that is, the value prior to the industry being locked in to the given standard, should be considered. The Commission also proposes that centrality and essentiality of the portfolio of the licensed IPRs to the given standard should be considered. The guidelines also suggest that comparable licenses are taken into account. *Id.* at ¶¶ 289–90.
[113]   OLG Düsseldorf v. 9.5.2016 – I-15 U 36/16 – *Saint Lawrence v. Vodafone* (Ger.).

a consequence, the SEP holder was, in that case, not obliged to submit a FRAND licensing offer at all since the implementer failed to signal its willingness to license.[114]

Some decisions rendered by German courts subsequent to *Huawei v. ZTE* elaborate on the conditions under which the level of royalties, which must be set forth in the SEP holder's licensing offer, can be considered "reasonable." In this respect, two alternative approaches should be distinguished (see, generally, discussion of monetary remedies under FRAND obligations in Section 5.2.4, above). Under the first approach, it is for the courts to determine whether the royalties offered by the SEP holder qualify as FRAND. For instance, the Düsseldorf District Court found in *Saint Lawrence v. Vodafone* that a worldwide licensing offer covering a whole SEP pool, at a rate of $0.26 per infringing device, and that was otherwise consistent with the SEP holder's existing licensing practices, to be FRAND under *Huawei v. ZTE*.[115] The findings of the court of first instance were confirmed in the subsequent judgment of the Düsseldorf Higher Regional Court.[116]

Under the second approach, it is not the court's task to determine whether the licensing conditions and royalties are FRAND. On the contrary, the judges should only assess, based on a summary assessment, whether the SEP holder's licensing offer and royalties evidently violate the FRAND concept (i.e., the offer is not obviously not FRAND). In this case, the Mannheim District Court held that the licensing offer complied with the procedures outlined in *Huawei v. ZTE*,[117] in particular because the SEP holder had explained its calculation of the licensing fee based on the percentage of patents in the WCMA/SIPRO and VIA patent pools held by the SEP holder. Comparable findings were made by the Mannheim District Court in *Pioneer v. Acer*.[118] The standard of review applied by the Mannheim court was criticized in subsequent proceedings before the Karlsruhe Higher Regional Court, which held that courts must determine whether licensing offers are FRAND and cannot limit their scrutiny to a summary assessment of whether such offers are obviously not FRAND.[119] Taking into account the opinion of the court of second instance, the Mannheim District Court did not resolve in *Philips v. Archos*[120] whether it is obliged to reconsider its standard of review. Nevertheless, it found that the SEP proprietor did not sufficiently substantiate why royalties of $1.00 per unit should be FRAND according to *Huawei*.

---

[114]   *Id.* at ¶ 2, b, cc.
[115]   LG Düsseldorf v. 31.3.2016 – 4a O 73/14 – *Saint Lawrence v. Vodafone,* ¶ 225 *et seq.* (Ger.); *cf.* LG Düsseldorf v. 31.3.2016 – 4a O 126/14 – *Saint Lawrence v. Vodafone.*
[116]   OLG Düsseldorf v. 9.5.2016 – I-15 U 36/16 – *Saint Lawrence v. Vodafone,* ¶ 2.b.ff. (Ger.); *cf.* OLG Düsseldorf v. 9.5.2016 – I-15 U 35/16 – *Saint Lawrence v. Vodafone* (Ger.).
[117]   LG Mannheim v. 29.1.2016 – 7 O 66/15 – *NTT DoCoMo v. HTC,* ¶ 70–72 (Ger.).
[118]   LG Mannheim v. 8.1.2016 – 7 O 96/14 – *Pioneer v. Acer* (Ger.).
[119]   OLG Karlsruhe v. 31.5.2016 – 6 U 55/16 – *Pioneer v. Acer* (Ger.).
[120]   LG Mannheim v. 1.7.2016 – 7 O 209/15 – *Philips v. Archos,* ¶ IV.1. (Ger.).

D) CALCULATION OF ROYALTIES. Furthermore, the German decisions elucidate the extent to which a SEP holder must specify the calculation of royalties in its licensing offer under *Huawei*. In general, the offer must specify the relevant conditions in a way that, in order to conclude a licensing agreement, the implementer has merely to state its acceptance.[121] Accordingly, the Mannheim District Court ruled in both *NTT DoCoMo v. HTC*[122] and *Philips v. Archos*[123] that the calculation of the license fee must be explained in a manner that enables the implementer to understand, on the basis of objective criteria, why the SEP holder considers its licensing offer to be FRAND. In the case of a quota license agreement, it is not sufficient merely to indicate the royalties per unit. The respective amount must be made sufficiently "transparent," e.g., by reference to an established standard licensing program or by indicating other reference values, such as a pool license fee.[124] In contrast, the court deemed a licensing offer sufficient if the calculation of royalties is explained based on the percentage of patents in the WCMA/SIPRO and VIA patent pools held by the SEP holder.[125] The Düsseldorf District Court stated in *Saint Lawrence v. Vodafone* that the SEP holder has to provide the information necessary to determine the amount of royalties to be paid, e.g., the royalty per unit and the products covered by the license. While the court left undecided whether additional indications, e.g., concerning the FRAND character of the licensing offer, are necessary to comply with *Huawei*, it found that the SEP holder's duty to inform should not be interpreted too strictly as FRAND does regularly encompass a *range* of terms and conditions.[126]

E) PORTFOLIO LICENSES. Several decisions discuss whether a (worldwide) portfolio license offered by the SEP holder is FRAND according to *Huawei v. ZTE*. The Mannheim District Court seems to favor the FRAND compatibility of such licenses in *Saint Lawrence v. Deutsche Telekom*,[127] but at first it did not come to a clear conclusion. In its subsequent decision in *Pioneer v. Acer*,[128] however, an offer of the SEP holder was considered sufficient,[129] in particular because a worldwide license granted to the parent of a group corresponded to recognized commercial practice in the field. Correspondingly, the Düsseldorf District Court said in *Saint Lawrence v. Vodafone*[130] that the more licensing agreements implementing comparable terms the SEP holder has already concluded, the stronger the presumption that these

---

[121] LG Mannheim v. 29.1.2016 – 7 O 66/15 – *NTT DoCoMo v. HTC* (Ger.).
[122] *Id.*
[123] LG Mannheim v. 1.7.2016 – 7 O 209/15 – *Philips v. Archos* (Ger.).
[124] *Id.* at ¶ IV, 1.
[125] LG Mannheim v. 29.1.2016 – 7 O 66/15 – *NTT DoCoMo v. HTC*, ¶ 70–72 (Ger.).
[126] LG Düsseldorf v. 31.3.2016 – 4a O 73/14 – *Saint Lawrence v. Vodafone*, ¶ 256 et seq. (Ger.).
[127] LG Mannheim v. 27.11.2015 – 2 O 106/14 – *Saint Lawrence v. Deutsche Telekom* (Ger.).
[128] LG Mannheim v. 8.1.2016 – 7 O 96/14 – *Pioneer v. Acer* (Ger.).
[129] For further details, *see id.* at ¶ 118–29.
[130] LG Düsseldorf v. 31.3.2016 – 4a O 73/14 – *Saint Lawrence v. Vodafone* (Ger.).

conditions are FRAND, unless factual reasons – which must be demonstrated by the implementer – justify modified terms. Recognized commercial practice in the relevant sector has to be considered when defining the admissible scope of the licensing agreement. The UK court in *Unwired Planet* v. *Huawei* also held that a license among global industry players should be worldwide, and that it was unreasonable for the potential licensee to insist on a United Kingdom-only license in this context.[131] Based on these cases, it appears that if patent portfolios are usually covered by group or worldwide licenses in the relevant market, a (worldwide) portfolio license will be FRAND for purposes of EU competition law unless the circumstances of the specific case, e.g., the SEP holders' or the implementer's market activity being limited to one geographic market, require a modification.

F) RESPONSE BY IMPLEMENTER – TIMING AND CONTENT. The German courts have also shed some light on the way an implementer ought to react to the SEP holder's licensing offer. In particular, the courts discuss whether there is an obligation of the implementer to respond to a licensing offer that is not FRAND. While the Düsseldorf District Court confirmed such an obligation at first in *Sisvel* v. *Haier*[132] and left this issue undecided in *Saint Lawrence* v. *Vodafone*,[133] the Düsseldorf Higher Regional Court explicitly denied in *NTT DoCoMo* v. *HTC*[134] that there is an obligation to respond if the SEP holder refrained from submitting a FRAND licensing offer. The question of whether the implementer may respond to a non-FRAND offer in a different manner than by submitting a specific counteroffer, in particular by merely demonstrating that the SEP holder's offer was not FRAND, remained unanswered.[135] In contrast, the Mannheim District Court found, in *NTT DoCoMo* v. *HTC*,[136] as well as *Saint Lawrence* v. *Deutsche Telekom*,[137] that even if the preceding licensing offer is not (fully) in compliance with FRAND, the implementer would still be under a duty to react diligently and to submit a corresponding FRAND counteroffer. In order to trigger the counteroffer obligation it is sufficient that the licensing offer contains all information, in particular regarding royalty calculation, which is necessary for the implementer to submit a counteroffer corresponding to FRAND terms.[138] Even though the Mannheim District Court recently reaffirmed, in *Philips* v. *Archos*,[139] the general findings of its previous decisions, it

[131]   *Unwired Planet Int'l Ltd.* v. *Huawei Techs. Co.* (Pat 2017) (UK). *See also Conversant Wireless Licensing SARL* v. *Huawei Technologies Co. Ltd & Ors* [2018] EWHC 808 (Pat), relying on *Unwired Planet* in holding that the English courts have jurisdiction to determine a global FRAND license.
[132]   LG Düsseldorf v. 3.11.2015 – 4a O 93/14 – *Sisvel* v. *Haier* (Ger.).
[133]   LG Düsseldorf v. 31.3.2016 – 4a O 73/14 – *Saint Lawrence* v. *Vodafone* (Ger.).
[134]   OLG Düsseldorf v. 13.1.2016 – I-15 U 66/15 – *Sisvel* v. *Haier* (Ger.).
[135]   LG Düsseldorf v. 3.11.2015 – 4a O 93/14 – *Sisvel* v. *Haier*, ¶¶ 98–101 (Ger.).
[136]   LG Mannheim v. 29.1.2016 – 7 O 66/15 – *NTT DoCoMo* v. *HTC* (Ger.).
[137]   LG Mannheim v. 27.11.2015 – 2 O 106/14 – *Saint Lawrence* v. *Deutsche Telekom* (Ger.).
[138]   *Id.*
[139]   LG Mannheim v. 1.7.2016 – 7 O 209/15 – *Philips* v. *Archos* (Ger.).

specified that an exception applies where it is established in the course of a summary examination that the licensing offer is evidently not FRAND and therefore constitutes an abuse of dominance.

As to the time limits for an adequate reaction of the implementer: In a more general manner, the Mannheim District Court held in *Philips* v. *Archos*[140] that the period of time in which the implementer has to react depends on the facts of the case as well as on the principles of good faith and recognized commercial practice.[141] More specifically, the same court found in *NTT DoCoMo* v. *HTC*[142] that the behavior of the implementer is considered insufficient if the counteroffer is made only one and a half years after receiving the licensing offer and half a year after the SEP holder filed suit.

Furthermore, the courts analyzed under which conditions a counteroffer meets the requirements of *Huawei* in terms of content. In the case of *Saint Lawrence* v. *Deutsche Telekom* the Mannheim District Court denied the existence of a specific counteroffer because the royalty was not specified in the document itself but was intended to be determined by an independent third party. Whether the limitation of the counteroffer to Germany was in compliance with FRAND terms remained undecided.[143] However, in *Saint Lawrence* v. *Vodafone* the Düsseldorf District Court decided that none of the counteroffers of the intervenor were FRAND in terms of content. They were either inadmissibly limited to Germany, contained no precise royalty, were not submitted "promptly" because the standard user had waited until the oral pleadings in the parallel procedure, or they proposed royalties per device that the court considered as too low.[144] Correspondingly, the Mannheim District Court denied in *Pioneer* v. *Acer* the FRAND conformity of an implementer's offer because the intended limitation of the license to Germany would have been inappropriate given the facts of the case and recognized commercial practice in the respective market.[145]

3 Other European Law Principles

In addition to the EU procedural requirements under *Huawei* that are described above, national law may be implicated when a SEP holder seeks an injunction for a FRAND-committed SEP. For example, Polish law would analyze the seeking of injunctive relief by patentees who made prior FRAND commitments under an abuse of rights doctrine independent of EU competition law. This doctrine provides

---

[140] *Id.*
[141] *Id.* at ¶ IV.1.
[142] LG Mannheim v. 29.1.2016 – 7 O 66/15 – *NTT DoCoMo* v. *HTC* (Ger.).
[143] LG Mannheim v. 27.11.2015 – 2 O 106/14 – *Saint Lawrence* v. *Deutsche Telekom*, ¶¶ 158–64 (Ger.).
[144] LG Düsseldorf v. 31.3.2016 – 4a O 73/14 – *Saint Lawrence* v. *Vodafone*, ¶ 291 *et seq.* (Ger.).
[145] LG Mannheim v. 8.1.2016 – 7 O 96/14 – *Pioneer* v. *Acer*, ¶¶ 131–33 (Ger.).

a general defense based on the provisions of the Polish Civil Code,[146] which can be applied to abuses of all types of private rights,[147] including patents. This analysis would likely look to arguments such as reliance on FRAND promises made by SEP holders during the standard-setting process, an obligation to act in good faith toward other parties operating in the market.[148] Polish law would rather approach all types of FRAND pledges in a similar manner, whether they are made within or outside the standard-setting context. Implementers would base their defenses against injunctions on breaches of reliance, loyalty, or good faith.

The reasoning behind denying injunctions on the basis of the abuse of rights doctrine is supported by equitable arguments rather than economic factors or patent law – particularly the ability of the patent system to stimulate investment in innovation. The abuse defense would likely be effective only if raised by an implementer acting in good faith – a willing implementer.

4 Injunctions and Alternative Dispute Resolution in Europe

Despite its potential benefits, the procedural framework introduced by *Huawei* has not solved all the practical challenges and difficulties that can arise in FRAND disputes. For example, *Huawei* fails to offer a solution to the territorial fragmentation of FRAND disputes or to the proliferation of parallel local court proceedings. The continuing conduct of multiple parallel proceedings is not cost efficient or time efficient, in spite of the fact that many if not all FRAND disputes are global (and would ideally materialize in global FRAND licensing transactions as noted above).[149] Numerous complex jurisdictional issues arise in this context, including the risk that courts will engage in a "race to the bottom" in order to present an attractive venue for FRAND litigation, and parties will engage in a "race to the courthouse" to ensure that their case is heard in the most favorable jurisdiction.[150] As a result, it is important to (continue to) explore means for rationalizing remedies offered both by courts and alternative dispute resolution (ADR) mechanisms in this area.[151]

---

[146]   Kodeks cywilny [Civil Code], art. 5 (1964 r. Dz. U. Nr. 16 poz. 93 with amendments) (Pol.).

[147]   Gutowski 2016, 50.

[148]   Sikorski 2015, 460.

[149]   The UK court in *Unwired Planet Int'l Ltd.* v. *Huawei Techs. Co.* (Pat 2017) (UK) makes this observation explicitly, observing that a licensor and licensee acting reasonably in markets such as telecommunication equipment would agree on a worldwide license. *Id.* at ¶ 544. *See also* Contreras 2017b, 11–14 (discussing global implications of case).

[150]   Contreras 2017b.

[151]   *See* the policy proposals for an arbitration system formulated in the Geneva Internet Disputes Resolution Policies 1.0 project, University of Geneva 2015; for a discussion about the use of arbitration for FRAND disputes, *see* Contreras & Newman 2014; Carter 2014; De Werra 2014. In fact, several global ADR service providers, including the Geneva-based WIPO Arbitration and Mediation Center, have already developed tailored rules for FRAND disputes. WIPO 2017.

5.3.3 *Korea*

Unlike the United States, in which injunctions are granted under principles of equity, patentees in Korea are entitled to an injunction automatically in case of patent infringement.[152] Only in exceptional cases where patentees are regarded as having abused their rights, courts will deny an injunction.[153] Thus, the question is whether such abuse is likely to be found when a SEP holder has violated its FRAND commitment.

In *Samsung Electronics Co. Ltd. v. Apple Korea Ltd.*, the Seoul Central District Court held that it is an abuse of patent rights for a SEP holder to seek an injunction under a FRAND-committed patent if the SEP holder has violated its duty to negotiate in good faith with the implementer and tries to maintain its dominance over the market contrary to the policy goals of the patent law.[154] This duty to negotiate in good faith includes a duty to offer any potential licensees a FRAND license with FRAND terms. Korean courts have held, however, that a SEP holder does not have a duty to disclose detailed information about comparable licenses with third parties.

SEP holders in Korea have a duty to negotiate in good faith with a party willing to obtain a license under FRAND terms.[155] Yet, as discussed above in the context of "holdout," a good faith negotiation is impossible when a potential licensee has no intention of obtaining a FRAND license at all. It is reasonable to consider a willing licensee to be a potential licensee that engages in licensing negotiations and proposes a specific royalty rate with a reasonable calculation basis. In *Samsung Electronics Co. Ltd. v. Apple Korea Ltd.*, the Seoul Central District Court held that the potential licensee does not have to deposit royalties in advance to be qualified as a willing licensee.[156] Moreover, the court found that there was a large gap between royalty rate proposals made by Samsung and Apple and, also, that there were no serious and intensive licensing negotiations in good faith between them.[157] When both parties were to blame for the lack of a good faith negotiation, the court concluded that it was difficult to see any abuse of patent rights on the part of the SEP holder in seeking an injunction.[158] This shows the difficulty of proving abuse of a patent right in Korea.

5.3.4 *Japan*

Article 100(1) of the Japanese Patent Act states: "A patentee or exclusive licensee may demand a person who infringes or is likely to infringe the patent right or exclusive

---

152 *See* Patent Act, Act No. 14691, art. 126 (Kor.); *LG Electronics, Inc. v. Daewoo Electronics, Inc.* (S. Ct. 2012) (Kor.).
153 *See LG Electronics, Inc. v. Daewoo Electronics, Inc.* (S. Ct. 2012) (Kor.).
154 *Samsung Electronics Co. Ltd. v. Apple Korea Ltd.* (Dist. Ct. 2012) (Kor.).
155 *Id.*
156 *Id.*
157 *Id.*
158 *Id.*

license to stop or prevent such infringement."[159] Under this Article, Japanese courts award injunctions almost automatically when they find a likelihood of patent infringement. The abuse of rights doctrine, which is stipulated in Article 1(3) of the Civil Code of Japan,[160] is theoretically applicable to the exercise of patent rights. But in patent infringement cases, courts have rarely applied this doctrine. The IP High Court reversed this trend in *Samsung v. Apple Japan*.[161]

In *Samsung v. Apple Japan*, Samsung accused Apple of infringing Samsung's SEPs in the ETSI UMTS standard.[162] According to the IP High Court, implementers wishing to manufacture a product compliant with the UMTS standard have no choice but to practice the SEPs, as "it is impossible for them to adopt alternative technology or to change the product design."[163] "Therefore, if the patentee is unconditionally allowed to exercise the right to seek an injunction based on the [SEPs, the implementers] may be put into a situation where they are forced to pay a high royalty or agree to extremely unfavorable license conditions that are not FRAND Terms, or to abandon the business project itself, so as to avoid the damage that may arise from such injunction."[164] The court also observed that "the UMTS standard contains a large number of patents owned by different owners (1800 or more patent families declared essential by 50 or more patentees)."[165] It is difficult for an implementer to obtain licenses to such a large number of patents in advance, after confirming whether each of such patents is essential or not.[166] As the court explained:

> [I]f the patentee is unconditionally allowed to seek an injunction based on the [SEPs], the use of the UMTS standard would become practically impossible. [This] situation would have a negative impact on the dissemination of the UMTS standard and run counter to the purpose of the ETSI IPR Policy . . . Further, if such situation arises, the general public would be unable to enjoy a variety of benefits that would be available if the harmonization and dissemination of communication standards was achieved.[167]

Therefore, the court reasoned that in relation to a SEP, it is not appropriate to allow a party that made a FRAND declaration to seek an injunction based on the SEP against an implementer willing to obtain a license on FRAND Terms.[168] The court went on to reason that an injunction "should be allowed against an implementer engaged in manufacturing, sales, etc. of a . . . standard-compliant

---

[159] Tokkyo-hō [Patent Act], No. 121 of 1959, art. 100(1) (Japan).
[160] Minpō [Civ. C.] art. 1(3) (Japan) ("No abuse of rights is permitted.").
[161] *Samsung Elecs. Co. v. Apple Japan LLC* (IP High Ct. 2014) (Japan) (FRAND II).
[162] *Id.* at 2.
[163] *Id.* at 24.
[164] *Id.*
[165] *Id.*
[166] *Id.*
[167] *Id.* at 24–25.
[168] *Id.* at 25.

product without any intention of obtaining a FRAND license,"[169] as such implementer cannot be considered to be complying with its own end of the FRAND bargain, and the patentee would not be adequately protected if its ability to seek an injunction even against such parties is restricted.[170] Nevertheless, because allowing a SEP holder to seek an injunction involves potential adverse effects, the court must carefully consider whether the prospective licensee had no intention of entering into a FRAND license.[171]

On this basis, the court concluded that the exercise of the right to seek an injunction based on a SEP by a SEP holder who made a FRAND commitment would constitute abuse of right (Article 1(3) of the Civil Code) and therefore is not allowed, if the implementer successfully alleges and proves that the SEP holder made the FRAND commitment and the implementer intended to receive it.[172] As to the specific case at hand, the court found that Apple intended to receive a FRAND license, and denied Samsung's claim for injunction.[173]

5.3.5 *China*

Courts in China have recently considered injunctions in two cases involving FRAND-committed SEPs. In *Iwncomm v. Sony*,[174] the Beijing IP court issued an injunction against the implementer Sony for the infringement of a FRAND-committed SEP covering the Chinese WAPI wireless networking standard; and the Shenzhen Intermediate People's Court issued an injunction for the infringement of two FRAND-committed patents essential to the 4G standard in *Huawei v. Samsung*.[175] In both cases, the courts concluded that the patentee had been a willing licensor and the infringer an unwilling licensee.

In addition to these cases, two Chinese courts have recently released guidance regarding disputes relating to SEPs disclosed in recommended national, industrial, or local standards. In the *Interpretations (II) of the Supreme People's Court on Several Issues concerning the Application of Law in the Trial of Patent Infringement Dispute Cases* art. 24 (effective as of April 1, 2016), the Supreme People's Court of the People's Republic of China states that courts should not award injunctive relief when a SEP owner deliberately fails to comply with its obligation to grant a FRAND license to a manufacturer, and the manufacturer is not clearly at fault. Chinese

---

[169] *Id.*
[170] *Id.*
[171] *Id.*
[172] *Id.*
[173] *Id.* at 27.
[174] *Xian Xidian Jietong Wireless Commc'n Co., Ltd. (Iwncomm) v. SONY Mobile Commc'n Prods. (China) Co. Ltd.* (Beijing IP Ct. Mar. 22, 2017).
[175] For further discussion of *Iwncomm*, see Bharadwaj & Verma 2017. As of this writing, an English-language translation of the January 2018 *Huawei v. Samsung* decision is not available, but a summary of the court's reasoning can be found in Schindler 2018.

courts recently have begun to address how fault on the part of either the patentee or the prospective licensee impacts the availability of injunctive relief in FRAND cases.[176]

5.3.6 Discussion and Analysis: FRAND and Injunctions

U.S. courts have analyzed the question whether the holder of a FRAND-committed SEP may seek to enjoin unlicensed implementers from practicing the SEP under the *eBay* framework, focusing primarily on whether the FRAND commitment implies that the SEP holder has conceded that it will accept monetary damages in lieu of the exclusionary remedy of an injunction and thereby suffer no "irreparable harm" if an injunction is not issued. In addition, appeals to the fourth *eBay* prong have caused some to consider the public interest associated with the exclusion of standardized products from the market, as the USTR did in rejecting the ITC's exclusion order against Apple in 2013 (see Section 5.3.1 above). The U.S. FTC has also asserted that SEP holders' attempts to enjoin "willing" licensees (as variously defined) may violate the FTC Act and antitrust laws. In the FTC's settlement with Google and Motorola, a detailed procedure involving several negotiation stages was established before Google/Motorola was permitted to seek an injunction against a SEP implementer.

In jurisdictions, such as Germany and Korea, in which injunctions issue more or less automatically, recourse is more likely to be made to competition law.[177] Additionally in the European Union, the EU competition law, which benefits from the principles of direct effect and supremacy over EU member states' laws, is also perhaps more attractive as a tool for patent litigants than the national patent laws of the EU member states (though this distinction may be lessened in view of the EU Enforcement Directive).[178] Rather than focusing primarily on the content of a FRAND commitment, the CJEU's decision in *Huawei Techs. Co. Ltd. v. ZTE Corp.* established detailed procedural requirements for both SEP holders and implementers when a SEP holder seeks an injunction. When the procedure is not followed by the SEP holder, it is vulnerable to claims of abuse of dominance under Article 102 of the TFEU. When the *Huawei* procedure is followed by both parties, the result is either an agreement between the parties or an adjudicated or arbitrated FRAND royalty determination that the implementer must honor, lest an injunction be issued. And if the *Huawei* procedure is followed by the SEP holder but not by the implementer, the SEP holder may seek and obtain an injunction without

---

[176] *See* Cui 2018 (summarizing recent Chinese court cases and guidelines); Guangdong High People's Court 2018; Beijing High People's Court 2017, ¶¶ 149–53.

[177] *See* Chapter 6.

[178] *See* Chapter 1.

violating Article 102 of the TFEU. The *Huawei* procedure is apparently not simple for implementers to follow, as several post-*Huawei* cases have resulted in injunctions after an implementer failed to comply with some element of the procedure such as making a valid counteroffer or posting bond in the amount of the estimated royalty. As such, it is possible that the procedure in *Huawei* is over-specified and perhaps rewards litigation experience and procedural savvy rather than a genuine desire to enter into license transactions. On the other hand, the post-*Huawei* cases may reveal the occurrence of intentional holdout at higher rates than expected.

As noted by Advocate General Wathelet in his opinion in *Huawei*,[179] the matters in dispute "could adequately – if not better – be resolved in the context of other branches of law or by mechanisms other than the rules of competition law." What the Advocate General means by other branches of law is unclear. But one might assume that he has in mind general defenses – such as abuse of rights – and possibly the application of patent remedies itself. If the disputes over injunctions for FRAND-pledged patents could be resolved within the law on patent remedies then Directive 2004/48/EC on IPR enforcement would provide arguments against granting injunctions to holders of FRAND-pledged patents, on the general principles discussed in Chapter 4. First, proportionality as a general principle governing remedies could be used. Proportionality – as the directive provides (and as discussed in Chapter 4) – requires that remedies be applied in a fair and equitable manner and that there are safeguards against abuse in place. Second, the directive also explains that in the application of remedies circumstances of the case need to be considered and the nature of an IP right should be taken into account.

The standard for proving abusive conduct in Japan, as described in *Samsung v. Apple Japan*, appears to be much more straightforward, involving only the stated (or proven) willingness of the implementer to accept a license of the asserted SEPs. The courts in Korea may have split the difference between the formalistic EU approach and the relatively unspecified Japanese approach, holding in *Samsung Electronics Co. Ltd. v. Apple Korea Ltd.* that abusive conduct will not be found if the parties engage in good faith negotiation of a FRAND license. In order to be found to have acted in good faith, an implementer need only show that it engaged in licensing negotiations and proposed a specific royalty rate with a reasonable calculation basis. But if a failure of negotiation is attributable to the action or inaction of both parties, an abuse by the SEP holder will not be found when it obtains an injunction against the implementer.

In our view, each of these approaches can profitably be informed by the other. To observers from the United States and other common law jurisdictions,

---

[179] *Huawei Techs. Co. Ltd. v. ZTE Corp.* (CJEU 2014, ¶ 9) (EU).

the fact that in the European Union and other civil law jurisdictions injunctions typically issue automatically in patent cases, subject only to the violation of competition law, seems unusual. Patent law has developed independently of competition law and the abuse of rights doctrine, and it seems reasonable for patent remedies to be governed by an internally consistent and cohesive framework independent of other external legal regimes (particularly regimes that are imposed by extra-national authority such as the European Union). As such, we recommend that courts consider imposing reasonable conditions on the issuance of injunctive relief, such as are discussed in Chapter 4, even absent a violation of competition law. Because the issuance of injunctive relief is typically a binary decision (either an injunction is issued or not),[180] the types of moderation and proportionality that are available to adjust monetary damages for the parties' behavior is typically not available in the injunctive arena. Instead, some measure of judicial discretion in the *granting* of injunctive relief could more accurately fit this remedy to the actions and behavior of the parties. This is not to say that civil law jurisdictions should adopt an *eBay*-style equitable analysis for the assessment of injunctive remedies, or refuse injunctions at the rates seen in U.S. courts, but only that some measure of judicial discretion be exercised.[181] Our discussion as to how that discretion should be exercised is found in Chapter 4.

On the other hand, the equitable analysis of party behavior in the context of SEPs and FRAND under U.S. law still suffers from a lack of precision and definition. The Federal Circuit in *Apple, Inc.* v. *Samsung Elecs. Co., Ltd.* offers a three-way split opinion regarding the presumptions and conduct that should inform the decision to grant injunctive relief. Parties thus lack clear guidance in this critical area. U.S. courts analyzing injunction availability in SEP cases have focused largely on the prongs of the *eBay* test pertaining to irreparable harm and adequacy of monetary damages. We recommend that when balancing equities between the parties, courts start with the procedures modeling well-functioning party behavior as laid out by the CJEU in *Huawei Techs. Co. Ltd.* v. *ZTE Corp.* or under the law of Japan or Korea. While each of these procedural analyses was developed with potential violations of competition law or obligations of parties entering into a contract to negotiate in good faith in mind, at their root they are each intended to model a well-functioning bilateral relationship within the standard-setting context. As such, a full and fair assessment of the appropriateness of equitable relief would do well to consider such factors.

---

[180] *But see* the discussion of tailored injunctions in Chapter 4.
[181] As noted above, the EU Enforcement Directive requires that remedies be applied in a fair and equitable manner, thus introducing an element of "equity" even into the EU analysis. *See* Directive 2004/48/EC.

APPENDIX – NATIONAL LAW CONSIDERATIONS FOR MONETARY
FRAND DAMAGES

A. Germany

Under § 139 of the German Patent Law (PatG), a patent owner may recover monetary damages from an infringer that intentionally or negligently makes use of the respective patent in the sense of §§ 9, 10 PatG.[182] In order to determine the specific amount of monetary damages to be paid by the infringer, the patent owner can select between three different calculation methods pursuant to § 139(2) PatG. These ways of calculating damages can, however, neither be aggregated nor mixed.[183]

The first calculation approach, pursuant to § 139(2) PatG in conjunction with §§ 249, 252 of the German Civil Code (BGB), refers to the "difference in wealth" of the patent owner caused by the infringement ("Differenzmethode").[184] In order to be compensated, the patent owner has to show a financial loss and causality between this loss and the infringement.[185] If the action seeks to recover lost profits, it is for the patent owner to prove that it could have obtained the amount of profits claimed in the absence of the infringing activity.[186]

The second calculation method, laid down by the third sentence of § 139(2) PatG, often called the "objective calculation of damages" and being widely used in practice,[187] refers to the reasonable royalties that could be obtained from a third person for the use of the patent.[188] The approach is based on the assumption that the infringer should compensate for the pecuniary benefits it obtained from using the patent-in-suit. The precise calculation should follow the hypothetical contractual terms that would have been agreed upon by reasonable parties taking into account all relevant factors for the determination of the patent value, such as a potential monopolistic position of the patent owner, the economic importance of the patent, customary royalties, royalties already agreed upon, or standardized licensing agreements.[189]

The third approach, formulated in the second sentence of § 139(2) PatG, concerns the recovery of the infringer's profits. Since it is only a calculation method and not a stand-alone claim, it must be proven that the patent owner incurred actual

---

[182] Mes 2015, § 139 rec. 6, 121; *cf.* Benkard 2015, § 139 rec. 13 et seq.; Keukenschrijver 2016, § 139 rec. 97.
[183] Benkard 2015, § 139 rec. 61; Mes 2015, § 139 rec. 123, 177; Keukenschrijver 2016, § 139 rec. 140; LG Düsseldorf v. 19.1.2016 – 4b O 120/14 – *Unwired Planet* v. *Samsung*, ¶ VII.6.b.cc (Ger.).
[184] LG Düsseldorf v. 19.1.2016 – 4b O 120/14 – *Unwired Planet* v. *Samsung*, ¶ VII.6.b.cc (Ger.).
[185] Mes 2015, § 139 rec. 123; Keukenschrijver 2016, § 139 rec. 154; Benkard 2015, § 139 rec. 57 et seq.
[186] Keukenschrijver 2016, § 139 rec. 156.
[187] *Id.* at § 139 rec. 138.
[188] Mes 2015, § 139 rec. 123; Benkard 2015, § 139 rec. 61.
[189] Mes 2015, § 139 rec. 131 et seq., 134; Benkard 2015, § 139 rec. 66; Keukenschrijver 2016, § 139 rec. 164. This calculation methodology bears some resemblance to the *Georgia-Pacific* framework used in the United States.

losses.[190] Furthermore, the owner can claim only those profits that effectively resulted from the patent infringement.[191] As a general rule, the profits are calculated by subtracting the costs related to the patent infringement from the revenues of the infringer.[192] However, according to the German Federal Court (BGH) the infringer is not allowed to deduct any fixed costs together with the production costs that are directly related to the manufacturing of the infringing product.[193] Fixed costs can only be considered if they are *exclusively* related to the infringement.[194] Other costs ("business-as-usual-costs") that occur irrespective of the volume of production and supply as a consequence of the general business activity of the infringer are not relevant. The necessary evidence has to be provided by the infringer.[195]

Irrespective of the calculation method, courts are permitted to estimate the damages to be paid pursuant to § 287 of the German Code of Civil Procedure (ZPO) if the patent owner is not able to substantiate its financial losses.[196] As a consequence, damages can be related to the royalties under a FRAND license, in particular where the patent owner selects the "license analogy method" instead of other available calculation methods. However, the patent owner is not prevented from claiming further damages exceeding FRAND royalties, under the condition that they correspond to the enrichment of the infringer.[197]

Important aspects of the relation between the level of royalties under a FRAND license and monetary damages for patent infringement were illustrated by the Düsseldorf District Court in *Unwired Planet v. Samsung*.[198] As noted above, the *Huawei* obligations do not hinder a SEP holder from bringing an action for damages against an implementer and it can freely choose between said calculations methods.[199] However, the CJEU requirements indirectly influence the extent to which compensation for past acts of infringement can be sought. If the implementer, having demonstrated its willingness to take a license, is able to raise a counterclaim according to § 33 of the German Competition Act (GWB), in conjunction with Article 102 of the TFEU, because the SEP proprietor, having made a FRAND declaration for the patent-in-suit, abusively refused to grant a license, monetary damages can be limited to the maximum amount of FRAND royalties for the period after the refusal.[200] In *Unwired Planet*, no such cap on damages applied, because the standard implementer did not express his readiness to conclude a licensing

---

[190] Mes 2015, § 139 rec. 146.
[191] *Id.* at § 139 rec. 163.
[192] Benkard 2015, § 139 rec. 73.
[193] Mes 2015, § 139 rec. 148; Benkard 2015, § 139 rec. 73b.
[194] Benkard 2015, § 139 rec. 73c.
[195] *Id.* at § 139 rec. 73g.
[196] *Id.* at § 139 rec. 60.
[197] *Id.* at § 139 rec. 63a.
[198] LG Düsseldorf v. 19.1.2016 – 4b O 120/14 – *Unwired Planet v. Samsung* (Ger.).
[199] *Id.* at ¶ VII.6.b.bb.
[200] *Id.* at ¶ VII.6.b.dd.

agreement.[201] In contrast to actions for injunction, abusive behavior of the SEP holder will not be assumed if it fails to provide an infringement notification.[202]

B. Switzerland

1 Legal Status of FRAND Commitments under Swiss Law

A Swiss court deciding the issue of damages for FRAND-committed SEPs will first have to assess the legal nature of the FRAND commitment that is made by the SEP holder to the relevant SSO under the applicable contract law that governs such commitment. By way of illustration, the ETSI IPR Policy[203] provides a FRAND commitment by which the owners of standard-essential patents[204] commit to make their patents available to willing licensees under FRAND terms.[205] Section 6.1 of the ETSI IPR Policy provides that "[w]hen an ESSENTIAL IPR[206] relating to a particular STANDARD or TECHNICAL SPECIFICATION is brought to the attention of ETSI, the Director-General of ETSI shall immediately request the owner to give within three months an irrevocable undertaking in writing that it is prepared to grant irrevocable licenses on fair, reasonable and non-discriminatory ("FRAND") terms and conditions under such IPR . . . . " Appendix A to the ETSI IPR Policy (entitled "IPR Licensing Declaration Forms")[207] contains different forms[208] to be completed and signed by the owner of the relevant IP rights under which such IP owner is invited to make a formal and binding statement according to which "it and its AFFILIATES are prepared to grant irrevocable licenses under its/their IPR(s) on terms and conditions which are in accordance with Clause 6.1 of the ETSI IPR Policy . . . "[209]

---

[201] *Id.* at ¶ VII.6.b.ee.

[202] *Id.* at ¶ VII.6.b.dd.

[203] ETSI 2018, Annex 6; *see also* the webpage dedicated to IPR: ETSI, *Intellectual Property Rights* (last visited Apr. 30, 2018).

[204] Essential patents are defined in ETSI 2018, Annex 6 § 15.6 ("'ESSENTIAL' as applied to IPR means that it is not possible on technical (but not commercial) grounds, taking into account normal technical practice and the state of the art generally available at the time of standardization, to make, sell, lease, otherwise dispose of, repair, use or operate EQUIPMENT or METHODS which comply with a STANDARD without infringing that IPR. For the avoidance of doubt in exceptional cases where a STANDARD can only be implemented by technical solutions, all of which are infringements of IPRs, all such IPRs shall be considered ESSENTIAL.").

[205] *Id.* at Annex 6 § 6.1.

[206] Each of the capitalized terms is defined in *id.* at Annex 6 § 15.

[207] *Id.* at Annex 6 app. A.

[208] A "General IPR Licensing Declaration" and an "IPR Information Statement and Licensing Declaration." *Id.*

[209] The relevant portions of the "General IPR Licensing Declaration" include: "it and its AFFILIATES are prepared to grant irrevocable licenses under its/their IPR(s) on terms and conditions which are in accordance with Clause 6.1 of the ETSI IPR Policy, in respect of the STANDARD(S), TECHNICAL SPECIFICATION(S), or the ETSI Project(s), as identified above, to the extent that the IPR(s) are or become, and remain ESSENTIAL to practice that/those STANDARD(S) or

These documents provide that their "construction, validity and performance ... shall be governed by the laws of France."[210] The legal issue is consequently to analyze the nature and the enforceability of the commitments ("undertaking")[211] that are made by the owners of the relevant SEPs to the SSOs under the applicable governing law.

By stating that the owners of SEPs are "prepared to grant irrevocable licenses"[212] under their SEPs to third party implementers (in their formal undertaking that they make to the SSOs), the issue is whether third party beneficiaries can request the performance of such obligation, which in turn depends on whether these potential licensees (which have not directly entered into any contract with the owner of the relevant SEPs) can be considered as third party beneficiaries. This issue, which obviously depends on the interpretation of the relevant declaration under the applicable law, remains disputed,[213] it being noted that granting – by contract – rights to a third party is generally admitted from a transnational perspective.[214] Under French law, which is of particular relevance here (given that it is the law that governs the ETSI Declarations), the view has been expressed that the commitments made by owners of SEPs under the ETSI Declarations can qualify as "stipulation pour autrui" within the meaning of Article 1121 of the French Civil Code.[215]

Assuming that willing licensees (implementers of the technology standards covered by the SEPs) could be considered third party beneficiaries of these commitments under the relevant law, the next issue would be to define precisely the legal nature and the scope of the commitments made by the owners of SEPs: i.e., what is the contractual obligation that the owners of SEPs have accepted to perform for the benefit of the potential licensees and that such licensees could directly enforce as

---

TECHNICAL SPECIFICATION(S) or, as applicable, any STANDARD or TECHNICAL SPECIFICATION resulting from proposals or Work Items within the current scope of the above identified ETSI Project(s), for the field of use of practice of such STANDARD or TECHNICAL SPECIFICATION ... "; similarly, the "IPR Information Statement and Licensing Declaration" includes: "To the extent that the IPR(s) disclosed in the attached *IPR Information Statement Annex* are or become, and remain ESSENTIAL in respect of the ETSI Work Item, STANDARD and/or TECHNICAL SPECIFICATION identified in the attached *IPR Information Statement Annex*, the Declarant and/or its AFFILIATES are (1) prepared to grant irrevocable licenses under this/these IPR(s) on terms and conditions which are in accordance with Clause 6.1 of the ETSI IPR Policy ... " *Id.*

[210]   *Id.*

[211]   *Id.* (describing the grant of a license as an "undertaking").

[212]   *Id.*

[213]   For a contractual analysis of FRAND commitments, *see* Straus 2011; Brooks & Geradin 2010; for the opposite view (considering that (common law) contract theory does not constitute the proper legal basis for analyzing FRAND), *see* Contreras 2015c.

[214]   *See, e.g.,* Unidroit 2016, art. 5.2.1 (contracts in favor of third parties): "(1) The parties (the 'promisor' and the 'promisee') may confer by express or implied agreement a right on a third party (the 'beneficiary'). (2) The existence and content of the beneficiary's right against the promisor are determined by the agreement of the parties and are subject to any conditions or other limitations under the agreement."

[215]   *See* Straus 2011; Caron 2013, 1008 et seq.

third party beneficiaries? The specificity and the difficulty of this analysis results from the finding that the relevant obligation does not consist of a straightforward – i.e., easy to identify and thus to enforce – contractual obligation.[216] Quite to the contrary, the owners of SEPs commit to be prepared to license out their patents to third party licensees on FRAND terms and conditions, whereby there remains considerable room as to what shall constitute FRAND terms and conditions.[217]

Under Swiss law (assuming that it would apply), the commitment could be considered as an "agreement to conclude a contract" within the meaning of Article 22¶ 1 of the Swiss Code of Obligations (SCO), which provides that "[p]arties may reach a binding agreement to enter into a contract at a later date." Pursuant to this provision, one contracting party can promise to its contracting party that it shall enter into a contract with a third party, so that such third party can subsequently request the performance of this obligation (as a third party beneficiary), i.e., it can request that the contract shall be entered into or claim damages for breach of such obligation.[218] The validity of such a preliminary contract (i.e., the contract by which one party agrees to enter into another future contract) depends on whether the object of the contract is determined or is at least determinable.[219]

From this perspective, the enforceability of the obligation against an owner of SEPs (to execute a license agreement with a third party licensee) will depend on whether such obligation is sufficiently determinable in order to qualify as a valid contractual obligation, the performance of which could be requested and enforced.

If a Swiss court considers that (as a result of its interpretation of the FRAND commitment on the basis of the law that shall govern it) the FRAND commitment constitutes a binding obligation that could be enforced by an implementer against the patent owner and that would further prevent the patent owner from initiating any patent infringement litigation against an implementer including an action for damages, a FRAND commitment could limit or affect a patent holder's ability to recover monetary damages from an infringing implementer of a standard. The reason would be that by bringing an action for damages against an implementer, the patent owner would be in breach of its contractual obligation resulting from the

---

[216] By contrast (for the sake of comparison), a contractual obligation that would be simple to enforce by a third party beneficiary would be an obligation of the debtor to pay a given amount to such third party under certain circumstances; *see* this decision of the Swiss Federal Supreme Court: 4C.5/2003 (TF 2003) (Switz.) (interpreting the financial penalty clause of a noncompetition undertaking in a shareholders' agreement, which allowed enforcement by the company, as granting a direct enforcement right to a third party beneficiary (the company) by application of Obligationenrecht [OR] [Code of Obligations], SR 220, art. 112 ¶ 2 (Switz.) (Swiss Code of Obligations)).

[217] *See, e.g.*, Allensworth 2014.

[218] *See, e.g.*, BGE 98 II 305 (BGer 1972, ¶ 1) (Switz.) ("The ... clause between the parties to the contract of sale is a preliminary contract (Art. 22 OR) in favor of third parties, i.e. the plaintiffs. They were directly favored and could therefore, according to Art. 112 (2) OR, request from the defendant that he shall conclude the main contract ... " (translated)).

[219] BGE 118 II 32 (BGer 1992, ¶ 3b) (Switz.); BGE 98 II 305 (BGer 1972, ¶ 1) (Switz.).

FRAND commitment and would thus be liable for the damages resulting from such contractual breach.[220]

2. Patent Damages under Swiss Law

As reflected in the Swiss case law[221] and legal literature,[222] Swiss law is characterized by the lack of a special legal regime that would specifically regulate the damages resulting from the infringement of IP rights. Under Swiss law, the financial consequences of an infringement of an IP right are governed by general tort law,[223] which is regulated in the Swiss Code of Obligations ("SCO").[224] An IP infringement constitutes a tort that triggers the obligation to pay damages under the general principles of Swiss civil law, and specifically under Article 41 ¶ 1 SCO, which provides that "[a]ny person who unlawfully causes loss or damage to another, whether wilfully or negligently, is obliged to provide compensation."[225]

According to case law, there are three methods to calculate damages resulting from an IP infringement under Swiss law:[226] The first method requires the showing of an effective or direct damage ("effektiver oder direkter Schaden" according to the German terminology); the second method is based on the so-called license analogy ("Lizenzanalogie"); and the third method is based on an analogy to the income of the infringer ("Analogieschluss aus dem Gewinn des Verletzers").

The first method – based on the showing of an effective or direct damage – generally presupposes to show that the income of the victim has declined as a result of the infringement activities.[227]

The second method – license analogy – means that the infringer has to pay damages that correspond to the level of royalties that reasonable contracting parties would have agreed upon in a license agreement.[228] As reflected in case law,

---

[220]   This could be compared to a situation in which a licensor would claim damage from a licensee that would have complied with the contractual terms of use of the license.

[221]   BGE 132 III 379 (BGer 2005) (Switz.).

[222]   *See, e.g.,* Benhamou 2013.

[223]   This is achieved by a reference that is made in the Swiss IP statutes to the Swiss Code of Obligations; for Swiss patent law, *see* Schweizerisches Zivilgesetzbuch [ZBG] [Civil Code], SR 232.14, art. 73 ¶ 1 (Switz.) (Swiss Patent Act) which provides that "[a]ny person who performs an act referred to in Article 66 either wilfully or through negligence shall be required to pay damages to the injured party according to the provisions of the Code of Obligations."

[224]   Obligationenrecht [OR] [Code of Obligations], SR 220 (Switz.).

[225]   *Id.* at art. 41 ¶ 1.

[226]   BGE 132 III 379 (BGer 2005, ¶ 3.2) (Switz.).

[227]   *Id.* at ¶ 3.2.1.

[228]   *Id.* at ¶ 3.2.2 ("The damage quantification using the method of *license analogy* means that the infringer has to pay damages to the holder of the intellectual property right in the amount of the remuneration which would have been agreed upon by reasonable contracting parties when concluding a license agreement for the relevant intellectual property right." (translated)) (internal citations omitted).

the second method aims at assessing the lost profits of the victim.[229] The victim has the burden to show the damage in the form of lost license royalties that it has suffered as a result of the IP infringement. The victim must consequently establish or at least make it probable that it has lost licensing royalties as a result of the infringing activities. Quite interestingly, the Swiss Federal Court has specified that the amount of the royalties based on a hypothetical agreement between the licensor and the licensee must be established without reference to the appropriateness of the royalties:[230] What counts in other terms is the royalties that the parties would have (subjectively) agreed upon in the relevant circumstances and not whether such royalties are (objectively) appropriate.[231]

The case law of the Swiss Federal Court is however very restrictive so that the method of license analogy for calculating the damages for IP infringement is extremely difficult to apply successfully for the victim/IP owner. In the leading case,[232] the Swiss Federal Court refused to award damages for lost royalties in a case in which the IP owner had offered a license for a flat fee of CHF 90,000 to the infringer and in which the infringer refused such offer and subsequently started to infringe the patent. In this case, the Swiss Federal Court held that the victim/IP owner had not established with sufficient probability the damage that it would have suffered, i.e., it had not established that it could have obtained the license royalties.

The third method – analogy to the income of the infringer – is not based on damage suffered by the victim but is rather based on the disgorgement of profits made by the infringer.[233] This method is based on Article 423 SCO, which provides (in the chapter "Agency without authority")[234] that "[w]here agency activities were not carried out with the best interests of the principal in mind, he is nonetheless entitled to appropriate any resulting benefits."

On this basis and in light of the case law of the Swiss Federal Court defining the calculation of damages for patent infringement based on the method of the license analogy, monetary damages for patent infringement based on a license analogy

---

[229] *Id.* at ¶ 3.4; BGE 97 II 169 (BGer 1971, ¶ 3a) (Switz.).

[230] BGE 132 III 379 (BGer 2005, ¶ 3.4) (Switz.) ("However, the application of the method presupposes proof of an asset reduction for the injured person. If loss of profit is claimed, it must be assumed that the holder of the intellectual property right should have been able to obtain the lost profit. This is not the case if the holder of the intellectual property right did not use the intellectual property right at all. Only in so far as the holder of the property right is able to prove that, as a result of the act of infringement, a license agreement and thus a license fee have probably escaped him, is it a loss of profit. In this case, however, the amount of the license fee shall be determined in accordance with the hypothetical agreement between the licensor and the licensee, irrespective of the appropriateness of the license fee." (translated)) (internal citations omitted).

[231] This method evokes the hypothetical negotiation framework of the U.S. *Georgia-Pacific* framework. In addition, this approach appears to diverge from the German approach of making an objective determination of royalties based on objective reasonableness.

[232] BGE 132 III 379 (BGer 2005) (Switz.).

[233] *Id.* at ¶ 3.2.3, with reference to BGE 97 II 169 (BGer 1971) (Switz.); BGE 98 II 325 (BGer 1972) (Switz.).

[234] Obligationenrecht [OR] [Code of Obligations], SR 220, art. 419–24 (Switz.).

could theoretically be granted even if such damages are not "appropriate"[235] or reasonable. This could for instance be the case if the patent owner had successfully negotiated (but not yet signed) a license agreement with a third party with a very high royalty payment (which might not be appropriate or reasonable by objective standards) and if the infringing activity had caused such license agreement not to be entered into (for instance because the negotiating licensee would have stopped the negotiation because of the sudden appearance of infringing products on the market). If the IP owner could prove such facts with a sufficient level of probability, it could obtain damages in the amount of the lost royalties even if such royalties would not be appropriate or reasonable.

As noted above, a FRAND commitment can imply a contractual obligation for the IP owner for the benefit of the implementers (as third party beneficiaries). The key substantive element of such commitment is the obligation to license the relevant patents on fair, reasonable, and nondiscriminatory terms. On this basis, the first source for defining the meaning of "reasonable" is the FRAND commitment itself, which must be interpreted according to the methods of interpretation that apply under the law that governs the FRAND commitment (which may make it possible to take into account other sources that can be relevant for interpreting a contract/a contractual term). Under Swiss contract law, what prevails is the subjective intention of the contracting parties as reflected in Article 18 ¶ 1 SCO, which provides that "[w]hen assessing the form and terms of a contract, the true and common intention of the parties must be ascertained without dwelling on any inexact expressions or designations they may have used either in error or by way of disguising the true nature of the agreement."

Assuming that Swiss law would apply to a FRAND commitment and that a dispute would be submitted to a Swiss court in order to decide the royalties to be paid under a FRAND license, the Swiss court would have to define the term of "reasonable" (as used in the FRAND commitment) by application of the usual methods of contract interpretation under Swiss contract law. As a result, a patent owner would have the right to receive FRAND royalties from an implementer at the level the court would consider "reasonable" based on its interpretation of the meaning of "reasonable" as used in the FRAND commitment. The Swiss court may in this respect be inspired to look at sources of international law[236] or of foreign law from which it may be tempted to draw analogies in order to define the concept of "reasonable" royalties under a FRAND commitment.

---

[235] "angemessen."

[236] Reference could be made to the TRIPS Agreement, art. 31, which provides for a compulsory mechanism (compulsory licensing of patents) for which similarities may be found with the obligation to license under a FRAND commitment, under which "the right holder shall be paid *adequate remuneration* in the circumstances of each case, taking into account the economic value of the authorization" (italics added).

In any event, in contrast to damages for patent infringement based on the method of license analogy, which may diverge from appropriate (or reasonable) royalties (see above), the royalties due under a FRAND license are in essence supposed to be "reasonable" (or appropriate). On this basis, it is unlikely that royalties paid under a FRAND license would be the same as monetary damages for infringement of the same patent and that "reasonable" royalties for FRAND purposes shall be the same as standard monetary damages for patent infringement under Swiss patent law in the scenario in which the FRAND commitment constitutes a valid contractual obligation. This reflects the difference between a contract-based royalty fee that is supposed to be "reasonable" under the FRAND framework and a tort-based damage corresponding to a lost royalty fee that is supposed to compensate the victim for the actual damage that it has suffered, whereby the damage may not be objectively "reasonable" provided that it can be established that such damage was incurred/was likely to have been incurred.

C. Korea

Unlike the United States, the typical measure of damages in Korean patent infringement suits is "total profits of the infringer" rather than "a reasonable royalty." And when damages are calculated in the form of total profits of the alleged infringer, it is difficult to distinguish FRAND-committed SEPs from non-SEPs. This issue arose in *Samsung Electronics Co. Ltd.* v. *Apple Korea Ltd.*[237] As long as total profits of the infringer are concerned, it is difficult for a court to reflect a FRAND commitment in calculating damages. Even in the case of "total profits of the infringer," however, a general principle of remedies law requires the plaintiff to show some causal relation between the infringer's profits and the infringement. Accordingly, the amount of actual damages is limited to the infringer's total profits that are caused by infringing patents only. Once we take into account the causal relation between the infringer's profits and the infringing patents, we have to face a difficult question of apportionment. The Supreme Court of Korea has struggled to determine what proportion of the whole product the infringing patents cover in terms of their quantity, quality, and price. It is difficult to prove the proportional quantity, quality, and price of one out of so many patents in a multicomponent product whether or not the patent is a FRAND-committed one.

Theoretically, royalties paid under a FRAND license may be the same as monetary damages for infringement of the same patent. Unfortunately, however, there is no judicial decision yet on this issue. As Seoul Central District Court noted in *Samsung Electronics Co. Ltd.* v. *Apple Korea Ltd.*, it is almost impossible to get enough data on reasonable royalties for FRAND purposes simply because most

---

[237] *Samsung Electronics Co. Ltd.* v. *Apple Korea Ltd.* (Dist. Ct. 2012) (Kor.).

licensing agreements are subject to an obligation of confidentiality and prohibited from disclosure of their terms and conditions.[238]

D. Japan

In *Samsung v. Apple Japan*, the Japanese IP High Court analyzed the patent infringement damages to which Samsung was entitled due to Apple's alleged infringement of Samsung's SEPs covering the ETSI UMTS standard.[239] In its decision, the court held that Samsung was entitled to recover damages from Apple only up to the level of a FRAND royalty.[240] Seeking damages in excess of a FRAND royalty could constitute an abuse of right unless a SEP holder demonstrates that the implementer had no intention of obtaining a license on FRAND terms, in which case damages in excess of the FRAND rate may be available.[241]

With respect to the FRAND level of royalties, the court first determined the percentage of the total value of the infringing products contributed by the UMTS standard.[242] It then determined that an aggregate royalty rate of 5 percent should be applied to all patents covering the UMTS standard, based on an analysis of industry practices and prior royalty commitments made by the parties and other industry participants.[243] It then found the FRAND royalty for an individual SEP by dividing the total royalty for UMTS by the number of UMTS SEPs identified by an independent third party (529 out of the total 1,889 SEPs declared to be essential to the standard).[244]

E. China

Thus far, courts in China have rendered judgments in three cases involving FRAND-committed SEPs. The first was the 2013 decision of the Shenzhen Intermediate People's Court in *Huawei Tech. Co., Ltd. v. InterDigital Commc'ns, Inc.*,[245] which involved InterDigital's portfolio of Chinese patents essential to the WCDMA, CDMA2000, and TD-SCDMA 3G wireless communication standards. After negotiations between the parties failed, Huawei filed two complaints against InterDigital, one for violation of China's Anti-Monopoly Law, and another requesting the court to set a FRAND royalty.[246] The court concluded that InterDigital had

---

[238] *Id.*
[239] *Samsung Elecs. Co. v. Apple Japan LLC* (IP High Ct. 2014) (Japan) (FRAND I).
[240] *Id.* at 124–25.
[241] *Id.* at 123–24.
[242] *Id.* at 132–33.
[243] *Id.* at 135–36.
[244] *Id.* at 137–38.
[245] *Huawei Tech. Co., Ltd. v. InterDigital Commc'ns, Inc.* (Guangdong Higher People's Ct. Oct. 28, 2013) (China).
[246] *Id.*

breached its obligation to license its patents on FRAND terms and that, based on the royalty rates Samsung and Apple had paid InterDigital for similar licenses, a FRAND royalty rate for the patents-in-suit would be 0.019 percent of end-product prices. The decision was affirmed on appeal by the Guangdong High Court.[247]

Second, as discussed in Section 5.3.5 above, in *Iwncomm v. Sony*, the Beijing IP court issued an injunction for the infringement of a FRAND-committed SEP covering the Chinese WAPI standard relating to wireless networking.[248] In addition, the court issued an award of monetary damages to Iwncomm, the SEP holder, in the amount of RMB 8,629,173. On the issue of monetary compensation, according to Shen and Ge:

> The court fully adopted Iwncomm's damages theory, citing the fact that the invention is a basic invention in the WLAN security field and that Sony was at fault during the negotiation. The court did not analyse in detail whether the licenses in evidence are comparable, merely noting that the territorial scope and duration of these licenses suggest that they can be referred to. Further, despite the fact that Iwncomm's four licenses are all licenses for a portfolio of patents, the court held that the rate of 1 RMB per unit would be applicable for a single WAPI patent at issue.[249]

The court then (1) multiplied this rate by the number of infringing devices, and (2) trebled the resulting amount as permitted under Article 21 of China's Patent Trial Guidelines.[250] So understood, the decision does not appear to involve a judicial determination of a FRAND royalty as such, but rather simply a damages award.

Finally, as discussed in Section 5.3.5 above, the Shenzhen Intermediate People's Court recently issued an injunction for the infringement of two FRAND-committed patents essential to the 4G standard in *Huawei v. Samsung*.[251]

---

[247] *Id.*

[248] For further discussion of *Xian Xidian Jietong Wireless Commc'n Co., Ltd. (IWNComm)* v. SONY *Mobile Commc'n Prods. (China) Co. Ltd.* (Beijing IP Ct. Mar. 22, 2017) (China), *see* Bharadwaj & Verma 2017.

[249] Shen & Ge 2017.

[250] *Id.*

[251] As of this writing, an English-language translation of the January 2018 *Huawei v. Samsung* decision is not available, but a summary of the court's reasoning can be found in Schindler 2018.

6

The Effect of Competition Law on Patent Remedies

Alison Jones and Renato Nazzini[1]

6.1 INTRODUCTION

More than 130 jurisdictions around the world now have competition, or antitrust,[2] systems in place. Many of these, to prevent firms from distorting competition in a free market economy, stand upon three main substantive pillars:

  i. provisions prohibiting restrictive agreements (e.g., in the United States (U.S.) and the European Union (EU), Section 1 of the Sherman Act 1890 and Article 101 of the Treaty on the Functioning of the European Union (TFEU), respectively);
 ii. provisions prohibiting monopolization (or attempts to monopolize) or abusive conduct of dominant firms[3] (Sherman Act Section 2 and Article 102 TFEU); and
iii. provisions prohibiting mergers that will substantially lessen or significantly impede competition (Clayton Act 1914 Section 7 and the EU Merger Regulation, Council Regulation 139/2004).

This chapter considers the extent to which, in the area of complex products, competition laws can, or should, (i) affect remedies available for patent infringement; and/or otherwise (ii) limit the conduct of patentees, particularly when transferring or licensing their patents.

In examining the tensions that have arisen between patent and antitrust law in this sphere of complex products, this chapter scrutinizes issues that have arisen in a series of cases across the globe; these have principally emerged in relation to a subset of

---

[1] The authors would like to thank Jorge L. Contreras, Tom Cotter, Damien Geradin, Oskar Liivak, Norman V. Siebrasse, Nicolas Petit, and Peter Picht for their comments on earlier drafts of this chapter.
[2] The European Commission in the European Union (EU) describes the enforcement of TFEU arts. 101 and 102 as "antitrust" and distinguishes it from merger enforcement. In the United States (U.S.), the term "antitrust" encompasses both merger and nonmerger enforcement. In this chapter we use the term antitrust in the broader U.S. manner as encompassing all areas of competition law.
[3] Broadly, dominance in the European Union is defined as a position of economic strength on a market that allows the undertaking to act independently (significant market power), *see, e.g., United Brands Co. and United Brands Continental B.V. v. Commission of the European Communities* (CJEU 1978) (EU).

patents that are "essential" to the implementation of standardized technologies (standard-essential patents – SEPs). It explains that, in most jurisdictions, competition law accepts both the importance of patents to the competitive process and that standards are critical to innovation in industries where compatibility between manufacturers' products is expected by customers. Nonetheless, antitrust enforcers worldwide have been concerned about the potential anticompetitive consequences that may flow from standardization processes (particularly in relation to mobile communication standards) and especially the behavior of SEP owners.

Section 6.2 considers the objectives of both antitrust and patent law focusing on whether, and if so how, they respectively seek to increase efficiency and welfare in markets – through promoting competition that delivers lower prices, greater quality of products, greater consumer choice, and/or innovation and dynamic efficiency. Despite relatively broad acceptance of the complementary nature of the antitrust and IP laws, it examines the inherent tension arising from the different methods deployed by the two systems to increase efficiency – grant of exclusionary rights versus protecting competition – and interactions between them. Further, Section 6.2 considers whether competition law should simply assume that the protection conferred by IP law is required for the creation and commercialization of new technology or whether competition law should intervene where conduct based on patent law seems to go beyond what is necessary and, for example, may be distorting competition in a downstream market and/or allowing the patentee to exploit users of the technology.

Section 6.3 examines whether and when there might be scope for antitrust law to "override" patent law, in particular in two interconnected circumstances, by:

- preventing a patentee from seeking, or limiting when it may seek (restorative), patent remedies, for example, an injunction to prevent future infringement of its patent or damages for past infringement, and thus the judicial protection of its rights; and
- limiting the commercial exploitation of patents, for example, by controlling the pricing of patent licenses (price levels or methodologies and how the requirement in some antitrust systems that dominant firms may not charge excessive or exploitative prices for their products or discriminate in prices between customers relates to fair, reasonable, and nondiscriminatory (FRAND)[4] licensing requirements); the structure of patent licenses (e.g., portfolio licensing, the bundling of patents in licenses, or the level at which the license is granted); collective licensing through patent pools; and the splitting or sale of patent portfolios.

When examining the antitrust jurisprudence one question arising is whether some cases have arisen, partly at least, as a response to a perceived failure of the

---

[4] *See infra* note 35 and accompanying text.

patent system or as a result of concern that patent law has been unable to deal adequately or effectively with remedies and breakdowns in licensing negotiations. Broader questions, therefore, are whether there would be a need for competition law to play such an important supplemental role in this sphere if a more efficient and principled system of patent remedies is put in place, in line with that proposed in this book, or whether, even with such a system in place, competition law systems provide more flexible techniques for solving some of the problems arising in this sphere.

Finally, the chapter considers whether antitrust remedies allow competition law to be effectively enforced and thus serve as a helpful supplement to other patent law solutions without becoming too intrusive or regulatory in nature. The answer to this question may shape the contours of substantive antitrust liability.

6.2 OBJECTIVES OF INTELLECTUAL PROPERTY AND COMPETITION LAW

It is often said that patent law (and intellectual property (IP) law more broadly) and competition law "constitute complementary components of a modern industrial policy" that aims to improve innovation and consumer welfare.[5] However, because of the different approaches they employ to achieve their objectives – the conferral of exclusive rights compared to the maintenance of effective competition – sometimes patent and competition law solutions to an identical issue appear to collide. Furthermore, even if it is recognized that they strive to achieve complementary goals, it does not mean that antitrust law should not sometimes constrain patent law, or vice versa; these distinct areas of law must be interpreted to accommodate each other.

Before examining those apparent collisions in the subsequent sections, this part considers the ostensible tension[6] between competition and patent law, focusing on the question of whether they are designed to achieve the same objectives – that is to improve welfare[7] and solve the same basic economic problem. Do they both aim to optimize the use of scarce resources in pursuit of providing the things that consumers want and need?[8] If so, the systems should then work harmoniously together and yield to each other when required. Where exclusion or unrestrained exploitation is necessary for the creation and commercialization of a new technology, competition law should defer to patent law. In contrast, where unconstrained exercise of IP rights goes beyond what is necessary for the creation and commercialization of a new technology and is detrimental to competition and efficiency, patent law should defer to competition law. With their unified goals, such trade-offs and concessions should be quite natural. In practice, however, things are not so simple and harmonious for a number of reasons.

[5] *See, e.g.*, Anderman & Kallaugher 2006; DOJ & FTC 2007, 1; Gilbert & Shapiro 1997.
[6] Bowman 1973, vii.
[7] *Id.* at 1.
[8] *Id.* at 2.

First, although in some jurisdictions, including the United States, there has, until recently at least, been a growing consensus that competition law is "technocratic"[9] and built on the "broad professional and policy consensus" that surrounds the basic microeconomic model of perfect competition,[10] such an approach is by no means universal or without challenges.[11] Further, there is no broad consensus on objectives on the patent side. Rather it is generally recognized that the patent system is a welfare enhancing, multipurpose instrument serving a variety of objectives, including[12] the provision of incentives to innovation and technology development,[13] the promotion of technology dissemination,[14] and the coordination of "the search for technological and market enhancement" (like prospects signal territories of interest to mine developers).[15] Furthermore, despite broad accord that innovation is crucial to technological growth, some disagreement as to how to foster such growth exists. For example, it may be difficult to know how best to incentivize both innovation and follow-on innovation or improvements. Although conferral of patents may incentivize innovation, it is possible that in some circumstances, rights conferred may be used to stifle competition that uses those patents and, consequently, subsequent innovation.

Secondly, in each field, agreement is lacking on how to achieve the objectives pursued.[16] Even in jurisdictions where a competition consumer welfare goal is clearly pursued, there is still considerable scope for debate as to how to reflect that underpinning aim, and in particular how to balance competing economic factors and, for example, how allocative efficiency (e.g., price equals marginal cost or price efficiency), productive efficiency (e.g., cost optimization), and/or dynamic efficiency (e.g., supply of improved and or new products/services) can be ensured. For example, a policy of *ex post* antitrust enforcement that prioritizes allocative efficiency over dynamic efficiency would almost inevitably upset a patent policy that aimed *ex ante* to maximize innovators' rewards through extensive patent protection.[17]

Another important issue relevant in the context of complex products is whether competition law should ever "regulate" the conduct of a dominant firm (or IP holder) by preventing it from engaging in exploitative conduct, for example through extracting "unfair" licensing terms from a licensee or implementer.[18] This matter is

---

[9] Blair & Sokol 2013, 2505.

[10] Bohannon & Hovenkamp 2012, 45.

[11] Khan 2017; Nazzini 2011, 11–50.

[12] It is also argued that the purpose of the patent system is tied to the concept that natural law conveys to the inventor some sort of property right regarding the invention; *see* Machlup 1958, 19–80.

[13] Scherer 1980, 632.

[14] Gallini & Winter 1985.

[15] Kitch 1977, 276.

[16] We leave aside other, less consensual goals, like the promotion of consumer choice, the protection of small businesses, or the fight against inequality. For a catalogue of such goals and their analysis from a normative perspective, *see* Nazzini 2011, 11–50.

[17] *See* Chapter 2 and *infra* note 29 and accompanying text.

[18] Three main conceptual challenges suggesting a cautionary approach to excessive pricing cases are that the markets are self-correcting, the prohibition is tantamount to prohibiting the dominant

controversial not only from a competition perspective but also because it seems to go so fundamentally against the grain of patent law, which aims to incentivize by giving a patentee freedom to exploit the fruit of its invention for a limited period of time. Purely exploitative pricing behavior of dominant firms is not prohibited by monopolization laws set out in Section 2 of the Sherman Act in the United States,[19] but is specifically prohibited in the European Union and a number of other jurisdictions.[20] Although the European Commission (the Commission), like many other competition agencies, has to date rarely intervened in cases that purely involve unfair pricing,[21] and has generally preferred to focus its resources on exclusionary conduct (see Section 6.3), it is now clear that a number of competition agencies are becoming increasingly interested in such cases, especially in the sphere of SEPs and pharmaceutical products.[22]

Thirdly, antitrust and patent laws involve different processes and are not enforced by common institutions. Rather, antitrust agencies and patent offices generally operate at arm's length from each other. This may create an initial disconnect that needs to be resolved *ex post* when competition enforcement action is taken in individual cases or where patent issues are litigated in the courts.

As a result of these factors, the interface between patent and competition law can be mired in an uneasy stand-off. In an ideal world, there should not be such a disconnect. Rather a rational social planner should ensure wholesale consistency across policies in both fields and conflicts should not occur. Reality does not, however, match such an abstract model.

The tension between antitrust and patent laws should not be exaggerated, however. Competition law is case specific. It is generally respectful of patent rights and only prohibits certain types of conduct, leaving patent owners free to behave as they see fit outside of its strictures.[23] In particular, it generally only interferes with unilateral conduct of a patentee where that patentee is dominant or has a significant degree of market power.[24] This point means that innovation-minded patent practitioners should not overreact to antitrust enforcement.

---

position, and exploitative practices serve an important dynamic role, thereby increasing welfare: *see* Gal 2013.

[19] *Verizon Commc'ns, Inc. v. Law Offices of Curtis V. Trinko, LLP* (U.S. 2004) (U.S.). An important question, however, is the extent to which FTC Act, 15 U.S.C. § 45, which provides the FTC with a broad mandate to prohibit "[u]nfair methods of competition in or affecting commerce, and unfair or deceptive acts or practices in or affecting commerce," applies beyond the reach of practices prohibited by the Sherman (and other antitrust) statutes.

[20] *See* TFEU art. 102(a).

[21] Apart from the regulatory nature of any such intervention and, for example, broader concerns as to when intervention of this type is desirable, the difficulties involved in determining whether selling prices imposed are unfair (or excessive) are acute.

[22] *See, e.g., infra* note 81; Jones & Stothers 2018.

[23] Unlike alternative remedies like heavy-handed price regulation or blanket compulsory licensing legislation.

[24] *See* Section 6.1.

Indeed, coordination between competition law and patent law is, frequently, left to doctrinal tools and techniques that are designed to balance the laws on a case-by-case basis, such as:

a. **Division of competences.** Competition law application may recede in spheres that the legislature has previously covered with IP rights. The idea behind this doctrine is that there is a core of IP law with which competition law cannot interfere. For example, in the European Union, the case law has accepted that EU competition law cannot deprive the holder of an IP right of the specific subject matter of its IP right but can only regulate the exercise of the right.[25]

b. **An enhanced intervention threshold.** Competition law frequently sets the bar particularly high for a finding of breach of its rules when an IP right is involved (the rules of engagement of antitrust liability are set higher than in non-IP rights cases). Put differently, antitrust law is only likely to interfere with the exercise of IP rights in "exceptional circumstances." Exceptionalism has been the approach ordinarily followed in, for example, refusal-to-license cases, both in the United States[26] and the European Union, although the authorities in the European Union have arguably been more willing to find that exceptional circumstances exist than their U.S. counterparts. For example, in *Microsoft*[27] the General Court upheld the Commission's finding that Microsoft had unlawfully withheld essential interoperability information from rivals, in a bid to leverage its dominant position on the market for Operating Systems (OS) for PCs into the adjacent market for

---

[25] See, e.g., *Centrafarm BV v. Sterling Drug Inc.* (CJEU 1974) (EU); *Windsurfing Int'l Inc. v. Comm'n of the European Communities* (CJEU 1986, ¶¶ 45, 92) (EU).

[26] Although the Federal Circuit put in place a virtually irrebuttable presumption of legality for refusals to license, holding that the subjective motivation of a patentee in refusing to license its IP rights should be irrelevant (antitrust laws should not interfere with an IP rights holder's right to refusal to license, even if the conduct was adopted for an anticompetitive purpose, *unless* the IP right had been acquired through fraud, the lawsuit to enforce the patent was a sham, or the owner was seeking to extend its monopoly beyond the exclusivity granted, see *CSU, LLC v. Xerox Corp.* (Fed Cir. 2000, p.1327) (U.S.)). In *Image Tech. Servs. v. Eastman Kodak Co.* (9th Cir. 1997, p.1218–19) (U.S.) the Ninth Circuit held that a unilateral refusal to license a patent or copyright could constitute exclusionary conduct but that a monopolist's "desire to exclude others from its [protected] work is a presumptively valid business justification for any immediate harm to consumers." In this case, the court was willing to go behind the exercise of the IP right and look to the intent of the IP rights holder and determine whether the presumption should be rebutted on the grounds of "pretext." "Neither the aims of intellectual property law, nor the antitrust laws justify allowing a monopolist to rely upon a pretextual business justification to mask anticompetitive conduct." *Id.* at 1219.

[27] See *Microsoft Corp. v. Comm'n of the European Communities (Microsoft I)* (CJEU 2007, ¶ 331) (EU) ("It is only in exceptional circumstances that the exercise of the exclusive right by the owner of the intellectual property right may give rise to such an abuse."); *Microsoft Corp. v. European Comm'n (Microsoft II)* (CJEU 2012, ¶¶ 139–40) (EU) (though the General Court did not explicitly mention exceptional circumstances, it ruled that the *IMS Health* conditions were fulfilled in *Microsoft I*). See also *Radio Telefis Eireann (RTE) and Independent Television Publications Ltd. (ITP) v. Comm'n of the European Communities* (CJEU 1995) (EU); *IMS Health GmbH & Co. OHG v. NDC Health GmbH & Co. KG* (CJEU 2004) (EU).

work group servers OS. The theory of exceptionalism has also been applied to IP
remedy cases in the European Union.

c. **Complementarity.** Given their complementary goals, the *ex post* application
   of competition law generally takes into account the need to protect investment
   in a patented invention. Thus, competition law recognizes that dynamic
   efficiency, and in particular the need to preserve the incentives to innovate
   provided by patent and IP law, could, under certain circumstances, be
   a crucial factor in crafting a test to identify anticompetitive conduct or a valid
   business justification of conduct that would otherwise be held to be
   anticompetitive.[28] Indeed in the European Union, the Commission has
   published a Communication on SEPs that sets out two objectives pursued in
   this sphere, "incentivising the development and inclusion of top technologies
   in standards, by preserving fair and adequate return for these contributions,
   and ensuring smooth and wide dissemination of standardized technologies
   based on fair access conditions."[29]

d. **Patent Misuse.** In the United States, the patent/antitrust interface had,
   historically, been governed by the judge-made patent misuse doctrine. Today,
   the doctrine has been significantly narrowed. Congress explicitly removed some
   practices from patent misuse[30] and the remainder of the doctrine has been
   narrowly interpreted by the courts.[31]

e. **Misrepresentation by a patentee.** In some jurisdictions a relevant factor in
   determining whether antitrust liability should ensue may be whether a patentee
   has made misrepresentations to an authority (such as a patent office), for example
   to acquire IP protection or otherwise to exclude a competitor.[32]

---

[28] *See, e.g.,* Section 6.3.2; *Microsoft Corp.* v. *Comm'n of the European Communities (Microsoft I)* (CJEU 2007, ¶¶ 697–710) (EU).

[29] European Commission, at 2, COM (2017) 712 final (Nov. 29, 2017) (Commission Communication on SEPs). The Draft Council Conclusions on the IP rights Enforcement Package broadly endorses the Communication: *see* Council of the European Union, at ¶¶ 3, 11–13, 5753/18 (Jan. 29, 2018).

[30] *See* U.S. Patent Act, 35 U.S.C. § 271(d) ("No patent owner ... shall be denied relief or deemed guilty of misuse or illegal extension of the patent right by reason of his having done one or more of the following: (1) derived revenue from acts which if performed by another without his consent would constitute contributory infringement of the patent; (2) licensed or authorized another to perform acts which if performed without his consent would constitute contributory infringement of the patent; (3) sought to enforce his patent rights against infringement or contributory infringement; (4) refused to license or use any rights to the patent; or (5) conditioned the license of any rights to the patent or the sale of the patented product on the acquisition of a license to rights in another patent or purchase of a separate product, unless, in view of the circumstances, the patent owner has market power in the relevant market for the patent or patented product on which the license or sale is conditioned.").

[31] *See Princo Corp.* v. *Int'l Trade Comm'n* (Fed. Cir. 2010) (U.S.) (en banc).

[32] *See AstraZeneca* v. *Commission* (CJEU 2010) (EU) (it can be an abuse for a dominant undertaking to make misrepresentations to regulatory authorities or to take steps with regard to regulatory procedures in order to exclude competitors) and *Walker Process Equipment, Inc.* v. *Food Machinery & Chemical Corp.* 382 U.S. 172 (1965) (if a patent holder obtained its patent by knowingly and willfully misrepresenting facts, such behavior may be sufficient to strip it of an exemption from antitrust laws).

6.3 ANTITRUST LIABILITY FOR ENFORCEMENT OR EXPLOITATION OF PATENTS

6.3.1 *Background*

In the area of complex products, tensions arising at the interface of patent and antitrust law have largely emerged in relation to the exploitation, commercialization, or enforcement of SEPs. Many of these cases initially focused on the risk of capture of the standard-setting process or the conduct of a patentee that resulted in the nondisclosure of the existence of a relevant patent during a standardization process.[33] In more recent years, attention has concentrated on the risk that SEP holders might use market power acquired as a result of the standardization process to exploit customers and/or to hold up implementers of the standard and adversely impact on innovation and the quality, variety, and cost of products/services available in a downstream market. This could, for example, be through demanding unreasonable, excessive (in excess of the patentee's true contribution),[34] or discriminatory royalties/licensing terms or through seeking injunctive relief against an implementer that does not agree to the patentee's licensing demands.

It is true that to minimize such risks many, or most, standard-development organizations (SDOs) have for some time required participating firms to disclose SEPs and to commit, as a condition to having their technology integrated into the standard, to licensing of any SEPs on FRAND terms.[35] It is well known, nonetheless, that SDO rules, which mainly relate to technical issues, leave open the answer to a number of complex questions, including how valid patents can be identified and invalid assertions quickly weeded out; how infringement can be tested in relation to a portfolio of SEPs (how it can be determined whether over-declarations of essentiality have been made); whether and how FRAND commitments can be enforced, initially or following transfer of the SEP to a third party; exactly how a FRAND

---

[33] *See, e.g.*, the European Commission's and U.S. Federal Trade Commission's (FTC) proceedings against Rambus, Inc.: Commission Decision of 9 December 2009, COMP/38.636—RAMBUS; European Commission Press Release IP/09/1897; European Commission Memorandum MEMO/09/544 (frequently asked questions); and *Rambus, Inc.* (FTC Aug. 2, 2006) (Opinion of the Commission), *reversed by Rambus Inc. v. Fed. Trade Comm'n* (D.C. Cir. 2008) (U.S.). *See also infra* note 87 and accompanying text.

[34] Lemley & Shapiro 2007b, 1993.

[35] *See Unwired Planet Int'l Ltd. v. Huawei Techs. Co.* (Pat 2017, ¶ 92) (UK) ("The underlying purpose of the FRAND undertaking is to secure a proper reward for innovation whilst avoiding 'hold up', i.e., the ability of the owner of a SEP to hold implementers to ransom by reason of the incorporation of the invention into the standard by declining to grant them a licence at all or only granting one on unfair, unreasonable or discriminatory terms."). The FRAND commitment precludes private profit maximizing by a SEP owner that "could impede the success of the standard, reducing profits for other SEP owners and for implementers and decreasing consumer surplus through higher prices and reduced output. Because many SEP owners have this private incentive to charge royalties that in aggregate lower the welfare of SEP owners and implementers alike, these parties find themselves in a prisoners' dilemma-like strategic situation in which they are likely to be worse off unless SEP owners can credibly commit *ex ante* to restrain their *ex post* opportunism." Ratliff & Rubenfeld 2013, 5.

royalty can be assessed (whether an *ex ante* definition and specification of FRAND can be identified); and how a FRAND commitment deals with the potential risk of royalty stacking.[36] As a result of these open issues FRAND commitments have not been as effective as hoped, and negotiating firms have frequently been unable to agree on FRAND licensing arrangements. Many disputes have thus required resolution *ex post* not only before courts and in alternative dispute resolution, but also before competition agencies.[37] Amongst other things, such courts and agencies have frequently been asked to consider whether SEP owners who seek injunctions to prevent infringement of their patents or who pursue other ways to monetize their patents (e.g., through licensing practices or splitting portfolios) may be violating competition law.[38]

These types of action might be reduced if SDO rules and processes were improved. The Commission Communication on SEPs thus calls upon SDOs to improve their processes and policies in several respects, including by:

a. providing more detailed and accessible information on their databases to facilitate patentees, implementers, and third parties obtaining information on declared patents and their current status, for example, by providing links to information held by patent offices on patent status, ownership, and transfer;[39]
b. providing for the possibility, and incentives, for patentees and technology users to report cases on declared SEPs, particularly on essentiality and patent validity;[40]
c. providing for a balanced and proportionate system of essentiality checks by a qualified third party, at the request of patentees or implementers, limiting, for example, the checks to one patent per family or samples (with patent offices being well placed to carry out such essentiality checks);[41] and
d. introducing systems whereby SEPs may be certified as complying with transparency criteria.[42]

Although the Commission believes that its proposals may facilitate FRAND negotiations between SEP holders and implementers,[43] it remains to be seen whether, and to what extent, they will be followed. Further, even if SDOs were to accept such recommendations, which are not binding, the process improvements

---

[36] Resulting from the fact that numerous complementary SEPs read on a product, or a component of it, and each of the SEP holders charge a royalty that aggregated together, significantly exceeds the rate that would be charged by a single owner of all the patents (or the standard) involved and/or exceeds the level that would make it economically feasible to operate in the downstream market.

[37] Yet, the question that remains is (i) whether the *ex ante* specification of FRAND terms is a desirable policy option, and (ii) in turn, whether this falls within the remit of private ordering institutions *or of* public interest agencies like antitrust authorities and regulators.

[38] *Huawei Techs. Co. Ltd.* v. *ZTE Corp.* (CJEU 2015) (EU).

[39] European Commission, at 3, COM (2017) 712 final (Nov. 29, 2017).

[40] *Id.* at 4.

[41] *Id.* at 5.

[42] *Id.*

[43] *Id.* at 3–5.

proposed are unlikely to resolve, by themselves, the problems that are discussed in this chapter. No matter how transparent, accurate, and robust SDOs' processes and procedures are, competition law issues cannot be completely avoided or resolved *ex ante*, particularly because, in the current context, it is not the role of SDOs to set royalties and the terms and conditions of licenses or to make final and binding determinations on the validity and essentiality of SEPs, which is where most of the problems arise.

A preliminary issue in cases raising antitrust law arguments is, as discussed in Section 6.2, how antitrust law should interact with IP (and contract) law in this area and, in particular, whether there should be any role for antitrust law at all.[44] In many jurisdictions it has been accepted that competition law can play a role in certain circumstances, subject perhaps to application of the type of doctrinal tools described in Section 6.2 above. Thus in the European Union, in the 2015 landmark ruling of the Court of Justice of the European Union (CJEU) in *Huawei*,[45] the Court stressed that (i) a balance must be maintained between free competition and safeguarding IP rights, and their effective judicial protection,[46] and (ii) although the exercise of an exclusive IP right (e.g., seeking an injunction against an alleged infringer) cannot, in itself, constitute a violation of EU competition law, in exceptional circumstances competition law might constrain the conduct of a SEP holder that holds a dominant position.[47]

6.3.2 *Antitrust Limits on a Patent Holder Seeking Restorative Patent Remedies (and Judicial Exploitation of Patents)*

1 Seeking an Injunction Following a Failure of Licensing Negotiations

An explosion of disputes and worldwide litigation in the mobile communication sector has, in recent years, raised a plethora of patent, contract, and competition law issues. These cases followed the change in incentives and the shift in bargaining position between SEP holders and implementers created when, in particular:[48] (1) a number of implementers entered the market, for example, Apple (with the iPhone), Google (with its open-source Android operating system), and Microsoft

---

[44] These issues are, therefore, now frequently arising both before courts, in the context of civil litigation between private parties, and before competition agencies, the recipients of complaints about the conduct of SEP holders.

[45] *Huawei Techs. Co. Ltd. v. ZTE Corp.* (CJEU 2015) (EU).

[46] *Id.* at ¶ 42 ("Court must strike a balance between maintaining free competition . . . and the requirement to safeguard that proprietor's intellectual-property rights and its right to effective judicial protection.").

[47] *See supra* note 3 and 29. For the view that antitrust law should be applied in China, *see* Wang 2017.

[48] Initially, there was relatively little patent litigation in the mobile telephony markets; most of the core players, for example, Samsung, Nokia, Ericsson, Motorola, Alcatel-Lucent, and Qualcomm, were both SEP holders and implementers in the market and cross-licensed each other licenses to a portfolio of their patents, *see* Jones 2014.

(with Windows Mobile), which did not originally have the same number of patents essential to European Telecommunications Standards Institute (ETSI) standards[49] as their competitors (although Apple and Microsoft, for example, held a significant portfolio of design and software patents that are not standard-essential (non-SEPs)); and (2) some of the original players in the market either sold off their patent portfolios to patent assertion entities (PAEs) or their position in the final product market began to decline.

The cases have raised issues in relation both to the infringement of non-SEPs and SEPs, and have included the question of whether a SEP holder should be able to enforce its exclusive rights through the bringing of an injunction claim in court. A particular concern in such cases has been how to balance the risk of holdup against the risk that an implementer who operates on the market without a license, thus infringing the patent, will seek to hold out by refusing to bargain in good faith (identified by some commentators as the "reverse holdup" problem).[50] (Although there is no agreed definition of holdup, the term is used, for present purposes, to describe any anticompetitive consequence of a refusal to license or the extraction of excessive royalties.)[51] For example, there is a concern that SEP holders may be able to secure rewards for innovation beyond their true value to consumers; to preclude open and effective access to the standard, thus allowing competition to be distorted through the exclusion, elimination, or hampering of competition,[52] new entry, and innovation downstream; and/or to undermine confidence in, and the working of, the standard-setting process.

In a number of jurisdictions, including the United States, the United Kingdom, and the Netherlands,[53] courts have, without needing recourse to antitrust law,

---

[49] Although Google has subsequently acquired Motorola and its patent portfolio and Apple, Microsoft, RIM, and Oracle acquired, through their Rockstar consortium, Nortel.

[50] Such behavior arguably threatens open standardization; if holdout is perceived to be widespread patentees might choose consortia or de facto standardization instead. *See, e.g.*, Camesasca et al. 2013; Harkrider 2013; Kobayashi & Wright 2009; Cary et al. 2011; Kobayashi & Wright 2012.

[51] *See, e.g.*, Lemley and Shapiro's characterization of patent holdup as a form of market failure, Lemley & Shapiro 2007b, 2164. Farrell et al. argue that patent holdups might prevent implementers from using patented technology altogether or encourage them to adopt costly countermeasures to avoid holdup, Farrell et al. 2007, 622–23. *See also* Kattan 2013; Kattan & Wood 2013; Ratliff & Rubenfeld 2013; Petrovčič 2013.

[52] As in the case of a refusal to deal or margin squeeze, therefore, a core antitrust concern is that the seeking of an injunction may distort competition in downstream markets. This will create upward pricing pressure and prevent the development of the secondary market to the detriment of consumers.

[53] *See* Chapter 5. *See also, e.g.*, in the United States, *eBay Inc.* v. *MercExchange, L.L.C.* (U.S. 2006) (U.S.) (injunctions for patent infringements are not automatic but based on specified criteria); *Apple, Inc.* v. *Motorola, Inc.* (Fed. Cir. 2014) (U.S.); *but see* the FTC's intervention under FTCA section 5 to prevent a patentee's attempt to obtain injunctive relief in the face of a prior FRAND commitment in *In the Matter of Motorola Mobility LLC and Google Inc.* (FTC July 23, 2013) (Decision and Order) and *In the Matter of Robert Bosch GmbH* (FTC Apr. 23, 2013) (Decision and Order); Section 6.4 below; in the UK, *Nokia OYJ* v. *IPCom GmbH & Co KG* (Ch 2012) (UK) (Roth J declined to grant an injunction sought by IPCom (a PAE) against Nokia in relation to a patent essential to the 3G standard and that would exclude Nokia from selling its products in the United Kingdom (given that Nokia had

refused to grant injunctions to patentees, and, in particular, have been unwilling to exercise their discretion to grant them to FRAND-committed SEP holders where the implementer, against whom the injunction is sought, is "willing" to take a license on FRAND terms.

In other jurisdictions, such as Germany, Japan,[54] and Korea, however, where a stronger legal tradition of providing security to patentees prevails,[55] courts generally require injunctions to be granted to protect patents when infringed.[56] It is in these latter jurisdictions[57] that antitrust law has most often been raised as a possible mechanism for precluding the grant of the injunction on the basis that an injunction might harm competition and that the patentee's investment incentives can be protected, as envisaged, not through exclusion but through FRAND licensing. In 2012, the European Commission launched investigations against both Samsung and Motorola Mobility for possible breaches of Article 102,[58] in particular by seeking

declared itself willing to take, and to be entitled to, a license in relation to valid patents on FRAND terms and IPCom acknowledged that it had made a FRAND declaration, the judge failed to see why an injunction should be granted)); *Vringo Infrastructure, Inc. v. ZTE (UK) Ltd.* (Pat 2013, ¶¶ 44–46) (UK) (the alleged patent infringer has the right to have the patents' validity and infringement determined before it determines whether it will take a license and on what terms. Such a stance cannot be said to be unwillingness); in the Netherlands, *Samsung Elecs. Co. Ltd. v. Apple Inc.* (Rb.-Gravenhage 2012) (Neth.) (the District Court of the Hague rejected an application by Samsung for an injunction to prevent Apple's sales of iPhones and iPads in the Netherlands and damages). Other national courts in the European Union have also resolved these issues by applying principles of national law without reference to antitrust law, *see* Directive 2004/48/EC (stating that infringement of a European patent is to be dealt with by national law, but must ensure certain measures be made available). *See also* the Supreme People's Court of the People's Republic of China 2016 (revision to judicial interpretation on intellectual property disputes); Wang 2017.

54   *But see Samsung Elecs. Co. v. Apple Japan LLC* (IP High Ct. 2014) (Japan).

55   A significant amount of the EU litigation has occurred in Germany. Not only is Germany the biggest market in the European Union for mobile telephony products, but the patent litigation environment there has made it an especially attractive forum for patentees in general, and SEP holders in particular. Indeed, the procedure in Germany enables patent infringement cases to be resolved quickly, cheaply, and in a relatively patent-holder friendly way. *See* Jones 2014; Chapter 5.

56   The specialist patent chambers of the Higher District Courts have taken the view that German law, rather than permitting discretion to be exercised, requires the grant of an injunction to a patentee whose patent is found to have been infringed unless: (a) an extremely high degree of likelihood of invalidity before the Federal Patent Court can be established; or (b) an infringer can establish that by refusing to conclude a license the claimant has abused its dominant position (since conduct prohibited by antitrust law must not be ordered by state courts). In BGH v. 6.5.2009 – KZR 39/06 – *Orange-Book-Standard* (Ger.), the German Federal Court of Justice (Bundesgerichtshof) had accepted that such an abuse would occur only in very limited circumstances, where the party seeking a license makes, and remains bound by, an unconditional offer to conclude a license contract with the patent holder on terms which, if rejected by the patent holder, would amount to a violation of antitrust law (the implementer has to be willing to pay (into court deposit) as if it were a licensee and to render accounts).

57   *But see* cases applying competition law in the United States and the European Union, *supra* note 53. *See also, e.g., Samsung Electronics Co. Ltd. v. Apple Korea Ltd.* (Dist. Ct. 2012) (Kor.).

58   Commission Decision of 29 April 2014, Case AT.39939 – Samsung – Enforcement of UMTS Standard Essential Patents (Samsung agreed not to seek any injunctions in Europe on the basis of SEPs for mobile devices for a period of five years against any potential licensee of these SEPs who agrees to accept a specific licensing framework); Commission Decision of 29 April 2014, Case AT.39958 – Motorola – Enforcement of GPRS Standard Essential Patents (without fines).

injunctions to enforce the SEPs in Germany. It articulated concerns that in the exceptional circumstances of the case (involving a standard-setting process and Samsung's and Motorola's commitments to license their SEPs on FRAND terms and conditions), the seeking of preliminary and permanent injunctions against Apple might be incompatible with Article 102. These actions, which eventually culminated in, respectively a commitments and infringement decision,[59] fuelled concern that, in the context of SEPs at least, German law might be making injunctions available in circumstances in which the seeking, and subsequent enforcing, of the injunction violated Article 102.[60] It was for this reason that the Landgericht Düsseldorf stayed patent litigation between Huawei and ZTE and referred a number of questions to the CJEU relating to the application of Article 102 to the conduct of SEP holders. Essentially, the questions referred asked whether German law was sufficient to prevent abusive conduct by SEP holders or whether Article 102 applies more stringently to constrain the ordinary rights of patentees, at least where the IP at issue is a FRAND-committed SEP.

In its *Huawei* judgment, the CJEU confirmed that although antitrust does not generally interfere with the exercise of IP rights, it might constrain the behavior of an IP rightsholder that has a dominant position in exceptional circumstances. In addition, the Court clarified that such circumstances might exist in a case such as the one before it, involving *de jure* standardization and a dominant SEP holder[61] that had made a FRAND commitment. The Court held that such a patentee may infringe Article 102 if it seeks an injunction, or an order for recall of products, in patent litigation against the user of standardized technology in circumstances where it had not taken certain steps to comply with its FRAND commitment and to ensure a fair balance between the interests involved.[62] Such compliance requires as

---

[59] *Id.*

[60] And concern that the German courts might consequently be in breach of their duty of sincere cooperation to the European Union, their duty to guarantee real and effective judicial protection for EU rights, and their obligation not to apply provisions of national law that contravene EU law.

[61] In most jurisdictions the concept of dominance or monopoly power is equated with (a significant degree of) market power. There seems little doubt that the standard-setting process *can* confer market power and a dominant position on SEP holders. Owners of SEPs are likely to acquire market power after the standard is adopted if it subsequently becomes impossible for implementers to invent or design around the patent (the standard constitutes a barrier to entry to the market as it is commercially indispensable to comply with it). In the mobile telephony sector, manufacturers of 3G or 4G mobile devices are generally locked in and unable to design around standards as they must be able to certify that their product is standard compliant in order to operate on UMTS and LTE networks. It is also important to consider whether the exercise of market power is constrained by buyer power, for example where the implementer owns blocking patents, *see* O'Donoghue & Padilla 2013, 703. In *Unwired Planet Int'l Ltd. v. Huawei Techs. Co.* (Pat 2017) (UK), Birss J considered that the ability of a potential licensee to hold out was relevant to the question of whether the SEP holder possesses a dominant position.

[62] Where the patent at issue is essential to a standard (and indispensable to competitors manufacturing products complying with the standard) and where SEP status had been granted only because of owner's irrevocable FRAND commitment a SEP holder could, by bringing action for injunction/ recall, prevent competitors' products from appearing/remaining on the market and reserve to itself manufacture of products. Further the FRAND commitment created legitimate expectations that

a starting point that the SEP holder: (i) give the alleged infringer notice of its infringement (even if the latter was already using the teaching of the SEP); and, if the implementer expresses a willingness to conclude a FRAND license, (ii) present a specific, written FRAND offer specifying the royalty and the way it is to be calculated. If these steps are taken, the Court held that the implementer must diligently respond to that offer, in accordance with recognized commercial practices in the field and in good faith,[63] and, if it does not accept the offer, respond promptly and in writing with a specific counteroffer that corresponds to FRAND terms.[64] Where no FRAND agreement is reached following a counteroffer,[65] the parties may, by common agreement, request that the amount of the royalty be determined by an independent third party, by decision without delay.[66]

The Commission Communication on SEPs sheds light, taking account of subsequent case law in national courts, on the Commission's understanding of the *Huawei* criteria. In particular, it states:[67]

a. A prospective licensee is entitled to receive sufficiently detailed information to determine the relevance of the SEP portfolio and the compliance of the offer with FRAND requirements. Determination of whether this requirement has been met is fact sensitive and will vary from case to case. However, the Commission believes that clear explanations are necessary on such matters as "the essentiality for a standard, the allegedly infringing products of the SEP user, the proposed royalty calculation and the non-discrimination element of FRAND."

b. The prospective licensee's counteroffer "should be concrete and specific" and "cannot be limited to contesting the SEP holder's offer" and making "a general reference to third-party determination of the royalty." The counteroffer should also provide information "on the exact use of the standard in the specific product." The willingness of the parties to submit to a binding third-party FRAND determination is considered to be evidence of FRAND-compliant behavior.

c. No general benchmark can be established to determine the timeliness of the counteroffer by the prospective licensee. Relevant factors include "the number of

---

a FRAND license will be granted so refusal to do so may in principle constitute an abuse, *Huawei Techs. Co. Ltd. v. ZTE Corp.* (CJEU 2015, ¶¶ 15–53) (EU).

[63] The required conduct must be established on the basis of objective factors and implies, in particular, that there are no delaying tactics.

[64] *Huawei Techs. Co. Ltd. v. ZTE Corp.* (CJEU 2015, ¶ 6) (EU).

[65] Where the implementer is using the teachings of the SEP before a licensing agreement has been concluded, it must, from the point at which its counteroffer is rejected, provide appropriate security, for instance by providing a bank guarantee or by placing the amount necessary on deposit. The calculation of the security must include, inter alia, the number of the past acts of use of the SEP, and the alleged infringer must be able to render an account in respect of those acts of use, *Id.* at ¶ 67.

[66] *Id.* at ¶ 68.

[67] European Commission, at 9–10, COM (2017) 712 final (Nov. 29, 2017).

asserted SEPs and the details contained in the infringement claim." The
Commission considers that there may well be a "trade-off between the time
considered as reasonable for responding to the offer and the detail and quality of
the information provided in the SEP holder's initial offer." Furthermore, the
more (reliable and up-to-date) information available to the prospective licensee
through the SDO's database, the shorter the time required to make
a counteroffer.

d. The security to be provided by the implementer as protection for the SEP holder
   when a claim for an injunction is denied "should be fixed at a level that
   discourages patent hold-out strategies." The Commission considers that "similar
   considerations could apply when assessing the magnitude of damages."

The judgment in *Huawei*, complemented by national case law and the
Commission Communication on SEPs, thus seeks to craft, for the European
Union, some degree of operational guidance for both SEP owners and implementers to follow.[68] Not only do these allow SEP owners to ensure that their conduct is
compatible with Article 102 (compliance with the stipulated procedure provides an
antitrust safe harbor for them), but it clearly delineates steps that implementers must
take in the FRAND negotiation process (to prevent holdout).

Although the judgment is very fact specific, the Court stressed the salient features
of the case that contributed to its finding that, in exceptional circumstances, seeking
an injunction or an order for recall by a patentee may constitute an abuse of
a dominant position contrary to Article 102:

- The patents at issue only had SEP status because of the owner's irrevocable
  FRAND commitment.
- The SEPs were essential to the standard and, consequently, indispensable to
  competitors manufacturing products complying with the standard. This meant
  that a SEP holder could, by bringing an action for injunction or recall, prevent
  competitors' products from appearing or remaining on the market and reserve
  to itself the manufacture of products.
- The FRAND commitment created legitimate expectations that a FRAND
  license would be granted (so a refusal to do so may in principle constitute an
  abuse).[69]

The Court thus referred to some likely anticompetitive effects on products reading on the standard: Products manufactured by competitors could be prevented
from being launched or remaining on the market so that a vertically integrated SEP
holder could "reserve to itself the manufacture of the product in question."[70] This

---

[68]   The Court also accepts that FRAND imposes obligations on implementers. For the view that the
       ruling's theoretical foundation in competition law is not solid, and that legislative intervention might
       be preferable to harmonization through competition law in this way, *see* Larouche & Zingales 2017.
[69]   *Huawei Techs. Co. Ltd. v. ZTE Corp.* (CJEU 2015, ¶¶ 49–53) (EU).
[70]   *Id.* at ¶ 52.

identified concern thus relates to the parameters of product competition in the market for the products reading on the standard: price, innovation, and choice. The Court was not, however, explicit about the impact of the conduct under review on the standard-setting process itself.[71] Yet, the emphasis placed on the legitimate expectation that a FRAND commitment creates as one of the grounds or conditions for a potential finding of infringement[72] might suggest that the Court was also concerned, implicitly, about likely anticompetitive effects on the integrity of the standard-setting process and, ultimately, on the success of the standard. From a policy perspective, it would indeed appear that the undermining of the standard-setting process (and, ultimately, of the success of the standard) as a result of non-FRAND-compliant behavior by any SEP holder is capable of having the same type of a negative impact on price, innovation, and choice on the market for the products reading on the standard as non-FRAND-compliant behavior by a vertically integrated SEP holder who reserves to itself the manufacture of the product in question.

As regards the need to ensure an adequate protection of the SEP, the Court seemed to consider that the patentee's investment incentives would be protected by its ability to recover FRAND licensing terms and that by giving the FRAND commitment it had demonstrated its intention to monetize its patents in this way.[73] The benefits to competition safeguarded in the manufactured product market would not therefore be offset by damage to investment in the upstream market.

In some respects, however, the Court left certain matters, or the exact scope of its judgment, unclear. For example, national courts in the EU Member States have subsequently had to wrestle with the question of exactly how the procedure described within it is actually to be implemented and, consequently, when a SEP holder can seek an injunction without infringing Article 102 and when an implementer can resist an injunction application on competition law grounds.[74] Chapter 5 discusses cases that deal with the question of what each party needs to do to establish it has been engaged in good-faith licensing negotiations.[75]

---

[71] Contrast Commission Decision of 29 April 2014, Case AT.39958 – Motorola – Enforcement of GPRS Standard Essential Patents, where the European Commission placed greater emphasis on the anticompetitive effects through: exclusion of innovative products from the markets (including a temporary ban on the online sale of Apple's GPRS compatible products in Germany); anticompetitive, disadvantageous licensing terms imposed in settlement agreements; and that confidence in the standard setting process would be undermined – which was designed to promote the functioning of standard setting by ensuring accessibility of technology and by preventing holdup.

[72] *Huawei Techs. Co. Ltd. v. ZTE Corp.* (CJEU 2015, ¶¶ 51–53) (EU).

[73] The FRAND commitment "implicitly acknowledges that a [FRAND] royalty is adequate compensation for a license to use that patent." *Apple, Inc. v. Motorola, Inc.* (N.D. Ill. 2012, p.914) (U.S.).

[74] *See* Chapter 5; Colangelo & Torti 2017. It also left open the questions of whether or how the ruling would apply in the context of de facto (rather than *de jure*) standardization, where a FRAND commitment had not been given because the patentee did not participate in the standard-setting process or if the patentee sought damages rather than an injunction (*but see* Section 6.3.2 below).

[75] In relation to the content of infringement notice: when the SEP holder is obliged to submit a FRAND licensing offer and how it is determined whether this offer is FRAND (e.g., in terms of royalty terms and whether a worldwide portfolio license is FRAND); the time limits within which alleged infringer

In addition, by confining the scope of its judgment to the facts of the case, namely a situation where the SEP holder that had given the FRAND commitment manufactured and sold products on the basis of the licensed technology, and placing emphasis both on competition between the patentee and implementer in the manufactured product market and the giving of the FRAND commitment, the Court did not clarify whether the same obligations would bind a subsequent nonpracticing purchaser of the SEPs that does not compete in the market for products based on the licensed technology and that did not give the original FRAND commitment. Although in such cases the nature of the conduct is exploitative rather than exclusionary,[76] it is possible that the Court would reach the same conclusion on the question of whether the conduct is abusive. If a FRAND commitment is given by, or binds, the subsequent purchaser, that purchaser also agrees not to exploit the SEP's market power and to license only on FRAND terms. Further, the impact of the conduct on competition in the products market and on standardization is potentially the same – irrespective of whether the SEP holder competes in the product market or whether it was the PAE itself or its predecessor that created legitimate expectations that the technology would be licensed on FRAND terms.

Chapter 5 explains that competition authorities in other jurisdictions (including Korea) have also considered whether injunction actions by SEP holders might result in violations of both FRAND commitments and antitrust laws. For example, the Federal Trade Commission (FTC) in the United States has been concerned that seeking injunctive relief can be coercive and oppressive and an "unfair method of competition" contrary to Section 5 of the Federal Trade Commission Act of 1914.[77]

2 Monetary Damages and Future Licensing Terms

Even if a SEP holder is not permitted to seek an injunction against a willing licensee, it is still entitled to damages for past infringement of the patent and to royalties for future licensing.

Indeed, in the European Union the General Court in *ITT Promedia NV v. Commission* stressed the importance of the principle of access to court both as

---

   must express its willingness to conclude license; and how the implementer should respond to the offer.

[76] Even if they have the power to do so (*see supra* note 23 and accompanying text), competition agencies are reluctant to bring exploitative cases (given the regulatory nature of such proceedings, the difficulties involved in identifying such conduct, and because they come close to prohibiting a dominant position) unless the case has another dimension, such as an exclusionary effect, an internal market aspect (in the European Union) or where the interests of the consumers cannot otherwise be ensured, *see* Section 6.3.3.

[77] *See, e.g., In the Matter of Robert Bosch GmbH* (FTC Apr. 23, 2013) (Decision and Order); *In the Matter of Motorola Mobility LLC and Google Inc.* (FTC July 23, 2013) (Decision and Order); and Section 6.4 below. *See also* the discussion of the cases that have arisen in Japan and Korea in Chapter 5.

a fundamental right and a general principle ensuring the rule of law.[78] In *Huawei*, the CJEU also recognized the high level of protection conferred by EU law on patentees who could not in principle be deprived of their right to have recourse to legal proceedings to ensure effective enforcement of their exclusive rights. Its acceptance in that case that the seeking of an injunction by a FRAND-committed SEP holder might, exceptionally, constitute an abuse of a dominant position, did not deny the patentee access to court or the right to bring legal proceedings. On the contrary, it made clear that a SEP holder was not prohibited "from bringing an action for infringement against the alleged infringer of its SEP and seeking the rendering of accounts in relation to past acts of use of that SEP or an award of damages in respect of those acts of use";[79] if an injunction is not available the SEP holder may thus seek *other* remedies to safeguard its patent rights in the legal proceedings, including damages for past infringement and the determination of future licensing terms.

Chapter 5 discusses the extent to which principles governing damages awarded in cases where a SEP holder has given a FRAND commitment should differ from those generally governing damages awards in patent infringement cases and how damages should relate to any determination of future FRAND licensing terms.[80] The sections below consider whether competition law might, however, impose additional obligations that may affect SEP licensing arrangements above and beyond those imposed by the FRAND commitment, and hence the level of monetary damages to which a FRAND-committed SEP holder is entitled when an unlicensed implementer infringes the SEP. In particular, it considers whether, and if so when, competition law may control unfair royalty levels, the tying or bundling of SEPS, price discrimination, and the transfer of SEPs.

6.3.3 *Antitrust Limits on the Commercial Exploitation of Patents*

1 Pricing of Patent Licenses: Excessive or Unfair Pricing

Competition law may in certain circumstances constrain the ability of a SEP holder to set the royalty rate for its SEPs or to negotiate the licensing conditions that it thinks fit. This is particularly true in jurisdictions, such as the European Union, the People's Republic of China, and India, that prohibit not only exclusionary abuses

---

[78] Consequently, it is clear that Article 102 can deny the right to bring legal proceedings exceptionally only where (i) the legal action cannot reasonably be considered as an attempt to establish the rights of the undertaking concerned and can therefore only serve to harass the opposite party; and (ii) the action is conceived in the framework of a plan whose goal is to eliminate competition.

[79] *Huawei Techs. Co. Ltd.* v. *ZTE Corp.* (CJEU 2015, ¶ 76) (EU). *See also* Chapter 5.

[80] *See* Chapter 5 and the judgment of Birss J in *Unwired Planet Int'l Ltd.* v. *Huawei Techs. Co.* (Pat 2017, ¶ 92) (UK) (holding that as damages for patent infringement are compensatory, damages to be paid in a FRAND case are the sums that the SEP holder would have earned in licensing – that is a FRAND license that would have been agreed between it and a willing licensee).

by dominant firms but also exploitative conduct, consisting in the application of excessive or unfair prices or other unfair contractual conditions regardless of any exclusionary effect. The question of whether, and if so when, it should impact on exploitative conduct is likely to become more topical as 5G technology develops and standards relating to the Internet of Things are adopted.[81]

In the European Union, for example, Article 102 prohibits exploitative practices, including unfair prices, unfair trading conditions, and the provision of substandard products or services (Article 102(a);[82] and Article 102(b) prohibits the limitation of production, markets, or technical development to the prejudice of consumers.[83] It may therefore constitute an abuse for a dominant SEP holder to charge a price that has "no reasonable relation to the economic value of the product supplied"[84] or to impose "directly or indirectly … unfair trading conditions,"[85] whether or not it has made a FRAND commitment. In *Rambus*,[86] the Commission accepted commitments from Rambus, a patentee that had *not* made a FRAND commitment, but which it nonetheless accused of charging excessive royalties for the use of patented technology relating to dynamic random access memory (DRAM).[87] The Commission took the view that these royalties could not have been claimed if Rambus had not intentionally deceived the SSO, Joint Electron Device Engineering Council (JEDEC), and its members, by not disclosing the existence of patents and patent applications relating to technology relevant to the adopted standard[88] (because had it disclosed the existence of the patents and patent applications, another standard would probably have been adopted and Rambus's technologies would not have been essential to the standard).[89] Although the Commission

---

[81] *See, e.g.*, Margrethe Vestager, Speech: Protecting Consumers from Exploitation (Nov. 21, 2016); European Commission, at 1, 6, COM (2017) 712 final (Nov. 29, 2017), where the Commission emphasizes that divergent views and litigation over FRAND licensing risk delaying the roll-out of the Internet of Things in the European Union.

[82] *See, e.g., United Brands Co. and United Brands Continental B.V.* v. *Commission of the European Communities* (CJEU 1978, ¶ 248) (EU); *François Lucazeau* v. *SACEM* (CJEU 1989) (EU); *AKKA/LAA* v. *Konkurences padome* (CJEU 2017) (EU); and the European Commission's current investigation into *Aspen Pharma*, European Commission Press Release IP/17/1323.

[83] On excessive pricing, *see, e.g.*, Evans & Padilla 2005; Ezrachi & Gilo 2009; De Coninck & Koustoumpardi 2017. Most competition law systems also regulate "restrictive" licensing agreements, e.g., in the European Union under TFEU art. 101.

[84] *United Brands Co. and United Brands Continental B.V.* v. *Commission of the European Communities* (CJEU 1978, ¶ 250) (EU).

[85] *Belgische Radio en Televisie* v. *SV SABAM* (CJEU 1974, ¶ 6) (EU).

[86] Commitments decisions do not contain a finding of infringement and are generally considerably shorter than infringement decisions.

[87] Commission Decision of 9 December 2009, COMP/38.636—RAMBUS. The Commission considered Rambus to be dominant on the worldwide market for DRAM interface technology, comprising the technology needed for the interoperability between a DRAM chip and the other components of a personal computer, *see id.* at ¶¶ 16, 17, 26. Contrast the opinion in *Rambus Inc.* v. *Fed. Trade Comm'n* (D.C. Cir. 2008) (U.S.).

[88] Commission Decision of 9 December 2009, COMP/38.636—RAMBUS, at ¶ 27.

[89] *Id.* at ¶¶ 43–46.

did not state, in the commitments decision, its legal basis for believing that the conduct in question was abusive, it seems clear that a core concern was that the conduct was exploitative. Rambus's unilateral conduct in allegedly deceiving the SSO and its members, which could have excluded competing technologies from the standard, could not have infringed Article 102 because Rambus was not, at that point, alleged to be dominant (and EU law does not, unlike U.S. law, prevent attempts to monopolize or dominate a market). Rambus only became dominant following the alleged exclusion and the adoption of the standard. To bring the proceedings to an end, Rambus committed to offer licenses to DRAM manufacturers and manufacturers of memory controller products at royalties not exceeding a stipulated cap for a period of five years. Rambus also committed not to seek further royalties for the licensed patents from the licensee's customers.[90]

In *Unwired Planet*,[91] the English High Court also had to consider whether a breach of a FRAND commitment by an NPE could constitute an exploitative abuse contrary to Article 102. In considering this issue, Birss J distinguished three scenarios: a price advanced in negotiation, a price demanded by a vendor backed by a refusal to supply at any other price, and a price agreed upon and paid.[92] In relation to a price advanced in negotiations, the judge considered that it was normal that the prospective licensor would start from a position that is higher than FRAND. Simply offering a non-FRAND royalty could not therefore constitute an abuse; it only would be if the offered rate was so high that it would disrupt or prejudice the negotiations.[93] This did not mean, of course, that the actual imposition of such rates in the agreed license or a refusal to license other than at those rates could not be an abuse of dominance, especially if obtained under the threat of an injunction. Birss J considered, however, that a royalty rate would not be excessive unless it substantially exceeded the FRAND rate; in other words, a FRAND royalty could not be an abusive one and a royalty in excess of FRAND would not necessarily be abusive.[94]

The Commission Communication on SEPs sets out some high-level principles for the valuation of SEPs and the assessment of FRAND licensing terms:[95]

a. Licensing terms need to bear a clear relationship to the economic value of the patented technology.[96] Such a value should not include a premium resulting from the decision to include the technology in the standard.
b. Determining a FRAND value should require "taking into account the present value added of the patented technology." The present value added of the

---

90 *Id.* at final commitments.
91 *Unwired Planet Int'l Ltd. v. Huawei Techs. Co.* (Pat 2017) (UK).
92 *Id.* at ¶ 762.
93 Birss J found that offers three, five, or even ten times the FRAND rates were not such as to prejudice the negotiations and were, therefore, not an abuse of dominance, *id.* at ¶¶ 762–84.
94 *Id.* at ¶¶ 153, 757.
95 European Commission, at 6–7, COM (2017) 712 final (Nov. 29, 2017).
96 *See also supra* note 83 and accompanying text.

technology should be irrespective of the market success of the product that is unrelated to the patented technology.

c. FRAND valuation should ensure that SEP holders continue to have incentives to contribute their best available technologies to standards.

d. FRAND valuation should also depend on a reasonable aggregate royalty rate for the standard, to avoid royalty stacking.

What might be considered to be an unfairly high price has also been considered under the Chinese Antimonopoly Law, including by the National Development and Reform Commission (NDRC) of the People's Republic of China in *Qualcomm*.[97] In this case it held that Qualcomm had abused its dominant position in the markets for licensing SEPs covering CDMA, WCDMA, and LTE wireless communication, as well as in the market of baseband chips. In particular, the NDRC had concerns about the following conduct in relation to Chinese licensees: (1) refusing to disclose patent lists; (2) charging licensing fees for expired patents included in patent portfolio; (3) requiring a free cross-license of the Chinese licensees' own relevant patents (so refusing to deduct the value of such cross-licensed patents from its licensing fees); and (4) charging royalties on the basis of the net wholesale price of the device and imposing a relatively high royalty rate on licensees who had been forced to accept Qualcomm's packaged licensing of non-SEPs. The NDRC found that the combination of these different strands of conduct resulted in excessively high, and abusive, royalties and abusive terms. If a potential licensee did not agree to them, Qualcomm would simply refuse to supply baseband chips to it. The NDRC levied a fine of RMB 6 billion[98] and imposed a number of behavioral remedies on Qualcomm. In particular, following the proceedings, Qualcomm agreed to charge royalties for 3G and 4G Chinese SEPs for branded smartphones sold for use in China of 5 percent for 3G devices and 3.5 percent for 4G phones on a royalty base of 65 percent of the net selling price of the smartphone; to provide patent lists when entering into a license with Chinese licensees and not to charge licensing fees for expired patents; not to request a free cross-license from Chinese licensees; not to request that Chinese licensees enter into a patent-license agreement including unreasonable conditions when selling baseband chips; and not to condition the supply of baseband chips to Chinese licensees on the obligation not to challenge such patent-license agreement.[99]

---

[97] NDRC Press Release (Feb. 10, 2015); Wang 2017. *See also Qualcomm Inc. v. Korea Fair Trade Commission* (KFTC 2009), in which the KFTC found that Qualcomm had infringed the Monopoly Regulation and Fair Trade Act by charging discriminatorily higher royalty rates for its standard-essential patents to non-Qualcomm chip users. In 2016, the KFTC further fined Qualcomm 1.03 trillion won for coercing licensing terms on handset makers and refusing to license competing chipset manufacturers to strengthen its monopoly power in the patent license market, *see* Yi & Kim 2017.

[98] By far the highest administrative penalty levied by Chinese authorities, *see* Wang 2017, 73.

[99] NDRC Press Release (Feb. 10, 2015). *See also* Emch & Zhang 2016.

Similarly, in *Huawei Technologies Co Ltd* v. *InterDigital Group*, the Shenzhen Intermediate People's Court found that InterDigital had abused its dominant position in certain markets concerning 3G wireless communications technology both in the People's Republic of China and in the United States by engaging in excessive and discriminatory abuses – by requiring Huawei to pay much higher royalties than those charged by InterDigital to Apple and Samsung and by forcing Huawei to give InterDigital a license to all Huawei's patents. It also held that it had abused its dominant position by tying SEPS to non-SEPS and imposing unreasonable licensing conditions on Huawei. The fact that InterDigital had made a FRAND commitment appeared central to the ruling of the Court that InterDigital had to adhere to principles of fairness, reasonableness, and nondiscrimination when negotiating, entering into, and performing a license agreement relating to its SEPs.[100]

In proceedings against Ericsson, the Competition Commission of India set out its preliminary view that Ericsson's practice of charging a royalty based on the value of the end product produced by the implementer is excessive, discriminatory, and contrary to FRAND terms. Following protracted litigation over the jurisdiction of the CCI in this case, the proceedings have still not been finalized.[101]

2 Tying, Bundling, and Price Discrimination

A number of other questions have also arisen in relation to contract, patent, and antitrust law in the sphere of SEPs and complex products. These include whether the following practices of a patentee might infringe a FRAND commitment or competition law (and whether the FRAND commitment is coextensive with, or distinct from, the competition law obligation): a decision by a SEP holder to require a licensee to take a global license, where the licensee is interested only in a license of more limited scope, and/or to take a license of both SEPs and non-SEPs, where the licensee is interested only in a license of SEPs; a decision to calculate licensing rates not by reference to the smallest saleable unit but to a percentage of net sales of the final product; a decision by a SEP holder to enforce its patents against entities at different levels of the vertical/production chain (e.g., against chipmakers, mobile phone manufacturers[102] and/or mobile phone network operators) and/or to charge

---

[100] The holding, which was affirmed by the Guangdong High People's Court, is summarized and analyzed in Yuan & Kossof 2015.

[101] *See* Sidak 2017.

[102] Patented Wi-Fi technology is typically implemented at chip level. The chip is then incorporated into the smartphone. A SEP holder may prefer to seek royalties from a mobile phone manufacturer than a chip maker. There may be many reasons for this. Firstly, if the license is granted to end-product manufacturers, the royalty can be based on the revenues from the sale of the end product. Although the royalty base should, in theory, make no difference to the calculation of the amount of a FRAND royalty, in practice the larger the royalty base the larger the royalty may eventually be. Secondly, the profits that end-product manufacturers may lose if the SEP holder obtains an injunction against them are higher than the profits that

different royalty rates to licensees at different levels of the chain;[103] or a decision by a SEP holder to license only mobile phone manufacturers but not chipmakers. Such practices could, in principle, be appraised as forms of excessive pricing tying,[104] bundling,[105] or price discrimination, which can infringe competition rules in some circumstances. Indeed, many jurisdictions have specific rules that target both tying/bundling[106] and price discrimination. In some, price discrimination laws may go beyond the aim of preventing exploitation of market power or the foreclosure of competitors and may be aimed at preventing market distortion, whether at the upstream or downstream level, for example by putting one buyer at a disadvantage vis-à-vis another.[107]

---

    a component manufacturer may lose. This suggests that SEP holders may obtain higher royalties from end-product manufacturers than they would from component manufacturers.

[103] *See* Nazzini 2017.

[104] Tying occurs when two products, A and B, are marketed so that customers buying A, the tying product, must also buy B, the tied product. B, however, can also be purchased as a stand-alone product. Tying can be technical or contractual. As the Commission Guidance on Article 102 explains, "technical tying occurs when the tying product is designed in such a way that it only works properly with the tied product (and not with the alternatives offered by competitors)" whereas "contractual tying occurs when the customer who purchases the tying product undertakes also to purchase the tied product (and not the alternatives offered by competitors)," *see* European Commission, at ¶ 48, 2009 O.J. (C45/02) 7 (Commission Guidance on Art. 102).

[105] Pure bundling occurs when two products are only sold jointly in fixed proportions. *Id. See, e.g.,* *Napier Brown – British Sugar* where the European Commission objected to British Sugar's practice to offer only delivered prices and not ex-factory prices, thereby forcing customers to use British Sugar's delivery services. Commission Decision of 18 July 1988, IV/30.178 Napier Brown – British Sugar. Because pure bundling is a form of reciprocal tying in that neither product is available alone, so that each is tied to the other, the assessment of pure bundling is not materially different to the assessment of tying. Mixed bundling occurs when "the products are also made available separately, but the sum of the prices when sold separately is higher than the bundled price." European Commission, at ¶ 48, 2009 O.J. (C45/02) 7. In *Coca-Cola*, the Commission took the view that the granting of rebates to customers purchasing a wide range of products in the on-premise and the take-home channels had the effect of making it more difficult for competitors to obtain sales space. The practice consisted of bundling together a number of stock keeping units (SKU), each corresponding to different products such as Coca-Cola and Fanta Orange, and making payments of up to 2 percent of total turnover to customers buying the whole bundle. Because the bestselling products generated significant turnover, the incentive for the customers to buy the whole bundle (10 to 20 SKUs on the on-premise channel and 20 to 60 SKUs on the take-home channel) was strong. Commission Decision of 22 June 2005, COMP/A.39.116/B2 – Coca-Cola.

[106] *See, e.g.,* in the European Union, TFEU arts. 101 and 102, and in Clayton Act § 3, 15 U.S.C. § 14 (U.S.) and Sherman Act, 15 U.S.C. § 1, § 2 (U.S.).

[107] *See, e.g.,* in the European Union, TFEU art. 102(c), which provides that it may be an abuse to apply dissimilar conditions to equivalent transactions with other trading parties, thereby placing them at a competitive disadvantage (three elements are necessary for a prima facie case of abuse to be established: (a) equivalent transactions; (b) dissimilar conditions; and (c) competitive disadvantage. Once these three elements have been established, it is for the dominant undertaking to adduce sufficient evidence tending to show that its conduct is objectively justified. This type of abuse can be defined as market-distorting discrimination given that its immediate anticompetitive effect is the distortion of downstream or upstream competition), *see* the Opinion of Advocate General Wahl and Court of Justice's judgement in *MEO* v. *Autoridade da Concorrência* (CJEU 2017 and 2018) (EU);

A number of these issues have arisen in a protracted battle between Apple and Qualcomm being played out in courts and competition agencies across the globe (in particular, before the English High Court,[108] as well as in the United States, Germany,[109] Japan, Korea, Taiwan, and China).

A) QUALCOMM. It has already been seen that the complaints against Qualcomm have alleged that it has engaged in a number of interrelated, anticompetitive exploitative and exclusionary licensing practices. Some complaints have alleged that Qualcomm has withheld baseband processors unless a customer accepts a license of its SEPs on Qualcomm's preferred terms ("no license-no chips" – resulting in non-FRAND licensing terms being extracted), a refusal to license SEPs to competing baseband processor manufacturers, and the bundling of SEPs and non-SEPs. In China, the NDRC in *Qualcomm*[110] supported the principle that a SEP holder is not permitted to bundle SEPs and non-SEPs in the same license.

B) UNWIRED PLANET. In *Unwired Planet*, Birss J also had to deal with claims of unlawful tying and discrimination. In so doing he held that an offer to grant a worldwide portfolio license, a common industry practice with potential efficiency benefits, instead of a license limited to the United Kingdom, was FRAND and did not automatically infringe Article 102; a worldwide license was not inherently likely to distort competition.[111] It might infringe Article 102, however, if three conditions were fulfilled:[112]

1. The components of the bundle were separate products.
2. The customer was coerced to obtain the tied product together with the tying product.

and in the United States the Robinson-Patman Act, 15 U.S.C. § 13 (U.S.) prohibits suppliers from charging different prices to different buyers where the effect may be to prevent or distort competition, for example with the supplier or a buyer. Although the Robinson-Patman Act is not enforced by federal agencies, it can still be relied upon by disfavored buyers in private litigation.

[108] *Unwired Planet Int'l Ltd.* v. *Huawei Techs. Co.* (Pat 2017) (UK).

[109] For a survey on these cases, *see* Chapter 5; Picht 2018.

[110] NDRC Press Release (Feb. 10, 2015). These cases appear to be ones of tying or pure bundling whereby the licensor refuses to license its SEPs unless the licensee also takes a license of the licensor's non-SEPs. More complex is the case in which the licensor offers two licenses: a SEP-only license and a global portfolio license bundling SEPs and non-SEPs. Presumably, provided that the SEP-only license is FRAND, there should be no objection to a licensor offering an alternative, bundled license, unless to do so forecloses competition for non-SEP technologies. This would require, at the very least, proof that competitors offering non-SEP technologies cannot overcome the advantage that the SEP holder obtains by virtue of being dominant with respect to its SEPs.

[111] If a licensor has a worldwide portfolio of SEPs, asking for a worldwide license is, therefore, unlikely to be abusive. *Unwired Planet Int'l Ltd.* v. *Huawei Techs. Co.* (Pat 2017, ¶ 535) (UK). Of course, a worldwide portfolio of SEPs does not mean that a licensor must have patents in every country. Unwired Planet had patents in forty-two countries and had limited coverage in Eastern Europe, South America, and Africa. *See id.* at ¶ 538. This did not invalidate the finding that a worldwide license was not abusive absent evidence of foreclosure

[112] *Id.* at ¶ 526, following *Microsoft Corp.* v. *Comm'n of the European Communities* (CJEU 2007, ¶¶ 842, 859, 862) (EU).

3. The tying must have an anticompetitive foreclosure effect; excluding equally efficient competitors and resulting in the acquisition, maintenance, or strengthening of market power on an affected market (the tying market, the tied market, or a related emerging market).

In relation to the bundling of SEPs and non-SEPs, however, Birss J was concerned that such conduct might foreclose competition for non-SEP technologies.[113] In addition, he held that the nondiscrimination limb of the ETSI FRAND undertaking meant that "a benchmark FRAND rate should be derived which is applicable to all licensees seeking the same kind of licence."[114] In so doing he indicated that the FRAND obligation may differ from the competition law one. In particular, the FRAND requirement may if anything be broader, applying even if the SEP holder is not dominant[115] and even if the discrimination does not cause a distortion of competition between licensees.

c) MULTILEVEL LICENSING AND LEVEL DISCRIMINATION. The teaching of a SEP may be utilized by the manufacturer of a product (e.g., a chip) that is incorporated into another product (e.g. a mobile phone), which is then sold by a provider of a service (e.g., a mobile network provider) to a final consumer.[116] The doctrine of patent exhaustion prohibits a SEP holder from demanding a license from each supplier down the chain. Nonetheless, the following questions have arisen, particularly in cases before the German courts:

(a) Which level of the chain should the patent license be granted – in particular, can the patentee choose the licensing point and/or can an implementer (e.g., an end-product manufacturer) refuse to take a license on the basis that the patentee should have licensed the SEP at a different level (e.g., a component manufacturer)?
(b) Can the level of licensing affect the level of the royalty to be paid? For example, might licensing further down the chain allow the SEP holder to extract higher licensing fees, because the royalty is calculated on the basis of a percentage of the (higher) value of the product or service sold by the licensee, or would that

---

[113] However, it did not follow that the making of an initial offer for a license of SEPs and non-SEPs was necessarily an abuse of dominance. On the facts, Unwired Planet had first made an offer for a license of SEPs and non-SEPs but had declared itself ready to discuss alternative arrangements. Huawei had then requested a SEP-only license and Unwired Planet had responded with an offer that related only to the SEPs. If Unwired Planet had insisted on bundling SEPs and non-SEPs, it might well have been the case that this conduct could have been found to be abusive even if an actual license bundling SEPs and non-SEPs had not been entered into. *Unwired Planet Int'l Ltd.* v. *Huawei Techs. Co.* (Pat 2017, ¶¶ 57–59) (UK).
[114] *Id.* at 503.
[115] Dominance is a requirement in the European Union (under TFEU art. 102) but not in the United States (under the Robinson-Patman Act, 15 U.S.C. § 13 (U.S.)).
[116] *See supra* notes 101–02 and accompanying text.

infringe the principle of fair and nondiscriminatory licensing required both by a FRAND commitment and some competition law systems?[117]

The general approach by the European Commission in the Guidelines on horizontal cooperation agreements and the enforcement practice so far arguably suggest that level discrimination may be problematic and that generally participants wishing to have their patent rights included in a standard should provide an irrevocable commitment to offer to license their essential patents to *all* (and any) third parties on FRAND terms.[118] The Commission has thus indicated concern that some suits arising in Germany may be designed to allow SEP holders to circumvent the obligations imposed on them by the CJEU's ruling in *Huawei* and has stated that it is monitoring the cases carefully. In the cases arising before the German courts, some SEP owners have commenced injunction proceedings not against phone manufacturers but against mobile network operators (which sell phones), alleging infringement of SEPs. The German courts have, to date, suggested that although in principle every market participant should be entitled to take a FRAND license, a patentee is free to choose which implementer in the chain it wishes to sue for infringement, unless it appears to be part of an undue strategy to extract non-FRAND licensing terms.[119] If there is a concern with level discrimination, however, such a concern would not result from the prohibition of discrimination by dominant undertakings under Article 102(c) TFEU. As the Commission Communication on SEPs points out, a SEP holder may not discriminate between licensees who are "similarly situated."[120] A final service provider or manufacturer is not, however, "similarly situated" to a component manufacturer. Level discrimination may, nevertheless, be problematic if the FRAND commitment is broadly framed as a commitment to license any third party and if component manufacturers were unable to manufacture components without a license. If such conditions occur, it is arguable that the broad *tenet*, if not the letter, of the *Huawei* judgment would require

---

[117] *See further* discussion in Chapter 1.

[118] European Commission, at ¶ 285, 2011 O.J. (C11/01) 1 (guidelines on horizontal cooperation agreements). *See also id.* at ¶ 279. *See also* the Commission's decisions in *Samsung* and *Motorola, supra* note 58 and accompanying text, which reinforce this view. Indeed, SSOs have generally adopted wide FRAND commitments in their policies, which appear not to permit level discrimination, *see, e.g.,* JEDEC Solid State Technology Association 2017, §§ 8.2.1, 8.2.4 (JEDEC IP Rights Policy envisages a RAND commitment to license "all Potential Licensees," which are defined as "[a]ll JEDEC Committee Members and non-members"); IEEE-SA Board of Governors 2017, §§ 6.1, 6.2(b) (IEEE IP Rights Policy provides that the licensing commitment of a SEP holder shall be to grant a license "to an unrestricted number of Applicants," which are defined as "any prospective licensee for Essential Patent Claims"); ETSI 2018, Annex 6 § 6.1 (ETSI IP Rights Policy is less clear as it does not identify who the licensee is to be).

[119] *See, e.g.,* LG Düsseldorf v. 31.3.2016 – 4a O 73/14 and 126/14 – *Saint Lawrence v. Vodafone* (Ger.), on appeal OLG Düsseldorf v. 9.5.2016 – I-15 U 35/16 and 36/16 – *Saint Lawrence v. Vodafone* (Ger.); LG Mannheim v. 8.1.2016 – 7 O 96/14 – *Pioneer v. Acer* (Ger.), on appeal OLG Karlsruhe v. 31.5.2016 – 6 U 55/16 – *Pioneer v. Acer* (Ger.).

[120] European Commission, at 7, COM (2017) 712 final (Nov. 29, 2017).

the SEP holder to grant a FRAND license to component manufacturers.[121] The issue is, however, still open.

A further question is whether a SEP holder that engages in multilevel licensing infringes discrimination provisions, if it discriminates between users on the basis of the utility of the patented technology to the licensee.[122] "Licensing only at the end-user product level and multi-level licensing are not rare, but there is a paucity of judicial authority as to how those strategies should be viewed under FRAND."[123] As explained above, the Commission Communication on SEPs considers that a SEP holder may treat differently licensees who are not "similarly situated."

3 Patent Pools

An important question in the sphere of complex products could be whether a technology or patent pool, an arrangement whereby two or more entities assemble a package of technology that is licensed both to contributors to the pool and third parties, might be a feasible mechanism for eradicating some of the more difficult problems that arise from individual licensing negotiations between SEP owners and implementers. Technology pools have often been used to support a *de jure* or *de facto* industry standard and may provide a convenient way for facilitating dissemination of technology through one-stop licensing of pooled technologies and reducing transaction costs and limiting cumulative royalties. In the mobile communications field, however, they have not been successfully used to date, perhaps because the largest SEP holders think they can extract better licensing terms outside of the pool.

Competition law systems generally recognize that technology pools may be procompetitive but are also concerned about the competitive risks that might arise from the licensing of substitute technologies (creating a risk of price-fixing or market-sharing) or as a result of a reduction of innovation from foreclosing alternative, competing technologies.[124] In assessing the compatibility of such arrangements with competition law rules therefore account is frequently taken of issues such as: the transparency of the pool creation process; the selection and nature of the pooled technologies; whether the technologies are complementary or substitutes, essential or nonessential; the institutional framework of the pool; the market position of the pool and whether it can foreclose third party technologies or limit the creation of alternative pools;[125] as well as the licensing terms. In the European Union, for

---

[121] Nazzini 2017.

[122] Belgum 2014, 1. The problem of multilevel licensing raises some questions in common with level discrimination, *see* Nazzini 2017, 215–16. *See also, e.g.,* Padilla & Wong-Ervin 2017.

[123] Belgum 2014, 1–2.

[124] *See, e.g.,* European Commission, 2014 O.J. (C89/03) 3 (guidelines on technology transfer agreements); DOJ & FTC 2017, § 5.5.

[125] European Commission, 2014 O.J. (C89/03) 3 also seeks to ensure that new technology is not foreclosed, for example by stating that restrictions on parties developing competing products or standards or on granting and obtaining licenses outside the pool should not be incorporated.

example, the Technology Transfer Guidelines state that "royalties and other licensing terms should be non-excessive and non-discriminatory and licences should be non-exclusive. These requirements are necessary to ensure that the pool is open and does not lead to foreclosure and other anti-competitive effects on down-stream markets."[126] The Commission has also, with the objective of encouraging the conclusion of procompetitive pools, set out a safe harbor for the creation of certain technology pools and subsequent licensing of the technology.[127] In particular, the Commission takes the view that the creation and operation of the pool, including the licensing out, generally falls outside Article 101(1) of the Treaty, irrespective of the market position of the parties, if all the following conditions are fulfilled:

a) participation in the pool creation process is open to all interested technology rights owners;
b) sufficient safeguards are adopted to ensure that only essential technologies (which therefore necessarily are also complements) are pooled;
c) sufficient safeguards are adopted to ensure that exchange of sensitive information (such as pricing and output data) is restricted to what is necessary for the creation and operation of the pool;
d) the pooled technologies are licensed into the pool on a nonexclusive basis;
e) the pooled technologies are licensed out to all potential licensees on FRAND terms;
f) the parties contributing technology to the pool and the licensees are free to challenge the validity and the essentiality of the pooled technologies; and
g) the parties contributing technology to the pool and the licensee remain free to develop competing products and technology.[128]

The Commission Communication on SEPs recognizes that patent pools and other licensing platforms may be procompetitive but does not go beyond a mere statement of principle, which could already be derived from general principles of EU competition law.[129]

4 Splitting Patent Portfolios: Sales of SEPs to PAEs in Return for a Share of Future Royalties

Apart from the difficulties involved in identifying competition-compliant FRAND licensing terms, further problems have arisen when owners of SEPs have sought to monetize their patent portfolio and increase revenue from it (so increasing their

---

[126] *Id.* at ¶ 244.
[127] *Id.* at ¶ 261.
[128] *Id.*
[129] European Commission, at 7–8, COM (2017) 712 final (Nov. 29, 2017).

competitors' costs), by splitting it[130] and selling part of the portfolio to a PAE that does not itself produce standardized equipment.[131]

In some such transfers the transaction has been structured not as a genuine clean sale of patents for a purchase price, but as one under which the PAE is essentially acting as a licensing (and litigation service) provider to the vendor whereby the PAE is obliged to pay a percentage of future royalties it obtains to the vendor (described by some as "privateering").[132] Instead of the vendor licensing its entire portfolio, therefore, it splits the portfolio, licensing the SEPs it retains and gaining a percentage of the royalties obtained by the NPE in respect of the SEPs transferred; the NPE and former patentee thus share the royalty income. This was the scenario that existed in relation to litigation in England involving Unwired Planet, an NPE[133] that acquired 2,400 wireless patents from Ericsson and sued Huawei, Google, and Samsung for infringement of six of the patents (five of which were claimed to be SEPs).[134] The alleged infringers in these cases raised defenses and counterclaims based on breaches of competition law. In particular, they argued that the master sales agreement (MSA) by which Unwired Patent acquired patents from Ericsson and under which Ericsson received a share of the royalties recovered by Unwired Planet, infringed Article 101 TFEU on the grounds that it was simply a device for increasing income over and beyond FRAND terms, thus rendering the transfer of the patents null and void. A further argument concerned the question of whether, if a valid transfer had taken place, Unwired Planet's license offers were FRAND and/or infringed Art 102 and thus whether they had abused their dominant position by bringing injunction proceedings; key battlegrounds centered around the royalty rate offered and the proper scope of any license.

The question of whether the MSA infringed Article 101 was not determined in the English proceedings.[135] Although Birss J refused an attempt by Ericsson to strike out this aspect of the action, holding that it was a properly arguable point that ought to go to trial, this aspect of the case was settled and a term in the MSA, which arguably put a floor on the royalty rate (the Applicable Royalty Rate) that Unwired Planet could

---

[130]   This may increase the revenue that can be obtained as when considering patent infringement cases courts are generally only prepared to consider a small number of patents.

[131]   Where the sale is of SEPs, this also of course raises FRAND issues. *See, e.g.,* Geradin 2016.

[132]   *See, e.g.,* Sokol 2017; Hovenkamp & Cotter 2016; Lundqvist 2014, 412.

[133]   Unwired Planet has a worldwide patent portfolio that includes numerous patents that are declared essential to various telecommunications standards (2G GSM, 3G UMTS, and 4G LTE). Most of the relevant portfolio was acquired from Ericsson. Unwired Planet's business is licensing those patents to companies that make and sell telecommunications equipment such as mobile phones and infra-structure. The action began in March 2014 when Unwired Planet sued Huawei, Samsung, and Google for infringement of six UK patents from their portfolio. Five were claimed to be SEPs. *Unwired Planet Int'l Ltd. v. Huawei Techs. Co.* (Pat 2017) (UK).

[134]   The patents were infringed by use in Google's Android operating system.

[135]   *See Unwired Planet Int'l Ltd. v. Huawei Techs. Co.* (Pat 2017, ¶ 5) (UK).

offer, was removed. In the German proceedings,[136] in contrast, the Düsseldorf Regional Court rejected the argument that the assignment of the patents was invalid under Art 101 or 102 and that the purpose of the assignment was to establish excessive pricing beyond FRAND. The Court in particular rejected the argument that this was by its very nature anticompetitive and that the object of the assignment was to establish excessive pricing in the market, in particular pricing that exceeds the FRAND benchmark. It did not agree that it was illegitimate for a SEP proprietor to seek to acquire a better position in the negotiation process by splitting up its SEP portfolio, or that the NPE[137] was obliged to continue the licensing practice of the former SEP owner; the only requirement was that its licensing should be FRAND. The Court thus held that targeting a fair remuneration for a patent portfolio was a legitimate and legal objective.

5 Patent Acquisitions

When conducting merger review, competition agencies have in some cases taken into account the impact the merger will have on the incentives of the merging firms to engage in anticompetitive behavior post-merger, including through the exploitation of SEPs.

For example, when reviewing Google's acquisition of Motorola and the acquisition by Apple, Microsoft, and Research in Motion (part of the Rockstar consortium) of Nortel and Apple's acquisition of certain Novell patents, the antitrust division of the U.S. Department of Justice (DOJ) considered the potential ability and incentives of the acquiring firms to use their patents, especially the SEPs that Nortel and Motorola had committed to license, to raise rivals' costs, to hold up rivals,[138] and to foreclose and substantially lessen competition. During the course of the investigation, several of the competitors, including Apple and Microsoft, made FRAND licensing commitments and committed not to seek injunctions in disputes involving SEPS, lessening the DOJ's concerns about the potential anticompetitive use of SEPs. In the end, the DOJ concluded that the transactions were not likely

---

[136] *See* L.G. Düsseldorf v. 19.1.2016 – 4b O 120/14, 4b O 122/14, and 4b O 123/14 – *Unwired Planet v. Samsung* (Ger.). The nontechnical trial thus focused on the question of whether the licensing offers made had been FRAND, whether Unwired Planet had abused their dominant position, and how remedies – injunction, damages, and declarations – should be dealt with.

[137] Further examples of German case law on NPEs in the SEP/FRAND area are the decisions OLG Düsseldorf v. 13.1.2016 – I-15 U 66/15 – *Sisvel v. Haier* (Ger.); LG Düsseldorf v. 31.3.2016 – 4a O 73/14 and 126/14 – *Saint Lawrence v. Vodafone* (Ger.). These decisions hold, inter alia, that there is no reason to treat NPEs per se differently than other patent owners when it comes to the FRAND licensing of SEPs.

[138] So preventing or inhibiting innovation and competition through, e.g., demanding supracompetitive licensing rates, compelling prospective licensees to grant the SEP holder the right to use the licensee's IP, charging licensees the entire portfolio royalty rate when licensing only a small subset of the SEPS, or seeking to prevent or exclude products practicing those SEPS from the market altogether, *see* (DOJ) Press Release 12–210 (Feb. 13, 2012).

substantially to lessen competition for wireless devices or change significantly existing market dynamics so did not challenge the merger. The DOJ made it clear, however, that it was concerned about the inappropriate use of SEPs, particularly by Google, post-merger and that it would continue to monitor their use to ensure that competition and innovation were unfettered.

During the course of this investigation the U.S. agency worked closely with other competition agencies, including in Australia, Canada, Israel, and Korea, and especially the European Commission. The Commission was also concerned by the fact that Google's open-source Android OS, one of the most popular mobile operating systems (OS), and a number of Motorola's SEPs were key inputs in smart mobile devices. However, it cleared the merger unconditionally in Phase I proceedings.[139] With regard to the SEPs, the Commission did not consider that the merger would significantly change the current position and was also influenced by Google's "legally binding" and "irrevocable" letter to standard-setting organizations to honor Motorola's pre-existing commitment to license them on FRAND terms. Further, it did not consider that Google would have the incentive to prevent Motorola's competitors from using its OS as that would stifle the spread of its other services. In China, the merger was approved only subject to conditions.[140]

6.4 ANTITRUST REMEDIES

Most competition law systems rely on a mixture of public and private enforcement in civil (or exceptionally criminal) proceedings to protect society's interest in the efficient working of markets and to ensure that victims can protect themselves from violations and receive compensation where necessary. A number rely (or have initially at least relied) heavily on public enforcement agencies to bring antitrust cases that define policy and prevent, deter, and punish serious violations of the law. Private litigation is now developing in many jurisdictions, and in the United States, the preponderance of antitrust enforcement occurs through private actions.

Remedies available for violations of antitrust and competition law broadly include monetary, behavioral, and injunctive remedies.[141] When actions are brought by enforcement agencies, monetary remedies typically take the form of penalties and fines intended to deter the particular harm in question and to punish the liable party. In private actions, monetary damages are typically compensatory, though in some jurisdictions, particularly in the United States, enhanced monetary awards (treble

---

[139]   Commission Decision of 13 February 2012, COMP/M.6381 – Google/Motorola Mobility.
[140]   Ministry of Commerce of the People's Republic of China Announcement No. 25 (May 31, 2012).
[141]   The importance of giving careful considerations to remedies at an early stage was something stressed by panelists in the DOJ/FTC single conduct hearings, *see* DOJ 2008, 143 ("Without a proper remedy, winning a judgment [in an antitrust case] is similar to winning a battle but losing the war.").

damages and attorneys' fees, this latter element as an exception to the general rule of non-recoverability of legal costs in that jurisdiction) may be available.[142]

In addition to compensatory damages, both private parties and enforcement agencies may seek behavioral remedies that are intended to deter, halt, and correct violations.[143] Injunctive relief in antitrust cases generally seeks to remedy a harm caused by anticompetitive conduct and to prevent its recurrence. Thus, in the case of price fixing between competitors, remedial measures may simply prohibit further price fixing. In monopolization or dominance cases, a remedial order may prohibit a dominant firm from carrying on a particular business within certain markets or, exceptionally, require a firm to divest certain business units or subsidiaries. The range of remedies in antitrust cases is thus quite broad, including cease and desist orders (for example, prohibiting the seeking of an injunction or the charging of exploitative royalties), affirmative obligations (e.g., an obligation to license or to license on competition compliant terms), structural remedies (such as structural separation of business units), and other sanctions. Such remedies may impact, or override, rights and remedies conferred by patent law by, for example, preventing a patent owner from seeking an injunction (through a cease and desist order), ordering a compulsory license, nullifying the sale of patent rights, or interfering with licensing arrangements or terms. They may also subsequently require close scrutiny or monitoring for compliance. In general, the scope of antitrust injunctive relief sought by enforcement agencies can be as broad as necessary "to bring about the dissolution or suppression of" the illegal conduct.[144] As such, these remedies, which must account for effects on the public and the marketplace, are considered to be more sweeping forms of relief than injunctive relief between private litigants.[145]

A decision-maker might be reluctant to intervene to prohibit certain conduct under competition law – for example, a refusal to license or the seeking of an injunction by a patentee – if it believes that a simple cease and desist order, prohibiting the unlawful conduct identified, and its recurrence, would be insufficient to ensure that the infringement is brought to an end. If an effective remedy requires more, the court or agency must undertake both a careful consideration of the appropriate terms of dealing (especially pricing) as well as the realistic prospects for monitoring of that behavior in the future. In the United States, for example, the Supreme Court has on some occasions expressed reluctance to find that a refusal to deal or a margin squeeze constitutes a substantive antitrust violation in

---

[142] *See, e.g.*, Clayton Act § 4, 15 U.S.C. § 15 (U.S.) (stating that "any person who shall be injured in his business or property by reason of anything forbidden in the antitrust laws may sue" for treble damages, prejudgment interest, and costs of suit, including attorneys' fees).

[143] In addition to its power to impose fines for violations of competition law rules, the European Commission may "impose on them any behavioural or structural remedies which are proportionate to the infringement committed and necessary to bring the infringement effectively to an end." Council Regulation (EC) 1/2003, art. 7, 2003 O.J. (L1) 1.

[144] *Northern Sec. Co. v. United States* (U.S. 1904, 346) (U.S.).

[145] Marcus 1945, 37.

circumstances where such a violation would require the courts to act as central planners, involved in the construction of "fair" access terms or the setting of "fair" prices or spreads between prices, a task to which the Supreme Court felt the courts were ill-suited.[146] In the European Union, the difficulty of ensuring the effectiveness of the antitrust intervention has also proved to be real. In the *Microsoft* case,[147] for example, the Commission and Microsoft, following the Commission's initial fining of Microsoft for its failure to supply interoperability information, wrangled for several years over the appropriate terms for supplying the interoperability information; eventually the Commission fined Microsoft a second time for its failure to comply.[148]

An important point in relation to remedies is that in many jurisdictions, mechanisms also exist to bring antitrust proceedings to an end by consent. These may allow for remedies to be agreed to more flexibly between an antitrust agency and investigated firms. For example, in the European Union the Commission has power to adopt decisions whereby, without a finding of infringement, commitments given by undertaking as to their future behavior are made binding upon them.[149] This procedure has been used quite frequently in dominance cases, and, arguably, has sometimes resulted in firms committing to behavioral or structural obligations that go beyond that which could have been imposed by the Commission in a final decision. Such commitments may involve a monitoring trustee mechanism to ensure their implementation. The commitments procedure was used by the Commission, in both *Rambus* and *Samsung*, to develop its use of Article 102 to SEPs, prior to its adoption of an infringement decision in *Motorola*.[150]

In the United States, both the DOJ and the FTC can also enter into consent decrees. The procedures differ, but if the DOJ and the defendant agree on the terms of a desired order prior to or during the course of litigation, they may stipulate the

---

[146]   *See, e.g., Verizon Commc'ns, Inc.* v. *Law Offices of Curtis V. Trinko* (U.S. 2004) (U.S.). In *Otter Tail Power Co.* v. *United States* (U.S. 1973) (U.S.) the Supreme Court required an integrated electric company to wheel bulk power over its lines to competitors at the distribution level. It did not however have the burden of itself dealing with the detail. Rather, the regulator, the Federal Power Commission, could regulate prices and scrutinize the terms of the contracts. *See also,* the approach to margin squeeze cases in the European Union and the United States, where many cases have arisen in regulated sectors where regulatory authorities may, for example, already be empowered to demand access and control pricing. The existence of this regulatory structure could therefore be considered to alter the calculus of antitrust harms and benefits likely to spring from the investigated conduct, in particular by diminishing the likelihood of antitrust harm and consequently the need for the behavior to be characterized as unlawful "exclusionary conduct." *See also Verizon Commc'ns, Inc.* v. *Law Offices of Curtis V. Trinko* (U.S. 2004) (U.S.).

[147]   European Commission Press Release IP/04/382 (Mar. 24, 2004).

[148]   *See* European Commission Press Release IP/06/979 (July 12, 2006) (Commission imposes penalty payment of €280.5m on Microsoft for continued noncompliance with March 2004 decision).

[149]   Council Regulation (EC) 1/2003, art. 9, 2003 O.J. (L1) 1.

[150]   Commission Decision of 9 December 2009, COMP/38.636—RAMBUS; Commission Decision of 29 April 2014, Case AT.39939 – Samsung – Enforcement of UMTS Standard Essential Patents, Commission Decision of 29 April 2014, Case AT.39958 – Motorola – Enforcement of GPRS Standard Essential Patents.

terms of a "consent decree," which will then be submitted to the court for approval and entry into the record. Though not fully adjudicated, a consent decree has the legal force of an adjudicated decision, enforceable upon pain of contempt.[151]

This procedure has also been relied upon quite frequently by the U.S. authorities in enforcement actions involving the anticompetitive licensing or exploitation of patents, particularly (in recent years) within the context of technical standard-setting. Thus, between World War II and the 1970s, the most aggressive period of U.S. antitrust enforcement,[152] U.S. courts issued more than one hundred antitrust decrees ordering patentees found to have engaged in anticompetitive conduct to license their patents on terms that were fair, reasonable, and nondiscriminatory.[153] Even in the more tempered modern era of antitrust enforcement, both the FTC and DOJ have utilized detailed behavioral remedies to address instances of antitrust violations involving patents, particularly in the area of standard-setting.[154] The first of these to gain significant attention was the FTC's 1996 consent decree with Dell Computer, in which Dell agreed to forfeit the enforcement of a patent that it improperly failed to disclose to a standard-setting organization, thereby exploiting an unfair method of competition in violation of Section 5 of the FTC Act.[155] In a case involving similar allegations, Unocal entered into an agreement with the FTC not to enforce a patent covering a standard for reduced gasoline emissions after it failed to disclose the patent to the relevant standards body.[156]

A different factual pattern was alleged in the FTC's action against Negotiated Data Solutions (N-Data) LLC. In that case, N-Data acquired a patent with knowledge of a prior patentee's commitment to license the patent to implementers of a technical standard at a flat rate of $1,000. When N-Data announced that it did not intend to honor that prior commitment, the FTC brought an action alleging violation of Section 5 of the FTC Act. N-Data settled the matter by agreeing to honor the prior patentee's royalty commitment.[157]

Finally, in 2013 the FTC settled two matters in which patentees were alleged to have violated Section 5 of the FTC Act by seeking injunctive relief against unlicensed implementers of a technical standard as to which they had made FRAND

---

[151] *United States v. Swift & Co.* (U.S. 1932, p.106) (U.S.). Though the use of consent decrees in antitrust cases can be traced to 1906 they did not come into widespread use until a new policy initiative by the Attorney General in 1938. Isenbergh & Rubin 1940, 387–88. By the end of the 1950s, consent decrees had become "the most widely used antitrust remedy in federal civil enforcement." Flynn 1968, 983–85 n.3.

[152] *See* Bohannan & Hovenkamp 2010, 908–09 (describing and critiquing expansionist U.S. antitrust enforcement policy during this period); Gavil 2012, 738.

[153] *See* Contreras 2015b (discussing and collecting these decrees).

[154] *See, generally,* Hesse & Marshall 2017.

[155] *In the Matter of Dell Computer Corp.* (FTC May 20, 1996, p.619–23) (Decision and Order).

[156] *In the Matter of Union Oil Co. of Cal.* (FTC July 27, 2005, p.161) (Decision and Order).

[157] *In the Matter of Negotiated Data Solutions LLC* (FTC Sept. 23, 2008) (Decision and Order).

commitments.[158] In settling these cases, each of the patentees agreed not to seek an injunction to prevent the infringement of a FRAND-committed standards-essential patent by a willing licensee unless and until the patentee engaged in a series of good-faith attempts to reach agreement with the infringer.[159]

These cases, taken together, demonstrate that the remedial orders fashioned by the U.S. antitrust agencies can be flexible mechanisms that are tailored to address specific forms of anticompetitive conduct. Remedies such as these arguably offer significantly more flexibility to improve competitive conditions than monetary damages or simple cease and desist orders such as those issued in private antitrust litigation.

6.5 CONCLUSIONS

Although competition and patent law pursue complementary goals, this chapter demonstrates that, in the sphere of complex products, tensions have arisen between the two systems, especially in situations where market power acquired by SEP owners as a result of a standardization process appears to have been used to exclude competition, hold up innovation, or exploit that market power to the detriment of consumers. In certain circumstances antitrust laws in some jurisdictions have been used to scrutinize mechanisms used by SEP holders to monetize their SEP portfolios – whether through the seeking of an injunction against an implementer, licensing arrangements, or through the sale of a portion of the patent portfolio. Its powerful mechanisms – formal and informal (e.g., through settlement processes) – to remedy infringements of its rules have also been used.

Section 6.2.1 discussed cases in which competition law has come directly into conflict with the patent system in some jurisdictions, by intervening to prevent a patentee from obtaining an injunction – its patent remedy of choice. This has been the case where the seeking of such an injunction has been found to be liable to hold up a willing licensee and impact on competition and innovation downstream and/or to compromise the standardization process, in circumstances where the SEP holder had committed to monetize its patent through FRAND licensing. These cases have, however, unleashed a number of other complex matters for resolution, including the scope of the obligations on the patentee and implementer and what each must do, respectively, to assert or avert injunctive relief. In the European Union, many of these questions have been working their way through the courts

---

[158]   *In the Matter of Robert Bosch GmbH* (FTC Apr. 23, 2013) (Decision and Order); *In the Matter of Motorola Mobility LLC and Google Inc.* (FTC July 23, 2013) (Decision and Order).

[159]   The DOJ expressed similar concerns with the ability of SEP holders to seek injunctions against implementers of technical standards in approving three proposed merger transactions in 2012. In considering three separate transactions, the agency assessed the potential for the merger parties to fail to honor the FRAND commitments made to various standards bodies, and particularly their ability to seek injunctions against implementers of their standards. The DOJ approved the mergers only after the parties each committed not to take such actions, *see supra* note 136 and accompanying text.

of Europe's biggest market, Germany. Solutions to these issues are crucial if further disputes are not to break out between SEP holders and potential licensees, especially as 5G technology is developed, together with the Internet of Things.

These cases, and FRAND commitments given during a standard-setting procedure, have also brought to the forefront the question of when licensing complies both with a FRAND commitment and competition law. These issues are crucial to the questions of what patent damages for past infringement should look like and what a competition-compliant FRAND license should look like. Although until recently few courts outside of the United States have tackled these matters, some cases are emerging across the globe that deal with the validity of global or portfolio licenses and the question of whether licensing rates are "fair" or "discriminatory" in both FRAND and competition law terms (to the extent that they differ) or otherwise infringe antitrust law. Although it still remains unclear whether competition law makes more onerous demands on patent holders than FRAND, some competition enforcers have indicated that they have some concerns about "exploitative" behavior of SEP holders and that they might be willing to intervene to control behavior, balancing the rewards of innovation with the interests of consumers.

The questions of whether, and if so when, dividing or selling a SEP portfolio violates antitrust law and whether the principle of nondiscrimination requires a purchaser of a patent portfolio – especially where the purchaser is an NPE – to adopt the same approach to licensing as the vendor, are also important ones requiring resolution.

Balancing the interests of SEP holders and implementers is proving to be an extremely difficult task that is eluding SDOs and policymakers[160] and creating complexity for courts charged with resolving the patent disputes arising. In some cases competition agencies are also being asked to help solve the problems occurring and to protect the competitive process from distortion by a multitude of SEP holders with significant market power. Although traditionally competition decision-makers have been reluctant to act as regulators, controlling the pricing and terms of dealing, they are increasingly drawn into these matters in the sphere of patents and the debate as to how the competing interests are to be balanced. This chapter illustrates that a number of difficult issues at the interface of patent and antitrust law remain to be resolved in the sphere of complex products. Given the central role of standardization to 5G and the Internet of Things it is crucial that solutions are found to these problems.

Accordingly, we propose further research on the following topics:

- the objectives of competition and patent law respectively and whether, and if so how, trade-offs between such objectives may be achieved or conflicts managed and resolved;

---

[160] *See, e.g.,* European Commission, COM (2017) 712 final (Nov. 29, 2017) (Commission Communication on SEPs).

- the steps that SEP holders must comply with to ensure that their seeking of an injunction does not infringe competition law, as well as the steps that implementers must take to allow them to lawfully resist an injunction;
- the extent to which competition law can impose additional constraints on SEP licensing terms beyond those demanded by a FRAND commitment, in particular whether it impacts on the scope and contours of the obligations of a patentee and an implementer when negotiating a FRAND license of the patentee's FRAND-committed patents and the consequences of breach of such obligations;
- whether competition agencies can do more to encourage the use of procompetitive patent pools or other licensing platforms to address licensing challenges and as a model for licensing complex product patents;
- the extent to which level discrimination, multilevel licensing, and the transfer of SEPs to PAEs may violate antitrust laws; and
- whether, and if so when, the antitrust system and the portfolio or antitrust remedies offer greater flexibility to deal with some of the patent issues arising in the sphere of complex products.

7

Holdup, Holdout, and Royalty Stacking: A Review of the Literature

Norman V. Siebrasse

7.1 INTRODUCTION

This chapter provides a critical review of the literature relating to remedies for patent infringement in the context of complex products, with a focus on the underlying theoretical issues of holdup, holdout, and royalty stacking.

A royalty can only be considered excessive when measured against some benchmark. Section 2 of this chapter considers the conceptually appropriate benchmark for a fair return to a patentee. Section 3 reviews the theory relating to "holdup," which is used generically to mean any mechanism by which a patentee, bargaining with the expectation of being able to enjoin any unlicensed use, might be able to extract a royalty that exceeds the benchmark. Section 4 reviews mechanisms by which holdup can be mitigated. Section 5 attempts to place this debate relating to holdup into the context of the general literature on property rules versus liability rules. Section 6 considers "holdout" mechanisms, which may allow implementers to force a patentee to accept a royalty that is lower than the fair benchmark. Royalty stacking refers generally to any mechanism by which the total royalty burden is unduly increased by the presence of multiple patentees. It is the focus of Section 7, while Section 8 considers empirical evidence relating to holdup and royalty stacking.

7.2 BENCHMARK RETURN TO PATENTEE

7.2.1 A Share of the Discounted Incremental Ex Ante Value: $\theta\beta v$

To decide whether a royalty is excessive or inadequate requires comparison with a benchmark. A prominent benchmark is that used by Lemley & Shapiro (2007a), namely a share of the incremental *ex ante* value of the invention as compared with the next best alternative, discounted by the probability of validity and infringement, where the patentee's share is determined by its bargaining power. This can be summarized as $r^* = \theta\beta v$, where r^* is the benchmark royalty, θ is the probability that the patent is valid and infringed, β is the patentee's bargaining power, and ν is the incremental *ex ante* value of the invention.[1]

7.2.2 *Incremental Value Over Best Alternative:* ν

1 Overview

On an instrumental view of the patent system, the patentee's incentive to invent should be commensurate with the social value of the invention,[2] and it is widely acknowledged that the social value of a technology is its incremental *ex ante* value over the next best alternative.[3]

The view that the value of an invention depends on its value over the best alternative is premised on the view that the patent system should incentivize the invention of socially beneficial products. If an already known drug treats pain effectively, and there is a new drug that is equally effective but no better in any respect, then it would be wasteful to spend social resources on the new drug that offers no advantages over the old drug. While this basic starting point is widely accepted, there are a number of details that are open to debate.[4]

---

[1]   Lemley & Shapiro 2007a, 1999.

[2]   Farrell et al. 2007, 610–11; Shapiro 2007.

[3]   *See, e.g.*, Swanson & Baumol 2005, 10–11; Farrell et al. 2007, 610–11; Elhauge 2008, 545; Denicolò et al. 2008, 577–78; Layne-Farrar et al. 2009, 448; Shapiro 2010, 282; Gilbert 2011, 642; Camesasca et al. 2013, 304; Cotter 2013a, 128; Carlton & Shampine 2013, 536, 545; Jarosz & Chapman 2013, 812; Cotter 2014a, 357; Sedona Conference 2014, 23–24; Contreras & Gilbert 2015, 1468–69, 1499–1500; Siebrasse & Cotter 2017a; Lee & Melamed 2016, 411–12.

   Golden 2007, 2144 n.119, challenges this, saying "The value of a patented invention is not necessarily merely its worth relative to that of an alternative. This can be appreciated by recognizing, for example, that my ability to purchase a bottle of Soda 2 for $1.00, rather than a bottle of Soda 1 for $1.25, does not mean that Soda 1 is worth only $0.25 – the difference between the values of the two choices." At first glance, this argument apparently fails to recognize the distinction between the value of the invention and the value of an embodiment of that invention. An invention is information, with zero marginal cost, while the embodiment of the invention may well have a substantial marginal cost. Suppose a consumer is indifferent between Soda 2 for $1 and Soda 1 for $1.25, and the cost of the ingredients for the two sodas is exactly the same, but Soda 1 has a flavor-enhancing technology, with a zero marginal cost. The value of the flavor-enhancing technology is $0.25, but the value of a bottle of Soda 1 is $1.25, because of the cost of the tangible ingredients. However, judging from the remainder of the passage, Golden's real concern may have been with cases where the alternative is also patented: *see* the discussion below in Section 7.2.2.a "Patented Alternatives." Golden 2007, 2138 also argues that the marginal value of an invention is difficult to determine. While this is no doubt often true, it is not a conceptual objection to the benchmark, but a practical one, which perhaps more properly goes to the point of whether a reasonable royalty is adequate compensation, which is discussed below in Section 5.1 "Inaccuracy of Damages Awards." Moreover, as Lemley & Shapiro 2007b, 2169 point out, it is not necessary to measure the marginal value to conclude that holdup allows the patentee to extract an excess.

[4]   Lemley & Shapiro 2007b, 2169, state that "[c]ertainly, [ν] is well defined conceptually." This is true only for the paradigmatic cases.

2 Incremental Value

A) PATENTED ALTERNATIVES. While it is widely acknowledged that the value of the invention is its incremental value over the best alternative, there is not a consensus when the best alternative is patented. Some authors explicitly identify the value of the patented technology as its incremental value over an unpatented alternative, and simply do not consider the case of a patented alternative,[5] but it is quite common to simply remain silent on the issue.[6]

What might be termed a "strict" interpretation of the incremental *ex ante* approach treats patented and unpatented alternatives in exactly the same way. Most prominently, Swanson & Baumol (2005) explicitly take the benchmark to be the strict incremental value of a patented invention over the best patented alternative, so that if two patented technologies are equally effective, the benchmark royalty is its marginal cost (potentially zero).[7] Siebrasse & Cotter (2017a) argue that this strict approach is wrong because if the royalty received by a patentee is equal to the marginal cost of manufacturing and licensing the technology, there will be an insufficient incentive to invest the sunk costs of invention in the first place. As they note: "The fact that two patentees develop equivalent technology at the same time does not mean that neither required the lure of a patent. Viagra and Cialis may be equally effective in treating erectile dysfunction, but that does not imply that they both would have been invented if pharmaceutical patents were not available."[8] Consequently, this strict interpretation of the incremental *ex ante* approach is inconsistent with the basic rationale of the patent system, which is to allow an inventor to recover some part of their sunk costs of invention.

Lemley & Shapiro (2007a) deal with the question of patented alternatives in a footnote, saying that when the best alternative is patented, "[t]he proper comparison is between the cost and value of the patentee's component and the cost and value of the alternative, including patent royalties that would have to be paid on the alternative where appropriate."[9] However, when there is no established royalty for the alternative it is not clear how Lemley & Shapiro would determine the royalty that would have to be paid on the

---

[5] Farrell et al. 2007, 612–15; Layne-Farrar et al. 2009, 456.

[6] *See, e.g.,* FTC 2011, 191–94; Shapiro 2010, 282.

[7] Swanson & Baumol 2005, 18–19; Layne-Farrar et al. 2007, 686 (expanding on the model of Swanson & Baumol 2005 and making the same assumption); Carlton & Shampine 2013, 541 n.25 (specifying that "[t]he alternatives could be patented or unpatented").

[8] Siebrasse & Cotter 2017a, 1192–93; *see also* Kieff & Layne-Farrar 2013, 1120 (leveling substantially the same criticism of the strict approach in the SEP context, noting it will result in "reduced SSO participation and suboptimal investment in innovation"); Golden 2007, 2144 n.119 (noting that "the fact that a patent has inspired the discovery of a [patented] substitute does not mean that the patented contribution should be considered to be devoid of value").

[9] Lemley & Shapiro 2007a, 2039 n.153; *see also* Contreras & Gilbert 2015, 1468 taking essentially the same position.

alternative.[10] Moreover, even if there were an established royalty for the alternative, competition from the new patented invention would presumably affect the royalty charged by the alternative patented technology. It is not clear whether the royalty to be taken into account for the alternative is the royalty that was actually being charged prior to the introduction of the new technology, or the royalty that would have been charged after the introduction of the new technology.

Consequently, Siebrasse & Cotter (2017a) suggest that there is, as yet, no satisfactory approach to determining the value of an invention in comparison to a patented alternative.[11]

B) INCREMENTAL VALUE TO DIFFERENT USERS. Epstein et al. (2012) argue that "it is a serious mistake to suppose that there is any such unique number that counts as the incremental value of a patent. Generally, different buyers will derive different benefits from implementing any particular technology," and consequently the incremental value "should not be given any prescriptive weight."[12] They appear to view this as both a conceptual and practical criticism of the incremental value approach. It is misplaced as a conceptual criticism, as the incremental social value of the invention is the aggregate of its incremental value to particular individuals.[13] While the incremental value benchmark faces substantial difficulties in implementation, this is true of any conceptual model. No method of assessing damages is perfect, and whether an explicit application of the incremental value approach is so impractical as to not be worth pursuing depends on the evidence available in the particular case and the feasible alternative methods.[14]

---

[10]   *See* Elhauge 2008, 564–65 (pointing out that Bertrand competition between the patentees implies that the royalty will be zero if both patented alternatives are equally valuable as compared with the unpatented alternative).

[11]   Siebrasse & Cotter 2017a (stating that "[w]e are not aware of any literature providing a thorough theoretical analysis of this problem, and the solution is not evident").

[12]   Epstein et al. 2012, 37.

[13]   Epstein et al. 2012, 37, suggest that in the context of SEPs such an interpretation, which would result in a different royalty to different users, would "violate the RAND policies without cause." Presumably they are referring to the nondiscrimination requirement. It is by no means settled that differing royalties to differently situated implementers would violate the nondiscrimination requirement: *see* Carlton & Shampine 2013, 546 (arguing that "non-discriminatory" means that similarly situated firms should pay the same royalty, where firms are similarly situated only "if ex ante they expect to obtain the same incremental value from the patented technology compared with the next best alternative"); *compare* Gilbert 2011, 875 (arguing that all licensees should be able to choose from the same schedule of royalties, even if they do not pay the same rate). In any event, even if there are good policy reasons why in the SEP context the nondiscrimination requirement should be interpreted as meaning that different implementers should pay the same royalty, the point remains that the value of a patented technology is the aggregate of its incremental value to particular individuals.

[14]   Epstein et al. 2012, 38 say that "[t]he complex institutional framework makes it apparent that no meaningful 'incremental value' calculation can be done." This is overstated. The courts have regularly attempted to assess the value of the invention at issue over the alternatives, and the results, while no doubt imperfect, have certainly been meaningful: *see, e.g., Microsoft Corp. v. Motorola, Inc.*

3 Ex Ante

A) WHY "EX ANTE"?. The fair benchmark royalty should relate to the value of the patented technology. As discussed in more detail below, there are situations in which the amount at stake in negotiations between a patentee armed with an injunction and an implementer[15] is more than just the value of the technology. For example, if the implementer has sunk costs in implementing the technology, the patentee might be able to "hold up" the implementer for some part of those costs that would be lost to the implementer if its use of the technology were enjoined. The incremental value is assessed before the potential for holdup arises – "*ex ante*" – on the view that the return due to holdup is not properly attributable to the invention.[16] The intuition is that the true incremental value of the patented technology over the best alternative is the most that a licensee would pay for license to the patented technology in pre-adoption negotiations, on the view that if the patentee demanded a higher royalty it would be more profitable for the user to adopt an unpatented alternative.[17] As Siebrasse & Cotter (2016) emphasize, the construct of an "ex ante negotiation" is only a mechanism for isolating the value of the patented technology from other value that might be appropriated by a patentee armed with an injunction, such as the implementer's sunk costs.

B) WHEN IS "EX ANTE"?. While there is general agreement that the appropriate benchmark is *ex ante* value, there is inconsistency on the specifics: "*ex ante*" is variously used to mean prior to sunk costs being incurred; prior to a standard being adopted (in the context of SEPs); or prior to first infringement.[18] Since the reason for an *ex ante* assessment is to avoid including holdup value, it follows that the precise meaning of "*ex ante*" turns on the type of holdup one is concerned with. If the concern is sunk costs holdup, then *ex ante* means before the implementer incurs sunk costs. If the concern is that a patentee should not be able to capture value

---

(W.D. Wash. 2013) (U.S.); *In re Innovatio IP Ventures, LLC Patent Litigation* (N.D. Ill. 2013) (U.S.); *Grain Processing Corp. v. Am. Maize-Prods. Co.* (N.D. Ind. 1995, p.1390–93) (U.S.).

[15] While the term "implementer" is often associated with the standards context, where it is used to mean a party implementing a standard, in this chapter I will use it more broadly, as a generic term for any party who might use or implement a patented technology. This includes both infringers and parties who may be infringers, though the action is settled because infringement is determined. It also includes noninfringers, such as licensees and potential licensees, parties who choose not to use the technology at all after failed negotiations.

[16] *See* Lemley & Shapiro 2007a, 1999 (describing the benchmark royalty as "the royalty rate that would be reasonable and expected in the ideal patent system without any element of holdup").

[17] Carlton & Shampine 2013, 540; Lee & Melamed 2016, 392.

[18] The general rule in U.S. law is that a reasonable royalty is assessed on the basis of a hypothetical negotiation taking place at the time of the first infringement; *see* Lee & Melamed 2016, 422–25 (reviewing the cases). However, some courts have said that in the context of SEPs the appropriate time is before the standard is adopted: *see Apple, Inc. v. Motorola, Inc.* (N.D. Ill. 2012, p.913) (U.S.); *In re Innovatio IP Ventures, LLC Patent Litigation* (N.D. Ill. 2013) (U.S.); *Microsoft Corp. v. Motorola, Inc.* (W.D. Wash. 2013) (U.S.). Some scholarship focusing on lock-in suggests the appropriate time is prior to lock-in occurring: *see, e.g.,* Lee & Melamed 2016.

arising from network effects on standardization, then *ex ante* should be taken to mean before a standard is adopted and network effects arise.

c) EX ANTE VS. EX POST INFORMATION. As noted above, it is widely accepted that the value of an invention is the amount that would be negotiated by willing parties *ex ante*. It is often assumed that this *"ex ante"* value must only take into account information actually available to the parties *ex ante*, so that if subsequent information (*"ex post* information") reveals that the invention was more or less valuable than would have been anticipated by the parties, that information should be ignored. Siebrasse & Cotter (2016) refer to this as a "pure" *ex ante* approach. They critique this approach, pointing out that the rationale for the *ex ante* nature of the benchmark royalty is to avoid providing the patentee with a return reflecting holdup, and this does not justify excluding *ex post* information. Building on a point made by Mariniello (2011), they argue that the incremental value of the invention should be determined on a "contingent *ex ante*" basis, under which the implementer is assumed not to have invested any sunk costs, but all available information is used to assess that value, including *ex post* information.[19] Siebrasse & Cotter (2016) argue that using all available information allows a more accurate assessment of the true social value of the invention and therefore more accurately aligns the patent incentive with the social value of the invention.[20]

Lee & Melamed (2016) provide the most sustained scholarly argument in favor of a pure *ex ante* approach, in which all *ex post* evidence is excluded except to the extent that it may be used to establish what the parties would have agreed to based purely on *ex ante* information.[21] They have three main objections to the use of *ex post* information: (1) "the rationale [for using *ex post* evidence] assumes that the actual profits would have been unforeseen entirely at the time of the hypothetical negotiation"; (2) "a royalty determined on the basis of ex post evidence will generally include a premium based on ex post economic developments that increase the infringer's reliance on the patent – in particular, lock-in costs – and that are unrelated to the incremental benefit the patent confers"; and (3) "[b]ecause the rationale is meant to avoid undercompensating the patent holder, often the only ex

[19] Carlton & Shampine 2013, 545 n.40, characterize Mariniello 2011 as disagreeing with the *ex ante* approach, when in fact he only disagree with using only *ex ante* information. That is, Carlton & Shampine implicitly assume that if the negotiation is *ex ante* for purposes of sunk costs, it must necessarily also be *ex ante* for the purposes of information.

[20] *See also* Jarosz & Chapman 2013 (arguing that assessment of reasonable royalty damages should consider all available evidence, including information generated after the date of the hypothetical negotiation); Geradin & Layne-Farrar 2007, 98 (criticizing "any ex ante approach" on the basis that for that matter, "it may hinder innovation in those cases in which the value of an invention is unclear at the moment of standardization." This implicitly assumes that all *ex ante* approaches must use only *ex ante* information); Epstein et al. 2012, 34 (arguing that a measure of damages fixed at the time the standard is adopted will fail to recognize changes in the value of technology over time).

[21] *See also* Gooding 2014.

post information considered is that which tends to increase the royalty rate."[22] The analysis provided by Siebrasse & Cotter (2016) does not turn on point (1). With respect to point (2), Siebrasse & Cotter (2016) agree that value arising from lock-in cost should be excluded, but they argue that this does not require excluding *ex post* information generally. And point (3) is not an argument against the use of *ex post* information as such, as opposed to an argument against the one-sided use of *ex post* information. Siebrasse & Cotter emphasize that the rationale for using *ex post* information is that it allows more accurate assessment of the true value of the invention, whether that true value is higher or lower than would have been anticipated by the parties *ex ante*.

In summary, while it is widely accepted that the value of an invention is the amount that would be negotiated by willing parties *ex ante*, there is relatively little scholarship that distinguishes an *ex ante* negotiation from the use of *ex post* information, and there is no consensus as to whether *ex post* information should be used.

D) FULL EX ANTE APPROACH. One criticism of the standard *ex ante* approach is that the hypothetical negotiation is assumed to take place before the implementer has sunk costs into implementing the invention, but after the patentee has invested sunk costs into inventing the patented technology. Epstein et al. (2012) point out that since the purpose of the patent system is to provide an incentive to invent, it is wrong to assume that the invention has already been invented. Instead, they argue that we should consider what bargain would be arrived at in "a truly 'ex ante' setting – that is, at the outset of a new technology, before either inventors or manufacturers have made the investments necessary to the success of that technology."[23] While Epstein et al. (2012) make this point as a criticism of the standard *ex ante* approach, they do not explain how the "truly" *ex ante* approach would differ from the standard *ex ante* approach. As they point out themselves, *ex ante* licensing in the sense used by the standard approach, after the patentee has invented but before the implementer has sunk costs, is common in practice, and voluntary *ex ante* licensing of this type provides the primary return to the patentee, and so the primary incentive to invent, in many, perhaps most areas of technology.[24] Prima facie, the "true" *ex ante* approach reflects this practical bargain; the patentee sinks costs of invention in return for the right to negotiate a license before the implementer has sunk costs of implementation. The incremental *ex ante* benchmark for reasonable royalty damages simply attempts to replicate this bargain. This implies that the standard *ex ante* model corresponds to the "true" *ex ante* model advocated by Epstein et al.

---

[22] Lee & Melamed 2016, 416.

[23] Epstein et al. 2012, 10 (referring specifically to FTC 2011, the FTC "*ex ante*" model; but the point is equally applicable to Lemley & Shapiro's model; *see also* Layne-Farrar et al. 2014, 29 n.14 (noting that the *ex ante* terminology, though standard, "might be misleading. That period is ex ante for implementers, but it is ex post for patent holders, who have already sunk their R&D investments at that time. A better term would be 'medio amne' or midstream.").

[24] Epstein et al. 2012, 17.

(2012). Of course, it is possible that the voluntary *ex ante* licenses that are in fact the primary source of the incentive to invent do not provide an optimal incentive to invent. If that is the case, it is a problem for the larger patent system to address, perhaps by adjusting the patent term or scope.

7.2.3 *Bargaining Power Discount:* β

1 What is "Bargaining Power"?

"Bargaining power" or "bargaining skill" is a term used in two related but distinct ways.[25] Theoretically, it is used in the context of the solution to the bargaining problem, as initially set out in Nash's famous paper of that name.[26] If two parties with the opportunity to collaborate for mutual benefit are rational, they will engage in an exchange that maximizes the total net benefit to the parties jointly.[27] This net benefit is often referred to as the gains from trade.[28] The bargaining power discount, β, represents the way in which the parties to a negotiation split the gains from trade.[29] So, if the patentee appropriates the entire gains from trade we would say $\beta = 1$, and if the bargaining power is equal the parties will split the gains equally, then $\beta = 0.5$.

Based on this theory, a patent licensing negotiation is often modeled as a bargaining problem in which the gains from trade are the difference between the patentee's minimum willingness to accept and the implementer's maximum willingness to pay (also sometimes referred to as the threat point).[30] In an *ex ante* negotiation over an ironclad patent, the implementer's maximum willingness to pay is normally taken to be the value of the invention, v, as its threat point is to walk away from the negotiation and use the best noninfringing alternative. In assessing a reasonable royalty, the patentee's minimum willingness to accept is normally taken to be its marginal cost.[31]

---

[25]   The term bargaining "skill" is often used to mean what I have been referring to as bargaining "power," as encompassing all residual factors that might affect the split in the gains to trade: Nash 1950 refers only to bargaining "skill," not bargaining "power." Lemley & Shapiro 2007a, use "skill" to refer to the general division of gains from trade, and "negotiating power" or similar terms to refer to specific factors, such as holdup, which affect the negotiated royalty. In my view it is more natural to use "skill" to refer to negotiation skills, as a small cash-constrained patentee might have to settle for a small share of the gains from trade even if its chief negotiator is a very skillful bargainer. However, when factors such as discount rates are modeled explicitly, then it is useful to use "skill" to refer to any residual factors affecting the split.

[26]   Nash 1950.

[27]   *Id.* at 155, 159.

[28]   *See, e.g.,* Lemley & Shapiro 2007a, 1997; Elhauge 2008, 538.

[29]   *See, e.g.,* Lemley & Shapiro 2007a, 1995–98 (citing Nash 1950).

[30]   *See, e.g., id.* at 1997–98.

[31]   Strictly the minimum willingness to accept is equal to the patentee's marginal cost only if it could not exploit the invention itself. If it could exploit the invention, its minimum willingness to accept is its opportunity cost of doing so, but in such a case lost profit damages would normally be appropriate.

In light of this model, bargaining power is also often used to mean that part of the difference between the value of the invention and the patentee's marginal cost that will be captured by the patentee in an actual license negotiation. This practical meaning of bargaining power and the theoretical meaning correspond only if the bargaining model just discussed accurately describes real-world negotiations. In particular, the Nash Bargaining Solution is strictly applicable only to negotiations over pure gains from trade. It is well understood that invention is only the first step toward commercialization, and that an implementer normally must make product specific investments in manufacturing, advertising, and distribution, and so on, in order for a product to be successfully commercialized. A number of authors have suggested that in practice the implementer's share of the profits is, at least in part, a return to the implementer for its contribution to that joint value.[32] If that is correct, then the split in profits negotiated by parties to a real-world agreement does not correspond exactly to the split in gains from trade in the theoretical Nash Bargaining Model.[33]

Returning to the basic theoretical bargaining model, the literature as to what determines bargaining power is thin. Nash's famous paper setting out what is now known as the Nash Bargaining Solution, took equality of bargaining power as a premise, and did not consider any of the factors that might affect it.[34] Formal game theory has added little to the concept to give it more real-world content. The main theoretical refinement is by Rubinstein (1982), who shows that under certain conditions, a party with a higher discount rate (higher time value of money) will have less bargaining power. This supports the informal view that resource constraints

---

[32] *See* Goldscheider et al. 2002, 130 (noting that "typically 75 per cent of the work needed to develop and commercialize a product must be done by the licensee"); Cotter 2009, 1169 (noting that "[i]n a sense, producers of end products are not merely users of the patented invention, but rather might be thought of as sequential innovators"); Lemley & Shapiro 2007b, 2167 (explaining that the value of the innovation is "jointly created" by various parties "including other patent holders and the downstream firm itself"); Siebrasse & Cotter 2016, 954–55 ("In an actual license agreement, both parties bring something to the table in the process of turning an invention into a commercially valuable revenue-generating product. The patentee's most obvious contribution is the invention, but bringing the final product to market will generally require further development and technical implementation, such as clinical trials, as well as marketing, manufacturing, and distribution, all of which require further investment at risk beyond the investment made by the patentee in the invention itself. These further services may be provided by either of the parties, and the way the parties split the incremental profit in an actual negotiation depends on who provides what services and on the relative importance and cost of those services.").

[33] To the extent that the implementer's share of the profits reflects a return to these kinds of transaction-specific investments, this could in principle be reflected in the bargaining model by adjusting the implementer's maximum willingness to pay accordingly. And to the extent that the bargaining power discount in a particular case is determining by looking to what similarly situated parties actually negotiated, any returns to the implementer that are necessary in the real world will automatically be included. The point remains that the familiar theoretical bargaining problem is probably not a complete model of actual patent license negotiations.

[34] Nash 1950, 159. More precisely, Nash assumes (Proposition 8) that similarly situated parties would split the gains from trade equally, and showed that rational parties would arrive at an agreement that maximizes the gains from trade.

affect bargaining power. Many other factors doubtless also affect real-world bargaining power, such as the ability to drive a hard bargain by psychological negotiating tactics (which might be termed bargaining skill), or repeat play and reputation effects.

The Nash Bargaining Solution is applicable only when there is some degree of bilateral monopoly, at least in the sense of the object of exchange having unique value to one of the parties.[35] This means that the market structure is also relevant to bargaining power. For example, a party negotiating with a counterparty in a competitive market will be able to extract the entire surplus by threatening to license to a different counterparty.

On the whole, the elegance and simplicity of the Nash Bargaining Model has made it a very attractive modeling construct, but a richer description of the factors that affect real-world bargaining power would be useful.

2 Justification for Bargaining Power Discount

The main justification provided by Lemley & Shapiro for using $\theta\beta v$ as the benchmark is that it reflects the royalty that would be negotiated by parties if they negotiated *ex ante*, and the return to voluntary market negotiations is theoretically appropriate in the absence of any known market failure.[36] So, as noted immediately above, the implementer's share of the profits may represent in part a return to investments made by the implementer to commercialize the invention. If so, voluntary market negotiations will provide an appropriate return to that investment, as will a benchmark that mimics the market.

As well as looking to the incentive to invent, the royalty also affects implementer incentives. To the extent that the gains from trade represent pure economic rents, then the particular split does not in principle affect the incentive to implement because any positive share provides a greater return to the implementer than does the best alternative.[37] However, to the extent that the implementer's share of the profits is a return to the implementer's technology-specific investments, holdup is inefficient, even if the royalty is less than θv, because the implementer may have to pay more for the patented technology than the value the implementer derives from the technology. When that is the case, the implementer may avoid implementing

---

35 *Id.* at 155 (noting that the article treats "the classical problem of exchange, and, more specifically, of bilateral monopoly").

36 Lemley & Shapiro 2007a, 1999 (stating that the benchmark is intended "to reflect the royalty rate that would be negotiated, prior to any infringement, if the patent were known to be valid"); *see also* Lemley & Shapiro 2007b, 2165; Cotter 2009, 1182 (preferring Lemley and Shapiro's use of the bargaining power discount over Elhauge's approach for this reason).

37 Elhauge 2008, 538, says explicitly that in Lemley & Shapiro's model, β reflects only a split in the joint gains from trade, and not any reward for relative contribution of the parties to the creation of that joint value. However, it is not clear that this is an accurate characterization of Lemley & Shapiro's model in particular, or of models of how parties split the value of the invention more generally.

the technology, even though the technology itself would have a net social benefit.[38] It is the avoidance of efficient investments by implementers that is the real downside of holdup.[39]

3 Criticism of Bargaining Power Discount

A) OPTIMAL RETURN TO PATENTEE. Elhauge (2008) argues that the bargaining power discount is inappropriate in principle.[40] His basic argument is that if the return to the patentee is less than the full social value of the invention there will be socially valuable inventions that the patentee will not have an incentive to invent.[41] The bargaining power discount, β, arbitrarily depresses the return to the patentee. Elhauge therefore takes θv to be the benchmark return.[42] Consequently, he argues that the risk of holdup is much less than is suggested by Lemley & Shapiro.

The main objection to Elhauge's analysis is that it is doubtful that full appropriability of the social value of the invention is the appropriate benchmark. As just discussed, the main justification for the bargaining power discount provided by Lemley & Shapiro is that it mimics the market. If parties to a voluntary transaction would include such a discount, then prima facie that is efficient.

Elhauge's implicit response is that there is market failure, because the bargaining discount, even if voluntarily negotiated, provides an inadequate incentive to invent. As noted, the thrust of his argument is that if the patentee cannot capture the full social value of the invention, there will be inventions that would be socially beneficial for which inventors will not have an adequate incentive to invent.[43] However, the dominant view is that full appropriability is probably not optimal and certainly it is not so clearly optimal as to justify a departure from the prima facie benchmark of a voluntary market transaction.[44]

---

[38] If the implementer knows with certainty that it will have to pay more than the value it can extract from the invention, it will avoid implementing the invention entirely. More generally, the potential for of holdup makes the investment riskier and inefficiently depresses the degree of investment.

[39] Lemley & Shapiro 2007b, 2164 (explaining that "holdup is recognized as a form of market failure that leads to inefficiency, primarily by discouraging what would otherwise be socially desirable investments").

[40] *See also* Denicolò et al. 2008, 577 n.27 (saying that they consider it "more natural to assume that the negotiating parties would agree on a license fee of v, remunerating the patent holder fully for the value its innovation contributes to the product," but they do not explain exactly why they consider this more natural, and in any event their analysis uses the β discount).

[41] Elhauge 2008, 541.

[42] *Id.* at 545.

[43] *Id.* at 543 (arguing that the Lemley-Shapiro model is wrong to ignore this); *see also* Shavell & van Ypersele 2001, 535 (suggesting that full appropriability of the social value of the invention by the patentee is the appropriate baseline).

[44] *See, e.g.,* Frischmann & Lemley 2007, 268–71; Golden 2010, 529–31; Scotchmer 1991, 31; Shapiro 2007, 114–77. *See also* Sichelman 2014 (arguing that traditional remedies may either over- or undercompensate patentees as compared to the socially optimal return, depending on the circumstances).

Elhauge's arguments for full appropriability are not sufficiently persuasive to displace the dominant view. It is true that on the one hand the problem of imperfect appropriability tends to result in too little investment in invention. But on the other hand, the so-called patent race problem tends to lead to excessive research. The patent race arises when multiple parties try to capture the winner-take-all prize of a patent. The marginal social benefit of additional research is the benefit of an earlier invention date, but the marginal private benefit is the increased chance of capturing the entire value of the patented technology, not just the marginal benefit of an earlier patent date. This divergence between social and private benefit tends to lead to wastefully duplicative research by firms competing for the patent prize, or excessively rapid invention, or both.

These two problems tend in different directions, and, in a leading article, Dasgupta & Stiglitz (1980) conclude that "there is no clear presumption whether … there will be excessive or inadequate research" when the patentee is able to capture the full appropriable surplus.[45] While Elhauge acknowledges this literature, he cites Dasgupta & Stiglitz (1980) for the proposition that an optimal patent term can be set to provide optimal incentives to invent and, "for *small inventions the market always provides inadequate research*."[46] However, that statement was made by Dasgupta & Stiglitz (1980) "within the confines of our simple model," and "for particular parameterizations," which includes in particular patents with an infinite life.[47] They do not suggest that this conclusion is generalizable.

Elhauge (2008) also quotes Dasgupta & Stiglitz (1980) as saying "where, with an infinite-lived patent, there is excessive expenditure on R&D, there is an optimal patent life."[48] He argues "if we assume, as makes sense to isolate the remedial issues at hand, that substantive patent law on issues such as patent length has been optimally set, then this literature supports awarding patent holders the full θv rather than discounting that amount by β."[49] However, the point being made by Dasgupta & Stiglitz is that the patent race problem is driven by the appropriable value of the invention, which increases with the patent term, which means that the patent race problem is at its worst if the term of the patent is infinite. If the patent race problem dominates the problem of an inadequate incentive to invent due to uncaptured social surplus, the patent race problem can be mitigated by reducing the patent term until an optimal balance is achieved. The rest of Dasgupta & Stiglitz's sentence – not

---

[45] Dasgupta & Stiglitz 1980, 21 (with an infinite-lived patent in markets with free entry into R&D); *see also* Tandon 1983, 156–57 (patent races might result in underinvestment or overinvestment in research).

[46] Dasgupta & Stiglitz 1980, 19 (their emphasis), quoted by Elhauge 2008, 544.

[47] Dasgupta & Stiglitz 1980, 1819. In particular, they assume constant elasticity demand curves, with elasticity less than unity, and an infinite life of a patent. *Id.* at 19. Shapiro 2007 also provides two simple models in which full appropriability is optimal, and again the restrictive requirement of these models illustrate the limits of full appropriability as a benchmark

[48] Dasgupta & Stiglitz 1980, 21, quoted by Elhauge 2008, 544.

[49] Elhauge 2008, 544.

quoted by Elhauge – concludes that "the optimal life of the patent will, however, vary depending on the size of invention and the elasticity of demand in the industry," and they conclude that "there is no simple intervention into the market allocation – no uniform rule applicable for all inventions and industries – which will attain the social optimum."[50] Since we know that the patent term does not, in fact, vary with those parameters, the proper conclusion from Dasgupta & Stiglitz is that we know that the patent term is not optimal, which implies that full appropriability is generally not optimal.

Elhauge (2008) also argues that θv understates the social value of the invention because v does not include social value arising after the patent term expires.[51] However, the patent reward should reflect the value of the inventor's contribution, which is only the earlier date of invention as compared with when the invention would have arisen even without the lure of a patent, as a result of general technological progress. If the patent term is set optimally the consumer surplus after expiry of the patent will not reflect any of the inventor's contribution, because the invention would have arisen anyway. While there is no particular reason to believe that the patent term is optimal, either on average or in any particular industry, neither do we know whether it is generally too long or too short.

In summary, the simple fact that the patentee cannot capture the full social value of the invention does not in itself allow us to conclude that the benchmark return proposed by Lemley & Shapiro, including the bargaining power discount, provides an inadequate incentive to invent.

B) CIRCULARITY. On a related point, Golden (2007) argues that Lemley & Shapiro's argument for the $\theta \beta v$ benchmark is "fundamentally circular," because their justification that it represents "the royalty rate that would be reasonable and expected in the ideal patent system without any element of holdup" assumes that a patent holder "should obtain no more than it would receive if an injunction were unavailable."[52] However, this is not really a circularity problem, because Lemley & Shapiro's main point is that the appropriate benchmark reflects the royalty rate that would be negotiated in the absence of market failure, and injunctive relief, in some circumstances, can give rise to holdup, which is a well-known source of market failure.[53] The benchmark is therefore not simply the assumption that injunctions are unavailable, but rather that they do not give rise to holdup. Indeed, their benchmark implicitly assumes that when parties negotiate *ex ante*, they negotiate with the understanding that if they cannot agree, an injunction will be granted to restrain

---

[50] Dasgupta & Stiglitz 1980, 21.

[51] Elhauge 2008, 543 (arguing that the Lemley-Shapiro model is wrong to ignore this); *see also* Golden 2007, 2138 (noting that the limited patent term means that the patentee cannot capture the full social value of the invention).

[52] Golden 2007, 2139–40, quoting Lemley & Shapiro 2007a, 1999.

[53] *See* Lemley & Shapiro 2007a, 1999 (stating that the benchmark is intended "to reflect the royalty rate that would be negotiated, prior to any infringement, if the patent were known to be valid").

the user from infringing; it is that assumption that sets the user's maximum willingness to pay at the incremental value of the invention over the best alternative.

With that said, while Golden frames the issue as being a problem of circularity, his key point is that Lemley & Shapiro do not adequately recognize the benefits of injunctive relief that might justify its use despite giving rise to holdup.[54] Certainly Golden is right to say that the mere fact that injunctive relief might, or even certainly would, give rise to holdup in a particular case, is not a sufficient justification for denying injunctive relief without consideration of its countervailing benefits.

c) INDEPENDENT CREATION. Lemley & Shapiro (2007b) respond to the argument that patentees are under-rewarded because they cannot capture the social value of the invention after the term expires by saying "this argument is plainly incorrect in the central case where the infringing party independently develops the patented invention, which is common in holdup situations. In those situations, the patent holder's reward typically exceeds its social contribution, the finite patent lifetime notwithstanding."[55] This is a curious response. On its face, the main result from Lemley & Shapiro (2007a) is that, because of holdup, the patent holder's reward typically exceeds its social contribution, even when the invention *was* copied by the infringer. To say that, if the infringing party independently developed the invention, the patentee's reward will exceed its social contribution even when there is no holdup at all is an entirely different argument. Lemley & Shapiro (2007a) do say that "[a]n additional prerequisite for denying an injunction should be that the defendant developed the technology independently rather than copying it from the plaintiff,"[56] but that explicitly turns on what they see as countervailing considerations, and not on the view that there is no holdup if the infringer copied.

If the implementer independently developed the technology covered by the patent, the social value of the patentee's contribution will certainly be less than v, the value of the invention as compared with the best alternative. The discounts for validity and bargaining power are irrelevant to the true value of the patentee's contribution, so that value may well be less than $\theta\beta v$.[57] This may be taken to suggest that in cases of independent creation the benchmark royalty should be discounted by some entirely different factor to reflect the patentee's true contribution. However, this observation really supports the view that an independent invention defense should be introduced into patent law, as the patentee's contribution to the infringer's

---

[54] Golden 2007, 2140 ("A more satisfactory analysis would at least acknowledge long-recognized benefits of injunctions against infringement and would engage in some substantial analysis of whether their costs nonetheless outweigh their benefits.").

[55] Lemley & Shapiro 2007b, 2169. They attribute this argument to Golden 2007, 2136, though its main point is that the optimal reward to the patentee is indeterminate, not that the patentee is under-rewarded. In any event, Elhauge 2008 does make that argument, and the more significant point here is Lemley & Shapiro's response.

[56] Lemley & Shapiro 2007a, 2036–37.

[57] Shapiro 2007, 115–17; Shapiro 2010, 304.

product is always zero if the infringer develops the technology independently.[58] An independent invention defense would effectively "discount" the royalty – to zero – on a case-by-case basis, and this is more sensible than applying a general discount to all royalties to reflect the general percentage of cases in which the infringer did not copy. While introducing an independent invention defense has considerable theoretical appeal, it is of course not part of patent law. There have been a number of suggestions that an independent invention defense should be introduced into patent law, but the debate is not yet sufficiently developed to decide whether the absence of an independent invention defense is a defect of patent law that should be rectified as a matter of policy, or whether there is some good counterargument against an independent invention defense. Consequently, this is a situation in which we should assume for remedial purposes that substantive patent law is optimal; either it is in fact optimal, or the best solution is to amend substantive patent law. With that said, there is a separate question, as to whether independent invention should be a factor in determining whether injunctive relief is granted. That is different from the question of an independent invention defense, because even if injunctive relief is denied, the patentee would still be entitled to a reasonable royalty in the amount of the benchmark; however, that benchmark will not be adjusted to reflect independent creation.

d) ASYMMETRIC INFORMATION. Golden (2007) suggests that a patent holder will likely approach negotiations at a significant informational disadvantage that may "appear to tilt the likely result of negotiations toward an outcome corresponding to a low value for [β]."[59] However, it is not clear that information asymmetries will systematically favor the infringer.[60] And even if information asymmetries do favor the infringer, it is not clear that this will tilt the result to a lower share of value for the patentee. The patentee's ignorance might cause it to ask for too much, rather than too little, and the main effect of information asymmetry may be only to reduce the chance of settlement and increase litigation rates.[61]

---

[58] See Shapiro 2007, 127–35 (arguing for an independent invention defense for this reason).

[59] Golden 2007, 2132–33; *see also* Elhauge 2008, 549–50.

[60] Golden 2007, 2132 notes that the implementer will have better information about its costs and profit margin, but the patentee will likely have better information about its patent's validity, Lemley & Shapiro 2007b, 2170, and the patentee will likely have better information about previous licenses it has granted that are likely to affect the royalty awarded in litigation. The patentee will also have superior information if it is entitled to lost profit damages. Further, as Lemley & Shapiro 2007b, 2170 point out, and Golden 2007, 2130 acknowledges, any information asymmetry will be reduced by discovery, at least in the U.S. litigation system.

[61] Lemley & Shapiro 2007b, 2170. Elhauge 2008, 550 responds that the implementer "will accept when the patent holder demands too little ... but won't accept when the patent holder demands too much," and therefore "the actual negotiated royalties will be lower than they predict." This is a variant on the "Option Effect" argument, discussed below, Section 7.5.4.2.b "Option Effect." Even if the option effect does depress the patentee's return (on the assumption that there is a systematic information asymmetry favoring the implementer), this does not affect the point that the problem is difficult to solve by changing legal rules related to remedies.

4 θ: Patent Strength

The benchmark fair royalty rate requires the value of the patented technology to be discounted by the strength of the patent, which is to say, the probability that it is valid and infringed. Otherwise, the implementer will be paying for a technology that it did not use, or for which no patent should have been granted. In U.S. law, a reasonable royalty is in principle awarded on the assumption that the patent was known to be valid and infringed – that is, without any discount for patent strength, since damages are only awarded if the patent has been held to be valid and infringed. This is not inconsistent with the principle that a fair royalty requires a discount for patent strength; on the contrary, it is necessary to avoid double discounting.[62] While these principles are not controversial, the extent to which the courts appropriately apply or ignore the patent strength discount is another question. The most complete analysis of that issue is Masur (2015), who characterizes existing U.S. law on this point as "both incoherent and backwards."[63]

7.3 HOLDUP

7.3.1 *Varieties of Holdup*

Despite the centrality of the concept of "holdup," it does not have any precise definition – or rather, it has a variety of precise definitions. In the broadest sense, holdup is used to mean any mechanism by which a patentee can extract a royalty that is higher than a fair benchmark royalty. In a slightly narrower sense holdup is used to mean any mechanism by which the royalty that might be demanded by a patentee *ex post* is higher than that which might be demanded *ex ante*, where *ex ante* is defined variously as the time at which infringement began, or sunk costs were

---

[62] Suppose that the parties would agree to a $1 million royalty *ex ante* if they knew the patent to be valid and infringed, but they each believe there is only a 70 percent probability of validity. The license they would actually negotiate would be appropriately discounted, to $700,000. If there is infringement and the patentee files suit, the patentee knows that it only has a 70 percent chance of obtaining a favorable judgment. If the amount of a favorable judgment is the actual $700,000 the parties would have negotiated, the patentee's expected pay-off from going to trial is only $490,000 (70 percent of $700,000), which means that the patentee will be worse off as a result of the infringement than if the infringer had licensed. The assumption of validity and infringement corrects for this problem by awarding the patentee $1 million if she prevails, so that her expectation pretrial is $700,000, exactly the amount she would have agreed to *ex ante*: for further discussion, *see* Cotter 2009, 1183; Taylor 2014, 115–16.

[63] Masur 2015, 127 (arguing that it is generally very difficult to apply an appropriate adjustment for patent strength because estimates of patent strength are private information not normally available to the courts, and further that licenses that are negotiated as litigation settlements in circumstances where the infringer was losing at trial are the best gauge of patent value, and yet such licenses are system-atically excluded).

incurred by the implementer, or, in the SEP context, as the time at which the standard was adopted.[64]

Focusing on the *ex ante/ex post* version of holdup, Siebrasse & Cotter (2017a) note that there are three different mechanisms by which *ex post* royalties may be higher than *ex ante* royalties. They refer to these as (1) sunk costs holdup, (2) network value appropriation, and (3) the apportionment problem. These are discussed subsequently in this section. Lemley & Shapiro (2007a) provide a very influential model of holdup, which extends the holdup analysis to probabilistic patents. All of these mechanisms are said to be a potential source of excess returns to the patentee. High litigation costs are also said to be another potential source of holdup. However, the effect of the distortion due to litigation costs is ambiguous, as is discussed in Section 6 "Holdout/Reverse Holdup."

1 Sunk Costs Holdup

Farrell et al. (2007) describe "opportunism" or "holdup" as follows: Holdup can arise, in particular, when one party makes investments specific to a relationship before all the terms and conditions of the relationship are agreed upon.[65]

They provide the following example of holdup in a case where the patented technology costs $40 to implement, exclusive of any royalty, and the best alternative technology costs $50, so that the inherent advantage of the patented technology is $10, and a benchmark reasonable royalty is any amount less than this:

> [S]uppose that, of the $40 cost of using the patented technology, $25 was spent before the royalty was negotiated and that this $25 is specific to the patented technology, i.e., would be wasted if the user later decided against adopting that technology. Then, at the time of negotiations, the forward-looking cost of using the patented technology (exclusive of royalty) is $40 – $25 = $15, while the cost of using the unpatented technology remains $50 (the $25 already spent has no value if the user adopts the alternative technology) ... [T]he maximum royalty that the user is willing to pay remains the added value of the patented technology, but with the key difference that this amount is now $50 – $15 = $35, or $25 more than in our first calculation. Ex post negotiation increases the user's willingness to pay for the patented technology because the user finds the alternative relatively less attractive after spending $25 on the patented technology. The patented technology's ex post advantage ... exceeds its inherent advantage ... by an amount equal to the user's $25 investment ... The patent holder thus captures a share (proportional to its bargaining skill) of sunk investments by the user.[66]

---

[64] These concepts may be related, because one definition of a benchmark fair royalty is the royalty that would have been negotiated *ex ante*.

[65] Farrell et al. 2007, 604.

[66] *Id.* at 612–13.

That is, the fact that the user has made transaction-specific investments prior to negotiating for the right to use the technology means that the patentee can capture part of the user's sunk costs, in addition to the inherent advantage of the patented technology. (This analysis implicitly assumes that the successful patentee will be granted an injunction.) It is convenient to refer to holdup arising from such transaction-specific investments as "sunk costs holdup" where the transaction specificity is left implicit.[67]

Sunk costs holdup relies centrally on the transaction-specific investment being sunk before any negotiations take place. It does not turn on the product being complex, as it can arise when only one patent covers the product. Nor does it turn on the probabilistic nature of the patent, or on the cost of litigation – in the above example, litigation costs are assumed to be zero.

If sunk costs holdup does occur, it has adverse effects on both patentee and implementer behavior. It allows the patentee to capture more than the value of the invention, thus creating an excessive incentive to invest in patented technologies; and the prospect of being held up increases the *ex ante* risk to the implementer, thus reducing the attractiveness of investments in products that are potentially subject to sunk costs holdup.

2 Network Effect Appropriation

Another type of holdup, applicable primarily in the context of standards, is referred to by Siebrasse & Cotter (2017a) as network effect appropriation, which they define as follows:

> [N]etwork value appropriation, arises whenever the value of a particular technology increases upon standardization due to the presence of network effects. As with sunk costs holdup, an injunction would enable the patentee to extract a higher royalty ex post than it could have negotiated ex ante, and thus again might be described as resulting in the capture of some of the value of the standard – though in this context, the increase in value is due to network effects and does not depend on the presence of transaction-specific sunk costs.[68]

---

[67] The general analysis of this type of opportunism, which arises whenever a transaction is subject to "durable investments in transaction specific human or physical assets" is associated with Williamson 1985, 61. It is not specific to patent law, or even intellectual property; Williamson originally discussed it in the context of contracts. Williamson famously defined "opportunism" as "self-interest seeking with guile," *id.* at 47, and he emphasized the investment of sunk costs (which he referred to as "the fundamental transformation," *id.* at 61) as giving rise to the possibility of opportunism. However, as Farrell et al. 2007, 604, point out, "[t]he pure economics are largely unaffected by whether or not guile is involved . . . ." While guile is involved in some cases of sunk costs holdup, for example in case of so-called patent ambush, many holdup scenarios of central concern to authors such as Lemley & Shapiro 2007a, Farrell et al. 2007, and Lee & Melamed 2016, do not turn on any deceitful behavior by the patentee.

[68] Siebrasse & Cotter 2017a, 1166.

U.S. courts have consistently held that a reasonable royalty should not reflect "any value added by the standardization of that technology."[69] On its face this appears to say that a patentee should not be able to capture any value arising from network effects, though as Siebrasse & Cotter (2017a) point out, courts routinely award damages, including ongoing royalties in lieu of an injunction, in the form of running royalties, which do allow the patentee to capture value arising from network effects.[70]

From a policy perspective, Siebrasse & Cotter (2017a) argue that allowing the patentee to capture some part of the value of a patented technology that arises due to network effects is desirable from a dynamic efficiency perspective, because it provides the correct incentive to invent, and it is not undesirable from a static efficiency perspective, as it has no adverse effects on implementer incentives.[71] While there are many articles arguing that a patentee should not be able to extract a higher royalty *ex post* than it could have obtained *ex ante*, which suggests that the patentee should not be able to capture any value arising from network effects, such articles typically do not distinguish between sunk costs and value arising from network effects. The two often go hand in hand, because adopting a standard and the consequent network effects, is often accompanied by substantial sunk costs. Two exceptions are Swanson & Baumol (2005) and Lee & Melamed (2016), which both specifically assert that the patentee should not be able to capture value arising from network effects. However, both treat network effect appropriation equivalently to sunk costs holdup, and they do not offer independent policy justification for not allowing the patentee to capture any of the value arising from network effects.[72] Chao (2016) also takes issue with Siebrasse & Cotter (2017a) on this point, but his discussion turns on what Siebrasse & Cotter (2017a) characterize as the distinct problem of apportionment, which is discussed in the next section.[73]

---

[69] See *Ericsson, Inc.* v. *D-Link Sys.* (Fed. Cir. 2014, p.1232) (U.S.); *see also CSIRO* v. *Cisco Sys., Inc.* (Fed. Cir. 2015, p.1304) (U.S.).

[70] Siebrasse & Cotter 2017a, 1220. They also note that there is some ambiguity in these statements, as the courts do not clearly distinguish value arising from network effects from sunk costs or problems of appropriation.

[71] *See also* Geradin & Layne-Farrar 2007, 93 (suggesting that it is not clear why the essential patent holder should not capture part of the value arising on standardization).

[72] Swanson & Baumol 2005, 8–10; Lee & Melamed 2016, 429–30.

[73] Chao 2016, 304 (stating that a patentee should not be able to capture any part of what he calls "ex ante compatibility value"). While Chao states that he disagrees with Siebrasse & Cotter 2017a on this point, the example he gives to illustrate this point is of a patented technology that does not make the standard any better as compared with existing alternatives. Chao does not specify whether the alternatives were unpatented. In a case in which the patented technology included in the standard was no better than an unpatented alternative, this would be an example of what Siebrasse & Cotter 2017a describe as the problem of apportionment, and in their analysis such a patent would receive a royalty of zero.

3 The Apportionment Problem

Another type of holdup may arise when a patent claims a relatively minor feature of a complex product. If the patentee can get an injunction that prevents sale of the entire product, it can extract part of the value of the entire product, even though the patented technology contributes little to that value. This point is explored at length by Lemley & Shapiro's model, which is addressed next.

The apportionment problem, when it exists, has the same adverse incentive effects on patentee and implementer incentives as does sunk costs holdup. It allows the patentee to capture more than the value of the invention, creating an excessive incentive to invest in minor patented technologies. The prospect of being held up in this manner increases the *ex ante* risk to the implementer, thus reducing the attractiveness of investments in products that are potentially subject to the apportionment problem.

The apportionment problem is exacerbated in the context of a standard. As discussed in more detail below, the excessive royalty that can be extracted by a patentee armed with an injunction is generally capped by the losses that would be suffered while the technology is designed around. This implies that if the technology can quickly and easily be removed or designed around, then the royalty overcharge will be small. However, this is not true in the SEP context because licensing terms of SEPs almost always specify that the SEPs are only licensed for use in the products that comply with the standard.[74] That means that if the technology covered by a SEP could easily be designed around or removed as a technical matter, the product would no longer be compliant with the standard and the other licenses to the truly important SEPs would lapse. This would allow the owner of the unimportant SEP to capture the value of the standard as a whole.[75] It is not enough to design around a SEP technically; instead, the implementer would have to be able to lobby the standards organization to remove the technology in question from the standard. While not necessarily impossible, this will certainly be a very lengthy process.[76] In such a case, the "redesign period" referred to in the discussion below

---

[74] *See* American Bar Association (ABA) 2007, 60–61 .

[75] Alternatively, the design-around costs would include the cost of lobbying the relevant standard development organization to adopt a new version of the standard that excluded the controversial technology, and the lost profits during that period. If the licenses for the other SEPs do not contain such a term, the problem might still arise if it was necessary for marketing purposes to advertise that the product was compliant with the standard. In other cases, the holdup effect would relate primarily to the lost profits during the period of redesign, as identified by Lemley & Shapiro 2007a.

[76] Consider, for example, the interlaced video SEPs at issue in *Microsoft Corp. v. Motorola, Inc.* (W.D. Wash. 2013) (U.S.). On the evidence, these added little to the value of the standard, and presumably it would have been relatively simple to remove support from interlaced video from Microsoft's products, since it involved disabling a feature rather than adding one, but doing so would have rendered Microsoft's products noncompliant with the standard. Support for interlaced video was eventually removed from the standard.

should be interpreted to mean the time needed to get the SEP removed from the standard, rather than the time needed for a technical redesign.

4 Probabilistic Holdup: Lemley & Shapiro Model

Lemley & Shapiro (2007a) and Shapiro (2010) provide a widely discussed model of holdup.[77] Their model incorporates both sunk costs holdup and the apportionment problem, and additionally addresses the effect of the probabilistic nature of patents; that is, the fact that the validity and scope of granted patents is uncertain until they are litigated.[78] Their model extends the simple sunk costs holdup model in two other respects. First, in the simple sunk costs model the implementer's option is to license or redesign its product to avoid using the patented technology; Lemley & Shapiro develop a more explicit model of the litigation process in which the implementer may choose to redesign either during the litigation period, or after the end of litigation. Second, in the simple model, the implementer is at risk of being held up for transaction-specific sunk costs that are generally conceptualized as being machinery or other tangible goods. Lemley & Shapiro point out that the implementer is also at risk of being held up for lost profits during the period that its product is being redesigned to avoid infringement. Lemley & Shapiro also focus on redesign costs (sometimes referred to as switching costs), rather than sunk costs. (The relationship between switching costs and sunk costs is discussed below.)

They consider two scenarios: a "surprise" scenario in which the implementer is already selling its product when it learns of the patent, and an "early negotiation" scenario in which negotiations take place before the product is designed.[79] For "ironclad" patents – those that are certainly valid – their model is a variant on the standard sunk costs model of holdup; there is no overcharge when *ex ante* negotiations are possible, and in the *ex post* scenario the patentee extracts part of the costs of switching to a noninfringing alternative.

When considering probabilistic patents, Lemley & Shapiro further distinguish between two scenarios. If the patent is relatively weak, it will make more sense for the implementer to refrain from redesigning until after it has lost in litigation, in which case its threat point is determined by the sunk costs plus the lost profits on the entire product during the period of redesign. This is the "Litigate" scenario. On the other hand, if the patent is relatively strong, the implementer's best negotiating strategy is to threaten to redesign its product during litigation ("Redesign and Litigate"), in which case its threat point is determined by the redesign costs. This means that a weak patent will have a higher relative overcharge because it can extract not just redesign costs, but also lost profits on the entire product during the period of

---

[77] Lemley & Shapiro 2007a, 1995 n.7 (noting that their technical economic analysis is based on a working draft of Shapiro 2010).

[78] Regarding probabilistic patents, *see generally* Lemley & Shapiro 2005.

[79] These terms are taken from Shapiro 2010.

redesign. The overcharge is discounted by the probability of validity, so the absolute overcharge for a weak patent will normally be smaller than for a strong patent covering the same technology.

Lemley & Shapiro show that the probabilistic nature of patents can result in an overcharge even when *ex ante* negotiations are possible. This is because the implementer's threat is to avoid using the patented technology entirely, and adopt the best noninfringing alternative instead. This is appropriate for an ironclad patent because it allows the patentee to obtain part of the true value of the invention. The problem is that the implementer's threat is exactly the same, and so the outcome of the negotiation is exactly the same, even if the patent is potentially invalid. This implies an overcharge, because the royalty should be discounted by the probability of invalidity. The problem, as they put it, is that "the accused infringer has chosen to give up without a fight, effectively agreeing to treat a possibly invalid patent as certainly valid, and so the chance that it would have invalidated the patent will not be reflected in the negotiated royalty."[80] (Because the overcharge can be extracted even when an *ex ante* negotiation takes place, it is perhaps not strictly correct to refer to it as "holdup," which normally implies that a higher royalty can be extracted *ex post*, than could have been negotiated *ex ante*.)

To summarize their results:

Scenario 1 – Surprise – "Litigate" strategy
- Applicable when patent is weak, redesign costs are high.
- Overcharge because patentee can extract lost profits on the entire product during redesign, plus redesign costs, both discounted by probability of validity. Because of the discount the absolute value of the overcharge will be small, but because of the lost profits on the entire product, the percentage overcharge will be large.
- Overcharge increases with (a) redesign costs; (b) lost profits during redesign period; and (c) value of the product relative to the value of the invention.

Scenario 2 – Surprise – "Litigate & Redesign" strategy
- Applicable when patent is strong, redesign costs are low.
- Overcharge because P can extract redesign costs, <u>not</u> discounted.
- Percentage overcharge (a) increases with redesign costs, and (b) decreases with probability of validity (i.e., is greater for weak patents).

Scenario 3 – Early Negotiation
- Either just like surprise case,
  or
- Overcharge because implementer's threat is not to use the invention with certainty, in which case percentage overcharge decreases with the probability of validity.

---

[80] Lemley & Shapiro 2007a, 2005.

Their results do not turn directly on the complex nature of the product, but complex products are likely to be subject to a greater overcharge because they are likely to face Scenario 1, in which a weak patent with relatively little value to the product can nonetheless extract a portion of the value of the entire product.

The adverse economic effects of holdup in Lemley & Shapiro's model in the surprise scenario are the same as for sunk costs holdup (though the mechanism is somewhat different). The economic effects of probabilistic holdup in the early negotiation scenario are slightly different. Again, the patentee is capturing more than the value of its contribution, which creates an excessive incentive to invest in patenting. But in principle the overcharge will not increase the risk to the implementer, because it knows how much it has to pay *ex ante*. Nor will it cause the implementer to avoid using the patented technology, because the patentee will not charge so much that the implementer would prefer to use the alternative. It will in principle reduce the implementer's expected profit, thus creating a distortion in the direction of investments. The degree of the distortion will presumably depend on the market structure.

While this model is well-known and influential for its implications respecting injunctive relief, within the context of remedies, and particularly the withholding of injunctive relief, another implication is that additional effort should be devoted to weeding out weak patents before they are licensed or litigated.[81]

5 Sunk Costs, Switching Costs, and Lock-in

Holdup is sometimes described as involving switching cost, on the view that once one technology is selected, it may be that the cost of switching to the alternative technology is prohibitively expensive.[82] This characterization is used most often in the standards context, where the implementer is said to be "locked in" to the standard once it is chosen, but similar reliance on switching costs as giving rise to holdup is also found in other contexts.[83] This contrasts with the traditional focus of the general economic holdup literature on sunk costs, in which holdup occurs when a party tries to charge a higher price than it would have been able to before those sunk costs were incurred. The puzzle is that sunk costs were necessarily incurred in the past – a party cannot be held up for costs that it has not yet incurred – while "switching costs" on the other hand, imply costs that would take place in the future, after failed negotiations, to switch to an alternative, nonstandard technology.

Cotter et al. (2018) provide a general framework for reconciling concepts of switching costs and sunk costs. They explain that the threat of adopting the next best alternative always disciplines the royalty that can be extracted by the

---

[81] Shapiro 2010, 307.
[82] *See, e.g.,* Gilbert 2011, 862; DOJ & FTC 2007, 35; FTC 2011, 5.
[83] *See, e.g.,* Lemley & Shapiro 2007a, 2037.

patentee, but the value of both the patented technology and the alternative may change. After costs are sunk, the selected technology is more profitable going forward, because the costs of implementation have already been incurred. So sunk costs holdup can be thought of as representing holdup due to the differential profitability of the selected technology *ex ante* versus *ex post*. The differential profitability of the alternative technology represents a separate source of holdup. If the profitability of the alternative technology changes, either because its costs change, or because its revenues change – as when it is not selected to be the standard – the disciplining value of the user's threat to switch also changes. Switching costs as such, in the sense of the forward-looking cost of implementing the alternative technology, are irrelevant to holdup. If the cost of implementing the alternative technology is the same *ex ante* or *ex post*, any amount that could be extracted by the patentee *ex post*, because the implementer wants to avoid incurring those costs, could also have been extracted *ex ante*. Implementers become "locked in" to a standard, not because of the costs of switching, but because the expected revenue from the alternative technology will have been reduced once the original technology was adopted as part of the standard.

This has practical implications. Lemley & Shapiro (2007a) recommend that "the court should evaluate the cost that the infringing firm would have to incur to redesign its product to avoid infringing the patent. If this cost is high relative to the value that the patented technology has added to the infringing firm's product, no permanent injunction should be issued."[84] But as Denicolò et al. (2008) point out, the relevant comparison is not the cost of redesign, but the additional cost of adopting the alternative technology *ex post* as compared with *ex ante*. Looking only to the cost of redesign risks penalizing "the most valuable patents – precisely, those that are most difficult to circumvent even with full knowledge of the patent."[85] They note that instead "the policy should indicate that to avoid injunctive relief an infringer must show not only that it is costly to redesign the product in a non-infringing way ex post, but also that it could easily have designed the product in a non-infringing way ex ante if only it had been aware of [the patent holder's] patent (which again emphasizes the importance of the inadvertent infringement assumption)."[86] The point made by Denicolò et al. (2008) is consistent with the analysis provided by Cotter et al. (2018); it is not the cost of switching to the alternative that is important, but whether the cost of switching has changed.[87]

---

[84] Lemley & Shapiro 2007a, 2037.
[85] Denicolò et al. 2008, 596.
[86] *Id.*
[87] It should be emphasized that this analysis of the source of the differential between *ex ante* and *ex post* royalties does not imply that all of that difference constitutes undesirable "holdup." Their analysis helps identify the specific source of the differential; whether allowing the patentee to capture part of that differential is undesirable is a separate question.

6 Caveats and Critiques

A) OVERVIEW. A number of theoretical critiques of the holdup model are discussed in the remainder of this section. While most of these points were directed at Lemley & Shapiro's model in particular, several are applicable to sunk costs holdup and the apportionment problem generally, as their model is in some respects simply the best known elaboration of these general problems. There is another general critique of the holdup argument, to the effect that even though holdup might be a problem in theory, there are a number of countervailing mechanisms, such as the potential for *ex ante* bargaining, that mean it is not a substantial problem in practice. These arguments are discussed subsequently in Section 4 "Mitigating Mechanisms." The empirical evidence is reviewed in Section 8 "Empirical Evidence."

B) LITIGATION COSTS AND WEAK PATENTS. Golden (2007) argues that "for a weak infringement case for which θ is sufficiently near 0, litigation costs can again be expected to dominate the potential infringer's concerns."[88] The intuition is that the implementer's exposure due to holdup is discounted by probability of validity, while litigation costs, under the U.S. rule (each party bears its own costs), are not. Therefore, for weak patents litigation costs will dominate (so long as litigation costs are roughly independent of the strength of the patent).[89] Recall that in Lemley & Shapiro's analysis, the overcharge factor – the overcharge as a percentage of the benchmark royalty – is very high for weak patents, but the absolute amount of the overcharge may be relatively small, because the overcharge due to holdup is discounted by the probability of validity, and so is small for a weak patent. One response to this might be that litigation costs drop out of Lemley & Shapiro's formal model, as they are assumed to be symmetric.[90] But costs are not necessarily symmetric in fact, and in practice negotiations might be driven by litigation costs. In that case, the transaction cost analysis discussed below in Section 7.5.2 would be more pertinent to the potential for holdup (or holdout).[91]

C) PATENTS CENTRAL TO THE PRODUCT. Denicolò et al. (2008) say that "[w]hen the infringed patent is essential to the innovative product . . . the logic of the holdup problem changes significantly."[92] They note that "for holdup to be a significant threat not only must the patent cover a single component of a larger complex product, but that one component must be minor (v small) and a stand-alone product

---

[88] Golden 2007, 2131.
[89] *See* Golden 2007, 2130–31 (discussing separately the cases in which the implementer's best strategy is to design around only if found liable, and in which the implementer would design around in any event).
[90] Lemley & Shapiro 2007b do not specifically respond to this point in their reply to Golden.
[91] *See* Section 6 "Holdout/Reverse Holdup."
[92] Denicolò et al. 2008, 593.

excluding v must have been commercially and technically feasible ex ante."[93] This is not really a challenge to Lemley & Shapiro's central point, which is precisely that holdup is especially severe for a complex product with a minor patented feature.[94] It is true that when the patent is more central to the product, the holdup in Lemley & Shapiro's *ex post* scenario is driven by sunk costs (as opposed to the loss of profits from the entire product being held off the market), and in the "early negotiation" case it is driven by the probabilistic nature of the patent. The question then is whether Denicolò et al. (2008) show that these factors do not result in holdup for essential patents. The answer is no.

To support their argument they give the example of the case in which the patentee and the implementer both have technology that is strictly complementary in the sense that both technologies are necessary to the success of the product. The proper benchmark in such a case is the royalty the parties would have negotiated prior to either sinking costs into their respective technologies.[95] If the parties negotiate *ex post*, and the patentee can obtain an injunction in the case of breakdown, their positions will not have changed much, since either will be able to block the project. The difference is that both will have sunk R&D costs into their technologies, but if those costs are similar, and the bargaining power does not change, then the *ex post* bargain will be the same as the *ex ante* bargain.[96]

This argument is evidently directed primarily at the "early negotiation" scenario in which sunk costs are the driver of holdup. While their example is correct so far as it goes, it is not strong support for their proposition. First, there is no particular reason to believe that the R&D costs will generally be similar. An example that approximates the situation they describe is *NTP v. Research in Motion*.[97] NTP had a patent on a technology essential to RIM's principal products, but RIM had spent substantial amounts implementing the technology, and there is no reason to believe that NTP's patent, which was a paper invention never commercialized by the inventor or NTP,[98] had been particularly costly to develop. No doubt there are cases where the patentee's R&D costs are roughly on the order of the implementer's technology-specific sunk costs, but that does not justify granting an injunction in cases like *NTP v. RIM*, simply on the basis that NTP's technology was essential to the product. The centrality of the patented technology to the product is not a good proxy for symmetry of investment between the patentee and implementer.

---

[93] *Id.* at 596.
[94] Lemley & Shapiro 2007a, 2001 (noting high holdup for lost profits during redesign "[f]or a complex product and a minor patented feature"); *Id.* at 2002–03 (noting the holdup potential when "the patented feature is nothing special").
[95] Denicolò et al. 2008, 594. The benchmark they give is equivalent to the Shapley pricing solution advocated by Siebrasse & Cotter 2017a.
[96] Denicolò et al. 2008, 593–94.
[97] *NTP, Inc. v. Research in Motion, Ltd.* (E.D. Va. 2003) (U.S.).
[98] Lohr 2010.

Secondly, the example of an implementer that has a strictly complementary technology is largely unrelated to the scenario in which the infringed patent is essential to the innovative product. Denicolò et al. (2008) argue that Lemley & Shapiro are wrong to focus on the implementer's sunk costs without considering the costs that the patentee had sunk into R&D.[99] This reflects the "true *ex ante*" argument discussed above. But how does this generalize to a case in which the patentee has a patent that is essential to the product? They say that "since both firms must sink a specific investment before they can contract, both may actually be subject to a hold up problem."[100] But that is true only if the patentee has no option other than to negotiate with that particular implementer. This emerges from their model because they assume that the patentee and the implementer have strictly complementary technologies. But that is a special case. As Denicolò et al. (2008) themselves point out, if the implementer market is perfectly competitive the patentee will be able to extract the full value of the invention. At the other extreme, if there is a monopsony in the implementer market, then the implementer does indeed have additional leverage, on standard monopsony pricing theory. But that arises from the structure of the implementer market, not because the patented technology is essential or otherwise to the product. In effect, Denicolò et al. (2008) are arguing that when the patentee has a patent that is essential to the product and the implementer is a monopsonist, the patentee should be entitled to an injunction in order to counterbalance that monopsony power. But recall that they are arguing that holdup is only significant when the patent covers a single component of a larger complex product, and one component is minor, and a stand-alone product was commercially and technically feasible *ex ante*, or, more generally, the infringed patent is essential to the innovative product. It is not clear how any of these are related to a case in which the implementer has monopsony power, whether because it has complementary technology, or for some other reason.

A model of parties with proprietary rights to complementary technologies is entirely appropriate when discussing multiple patentees with patents reading on a product sold by an implementer, as is notoriously the case with SEPs. This does indeed raise a difficult question of how to allocate royalties, and whether any party should be entitled to an injunction. It is not uncommon that one of those patentees with complementary technology might also be an implementer, but it does not follow that all patentees should be entitled to injunctions against all implementers in order to give them appropriate leverage against a particular implementer that happens to also be a patentee.[101]

---

[99] Denicolò et al. 2008, 594.
[100] *Id.*
[101] Denicolò et al. 2008, 595, also dispute the assertion by Lemley & Shapiro that the magnitude of the holdup problem increases approximately linearly with the number of infringed patents; they conclude instead that the increase in holdup is less than linear. That point is discussed in more detail below in Section 7.7.2 "Cumulative Effect of Holdup." In the present context, their point is

D) MARKET STRUCTURE. The Lemley & Shapiro model assumes a patentee negotiating with a single downstream firm, and while they make some observations
respecting markets with multiple downstream firms, they acknowledge that
a thorough discussion is beyond the scope of their article.[102] Elhauge (2008) argues
that "there is every reason to think the results are totally different if the downstream
market is competitive."[103] The gist of his argument seems to be that in a competitive
market the patentee will extract the entire expected value of the invention,[104] and so
there cannot be any overcharge because an implementer would prefer to exit the
market entirely.[105] He then argues that the royalty the patentee can charge is
constrained to no more than $v\theta$:

> Assuming damages are properly set at v times X_i [number of units sold] for any
> infringing seller, the expected damages for infringement will be $v\theta X_i$. Thus, if the
> patent owner tried to charge a royalty of more than $v\theta$, all the downstream firms
> would decline the license because they would incur expected losses from
> agreeing.[106]

That is not correct, or at least it is overly simplistic. This statement is addressed at the
early negotiation scenario, and in that case the implementer's threat point is to use
the best noninfringing alternative. Suppose the value of the patent is reflected in
a cost saving, and the patentee negotiates with one implementer. If the other
implementers do not take a license, their costs will be higher than that of the
licensee by v (by the definition of v). The licensee can afford to pay more than $v\theta$
and still undercut the other implementers. On the other hand, if the patentee makes
the same offer to all implementers simultaneously, we are essentially back in the
scenario of a single downstream firm. If the patentee demands more than v, they will
all prefer to use the alternative, but otherwise they will be willing to pay more than
$v\theta$, because they all have to pay the same amount, and so all will earn the same zero
economic return that is standard in a competitive market.

  Elhauge then says, "[e]ven if the downstream firms had already used the technology inadvertently, the patent owner could not charge more than $v\theta$ by trying to
holdup the downstream firm for some of the costs of redesign, because if it did so the
downstream firm would expect to lose money and prefer to exit the market."[107] If the

---

apparently that stacking will not result in significant holdup if the patents involved are not essential to
    the product. Given my discussion in the text, this point need not be addressed here.

[102] Lemley & Shapiro 2007a, 2005–08.

[103] Elhauge 2008, 561.

[104] *Id.* at 562 (noting that the patentee can play one implementer off against another, so that in effect "β =
    1 if the downstream market is competitive"). This is subject to the point that splitting the value of the
    invention may amount to paying the implementer for product-specific services, in which case the
    value would be split even in a competitive market; but the implementer's expected profit would still
    be zero.

[105] *Id.*

[106] *Id.*

[107] *Id.*

implementers were not aware of the patent *ex ante*, their expected profit in the competitive market would be zero, and all the cost saving of the technology would be passed on to consumers. If the patentee then emerges, *any* positive royalty, even a royalty of less than $v\theta$, will result in the implementers losing money, unless they raise their prices. If the patentee approaches only one implementer, it will lose money if it takes a license and none of the others do, so it will exit the market and the patentee will get no revenue. If the patentee then approaches another implementer, this process will continue until there are so few implementers left that the market is no longer competitive and the remaining implementer can take a license and raise its prices. In effect, by selectively licensing, the patentee will have transformed a perfectly competitive downstream market into an imperfectly competitive market. There may be circumstances in which that strategy would be rational, but on this route we are no longer dealing with a competitive market, so Elhauge's point would not apply. Alternatively, the patentee might license all implementers at the same royalty, in which case each implementer could raise its price by the same amount without losing its market. Each implementer would be willing to pay the royalty and stay in the market (strictly, it is indifferent between leaving and staying in the market, but that was also true under *ex ante* negotiations) until the royalty is so high it would be preferable to redesign the product – which is the standard point that the implementer can be held up for the redesign costs. The implementers would lose money, but they would lose less money than if they left the market; that is the standard sunk costs holdup result.[108] The only real difference is that the implementers cannot be held up for lost economic profits during the redesign phase, because they are not making any economic profits. But if they are making accounting profits because they have fixed costs, they could be held up for those profits.

This is not to say that the market structure does not affect Lemley & Shapiro's result at all; a thorough discussion is beyond the scope of this chapter, just as it was beyond the scope of Lemley & Shapiro's original article. But Elhauge's critique does not give any reason to think that the basic result does not extend to different market structures.

E) ELASTIC DEMAND. Elhauge (2008) asserts "the Lemley–Shapiro model would overstate royalties because it assumes inelastic output."[109] It is true that inelastic demand is a dubious assumption. It is also true that the overcharge will be less when demand increases in the presence of the patented technology; the intuition is that when the patented technology adds value to the product, the implementer will

---

[108] *Id.* at 563 (noting that "[t]he same is true if the market downstream is marked by recurring fixed costs or product differentiation, making models of "monopolistic competition" more appropriate," and the same counterargument is applicable).

[109] *Id.* at 547 ("Third, even with the above problems, their assumption of inelastic output is unrealistic and inflates predicted royalties"); *id.* at 551 ("[T]he Lemley–Shapiro model would overstate royalties because it assumes the downstream output X is constant and totally unaffected by whether D incorporates a patented feature that increases product value.").

normally get value from the patent in the form of increased sales, as well as in the form of a higher price, and the increased profit from increased sales partially offsets the overcharge. But Lemley & Shapiro's model does not turn on the assumption of inelastic output. That is merely an example they provide by way of illustration.[110] Elasticity of demand will mitigate the overcharge problem to some degree, but it seems unlikely to provide significant relief in the context of complex products, where thousands of patents may read on a single product.

7 Competing Patentees

Lemley & Shapiro state that their analysis is limited to situations in which the patentee's predominant commercial interest in bringing a patent infringement case is to obtain licensing revenues and it does not apply to settings in which the patent holder practices the invention and seeks to use the patent to exclude a competitor from the market in order to preserve its profit margins.[111] Golden (2007) and Elhauge (2008) argue that Lemley & Shapiro's distinction is not compelling, and they indicate that even patentees seeking only royalties should be entitled to injunctive relief.[112]

The holdup problem faced by the implementer is just as severe whether the patentee competes in the market or not.[113] The key question is therefore whether there are countervailing considerations that imply that a patentee who competes in the market should be granted injunctive relief notwithstanding these holdup concerns.

Lemley & Shapiro's model considers only reasonable royalty damages, and they equivocate when considering a patent holder who would be entitled to lost profit damages, saying in cases involving "significant" lost profits, they favor a presumption that the patent holder will be granted a permanent injunction,

> perhaps with a stay to allow the infringing firm to redesign its product. The presumptive right to a permanent injunction in these cases is justified in part for reasons of equity and in part because of the grave difficulties associated with calculating and awarding lost profits on an ongoing basis.[114]

---

[110]   Lemley & Shapiro 2007a, 2046 Appendix – A.

[111]   Lemley & Shapiro 2007a.

[112]   After making the point that there is no evident basis for distinguishing between a patentee who seeks lost profit and one who seeks reasonable royalties, Golden 2007, 2155 asks "[w]hy not simply curtail injunctive relief for all patent holders?," but he appears to be asking the question rhetorically.

[113]   *See* Denicolò et al. 2008, 588–89.

[114]   Lemley & Shapiro 2007a, 2036. Lemley & Shapiro 2007b, 2171–73 also address this point, but they do not develop the substantive rationale for the distinction beyond saying that what matters is "the nature of the patent holder's contribution and how it seeks compensation in the marketplace." However, it is not clear exactly what Lemley & Shapiro mean by "the patent holder's contribution" or why it should vary systematically between practicing and nonpracticing entities, and they do not elaborate on why the availability of injunctive relief should depend on how the patentee seeks compensation in the

This suggests that the costs of denying injunctive relief, in the form of increased error costs of damages calculation, are greater in the context of lost profits.[115] There are two problems with this argument.

First, while it is no doubt difficult to assess lost profits on an ongoing basis, it is not easy to accurately quantify a reasonable royalty either. It is not evident that lost profit calculations are generally so much more difficult than reasonable royalty calculations, particularly in the case of complex products, as to justify a sharp distinction between cases in which the patentee is seeking lost profits and those in which it is not.[116]

Moreover, Golden (2007) points out that the difficulty in assessing reasonable royalty damages has traditionally been one of the principal rationales for granting permanent injunctions.[117] Lemley & Shapiro respond by noting that "all that is required for reasonable royalties to play their role in guiding parties to a negotiated settlement in the shadow of litigation is that they be unbiased."[118] But this same point undermines their distinction between reasonable royalties and lost profits; even if lost profits are more difficult to assess, that makes no difference so long as the errors are unbiased. The important question is not whether lost profit damages are more difficult to assess than reasonable royalties, but whether they are more likely to be biased against the patentee. There is no obvious reason why errors in lost profit damages are less likely to be unbiased than reasonable royalty damages.

Apart from the relative accuracy of the two types of damages, Elhauge (2008), and Denicolò et al. (2008) suggest that the holdup problem might be worse when the patentee is able to seek lost profit damages because it competes in the downstream market. In that case the patentee may hold up the implementers even more because higher royalties provide it with increased market share in the downstream market, as well as directly benefiting from high royalties itself.[119] In effect, the patentee has increased bargaining power when it competes in the downstream market; when it

---

marketplace. Shapiro 2010, 304, similarly adverts to the difficulty of determining lost profits on a forward-looking basis.

[115] Lemley & Shapiro's reference to "equity," is obscure. They do not refer to any particular equitable principles, which suggests they mean equity in the sense of fairness rather than equity as a legal term of art, but neither do they elaborate on any relevant fairness intuitions.

[116] Golden 2007, 2155. Reasonable royalties are often based on comparable licenses, but as Lemley & Shapiro 2007a themselves point out, at 2022, information about comparable licenses is limited and biased. *See also* Masur 2015 (explaining the difficulties associated with assessing reasonable royalties based on comparable licenses).

[117] Golden 2007, 2152.

[118] *See* Lemley & Shapiro 2007b, 2172. By the same token, the incentive to innovate is maintained if lost profit damages are accurate and unbiased. Lemley & Shapiro give no reason to think that lost profit damages are less likely to be unbiased than reasonable royalty damages. *Id.* (acknowledging that sometimes nonpracticing entities should be able to get injunctive relief and vice versa, but their examples are tied to whether the entity suffers lost sales, which begs the question of why that should be a determinative factor).

[119] Elhauge 2008, 560–61; *see also* Denicolò et al. 2008, 588–89. Elhauge views this point as a criticism of Lemley & Shapiro's model, but it is more properly viewed as an extension.

only licenses, the royalty is constrained because it will make nothing if the royalties are so high as to unduly restrict sales, but if the patentee competes in the downstream market that constraint is lifted, as the patentee might anticipate capturing those sales itself.

A distinct reason for preferring injunctive relief in the case of a patentee that practices the invention is that in such a case we should expect the patentee to be more efficient, because if the infringer were more efficient than the patentee, the patentee would have been willing to license. Allowing the patentee to exclude the infringer in such circumstances gives the market to the more efficient producer.[120] However, granting an injunction to a nonpracticing patentee should have the same effect, and the patentee would license to the more efficient producer.

As a final point on this issue, Geradin (2010a) argues that Lemley & Shapiro's distinction between patentees seeking lost profits and those seeking reasonable royalties "would unduly affect innovators which have opted for a licensing business model for perfectly legitimate reasons, such as for instance the fact that they do not have the skills or the resources to develop and manufacture products embedding their technologies," and "effectively tip the market in favor of vertically-integrated incumbents ... [, which] would impede efficiency-enhancing specialization allowing firms to focus on what they do best and harm innovation."[121] However, it is not clear that the lost profit damages per unit, properly assessed, will be greater than the royalties per unit. That will only be true, in an economic sense, if the vertically integrated firm has the capacity to satisfy the market and is a more efficient producer than the implementer, in which case it is not inefficient to give the patentee extra leverage against the implementer. If the vertically integrated firm is actually worse at commercializing the invention, this implies that its lost profits will be less than the reasonable royalty it could have obtained from licensing to a more efficient implementer; as Geradin (2010a) points out, the innovator is more likely to opt for a licensing model when it does not have the skills or resources to manufacture the product, and the lower return from a royalty reflects these shortcomings. While this follows as a matter of economic logic, it requires that the lost profits calculation properly accounts for the patentee's costs of production, including fixed costs. If lost profits calculations are excessively generous to the patentee, then the vertically integrated patentee will have greater leverage because of the excessive damages for past infringement whether or not it is granted an injunction. As discussed above, the implementer's share of the surplus may be best understood as compensation for its investment in the success of the product, through marketing and distribution, etc., which would represent costs to the patentee.

In summary, despite their protestations, Lemley & Shapiro's holdup model does prima facie apply to patentees who compete with the infringer. This does not imply

---

[120]   Blair & Cotter 1998, 1626–28.
[121]   Geradin 2010a, 126–27. To the same effect, *see also* the second point made by Elhauge 2008, 561.

that their model should be rejected, but it does suggest that their model is incomplete,[122] and/or that the holdup problem needs to be taken seriously in that context as well.

7.4 MITIGATING MECHANISMS

7.4.1 *Introduction*

There are a variety of mechanisms that have been suggested as being effective in mitigating the effects of holdup in a variety of contexts. This section discusses the theoretical plausibility of those mechanisms. Whether they are effective to mitigate the effects of holdup (if any) is an empirical question that is discussed below in Section 8 "Empirical Evidence."

It is sometimes suggested that holdup is not a serious problem in practice because legal constraints, such as the FRAND commitment or oversight by competition authorities, are effective in preventing abuse of patent power.[123] While this may be true, it is not helpful to consider such legal constraints to be relevant mitigating mechanisms. The ultimate question is how to interpret the FRAND commitment when faced with a decision as to whether to grant injunctive relief, and to say the FRAND commitment helps prevent abuse tells us nothing about how to interpret that commitment. If anything, the implicit suggestion that the FRAND commitment and competition law oversight are necessary implies that holdup would be a problem in their absence.

7.4.2 Ex Ante *Licensing*

If *ex ante* licensing is possible, the holdup problem is substantially mitigated.[124] In the SEP context the dominant view appears to be that licensing prior to the standard being adopted is rare and generally impractical,[125] though it does appear that *ex ante*

---

[122] *See* Section 7.5 "Property Rules and Liability Rules" (suggesting that the theory presented by Smith 2004 might provide the basis for a distinction between the two scenarios).

[123] *See, e.g.,* Nokia Corp. 2011 (stating that "[e]specially for complex standards as in telecoms, Nokia believes that (F)RAND is the only workable solution to prevent patent hold up"); Denicolo et al. 2008, 597 n.80 (referring to Rambus's attempt to hold up its licensees, which was struck down by the FTC).

[124] *See* Lee & Melamed 2016, 460–61. However, it is not necessarily eliminated entirely. As Lemley & Shapiro 2007a show, *ex ante* licensing only avoids holdup entirely for ironclad patents. For probabilistic patents, holdup may occur even with *ex ante* bargaining: *see* above Section 3.1.4 "Probabilistic Holdup: Lemley & Shapiro Model." Further, royalty stacking is not addressed by *ex ante* licensing as such.

[125] *See* Contreras 2013, 59 (stating that "*very few* [FRAND] licenses are negotiated prior to market adoption") (emphasis in original); Intel Corp. 2011, 9 (stating that "ex ante licensing is unlikely to occur in the most common licensing scenarios: those involving new technologies, new product markets, and/or early versions of standards"); Nokia Corp. 2011, 6 (stating that in the telecoms

licensing is at least occasionally possible, and the view is also sometimes expressed that it is common and generally feasible.[126] The extent to which *ex ante* licensing is feasible is an empirical question that this chapter cannot resolve.[127]

Outside of the SEP context whether *ex ante* negotiations are possible will depend on the ability of an implementer to undertake an effective preclearance search. For some types of products, preclearance searches may be generally feasible and costs-effective. However, for complex products, effective *ex ante* negotiation may be even more difficult than in the SEP context. In the SEP the development of the standard will be well-known to those in the industry, and the identity of the patentees will be known, and the hurdle to *ex ante* negotiations is primarily the cost and delay associated with actually negotiating the agreements.[128] For equivalently complex products outside the SEP context, implementers will face the same difficulty, plus the additional burden of actually identifying all the relevant patents.[129]

7.4.3 Ex Ante *Validity Challenge*

Denicolò et al. (2008) note that in Lemley & Shapiro's model, holdup can occur even if the implementer had the opportunity to negotiate *ex ante*, because of the probabilistic nature of the patent. They argue that this result is based on the

---

environment "[i]t is simply not possible to determine a meaningful value/price long before it is known what kind of products will eventually implement the standard").

[126] Qualcomm Inc. 2011, 11 (stating that Qualcomm entered into *ex ante* WCDMA licenses with firms representing more than 60 percent of royalty-bearing unit sales in 2005); Epstein et al. 2012, 17–18 ("Manufacturers can, and do, engage in bilateral patent licensing before seriously investing in patented technology, both in settings in which SSOs are deployed and those in which they are not" (citing Qualcomm Inc. 2011, 8)); Geradin & Layne-Farrar 2007, 91 ("[V]oluntary ex ante disclosure of licensing terms by IPR owners and ex ante negotiations of license agreements with IPR owners are already regular occurrences" (citing Holleman 2002, 2)); Geradin 2010a, 111 (stating that "the majority of key patent owners and standard implementers commonly engage in ex ante licensing negotiations – that is, they routinely negotiate patent portfolio licenses or cross-licenses pertaining to an anticipated standard, or to a standard under development, well before the standard is finalised," though without citing supporting sources); Microsoft 2011, 14 (noting that potential implementers can sometimes negotiate with SEP holders before the standard is finalized).

Ganglmair et al. 2012, 251 n.5–6 assert that "[o]ption contracts have been shown to be a robust solution to hold-up problems," and that "[c]ontracts with an option feature were used by Qualcomm with its innovative CDMA technology for mobile telephony"). However, this is effectively a type of *ex ante* licensing, as it requires entering into an option-to-license contract before the implementer incurs sunk costs, *id.* at 252, so the feasibility of this solution turns on the feasibility of *ex ante* negotiations.

[127] *Ex ante* negotiation is clearly not possible if the implementer only enters the industry after the standard has issued. *See* Gilbert 2011, 860. In principle the "non-discrimination" branch of the FRAND requirement would protect against holdup in such circumstances, though in practice it might not be possible for the late entrant to find out the terms that were offered to others.

[128] *See* Contreras 2013, 59–62 (explaining the practical factors making *ex ante* negotiations difficult in the standards context).

[129] *See* Lee & Melamed 2016, 405–08; Kieff & Layne-Farrar 2013, 1105–08 (suggesting that *ex ante* licensing is often possible if implementers exercise due diligence, though not always).

assumption that the implementer cannot contest the validity of the patent before designing its product.[130] However, this critique turns on the validity challenge being costless and immediate. Denicolò et al. (2008) assert that "similar conclusions also hold with costly litigation,"[131] but it is not clear that this is true. Apart from the cost, litigation takes time, and the point made by Lemley & Shapiro is that the implementer can be held up for redesign costs and lost profits on its product during the period of redesign, because the implementer's threat point in the negotiation is not to use the invention at all. All of these sources of holdup will arise unless the validity can be determined before the implementer begins to produce the product. If the implementer holds off on selling until validity is decided, it can be held up for the opportunity cost of its foregone profits during that period. Lemley & Shapiro's model gives the same results whether the litigation is assumed to be an infringement action by the patentee, or a declaratory judgment action by the implementer.

7.4.4 *Norms*

Elhauge (2008) suggests that even in a single-shot game, fairness-based norms may help prevent or mitigate excessive royalties by making the implementer's threat to reject such royalties credible.[132] However if fairness norms anchor negotiations even between sophisticated parties, that can only lead to a fair royalty if the norm itself is fair. He says that "[i]f parties believed that $\theta\beta v$ was the fair benchmark, as Lemley and Shapiro argue, then they are likely to refuse royalties above that, making royalties even more undercompensatory."[133] Given that Elhauge is of the view that $\theta\beta v$ is unfair, it is not clear why he believes that it would be adopted as the fairness norm.

More generally, as discussed at the outset of this section, the theory of how parties to a negotiation split the gains to trade is incomplete, and it is certainly possible that fairness norms play a role. But if fairness norms are thought only to influence β, that would affect the degree of holdup – one way or the other – but it would not affect the fact of holdup, unless the fairness norm is so powerful as to displace the standard assumption that the parties negotiate in the shadow of the litigation outcome. A much more substantial argument than is provided by Elhauge would be required to make either point.

7.4.5 *Repeat Play*

Lemley & Shapiro's model of holdup considers a one-shot game. Elhauge (2008) argues that if negotiations over patent royalties are repeated between an

---

[130]   Denicolò et al. 2008, 590, suggest that the implementer might contest the validity when it is aware the patent is weak, but the general point applies regardless of the strength of the patent.
[131]   *Id.*
[132]   Elhauge 2008, 549–51.
[133]   *Id.* at 550–51.

implementer and multiple sequential patent holders, the equilibrium royalty will be lower than the rates predicted by Lemley & Shapiro, essentially because the implementer can improve its bargaining position by developing a credible reputation as a hard negotiator.[134] Elhauge argues that the bargaining is more appropriately modeled as being between an implementer and multiple patentees because the implementer of a complex product necessarily faces multiple patentees, and it will therefore be in the implementer's interest to develop a reputation as a tough negotiator. However, the conclusion that a repeated game will lead to a lower royalty does not appear to be robust to the details of the way in which the game is modeled. For example, similar reasoning suggests that if the negotiations took place between a single patentee and multiple implementers, the royalty might be higher than the rates predicted by Lemley & Shapiro, because the patentee can improve its bargaining position by developing a credible reputation as a hard negotiator. And in many cases, it will be realistic to model both parties as repeat players, as when negotiations are between NPEs with a large portfolio and large implementers who are often targeted by NPEs.[135] On the other hand, patents may be asserted by a special-purpose entity formed solely to assert a single patent portfolio, which is, by definition, not a repeat player, and does not have a market reputation to defend.[136] Also, Elhauge's formal model considers an implementer and multiple sequential patent holders, not simultaneous patent holders, and it is not obvious that there will be a reputational effect when the negotiations are simultaneous. On the whole, there is little doubt that repeat play and reputation effects can have a significant effect on bargaining outcomes, but it is difficult to generalize about exactly what that effect might be.

1 Modified Injunction

A) STAY OF INJUNCTION. A modified injunction may mitigate holdup problems. Lemley & Shapiro (2007a) recommend that if the cost of designing around the patent is moderate or low, the permanent injunction be granted with a stay that is long enough to permit the infringing firm to complete the redesign.[137] The option of a stay is attractive because it reduces the risk of holdup in cases where redesign is not too costly, while also minimizing the risk of undercompensation, because even if damages are undercompensatory, the marginal effect of that undercompensation is felt only during the period of the stay.[138] This option has at least occasionally been

---

[134]   *Id.* at 547–49.
[135]   *See* Qualcomm Inc. 2011, 25–26 (suggesting informally that demands will be moderated if both parties are repeat players).
[136]   Chien 2014, 31.
[137]   Lemley & Shapiro 2007a, 2038.
[138]   Of course, damages for pretrial infringement may be undercompensatory, but this is not affected by staying the permanent injunction. Denicolò et al. 2008, 602–03 accuse Lemley & Shapiro of ignoring litigation delays in making this suggestion for a stay, saying patent infringement cases "can take years to wend their way through the courts." This criticism conflates the effect of the stay with the

employed by U.S. courts,[139] but apart from the recommendation by Lemley & Shapiro, it has not featured prominently in the scholarly literature.[140] A stay will not be effective in preventing holdup where the cost of redesign is high relative to the value of the invention.[141]

B) PATENTEE PAYS SWITCHING COSTS. Lee & Melamed (2016) propose a novel form of modified injunction. They distinguish between a willing licensor, who would have been willing to license to the infringer, and unwilling licensors, which includes both patent holders who wanted to practice the patents themselves, as well as those who wanted to license a limited number of others, and so would not have been willing to license the infringer.[142] They propose that an unwilling licensor should generally be able to obtain an injunction against a "guilty" infringer, who could in practice have entered into *ex ante* licensing negotiations, thereby avoiding any holdup problem. In a case involving an unwilling licensor and an "innocent" infringer, who could not as a practical matter have negotiated *ex ante*, they propose as a prospective remedy that the licensor be provided with a choice between an ongoing royalty[143] and an injunction, but the injunction would be available only on the condition that the patentee would pay the infringer's cost of switching to a noninfringing alternative.[144]

This type of injunction protects the implementer from holdup based on switching costs even more effectively than a stay because the patent holder rather than the implementer would bear the costs of switching. As a result, their proposal would protect the implementer even when switching costs are high relative to the value of the invention.

One caveat is that Lee & Melamed do not specify whether a stay of the injunction would also be granted to the implementer.[145] If not, the implementer might be subject to holdup based on lost profits on the product during the redesign period, as argued by Lemley & Shapiro (2007a). It may be that Lee & Melamed would consider such lost profits to be part of the cost of switching, in which case it would

---

independent effect of litigation delay; it is more properly directed at the U.S. practice of rarely granting preliminary injunctions.

[139] *See* FTC 2011, 238 (citing *i4i Ltd. Partnership v. Microsoft Corp.* (Fed. Cir. 2010) (U.S.)).

[140] *But see* Shapiro 2016, 27 (reiterating the stay recommendation).

[141] Lee & Melamed 2016, 458 n.332. In that case, Lemley & Shapiro 2007a, 2036, recommend denying the permanent injunction entirely.

[142] Lee & Melamed 2016, 445.

[143] The royalty would be at the same rate as past compensatory damages. If the patentee would have been entitled to lost profits for past infringement, the ongoing royalty would be at the same rate; otherwise, it would be equal to a reasonable royalty: *id.* at 445.

[144] *See id.* at 390, table 1 (summarizing their proposal); *id.* at 457–60 (discussing the proposal in more detail).

[145] Lee & Melamed 2016, 458 n.332 discuss the possibility of a stay without mentioning it as part of their proposal. This indicates that under their proposal injunctive relief would not be conditioned on a stay.

either be borne by the patentee, or the patentee would agree to a stay voluntarily to avoid having to bear those costs.

Their proposal also captures the intuition that a patentee who practices the invention, and so would normally be entitled to lost profits, should have a stronger entitlement to injunctive relief; but their distinction between willing and unwilling licensors avoids the difficulties associated with distinguishing competing patentees as such.[146]

7.5 PROPERTY RULES AND LIABILITY RULES

7.5.1 Inaccuracy of Damages Awards

In their landmark article, Calabresi & Melamed (1972) introduced the now standard distinction between property rules and liability rules. A property rule, in which an entitlement is protected by injunctive relief, gives an individual the right to keep an entitlement unless he chooses to part with it voluntarily. In contrast, if the entitlement is protected by a liability rule, the owner of the entitlement must give it up to another who is willing to pay its fair value, as objectively determined by the court. According to Calabresi & Melamed, the disadvantage of a property rule is that it allows the owner of the entitlement to hold out for an excessive price when there is market failure; the corresponding advantage of a liability rule is that it avoids such holdup.[147] Conversely, the advantage of a property rule is that the owner of the entitlement determines its value, and having the court assess the value of the right, as under the liability rule, is inherently less accurate. This implies that the decision as to whether the patent holder should be granted an injunction turns on whether the holdup problem is worse than the valuation problem.[148]

This analysis transfers directly to the context of patents for complex products. Golden (2007) points out that "[t]he difficulty of assessing a reasonable royalty has in fact been one of the principal rationales for granting permanent injunctions."[149] He notes that "[t]he difficulty of assessing even a retrospective reasonable royalty is notorious," and expert evidence may differ by an order of magnitude.[150]

---

[146] See Section 3.1.7 "Competing Patentees."

[147] Calabresi & Melamed 1972, 1107–08, refer to the "holdout" problem, and their examples turn on collective action problems rather than sunk costs, but their insight applies whenever voluntary bargaining does not result in an exchange based on the true value of the right, and so encompasses what is referred to as "holdup" in the patent context.

[148] See Epstein 1997, 2094 ("Stated formally, the task of a legal system is to minimize the sum of errors that arise from expropriation and undercompensation, where the two are inversely related.").

[149] Golden 2007, 2152.

[150] Id., 2150–51 (also noting that the difficulty is compounded in assessing a reasonable royalty going forward, where the market for the invention may be permanently distorted by the infringement); see also Cotter 2013a, 54–56 (arguing that the difficulty of accurately valuing patent rights is an important justification for granting injunctive relief).

However, there are a variety of other possible justifications for the use of property rules apart from inaccuracy of damages, and the argument based on inaccuracy of damages is itself problematic. These points are discussed in turn below.

7.5.2 *Transaction Cost Arguments*

One solution to the puzzle is that injunctive relief might be justified on a variety of other grounds broadly related to transaction costs. Injunctive relief might save the litigation costs associated with quantifying damages; reduce administrative costs associated with judicial supervision of the ongoing royalties; encourage development of transaction cost-reducing institutions; provide an incentive to avoid litigation in the first place; and/or avoid the risk of the implementer otherwise holding out through manipulation of delays in the litigation system.[151]

The problem with this solution is that these second-order arguments require a difficult empirical assessment of the relative severity of these various factors if they are to serve either as a normative basis for recommendations regarding injunctive relief, or as a descriptive theory of current trends and practices. For example, courts are far more likely to grant injunctive relief to a patentee that competes with the infringing firm.[152] As discussed above, Lemley & Shapiro argue that such a preference is justified in order to avoid the costs of damages calculations,[153] but it is far from clear that this justifies a distinction between patentees who would be entitled to lost profits and those entitled only to a reasonable royalty, as it is not evident that there is a substantial difference in the difficulty of the two calculations.[154]

7.5.3 *Generating Information Regarding Potential Use*

Smith (2004) argues that the basic flaw in the pro-liability rules literature is the assumption that the underlying risk distribution is known.[155] He argues that the problem with liability rules is not so much undercompensation for loss of known uses, but failure to compensate the owner of the entitlement for uses that are themselves speculative.[156] While Smith presents this as an argument in favor of

---

[151] *See* Cotter 2009, 1175–76 (reviewing a variety of justifications for injunctive relief, while nonetheless stating that the valuation advantage is the "first" reason for preferring injunctive relief); *see also* Cotter 2013a, 54–56.

[152] *See* Seaman 2016, 1990, figure 4.

[153] Lemley & Shapiro 2007b, 2172; *see also* Kaplow & Shavell 1996, 741–42 (making a similar point in the context of the general debate about the proper use of property and liability rules).

[154] *See* Section 3.1.7 "Competing Patentees."

[155] Smith 2004, 1721–22.

[156] That is, the value of a property right depends on the range of its potential future uses, as well as the expected value of each of those uses. If some potential future uses are not known to the court, then the assessment of the value of the right will be inaccurate, even if the assessment of the value of the known uses is correct in expectation. Since any positive value potential future use (as opposed to

property rights generally, it does not particularly support injunctive relief for patent infringement in contexts in which the patentee would have been willing to license. In such cases the use itself is known, and any uncertainty relates only to the value of the use. Smith's argument might be relevant to the question of whether there is a sound distinction between a patentee who exploits the patent by practicing the technology and one who seeks only to license it.[157]

7.5.4 *Inaccuracy of Damages Assessment*

1 Inaccuracy v. Biased Damages

It is largely uncontroversial that the assessment of damages for patent infringement is likely to be inaccurate, as Lemley & Shapiro acknowledge in their reply to Golden.[158] They say, however, that

> all that is required for reasonable royalties to play their role in guiding parties to a negotiated settlement in the shadow of litigation is that they be unbiased, so that deviations from the benchmark royalty are not systematic one way or the other.[159]

This exchange reflects a similar debate in the general literature on property rules versus liability rules. There has been a substantial literature responding to Calabresi & Melamed, arguing that liability rules are superior to injunctive relief in a range of circumstances, to the point that "[p]roperty rules find relatively few defenders among legal economists."[160] Smith (2004) points out that the pro-liability rule literature turns on two basic assumptions: that the risk distribution is known; and that errors in judicial determination of damages are unbiased.[161] Lemley & Shapiro's response to Golden reflects the second assumption in particular.

a potential liability), will necessarily increase the expected value of the property, failure to take into account a potential use will result in an assessment of the expected value of the right that is biased downward. Property rules, according to Smith, solve this problem by giving the owner of the right a generalized entitlement to all future uses. This allows the owner to assess the potential future uses herself, without having to convince a court. A second advantage is that a potential use that is not known even to the owner of the right cannot affect the value of the right even under a property rule, but a property right gives the owner an incentive to investigate and discover potential uses, whether or not the value of those potential uses can be proven to a court.

[157] *See* Section 3.1.7 "Competing Patentees." Smith 2007, applies his theory to various issues in intellectual property law, and at 1781–82, discusses the standard for injunctions in patent law, but the discussion is so brief as to add little on this issue to his general theory. Smith does not argue that damages assessments are indeed unbiased; his theory is an alternative justification for property rules, which is not necessarily inconsistent with the view that damages are generally undercompensatory.

[158] See, for example, Judge Learned Hand's observation in *Cincinnati Car Co.* v. *New York Rapid Transit Corp.* (2d Cir. 1933, p.595) (U.S.) (quoted by Golden 2007, 2123, 2152) that assessment of the patentee's loss "is really incalculable" and a damages assessment can be no more than an approximation.

[159] Lemley & Shapiro 2007b, 2172.

[160] Smith 2004, 1721–22. *See also* Kaplow & Shavell 1996; Smith 2004, 1741–48 (reviewing the literature).

[161] Smith 2004, 1725–26, 1746.

If the courts can reliably award damages that are equal to the loss suffered by the patentee, at least in expectation, the basic argument for injunctive relief would be much weaker, as the assessment of damages would perfectly compensate the patentee while avoiding the holdup problem. The puzzle is that this proves too much: If damages are accurate in expectation, then even a slight possibility of holdup would be enough to warrant denying injunctive relief, given that there will be no impact on the incentive to invent. One response to this puzzle is to say that injunctive relief is justified on the basis of the transaction cost arguments or Smith's theory, discussed in the preceding sections.

Another response is to posit that damages are systematically undercompensatory, apart from any feedback effects from holdup and the availability of injunctive relief, that would tend to make damages overcompensatory.[162] If so, this would not in itself imply that injunctive relief should routinely be granted. Indeed, that would provide a ready explanation, at least in principle, for the observed pattern of injunctive relief in patent cases. Ever since Calabresi & Melamed, the pro-property rights literature has acknowledged that a liability rule is justified when there is a serious risk of holdup. The shift in patent law can be reconciled with the traditional dominance of property rules, and traditional property rights theory, on the basis that shifting realities, such as the rise in patent NPEs and SEPs, and perhaps also a general increase in patents for complex products, have substantially increased the circumstances in which there is a serious risk of holdup.

If damages are systematically undercompensatory, the difficulty is not conceptual, but practical. As Lemley & Shapiro point out, "all advantages are comparative." They argue that "since, as we have demonstrated, injunctive relief will systematically overcompensate patent owners in component industries, there is a strong reason to prefer damages rules in those cases."[163] But this observation cuts both ways. Even if it is true that injunctive relief will systematically overcompensate patent owners, that in itself only gives a strong reason to prefer damages rules if there is no counterbalancing reason to prefer property rights. It is not enough to simply point to a risk of undercompensation to justify a property rule, but neither is it enough to simply point to the risk of holdup to justify a liability rule. Instead, the question would turn on whether the problem of undercompensation is outweighed by the holdup problem. If damages are undercompensatory, this kind of balancing inquiry is inherently difficult, as it turns not just on the existence of undercompensation or holdup, but also on an estimate of the relative severity of each.

---

[162] *See, e.g.*, Lemley & Shapiro 2007a; Lee & Melamed 2016.
[163] Lemley & Shapiro 2007b, 2172.

2 Are Damages Biased?

a) Direct Evidence

I am not aware of any direct evidence assessing whether damages awards are biased, in the form of a comparison between damages awards and the plaintiff's true loss. It is difficult to imagine how such a comparison could be carried out, given that a legal damages assessment, at least when carried out by a judge, is the most rigorous method we have for assessing the plaintiff's true loss.

b) Option Effect

Denicolò et al. (2008) and Elhauge (2008) argue that even unbiased errors in determining the reasonable royalty rate could favor the infringer, as the downstream firm could pay the court-determined royalties when they are too low and redesign the product when they are too high.[164] For convenience, I will refer to this as an "option effect," as the argument is that the court-determined royalties effectively provide the infringer with an option that can be exercised when it is in the money. Shapiro (2010) agrees with this basic point, but he states that sufficiently small errors will not affect the basic model and its implications so long as the court-determined royalties are unbiased, and further, the option effect "might not arise, even for fairly large errors, for patents covering a small feature of a high-margin product: the downstream firm would pay greatly excessive royalties rather than withdraw its product from the market while engaging in the redesign."[165] However, Shapiro (2016) provides a model in which the option effect is the only source of under-compensation to the patentee when the patentee would be willing to license, and recommends that injunctive relief should sometimes be granted for this reason.[166]

The option effect will be larger if the damages error is large and the intrinsic holdup is small. It also seems that the option effect will be relatively larger for a stronger patent, because it is important only if the patentee wins and is awarded damages. On the other hand, the option effect will have no impact in the early negotiation scenario, where the implementer's threat point is to avoid using the invention entirely, though presumably it would affect the exact probability of

---

[164] Denicolò et al. 2008, 578–80; Elhauge 2008, 557–58. *See also* Kaplow & Shavell 1996, 761–62 (making essentially the same point to argue that property rights are appropriate for protecting entitlements to things).

[165] Shapiro 2010, 305–06.

[166] Shapiro 2016, 11–12 (describing the option effect), 22 (noting that "the value of the downstream firm's option to negotiate rather than pay the court-awarded royalties declines as the switching costs grow," and discussing when injunctive relief should consequently be awarded). Shapiro 2016, 13–14, also describes a variant of the option effect that arises when the implementer would not have found it worthwhile to use the invention *ex ante*, but the royalty awarded by the court is sufficiently low to make it worthwhile *ex post*. In the absence of reverse payments from the patentee to the implementer, the implementer may pay the unduly low royalty, and the patentee will be undercompensated.

validity at which that becomes the relevant threat point. It is at least clear that the size of the option effect depends on the magnitude of the variance in the error in damages awards, and without empirical evidence on this point, it is difficult to know how important this effect might be in practice.

Further, Cotter (2014a) adds that this strategy "seems to require a good deal of foresight on the part of infringers, as well as a willingness to ignore the high cost of attorney fees and (in some countries) the risk of enhanced damages if the defendant knowingly infringes."[167]

On the whole, it is plausible in principle that the option effect might result in undercompensation if damages are awarded in lieu of an injunction, but it is not clear how significant the effect will be in practice. It would be helpful to be able to estimate the variance in the error of damages awards, but that will be very difficult given that it is not even clear how we could estimate the error term itself.

c) Burden of Proof

Kieff & Layne-Farrar (2013) point out that putting the burden on the patentee to prove its loss may be problematic in the context of reasonable royalty damages because the royalty is often assessed as a portion of the value to the infringer, which requires the patentee "to adduce evidence about a decision made long ago inside the secret business workings of the infringer's enterprise to select the infringing technology over any alternatives that may or may not have existed at that time."[168] More generally, the general principle that the plaintiff must prove its loss may in principle result in undercompensation. The plaintiff's actual losses will be supported by a range of evidence, with some losses supported by more evidence than others. This directly implies that in at least some cases the plaintiff will suffer actual losses that it cannot recover, and that in turn implies that damages are normally undercompensatory.[169] This is not to say that it is wrong to put the burden on the plaintiff to prove its loss, as the opposite rule would result in systematic overcompensation, but the point remains that the rule implies that the plaintiff will be systematically undercompensated.

---

[167] Cotter 2014a, 345.

[168] Kieff & Layne-Farrar 2013, 1117.

[169] This result follows because proof on the balance of probabilities is a threshold that cuts off some losses entirely. In contrast, under an alternative rule in which damages would be awarded for all losses for which there is evidence, but discounting for the strength of the evidence, difficulty of proof would not in principle be a source of undercompensation. That is, if the plaintiff identified a $1 million loss, but could only establish a 10 percent probability that the loss was caused by the tort, it would be awarded $100,000. To be clear, I am not advocating such a rule, but merely using it to illustrate why the rule that the plaintiff must prove its loss results in undercompensation, at least in principle. No doubt the plaintiff will often attempt to prove losses that did not occur, but it is reasonable to suppose that the evidence supporting losses that did not occur will systematically be weaker than that supporting losses that did occur. This implies that unwarranted compensation for loss that did not occur will not be sufficient to offset denial of compensation for actual losses.

d) Hindsight Bias

Elhauge (2008) suggests that damages might be systematically undercompensatory due to hindsight bias, on the view that juries may underestimate the value of the invention because inventions often seem more obvious after they have been created. However, as Cotter (2013a) points out, hindsight bias might just as plausibly lead to overcompensation.[170] More generally, behavioral economics has identified a variety of psychological mechanisms that give rise to systematic biases in decision-making, so it is plausible that such mechanisms might lead to systematically biased damages, but these mechanisms turn on the details of the decision-making context, and it is not clear how these effects will play out in the context of patent damages.

e) Jury Bias

Jury trials are often used in the U.S. system. Juries are more sympathetic toward patentees than judges, and are more likely to award greater damages.[171] It is not uncommon for jury awards to be overturned on appeal as not being adequately supported by the evidence, and this suggests that jury awards are systematically overcompensatory. Even if jury awards are systematically overcompensatory, this does not imply that awards made by a judge alone are unbiased. Since damages awarded by judges and juries appear to be systematically different, both cannot be unbiased, but it is possible that both are biased.

f) Interest

Damages will be undercompensatory if interest is not awarded, as is the case in some jurisdictions.[172] This may lead to holdout, but it is a problem that impacts patent litigation, and indeed all litigation, well beyond patents for complex products, and the obvious solution is to award interest at compensatory rates.

g) Presumption of Unbiased Damages

Lemley & Shapiro give no reason for believing that errors in reasonable royalty damages (or any other damages) are unbiased. They are not alone in this; I am unaware of any scholarship in the general property and liability rules literature that makes a positive case for the view that damages assessments are unbiased, as opposed to simply assuming it. The implication is that we should presume that damages are unbiased in the absence of any evidence to the contrary, so that the burden of proof

---

[170] Cotter 2013a, 345.
[171] *See* Chien 2014, 22 and sources cited therein.
[172] *See* Cotter 2013a, 276 (noting that interest is routinely awarded in some jurisdictions, but not in others); Denicolò et al. 2008, 602–03 (suggesting that damages are likely to be undercompensatory for this reason).

lies with those who suggest damages tend to be undercompensatory.[173] As discussed above in this section, the direct arguments as to whether damages assessments are biased are not conclusive, so the presumption matters.

One possible reason for presuming that damages are fully compensatory in expectation is that full compensation is the stated goal of the law of damages generally, and the law of patent damages in particular. But in legal scholarship the fact that the courts say that they are doing something is not usually taken as particularly good evidence that they are succeeding.

On the other hand, descriptively, "[t]he standard practice in virtually all legal systems assumes the dominance of property rules over liability rules," except in circumstances in which there is a serious risk of holdup.[174] To the extent one believes that the common law tends toward efficiency, this would suggest that there is one fundamental and general concern reflected by property rights. One candidate for such a general concern is that damages are undercompensatory. That is, rather than saying that property rules are justified by undercompensatory damages, it might be suggested that the prevalence of property rights is itself reason to believe that damages are undercompensatory. However, this inference is not very strong, given that there are plausible alternative explanations for the dominance of property rules, and considering that the theory of property rights and liability rules remains unsettled.

Smith notes that, in the general literature, "[p]ro-liability rule commentators also tend to disagree with those in the pro-property rule camp on the relative magnitudes of both the hold-out and undercompensation problems,"[175] and the same appears to be true in the patent literature. This is even though the two problems are independent; there is no particular reason to believe that holdup will be large if valuation is accurate, or vice versa. It is just as plausible that both problems are large, or both are small. This suggests that intuitions on whether damages assessments are accurate may turn on general intuitions about the desirability of injunctive relief, rather than the other way around.

7.5.5 *Summary*

In the general property rights scholarship, inaccuracy of damages has been a prominent justification for injunctive relief. However, this justification is most

---

[173] *See, e.g.*, Hovenkamp & Cotter 2016, 903–04 (suggesting that "[a]bsent some reason to believe that courts systematically are likely to err in favor of defendants," there is no obvious reason to suppose that damages are undercompensatory in expectation). *See also* Shapiro 2016 (providing a model in which judicial errors are unbiased, and noting that if this is so, the errors will not affect the incentive to innovate, but without providing any support for the assumption).

[174] Epstein 1997, 2092; *see also* Smith 2004, 1731–40 (describing the "long tradition of preference for property rules in the law," except in situations involving very high transaction costs or holdout and strategic behavior).

[175] Smith 2004, 1746.

powerful when errors in damages awards are systematically undercompensatory, rather than inaccurate but unbiased. It is often assumed that errors in damages are unbiased, but there appears to be no sound justification for this assumption; but on the other hand, neither is there any compelling general reason to suppose damages are systematically significantly undercompensatory. Given the centrality of this issue to property rights generally and the question of injunctive relief for patents for complex products more specifically, the issue warrants further research.

7.6 HOLDOUT/REVERSE HOLDUP

7.6.1 *General*

Holdout, or reverse holdup, refers generally to efforts by an implementer to pay a royalty that is unfairly low. In contrast to holdup, holdout is generally undertheorized.[176] The holdout argument is typically stated informally, leaving considerable ambiguity as to the precise mechanism, with consequent lack of clarity as to the circumstances in which holdout is likely to be a problem. Once unpacked, the factors are generally ambiguous. A notable exception is Langus et al. (2013) who provide a very detailed model of holdout in the context of European law. The drawback of their model is that its very specificity makes it unclear how widely their results can be generalized.

The difficulty of enforcing patents is commonly suggested as the primary source of holdout, on the view that when damages are compensatory, the threat of an order to pay damages (and costs) does not act as an effective deterrent, because the implementer will be no worse off if it resists and is ultimately held liable than if it licenses *ex ante*. For example, Epstein et al. (2012) say that if reasonable royalty damages are capped at the amount the infringer would pay in *ex ante* negotiations,

> the blithe infringer – the infringer who for any reason falls short of "willful" – is to pay no more, if identified, sued, and defeated, than he would have had to pay if he had in fact negotiated a license at the time the standard was set. The situation is difficult enough if the patentee is in a position to identify and pursue, often at great cost, the large number of infringers. But, these assumptions ignore the high costs in the detection and enforcement of these rights.[177]

---

[176]   *See* Chien 2014, 20 (noting that holdout is "arguably undertheorized").

[177]   Epstein et al. 2012, 26–27. Kieff & Layne-Farrar 2013, 1113 argue that if a RAND commitment were interpreted as preventing SEP holders from ever seeking an injunction, "infringers would rationally consider the benefits of simply avoiding any up-front offer to take a license on any terms, RAND or not, knowing that on the back end they will not have to face an injunction for any patent that makes its way into any RAND commitment from within an SSO." However, they do not explain why it would be rational for an implementer to avoid an *ex ante* license on RAND terms if the probability of detection is high and they would eventually be required to take a license on RAND terms and pay the same RAND royalty for pre-license infringement. *See also* Wright 2014, 807 (stating that "it is well understood that weakening the availability of injunctive relief for infringement . . . may increase the

This is sometimes referred to as the "catch-me-if-you-can" problem.[178]

Comments such as these raise three distinct issues: (1) litigation costs; (2) underdetection; and to a lesser extent (3) undercompensatory damages.[179] Oligopoly power on the part of implementers is also sometimes put forward as a fourth distinct source of holdout, particularly in the context of SSOs.

1 Litigation Costs and Resource Constraints

To isolate the role of litigation costs, suppose that detection is certain and damages are fully compensatory. The basic rejoinder to the argument that implementers will take advantage of high litigation costs to force an unfair settlement is that this strategy is expensive for the implementer as well. If litigation costs are symmetric, costs drop out of most formal models, as the parties will settle in order to avoid them, and symmetric costs do not give either party an advantage in the negotiations. Indeed, it is normally suggested that high litigation costs will encourage early licensing, rather than holdout, in order to avoid the litigation costs.[180] This reasoning implies that there must be some kind of asymmetry between the parties before litigation costs can distort the royalty settlement, though when asymmetry does exist, it can result in unfair settlements.[181] The same is true if there are asymmetries in risk aversion, perhaps because of resource constraints.

probability of reverse holdup and weaken any incentives implementers have to engage in good faith negotiations with the patent holder," and that in the absence of injunctive relief "a potential licensee can delay good faith negotiation of a F/RAND license, and the patent holder can be forced to accept less than fair market value for the use of the patent," though without explaining the mechanism); Geradin 2010a, 125 (arguing that without the threat of an injunction "any firm wishing to implement a standard would be invited to begin immediately using the invention without even trying to obtain a license from the IP owner and take its chances in court later," though again without elaborating on the mechanism); Egan & Teece 2015, 13 ("Implementers can simply use the invention covered by a patent and wait to get sued, using as many diversionary tactics in the courts as is possible, knowing that it is hard, time-consuming, and expensive for a patentee to get an injunction."); Sidak 2008, 736–43; Camesasca et al. 2013, 300.

[178] Golden 2007, 2135.

[179] Note that in actual *ex ante* negotiations the royalty is presumably discounted by the probability of validity, while in U.S. law, at least, reasonable royalty damages are assessed on the basis that the patent was known to be valid and infringed. Thus, it is not strictly correct to say that the implementer who is caught will pay no more than it would have had to pay had it actually negotiated a license in the first place. However, it is true that the expected royalty (if calculated accurately) is the same whether the licensee negotiates a discounted royalty, or gambles on paying a non-discounted royalty.

[180] That is obviously true if each party bears its own costs, but even with full fee shifting in favor of the successful party, expected litigation costs will be positive, and the licensee will strictly prefer to license *ex ante*. Moreover, litigation costs are never fully shifted, particularly if one takes into account business disruption. Camesasca et al. 2013, 300, call costs "more or less irrelevant," but even very small costs are enough to make the implementer prefer to license, all else being equal.

[181] *See* Morton & Shapiro 2016 (discussing the distortion caused if litigation costs are highly asymmetric as between the patent holder and the target firm); Chien 2014 (discussing asymmetry arising when small firms are involved in litigation); Denicolò et al. 2008, 594 (noting asymmetric litigation costs may lead to holdup problem in either direction). In Lemley & Shapiro 2007a, 1999 n.16, litigation

Litigation costs may undoubtedly be asymmetric in particular cases, but there seems to be little reason to believe that litigation costs systematically favor the accused infringer either in general, or in the category of patents for complex products. Indeed, it may be that patent holders have a systematic cost advantage because litigation may impose substantial discovery costs on alleged infringers without an equivalent burden on the patent holder.[182] Similarly, patent assertion entities likely have a cost advantage over end users.[183] Nor is there any particular reason to believe infringers have a systematic resource advantage over patentees.[184]

With that said, there is no doubt that cost or resource asymmetries may cause significant distortions in some individual cases, and potentially in some categories of cases. However, it is not clear that granting injunctive relief in such cases will effectively address the problem in those cases where costs consideration favor the implementer. Litigation cost asymmetries tend to lead to unfair settlements when those costs are high relative to the value of the invention, so that the implementer's main leverage is the threat to impose high litigation costs on the patentee. The prospect of injunctive relief as a remedy, as opposed to an ongoing royalty, will shift that balance only when the extra costs imposed on the implementer by injunctive relief as opposed to an ongoing royalty – that is, the holdup costs – are large enough to counterbalance the litigation cost asymmetry. This means granting injunctive relief would not help the patentee in those cases in which the holdup threat is relatively small. With extremely high costs and delay, injunctive relief becomes entirely irrelevant.[185]

Injunctive relief might tilt the balance substantially, even in the face of high litigation costs, if there is a very large potential for holdup. But allowing holdup may not be a proportionate response, for example if the implementer was not aware of the patent when it infringed, or if the implementer had a good-faith belief that the patent

---

costs drop out of the analysis because of their focus on a percentage overcharge. However, in their model asymmetric litigation costs still result in an absolute over/undercharge.

[182] Morton & Shapiro 2016, 13; Golden 2007, 2133.

[183] Chien 2014, 13 (noting specialized PAEs have been able to drive down the costs of bringing patent cases without a corresponding reduction in the cost of defense, and "[t]he resulting gap between the cost of defense and cost of assertion has created compelling patent nuisance fee economics").

[184] Golden 2007, 2132, suggests that "a patent holder's resources for litigation might also be substantially less than those of the potential infringer," but without noting the opposite is also plausible. Golden goes on to say that the infringer enjoys an additional advantage because it will, "if it chooses, likely be able to enjoy the benefit of the invention for years before the typically tortuous process of patent litigation can produce favorable returns for the patent holder." However, if the successful patentee is fully compensated for the past infringement, and it has the resources to fund the litigation, then the fact that the patentee was not receiving royalties during the litigation period will not affect the bargaining outcome.

[185] See Golden 2007, 2134–35 ("The potential infringer may very well have a plausible claim that the threat of a permanent injunction is no real threat at all – that by the time a permanent injunction could issue, the accused product will have long since, and in the regular course of business, been either discontinued or substantially redesigned in a way that nullifies any possible claim of ongoing infringement.").

was invalid. This suggestion is more justifiable where *ex ante* negotiations were feasible, so that the result of granting injunctive relief is to induce negotiation. But in that case the holdout argument is primarily a supporting rationale for the view that injunctive relief should be preferred when *ex ante* negotiations are possible.

Most of the analysis of litigation costs in the holdup context has assumed the American rule that each party bears its own costs. Fee shifting may be a more effective way of addressing the holdout problem raised by asymmetric litigation costs, though it raises its own problems.[186]

2 Asymmetric Stakes

Golden (2007) suggests that there is an inherent asymmetry in the amount at stake in patent litigation because a patentee who is unsuccessful in litigation will lose not just the revenue from that one deal, but also from other potential licenses if the patent is held to be invalid.[187] However, this does not reflect undesirable leverage; it merely reflects the point that the negotiated royalty should reflect the probability that the patent is invalid.

7.6.2 *Underdetection*

Denicolò et al. (2008) note that implementers may infringe intentionally without seeking a license "hoping that patent holders do not have the will or the resources needed to detect or pursue each and every instance in which their patents are infringed."[188] If the probability of detection is sufficiently small, the expected royalty may be undercompensatory even in the presence of some degree of holdup; the royalties that are paid will be too high, but many will not be paid at all. Consequently, if there is a significant likelihood of underdetection, a holdout problem may arise in the sense that the implementer may choose not to negotiate a license *ex ante*, even though it anticipates that it will be held up for an excessive royalty if it has to negotiate *ex post* under the threat of an injunction. If injunctive relief is routinely denied, then the problem is exacerbated because the downside to the implementer of holding out is reduced, and so there will be more situations in which it is rational to hold out.

In the general remedies context, Polinsky & Shavell (1998) argue that the problem of underdetection justifies an award of enhanced damages under which the multiplier reflects the probability of the infringer escaping detection.[189] However, as Blair

---

[186] *See, e.g.,* Chien 2014, 40–41, for a brief discussion with citations to some of the general fee-shifting literature.

[187] Golden 2007, 2134 (noting also that even short of invalidation, failure to reach agreement might make agreement with others less likely).

[188] Denicolò et al. 2008, 591.

[189] Polinsky & Shavell 1998, 887–96.

& Cotter (2005) note, calculating the multiplier with any degree of accuracy may be impossible.[190] And as Cotter (2013a) notes, "most nations generally do not authorize awards of enhanced damages," and in the United States, which does, the availability of enhanced damages depends upon state-of-mind criteria that have relatively little to do with the underdeterrence rationale.[191]

Less attention has been focused on the implications of underdetection for injunctive relief.[192] In principle, the holdup value that a patentee, armed with the prospect of an injunction, might extract could serve as a kind of enhanced damages that would counterbalance the problem of underdetection. Even though the individual implementers who were detected would be held up, in principle this would not adversely affect implementer behavior, because the expected rate of return would not be depressed below that which would be expected if there were no holdup and no underdetection. However, there are no evident structural or institutional considerations that suggest that the problems of holdup and underdetection are likely to balance each other, even roughly, and in contrast with enhanced damages, there is no adjustable multiplier, which might, at least in principle, allow the court to balance the two factors, even if the court could assess the probability of underdetection.

7.6.3 *Undercompensatory Damages*

To isolate the issue of undercompensatory damages from that of litigation costs and underdetection, suppose that detection is certain and litigation costs are symmetric, but damages are undercompensatory. In that case, it will only be in the interest of the implementer to hold out by delaying trial if injunctive relief *is* routinely granted, in which case it will be in the interest of the implementer to delay proceedings because the effective royalty paid prior to trial, in the form of damages, will be less than the royalty it pays after trial when it has to bargain under the threat of an injunction. On the other hand, if injunctive relief is routinely denied, and the same reasonable royalty is granted post-trial as an ongoing royalty as for pretrial damages, then the implementer has no reason to delay trial, because its liability is the same before and after. On the contrary, in that case the implementer would prefer to settle early – for the undercompensatory rate that both parties anticipate being awarded in litigation – in order to avoid litigation costs. Thus, if the only concern is undercompensatory damages, routinely granting injunctive relief is the source of holdout, not a cure for it.

---

[190] Blair & Cotter 2005, 45–49 (analyzing the issue), 58 (summarizing by noting that "calculating the appropriate amount of the multiplier may be impossible").

[191] Cotter 2013a, 73.

[192] Denicolò et al. 2008, 592, raise the issue in the context of an article on injunctive relief, but they conclude only that "policy should be concerned not only with the possibility of holdup, but also with manufacturers' incentives to behave opportunistically, purposefully infringing a known patent or failing to adequately search for patents."

7.6.4 *Oligopoly Pricing in SSOs*

There is a substantial literature addressing the possibility that implementers, particularly when operating through the framework of SSOs, may exercise oligopoly power to depress royalties that would otherwise be obtained by patentees.[193] These concerns are addressed primarily through competition law. Addressing that literature is beyond this scope of this chapter, as it does not have direct implications for patent remedies.

7.6.5 *Summary*

The basic intuition behind the catch-me-if-you-can argument is that without the threat of injunctive relief, the implementer has no particular incentive to seek a license, and the burden of seeking out the implementer and initiating negotiations lies with the patentee. Injunctive relief levels the playing field (or tilts it the other way), by giving the implementer an incentive to seek out a license early on, or risk being held up. This argument is most powerful when *ex ante* licensing is feasible, in which case it supplements other arguments for injunctive relief, such as the valuation problem and the desirability of reducing transaction costs.

When *ex ante* negotiations are not feasible, so that the catch-me-if-you-can argument must stand on its own, it is less persuasive as a justification for injunctive relief as it is not clear that the specific mechanism at issue systematically favors the implementer. Holdout and holdup are normally portrayed as opposing arguments, in favor of or against injunctive relief. But as Chien (2014) argues, in many respects both can be seen as consequences of transaction costs and asymmetries in the patent litigation system, which implies that both can be addressed simultaneously by reforms that target those fundamental problems. Consequently, reforms aimed directly at these problems are desirable, such as early dispositive rulings, institutional coordination, and fee- and cost-shifting, along with other procedural reforms.[194]

7.7 ROYALTY STACKING

7.7.1 *Introduction*

Royalty stacking refers generally to any mechanism by which the total royalty burden is unduly increased by the presence of multiple patentees.[195] The term may refer to two distinct phenomena: first, where the presence of multiple patentees exacerbates the effect of one of the forms of holdup described above; and second, the Cournot

---

[193] *See, e.g.*, Sidak 2009; Farrell et al. 2007, 632; Gilbert 2011; Kieff & Layne-Farrar 2013, 1107–09; for a review of some of the literature, *see* Cotter 2009, 1200–06.

[194] Chien 2014; Morton & Shapiro 2016; Golden 2007, 2125.

[195] *See* Lemley & Shapiro 2007a, 1993 ("Royalty stacking refers to situations in which a single product potentially infringes on many patents, and thus may bear multiple royalty burdens.").

complements problem, which may arise even in the absence of holdup. The term is also commonly used to refer to any situation in which the cumulative royalty seems too high. However, a high aggregate royalty is not problematic in itself, as it may simply indicate that the licensed technologies are valuable.

7.7.2 Cumulative Effect of Holdup

Lemley & Shapiro (2007a) note that "the existence of such 'royalty stacking' exacerbates the holdup problem," and "[a]s a first approximation, the magnitude of the [holdup] problem is multiplied by the number of patents that read on the product."[196] However, Denicolò et al. (2008) point out that this is true only if the cost of redesign is independent. If the cost of designing around two patents at once is less than the sum of designing around each of the patents separately, then the holdup problem is less than additive. In the extreme case where the cost of designing around two patents at once is the same as the cost of designing around one of them, then any cumulative effect is due only to the difficulty of bargaining with two patentees rather than one, and not due to an increase in holdup itself.[197] It is not clear whether the costs of redesign are generally independent. Moreover, even if two patents could be designed around as easily as one, if the implementer faces sequential demands, independent redesign costs may arise.

7.7.3 Cournot Complements

1 Theory

The problem of Cournot complements arises in principle whenever multiple independent suppliers with market power sell complementary inputs; Cournot's example was suppliers of copper and zinc, which is combined to make brass.[198] The price decisions of each supplier impose a negative externality on other suppliers; as one supplier raises its price, demand for the product decreases, thus decreasing revenue for the other suppliers. If the suppliers price independently they will not take this externality into account, and the resultant aggregate price will be higher

---

[196] Lemley & Shapiro 2007a, 2011; *id.* at 1993 ("As a matter of simple arithmetic, royalty stacking magnifies the problems associated with injunction threats and holdup, and greatly so if many patents read on the same product.").

[197] Denicolò et al. 2008 assume symmetric bargaining power, so that the implementer would get only one-third of the total rent if it negotiated with two patentees, whereas it would get half if it negotiated with them individually; but these assumptions about bargaining power and the split of the surplus are not theoretically robust. This is not to dispute the basic point made by Denicolò et al. 2008, but rather to reinforce it; in their example and with other plausible assumptions regarding bargaining power, there might not be any stacking effect at all.

[198] Cournot 1838, 99–116.

than would be charged by a single supplier that owned all the inputs.[199] Consumers will be worse off, and the suppliers (patentees) themselves will also be worse off than if all the inputs were supplied by a single firm.

The Cournot problem does not arise unless there are multiple input owners, and it becomes worse as there are more independent input suppliers. In the patent context, the problem does not turn on the number of complementary patents, but on the number of independent price-setting owners of those patents. This implies that there will be no Cournot complements problem in an industry in which a single entity owns all the complementary patents. By the same token, the problem is mitigated or eliminated if some or all of the input owners coordinate their prices. That is, the extent of the problem depends on the number of patent owners who are independently price-setting.[200]

The Cournot complements problem does not require that the inputs are strict complements; it arises to some degree whenever the demand for one input depends on the demand for the other, so that an increase in the price of one affects demand for the other.[201]

Nor does the problem of Cournot complements turn on the presence of sunk costs holdup. However, in the absence of sunk costs holdup, Cournot price-setting alone cannot result in prices greater than the value of the patented technology. If the inputs are strict complements, then the aggregate royalty cannot exceed the combined value of the patented technology to the product to at least some users,[202] though other users will be priced out of the market. The royalty is nonetheless excessive in the sense that it is higher than the price that would be set by a single firm holding all the relevant patents.

In principle then, the loss to society comes from reduced output, rather than implementers refusing to enter the market at all. However, to the extent that

---

[199] A fortiori, it will be higher than the competitive price (marginal cost); but competitive price is not usually used as a benchmark in the patent context, as that will not provide an adequate incentive to invent.

[200] Geradin et al. 2008.

[201] For example, copper and zinc are not strict complements in making brass as they can be combined in varying proportions to create brasses with different properties.

[202] Lemley & Shapiro 2007a, 2048, do suggest that the royalty charged by an individual patentee will exceed the value of its contribution "if and only if" the value of the product without the patented technology, minus the marginal cost of the product, is greater than the value of the patented technology, which they describe as "a relatively weak condition." However, Lemley & Shapiro 2007a, 2047–48 qualify this by stating that "in the presence of holdup and opportunism, each patent has the ability to charge a royalty that exceeds the value of its patented technology," and "there is no reason why the constraint $r_i \leq v_i$, must hold if redesign costs are significant." Thus, Lemley & Shapiro have incorporated sunk costs holdup into their royalty stacking discussion. Elhauge 2008, 565, critiques Lemley & Shapiro's suggestion that where there are multiple patent owners facing one downstream firm "a 'royalty stacking' problem will be created in which each patent owner charges more than the value of its product." Elhauge 2008 says the source of this error is their failure to recognize that the implementer can "simply decline to use the overpriced technologies at all," but it is perhaps more accurate to say that Lemley & Shapiro assume sunk costs.

Cournot price-setting exacerbates sunk costs holdup, then it may result in implementers not entering the market at all.

2 Mitigating Mechanisms

A) INPUT PRICE COORDINATION. As just discussed, the extent of the Cournot
complements problem depends on the number of rights holders who set their
prices independently. Consequently, the problem is mitigated if owners of the
complementary inputs can coordinate prices, so that they are no longer
setting prices independently. Under Cournot price-setting the input owners
cumulatively make less than would a single monopolist who owned all the
inputs, so it would be in the interest of the input owners to coordinate prices
so that the cumulative price for the inputs will be the same as would be
charged by a monopolist, assuming the collective action problem can be
overcome.

Some coordination mechanisms include cross-licensing among vertically integrated firms and patent pools.[203] When vertically integrated firms cross-license on
the basis that each will charge the other the same rate for equivalent patents, then if
firm A raises its rate, it knows that firm B will raise its rate in return, and the demand-
effect externality will be internalized. If all firms are vertically integrated and
symmetrical, the Cournot complements problem will be solved.[204] More generally,
the complements problem depends not on the number of entities holding patents on
complementary inputs, but on the entities who are independently setting the input
prices, and vertically integrated firms that cross-license are effectively not independent input price-setters. However, nonintegrated upstream firms will have no interest in cross-licensing and "prefer a royalty rate that is somewhat higher than the
monopoly rate," which means that the Cournot complements problem will persist if
there are nonintegrated upstream firms.[205]

Coordination can in principle also be achieved by a patent pool, even in the
presence of non-vertically integrated upstream patent holders.[206] A pool will license
the pooled patents at a rate that maximizes profits by balancing higher royalties
against lower volumes. That is, the pool internalizes the externality in the form of
reduced volumes, which gives rise to the Cournot complements problem. Because
the price with Cournot stacking is higher than the profit-maximizing price, it is
advantageous for all patent holders to solve the problem, whether or not they are
vertically integrated. However, because of high up-front expenses associated with
their formation collective action problems, a pool will not necessarily be formed

---

[203] Layne-Farrar & Schmidt 2010, 1132–36; *see also* Contreras 2015a (discussing patent pledges as another
       coordination mechanism).
[204] Layne-Farrar & Schmidt 2010, 1135–36.
[205] *Id.* at 1136.
[206] *Id.* at 1135; Geradin et al. 2008; Lemley & Shapiro 2007a, 2014–15.

even if a successful pool would increase the patent owner's revenue.[207] These problems in pool formation mean we cannot be confident that pools will generally form so as to solve the Cournot complements problem.

B) TACIT COORDINATION THROUGH GENERALIZED BARGAINING STRATEGIES. Tacit coordination through more general bargaining strategies may also solve the Cournot complements problem. In the model generating the Cournot complements problem, each patentee sets its own per unit price while taking the prices of other patentees as given, and implementers choose quantities based on the offered price. In contrast with Cournot's single-stage price-setting model, Spulber (2016) develops a two-stage quantity-setting model. In the first stage, each input supplier (e.g., patentee), makes a binding commitment to provide whatever quantity of its input the implementers demand, up to a specified maximum. In the second stage, implementers and patentees bargain over price, resulting in a price that clears the market at the specified quantity. The result in Spulber's model is that the quantity of complementary inputs supplied is equal to the quantity that would be offered by a monopolist selling the inputs as a bundle; in other words, the royalty stacking problem disappears. The reason is that quantity-setting results in tacit coordination between patentees. Because inputs are complementary, each patentee can unilaterally set the maximum total output quantity by limiting its own input quantity offer. Because each patentee recognizes the effect of its offer on overall output, it will offer the quantity that maximizes joint profits in order to maximize the total value to be bargained over in the second stage.

The general insight from Spulber's work is that the Cournot complements problem arises because Cournot's model restricts the available strategies, and not simply from the fact of complementary input monopolies. It is of course likely that real-world licensing does not follow either Cournot's model or Spulber's, both of which assume an equilibrium outcome. For example, if patentees in fact approach the implementer sequentially, rates negotiated in earlier deals may be effectively taken as given in subsequent negotiations, and the overall equilibrium outcome will only be achieved if in the early negotiations the implementer correctly anticipates the subsequent royalty demands and bargains accordingly.

More generally, the extent of the Cournot complements problem depends on how patent holders set royalty rates in practice. A more detailed understanding of real-world royalty negotiation practices would help build a more accurate model of royalty stacking and would help identify industries in which the Cournot complements problem is likely to be important.

---

[207] *See, e.g.*, Contreras 2013, 76–77 (describing high upfront costs associated with pool formation); Lemley & Shapiro 2007a, 2014 (noting that potential pool member might try to hold out for a larger share of the pool, thus preventing the pool from forming at all).

7.8 EMPIRICAL EVIDENCE

7.8.1 *General*

Given that there are mechanisms that could plausibly mitigate the effects of both holdup and royalty stacking, at least in some circumstances, it is an empirical question as to whether these problems are "common enough and costly enough in actuality to warrant policy changes."[208] Three types of evidence are advanced: case studies, testing of quantitative models, and analysis of the industry structure.

On the whole, there is little evidence that holdup and royalty stacking are systemic problems, but there are some individual cases that are strongly suggestive of attempted holdup. Presumably there are other such cases that have settled and remain confidential.

7.8.2 *Case Studies*

1 Overview

Case studies in which arguably excessive royalties were demanded are often advanced as evidence of holdup or royalty stacking. There are two general concerns with case studies. One is that without a sound benchmark for the optimal royalty on the facts of a particular case, it may be difficult to say whether any particular royalty is too much. A second concern is that even if a particular case does illustrate pernicious royalty demands, a single example does not establish that there is a systemic problem. With that said, identifying what might be isolated instances of holdup or royalty stacking remains important as the courts may wish to respond to holdup or royalty stacking if established on the facts of a particular case, even if the problem is not systemic.

2 Distinguishing Holdup and Stacking

In case studies it can be difficult to distinguish holdup from royalty stacking. We may be able to conclude that a particular royalty is excessive because it implies an aggregate royalty for multiple patented technologies that would be excessive. But the royalty may be excessive, even without the Cournot complements problem, because the individual royalties are excessive due to holdup, or it may be excessive even without holdup as a result of the Cournot complements problem. And of course a combination is possible, in which the Cournot complements problem exacerbates individual holdup. The fact that the aggregate royalty is excessive does not in itself allow us to distinguish between these cases.[209]

---

[208] Geradin et al. 2008, 145.
[209] For example, the court in *Microsoft Corp.* v. *Motorola, Inc.* (W.D. Wash. 2013, p.73, 86) (U.S.) found that royalty stacking, rather than holdup, was the primary constraint on the upper bound of a RAND

The main problem in identifying royalty stacking in a particular case is to establish a sound benchmark for what is a reasonable aggregate royalty on the facts. The appropriate benchmark to address the Cournot complements problem is the royalty that would be charged by a single patentee holding all the relevant patents. This benchmark can be approximated by a successful patent pool. Like a single patentee, a pool will seek to maximize its revenue by considering the trade-off between a high royalty and widespread adoption of the standard. But, as noted above, pools face significant hurdles to their formation, and a relevant pool often doesn't exist. Moreover, patents that are excluded from a pool may be systematically different from those that are included. For example, if the pool in question distributes the royalties to individual patentees purely on a numerical basis, without consideration of the value of the particular patent, patents that are particularly valuable to the standard may not be adequately compensated by the pool rate. When a patentee stays out of a pool and demands a higher than pool rate, this might be because it had an average or weak patent and it was seeking to hold up implementers, but it might also be because it had a particularly valuable patent and the pool rate was not adequate. An assessment of patent quality is needed to distinguish between these possibilities.

3 Case Studies

Lemley & Shapiro (2007a) provide two examples of holdup. The first is Rambus charging "a 0.75% royalty rate for patents that do not cover industry standards and 3.50% for patents that do cover industry standards."[210] However, as Denicolò et al. (2008) point out, this misunderstands the facts in the Rambus litigation; both sets of patents covered standards, and the difference in royalty rates was due to the fact that the latter incorporated more patented components.[211]

Their second example, RIM's settlement with NTP for $612.5 million, is more persuasive.[212] The settlement was eighteen times the jury award, and the parties

royalty, but the evidence of stacking was simply an intuitive assessment that the cumulative royalty was excessive.

[210] Lemley & Shapiro 2007a, 2009 (citing Patterson 2003, 2001 n.33). Patterson in turns cites Smith 2001 as reporting that Rambus was charging a royalty of 3.5 percent of sales for rights to patents that had been incorporated in a standard, as compared with a 0.75 percent rate "for some of its other patents." Neither Patterson nor Smith stated that the other patents did not cover industry standards.

[211] Lemley & Shapiro 2007a, 2016 n.57 (citing *Rambus, Inc.* (FTC Feb. 23, 2004, ¶¶ 1262, 1390) (U.S.) (Initial Decision)). While the factual findings of the Initial Decision were vacated by the subsequent FTC Liability Opinion, *Rambus, Inc.* (FTC Aug. 2, 2006) (U.S.) (Opinion of the Commission), the Commission would still have granted a higher royalty in one respect of one standard: *see Rambus Inc. v. Fed. Trade Comm'n.* (D.C. Cir. 2008, p.462) (U.S.) (noting two standards were at issue, with a higher royalty for one than the other).

[212] Lemley & Shapiro 2007a, 2009 (citing *NTP, Inc. v. Research in Motion, Ltd.* (E.D. Va. 2003) (U.S.) (awarding reasonable royalty damages in the amount of about $33.5 million) and noting the 2006 settlement of $612.5 million).

would have had to anticipate a twelve-fold increase in sales going forward for the settlement to correspond to the reasonable royalty damages awarded by the jury.[213] Unless an extremely rapid growth in sales was plausible, or if the jury had grossly underestimated the value of the patented technology in its reasonable royalty award, this is very suggestive of holdup.

Lemley & Shapiro (2007a) also provide two case studies relating to standards, in addition to Rambus. The first relates to 3G Cellular Technology, in particular the WCDMA (3GPP) and CDMA2000 (3GPP2) standards.[214] They note the large number of patent families associated with each standard, owned by at least forty-one different companies.[215] This indicates that the structural requirements for royalty stacking are satisfied. Lemley & Shapiro then cite estimates in the range of 20 percent of the price of the phone as the total cost of the relevant licenses. Denicolò et al. (2008) dispute the accuracy of the aggregate rate, citing sources suggesting it is close to 5 percent.[216] More fundamentally, they note that even if 20 percent were the true aggregate rate, this figure in itself does not tell us that the royalty stack is excessive. Much of the value of a cell phone lies in the patented technology, and it is not obvious that 20 percent is too high for the central function-ality of a phone. The value of the intellectual property in a book is not excessive simply because it is a multiple of the value of the physical medium in which it is embodied, even if that multiple is very large. The rates themselves, without any objective estimate of the value of the patented technology, are not helpful. Further, the 3G technology at issue was widely licensed and achieved substantial market penetration,[217] which suggests that holdup and stacking did not have serious adverse effects; though, as always with case studies, it might be said that uptake would have been even greater in the absence of stacking.

The second case study provided by Lemley & Shapiro (2007a) is of the IEEE 802.11 family of Wi-Fi standards.[218] Again they note that numerous patents held by multiple companies are essential to this standard, which suggests that stacking is potentially a problem, but the only evidence they give that the stacked royalties are actually excessive is that one patentee was awarded a 6 percent royalty after litigation.[219] Geradin et al. (2008) point out that without knowing how important the patent was to the standard, we can't say from the rate alone whether the royalty was excessive.[220] More generally,

---

[213]   This is after adjusting for the fact that the jury award covered approximately six years and nine years were left on the patent. Denicolò et al. 2008, 597, argue that the settlement might have anticipated increased sales, but a twelve-fold increase seems implausibly high on its face.

[214]   Lemley & Shapiro 2007a, 2025–27.

[215]   *Id.* at 2026 (noting 732 patent families for WCDMA and 527 for CDMA2000; and noting that there are probably other unlisted SEPs).

[216]   Denicolò et al. 2008, 599–600.

[217]   Geradin et al. 2008, 160–61.

[218]   Lemley & Shapiro 2007a, 2027–28.

[219]   *Id.* at 2028 (referring to an award in favor of Symbol Technologies).

[220]   Geradin et al. 2008, 161.

this verdict may have been an outlier.[221] Courts, and juries, sometimes make mistakes. As Lemley & Shapiro (2007b) point out, only systematic errors will affect negotiating incentives.[222] A single error, even if it is a significant outlier, will not substantially affect expected outcomes or negotiated royalties.

Cotter (2009) provides several other possible examples of "patent ambush," in which patentees were alleged to have induced an SSO to adopt a standard that incorporated patented or soon-to-be patented technology, "and then, once lock-in has occurred, demanding higher royalties than the patentees would have been able to negotiate ex ante."[223] It seems clear that in these cases the patentees were attempting to get a higher royalty by negotiating after the standard was adopted, but this does not necessarily illustrate sunk costs holdup, as opposed to network value appropriation.[224] As discussed above, the value of a patented technology increases after it is adopted as part of a standard even in the absence of any sunk costs, simply because the technology is more likely to be widely adopted. Siebrasse & Cotter (2017a) argue that allowing a patentee to capture some part of this network effect value is unobjectionable from a policy perspective. It is, in any event, a distinct effect, as holdup may allow a patentee to capture more than the value of its technology to the implementer, while the network effect does not. Without a more detailed assessment of the facts, we cannot say whether the *ex post* increase in royalty demanded was due to network effect appropriation or sunk costs holdup.

Other suggestive examples are provided by recent litigation. In *Microsoft Corp. v. Motorola, Inc.*,[225] Motorola had asked for a royalty of 2.25 percent of the end-product selling price for licenses to its patents that were essential to Wi-Fi and video standards. This would have amounted to a royalty of $5.85 for an Xbox, for the Wi-Fi SEPs alone.[226] Judge Robart found that a reasonable royalty was only 3.5 cents per

---

[221]   Geradin et al. 2008 make the distinct point that "this one rate may be an outlier in comparison to non-litigated rates" because "court awarded royalty rates often include an element of punishment to ensure that future infringement is deterred." This point is speculative, and in any event it is misplaced as a critique of Lemley & Shapiro; if courts systematically add a deterrent sanction on top of the true value of the patent, this will exacerbate the holdup problem, unless the deterrent sanction is imposed only in those cases in which *ex ante* licensing was feasible.

[222]   Lemley & Shapiro 2007b, 2172.

[223]   Cotter 2009, 1188–89 (discussing *Rambus Inc. v. Fed. Trade Comm'n* (D.C. Cir. 2008) (U.S.); *Broadcom Corp. v. Qualcomm Inc.* (3d Cir. 2007) (U.S.); Negotiated Data Solutions, LLC, Analysis of Proposed Consent Order to Aid Public Comment, 73 Fed. Reg. 5846–01 (Jan. 31, 2008); *Union Oil Co. of Cal.* (FTC July 6, 2004) (U.S.) (Opinion of the Commission); *Dell Computer Corp.* (FTC May 20, 1996) (U.S.) (Consent Order); and related orders and litigation).

[224]   Denicolò et al. 2008, 597 n.80 say that "there seems little doubt that Rambus tried to holdup its licensees, but its attempt was struck down by the FTC," but they are evidently not distinguishing between sunk costs holdup and network value appropriation.

[225]   *Microsoft Corp. v. Motorola, Inc.* (W.D. Wash. 2013) (U.S.).

[226]   *See id.* at 65 (discussing evidence related to the 802.11 portfolio). The Xbox was the only Microsoft product that used Motorola's 802.11 SEPs. *Id.* at 54. The royalty actually proposed by Motorola was $3.00 to $4.50 per Xbox, because Motorola also wanted a cross-license to Microsoft's portfolio. *Id.* at 65. This corresponds to $5.85 when the value of the cross-license is added; that is the appropriate

unit, and an upper bound on a reasonable rate was 19.5 cents.[227] Therefore, Motorola's demand for the Xbox was a minimum of thirty times greater than what Judge Robart found to be reasonable, and perhaps as much as sixteen hundred times greater.[228] Not surprisingly, the U.S. Court of Appeals for the Ninth Circuit said that there was "evidence from which the jury could infer that demanding a 2.25% royalty rate was not a good-faith effort to realize the value of the technology, but rather an attempt to capitalize on the value of the standard itself – that is, to obtain the hold-up value."[229] If we accept Judge Robart's FRAND rate determination as even roughly accurate, it is difficult not to see this as an instance of holdup of some kind. The video SEPs are a particularly compelling example, because the patents related to interlaced video, which is largely obsolete, and so the technology added very little value to the standard.[230]

Lemley & Shapiro also note that a patent pool, Via Licensing, has been set up "[i]n an attempt to deal with the problem of patent stacking for 802.11 products." That is, they cite the existence of a patent pool as evidence of the royalty stacking problem. On the other hand, in their review of the evidence, Geradin et al. (2008) find there is little evidence of systemic problems of royalty stacking within standard setting "that are not already adequately dealt with through existing mechanisms, including . . . patent pools" among other mechanisms. In effect, Lemley & Shapiro cite the existence of a pool as evidence that there is a problem, and Geradin et al. (2008) cite the existence of a pool as evidence that there is not a problem. More accurately, Geradin et al. (2008) do not deny the existence of the problem,[231] but they argue it has been adequately addressed.

Even those who are skeptical of whether holdup and royalty stacking are systemic problems generally do not deny that they may occur in individual cases. It is therefore somewhat surprising that there are not more clear-cut individual cases, though that may be in part because the difficulty of assessing whether a royalty is excessive cuts both ways, and because most negotiations remain confidential. With that said, the individual cases taken together are at least strongly suggestive that excessive royalty demands resulting from holdup and/or royalty stacking do occur, at least on occasion.

comparison, because the FRAND rates found by Judge Robart did not reflect any value for cross-licenses.

[227] *Id.* at 101.

[228] The discrepancy for Motorola's video (H.264) patent portfolio was even greater, as Motorola asked for the same 2.25 percent royalty, and the FRAND rate found by Judge Robart was only 0.555 cents per unit, with an upper bound of 16.389 cents per unit.

[229] *Microsoft Corp. v. Motorola, Inc.* (9th Cir. 2015, p.1053) (U.S.).

[230] A caveat is that Motorola's portfolio included twenty-four patents, and the FRAND royalty was based on only eleven that were found to have been used. Motorola's initial demand might have reflected a good faith belief that those patents were also valid and infringed, but even if Motorola had been right, at most this would have doubled the FRAND royalty.

[231] Geradin et al. 2008, 149 ("Certainly the complements theory behind royalty stacking has stood the test of time.").

7.8.3 *Testing of Empirical Models*

1 General

Empirical studies generally do not establish that holdup and royalty stacking are serious systemic problems. Geradin et al. (2008) review the empirical evidence relating to the semiconductor, software, and biomedical device industries, and find no clear evidence that anti-commons and royalty stacking are significant problems.[232]

2 Holdup

The most important recent study is that of Galetovic et al. (2015), which examines SEPs in particular. They examine two empirical implications of the SEP holdup hypothesis. First, if holdup in the standards context is slowing the rate of innovation, then products that are highly reliant upon SEPs will experience slower rates of decrease in quality-adjusted prices than similar products that do not. Second, they consider the quasi-natural experiment resulting from the 2006 Supreme Court of the United States decision in *eBay Inc.* v. *MercExchange, LLC*,[233] which made it more difficult for SEP holders to obtain injunctions against infringers than for the holders of non-SEP patents. They find no evidence of SEP holdup on either test. With respect to the comparison between industries, they find:

> [P]roducts that are SEP-reliant have experienced faster price declines than any other good in the Consumer Price Index (CPI) over the past 16 years . . . The prices of SEP-reliant products have fallen at rates that are not only fast relative to a classic holdup industry, they are fast relative to other patent-intensive products that benefit from Moore's Law but are not SEP-reliant.[234]

On the second test, they use a difference in differences specification to test whether quality-adjusted prices fall faster in SEP-reliant industries after *eBay*, while controlling for industry and year effects. Their analysis does not allow them to reject the null hypothesis that *eBay* did not differentially affect SEP-reliant industries.

These results imply that holdup is not systemically impeding innovation in SEP-reliant industries. There are two caveats to these results that are potentially relevant to remedial issues. First, they do not claim that individual firms never attempt to engage in behavior that can be characterized as holdup.[235] Courts may wish to respond to individual instances of holdup, even if it is not a systemic problem.

---

[232] Geradin et al. 2008, 155–59. They also consider the examples of WCDMA and Wi-Fi in mobile telephony, that are discussed above, with the same conclusion. *Id.* at 159–63.
[233] *eBay Inc.* v. *MercExchange, L.L.C.* (U.S. 2006) (U.S.).
[234] Galetovic et al. 2015, 554.
[235] *Id.* at 555.

Secondly, they do not take issue with the view that the theoretical conditions for holdup exist in SEP-reliant industries, which suggests that it is some mitigating mechanism that explains their results. One possibility is that systemic holdup has been avoided as a result of structural factors such as the prevalence of *ex ante* bargaining or repeat play mechanisms. On the other hand, we have seen that it is sometimes suggested that it is legal constraints, such as the FRAND commitment, that mitigate the effect of holdup. That hypothesis is broadly consistent with the result that the prices of SEP-reliant products have fallen at rates that are fast relative to other patent-intensive products that are not SEP-reliant. It is more difficult to reconcile with the result that *eBay* has had no observable effect on holdup, but it is possible that *eBay* was effectively anticipated in the context of SEPs. That is, it may be that even before *eBay*, implementers understood that the FRAND commitment meant what it said and that they would be able to use standards subject to the FRAND commitment without fear of being held up by injunctions or excessive royalties.

From a remedial perspective, it matters what the particular mechanism might be. If structural factors are at play, this would suggest that the courts should be relatively reluctant to withhold injunctive relief to a successful patentee. On the other hand, if it is the FRAND commitment that is avoiding holdup in SEP-reliant industries, the results of Galetovic et al. (2015) show that the FRAND system is working, but it might suggest that the courts should continue to apply the FRAND principles relatively aggressively in order to ensure that the system keeps working. This might also suggest that the courts should apply a similar reluctance to grant injunctions even in respect of patents that are not FRAND committed, if the potential for holdup is otherwise present. The other side of that coin is that it is also possible that the FRAND commitment has been applied too aggressively, resulting in an inadequate incentive to invent. There appear to be no systemic studies addressing that possibility, though it is likely too soon for incentive effects to have manifested themselves.

3 Royalty Stacking

Galetovic & Gupta (2017) empirically investigate royalty stacking, and the Cournot complements problem in particular, in the world mobile wireless industry, focusing on third generation (3G) and fourth generation (4G) wireless cellular standards defined by the third generation partnership project (3GPP). Their paper draws on the fact that the number of SEP holders and the number of SEPs have grown dramatically over the life of this technology: "During the last 20 years the number of SEP holders for 3G and 4G standards grew from 2 in 1994 to 130 in 2013 and the number of SEPs rose from fewer than 150 in 1994 to more than 150,000 in 2013."[236] Cournot complements theory implies that with the increase in the number of SEP

---

[236] Galetovic & Gupta 2017, 19–20, figure 2.

holders, royalty stacking would have gotten worse. In particular, they note that the price of phones should increase or (if quality increases demand) at least stagnate; that margins of SEP holders and downstream manufacturers will fall; and that the number of device manufacturers will decrease and industry concentration will rise. They find none of these effects. On price, for example, they find that "between 1994 and 2013 and controlling for technological generation, the real average selling price of a device fell between −11.4% to −24.8% per year. Moreover, the introductory average selling price of successive generations fell."[237] They also find no trend in margins, and that industry concentration fell.[238] There are many other variables that might also affect the price of phones. Most obviously, the quality of phones has increased, raising willingness to pay, and manufacturing costs have probably decreased, and other factors such as incomes, substitute prices, and downstream intensity of price competition have also changed.[239] However, in their model, such changes cannot explain the price decrease and other observed effects, because when stacking is severe, the stacked royalty will increase to extract any benefit from cost reductions or increased demand.[240]

Galetovic & Gupta portray these results as indicating that royalty stacking has not been a systemic problem in the wireless industry, despite the large number of SEP owners. This raises a puzzle: How is this result to be reconciled with Cournot complements theory? The general Cournot complements model developed by Galetovic & Gupta (2017) shows that "even with a modest number of SEP holders, the effect of royalty stacking on output is severe and eventually, output collapses."[241] As they observe, the modern wireless industry has a large number of complementary inputs in the form of SEPs, held by independent owners. This implies that the market should "nearly disappear" and yet, as they also observe, the modern wireless industry is very healthy.

Galetovic & Gupta do not attempt to resolve this puzzle. As discussed above, the Cournot complements problem might be mitigated or solved by wide-scale price coordination, perhaps through patent pools, or possibly by specific pricing strategies or practices, but it is not obvious that such factors can explain the apparent lack of royalty stacking in the wireless industry. If Galetovic & Gupta's basic results are replicated, it is of pressing interest to explain why the wireless industry is so robust, as this might shed entirely new light on the Cournot complements problem. While Galetovic & Gupta present their work as challenging the claim that royalty stacking is a problem in complex product industries such as cellular phones, their work can also be seen as a challenge to Cournot complements theory itself.

---

[237] *Id.* at 5.
[238] *Id.* at 24–25.
[239] *Id.* at 20–21.
[240] *Id.* at 22.
[241] *Id.* at 16, referring to a scenario in which additional SEP holders do not add value. Their model produces similar results when additional SEP holders do add value: *id* at 16–17.

7.8.4 *Industry Structure*

In the general economic literature on holdup, the existence of holdup is often inferred from its institutional effects. For example, vertical integration may be a response to a potential holdup problem.[242] It is possible that the FRAND commitment can be understood as an institutional response to the holdup problem in the standards context. However, there are few studies that explore this analysis in depth, and it is not clear what remedial implications it might have.

7.8.5 *Summary*

On the whole, there is little evidence that holdup and royalty stacking are systemic problems, but there are some individual cases that are strongly suggestive of attempted holdup. The remedial implications of this conclusion are not clear, as the exact mechanism by which holdup is being kept in check is not clear. It may be that holdup is rare because of structural factors, such as repeat play, or because of legal factors such as the FRAND commitment and the threat of intervention by competition authorities; the first hypothesis suggests a general willingness to grant injunctive relief is appropriate, while the latter suggests that the courts should be vigilant to ensure than injunctions do not result in holdup. It is also reasonable to suggest that even though structural factors generally prevent holdup, the courts should be willing to deny injunctive relief in those cases where holdup is attempted. It is therefore important to distinguish these scenarios, and the factors that should consequently be considered in granting injunctive relief.

---

[242]   *See generally* Masten 1996.

Bibliography

CASES:

Australia:

Dart Indus. Inc. v. Decor Corp. Pty Ltd., [1993] 179 CLR 101 (High Ct.)
Pacific Enter. (Aust) Pty Ltd. v. Bernen Pty Ltd., [2014] FCA 1372 (Fed. Ct.)

Canada:

AbbVie Corp. v. Janssen Inc., [2014] FC 489 (Fed. Ct.)
AbbVie Corp. v. Janssen Inc., [2014] FCA 241 (Fed. Ct. App.)
Airbus Helicopters, S.A.S. v. Bell Helicopter Textron Canada Ltée, [2017] FC 170 (Fed. Ct.)
AlliedSignal Inc. v. DuPont Canada Inc., [1998] 78 CPR(3d) 129 (Fed. Ct.)
Apotex Inc. v. ADIR, [2017] FCA 23 (Fed. Ct. App.)
Apotex Inc. v. Merck & Co., [2015] FCA 171 (Fed. Ct. App.)
Eli Lilly and Co. v. Apotex Inc., [2009] FC 991 (Fed. Ct.)
Eli Lilly and Co. v. Apotex Inc., [2014] FC 1254 (Fed. Ct.)
Eurocopter v. Bell Helicopter Textron Canada Ltée, [2012] FC 113 (Fed. Ct.)
Eurocopter v. Bell Helicopter Textron Canada Ltée, [2013] FCA 219 (Fed. Ct. App.)
Frac Shack Inc. v. AFD Petroleum Ltd., [2017] FC 104 (Fed. Ct.)
J.M. Voith GmbH v. Beloit Corp., [1997] 3 FC 497 (Fed. Ct. App.)
Jay-Lor Int'l Inc. v. Penta Farm Sys. Ltd., [2007] FC 358 (Fed. Ct.)
Monsanto Canada Inc. v. Rivett, [2009] FC 317 (Fed. Ct.)
Monsanto Canada Inc. v. Rivett, [2010] FC 207 (Fed. Ct. App.)
Monsanto Canada Inc. v. Schmeiser, [2004] SSC 34 (Sup. Ct.)
Philip Morris Prod. S.A. v. Marlboro Canada Ltd., [2015] FC 364 (Fed. Ct.)
Varco Canada Ltd. v. Pason Systems Corp., [2013] FC 750 (Fed. Ct.)
Whiten v. Pilot Ins. Co., [2002] 1 S.C.R. 595 (Sup. Ct.)

China:

WatchData Co. Ltd. v. Hengbao Co. Ltd. (Beijing IP Ct. Dec. 8, 2016)
Huawei Technology Co., Ltd. v InterDigital Commc'ns, Inc. (Guangdong Higher People's Ct. Oct. 28, 2013)

Xian Xidian Jietong Wireless Commc'n Co., Ltd. (IWNComm) v. SONY Mobile Commc'n
    Prods. (China) Co. Ltd. (Beijing IP Ct. Mar. 22, 2017)

European Union:

Case C-177/16, *Autortiesību un komunicēšanās konsultāciju aģentūra/Latvijas Autoru
    apvienība (AKKA/LAA)* v. *Konkurences padome*, ECLI:EU:C:2017:689 (CJEU 2017)
Case C-15/74, *Centrafarm BV* v. *Sterling Drug Inc.*, 1974 E.C.R. 1148, ECLI:EU:C:1974:114
    (CJEU 1974)
Case C-127/73, *Belgische Radio en Televisie* v. *SV SABAM*, 1974 E.C.R. 313, ECLI:EU:
    C:1974:25 (CJEU 1974)
Case C-110/88, C-241/88 and C-242/88, *François Lucazeau* v. *Société des Auteurs, Compositeurs
    et Editeurs de Musique (SACEM)*, 1989 E.C.R. 2811, ECLI:EU:C:1989:326 (CJEU 1989)
Case C-170/13, *Huawei Techs. Co. Ltd.* v. *ZTE Corp.*, ECLI:EU:C:2014:2391 (CJEU 2014)
Case C-170/13, *Huawei Techs. Co. Ltd.* v. *ZTE Corp.*, ECLI:EU:C:2015:477 (CJEU 2015)
Case C-418/01, *IMS Health GmbH & Co. OHG* v. *NDC Health GmbH & Co. KG*, 2004 E.C.
    R. I-5069, ECLI:EU:C:2004:257 (CJEU 2004)
Case C-525/16, MEO – *Serviços de Comunicações e Multimédia SA (MEO)* v. *Autoridade da
    Concorrência*, ECLI:EU:C:2017:1020 (CJEU 2017)
Case T-201/04, *Microsoft Corp.* v. *Comm'n of the European Communities (Microsoft I)*, 2007
    E.C.R. II-3619, ECLI:EU:T:2007:289 (CJEU 2007)
Case T-167/08, *Microsoft Corp.* v. *European Comm'n (Microsoft II)*, ECLI:EU:T:2012:323
    (CJEU 2012)
Case C-99/15, *Liffers* v. *Producciones Mandarina SL*, ECLI:EU:C:2016:173 (CJEU 2016)
Case C-241/91 P and C-242/91 P, *Radio Telefis Eireann (RTE) and Independent Television
    Publications Ltd. (ITP)* v. *Comm'n of the European Communities*, 1995 E.C.R. I-808, ECLI:
    EU:C:1995:98 (CJEU 1995)
Case C-27/76, *United Brands Co. and United Brands Continental BV* v. *Comm'n of the
    European Communities*, 1978 E.C.R. 207, ECLI:EU:C:1978:22 (CJEU 1978)
Case C-57/15, *United Video Properties, Inc.* v. *Telenet NV*, ECLI:EU:C:2016:611 (CJEU 2016)
Case C-193/83, *Windsurfing Int'l Inc.* v. *Comm'n of the European Communities*, 1986 E.C.R.
    611, ECLI:EU:C:1986:75 (CJEU 1986)

France:

Cour d'appel [CA] [regional court of appeal] Paris, 23 Jan. 2013, 10/13867 – *TYC Europe*
    v. *Valeo*
Tribunal de grande instance [TGI] [ordinary court of original jurisdiction] Paris, June 25,
    2010, 01/00035 – *S.A. Technogenia* v. *S.A.R.L. Martec*
Tribunal de grande instance [TGI] [ordinary court of original jurisdiction] Paris, 24 Jan. 2013,
    10/14541 – *Hydr Am* v. *Gimaex and Weber Hydraulik*
Tribunal de grande instance [TGI] [ordinary court of original jurisdiction] Paris, 13 Nov. 2013,
    11/16713 – *Time Sport International* v. *JCR*
Tribunal de grande instance [TGI] [ordinary court of original jurisdiction] Paris, 11
    Oct. 2013, 11/14587 – *Saint Dizier Environment* v. *Materiel Santé Environment
    and CME*

Germany:

Bundesgerichtshof v. 14.3.2000 – X ZR 115/98 – GRUR 2000, 685 = NJW 2001, 1332

Bundesgerichtshof v. 6.3.1980 – X ZR 49/78 – *Tolbutamid*, GRUR 1980, 841 = NJW 1980, 2522

Bundesgerichtshof v. 2.11.2000 – I ZR 246/98 – *Gemeinkostenanteil*, GRUR 2001, 329 = NJW 2001, 2173

Bundesgerichtshof v. 24.7.2012 – X ZR 51/11 – *Flaschenträger*, GRUR 2012, 1226

Bundesgerichtshof v. 6.5.2009 – KZR 39/06 – *Orange-Book-Standard*, GRUR 2009, 694 = NJW-RR 2009, 1047

Bundesgerichtshof v. 13.7.2004 – KZR 40/02 – *Standard-Spundfass*, GRUR 2004, 966 = NJW-RR 2005, 269

Bundesgerichtshof v. 10.5.2016 – X ZR 114/13 – GRUR 2016, 1031

Landgericht Düsseldorf v. 31.3.2016 – 4a O 73/14 – *Saint Lawrence v. Vodafone*, BeckRS 2016, 08353

Landgericht Düsseldorf v. 31.3.2016 – 4a O 126/14 – *Saint Lawrence v. Vodafone*, BeckRS 2016, 08040

Oberlandesgericht Düsseldorf v. 9.5.2016 – I-15 U 35/16 – *Saint Lawrence v. Vodafone*, GRUR-RS 2016, 9322

Oberlandesgericht Düsseldorf v. 9.5.2016 – I-15 U 36/16 – *Saint Lawrence v. Vodafone*, GRUR-RS 2016, 9323

Landgericht Mannheim v. 8.1.2016 – 7 O 96/14 – *Pioneer v. Acer*, LSK 2016, 102907

Oberlandesgericht Karlsruhe v. 31.5.2016 – 6 U 55/16 – *Pioneer v. Acer*, GRUR-RS 2016, 10660

Landgericht Düsseldorf v. 19.1.2016 – 4b O 120/14 – *Unwired Planet v. Samsung*, GRUR-RS 2016, 08288

Landgericht Düsseldorf v. 19.1.2016 – 4b O 122/14 – *Unwired Planet v. Samsung*, BeckRS 2016, 08379

Landgericht Düsseldorf v. 19.1.2016 – 4b O 123/14 – *Unwired Planet v. Samsung*, BeckRS 2016, 14979

Landgericht Düsseldorf v. 3.11.2015 – 4a O 93/14 – *Sisvel v. Haier*, GRUR-RS 2016, 04073

Oberlandesgericht Düsseldorf v. 13.1.2016 – I-15 U 66/15 – *Sisvel v. Haier*, GRUR-RS 2016, 01680

Landgericht Mannheim v. 29.1.2016 – 7 O 66/15 – *NTT DoCoMo v. HTC*, BeckRS 2016, 4228

Landgericht Mannheim v. 1.7.2016 – 7 O 209/15 – *Philips v. Archos*, GRUR-RS 2016, 18389

Landgericht Mannheim v. 27.11.2015 – 2 O 106/14 – *Saint Lawrence v. Deutsche Telekom*, GRUR-RS 2015, 20077

Japan:

Fulta Elec. Machinery Co. v. Watanabe Kikai Kogyo K. K., Chiteki Zaisan Kōtō Saibansho [Intellectual Prop. High. Ct., Fourth Division] Nov. 12, 2015, Hei 27 (ne) No. 10048, Chiteki Zaisan Kōtō Saibansho Hanketsu Shōkai Hanrei Kensaku Shisutemu [*Chizai Kōsai Web*] 1 www.ip.courts.go.jp/app/files/hanrei_en/923/001923.pdf

Northcon I v. Mansei Kogyo, Saikō Saibansho [Sup. Ct.] July 11, 1997, Hei 5 (o) No. 1762, 51 Saikō Saibansho Minji Hanreishū [*Minshū*] 2573

Samsung Elecs. Co. v. Apple Japan LLC, Chiteki Zaisan Kōtō Saibansho [Intellectual Prop. High. Ct., Special Division] May 16, 2014, Hei 25 (ne) No. 10043, Chiteki Zaisan Kōtō Saibansho Hanketsu Shōkai Hanrei Kensaku Shisutemu [*Chizai Kōsai Web*] 1 (FRAND I) www.ip.courts.go.jp/eng/vcms_lf/25ne10043full.pdf

Samsung Elecs. Co. v. Apple Japan LLC, Chiteki Zaisan Kōtō Saibansho [Intellectual Prop. High. Ct., Special Division] May 16, 2014, Hei 25 (ne) No. 10007, CHITEKI ZAISAN KŌTŌ SAIBANSHO HANKETSU SHŌKAI HANREI KENSAKU SHISUTEMU [*Chizai Kōsai Web*] 1 (FRAND II) www.ip.courts.go.jp/app/files/hanrei_en/140/001140.pdf

Samsung Elecs. Co. v. Apple Japan LLC, Chiteki Zaisan Kōtō Saibansho [Intellectual Prop. High. Ct., Special Division] May 16, 2014, Hei 25 (ne) No. 10008, CHITEKI ZAISAN KŌTŌ SAIBANSHO HANKETSU SHŌKAI HANREI KENSAKU SHISUTEMU [*Chizai Kōsai Web*] 1 (FRAND III) www.ip.courts.go.jp/app/files/hanrei_en/141/001141.pdf

Sangenic Int'l Ltd. v. Aprica Children's Prod. Inc., Chiteki Zaisan Kōtō Saibansho [Intellectual Prop. High. Ct., Special Division] Feb. 1, 2013, Hei 25 (ne) No. 10015, CHITEKI ZAISAN KŌTŌ SAIBANSHO HANKETSU SHŌKAI HANREI KENSAKU SHISUTEMU [*Chizai Kōsai Web*] 1 www.ip.courts.go.jp/eng/vcms_lf/10015_zen.pdf

Chiteki Zaisan Kōtō Saibansho [Intellectual Prop. High. Ct., Third Division] Sept. 11, 2014, Hei 26 (ne) 10022, CHITEKI ZAISAN KŌTŌ SAIBANSHO HANKETSU SHŌKAI HANREI KENSAKU SHISUTEMU [*Chizai Kōsai Web*] 1 www.ip.courts.go.jp/app/files/hanrei_en/433/001433.pdf

Saikō Saibansho [Sup. Ct.] Apr. 11, 2000, Hei 10 (o) No. 364, 54 SAIKŌ SAIBANSHO MINJI HANREISHŪ [*Minshū*] 1368 (Kilby patent case) www.ip.courts.go.jp/app/files/hanrei_en/647/001647.pdf

Tōkyō Chihō Saibansho [Tokyo Dist. Ct.] Jan. 22, 2015, Hei 24 (Wa) 15621, CHITEKI ZAISAN KŌTŌ SAIBANSHO HANKETSU SHŌKAI HANREI KENSAKU SHISUTEMU [*Chizai Kōsai Web*] 1 (Cu-Ni-Si Alloy) www.ip.courts.go.jp/app/files/hanrei_en/942/001942.pdf

Korea:

LG Electronics, Inc. v. Daewoo Electronics, Inc., Supreme Court [S. Ct.], 2010da95390, Jan. 19, 2012

Samsung Electronics Co. Ltd. v. Apple Korea Ltd., Seoul Central District Court [Dist. Ct.], 2011GaHap39552, Aug. 24, 2012

Netherlands:

Rb.-Gravenhage, Mar. 14, 2012, Case No. 400367 / HA ZA 11–2212, 400376 / HA ZA 11–2213, 400385 / HA ZA 11–2215 (*Samsung Elecs. Co. Ltd. v. Apple Inc.*)

Switzerland:

Bundesgericht [BGer] [Federal Supreme Court] Mar. 16, 1971, BGE 97 II 169
Bundesgericht [BGer] [Federal Supreme Court] Jun. 27, 1972, BGE 98 II 325
Bundesgericht [BGer] [Federal Supreme Court] Oct. 3, 1972, BGE 98 II 305
Bundesgericht [BGer] [Federal Supreme Court] Mar. 6, 1992, BGE 118 II 32
Bundesgericht [BGer] [Federal Supreme Court] Dec. 19, 2005, BGE 132 III 379
Tribunal Fédéral [TF] [Federal Supreme Court] Mar. 11, 2003, 4 C.5/2003

United Kingdom:

Am. Cyanamid Co. v. Ethicon Ltd., [1975] 1 All ER 504 (HL)

Am. Cyanamid Co. v. Ethicon Ltd., [1979] RPC 215 (Ch)

Attorney General v. Blake, [2000] 4 All ER 385 (HL)

Banks v. EMI Songs Ltd. (No 2), [1996] EMLR 452 (Ch)

Cassell & Co. Ltd. v. Broome, [1972] 1 All ER 801 (HL)

Celanese Int'l Corp. v. BP Chemicals Ltd., [1999] RPC 203 (Pat)

Catnic Components Ltd. v. Hill & Smith Ltd., [1983] FSR 512 (Pat)

Design & Display Ltd. v. OOO Abbott & Anor, [2016] EWCA Civ 95 (appeal taken from IPEC)

Films Rover Int'l Ltd. v. Cannon Film Sales Ltd. [1986] 3 All ER 772 (Ch)

Gafford v. Graham, [1999] 77 P & CR 73 (Civ)

General Tire & Rubber Co. Ltd. v. Firestone Tyre & Rubber Co. Ltd., [1975] 2 All ER 173 (HL)

Gerber Garment Tech. Inc. v. Lectra Systems Ltd., [1997] RPC 443 (Civ) (appeal taken from Pat)

Glaxosmithkline UK Ltd. v. Wyeth Holdings LLC, [2017] EWCH 91 (Pat)

Hollister Inc. & Dansac A/S v. Medik Ostomy Supplies Ltd., [2011] EWPCC 024 (PCC)

Hollister Inc. & Dansac A/S v. Medik Ostomy Supplies Ltd., [2012] EWCA Civ 1419 (appeal taken from PCC)

HTC Corp. v. Nokia Corp., [2013] EWHC 3778 (Pat)

Illinois Tool Works Inc. v. Autobars Co. (Servs.) Ltd., [1974] RPC 337 (Ch)

Isenberg v. East India House Estate Co. Ltd., [1863] 3 De GJ S 263, 46 ER 637 (Ct Ch)

Island Records Ltd. v. Tring Int'l Plc., [1995] 3 All ER 444 (Ch)

Jaggard v. Sawyer, [1993] 1 EGLR 197 (Co Ct)

Jaggard v. Sawyer, [1995] 2 All ER 189 (Civ) (appeal taken from Co. Ct.)

Knight v. AXA Assurance, [2009] EWHC 1900 (QB)

Kuddus v. Chief Constable of Leicestershire Constabulary, [2001] UKHL 29

Navitaire Inc. v. easyJet Airline Co. Ltd. (No.2), [2006] RPC 4 (Ch)

Nokia OYJ v. IPCom GmbH & Co KG, [2012] EWHC 1446 (Ch)

Rookes v. Barnard, [1964] AC 1129 (HL)

Shelfer v. City of London Elec. Lighting Co., [1891–4] All ER Rep 838 (Civ)

Siddell v. Vickers, [1892] 9 RPC 152 (Civ) (appeal taken from Ch)

Ultraframe Ltd. v. Eurocell Building Plastics Ltd., [2006] EWCH 1344 (Pat)

United Horse-Shoe and Nail Co. Ltd. v. John Stewart and Co., [1888] 5 RPC 260 (HL)

Unwired Planet Int'l Ltd. v. Huawei Techs. Co., [2017] EWHC 711 (Pat)

Unwired Planet Int'l Ltd. v. Huawei Techs. Co., [2017] EWHC 1304 (Pat)

Vestergaard Frandsen A/S v. Bestnet Europe Ltd., [2011] EWCA Civ 424

Virgin Atlantic v. Premium Aircraft, [2009] EWCA Civ 1513

Vringo Infrastructure, Inc. v. ZTE (UK) Ltd., [2013] EWHC 1591 (Pat)

Wrotham Park Estate Co. v. Parkside Homes Ltd., [1974] 2 All ER 321 (Ch)

United States:

ActiveVideo Networks, Inc. v. Verizon Comm'ns, Inc., Case No. 2:10cv248, 2011 WL 4899922 (E.D. Va. 2011)

All. for the Wild Rockies v. Cottrell, 632 F.3d 1127 (9th Cir. 2011)

Alyeska Pipeline Serv. Co. v. Wilderness Soc'y, 421 U.S. 240 (1975)

Am. Hosp. Supply Corp. v. *Hosp. Prods. Ltd.*, 780 F.2d 589 (7th Cir. 1986)

Am. Safety Table Co. v. *Schreiber*, 415 F.2d 373 (2d Cir. 1969)

Am. Seating Co. v. *USSC Group, Inc.*, 513 F.3d 1262 (Fed. Cir. 2008)

Apple, Inc. v. *Motorola, Inc.*, 869 F.Supp.2d 901 (N.D. Ill. 2012)

Apple, Inc. v. *Motorola, Inc.*, 757 F.3d 1286 (Fed. Cir. 2014)

Apple, Inc. v. *Samsung Elecs. Co., Ltd.*, 678 F.3d 1314 (Fed. Cir. 2012) (*Apple I*)

Apple, Inc. v. *Samsung Elecs. Co., Ltd.*, 695 F.3d 1370 (Fed. Cir. 2012) (*Apple II*)

Apple, Inc. v. *Samsung Elecs. Co., Ltd.*, 735 F.3d 1352 (Fed. Cir. 2013) (*Apple III*)

Apple, Inc. v. *Samsung Elecs. Co., Ltd.*, 786 F.3d 983 (Fed. Cir. 2015)

Apple, Inc. v. *Samsung Elecs. Co., Ltd.*, 809 F.3d 633 (Fed. Cir. 2015) (*Apple IV*)

Apple, Inc. v. *Samsung Elecs. Co., Ltd.*, 258 F.Supp.3d 1013 (N.D. Cal. 2017)

Arctic Cat Inc. v. *Bombardier Recreational Prod., Inc.*, Case No. 14-cv-62369, 2017 WL 7732873 (S.D. Fla. 2017)

Aro Mfg. Co. v. *Convertible Top Replacement Co.*, 377 U.S. 476 (1964)

B. Braun Melsungen AG v. *Terumo Med. Corp.*, 778 F. Supp. 2d 506 (D. Del. 2011)

Bard Peripheral Vascular, Inc. v. *W. L. Gore & Assocs., Inc.*, 682 F.3d 1003 (Fed. Cir. 2012)

Bard Peripheral Vascular, Inc. v. *W. L. Gore & Assocs., Inc.*, 776 F.3d 837 (Fed. Cir. 2015)

BIC Leisure Prod., Inc. v. *Windsurfing Int'l, Inc.*, 1 F.3d 1214 (Fed. Cir. 1993)

Birdsall v. *Coolidge*, 93 U.S. 64 (1876)

Blitzsafe Texas, LLC v. *Volkswagen Grp. of Am., Inc.*, Case No. 2:15-CV-1274-JRG-RSP, 2016 WL 4778699 (E.D. Tex. 2016)

BMW of N. Am., Inc. v. *Gore*, 517 U.S. 559 (1996)

Braun Inc. v. *Dynamics Corp. of Am.*, 975 F.2d 815 (Fed. Cir. 1992)

Broadcom Corp. v. *Emulex Corp.*, Case No. SACV 09–1058 JVS (ANx); SACV 10–3963 JVS (ANx), 2012 U.S. Dist. LEXIS 129524 (C.D. Cal. 2012)

Broadcom Corp. v. *Emulex Corp.*, 732 F.3d 1325 (Fed. Cir. 2013)

Broadcom Corp. v. *Qualcomm Inc.*, 501 F.3d 297 (3d Cir. 2007)

Broadcom Corp. v. *Qualcomm Inc.*, Case No. SACV 05–467 JVS (RNBx), 2007 U.S. Dist. LEXIS 97647 (C.D. Cal. 2007)

Broadcom Corp. v. *Qualcomm Inc.*, 543 F.3d 683 (Fed. Cir. 2008)

Brooks Furniture Mfg., Inc. v. *Dutailier Int'l, Inc.*, 393 F.3d 1378 (Fed. Cir. 2005)

Carborundum Co. v. *Molten Metal Equip. Innovations, Inc.*, 72 F.3d 872 (Fed. Cir. 1995)

Carson et al. v. *American Smelting & Refining Co.*, 25 F.2d 116 (W.D. Wash. 1928)

CG Tech. Dev., LLC v. *Big Fish Games, Inc.*, Case No. 2:12-CV-00857-RCJ-VCF, 2016 WL 4521682 (D. Nev. 2016)

Cincinnati Car Co. v. *New York Rapid Transit Corp.*, 66 F.2d 592 (2d Cir. 1933)

Citigroup Glob. Mkts., Inc. v. *VCG Special Opportunities Master Fund Ltd.*, 598 F.3d 30 (2d Cir. 2010)

Commil USA, LLC v. *Cisco Sys., Inc.*, 135 S. Ct. 1920 (2015)

Commonwealth Sci. and Indus. Research Org. (CSIRO) v. *Cisco Sys., Inc.*, 809 F.3d 1295 (Fed. Cir. 2015)

Consol. Rubber Tire Co. v. *Diamond Rubber Co. of NY*, 226 F. 455 (S.D.N.Y. 1915)

Cont'l Circuits LLC v. *Intel Corp.*, Case No. CV16-2026 PHX DGC, 2017 WL 679116 (D. Ariz. 2017)

Core Wireless Licensing S.A.R.L. v. *LG Electronics, Inc.*, Case No. 2:14-CV-911, 2016 WL 4596118 (E.D. Tex. 2016)

Crosby Steam Gage & Valve Co. v. *Consol. Safety Valve Co.*, 141 U.S. 441 (1891)

CSU, LLC v. *Xerox Corp.*, 203 F.3d 1322 (Fed Cir. 2000)

Datascope Corp. v. *SMEC, Inc.*, 879 F.2d 820 (Fed. Cir. 1989)

Daubert v. Merrell Dow Pharm. Inc., 509 U.S. 579 (1993)

Dominion Res. Inc. v. Alstom Grid, Inc., Case No. 15–224, 2016 WL 5674713 (E.D. Pa. 2016)

Dowagiac Mfg. Co. v. Minn. Moline Plow Co., 235 U.S. 641 (1915)

Dowling v. U.S., 473 U.S. 207 (1985)

E.I. DuPont De Nemours & Co. v. Phillips Petroleum Co., 835 F.2d 277 (Fed. Cir. 1987)

eBay Inc. v. MercExchange, L.L.C., 547 U.S. 388 (2006)

Egry Register Co. v. Standard Register Co., 23 F.2d 438 (6th Cir. 1928)

Ericsson, Inc. v. D-Link Sys., 773 F.3d 1201 (Fed. Cir. 2014)

Finjan, Inc. v. Cisco Sys. Inc., Case No. 17-CV-00072-BLF, 2017 WL 2462423 (N.D. Cal. 2017)

Fromson v. W. Litho Plate & Supply Co., 853 F.2d 1568 (Fed. Cir. 1988) *overruled by* Knorr-Bremse Systeme Fuer Nutzfahrzeuge GmbH v. Dana Corp., 383 F.3d 1337 (Fed. Cir. 2004)

Garretson v. Clark, 111 U.S. 120 (1884)

Genband US LLC v. Metaswitch Networks Corp., 861 F.3d 1378 (Fed. Cir. 2017)

General Motors Corp. v. Devex Corp., 461 U.S. 648 (1983)

Georgia-Pacific Corp. v. U.S. Plywood Corp., 318 F. Supp. 1116 (S.D.N.Y. 1970)

Georgia-Pacific Corp. v. U.S. Plywood Corp., 446 F.2d 295 (2d Cir. 1971)

Glaxo Group Ltd. v. Apotex, Inc., 376 F.3d 1339 (Fed. Cir. 2004)

Global-Tech Appliances, Inc. v. SEB S.A., 563 U.S. 754 (2011)

Golden Blount, Inc. v. Robert H. Peterson Co., 438 F.3d 1354 (Fed. Cir. 2006)

Grain Processing Corp. v. Am. Maize-Prods. Co., 893 F. Supp. 1386 (N.D. Ind. 1995), *rev'd on other grounds*, 108 F.3d 1392 (Fed. Cir. 1997)

Grain Processing Corp. v. Am. Maize-Prods. Co., 185 F.3d 1341 (Fed. Cir. 1999)

Halo Elec., Inc. v. Pulse Elec., Inc., 136 S.Ct. 1923 (2016)

Hanson v. Alpine Valley Ski Area, Inc., 718 F.2d 1075 (Fed. Cir. 1983)

Highmark Inc. v. Allcare Health Mgmt. Sys., Inc., 134 S. Ct. 1744 (2014)

Hilton v. Braunskill, 481 U.S. 770 (1987)

Humanscale Corp. v. CompX Int'l Inc., Case No. 3:09–CV–86, 2010 WL 3397455 (E.D. Va. 2010)

i4i Ltd. Partnership v. Microsoft Corp., 598 F.3d 831 (Fed. Cir. 2010)

Illinois Tool Works Inc. v. Independent Ink, Inc., 547 U.S. 28 (2006)

Image Tech. Servs. V. Eastman Kodak Co., 125 F.3d 1195 (9th Cir. 1997)

Imperium IP Holdings (Cayman), Ltd. v. Samsung Elecs. Co., 203 F.Supp.3d 755 (E.D. Tex. 2016)

In re Innovatio IP Ventures, LLC Patent Litigation, Case No. 11 C 9308, 2013 WL 5593609 (N.D. Ill. 2013)

In re Seagate Tech., LLC, 497 F.3d 1360 (Fed. Cir. 2007) (en banc)

In the Matter of Mahurkar Double Lumen Hemodialysis Catheter Patent Litig., 831 F.Supp. 1354 (N.D. Ill. 1993), *aff'd*, 71 F.3d 1573 (Fed. Cir. 1995)

Integrated Tech. Corp. v. Rudolph Tech., Inc., 734 F.3d 1352 (Fed. Cir. 2013)

Interactive Pictures Corp. v. Infinite Pictures, Inc., 274 F.3d 1371 (Fed. Cir. 2001)

Kaufman Co. v. Lantech, Inc., 926 F.2d 1136 (Fed. Cir. 1991)

Kimberly-Clark Worldwide, Inc. v. First Quality Baby Prod., LLC, 660 F.3d 1293 (Fed. Cir. 2011)

King Instrument Corp. v. Otari Corp., 767 F.2d 853 (Fed. Cir. 1985)

King Instruments Corp. v. Perego, 65 F.3d 941 (Fed. Cir. 1995)

Kori Corp. v. Wilco Marsh Buggies & Draglines, Inc., 761 F.2d 649 (Fed. Cir. 1985)

Lam, Inc. v. Johns-Manville Corp., 668 F.2d 462 (10th Cir. 1982)

Lam, Inc. v. Johns-Manville Corp., 718 F.2d 1056 (Fed. Cir. 1983)

Lands Council v. McNair, 537 F.3d 981 (9th Cir. 2008)

LaserDynamics, Inc. v. Quanta Comp., Inc., 694 F.3d 51 (Fed. Cir. 2012)

Leesona Corp. v. United States, 599 F.2d 958 (Ct. Cl. 1979)

Lear, Inc. v. Adkins, 395 U.S. 653 (1969)

Livesay Window Co., Inc. v. Livesay Indus., Inc., 251 F.2d 469 (5th Cir. 1958)

Lucent Techs., Inc. v. Gateway, Inc., 580 F.3d 1301 (Fed. Cir. 2009)

Maxwell v. J. Baker, Inc., 86 F.3d 1098 (Fed. Cir. 1996)

Mentor Graphics Corp. v. EVE-USA, Inc., 851 F.3d 1275 (Fed. Cir. 2017), *denying rehearing and rehearing en banc*, 870 F.3d 1298 (Fed. Cir. Sep. 1, 2017).

MercExchange, LLC v. eBay, Inc., 401 F.3d 1323 (Fed. Cir. 2005)

Metso Minerals, Inc. v. Powerscreen Int'l Distribution Ltd., 788 F. Supp. 2d 71 (E.D.N.Y. 2011)

Micro Chem., Inc. v. Lextron, Inc., 318 F.3d 1119 (Fed. Cir. 2003)

Microsoft Corp. v. Motorola, Inc., Case No. C10-1823JLR, 2013 WL 2111217 (W.D. Wash. 2013)

Microsoft Corp. v. Motorola, Inc., 795 F.3d 1024 (9th Cir. 2015)

Minks v. Polaris Indus., 546 F.3d 1364 (Fed. Cir. 2008)

Minn. Min. & Mfg. Co. v. Johnson & Johnson Orthopaedics, Inc., 976 F.2d 1559 (Fed. Cir. 1999)

Monsanto Co. v. E.I. DuPont De Nemours & Co., Case No. 4:09-CV-00686-ERW, 2013 WL 10300977 (E.D. Mo. 2013)

NTP, Inc. v. Research in Motion, Ltd., Case No. Civ. A. 3:01CV767, 2003 WL 23100881 (E.D. Va. 2003)

Nichia Corp. v. Everlight Ams., Inc., 855 F.3d 1328 (Fed. Cir. 2017)

Nickson Indus., Inc. v. Rol Mfg. Co., 847 F.2d 795 (Fed. Cir. 1988)

Northern Sec. Co. v. United States, 193 U.S. 197 (1904)

Octane Fitness, LLC v. ICON Health & Fitness, Inc., 134 S.Ct. 1749 (2014)

Otter Tail Power Co. v. United States, 410 U.S. 366 (1973)

Paper Converting Mach. Co. v. Magna-Graphics Corp., 745 F.2d 11 (Fed. Cir. 1984)

Panduit Corp. v. Stahlin Bros. Fibre Works Inc., 575 F.2d 1152 (6th Cir. 1978)

PPC Broadband v. Corning Optical Commc'ns RF, LLC, Case No. 5:11-CV-761, 2016 WL 6537977 (N.D.N.Y. 2016)

Presidio Components, Inc. v. Am. Tech. Ceramics Corp., 875 F.3d 1369 (Fed. Cir. 2017)

Princo Corp. v. Int'l Trade Comm'n, 616 F.3d 1318 (Fed. Cir. 2010)

Prism Techs, LLC v. Sprint Spectrum L.P., 849 F.3d 1360 (Fed. Cir. 2017)

R-BOC Reps., Inc. v. Minemyer, 233 F. Supp. 3d 647 (N.D. Ill. 2017)

Rambus Inc. v. Fed. Trade Comm'n, 522 F.3d 456 (D.C. Cir. 2008), *cert. denied*, 129 S. Ct. 1318 (2009)

Read Corp. v. Portec, Inc., 970 F.2d 816 (Fed. Cir. 1992)

Realtek Semiconductor Corp. v. LSI Corp., 946 F. Supp.2d 998 (N.D. Cal. 2013)

Rembrandt Wireless Tech., LP v. Samsung Elects. Co., Ltd., Case No. 2:13-CV-213-JRG, 2016 WL 362540 (E.D. Tex. 2016)

ResQNet.com, Inc. v. Lansa, Inc., 594 F.3d 860 (Fed. Cir. 2010)

Ristvedt-Johnson, Inc. v. Brandt, Inc., 805 F. Supp. 557 (N.D. Ill. 1992)

Rite-Hite Corp. v. Kelley Co., 56 F.3d 1538 (Fed. Cir. 1995) (en banc)

Rude v. Westcott, 130 U.S. 152 (1889)

Samsung Elecs. Co., Ltd. v. Apple, Inc., 137 S. Ct. 429 (2016)

SCA Hygiene Prod. Aktiebolag v. First Quality Baby Prod., LLC, 807 F.3d 1311 (Fed. Cir. 2015)

SCM Corp. v. Xerox Corp., 645 F.2d 1195 (2d Cir. 1981)

Seymour v. McCormick, 57 U.S. 480 (1853)

Spansion, Inc. v. Int'l Trade Comm'n, 629 F.3d 1331, 1359 (Fed. Cir. 2010)

Spine Sol., Inc. v. Medtronic Sofamor Danek USA, Inc., 620 F.3d 1305 (Fed. Cir. 2010)

Sinclair Ref. Co. v. Jenkins Petroleum Process Co., 289 U.S. 689 (1933)

SmithKline Diagnostics, Inc. v. Helena Labs. Corp., 926 F.2d 1161 (Fed. Cir. 1991)

St. Lawrence Comm'ns LLC v. ZTE Corp., Case No. 2:15-cv-349-JRG, 2017 WL 679623 (E.D. Tex. 2017)

State Indus., Inc. v. Mor-Flo Indus., Inc., 883 F.2d 1573 (Fed. Cir. 1989)

Stevens v. Gladding, 58 U.S. 447 (1854)

Summit 6, LLC v. Samsung Electronics Co., 802 F.3d 1283 (Fed. Cir. 2015)

Sundance, Inc. v. DeMonte Fabricating Ltd., Case No. 02–73543, 2007 WL 37742 (E.D. Mich. 2007)

Tate Access Floors, Inc. v. Maxcess Techs., Inc., 222 F.3d 958 (Fed. Cir. 2000)

TCL Commc'ns Tech. Holdings, Ltd. v. Telefonaktiebolaget LM Ericsson, Case No. SACV 14–341 JVS (DFMx), 2017 WL 6611635 (C.D. Cal. 2017)

Telcordia Tech., Inc. v. Cisco Sys., Inc., 592 F.Supp.2d 727 (D. Del. 2009)

Tights, Inc. v. Kayser-Roth Corp., 442 F. Supp. 159 (M.D.N.C. 1977)

Tilghman v. Proctor, 125 U.S. 136 (1888)

TWM Mfg. Co., Inc. v. Dura Corp., 789 F.2d 895 (Fed. Cir. 1986), *cert. denied* 479 U.S. 852 (1986)

U.S. Frumentum Co. v. Lauhoff, 216 F. 610 (6th Cir. 1914)

Underwater Devices Inc. v. Morrison-Knudsen Co., 717 F.2d 1380 (Fed. Cir. 1983), *overruled by In re Seagate Tech., LLC*, 497 F.3d 1360 (Fed. Cir. 2007) (en banc)

Uniloc USA, Inc. v. Microsoft Corp., 632 F.3d 1292 (Fed. Cir. 2011)

United States v. Swift & Co., 286 U.S. 106 (1932)

Varian Med. Sys., Inc. v. Elekta AB, Case No. 15–871-LPS, 2016 WL 3748772 (D. Del. 2016)

Verizon Commc'ns, Inc v. Law Offices of Curtis V. Trinko, LLP, 540 U.S. 398 (2004)

Verizon Servs. Corp. v. Vonage Holdings Corp., 503 F.3d 1295 (Fed. Cir. 2007)

VirnetX, Inc. v. Apple Inc., 767 F.3d 1308 (Fed. Cir. 2014)

VirnetX, Inc. v. Apple Inc., Case No. 6:10-cv-00417-RWS, Doc. 1086 (E.D. Tex. 2017)

WPIB, LLC v. Kohler Co., 829 F.3d 1317 (Fed. Cir. 2016)

W. L. Gore and Assoc., Inc. v. Carlisle Corp., 1978 WL 21430, 198 U.S.P.Q. 353 (D. Del. 1978)

Wedgetail, Ltd. v. Huddleston Deluxe, Inc., 576 F.3d 1302 (Fed. Cir. 2009)

Westinghouse Electric & Mfg. Co. v. Wagner Electric & Mfg. Co., 225 U.S. 604 (1912)

Whitserve, LLC v. Computer Packages, Inc., 694 F.3d 10 (Fed. Cir. 2012)

Winter v. Natural Resources Defense Council, Inc., 555 U.S. 7 (2008)

Yale Lock Mfg. Co. v. Sargent, 117 U.S. 536 (1886)

Zegers v. Zegers, Inc., 458 F.2d 726 (7th Cir. 1972)

REGULATORY AND LEGISLATIVE MATERIALS:

Multinational:

TRIPS: Agreement on Trade-Related Aspects of Intellectual Property Rights, Apr. 15, 1994, Marrakesh Agreement Establishing the World Trade Organization, Annex 1 C, 1869 U.N. T.S. 299, 33 I.L.M. 1197 (as amended on Jan. 23, 2017)

Australia:

Patents Act 1990

Canada:

Patent Act, R.S.C. 1985, c. P-4

China:

Zhōnghuá rénmín gònghéguó zhuānlì fǎ (中华人民共和国专利法) [Patent Law of the People's Republic of China] (promulgated by the Standing Comm. Nat'l People's Cong., Dec. 27, 2008, effective Oct. 1, 2009) 2008 China Law LEXIS 7207

Ministry of Commerce of the People's Republic of China Announcement No. 25, Announcement of Approval with Additional Restrictive Conditions of the Acquisition of Motorola Mobility by Google (May 31, 2012). http://english.mofcom.gov.cn/article/policy release/domesticpolicy/201206/20120608199125.shtml

National Development and Reform Commission (NDRC) Press Release, National Development and Reform Commission Ordered Rectification of Qualcomm's Monopolistic Behavior and Fined 6 Billion Yuan (Feb. 10, 2015). www.ndrc.gov.cn/xwzx/xwfb/201502/t20150210_663822.html

European Union:

Commission Decision of 18 July 1988 relating to a proceeding under Article 86 of the EEC Treaty: Case No. IV/30.178 Napier Brown – British Sugar, 1988 O.J. (L284) 41. https://eur-lex.europa.eu/legal-content/EN/TXT/?uri=uriserv:OJ.L_.1988.284.01.0041.01.ENG

Commission Decision of 22 June 2005 relating to a proceeding pursuant to Article 82 of the EC Treaty and Article 54 of the EEA Agreement: Case COMP/A.39.116/B2 – Coca-Cola, 2005 O.J. (L253) 21. https://eur-lex.europa.eu/legal-content/EN/TXT/?uri=uriserv:OJ.L_.2005.253.01.0021.01.ENG

Commission Decision of 13 February 2012 declaring a concentration to be compatible with the common market according to Council Regulation (EC) No. 139/2004: Case COMP/M.6381 – Google/Motorola Mobility, 2012 O.J. (C75/01) 1. http://eur-lex.europa.eu/legal-content/EN/TXT/?uri=uriserv:OJ.C_.2012.075.01.0001.01.ENG (full decision available at http://eur-lex.europa.eu/legal-content/EN/TXT/?uri=CELEX:32012M6381)

Council Regulation (EC) 1/2003 of Dec. 16, 2002 on the implementation of the rules on competition laid down in Articles 81 and 82 of the Treaty, 2003 O.J. (L1) 1. http://eur-lex.europa.eu/legal-content/en/ALL/?uri=CELEX:32003R0001

Consolidated Version of the Treaty on the Functioning of the European Union (TFEU), 2012 O.J. (C326) 47. https://eur-lex.europa.eu/legal-content/EN/TXT/?uri=CELEX%3A12012E%2FTXT

Council of the European Union, *Draft Council Conclusions on the IPR Enforcement Package,* 5753/18 (Jan. 29, 2018). http://data.consilium.europa.eu/doc/document/ST-5753–2018-INIT/en/

Directive 2004/48/EC, of the European Parliament and of the Council of 29 April 2004 on the enforcement of intellectual property rights, 2004 O.J. (L195) 16. http://eur-lex.europa.eu/legal-content/EN/TXT/?uri=uriserv:OJ.L_.2004.195.01.0016.01.ENG

European Commission, *Communication from the Commission – Guidance on the Commission's Enforcement Priorities in Applying Article 82 of the EC Treaty to Abusive Exclusionary Conduct by Dominant Undertakings*, 2009 O.J. (C45/02) 7. http://eur-lex.europa.eu/legal-content/EN/TXT/?uri=uriserv:OJ.C_.2009.045.01.0007.01.ENG

Analysis of the application of Directive 2004/48/EC of the European Parliament and the Council of 29 April 2004 on the enforcement of intellectual property rights in the Member States, COM (2010) 779 final (Dec. 22, 2010). http://eur-lex.europa.eu/legal-content/EN/TXT/?uri=CELEX%3A52010SC1589

Communication from the Commission – Guidelines on applicability of Article 101 of the Treaty on the Functioning of the European Union to horizontal co-operation agreements, 2011 O.J. (C11/01) 1. https://eur-lex.europa.eu/legal-content/EN/ALL/?uri=CELEX:52011XC0114(04)

Communication form the Commission – Guidelines on the application of Article 101 of the Treaty on the Functioning of the European Union to technology transfer agreements, 2014 O.J. (C89/03) 3. http://eur-lex.europa.eu/legal-content/EN/TXT/?uri=uriserv:OJ.C_.2014.089.01.0003.01.ENG

Communication from the Commission to the European Parliament, the Council and the European Economic and Social Committee: Setting Out the EU Approach to Standard Essential Patents, COM (2017) 712 final (Nov. 29, 2017). http://eur-lex.europa.eu/legal-content/EN/TXT/?uri=CELEX:52017DC0712

Communication from the Commission to the European Parliament, the Council and the European Economic and Social Committee: Guidance on Certain Aspects of Directive 2004/48/EC of the European Parliament and of the Council on the Enforcement of Intellectual Property Rights, COM (2017) 708 final (Nov. 29, 2017). http://eur-lex.europa.eu/legal-content/EN/TXT/?uri=CELEX:52017DC0708

European Commission Press Release IP/04/382, Commission concludes on Microsoft investigation, imposes conduct remedies and a fine (Mar. 24, 2004). http://europa.eu/rapid/press-release_IP-04-382_en.htm

IP/06/979, Competition: Commission imposes penalty payment of €280.5 million on Microsoft for continued non-compliance with March 2004 Decision (July 12, 2006). http://europa.eu/rapid/press-release_IP-06-979_en.htm

IP/09/1897, Antitrust: Commission accepts commitments form Rambus lowering memory chip royalty rates (Dec. 9, 2009). http://europa.eu/rapid/press-release_IP-09-1897_en.htm

IP/17/1323, Antitrust: Commission opens formal investigation into Aspen Pharma's pricing practices for cancer medicines (May 15, 2017). http://europa.eu/rapid/press-release_IP-17-1323_en.htm

European Commission Memorandum MEMO/09/544, Antitrust: Commission accepts commitments from Rambus lowering memory chip royalty rates – frequently asked questions (Dec. 9, 2009). http://europa.eu/rapid/press-release_MEMO-09-544_en.htm

Margrethe Vestager, European Commissioner for Competition, European Commission, Speech at the Chillin' Competition Conference, Brussels: Protecting Consumers from Exploitation (Nov. 21, 2016). https://ec.europa.eu/commission/commissioners/2014–2019/vestager/announcements/protecting-consumers-exploitation_en

Summary of Commission Decision of 9 December 2009 relating to a proceeding under Article 102 of the Treaty on the Functioning of the European Union and Article 54 of the

EEA Agreement: Case COMP/38.636—RAMBUS, 2010 O.J. (C030/09) 17. http://eur-lex.europa.eu/legal-content/EN/TXT/?uri=uriserv:OJ.C_.2010.030.01.0017.01.ENG (full decision available at http://ec.europa.eu/competition/antitrust/cases/dec_docs/38636/38636_1203_1.pdf)

Summary of Commission Decision of 29 April 2014 relating to a proceeding under Article 102 of the Treaty on the Functioning of the European Union and Article 54 of the EEA Agreement: Case AT.39939 – Samsung – Enforcement of UMTS Standard Essential Patents, 2014 O.J. (C350/08) 8. http://eur-lex.europa.eu/legal-content/EN/TXT/?uri=uriserv:OJ.C_.2014.350.01.0008.01.ENG

Summary of Commission Decision of 29 April 2014 relating to a proceeding under Article 102 of the Treaty on the Functioning of the European Union and Article 54 of the EEA Agreement: Case AT.39958 – Motorola – Enforcement of GPRS Standard Essential Patents, 2014 O.J. (C344/06) 6. http://eur-lex.europa.eu/legal-content/EN/TXT/?uri=uriserv:OJ.C_.2014.344.01.0006.01.ENG

France:

Code Civil [C. civ.] [Civil Code] art. 1121, 1153–1.

Germany:

Bürgerliches Gesetzbuch [BGB] [Civil Code], Jan. 2, 2002, Bundesgesetzblatt, Teil I [BGBl I] 2003, 738, last amended by Act of Oct. 1, 2013, Bundesgesetzblatt, Teil I [BGBl I] 3719. www.gesetze-im-internet.de/englisch_bgb/index.html

Gesetz gegen Wettbewerbsbeschränkungen [GWB] [Competition Act], June 26, 2013, Bundesgesetzblatt, Teil I [BGBl I] 2013, 1750, last amended by Act of July 21, 2014, Bundesgesetzblatt, Teil I [BGBl I] 1066. www.gesetze-im-internet.de/englisch_gwb/index.html

Patentgesetz [PatG] [Patent Act], Dec. 16, 1980, Bundesgesetzblatt, Teil I [BGBl I] 1981, 1, as amended by Act of Apr. 4, 2016, Bundesgesetzblatt, Teil I [BGBl I] 2016, 558, art. 2. www.gesetze-im-internet.de/englisch_patg/index.html

Zivilprozessordnung [ZPO] [Code of Civil Procedure], Dec. 5, 2005, Bundesgesetzblatt, Teil I [BGBl I] 2007, 1781, last amended by Act of Oct. 10, 2013, Bundesgesetzblatt, Teil I [BGBl I] 3786. www.gesetze-im-internet.de/englisch_zpo/index.html

India:

Patents Act, No. 39 of 1970.

Italy:

Art. 833 Codice civile [C.c.]

Japan:

Minpō [Civ. C.] art. 404.
Tokkyo-hō [Patent Act], No. 121 of 1959.

Korea:

Patent Act, Act No. 14691, March 31, 2017.

Netherlands:

Artikel 3:13 BW.

Poland:

Kodeks cywilny [Civil Code] (1964 r. Dz. U. Nr. 16 poz. 93). http://prawo
.sejm.gov.pl/isap.nsf/DocDetails.xsp?id=WDU19640160093

Switzerland:

Obligationenrecht [OR] [Code of Obligations] Mar. 30, 1911, SR 220, art. 112. www.admin.ch
/opc/en/classified-compilation/19110009/index.html
Schweizerisches Zivilgesetzbuch [ZBG] [Civil Code] Dec. 10, 1907, SR 210, art. 2. www
.admin.ch/opc/en/classified-compilation/19070042/index.html
Schweizerisches Zivilgesetzbuch [ZBG] [Civil Code] June 25, 1954, SR 232.14, art. 73. www
.admin.ch/opc/en/classified-compilation/19540108/index.html

United Kingdom:

Chancery Amendment Act, 1858, 21 & 22 Vict. c. 27
Patents Act, 1977, c. 37

United States:

Act of Feb. 1, 1793, ch. 11, 1 Stat. 318.
Act of July 4, 1836, ch. 357, 5 Stat. 117.
Act of July 8, 1870, ch. 230, 16 Stat. 198.
Act of Feb. 4, 1887, ch. 105, 24 Stat. 387.
Act of Aug. 1, 1946, ch. 726, 60 Stat. 778.
Amendment to the U.S. Patent Act, H.R. Rep. No. 79–1587 (1946)

Clayton Act § 3, 15 U.S.C. § 14.

In the Matter of Dell Computer Corp., 121 F.T.C. 616 (FTC May 20, 1996) (Consent Order). www.ftc.gov/system/files/documents/cases/960617dellconsentorder.pdf

Federal Trade Commission (FTC). 2012. Third Party United States Federal Trade Comission's Statement on the Public Interest, In the Matter of Certain Electronic Devices, Including Wireless Communication Devices, Portable Music and Data Processing Devices, and Tablet Computers, Inv. No. 337-TA-794 (Jun. 6, 2012). www.ftc.gov/sites/default/files/documents/advocacy_documents/ftc-comment-united-states-international-trade-commission-concerning-certain-wireless-communication/1206ftcwirelesscom.pdf

FTC Act, 15 U.S.C. § 45

Froman, Michael B. G. 2013. "RE: Disapproval of the U.S. International Trade Commission's Determination in the Matter of Certain Electronic Devices, Including Wireless Communication Devices, Portable Music and Data Processing Devices, and Tablet Computers, Investigation No. 337-TA-794," Letter to the Honorable Irving A. Williamson, *Executive Office of the President, The United States Trade Representative* (Aug. 3, 2013). https://ustr.gov/sites/default/files/08032013%20Letter_1.PDF

Holleman, Richard J. 2002. "Comments on Standards Setting and Intellectual Property," *FTC/DOJ Hearings on Competition Law and Intellectual Property Law and Policy* (unpublished statement, April 10, 2002). http://web.archive.org/web/20060915153543/ and www.ftc.gov:80/opp/intellect/020418richardjholleman.pdf

In the Matter of Certain Electronic Devices, Including Wireless Communication Devices, Portable Music and Data Processing Devices, and Tablet Computers, Inv. No. 337-TA-794, 2013 WL 2453722 (ITC June 4, 2013)

In the Matter of Dell Computer Corp., 121 F.T.C. 616 (FTC May 20, 1996) (Decision and Order)

In the Matter of Motorola Mobility LLC and Google Inc., 156 F.T.C. 147 (FTC July 23, 2013) (Decision and Order)

In the Matter of Negotiated Data Solutions LLC, Case No. 051–0094 (FTC Sept. 23, 2008) (Decision and Order)

In the Matter of Robert Bosch GmbH, 155 F.T.C. 713 (FTC Apr. 23, 2013)

In the Matter of Union Oil Co. of Cal., 140 F.T.C. 123 (FTC July 27, 2005) (Decision and Order)

Innovation Act, H.R. 3309, 113th Cong. (2013)

Innovation Act, H.R. 9, 114th Cong. (2015)

Intel Corp. 2011. *Response of August 5, 2011 to Fed. Trade Comm'n Request for Comments on the Role of Patented Technology in Collaborative Industry Standards*, Project No. P111204 #00042. www.ftc.gov/policy/public-comments/comment-00042–11

Judiciary and Judicial Procedure, 28 U.S.C. § 1961

Machlup, Fritz. 1958. "An Economic Review of the Patent System," *Study of the Subcommittee on Patents, Trademarks, and Copyrights of the Committee on the Judiciary*, 85th Cong., 2d Sess., Study No. 15.

Microsoft. 2011. *Response of June 13, 2011 to Fed. Trade Comm'n Request for Comments on the Role of Patented Technology in Collaborative Industry Standards*, Project No. P111204 #00009. www.ftc.gov/policy/public-comments/comment-00009–28

Negotiated Data Solutions LLC, Analysis of Proposed Consent Order to Aid Public Comment, 73 Fed. Reg. 5846–01 (Jan. 31, 2008)

Netgear, Inc., Annual Report (Form 10-K) (Feb. 16, 2018). www.sec.gov/Archives/edgar/data/1122904/000112290418000076/ntgr20171231-10k.htm

Nokia Corp. 2011. *Response of July 8, 2011 to Fed. Trade Comm'n Request for Comments on the Role of Patented Technology in Collaborative Industry Standards*, Project No. P111204 #00032. www.ftc.gov/policy/public-comments/comment-00032-10

Patent Reform Act of 2009: Hearing on H.R. 1260 Before the H. Comm. on the Judiciary, 111th Cong. 75 (2009) (prepared statement of Professor John R. Thomas, Georgetown University Law School).v

Qualcomm Inc. 2011. *Response of June 13, 2011 to Fed. Trade Comm'n Request for Comments on the Role of Patented Technology in Collaborative Industry Standards*, Project No. P111204 #00011. www.ftc.gov/policy/public-comments/comment-00011–26

In the Matter of Rambus, Inc., 2004 WL 390647 (FTC Feb. 23, 2004) (Initial Decision). www .ftc.gov/sites/default/files/documents/cases/2004/02/040223initialdecision.pdf

In the Matter of Rambus, Inc., 2006 WL 2330117 (FTC Aug. 6, 2006) (Opinion of the Commission). www.ftc.gov/sites/default/files/documents/cases/2006/08/060802commissio nopinion.pdf

Tariff Act of 1930, 19 U.S.C. § 1337

The Evolving IP Marketplace: Hearing before the Fed. Trade Comm'n, Matter No. P093900, 15 (Feb. 11, 2009) (testimony of Professor Paul M. Janicke, University of Houston Law Center).

Robinson-Patman Act, 15 U.S.C. § 13.

Sherman Act, 15 U.S.C. § 1, § 2

U.S. Department of Justice (DOJ) Press Release 12–210, Statement of the Department of Justice's Antitrust Division on Its Decision to Close Its Investigations of Google Inc.'s Acquisition of Motorola Mobility Holdings Inc. and the Acquisitions of Certain Patents by Apple Inc., Microsoft Corp. and Research in Motion Ltd. (Feb. 13, 2012). www.justice.gov/opa/pr/statement-department-justice-s-antitrust-division-its-decision-close-its-investigations

U.S. Patent Act, 35 U.S.C. § 271, § 283, § 284, § 287, § 289.

In the Matter of Union Oil Co. Of Cal., 138 F.T.C. 1 (FTC July 6, 2004) (Opinion of the Commission). www.ftc.gov/sites/default/files/documents/cases/2004/07/040706commissio nopinion.pdf

SSO MATERIALS:

CEN-CENELEC. 2015. *CEN-CENELEC Guidelines for Implementation of the Common Policy on Patents (and other statutory intellectual property rights based on inventions)*, Brussels: CEN-CENELEC. www.cencenelec.eu/standards/Guides/Pages/default.aspx

ETSI. 2018. "Rules of Procedure of the European Telecommunications Standards Institute," in *ETSI Directives: Version 38*, Valbonne, Fr.: European Telecommunications Standards Institute. https://portal.etsi.org/directives/38_directives_feb_2018.pdf

Intellectual Property Rights (IPRs), European Telecommunications Standards Institute, www .etsi.org/about/how-we-work/intellectual-property-rights-iprs (last visited Apr. 30, 2018).

IEEE-SA Board of Governors. 2017. *IEEE-SA Standards Board Bylaws*, New York, NY: Institute of Electrical and Electronics Engineers, Inc. https://standards.ieee.org/develop/ policies/bylaws/sb_bylaws.pdf

JEDEC Solid State Technology Association. 2017. *JEDEC Manual of Organization and Procedure*, Arlington, VA: JEDEC Solid State Technology Association. www.jedec.org /sites/default/files/JM21S.pdf

BOOKS, ARTICLES AND ONLINE MATERIALS:

Allensworth, Rebecca Haw. 2014. "Casting a FRAND Shadow: The Importance of Legally Defining 'Fair and Reasonable' and How *Microsoft v. Motorola* Missed the Mark," *Texas Intellectual Property Law Journal* 22(3): 235–52.

American Bar Association (ABA). 2007. *Standards Development Patent Policy Manual* (Jorge L. Contreras, ed.), Chicago: ABA Publications.

American Intellectual Property Law Association (AIPLA). 2015. *2015 Report of the Economic Survey*, Arlington, VA: American Intellectual Property Law Association.

2017. *2017 Report of the Economic Survey*, Arlington, VA: American Intellectual Property Law Association.

American Law Institute (ALI). 1939. *Restatement (Second) of Torts.*

2011. *Restatement (Third) of Restitution and Unjust Enrichment.*

Anderman, Steven D. & John Kallaugher. 2006. *Technology Transfer and the New EU Competition Rules: Intellectual Property Licensing after Modernisation*, New York.: Oxford University Press.

Anderson, Roy Ryden. 2015. "The Compensatory Disgorgement Alternative to Restatement Third's New Remedy for Breach of Contract," *Southern Methodist University Law Review* 68(4): 953–1020.

Balganesh, Shyamkrishna. 2008. "Demystifying the Right to Exclude: Of Property, Inviolability, and Automatic Injunctions," *Harvard Journal of Law & Public Policy* 31 (2): 593–661.

Bartlett, Jason R. & Jorge L. Contreras. 2017. "Rationalizing FRAND Royalties: Can Interpleader Save the Internet of Things?," *The Review of Litigation* 36(2): 285–334.

Bayliss, Geoffrey, Daniel Brook, Trevor Cook, Matthew Felwick, Nick Gardner, Neil Jenkins, Nicholas MacFarlane, Roland Mallinson, Jocelyn Man, Christopher Morcom, David Musker, Doris Myles, David Perkins, John Reid, Tony Rollins, Ashley Roughton, Peter Smith, Edward Stanford, Jonathan Turner, Jan Vleck & Ian Wood. 2005. *Punitive Damages as a Contentious Issue of Intellectual Property Rights (Report Q186): United Kingdom*, A.I.P.P.I.: United Kingdom Group. https://aippi.org/download/commi tees/186/GR186uk.pdf

Beijing High People's Court. 2017. *Guidelines for Patent Infringement Determination.* www .cpahkltd.com/en/info.aspx?n=20170424155321600369

Belgum, Karl D. 2014. "The Next Battle over FRAND: The Definition of FRAND Terms and Multilevel Licensing," *New Matter* 39(2).

Benhamou, Yaniv. 2013. *Dommages-intérêts suite à la violation de droits de propriété intellectuelle: Etude de la méthode des redevances en droit suisse et comparé*, Zürich: Schulthess.

Benkard, Georg. 2015. *Patentgesetz*, Munich: C.H. Beck.

Bensen, Eric E. 2005. "Apportionment of Lost Profits in Contemporary Patent Damages Cases," *Virginia Journal of Law & Technology* 10(8): 1–46.

Bernstein, David E. & Eric G. Lasker. 2015. "Defending Daubert: It's Time to Amend Federal Rule of Evidence," *William & Mary Law Review* 57(1): 1–48.

Berry, Chris, Ronen Arad, Landan Ansell, Meredith Cartier & HyeYun Lee. 2015. *2015 Patent Litigation Study: A Change in Patentee Fortunes*, PricewaterhouseCoopers. www.pwc.com/us/en/forensic-services/publications/assets/2015-pwc-patent-litigation-study.pdf

2016. *2016 Patent Litigation Study: Are We at an Inflection Point?,* PricewaterhouseCoopers. www.pwc.com/us/en/forensic-services/publications/assets/2016-pwc-patent-litigation-study.pdf

2017. *2017 Patent Litigation Study: Change on the Horizon?,* PricewaterhouseCoopers. www.pwc.com/us/en/forensic-services/publications/assets/2017-patent-litigation-study.pdf

Bharadwaj, Ashish & Dipinn Verma. 2017. "China's First Injunction in Standard Essential Patent Litigation," *Journal of Intellectual Property Law & Practice* 12(9): 717–19.

Birss, Hon. Colin, Andrew Waugh, Tom Mitcheson, Douglas Campbell, Justin Turner & Tom Hinchliffe. 2016. *Terrell on the Law of Patents: Eighteenth Edition,* London: Sweet & Maxwell.

Blair, Roger D. & Thomas F. Cotter. 1998. "An Economic Analysis of Damages Rules in Intellectual Property Law," *William and Mary Law Review* 39(5): 1585–1694.

2001. "Rethinking Patent Damages," *Texas Intellectual Property Law Journal* 10(1): 1–94.

2005. *Intellectual Property: Economic and Legal Dimensions of Rights and Remedies,* New York: Cambridge University Press.

Blair, Roger D. & D. Daniel Sokol. 2013. "Welfare Standards in U.S. and E.U. Antitrust Enforcement," *Fordham Law Review* 81(5): 2497–2541.

Bohannon, Christina & Herbert Hovenkamp. 2010. "IP and Antitrust: Reformation and Harm," *Boston College Law Review* 51(4): 905–92.

2012. *Creation without Restraint: Promoting Liberty and Rivalry in Innovation,* New York: Oxford University Press.

Bowman, Ward S. 1973. *Patent and Antitrust Law: A Legal and Economic Appraisal,* Chicago: University of Chicago Press.

Brooks, Roger G. & Damien Geradin. 2010. *Interpreting and Enforcing the Voluntary FRAND Commitment.* https://ssrn.com/abstract=1645878

Byrd, Owen, Brian C. Howard & Jason Maples. 2014. *2014 Lex Machina Patent Litigation Damages Report,* Menlo Park, CA: Lex Machina.

Caffarra, Cristina. 2014. "Patent Explosion and Patent Wars: Holdup, Royalties and Misunderstandings over 'Market Value'," *European Competition Law Annual* 2012: 307–29.

Calabresi, Guido & A. Douglas Melamed. 1972. "Property Rules, Liability Rules, and Inalienability: One View of the Cathedral," *Harvard Law Review* 85: 1089–1128.

Camesasca, Peter, Gregor Langus, Damien Neven & Pat Treacy. 2013. "Injunctions for Standard-Essential Patents: Justice Is Not Blind," *Journal of Competition Law & Economics* 9(2): 285–311.

Campbell, John E., Bernard Chao, Christopher T. Roberson & David V. Yokum. 2016. "Countering the Plaintiff's Anchor: Jury Simulations to Evaluate Damages Arguments," *Iowa Law Review* 101(2): 543–71.

Carlton, Dennis W. & Allan L. Shampine. 2013. "An Economic Interpretation of FRAND," *Journal of Competition Law & Economics* 9(3): 531–52.

Caron, Christophe. 2013. "L'efficacité des licences FRAND: entre droit des brevets, droit civil et normalisation," *La Semaine Juridique, Edition Générale* 2013(21): 1006–13.

Carter, James H. 2014. "FRAND Royalty Disputes: A New Challenge for International Arbitration?," in Arthur W. Rovine, ed., *Contemporary Issues in International Arbitration and Mediation – the Fordham Papers 2013,* Boston: Brill Nijhoff.

Cary, George S., Mark W. Nelson, Steven J. Kaiser & Alex R. Sistla. 2011. "The Case for Antitrust Law to Police the Patent Holdup Problem in Standard Setting," *Antitrust Law Journal* 77(3): 913–45.

Chao, Bernard. 2012. "The Case for Contribution in Patent Law," *University of Cincinnati Law Review* 80(1): 113–59.

  2016. "Horizontal Innovation and Interface Patents," *Wisconsin Law Review* 2016(2): 287–336.

  2018. "Lost Profits in a Multicomponent World," *Boston College Law Review* 59(4): 1321–56.

Chao, Bernard & Jonathan Gray. 2013. "A $1 Billion Parable," *Denver University Law Review* 90: 185–91.

Chapman, Gretchen B. & Brian H. Bornstein. 1996. "The More You Ask For, the More You Get: Anchoring in Personal Injury Verdicts," *Applied Cognitive Psychology* 10 (6): 519–40.

Chiang, Tun-Jen. 2017. "The Information-Forcing Dilemma in Damages Law," *William & Mary Law Review* 59(1): 81–145.

Chien, Colleen V. 2014. "Holding Up and Holding Out," *Michigan Telecommunications & Technology Law Review* 21(1): 1–41.

  2016. "Contextualizing Patent Disclosure," *Vanderbilt Law Review* 69(6): 1849–90.

Chien, Colleen V. & Mark A. Lemley. 2012. "Patent Holdup, the ITC, and the Public Interest," *Cornell Law Review* 98(1): 1–46.

Chisum, Donald S. 2017. *Chisum on Patents*, Binghamton, NY: Matthew Bender & Company, Inc.

Choi, Jay Pil. 2009. "Alternative Damage Rules and Probabilistic Intellectual Property Rights: Unjust Enrichment, Lost Profits, and Reasonable Royalty Remedies," *Information Economics & Policy* 21(2): 145–57.

Colangelo, Giuseppe & Valerio Torti. 2017. "Filling Huawei's Gaps: The Recent German Case Law on Standard Essential Patents," *European Competition Law Review* 2017 38 (12): 538–46.

Conley, Ned L. 1987. "An Economic Approach to Patent Damages," *AIPLA Quarterly Journal* 15(4): 354–90.

Contreras, Jorge L. 2012. "The February of FRAND," *Patently-O*, Mar. 6, 2012. https://patentlyo.com/patent/2012/03/february-of-frand.html

  2013. "Fixing FRAND: A Pseudo-Pool Approach to Standards-Based Patent Licensing," *Antitrust Law Journal* 79(1): 47–97.

  2015a. "Patent Pledges," *Arizona State Law Journal* 47(3): 543–608.

  2015b. "A Brief History of FRAND: Analyzing Current Debates in Standard Setting and Antitrust Through a Historical Lens," *Antitrust Law Journal* 80(1): 39–120.

  2015c. "A Market Reliance Theory for FRAND Commitments and Other Patent Pledges," *Utah Law Review* 2015(2): 479–558.

  2016. "When a Stranger Calls: Standards Outsiders and Unencumbered Patents," *Journal of Competition Law & Economics* 12(3): 507–39.

  2017a. "Aggregated Royalties for Top-Down FRAND Determinations: Revisiting Joint Negotiation," *Antitrust Bulletin* 62(4): 690–709.

  2017b. "Global Markets, Competition, and FRAND Royalties: The Many Implications of *Unwired Planet v. Huawei*," *The Antitrust Source* 17(1): 1–14.

Contreras, Jorge L., Colleen Chien, Thomas F. Cotter & Brad Biddle. 2016. "Study Proposal – Commercial Patent Licensing Data." https://papers.ssrn.com/abstract_id=2755706

Contreras, Jorge L. & Michael A. Eixenberger. 2016. "Model Jury Instructions for Reasonable Royalty Patent Damages," *Jurimetrics* 57(1): 1–24.

Contreras, Jorge L. & Richard J. Gilbert. 2015. "A Unified Framework for RAND and Other Reasonable Royalties," *Berkeley Technology Law Journal* 30: 1451–1504.

Contreras, Jorge L. & David L. Newman. 2014. "Developing a Framework for Arbitrating Standards-Essential Patent Disputes," *Journal of Dispute Resolution* 2014(1): 23–50.

Contreras, Jorge L. & Peter Georg Picht. 2017. "Patent Assertion Entities and Legal Exceptionalism in Europe and the United States, A Comparative View," *Max Planck Institute for Innovation and Competition Research Paper No. 17–11*. https://ssrn.com /abstract=3036578

Cotropia, Christopher A. 2008. "Compulsory Licensing Under TRIPS and the Supreme Court of the United States' Decision in *eBay* v. *MercExchange*," in Toshiko Takenaka, ed., *Patent Law and Theory: A Handbook of Contemporary Research*, Northampton, MA: Edward Elgar Publishing, Inc.

Cotropia, Christopher A., Jay P. Kesan & David L. Schwartz. 2014. "Unpacking Patent Assertion Entities (PAEs)," *Minnesota Law Review* 99(2): 649–703.

Cotropia, Christopher A. & Mark A. Lemley. 2009. "Copying in Patent Law," *North Carolina Law Review* 87(5): 1421–66.

Cotter, Thomas F. 2004. "An Economic Analysis of Enhanced Damages and Attorney's Fees for Willful Patent Infringement," *Federal Circuit Bar Journal* 14: 291–331.

2009. "Patent Holdup, Patent Remedies, and Antitrust Responses," *Journal of Corporation Law* 34: 1151–1207.

2011. "Four Principles for Calculating Reasonable Royalties in Patent Infringement Litigation," *Santa Clara Computer and High Technology Law Journal* 27(4): 725–61.

2013a. *Comparative Patent Remedies: A Legal and Economic Analysis*, New York: Oxford University Press.

2013b. "Reining in Remedies in Patent Litigation: Three (Increasingly Immodest) Proposals," *Santa Clara High Tech Law Journal* 30: 1–30.

2013c. "After a Six-Month Hiatus, Enhanced Damages for Patent Infringement in Taiwan Are Back," *Comparative Patent Remedies*, Aug. 6, 2013. http://comparativepatentreme dies.blogspot.com/2013/08/after-six-month-hiatus-enhanced-damages.html

2013d. "Kleinheyer and Hartwig on Allocation of Defendant's Profits in Germany," *Comparative Patent Remedies*, Sep. 18, 2013. http://comparativepatentremedies .blogspot.jp/2013/09/kleinheyer-and-hartwig-on-allocation-of.html

2013e. "The Draft Fourth Amendment of the Chinese Patent Act Would Authorize Treble Damages for Willful Infringement," *Comparative Patent Remedies*, Oct. 31, 2013. http://comparativepatentremedies.blogspot.com/2013/10/the-draft-fourth-amendment-of-chinese.html

2013f. "Punitive Damages for Patent Infringement in the UK?," *Comparative Patent Remedies*, Nov. 27, 2013. http://comparativepatentremedies.blogspot.com/2013/11/puni tive-damages-for-patent.html

2013g. "Article by Meier-Beck on Infringement Damages Under German Law," *Comparative Patent Remedies*, Dec. 11, 2013. http://comparativepatentremedies .blogspot.jp/2013/12/article-by-meier-beck-on-infringement.html

2014a. "Comparative Law and Economics of Standard-Essential Patents and FRAND Royalties," *Texas Intellectual Property Law Journal* 22: 311–63.

2014b. "*Bobst* v. *Heidelberg*: A Recent French Case on Lost Profits," *Comparative Patent Remedies*, Jan. 24, 2014. http://comparativepatentremedies.blogspot.com/2014/01/bobst-v-heidelberg-recent-french-case.html

2014c. "Setting the Amount of an Injunction Bond (and a Brief Digression about the Wright Brothers)," *Comparative Patent Remedies*, Apr. 18, 2014. http://comparative patentremedies.blogspot.com/2014/04/setting-amount-of-injunction-bond-and.html

2015. "A Study of Reasonable Royalty Awards in Japan," *Comparative Patent Remedies*, Mar. 23, 2015. https://comparativepatentremedies.blogspot.com/2015/03/a-study-of-reasonable-royalty-awards-in.html

2016a. "A Recent English Decision on Accountings of Profits," *Comparative Patent Remedies*, Feb. 29, 2016. http://comparativepatentremedies.blogspot.jp/2016/02/a-recent-english-decision-on.html

2016b. "Infringer's Profits as a Proxy for Plaintiff's Lost Profits in Japan," *Comparative Patent Remedies*, June 8, 2016. http://comparativepatentremedies.blogspot.com/2016/06/infringers-profits-as-proxy-for.html

2016c. "Damages for Moral Prejudice in Spain and Elsewhere," *Comparative Patent Remedies*, June 20, 2016. http://comparativepatentremedies.blogspot.com/2016/06/damages-for-moral-prejudice-in-spain.html

2016d. "CJEU Rules on Recovery of Attorney's Fees and Other Costs," *Comparative Patent Remedies*, Aug. 22, 2016. http://comparativepatentremedies.blogspot.com/2016/08/cjeu-rules-on-recovery-of-attorneys.html

2016e. "A Couple of Commentaries on Genentech v. Hoechst," *Comparative Patent Remedies*, Nov. 18, 2016. http://comparativepatentremedies.blogspot.com/2016/11/a-couple-of-commentaries-on-genentech-v.html

2016f. "From Around the Blogs: Lost Profits in China, Accountings of Profits in Canada, and Reasonable Royalties in the U.S.," *Comparative Patent Remedies*, Dec. 15, 2016. http://comparativepatentremedies.blogspot.com/2016/12/from-around-blogs-lost-profits-in-china.html

2017. "Stays Pending Design-Around in Germany?," *Comparative Patent Remedies*, Feb. 16, 2017. http://comparativepatentremedies.blogspot.com/2017/02/stays-pending-design-around-in-germany.html

2018. "Patent Damages Heuristics," *Texas Intellectual Property Law Journal* 25(2): 159–213.

Cotter, Thomas F. & John M. Golden. 2018. "Empirical Studies Relating to Patents: Remedies," in Peter S. Menell and David L. Schwartz, eds., *Research Handbook on the Economics of Intellectual Property Law: Analytical Methods*, Cheltenham: Edward Elgar, https://papers.ssrn.com/sol3/papers.cfm?abstract_id=2665680 (forthcoming).

Cotter, Thomas F., Erik Hovenkamp & Norman V. Siebrasse. 2019. "Switching Costs, Path Dependence and Patent Holdup," *Washington and Lee Law Review* (forthcoming).

Cournot, Augustin. 1838. *Researches into the Mathematical Principles of the Theory of Wealth*, Nathaniel T. Bacon trans., New York: Augustus M. Kelley Publishers.

Covington & Burling LLP. 2015. "China's Draft Patent Law Seeks Five Fold Increase on Damages Cap for Patent Infringement Cases," *Covington Alert*, Dec. 9, 2015. www.cov.com/-/media/files/corporate/publications/2015/12/chinas_draft_patent_law_seeks_five_fold_increase_on_damages_cap_for_patent_infringement_cases.pdf

Cox, Alan. 2017. "The Limited Role of Analytical Approach to Reasonable Royalty," *Law360*, Apr. 13, 2017.

Cremers, Katrin, Fabian Gaessler, Dietmar Harhoff, Christian Helmers & Yassine Lefouili. 2016. "Invalid but Infringed? An Analysis of the Bifurcated Patent Litigation System," *Journal of Economic Behavior & Organization* 131(1): 218–42.

Crowne, Emir. 2015. "Non-Infringing Alternatives Make Their Way into Canadian Law," *Journal of Intellectual Property Law & Practice* 10(12): 889–90.

Cui, Xiaoguang & Lena (Lanying) Shen. 2016. "China," in Michael C. Elmer & C. Gregory Gramenopoulos, eds., *Global Patent Litigation: How and Where to Win, Second Edition*, Arlington VA: Bloomberg BNA.

Cui, Yabing. 2018. "Across the Faulty Lines: Chinese Judicial Approaches to Injunctions and SEPs," *China IPR*, Jun. 5, 2018. https://chinaipr.com/2018/06/05/across-the-fault-lines-chinese-judicial-approaches-to-injunctions-and-seps/

Dasgupta, Partha & Joseph Stiglitz. 1980. "Uncertainty, Industrial Structure, and the Speed of R&D," *Bell Journal of Economics* 11(1): 1–28.

De Coninck, Raphaël & Elina Koustoumpardi. 2017. "Excessive Pricing Cases in the Pharmaceutical Industry: Economic Considerations and Practical Pitfalls," *Concurrences* 2017(3): 9–16.

De Werra, Jacques. 2014. "The Expanding Significance of Arbitration for Patent Licensing Disputes: From Post-Termination Disputes to Pre-Licensing FRAND Disputes," *ASA Bulletin* 32(4): 692–706.

Delrahim, Makan. 2017. "Take It to the Limit: Respecting Innovation Incentives in the Application of Antitrust Law," *Remarks Prepared for Delivery at USC Gould School of Law – Application of Competition Policy to Technology and IP Licensing*, Nov. 10, 2017. www.justice.gov/opa/speech/assistant-attorney-general-makan-delrahim-delivers-remarks-usc-gould-school-laws-center

Denicolò, Vincenzo, Damien Geradin, Anne Layne-Farrar & A. Jorge Padilla. 2008. "Revisiting Injunctive Relief: Interpreting eBay in High-Tech Industries with Non-Practicing Patent Holders," *Journal of Competition Law & Economics* 4(3): 571–608.

Di Pietro, Susanne, Teresa W. Carns, & Pamela Kelley. 1995. "Alaska's English Rule: Attorney's Fee Shifting in Civil Cases," *Report to the Alaska Judicial Council*. www.ajc.state.ak.us/reports/atyfee.pdf

Dobbs, Dan B. 1993. *Dobbs Law of Remedies: Second Edition, Volume 1*, St. Paul, MN: West Publishing Co.

Dumont, Béatrice. 2015. "Does Patent Quality Drive Damages in Patent Lawsuits? Lessons from the French Judicial System," *Review of Law & Economics* 11(2): 355–83.

Durie, Daralyn J. & Mark A. Lemley. 2010. "A Structured Approach to Calculating Reasonable Royalties," *Lewis & Clark Law Review* 14: 627–50.

Egan, Edward J. & David J. Teece. 2015. "Untangling the Patent Thicket Literature," *Tusher Center for the Management of Intellectual Capital*, Working Paper No. 7. http://innovation-archives.berkeley.edu/businessinnovation/documents/Tusher-Center-Working-Paper-7.pdf

Eisenberg, Melvin A. 2006. "The Disgorgement Interest in Contract Law," *Michigan Law Review* 105(3): 559–602.

Elhauge, Einer. 2008. "Do Patent Holdup and Royalty Stacking Lead to Systematically Excessive Royalties?," *Journal of Competition Law & Economics* 4(3): 535–70.

Elmer, Michael C. & C. Gregory Gramenopoulos. 2016. *Global Patent Litigation: How and Where to Win, Second Edition*, Arlington VA: Bloomberg BNA.

Emch, Adrian & Jiaming Zhang. 2016. "Chinese Competition Law – The Year 2015 in Review," *Global Competition Litigation Review* 2016(1): 30–37.

Epstein, Richard A. 1997. "A Clear View of the Cathedral: The Dominance of Property Rules," *Yale Law Journal* 106(7): 2091–2120.

　　2010. "The Disintegration of Intellectual Property? A Classical Liberal Response to a Premature Obituary," *Stanford Law Review* 62(2): 455–522.

Epstein, Richard A. & David J. Kappos. 2013. "Legal Remedies for Patent Infringement: From General Principles to FRAND Obligations for Standard Essential Patents," *Competition Policy International* 9(2): 69–89.

Epstein, Richard A., F. Scott Kieff, & Daniel F. Spulber. 2012. "The FTC, IP, and SSOs: Government Hold-Up Replacing Private Coordination," *Journal of Competition Law & Economics* 8(1): 1–46.

Epstein, Roy. 2006. "Prejudgment Interest Rates in Patent Cases: Don't Compound an Error," *IPL Newsletter* 24(2): 1–12. www.royepstein.com/Epstein_ipl_winter_2006.pdf

Epstein, Roy J. & Alan J. Marcus. 2003. "Economic Analysis of the Reasonable Royalty: Simplification and Extension of the Georgia-Pacific Factors," *Journal of the Patent and Trademark Office Society* 85(7): 555–81.

Europe Economics. 2016. *JRC Science for Policy Report: Patent Assertion Entities in Europe: Their Impact on Innovation and Knowledge Transfer in ICT Markets* (Nikolaus Thumm & Garry Gabison eds.), Luxembourg: Publications Office of the European Union. http://publications.jrc.ec.europa.eu/repository/bitstream/JRC103321/lfna28145enn.pdf

Evans, David S. & A. Jorge Padilla. 2005. "Excessive Prices: Using Economics to Define Administrable Legal Rules," *Journal of Competition Law & Economics* 1(1): 97–122.

Ezrachi, Ariel & David Gilo. 2009. "Are Excessive Prices Really Self-Correcting?," *Journal of Competition Law & Economics* 5(2): 249–68.

Faigman, David L. & Edward J. Imwinkelreid. 2013. "Wading into the Daubert Tide: *Sargon Enterprises, Inc. v. University of Southern California*," *Hastings Law Journal* 64(6): 1665–96.

Fairfield Resources International. 2007. *Analysis of Patents Declared as Essential to GSM as of June 6, 2007.* http://frlicense.com/GSM_FINAL.pdf

   2010. *Review of Patents Declared as Essential to LTE and SAE (4G Wireless Standards) Through June 30, 2009.* www.frlicense.com/LTE%20Final%20Report.pdf

Farrell, Joseph, John Hayes, Carl Shapiro & Theresa Sullivan. 2007. "Standard Setting, Patents, and Hold-Up," *Antitrust Law Journal* 74: 603–70.

Federal Circuit Bar Association (FCBA). 2016. "Model Patent Jury Instructions." https://fedcirbar.org/IntegralSource/Model-Patent-Jury-Instructions

Federal Trade Commission (FTC). 2003. *To Promote Innovation: The Proper Balance of Competition and Patent Law and Policy.* www.ftc.gov/reports/promote-innovation-proper-balance-competition-patent-law-policy

   2011. *The Evolving IP Marketplace: Aligning Patent Notice and Remedies with Competition.* www.ftc.gov/reports/evolving-ip-marketplace-aligning-patent-notice-remedies-competition

Fennell, Lee Anne. 2006. "Efficient Trespass: The Case for Bad Faith Adverse Possession," *Northwestern University Law Review* 100(3): 1037–96.

Fish & Richardson, P.C. 2018. "Prejudgment and Post-Judgment Interest," *Patent Damages Services.* www.fr.com/services/litigation/patent/patent-damages/prejudgment-and-post-judgment-interest/

Flanz, Scott M. 2016. "*Octane Fitness*: The Shifting of Patent Attorneys' Fees Moves into High Gear," *Stanford Technology Law Review* 19(2): 329–63.

Flynn, John J. 1968. "Consent Decrees in Antitrust Enforcement: Some Thoughts and Proposals," *Iowa Law Review* 53(5): 983–1019.

Fournier, Gary M. & Thomas W. Zuehlke. 1989. "Litigation and Settlement: An Empirical Approach," *The Review of Economics and Statistics* 71(2): 189–95.

Fox, Nicholas, Bas Berghuis, Ina vom Feld & Laura Orlando. 2015. "Accounting for Differences: Damages and Profits in European Patent Infringement," *European Intellectual Property Review* 37(9): 566–74.

Frischmann, Brett M. & Mark A. Lemley. 2007. "Spillovers," *Columbia Law Review* 107: 257–301.

Furnham, Adrian & Hua Chu Boo. 2011. "A Literature Review of the Anchoring Effect," *The Journal of Socio-Economics* 40(1): 35–42.

Gal, Michal S. 2013. "Abuse of Dominance – Exploitative Abuses," in Ioannis Lianos & Damien Geradin, eds., *Handbook on European Competition Law: Substantive Aspects*, Northampton, MA: Edward Elgar Publishing, Inc.

Galetovic, Alexander & Kirti Gupta. 2017. "Royalty Stacking and Standard Essential Patents: Theory and Evidence from the World Mobile Wireless Industry." https://papers.ssrn.com/sol3/papers.cfm?abstract_id=2790347

Galetovic, Alexander, Stephen Haber & Ross Levine. 2015. "An Empirical Examination of Patent Holdup," *Journal of Competition Law & Economics* 11(3): 549–78.

Gallini, Nancy T. & Ralph A. Winter. 1985. "Licensing in the Theory of Innovation," *The RAND Journal of Economics* 16(2): 237–52.

Ganglmair, Bernhard, Luke M. Froeb & Gregory J. Werden. 2012. "Patent Hold-Up and Antitrust: How a Well-Intentioned Rule Could Retard Innovation," *The Journal of Industrial Economics* 60(2): 249–73.

Gavil, Andrew I. 2012. "Moving Beyond Caricature and Characterization: The Modern Rule of Reason in Practice," *Southern California Law Review* 85(3): 733–82.

Ge, Yijun (Jill). 2017. "The Beijing IP Court's 50 Million RMB Judgment in WatchData v. Hengbao," *Comparative Patent Remedies*, Jan. 23, 2017. http://comparativepatentremedies.blogspot.com/2017/01/the-beijing-ip-courts-50-million-rmb.html

Geradin, Damien. 2010a. "Reverse Hold-Ups: The (Often Ignored) Risks Faced by Innovators in Standardized Areas," in Konkurrensverket: Swedish Competition Authority, ed., *The Pros and Cons of Standard Setting*, Västerås, Sweden: Edita Västra Aros AB. www.konkurrensverket.se/globalassets/english/research/read-the-book-14mb.pdf

  2010b. "Reverse Hold-Ups: The (Often Ignored) Risks Faced by Innovators in Standardized Areas," presentation delivered at *The Pros and Cons of Standard Setting 2010* at Konkurrensverket: Swedish Competition Authority, Nov. 12, 2010. www.konkurrensverket.se/globalassets/english/research/presentation-by-damien-geradin-reverse-hold-ups-theften-ignored-risks-faced-by-innovators-in-standardized-areas.pdf

  2016. "Patent Assertion Entities and EU Competition Law," *George Mason University Law and Economics Research Paper Series* No. 16–08. https://ssrn.com/abstract=2728686

Geradin, Damien & Anne Layne-Farrar. 2007. "The Logic and Limits of Ex Ante Competition in a Standard Setting Environment," *Competition Policy International* 3 (1): 79–106.

  2010. "Patent Value Apportionment Rules for Complex Multi-Patent Products," *Santa Clara High Technology Law Journal* 27(4): 763–92.

Geradin, Damien, Anne Layne-Farrar & Jorge Padilla. 2008. "The Complements Problem Within Standard Setting: Assessing the Evidence on Royalty Stacking," *Boston University Journal of Science & Technology Law* 14(2): 144–76.

Gergen, Mark P., John M. Golden & Henry E. Smith. 2012. "The Supreme Court's Accidental Revolution – The Test for Permanent Injunctions," *Columbia Law Review* 112(2): 203–249.

Gilbert, Richard J. 2011. "Deal or No Deal? Licensing Negotiations in Standard-Setting Organizations," *Antitrust Law Journal* 77: 855–88.

Gilbert, Richard J. & Carl Shapiro. 1997. "Antitrust Issues in the Licensing of Intellectual Property: The Nine No-No's Meet the Nineties," *Brookings Papers on Economic Activity: Microeconomics* 1997: 283–349.

Glänzel, Wolfgang & Martin Meyer. 2003. "Patents Cited in the Scientific Literature: An Exploratory Study of 'Reverse' Citation Relations," *Scientometrics* 58(2): 415–28.

Golden, John M. 2007. "Commentary, 'Patent Trolls' and Patent Remedies," *Texas Law Review* 85(7): 2111–61.

2010. "Principles for Patent Remedies," *Texas Law Review* 88(3): 505–92.

2012. "Injunctions as More (or Less) than off Switches: Patent-Infringement Injunctions' Scope," *Texas Law Review* 90(6): 1399–1472.

2017. "Reasonable Certainty in Contract and Patent Damages," *Harvard Journal of Law & Technology* 30: 257–78.

Golden, John M. & Karen E. Sandrik. 2017. "A Restitution Perspective on Reasonable Royalties," *The Review of Litigation* 36(2): 335–77.

Goldscheider, Robert, John Jarosz & Carla Mulhern. 2002. "Use of The 25 Per Cent Rule in Valuing IP," *les Nouvelles* 37: 123–33.

Gooding, Martha K. 2012. "Analyzing the 'Analytic Method' of Calculating Reasonable Royalty Patent Damages," *Patent, Trademark & Copyright Law Daily* (Bloomberg BNA), May 14, 2012.

2014. "Reasonable Royalty Patent Damages: A Proper Reading of the Book of Wisdom," *Patent, Trademark & Copyright Law Daily* (Bloomberg BNA), Apr. 21, 2014.

Goodman, David J. & Robert A. Myers. 2005. "3D Cellular Standards and Patents," *2005 International Conference on Wireless Networks, Communications and Mobile Computing.* https://doi.org/10.1109/WIRLES.2005.1549445

Grabinski, Klaus. 2009. "Gewinnherausgabe nach Patentverletzung: Zur gerichtlichen Praxis acht Jahre nach dem „Gemeinkostenanteil" Urteil des BGH," *Gewerblicher Rechtsschutz und Urheberrecht* 3–4: 260–65.

Greene, Edie & Brian H. Bornstein. 2003. *Determining Damages: The Psychology of Jury Awards*, Washington, D.C.: American Psychological Association.

Grosskopf, Ofer & Barak Medina. 2009. "Remedies for Wrongfully-Issued Preliminary Injunctions: The Case for Disgorgement of Profits," *Seattle University Law Review* 32 (4): 903–42.

Guangdong High People's Court. 2018. *Trial Adjudication Guidance for Standard Essential Patent Dispute Cases.* www.iprdaily.cn/article_18855.html

Gupta, Kirti & Jay P. Kesan. 2016. "Studying the Impact of *eBay* on Injunctive Relief in Patent Cases," *University of Illinois College of Law Legal Studies Research Paper No.* 17–03: 1–45. https://papers.ssrn.com/sol3/papers.cfm?abstract_id=2816701

Gutowski, Maciej. 2016. *Kodeks Cywilny, Tom I: Komentarz – Art. 1–449*", Warsaw: C.H. Beck.

Hall, Bronwyn H. & Dietmar Harhoff. 2012. "Recent Research on the Economics of Patents," *Annual Review of Economics* 4: 541–65.

Harkrider, John D. 2013. "Seeing the Forest Through the SEPs," *Antitrust* 27(3): 22–29.

Hastie, Reid, David A. Schkade & John W. Payne. 1999. "Juror Judgments in Civil Cases: Effects of Plaintiff's Requests and Plaintiff's Identity on Punitive Damage Awards," *Law & Human Behavior* 23(4): 445–70.

Heald, Paul J. 2008. "Optimal Remedies for Patent Infringement: A Transactional Model," *Houston Law Review* 45(4): 1165–1200.

Heath, Christopher. 2008. "Wrongful Patent Enforcement: Threats and Post-Infringement Invalidity in Comparative Perspective," *International Review of Intellectual Property and Competition Law* 39(3): 307–22.

2015. *Patent Enforcement Worldwide: Writings in Honour of Dieter Stauder, Third Edition*, Portland, OR: Hart Publishing.

Helmers, Christian, Yassine Lefouili, Brian Love, & Luke McDonagh. 2018. "Incentives to Litigate: Evidence from a Court Reform in the UK," *Working Paper* (On file with authors).

Helmers, Christian, Brian Love, & Luke McDonagh. 2014. "Is There a Patent Troll Problem in the U.K.?," *Fordham Intellectual Property, Media & Entertainment Law Journal* 24(2): 509–54.

Henrich, Joseph. 2015. *The Secret of Our Success: How Culture Is Driving Human Evolution, Domesticating Our Species, and Making Us Smarter*, Princeton, NJ: Princeton University Press.

Hesse, Renata & Frances Marshall. 2017. "U.S. Antitrust Aspects of FRAND Disputes," in Jorge L. Contreras, ed., *The Cambridge Handbook of Technical Standardization Law*, Cambridge: Cambridge University Press.

Holte, Ryan T. & Christopher B. Seaman. 2017. "Patent Injunctions on Appeal: An Empirical Study of the Federal Circuit's Application of *Ebay*," *Washington Law Review* 92(1): 145–212.

Hoshi, Katsuhiro. 1998. "Research and Study on the Way of Damages Compensation and Penal Regulations in Cases of Intellectual Properties Infringement," *Institute of Intellectual Property Bulletin* 7: 1–15.

Hovenkamp, Erik & Thomas F. Cotter. 2016. "Anticompetitive Patent Injunctions," *Minnesota Law Review* 100(3): 871–920.

Hovenkamp, Erik & Jonathan S. Masur. 2017. "How Patent Damages Skew Licensing Markets," *The Review of Litigation* 36(2): 379–416.

Howard, Brian C. & Jason Maples. 2017. "Lex Machina Patent Litigation Year in Review 2016," Menlo Park, CA: Lex Machina.

Hu, Jingjing. 2016. "Determining Damages for Patent Infringement in China," *International Review of Intellectual Property & Competition Law* 47(1): 5–27.

Hughes, James W. & Edward A. Snyder. 1995. "Litigation and Settlement Under the English and American Rules: Theory and Evidence," *Journal of Law & Economics* 38(1): 225–50.

Inglis, Laura, Kevin McCabe, Steve Rassenti, Daniel Simmons, & Erik Tallroth. 2005. "Experiments on the Effects of Cost Shifting, Court Costs, and Discovery on the Efficient Settlement of Tort Claims," *Florida State University Law Review* 33(1): 89–117.

Isenbergh, Maxwell S. & Seymour J. Rubin. 1940. "Antitrust Enforcement Through Consent Decrees," *Harvard Law Review* 53(3): 386–414.

Janicke, Paul M. 1993. "Contemporary Issues in Patent Damages," *American University Law Review* 42: 691–736.

Jarosz, John C. & Michael J. Chapman. 2013. "The Hypothetical Negotiation and Reasonable Royalty Damages: The Tail Wagging the Dog," *Stanford Technology Law Review* 16: 769–830.

Jiam, Hannah. 2015. "Fee-Shifting and Octane Fitness: An Empirical Approach Toward Understanding 'Exceptional'," *Berkeley Technology Law Journal* 30 (Annual Review 2015): 611–74.

Jones, Alison. 2014. "Standard-Essential Patents: Frand Commitments, Injunctions and the Smartphone Wars," *European Competition Journal* 10(1): 1–36.

Jones, Alison & Christopher Stothers. 2018. "Establishing Unfairly High Prices: The Implications of the CAT's Judgment in Flynn and Pfizer v Competition and Market Authority," *Bio-Science Law Review* 17(1): 19–26.

Kamlah, Dietrich. 2014. "Legal Consequences of Patent Infringement," in Maximilian Haedicke & Henrik Timmann, eds., *Patent Law: A Handbook on European and German Patent Law*, Munich: C.H. Beck oHG.

Kapczynski, Amy. 2009. "Harmonization and Its Discontents: A Case Study of TRIPS Implementation in India's Pharmaceutical Sector," *California Law Review* 97(6): 1571–1650.

Kaplow, Louis & Steven Shavell. 1996. "Property Rules v. Liability Rules: An Economic Analysis," *Harvard Law Review* 109(4): 713–90.

Kattan, Joseph. 2013. "FRAND Wars and Section 2," *Antitrust* 27(3): 30–35.

Kattan, Joseph & Chris Wood. 2013. "Standard-Essential Patents and the Problem of Hold-Up," in Nicolas Carbit & Elisa Ramundo, eds., *William E. Kovacic – An Antitrust Tribute: Liber Amicorum – Volume II*, New York: Institute of Competition Law.

Kelley, Anne. 2011. "Practicing in the Patent Marketplace," *University of Chicago Law Review* 78(1): 115–38.

Keukenschrijver, Alfred. 2016. "Unterlassungsanspruch; Schadensersatz," in Rudolf Busse & Alfred Keukenschrijver, eds., *Patentgesetz*, Berlin: de Gruyter.

Keyhani, Dariush. 2008. "Permanent Injunctions in Patent Cases," *Buffalo Intellectual Property Law Journal* 6(1): 1–12.

Khan, Lina M. 2017. "Amazon's Antitrust Paradox," *Yale Law Journal* 126(3): 710–805.

Kidd, George David. 2014. "Accuracy or Efficiency: Has *Grain Processing* Made a Difference?," *Minnesota Journal of Law, Science & Technology* 15(1): 653–88.

Kieff, F. Scott & Anne Layne-Farrar. 2013. "Incentive Effects from Different Approaches to Holdup Mitigation Surrounding Patent Remedies and Standard-Setting Organizations," *Journal of Competition Law & Economics* 9(4): 1091–1123.

Kim, Byungil. 2015. "Patent Enforcement in China," in Christopher Heath, ed., *Patent Enforcement Worldwide: Writings in Honour of Dieter Stauder, Third Edition*, Portland, OR: Hart Publishing.

Kim, Jay J., Duck Soon Chang, Tae-Jun Suh, & Cy C. Kim. 2016. "South Korea," in Michael C. Elmer & C. Gregory Gramenopoulos, eds., *Global Patent Litigation: How and Where to Win, Second Edition*, Arlington VA: Bloomberg BNA.

Kitch, Edmund W. 1977. "The Nature and Function of the Patent System," *Journal of Law & Economics* 20(2): 265–90.

Kobayashi, Bruce H. & Joshua D. Wright. 2009. "Federalism, Substantive Preemption, and Limits on Antitrust: An Application to Patent Holdup," *Journal of Competition Law & Economics* 5(3): 469–516.

2012. "The Limits of Antitrust and Patent Holdup: A Reply to Cary et al.," *Antitrust Law Journal* 78(2): 505–26.

Kritzer, Herbert M. 2002. "Lawyer Fees and Lawyer Behavior in Litigation: What Does the Empirical Literature Really Say?," *Texas Law Review* 80(7): 1943–83.

Kühnen, Thomas. 2015. *Patent Litigation Proceedings in Germany: A Handbook for Practitioners*, Cologne, Ger.: Carl Heymanns Verlag.

2017. *Handbuch der Patentverletzung*, Cologne, Ger.: Carl Heymanns Verlag.

La Belle, Megan M. 2012. "Patent Law as Public Law," *George Mason Law Review* 20(1): 41–104.

Landes, William M. & Richard A. Posner. 1983. "Causation in Tort Law: An Economic Approach," *Journal of Legal Studies* 12(1): 109–34.

Langus, Gregor, Vilen Lipatov & Damien Neven. 2013. "Standard-Essential Patents: Who Is Really Holding up (And When)?" *Journal of Competition Law & Economics* 9(2): 253–84.

Larouche, Pierre & Nicolo Zingales. 2017. "Injunctive Relief in FRAND Disputes in the EU – Intellectual Property and Competition Law at the Remedies Stage," *Tilburg Law School Legal Studies Research Paper Series No. 01/2017*. https://ssrn.com/abstract=2909708

Laycock, Douglas. 1991. *The Death of the Irreparable Injury Rule*, New York: Oxford University Press.

2002. *Modern American Remedies: Cases and Materials*, New York: Aspen Law & Business.

Layne-Farrar, Anne. 2014. "Moving Past the SEP RAND Obsession: Some Thoughts on the Economic Implications of Unilateral Commitments and the Complexities of Patent Licensing," *George Mason Law Review* 21: 1093–1110.

2017. "The Patent Damages Gap: An Economist's Review of U.S. Patent Damages Apportionment Rules," Working Paper (Apr. 8, 2017). http://papers.ssrn.com/abstract_id=2911289

Layne-Farrar, Anne, Gerard Llobet & A. Jorge Padilla. 2009. "Preventing Patent Holdup: An Economic Assessment of Ex Ante Licensing Negotiations in Standard Setting," *AIPLA Quarterly Journal* 37(4): 445–78.

2014. "Payments and Participation: The Incentives to Join Cooperative Standard Setting Efforts," *Journal of Economics & Management Strategy* 23(1): 24–49.

Layne-Farrar, Anne, A. Jorge Padilla & Richard Schmalensee. 2007. "Pricing Patents for Licensing in Standard-Setting Organizations: Making Sense of FRAND Commitments," *Antitrust Law Journal* 74(3): 671–706.

Layne-Farrar, Anne & Klaus M. Schmidt. 2010. "Licensing Complementary Patents: Patent Trolls, Market Structure, and Excessive Royalties," *Berkeley Technology Law Journal* 25 (2): 1121–44.

Lee, William F. & A. Douglas Melamed. 2016. "Breaking the Vicious Cycle of Patent Damages," *Cornell Law Review* 101: 385–466.

Lemley, Mark A. 2005. "Property, Intellectual Property, and Free Riding," *Texas Law Review* 83: 1031–75.

2007. "Ten Things to Do About Patent Holdup of Standards (and One Not to)," *Boston College Law Review* 48(1): 149–68.

2009. "Distinguishing Lost Profits from Reasonable Royalties," *William & Mary Law Review* 51(2): 655–74.

2011. "The Ongoing Confusion over Ongoing Royalties," *Missouri Law Review* 76(3): 695–707.

2013. "A Rational System of Design Patent Remedies," *Stanford Technology Law Review* 17: 219–38.

Lemley, Mark A. & Nathan Myhrvold. 2007. "How to Make a Patent Market," *Hofstra Law Review* 36(2): 257–60.

Lemley, Mark A. & Carl Shapiro. 2005. "Probabilistic Patents," *Journal of Economic Perspectives* 19(2): 75–98.

2007a. "Patent Holdup and Royalty Stacking," *Texas Law Review* 85(7): 1991–2049.

2007b. "Patent Hold-Up and Royalty Stacking: Reply," *Texas Law Review* 85(7): 2163–74.

Lemley, Mark A. & Philip J. Weiser. 2007. "Should Property or Liability Rules Govern Information," *Texas Law Review* 85(4): 783–842.

Léonard, Amandine. 2016. "'Abuse of Rights' in Belgian and French Patent Law – A Case Law Analysis," *Journal of Intellectual Property, Information Technology and Electronic Commerce Law* 7(1): 1–21.

2017. "L'abus de droit dans le contentieux des brevets – Entre divergences nationales et voeu d'harmonisation de la juridiction unifiée du brevet – une piste à suivre?," *Propriété Industrielle* 2017(1): Etude 2.

Leubsdorf, John. 1978. "The Standard for Preliminary Injunctions," *Harvard Law Review* 91 (3): 525–66.

Li, Xiaowu & Don Wang. 2017. "Chinese Patent Law's Statutory Damages Provision: The One Size That Fits None," *Washington International Law Journal* 26(2): 209–46.

Lichtman, Douglas. 2003. "Uncertainty and the Standard for Preliminary Relief," *University of Chicago Law Review* 70(1): 197–214.

Lohr, Steve. 2010. "Smartphone Patent Suits Challenge Big Makers," *The New York Times,* July 9, 2010. www.nytimes.com/2010/07/09/technology/09patent.html

Love, Brian J. 2007. "Patentee Overcompensation and the Entire Market Value Rule," *Stanford Law Review* 60(1): 263–94.

2009. "The Misuse of Reasonable Royalty Damages as a Patent Infringement Deterrent," *Missouri Law Review* 74(4): 909–48.

Love, Brian J., Christian Helmers & Markus Eberhardt. 2016. "Patent Litigation in China: Protecting Rights or the Local Economy," *Vanderbilt Journal of Entertainment & Technology Law* 18(4): 713–42.

Love, Brian J., Christian Helmers, Fabian Gaessler, & Maximilian Ernicke. 2017. "Patent Assertion Entities in Europe," in D. Daniel Sokol, ed., *Patent Assertion Entities and Competition Policy*, New York: Cambridge University Press.

Love, Brian J. & James C. Yoon. 2013. "Expanding Patent Law's Customer Suit Exception," *Boston University Law Review* 93(5): 1605–41.

Lundqvist, Björn. 2014. *Standardization Under EU Competition Rules and US Antitrust Laws,* Northampton, MA: Edward Elgar Publishing, Inc.

Mace, Andrew C. 2009. "TRIPS, eBay, and Denials of Injunctive Relief: Is Article 31 Compliance Everything?," *Columbia Science and Technology Law Review* 10: 232–66.

Malbon, Justin, Charles Lawson & Mark Davison. 2014. *The WTO Agreement on Trade-Related Aspects of Intellectual Property Rights: A Commentary*, Northampton, MA: Edward Elgar Publishing, Inc.

Manta, Irina D. 2011. "The Puzzle of Criminal Sanctions for Intellectual Property Infringement," *Harvard Journal of Law & Technology* 24(2): 469–518.

Marchese, Christopher S. 1994. "Patent Infringement and Future Lost Profits Damages," *Arizona State Law Journal* 26(3): 747–95.

Marcus, Philip. 1945. "Patents, Antitrust Law and Antitrust Judgments Through *Hartford-Empire*," *Georgetown Law Journal* 34(1): 1–63.

Mariniello, Mario. 2011. "Fair, Reasonable and Non-Discriminatory (FRAND) Terms: A Challenge for Competition Authorities," *Journal of Competition Law & Economics* 7 (3): 523–41.

Masten, Scott E., ed. 1996. *Case Studies in Contracting and Organization*, New York: Oxford University Press.

Masur, Jonathan S. 2015. "The Use and Misuse of Patent Licenses," *Northwestern University Law Review* 110: 115–57.

Matsunaka, Masahiko. 2004. "FY 2003 Study Report on the Japanese Economic Structure from a Competition Policy Perspective—Court Judgments Concerning Calculation of the Amount of Damages in Intellectual Property Infringement Litigation," *Institute of Intellectual Property Bulletin* 13: 168–77.

McGowan, David. 2010. "Irreparable Harm," *Lewis & Clark Law Review* 14: 577–96.

McManis, Charles R. & Jorge L. Contreras. 2014. "Compulsory Licensing of Intellectual Property: A Viable Policy Lever for Promoting Access to Critical Technologies?," in Gustavo Ghidini, Rudolph J. R. Peritz & Marco Ricolfi, eds., *TRIPS and Developing*

Countries: Towards a New IP World Order?, Northampton, MA: Edward Elgar Publishing, Inc.

Means, Samuel Chase. 2013. "The Trouble with Treble Damages: Ditching Patent Law's Willful Infringement Doctrine and Enhanced Damages," *University of Illinois Law Review* 2013(5): 1999–2046.

Melullis, Klaus-J. 2008. "Zur Ermittlung und zum Ausgleich des Schadens bei Patentverletzungen," *Gewerblicher Rechtsschutz und Urheberrecht Internationaler Teil* 8–9: 679–85.

Merges, Robert P. 1994. "Of Property Rules, Coase, and Intellectual Property," *Columbia Law Review* 94(8): 2655–73.

Mes, Peter. 2015. *Patentgesetz, Gebrauchsmustergesetz: Kommentar*, Munich: C.H. Beck.

Michel, Hon. Paul R., ed. 2010. *Compensatory Damages Issues in Patent Infringement Cases: A Handbook for Federal District Court Judges.* www.law.berkeley.edu/files/bclt_PatentDamages_Ed.pdf

Montañá, Miquel. 2013. "Court Sheds Light on Damages Caused by Preliminary Injunctions," *Kluwer Patent Blog*, May 17, 2013. http://patentblog.kluweriplaw.com/2013/05/17/court-sheds-light-on-damages-caused-by-preliminary-injunctions/

Morton, Fiona Scott & Carl Shapiro. 2016. "Patent Assertions: Are We Any Closer to Aligning Reward to Contribution?" *Innovation Policy and the Economy* 16(1): 89–133.

Mueller, Christopher B. & Laird C. Kirkpatrick. 1999. "§ 3.5 — Underlying Reasons and Examples," *Evidence*, New York: Aspen Law & Business.

Mulligan, Christina & Timothy B. Lee. 2012. "Scaling the Patent System," *NYU Annual Survey of American Law* 68(2): 289–318.

Nagakoshi, Yuzuki & Katsuya Tamai. 2016. "Japan Without FRANDS? Recent Developments on Injunctions and FRAND-Encumbered Patents in Japan," *AIPLA Quarterly Journal* 44 (2): 243–93.

Nakamura, Nodoka. 2014. "Recent Trends in Court Judgments Concerning Damages in Japanese Patent Infringement Litigations," *A.I.P.P.I. — Japan* 39: 389–410.

Narechania, Tejas N. & Jackson Taylor Kirklin. 2012. "An Unsettling Development: The Use of Settlement-Related Evidence for Damages Determinations in Patent Litigation," *University of Illinois Journal of Law, Technology & Policy* 2012(1): 1–44.

Nash, John F. 1950. "The Bargaining Problem," *Econometrica* 18(2): 155–62.

Nazzini, Renato. 2011. *The Foundations of European Union Competition Law: The Objective and Principles of Article 102*, New York: Oxford University Press.

2017. "Level Discrimination and FRAND Commitments Under EU Competition Law," *World Competition* 40(2): 213–39.

Nicholson, Walter & Christopher Snyder. 2008. *Microeconomic Theory: Basic Principles and Extensions, Tenth Edition*, Mason, OH: Thomson South-Western.

Noguchi, Yuki. 2005. "Government Enters Fray over BlackBerry Patents," *The Washington Post*, Nov. 12, 2005. www.washingtonpost.com/wp-dyn/content/article/2005/11/11/AR2005111101789.html

Noll, Roger G. 2005. "'Buyer Power' and Economic Policy," *Antitrust Law Journal* 72(2): 589–624.

O'Donoghue, Robert & A. Jorge Padilla. 2013. *The Law and Economics of Article 102 TFEU, Second Edition*, Oxford: Hart Publishing.

Ohly, Ansgar. 2009. "Three Principles of European IP Enforcement Law: Effectiveness, Proportionality, Dissuasiveness," in Josef Drexl, Reto M. Hilty, Laurence Boy, Christine Godt & Bernard Remiche, eds., *Technology and Competition: Contributions in Honour of Hanns Ullrich*, Brussels: Larcier.

Oppenheimer, Max Stul. 2015. "Rethinking Compact Prosecution," *Albany Law Journal of Science & Technology* 25(2): 257–88.

Osterrieth, Christian. 2015. "Patent Enforcement in Germany," in Christopher Heath, ed., *Patent Enforcement Worldwide: Writings in Honour of Dieter Stauder, Third Edition*, Portland, OR: Hart Publishing.

Ouellette, Lisa Larrimore. 2017. "Who Reads Patents?," *Nature Biotechnology* 35(5): 421–24.

Padilla, A. Jorge & Koren W. Wong-Ervin. 2017. "Portfolio Licensing to Makers of Downstream End-User Devices: Analyzing Refusals to License FRAND-Assured Standard-Essential Patents at the Component Level," *Antitrust Bulletin* 62(3): 494–513.

Page, William H. 2014. "Judging Monopolistic Pricing: F/RAND and Antitrust Injury," *Texas Intellectual Property Law Journal* 22: 181–208.

Parr, Russell L. & Gordon V. Smith. 2005. *Intellectual Property: Valuation, Exploitation, and Infringement Damages*, Hoboken, NJ: John Wiley & Sons, Inc.

Patterson, Mark R. 2003. "Antitrust and the Costs of Standard-Setting: A Commentary on Teece & Sherry," *Minnesota Law Review* 87(6): 1995–2018.

Pattloch, Thomas. 2015. "Patent Enforcement in China," in Christopher Heath, ed., *Patent Enforcement Worldwide: Writings in Honour of Dieter Stauder, Third Edition*, Portland, OR: Hart Publishing.

Pedigo, Mark. 2017. "Determining Reasonable Royalties with Analytical Approach," *Law360*, Mar. 3, 2017.

Pentheroudakis, Chryssoula & Justus A. Baron. 2017. *JRC Science for Policy Report: Licensing Terms of Standard Essential Patents: A Comprehensive Analysis of Cases* (Nikolaus Thumm ed.), Luxembourg: Publications Office of the European Union. http://publications.jrc.ec.europa.eu/repository/bitstream/JRC104068/jrc104068%20online.pdf

Petit, Nicolas. 2016. "The Smallest Saleable Patent-Practicing Unit (SSPU) Experiment: General Purpose Technologies and the Coase Theorem," Working Paper (Feb. 18, 2016). https://papers.ssrn.com/sol3/papers.cfm?abstract_id=2734245

 2017. "EU Competition Law Analysis of FRAND Disputes," in Jorge L. Contreras, ed., *The Cambridge Handbook of Technical Standardization Law*, Cambridge: Cambridge University Press.

Petrovčič, Urška. 2013. "Patent Hold-Up and the Limits of Competition Law: A Trans-Atlantic Perspective," *Common Market Law Review* 50(5): 1363–86.

Pfenningstorf, Werner. 1984. "The European Experience with Attorney Fee Shifting," *Law and Contemporary Problems* 47(1): 37–124.

Picht, Peter Georg. 2018. "FRAND Wars 2.0: Survey of Court Decisions in the Aftermath of Huawei/ZTE," *Wettbewerb in Recht und Praxis* (Forthcoming). https://ssrn.com/abstract=2916544

Pindyck, Robert S. & Daniel L. Rubinfeld. 2013. *Microeconomics, Eighth Edition*, Boston: Pearson Education, Inc.

Pitz, Johann & Gerhard Hermann. 2007. "Germany: Enforcement of IP Rights by the National Courts," in *IP Value 2007: Building and Enforcing Intellectual Property Value*, London: Globe White Page Ltd.

Platt, S. Christian & Bob Chen. 2013. "Recent Trends and Approaches in Calculating Patent Damages: Nash Bargaining Solution and Conjoint Surveys," *Patent, Trademark & Copyright Law Daily* (Bloomberg BNA), Aug. 30, 2013.

Polinsky, A. Mitchell & Daniel L. Rubinfeld. 1998. "Does the English Rule Discourage Low-Probability-of-Prevailing Plaintiffs?," *Journal of Legal Studies* 27(1): 141–57.

Polinsky, A. Mitchell & Steven Shavell. 1998. "Punitive Damages: an Economic Analysis," *Harvard Law Review* 111(4): 869–962.

Posner, Richard A. 1999. "An Economic Approach to the Law of Evidence," *Stanford Law Review* 51: 1477–1546.

Posner, Eric A. & Cass R. Sunstein. 2005. "Dollars and Death," *University of Chicago Law Review* 72(2): 537–98.

Rabowsky, Brento 1996. "Recovery of Lost Profits on Unpatented Products in Patent Infringement Cases," *Southern California Law Review* 70(1): 281–336.

Rachlinski, Jeffery J., Andrew J. Wistrich & Chris Guthrie. 2015. "Can Judges Make Reliable Numeric Judgments? Distorted Damages and Skewed Sentences," *Indiana Law Journal* 90(2): 695–739.

Ratliff, James & Daniel L. Rubinfeld. 2013. "The Use and Threat of Injunctions in the RAND Context," *Journal of Competition Law & Economics* 9(1): 1–22.

Régibeau, Pierre, Raphaël De Coninck & Hanz Zengler. 2016. *Transparency, Predictability, and Efficiency of SSO-Based Standardization and SEP Licensing: A Report for the European Commission*, European Union.

Rennie, Douglas C. 2012. "Rule 82 and Tort Reform: An Empirical Study of the Impact of Alaska's English Rule on Federal Civil Case Filings," *Alaska Law Review* 29(1): 1–50.

Rennie-Smith, Christopher. 2015. "Patent Enforcement in the United Kingdom," in Christopher Heath, ed., *Patent Enforcement Worldwide: Writings in Honour of Dieter Staude, Third Editionr*, Portland, OR: Hart Publishing.

République Française, Ministère du Redressement Productifs. 2014. "Étude Comparée sur les Dommages et Intérêts Alloués dans le Cadre des Actions en Contrefaçon en France, Au Royaume-Uni et en Allemagne."

Risch, Michael. 2018. "(Un)reasonable Royalties," *Boston University Law Review* 98(1): 187–261.

Roberts, Caprice L. 2010. "The Case for Restitution and Unjust Enrichment Remedies in Patent Law," *Lewis & Clark Law Review* 14(2): 653–85.

Robinson, William C. 1890. *Law of Patents for Useful Inventions* 3, Boston: Little Brown.

Romet, Isabelle, Amandine Métier & Dora Talvard. 2015. "Patent Enforcement in France," in Christopher Heath, ed., *Patent Enforcement Worldwide: Writings in Honour of Dieter Stauder, Third Edition*, Portland, OR: Hart Publishing.

Rooklidge, William. 2014. "Infringer's Profits Redux: The Analytical Method of Determining Patent Infringement Reasonable Royalty Damages," *Patent, Trademark & Copyright Law Daily* (Bloomberg BNA), Nov. 5, 2014.

Rubinstein, Ariel. 1982. "Perfect Equilibrium in a Bargaining Model," *Econometrica* 50(1): 97–109.

Scherer, F. M. 1980. *Industrial Market Structure and Economic Performance: Second Edition*, Chicago: Rand McNally College Publishing Company.

Schindler, Jacob. 2018. "Huawei Scores SEP Injunction in Shenzhen Suit Against Samsung Electronics," *IAM Blog*, Jan. 11, 2018. www.iam-media.com/blog/Detail.aspx?g=6cc258a9-cc70-4f88-858b-228c05981776

Schlicher, John W. 2009. "Patent Damages, the Patent Reform Act, and Better Alternatives for the Courts and Congress," *Journal of the Patent and Trademark Office Society* 91: 21–76.

Schoenhard, Paul M. 2008. "Who Took My IP – Defending the Availability of Injunctive Relief for Patent Owners," *Texas Intellectual Property Law Journal* 16(2): 187–236.

Schönknecht, Markus. 2012. "Determination of Patent Damages in Germany," *International Review of Intellectual Property & Competition Law* 43(3): 309–32.

Scotchmer, Suzanne. 1991. "Standing on the Shoulders of Giants: Cumulative Research and the Patent Law," *Journal of Economic Perspectives* 5(1): 29–41.

Seaman, Christopher B. 2010. "Reconsidering the Georgia-Pacific Standard for Reasonable Royalty Patent Damages," *Brigham Young University Law Review* 2010(5): 1661–1727.

——— 2012. "Willful Patent Infringement and Enhanced Damages after *In re Seagate*: An Empirical Study," *Iowa Law Review* 97(2): 417–71.

——— 2015. "Ongoing Royalties in Patent Cases after eBay: An Empirical Assessment and Proposed Framework," *Texas Intellectual Property Law Journal* 23(3): 203–50.

——— 2016. "Permanent Injunctions in Patent Litigation after eBay: An Empirical Study," *Iowa Law Review* 101(5): 1949–2019.

Second Subcommittee of the Second Patent Committee. 2014. "Predictability of Monetary Damages under Article 102(3) of the Japanese Patent Law," *Intellectual Property Management* 64: 219–235 (in Japanese).

Sedona Conference. 2014. "Commentary on Patent Damages and Remedies: A Project of the Sedona Conference Working Group on Patent Damages and Remedies (WG9), Public Comment Version." https://thesedonaconference.org/download-publication?fid=3282

——— 2016. "Commentary on Patent Reasonable Royalty Determinations: A Project of the Sedona Conference Working Group on Patent Damages and Remedies (WG9), December 2016 Edition." https://thesedonaconference.org/download-publication?fid=571

Sganga, Caterina & Silvia Scalzini. 2017. "From Abuse of Right to European Copyright Misuse: A New Doctrine for EU Copyright Law," *International Review of Intellectual Property and Competition Law* 48(4): 405–35.

Shapiro, Carl. 2006. "Prior User Rights," *American Economic Review* 96(2): 92–96.

——— 2007. "Patent Reform: Aligning Reward and Contribution," *Innovation Policy and the Economy* 8: 111–56.

——— 2010. "Injunctions, Hold-Up, and Patent Royalties," *American Law & Economics Review* 12 (2): 280–318.

——— 2016. "Property Rules vs. Liability Rules for Patent Infringement." https://papers.ssrn.com /sol3/papers.cfm?abstract_id=2775307

Shavell, Steven. 1980. "An Analysis of Causation and the Scope of Liability in the Law of Torts," *Journal of Legal Studies* 9(3): 463–516.

Shavell, Steven & Tanguy van Ypersele. 2001. "Rewards Versus Intellectual Property Rights," *Journal of Law & Economics* 44(2): 525–48.

Shen, David & Jill Ge. 2017. "*IWNCOMM* v. *Sony*: First SEP-Based Injunction Granted in China," *Allen & Overy*, Apr. 10, 2017. www.allenovery.com/publications/en-gb/Pages/ Iwncomm-v-Sony-first-SEP-based-injunction-granted-in-China.aspx

Sichelman, Ted. 2014. "Purging Patent Law of 'Private Law' Remedies," *Texas Law Review* 92 (3): 517–72.

——— 2018. "Innovation Factors for Reasonable Royalties," *Texas Intellectual Property Law Journal* 25(2): 277–325.

Sidak, J. Gregory. 2008. "Holdup, Royalty Stacking, and the Presumption of Injunctive Relief for Patent Infringement: A Reply to Lemley and Shapiro," *Minnesota Law Review* 92(3): 714–48.

——— 2009. "Patent Holdup and Oligopsonistic Collusion in Standard-Setting Organizations," *Journal of Competition Law & Economics* 5(1): 123–88.

——— 2014. "The Proper Royalty Base for Patent Damages," *Journal of Competition Law & Economics* 10(4): 989–1037.

——— 2016a. "Apportionment, FRAND Royalties, and Comparable Licenses After Ericsson v. D-Link," *University of Illinois Law Review* 2016(4): 1809–70.

——— 2016b. "Enhanced Damages for Infringement of Standard-Essential Patents," *The Criterion Journal on Innovation* 2016(1): 1101–13.

2017. "FRAND in India," in Jorge L. Contreras, ed., *The Cambridge Handbook of Technical Standardization Law*, Cambridge: Cambridge University Press.

Sidak, J. Gregory & Jeremy O. Skog. 2016. "Using Conjoint Analysis to Apportion Patent Damages," *Federal Circuit Bar Journal* 25: 581–620.

Siebrasse, Norman V. 2001. "A Property Rights Theory of the Limits of Copyright," *University of Toronto Law Journal* 51(1): 1–62.

2013. "Opening the Door to Punitive Damages in Patent Law?," *Sufficient Description: Observations on Canadian Patent Cases*, Oct. 4, 2013. www.sufficientdescription.com /2013/10/opening-door-to-punitive-damages-in.html

2016. "No Presumption Against an Accounting of Profits," *Sufficient Description: Observations on Canadian Patent Cases*, Feb. 26, 2016. www.sufficientdescription.com /2016/02/no-presumption-against-accounting-of.html

2017. "Instantaneous Availability of Non-Infringing Alternative," *Sufficient Description: Observations on Canadian Patent Cases*, Feb. 10, 2017. www.sufficientdescription.com /2017/02/instantaneous-availability-of-non.html

Siebrasse, Norman V. & Thomas F. Cotter. 2016. "A New Framework for Determining Reasonable Royalties in Patent Litigation," *Florida Law Review* 68(4): 929–99.

2017a. "The Value of the Standard," *Minnesota Law Review* 101(3): 1159–1246.

2017b. "Judicially Determined FRAND Royalties," in Jorge L. Contreras, ed., *The Cambridge Handbook of Technical Standardization Law*, Cambridge: Cambridge University Press.

Siebrasse, Norman V., Alexander J. Stack & Cole & Partners IP Litigation Support Group. 2008. "Accounting of Profits in Intellectual Property Cases in Canada," *Canadian Intellectual Property Review* 24(1): 83–136.

Sikorski, Rafal. 2015. "Nadużycie patentu w świetle art. 5 KC," in Ewa Nowińska & Krystyna Szczepanowska-Kozłowska, eds., *System Prawa Handlowego, Tom 3: Prawo własności przemysłowej*, Warsaw: C.H. Beck.

Skenyon, John M., Christopher Marchese, John Land & Frank Porcelli. 2016. *Patent Damages Law and Practice*, 2016–2017 ed., Eagan, MN: Thomson Reuters.

Smith, Henry E. 2004. "Property and Property Rules," *New York University Law Review* 79(5): 1719–98.

2007. "Intellectual Property as Property: Delineating Entitlements in Information," *Yale Law Journal* 116(8): 1742–1823.

Smith, Tony. 2001. "Rambus' 'Very High' DDR Royalty Revealed," *The Register*, May 3, 2001. www.theregister.co.uk/2001/05/03/rambus_very_high_ddr_royalty/

Snyder, Edward A. & James W. Hughes. 1990. "The English Rule for Allocating Legal Costs: Evidence Confronts Theory," *Journal of Law, Economics, and Organization* 6(2): 345–80.

Sokol, D. Daniel. 2017. "Patent Privateering: The Rise of Hybrid Patent Assertion Entities," in D. Daniel Sokol, ed., *Patent Assertion Entities and Competition Policy*, New York: Cambridge University Press.

Spier, Kathryn E. 2007. "Litigation," in A. Mitchell Polinsky & Steven Shavell eds., *Handbook of Law & Economics, Volume 1*, Amsterdam: Elsevier B.V.

Spulber, Daniel F. 2017. "Complementary Monopolies and Bargaining," *Journal of Law & Economics* 60(1): 29–74.

State Intellectual Property Office of the P.R.C. (SIPO). 2016. "Beijing Court Hands Down Highest Ever Compensation Order," *IPR Special*, Dec. 15, 2016. http://english .sipo.gov.cn/news/iprspecial/920348.htm

Steppe, Richard & Amandine Léonard. 2017. "Catching Patent Trolls in the Net of Abuse of Rights: Applying the General Principle of Union Law in the Context of the Unitary Patent Package," *European Intellectual Property Review* 39(3): 163–72.

Sterk, Stewart E. 2008. "Property Rules, Liability Rules, and Uncertainty about Property Rights," *Michigan Law Review* 106(7): 1285–1336.

Stern, Richard H. 2015. "What Are Reasonable and Non-Discriminatory Terms for Licensing a Standard-Essential Patent?," *European Intellectual Property Review* 37: 549–57.

Stout, Lynn A. 2011. *Cultivating Conscience: How Good Laws Make Good People*, Princeton NJ: Princeton University Press.

Straus, Joseph. 2011. "Das Regime des European Telecommunications Standards Institute – ETSI: Grundsätze, anwendbares Recht und die Wirkung der ETSI gegenüber abgegebenen Erklärungen," *Gewerblicher Rechtsschutz und Urheberrecht, Internationaler Teil* 60(6): 469–80.

Supreme People's Court of the People's Republic of China. 2009. "Interpretation of the Supreme People's Court on Several Issues Concerning the Application of Law in the Trial of Patent Infringement Dispute Cases," No. 21 Judicial Interpretation.

2016. "Interpretation (II) of the Supreme People's Court on Several Issues Concerning the Application of Law in the Trial of Patent Infringement Dispute Cases."

Suzuki, Masabumi & Yoshiyuki Tamura. 2011. "Patent Enforcement in Japan," *Zeitschrift für Geistiges Eigentum/Intellectual Property Journal* 3(4): 435–74.

Swanson, Daniel G. & William J. Baumol. 2005. "Reasonable and Nondiscriminatory (RAND) Royalties, Standards Selection, and Control of Market Power," *Antitrust Law Journal* 73: 1–58.

Takenaka, Toshiko. 2009. "Harmonizing Patent Infringement Damages: A Lesson from Japanese Experiences," in Martin J. Adelman, Robert Brauneis, Josef Drexl, & Ralph Nack, eds., *Patent and Technological Progress in a Globalized World*, Heidelberg: Springer.

Tandon, Pankaj. 1983. "Rivalry and the Excessive Allocation of Resources to Research," *Bell Journal of Economics* 14(1): 152–65.

Taylor, David O. 2014. "Using Reasonable Royalties to Value Patented Technology," *Georgia Law Review* 49(1): 79–162.

Teece, David J., Peter C. Grindley & Edward F. Sherry. 2012. "SDO IPR Policies in Dynamic Industries," *National Academy of Sciences Symposium on RAND Patent Policies*.

Teece, David J. & Edward F. Sherry. 2016. "'Smallest Saleable Patent Practicing Unit' Doctrine: An Economic and Public Policy Analysis," *Working Paper Series No. 11*: 1–33. http://innovation-archives.berkeley.edu/businessinnovation/documents/Tusher-Center-Working-Paper-11.pdf

Thiele, Alan R., Judith R. Blakeway & Charles M. Hosch. 2010. *The Patent Infringement Litigation Handbook: Avoidance and Management*, Chicago: American Bar Association.

Unidroit. 2016. *Unidroit Principles of International Commercial Contracts*, Rome: International Institute for the Unification of Private Law. www.unidroit.org/instruments/commercial-contracts/unidroit-principles-2016

University of Geneva. 2015. "Topic 3: How shall disputes about the licensing of Standard Essential Patents (SEP) under Fair, Reasonable and Non-Discriminatory (FRAND) terms be solved?," *Geneva Internet Disputes Resolution Policies* 1.0. https://geneva-internet-disputes.ch/

U.S. Department of Justice (DOJ). 2008. *Competition and Monopoly: Single-Firm Conduct Under Section 2 of the Sherman Act*. www.usdoj.gov/atr/public/reports/236681.htm

U.S. Department of Justice (DOJ) & U.S. Federal Trade Commission (FTC). 2017. *Antitrust Guidelines for the Licensing of Intellectual Property*. www.justice.gov/atr/IPguidelines/download
2007. *Antitrust Enforcement and Intellectual Property Rights: Promoting Innovation and Competition*. www.ftc.gov/sites/default/files/documents/reports/antitrust-enforcement-and-intellectual-property-rights-promoting-innovation-and-competition-report.s.department-justice-and-federal-trade-commission/p040101promotinginnovationandcompetitionrpto704.pdf
U.S. Department of Justice (DOJ) & U.S. Patent and Trademark Office (USPTO). 2013. *Policy Statement on Remedies for Standards-Essential Patents Subject to Voluntary F/RAND Commitments*. www.justice.gov/atr/page/file/1118381/download
Verma, Rohit, Gerhard Plaschka & Jordan J. Louviere. 2002. "Understanding Customer Choices: A Key to Successful Management of Hospitality Services," *Cornell Hotel & Restaurant Administration Quarterly* 43(6): 15–24.
Vermont, Samson. 2006. "Independent Invention as a Defense to Patent Infringement," *Michigan Law Review* 105(3): 475–504.
Véron, Pierre. 2012. "Civil Liability Because of the Enforcement of a Preliminary Injunction," *Kluwer Patent Blog*, Feb. 29, 2012. http://patentblog.kluweriplaw.com/2012/02/29/civil-liability-because-of-the-enforcement-of-a-preliminary-injunction/
Wang, Xiaoye. 2017. "Why SEPs Have Been Involved in Antitrust Cases – From A Chinese Scholar's Perspective," *Zeitschrift für Wettbewerbsrecht* 15(1): 72–87.
Ward, Annesley Merele. 2017. "Is German SEP litigation set to increase with the "confidentiality club decision" of the Higher Regional Court of Düsseldorf?," *The IPKat*, Feb. 7, 2017. http://ipkitten.blogspot.com/2017/02/german-court-prowls-into-realm-of.html
Weinstein, Roy, Ken Romig & Frank Stabile. 2013. "Taming Complex Intellectual Property Compensation Problems," *Federal Circuit Bar Journal* 22(3): 547–61.
Williams, Jackson. 2001. "Effects of Attorney Fee Shifting Law on Claiming Behavior," *Policy Sciences* 34(3–4): 347–56.
Williamson, Oliver E. 1985. *The Economic Institutions of Capitalism: Firms, Markets, Relational Contracting*, New York: The Free Press.
World Intellectual Property Organization (WIPO). 2017. *Guidance on WIPO FRAND Alternative Dispute Resolution (ADR)*, WIPO Arbitration and Mediation Center. www.wipo.int/amc/en/center/specific-sectors/ict/frand/
Wright, Joshua D. 2014. "SSOs, FRAND, and Antitrust: Lessons from the Economics of Incomplete Contracts," *George Mason Law Review* 21(4): 791–810.
Wu, H. D. 2014. "The Presumption of Fault Principle and Determination in IPR Infringement Litigation," *Law Review (Faxue Pinglun)* 5: 124–30.
Yamaguchi, Kazuhiro. 2016. "Japanese Patent Litigation and Its Related Statistics–Current Environment and Future Agenda," *A.I.P.P.I.—Japan* 41: 128–42.
Yang, Zelin. 2014. "Damaging Royalties: An Overview of Reasonable Royalty Damages," *Berkeley Technology Law Journal* 29: 647–78.
Yi, Sang-Seung & Yoonhee Kim. 2017. "FRAND in Korea," in Jorge L. Contreras, ed., *The Cambridge Handbook of Technical Standardization Law*, Cambridge: Cambridge University Press.
Yuan, Xiuting & Paul Kossof. 2015. "Developments in Chinese Anti-Monopoly Law: Implications of Huawei v. InterDigital on Anti-Monopoly Litigation in Mainland China," *European Intellectual Property Review* 37(7): 438–41.

Index

9 781108 445498